CHOICE, BEHAVIOURAL ECONOMICS AND ADDICTION

CHOICE, BEHAVIOURAL ECONOMICS AND ADDICTION

EDITED BY

RUDY E. VUCHINICH

Department of Psychology, University of Alabama at Birmingham, Birmingham, AL, USA.

NICK HEATHER

School of Psychology and Sport Sciences, Northumbria University, UK

2003

Pergamon
An imprint of Elsevier

Amsterdam – Boston – Heidelberg – London – New York – Oxford – Paris
San Diego – San Francisco – Singapore – Sydney – Tokyo

ELSEVIER Ltd
The Boulevard, Langford Lane
Kidlington, Oxford OX5 1GB, UK

First edition 2003

Library of Congress Cataloging in Publication Data
A catalog record from the Library of Congress has been applied for.

British Library Cataloguing in Publication Data
A catalogue record from the British Library has been applied for.

ISBN: 0-08-044056-8

⊗ The paper used in this publication meets the requirements of ANSI/NISO Z39.48-1992 (Permanence of Paper).
Printed in The Netherlands.

Contents

Part II: Other Perspectives on Addiction

Part III: Empirical Studies of Addiction

Contributors

George Ainslie MD
116A Veterans Affairs Medical Center, Coatesville, PA 19320, USA

Thomas F. Babor Ph.D.
Department of Community Medicine and Health Care, University of Connecticut School of Medicine, 263 Farmington Avenue, Farmington, CT 06030-6325, USA

Warren K. Bickel Ph.D.
Department of Psychiatry, College of Medicine, University of Vermont, 38 Fletcher Place, Burlington, VT 05401, USA

Anne Line Bretteville-Jensen Ph.D.
National Institute for Alcohol and Drug Research (SIRUS), Øvre Slottsgate 2B, Box 565, Sentrum, 0105 Oslo, Norway

Rudolf N. Cardinal Ph.D., M.D.
Department of Experimental Psychology, University of Cambridge, Downing Street, Cambridge CB2 3EB, UK

Frank J. Chaloupka Ph.D.
Department of Economics, Health Research and Policy Centers, University of Illinois at Chicago, 850 W. Jackson Blvd, Suite 400, Chicago, IL 60607, USA

Sherry L. Emery Ph.D.
Health Research and Policy Centers, University of Illinois at Chicago, 850 W. Jackson Blvd, Suite 400, Chicago, IL 60607, USA

Barry J. Everitt Ph.D.
Department of Experimental Psychology, University of Cambridge, Downing Street, Cambridge CB2 3EB, UK

Olav Gjelsvik D.Phil.
Department of Philosophy, University of Oslo, P.O. Box 1024, Blindern, 0315 Oslo Norway

Nick Heather Ph.D.
School of Psychology and Sport Sciences, Northumbria University, Newcastle upon Tyne, NE1 8ST, UK

Gene M. Heyman Ph.D.
Behavioral Psychopharmacological Research Laboratory, McLean Hospital/Harvard University Medical School, 115 Mill Street, Belmont, MA 02478, USA

Keith Humphreys Ph.D.
Stanford University School of Medicine, 40 North Quarry Road, Stanford, CA 94305-5717, USA

Matthew W. Johnson M.A.
Department of Psychiatry and Psychology, University of Vermont, 38 Fletcher Place, Burlington, VT 05401, USA

Lan Liang Ph.D.
Department of Economics, University of Illinois at Chicago M/C, 144, UH2103, 601 S. Morgan Street, Chicago, IL 60607, USA

Robert MacCoun Ph.D.
Goldman School of Public Policy and Boalt Hall School of Law, University of California at Berkeley, 2607 Hearst Avenue Mc7320, Berkeley, CA 9472-7320, USA

Hans O. Melberg B.A. (Oxon)
SIRUS, Box 565 Sentrum, N-0105 Oslo, Norway

William R. Miller Ph.D.
Center on Alcoholism, Substance Abuse, and Addictions (CASAA), University of New Mexico, Albuquerque, NM 87131-1161, USA

Suzanne H. Mitchell Ph.D.
Department of Behavioral Neurosciences and Psychiatry, Department of Behavioral Neurosciences L-470, Oregon Health and Science University, 3181 SW Sam Jackson Road, Portland, OR 97239, USA

John Monterosso Ph.D.
UCLA School of Medicine, 760 Westwood Plaza C8-532, Los Angeles, CA 90024, USA

Michael A. Morrisey Ph.D.
Lister Hill Center for Health Policy, University of Alabama at Birmingham, Birmingham, AL 35294-0022, USA

Howard Rachlin Ph.D.
Psychology Department, State University of New York, Stony Brook, NY 11794, USA

Trevor W. Robbins Ph.D.
Department of Experimental Psychology, University of Cambridge, Downing Street, Cambridge CB2 3EB, UK

Charles R. Schuster Ph.D.
Department of Psychiatry and Behavioral Neurosciences, Wayne State University, 2761 East Jefferson, Detroit, MI 48207, USA

Cathy A. Simpson Ph.D.
Department of Psychology, Jacksonville State University, 700 Pelham Road North, Jacksonville, AL 36265, USA

Ole-Jørgen Skog Ph.D.
Centre for Advanced Studies, The Norwegian Academy of Science and Letters, Department of Sociology, University of Oslo, P.O. Box 1096, Blindern, 0317 Oslo, Norway

Jalie A. Tucker Ph.D., M.P.H.
Department of Health Behavior, School of Public Health, University of Alabama at Birmingham, 277 Ryals, Birmingham, AL 35294, USA

Rudy E. Vuchinich Ph.D.
Department of Psychology, University of Alabama at Birmingham, CH 415, 1530 3rd Ave S, Birmingham, AL 35294-1170, USA

Preface

This book is based on the proceedings of an invitation-only conference entitled, *Choice, Behavioural Economics and Addiction: Theory, Evidence and Applications*, which was held at the University of Alabama at Birmingham (UAB), USA, on March 15–17, 2002. The main sponsor of the conference was the National Institute on Alcohol Abuse and Alcoholism (NIAAA) in the USA, with contributions from the U.K. Society for the Study of Addiction, Elsevier Limited, the UAB Lister Hill Center for Health Policy, and the UAB Center for Health Promotion.

The conference was mainly concerned with applications to substance use and addiction of a confluence of theoretical and empirical developments in economic science and in behavioural economics within psychological science. The stated aims were as follows:

(1) To articulate the shared and distinctive elements of the four major theories of addiction that have been developed in the area of economic science/behavioural economics (rational addiction, hyperbolic discounting, melioration, and relative addiction: called for convenience here *behavioural choice theories*). Either the originator or one of the major developers of each of these theories participated in the conference. This was intended to allow: (a) theoretical integration where that was possible; (b) the development of empirical interpretations of theoretical concepts that have not yet been empirically evaluated; and (c) the identification of issues that may provide empirical evaluations of the relative merits of the different theoretical perspectives.

(2) To present and discuss the latest empirical work on substance use and addiction that is being conducted in this area. To that end, many of the most active basic and applied researchers with an interest in the theoretical perspectives under discussion agreed to participate in the conference.

(3) To articulate a range of applied implications of the behavioural economics perspective on addiction for clinical, public health and public policy initiatives. For this reason, leading clinical, public health and public policy scientists in the addiction field were invited to attend.

(4) To publish the conference proceedings in a book that will facilitate progress in this area by dissemination in the scholarly, research and professional substance use and addiction communities. This, obviously, resulted in the present volume.

For the reader who is not familiar with this body of work, Chapter 1 provides an introduction to the key concepts in the field of behavioural economics, as well as summaries of the four theories under discussion. Meanwhile, it may be helpful to elaborate on our reasons for organizing the Birmingham meeting and for editing this book.

First and foremost, it seemed to us that the four theories focused on at the meeting were full of promise for improving understanding of addiction but were virtually unknown to workers in the addictions field — not only unknown to clinicians, but also to those with more academic and research perspectives on addictions. A few psychologists have addressed the issue of self-control (or self-regulation) among addicts, with interesting results (e.g. Carey & Maisto 1985; Kanfer 1986; Maisto & Caddy 1981; Miller & Brown 1991), but even these writers seem unaware of the work in question. Indeed, in 1990 one of us was able, with William R. Miller and Janet Greeley, to organise a conference with the title, *Self-control and the Addictive Behaviours*, and edit a book of proceedings with the same title (Heather *et al.* 1991), without referring once to the work of George Ainslie, Gary Becker, Richard Herrnstein, or Howard Rachlin. No doubt this was remiss of these editors, but we are sure that it also reflected a wider ignorance in the addictions field. So we have taken it as a self-appointed task to remedy this situation by attempting to popularise these theories among our fellow addiction specialists.

When one comes to ask why these ideas have made so little impression on the addictions field, especially given what we see as their fundamental significance for a satisfactory explanation of addiction, a few possibilities suggest themselves. First, it is possible that the phenomena addressed by behavioural choice theories have not been of concern to those in the addiction field. That is, in the disease theory tradition that has dominated the field for so long, the very problems on which choice theories are focused, especially temporal inconsistency, are not seen as important questions. It is no doubt possible to discern several versions of a disease theory of addiction, but they all share the property we mention.

The leading symptom of the disease is an impaired control over the ingestion of the substance in question, but the nature of this impaired control and how it can best be conceptualised are largely ignored. More modern formulations such as the drug dependence syndrome (Edwards *et al.* 1981) have apparently renounced a thorough-going disease conception, but the nature of impaired control remains unanalysed. In short, the theories we are concerned with here have not grabbed the attention of addiction specialists because they apparently see no need to explain the very phenomena the theories were mainly developed to account for. Perhaps the old adage about scientific advances occurring when what was previously taken for granted is now seen as mysterious is relevant here.

A second possibility is that, in the positivist tradition within which the study of addiction is mainly ensconced, the basic concepts employed in behavioural economic accounts of addiction are seen as beyond the pale. As an obvious example, in Ainslie's (1992, 2001) theory, the concepts of "weakness of will" and "will-power" would be viewed by positivists as incapable of scientific expression (see Heather 1994). This may in part be due to a failure fully to understand what is being suggested by the use of these terms in the context of addiction theory. However, from a more general perspective, the assumption that addiction can be explained in terms of agents making choices, which forms the basis for economists' accounts of addiction, would seem strange and unacceptable to addiction researchers and clinicians alike. It might be objected against this that Rachlin's (1997, 2000a, b) behavioural theory has been similarly ignored by addiction specialists but, in addition to the more general insularity of addiction studies from mainstream psychology, it may be the "teleological" nature of his behaviourism that is the problem here.

In fairness to the addictions field, however, it may be a failure of behavioural choice theories that is mainly responsible for lack of interest in them. This is the failure to have obvious implications for new ways of responding to addictions, both in clinical and wider contexts. Some authors in the area (e.g. Vuchinich & Tucker 1988, 1998) have written about the relevance of behavioural economics to the treatment and prevention of addictive behaviours, but such writings apparently have been unpersuasive to a larger audience. It is also true that choice theories have reconceptualised and clarified the important behavioural processes in existing and popular forms of treatment — for example, the self-management techniques developed in the early 1970s (Mahoney & Thoresen 1974; Thoresen & Mahoney 1974) — and can perhaps do the same with the principles and techniques of motivational interviewing (Miller & Rollnick 1991). We nevertheless believe that behavioural choice theories have, on the whole, yet to offer addiction specialists unique and practical alternatives to the principles and methods they currently use. We do believe that these theories are capable eventually of making such an offer and hope that this book can help to further this objective.

Although ignored by addiction specialists, many of the ideas discussed at the conference have formed the subject matter of excellent volumes published in recent years. The philosophical, conceptual and theoretical underpinnings of the general area of intertemporal choice and irrationality have been brilliantly explored in the work of Jon Elster and his colleagues (Elster 1979, 1983, 2000; Loewenstein & Elster 1992). The application of the same concepts to addiction has been made in two edited volumes, including contributions by several of the chapter authors in this book, by Elster (1999) and Elster & Skog (1999). Given the existence of this rich literature, it is reasonable to ask what is distinctive about the present volume.

What is Distinctive About This Book?

The short answer is that we wished to focus more on empirical aspects of behavioural choice theories of addiction, aspects that arguably have been neglected in the literature cited above. While each of the four theories does already rest to some extent on empirical foundations, it is hardly contentious to claim that, without stronger support from studies of individuals showing addictive behaviours of various kinds, the theories are unlikely to have the influence on the addictions field we hope for them. This is particularly true in considering which among the four theories, or among developments or amalgamations of them, is likely to prove most practically useful. Thus, we asked all participants at the conference to emphasise, as far as this was possible, the empirical connotations of their views and work, as reflected in the stated aims of the meeting.

It should be added that two recent edited volumes concerned with the application of behavioural economics to substance use and abuse (Chaloupka *et al.* 1999) and health behaviour change in general (Bickel & Vuchinich 2000) have emphasised empirical enquiry. However, compared to the present volume, these works were either wider in their focus than on addictions or did not present empirical data within the theoretical frameworks employed here.

Another distinctive feature of this book that might be claimed is the disciplinary diversity of its contributors and the various scholarly, theoretical, empirical, and applied perspectives they bring to it. The disciplines represented at the conference and in this book include psychiatry, clinical psychology, basic behavioural science, economics, sociology, public policy analysis, public health/epidemiology, and philosophy. This diversity arose naturally both from the nature of the study of addiction itself and from the origins of the four theories we were interested in. It also reflected our plan to have leading researchers, clinicians and policy analysts in the addiction field comment on the practical implications of the theories under discussion.

Finally, we wished also at the meeting to provide a bridge and vehicle for communication between scientists from North America and from Europe. Most of the work on behavioural choice theories has been done in the USA. It so happens, however, that the European country that has shown most interest in them so far is Norway, and this is reflected in the substantial Norwegian contribution to this book. There are signs that scientists and scholars in the U.K. are beginning to pay attention to these theories of addiction and this accounts for the British input. We hope this interest will continue to flourish, not only in the countries represented at the conference but around the world.

Structure of the Book

The format of the conference is relevant to the structure of this book and was as follows. All presenters of main papers were asked to submit text versions of their presentations to the conference organizers one month before the conference began. These papers were copied and distributed to all conference participants prior to their arrival. Following the conference, presenters were given the opportunity to "polish" their papers but were asked not to make substantive changes to them. The polished versions are what appear in the book. For each primary paper, a discussant was identified who agreed to submit text versions of their comments to us upon arrival at the conference. These comments were distributed to all conference participants prior to the first session. Again, apart from minor corrections, these discussant comments are what appear in this book following each main chapter.

At the conference, each main presenter was given the opportunity to respond briefly to their discussant's comments but there was obviously no opportunity for these replies to be written down. After the meeting, however, the editors decided that it would be only fair to offer primary presenters the opportunity to respond to discussant comments in this book — perhaps because they felt that criticisms of parts of their paper were based on a misunderstanding or were factually incorrect but also, perhaps, because something in the comments was sufficiently interesting to remark upon. Not all main presenters felt the need to take advantage of this offer but, as will be seen, many did. We should also add that, quite apart from the more formal conference presentations that are reproduced here, the meeting generated many lively and fascinating interchanges between partici-pants, both in the meeting room and outside it. Unfortunately, it has not been possible, mainly for reasons of space, to include these conversations but we are sure they served a useful purpose in clarifying differences of view and moving forward the agenda of the meeting.

For the purposes of the book, we have divided the presentations at the conference into four parts. Part I contains a chapter on each of the four theories under consideration. In two cases (Ainslie & Rachlin) these are authored or co-authored by the originator of the theory; in the other two cases, the authors or co-authors are scientists who have done most to carry forward the implications of the theory and have become closely identified with it — Heyman for Herrnstein & Prelec's (1992) theory and Chaloupka for Becker & Murphy's (1988) theory. However, the chapters in Part I are not merely further presentations of the theories themselves. Rather, they all explore some chosen aspect or aspects of the study of addiction from their own theoretical viewpoint and thus can be described, as we say, as "views" of addiction from each theory.

Part II contains four alternative views of addiction, all within the framework of behavioural choice theories. First, Skog, who has already made a considerable contribution to this literature, explains his position of how addiction should be defined and then considers our four theories in the light of this definition. The next two chapters present perspectives of behavioural choice theories from two very different scholarly and scientific disciplines. Cardinal and colleagues, from a combined perspective of learning theory, neurochemistry and neuroanatomy, discuss the consequences of modern learning theories and of their own experimental work for an understanding of disorders of impulsivity. Then Gjelsvik, from the perspective of philosophy, provides an extended commentary on Ainslie's theory. Lastly in Part II, Bickel and Johnson apply evolutionary and cultural perspectives to perhaps the key concept in the behaviour economic account of addiction, temporal discounting.

Part III of the book is devoted to empirical studies of addiction. Bretteville-Jensen describes the research of colleagues and herself among heroin injectors in Norway and considers its implications for the adequacy of Becker & Murphy's (1988) rational theory of addiction. Other research in Norway is used by Melberg to comment on Rachlin's (2000a) relative theory of addiction. The last chapter in Part III, by Mitchell, is both a methodological and an empirical contribution to behavioural choice theories — exploring various ways in which the "cost" of behaviour can be conceptualised and measured, and presenting empirical data of her own that bear on these issues.

The last section of the book, Part IV, contains two chapters that attempt to review the practical implications of behavioural choice theories of addiction. Tucker & Simpson consider how behavioural economic and public health approaches might be merged to improve services for people with substance use disorders. MacCoun gives his views on the implications of the concept of addiction in general, and behaviour economic theories of addiction in particular, for policies on the prevention of drug-related problems.

In addition to the chapters themselves, each comes with a commentary by a distinguished scholar or scientist and sometimes a reply from the chapter authors. This additional material contributes in no small measure to aims of the conference and book and to the potential we hope for the book in advancing theory, research and practice in the addictions field. We conclude the book with some brief, general observations of our own.

Acknowledgements

There are several people we would like to thank for their generous assistance in this under-taking, including Drs. Harold Perl and Michael Hilton at NIAAA, Mary Frances Blanton in the Department of Psychology at UAB, Laura Reynolds at the Centre for Alcohol and Drug Studies, Newcastle upon Tyne, Diana Jones of Elsevier, and the anonymous reviewers of our first proposal for an edited book. We are also indebted, of course, to the sponsors whose support made the conference and this book possible — the National Institute on Alcohol Abuse and Alcoholism, the Society for the Study of Addiction, Elsevier Limited, the UAB Lister Hill Center for Health Policy, and the UAB Center for Health Promotion.

Rudy Vuchinich
Birmingham, Alabama, USA

Nick Heather
Newcastle upon Tyne, UK

January 2003

References

Ainslie, G. (1992). *Picoeconomics: The strategic interaction of successive motivational states within the person.* Cambridge, UK: Cambridge University Press.

Ainslie, G. (2001). *Breakdown of will.* Cambridge, UK: Cambridge University Press.

Becker, G. S., & Murphy, K. M. (1988). A theory of rational addiction. *Journal of Political Economy*, *96*, 675–700.

Bickel, W. K., & Vuchinich, R. E. (Eds) (2000). *Reframing health behavior change with behavioral economics.* Mehwah, NJ: Lawrence Erlbaum.

Carey, K. B., & Maisto, S. A. (1985). A review of the use of self-control techniques in the treatment of alcohol abuse. *Cognitive Therapy and Research*, *9*, 235–251.

Chaloupka, F. J., Grossman, M., Bickel, W. K., & Saffer, H. (Eds) (1999). *The economic analysis of substance use and abuse: An integration of econometric and behavioral economic research.* Chicago: University of Chicago Press.

Edwards, G., Arif, A., & Hodgson, R. (1981). Nomenclature and classification of drug- and alcohol-related problems. *Bulletin of the World Health Organization*, *59*, 225–242.

Elster, J. (1979). *Ulysses and the sirens: Studies in rationality and irrationality.* Cambridge, UK: Cambridge University Press.

Elster, J. (1983). *Sour grapes: Studies in the subversion of rationality.* Cambridge, UK: Cambridge University Press.

Elster, J. (Ed.) (1999). *Addiction: Entries and exits.* New York: Russell Sage Foundation.

Elster, J. (2000). *Ulysses unbound.* Cambridge, UK: Cambridge University Press.

Elster, J., & Skog, O. J. (Eds) (1999). *Getting hooked: Rationality and addiction.* Cambridge, UK: Cambridge University Press.

Heather, N. (1994). Weakness of will: A suitable topic for scientific study? (Editorial). *Addiction Research*, *2*, 135–139.

Heather, N., Miller, W. R., & Greeley, J. (Eds) (1991). *Self-control and the addictive behaviors.* Sydney, Australia: Maxwell Macmillan Publishing.

Herrnstein, R. J., & Prelec, D. (1992). A theory of addiction. In: G. Loewenstein, & J. Elster (Eds), *Choice over time* (pp. 331–360). New York: Russell Sage Foundation.

Kanfer, F. H. (1986). Implications of a self-regulation model of therapy for treatment of addictive behaviors. In: W. R. Miller, & N. Heather (Eds), *Treating addictive behaviors: Processes of change* (pp. 29–47). New York: Plenum.

Loewenstein, G., & Elster, J. (Eds) (1992). *Choice over time*. New York: Russell Sage Foundation.

Mahoney, M. J., & Thoresen, C. E. (1974). *Self-control: Power to the person*. Monterey, CA: Brooks/Cole.

Maisto, S. A., & Caddy, G. R. (1981). Self-control and addictive behavior: Present status and prospects. *International Journal of the Addictions, 16*, 109–133.

Miller, W. R., & Brown, J. M. (1991). Self-regulation as a conceptual basis for the prevention and treatment of addictive behaviors. In: N. Heather, W. R. Miller, & J. Greeley (Eds), *Self-control and the addictive behaviors* (pp. 3–79). Sydney, Australia: Maxwell Macmillan.

Miller, W. R., & Rollnick, S. (1991). *Motivational interviewing: Preparing people to change addictive behavior*. New York: Guilford.

Rachlin, H. (1997). Four teleological theories of addiction. *Psychonomic Bulletin and Review, 4*, 462–473.

Rachlin, H. (2000a). The lonely addict. In: W. K. Bickel, & R. E. Vuchinich (Eds), *Reframing health behavior change with behavioral economics* (pp. 145–166). Mehwah, NJ: Lawrence Erlbaum.

Rachlin, H. (2000b). *The science of self-control*. Cambridge, MA: Harvard University Press.

Thoresen, C. E., & Mahoney, M. J. (1974). *Behavioral self-control*. New York: Holt, Rinehart & Winston.

Vuchinich, R. E., & Tucker, J. A. (1988). Contributions from behavioral theories of choice to an analysis of alcohol abuse. *Journal of Abnormal Psychology, 97*, 181–195.

Vuchinich, R. E., & Tucker, J. A. (1998). Choice, behavioral economics and addictive behavior patterns. In: W. R. Miller, & N. Heather (Eds), *Treating addictive behaviors* (pp. 93–104). New York: Plenum.

Chapter 1

Introduction: Overview of Behavioural Economic Perspectives on Substance Use and Addiction

Rudy E. Vuchinich and Nick Heather

The key challenge for any theory of addiction is to explain why an individual would continue a behaviour pattern of excessive consumption when that pattern produces a variety of sometimes extremely negative consequences of which he or she is aware. In order to explain this puzzling phenomenon, the disease-based views that have dominated the field historically argue that consumption has somehow gotten outside the individual's volitional control. This "loss of control" feature of disease models is contained in some contemporary scientific views as well (e.g. Robinson & Berridge 1993). On the other hand, economic and behavioural economic views of addiction are fundamentally based on some model of choice, and appealing to non-volitional forces is not an option for a theory of addiction based on choice. Thus, the challenge of developing a theory of addiction is particularly acute in the choice literature because of the basic assumption that individuals choose their behavioural allocation patterns based on some function of the consequences of those patterns.

This book is about the theory, data, and applied implications of these choice-based models of substance use and addiction. The distinction between substance use and addiction obviously is important, because many individuals use substances but are not also addicted to them. The behavioural economic perspective has made contributions to the analysis of both of these phenomena and, while the major focus of the book is on theories of addiction, it is necessary also to consider the behavioural economic account of substance use in order to place the theories in their proper context and provide full coverage of the contribution of behavioural economics to this field of study.

The papers in this book are based on conference papers given by experts in the field, most of whom have long histories of dealing with this material. Although an appreciation of the contemporary material in the papers depends on knowledge of prior developments in the field, that prior knowledge often is not explicated in the papers themselves. The purpose of this introductory chapter is to provide a summary of the key conceptual and empirical developments that led to the current status of the area as represented in this

Choice, Behavioural Economics and Addiction
Copyright © 2003 by Elsevier Ltd.
All rights of reproduction in any form reserved
ISBN: 0-08-044056-8

volume. Beyond brief statements regarding the empirical support for various theories of addiction, this will be a non-critical explication of the relevant material.

The four primary theories discussed in this book are hyperbolic temporal discounting as applied to addiction, the melioration theory of addiction, the relative theory of addiction, and the theory of rational addiction. This introduction provides some background to the development of each of these four theories. Because the matching law (Herrnstein 1970) is a fundamental contribution from psychology to this literature, it will be described first. We then summarize two conceptual innovations produced by the matching law, and how those innovations connected with economics to produce behavioural economics. The next section summarizes some applications of behavioural economics to research on substance use. Because of its critical importance in this literature, we next devote a section to showing how hyperbolic temporal discounting is derived from the matching law. The final section summarizes the four theories of addiction.

Our discussion includes a fair amount of detail on basic science conceptual issues. This apparently arcane detail may challenge the reader's patience in making a possible connection to substance use and addiction, which comes later in the chapter and then throughout the book. We justify this level of initial detail with the belief that full appreciation of contributions of behavioural economics to studying addiction depends on a clear understanding of basic concepts. The reader, of course, is the final arbiter of the utility of this strategy. Our hope is that by the end of the book you will see how basic science innovations over the last several decades have led to a view of addiction with considerable explanatory power and breadth of applications.

The Matching Law

Initial Empirical Findings

The original behavioural theory of choice is the matching law (Herrnstein 1970), which produced subsequent conceptual and empirical developments that currently are theoretically, methodologically, and quantitatively quite complex and sophisticated (Grace 1994; Mazur 2001). The complexities of this current work are well beyond our present purpose. Fortunately for this purpose, the basic concepts concerning the matching law have been much more important than their nuances for extending these ideas to the addiction field.

The primary empirical arena of basic behavioural research on choice has been the operant laboratory with animal subjects, although virtually all of the empirical generalizations found regarding animal choice have also been found to hold regarding human choice (e.g. McDowell 1988; Rachlin 1987). In these studies, animals are exposed simultaneously to two response options, and they "freely" emit simple responses (e.g. key pecks for pigeons or bar presses for rats) that are occasionally reinforced with food according to the programmed contingencies. The relative frequency (rate) of responding to the two schedules is the primary dependent variable.

Herrnstein's (1961) seminal experiment held constant the combined total frequency of reinforcement that was available from both alternatives, as well as the amount of food per reinforcement, and varied the relative frequency of reinforcement from the two alternatives.

The critical issue in the experiment was how the relative frequency of responding was distributed across the two response alternatives as a function of how the relative frequency of reinforcement was distributed across the two alternatives. The result was the surprisingly simple Equation (1).

$$\frac{B_1}{B_2} = \frac{FR_1}{FR_2} \tag{1}$$

In Equation (1), B_1 and B_2 represent responses allocated to options one and two, respectively, and FR_1 and FR_2 represent reinforcements received from options one and two, respectively. Thus, behaviour was distributed to the response options in direct proportion to the frequency of reinforcement received from those options. For example, if one-fourth of the total reinforcements were received from option one, then one-fourth of responding was allocated to option one, and so on for different distributions of responding and reinforcement across the alternatives. Because the behaviour ratio "matched" the reinforcement ratio, this relation became known as the matching law.

Subsequent research investigated how variations in dimensions of reinforcement other than frequency, such as amount and delay, would affect relative behavioural allocation. Catania (1963) studied how behaviour is allocated between two schedules that provided the same frequency of reinforcement but different amounts of food per reinforcement. He found that behavioural allocation matched relative reinforcement amounts, as in Equation (2),

$$\frac{B_1}{B_2} = \frac{AR_1}{AR_2} \tag{2}$$

In Equation (2), B_1 and B_2 are as before and AR_1 and AR_2 represent the amounts of food received per reinforcement from options one and two, respectively. Thus, relative behavioural allocation was directly proportional to relative reinforcement amount. Chung & Herrnstein (1967) studied the effects of delay of reinforcement on behavioural allocation, and found that relative behavioural allocation matched the inverse of the relative delays of reinforcement, as in Equation (3).

$$\frac{B_1}{B_2} = \frac{DR_2}{DR_1} \tag{3}$$

In Equation (3), B_1 and B_2 are as before and DR_1 and DR_2 represent the delays of receipt of reinforcement from options one and two, respectively. Thus, behavioural allocation was inversely proportional to the relative delays of reinforcement.

The results of these and other early experiments on behavioural allocation were consistent enough for Herrnstein (1970) to propose the matching law as a general analytic framework for describing behavioural allocation to any activity in any situation. This general version of the matching law is expressed in Equation (4).

$$\frac{B_1}{B_0} = \frac{R_1}{R_0} \tag{4}$$

In Equation (4), B_1 and R_1 refer to behaviour allocated to and (the combined dimensions of) reinforcement received from a particular activity, and B_0 and R_0 refer to behaviour allocated to and reinforcement received from all other activities in that situation. Thus, Equation (4) states that the proportion of behaviour allocated to any given activity (B_1)

will be a joint function of reinforcement received from that activity (R_1) and reinforcement received from all other sources (R_0).

Two Conceptual Innovations Produced by the Matching Law

Although the matching law and its original empirical arena are simple, the conceptual innovations initiated by the matching law and the situations to which these ideas have been extended have not been simple. Quite the contrary, these innovations led to revisions of some fundamental assumptions about what controls behaviour. These two conceptual innovations derived from the relativistic and molar characteristics of the matching law.

The matching law is a relative account of behaviour   At the time the matching law was formulated, the principle of the reflex was the overarching concept in experimental psychology (cf. Rachlin & Laibson 1997). In an analysis based on reflexes, each particular response was thought to correspond to a particular environmental or internal stimulus. From this perspective, the determinants of any response were thought to reside in the eliciting or discriminative stimuli that immediately preceded it, the consequent stimuli that immediately followed it, or in some mechanism that mediated between stimuli, responses, and consequences. Little theoretical attention was paid to the more general context of other behaviour and other consequences that surrounded any particular response. But Herrnstein's (1970) equations clearly indicate that behaviour allocated to a particular response option could be altered by modifying the reinforcement for other response options as well as the reinforcement for that option itself. For example, according to Equation (4), we could increase the behaviour ratio (relatively more behaviour allocated to B_1) on the left side of the equation either by increasing R_1 or by decreasing R_0 on the right side of the equation. Both types of changes in reinforcement would realign the behaviour ratio on the left side of the equation so that B_1 constituted a larger fraction of behavioural output. Although changing B_1 by changing R_1 was easily incorporated by a reflex-based account, changing B_1 by changing R_0 was not so easily accommodated. Such indirect behaviour modification due to the relativism inherent in the matching law was not easily handled by accounts that focused on individual responses (Rachlin & Laibson 1997).

The matching law is a molar account of behaviour   The matching law is a molar account of behaviour in that it relates aggregates of behaviour to aggregates of reinforcement as measured over some extended temporal interval (cf. Vuchinich 1995). It cannot and does not attempt to account for the occurrence of particular B_1 or B_0 responses, which would be the goal of a molecular account of behaviour. Abandoning any theoretical effort aimed at accounting for the occurrence of particular responses was a significant departure from what was regarded as an acceptable explanation for behaviour at the time (Lacey & Rachlin 1978; Rachlin 1974). Other influential behavioural theories in that era (e.g. Hull *et al.*) were molecular and were designed, at least in principle, to explain the occurrence of particular responses. Rather than accounting for the occurrence of each particular response, the matching law is concerned with understanding the distribution of behaviour over time to response alternatives in relation to the contextually determined value of the consequences of those alternatives.

The Economic Connection

The conceptual and empirical implications of the relativism and molarity of the matching law (e.g. Baum 1973; Herrnstein 1969, 1970; Lacey & Rachlin 1978; Rachlin 1974; Staddon 1973) differed greatly from the issues raised by molecular accounts. Generally, each activity and its associated consequences were viewed not as a reflex but as a package with a given benefit/cost ratio derived from the consequences produced over time by a given level of behavioural output over time. Behaviour is seen as being allocated to a particular activity according to the value of its benefit/cost ratio relative to those of the set of activities. Theoretical and empirical issues became focused on measuring value and on identifying functional relations between value so measured and behavioural allocation (Lacey & Rachlin 1978). In general, increasing (decreasing) the benefit or decreasing (increasing) the cost of a particular alternative would raise (lower) its value relative to the set, which would increase (decrease) the behaviour allocated to it.

Given this new orientation, research became concerned with understanding the manner in which behavioural allocation over time entrains with the availability of valued consequences over time. Several scientists (e.g. Allison 1979; Hursh 1980; Rachlin *et al.* 1976; Staddon 1980) quickly recognized that this general type of question was very similar to those addressed by consumer demand theory in economics. That is, animals in operant experiments and human consumers in the economy both allocate limited resources (time, behaviour, money) to gain access to more or less valuable activities (eating, drinking, leisure) under conditions of variable environmental constraint. Recognizing this commonality led to a merger of the behavioural analysis of choice and of microeconomic theory, now known as behavioural economics (e.g. Green & Kagel 1987; Hursh 1980; Kagel *et al.* 1995; Staddon 1980).

Behavioural Economics of Substance Use

The potential relevance of behavioural economics for studying substance use was recognized early in its development (Allison 1979; Elsmore *et al.* 1980; Vuchinich 1982). To date there have been a number of research applications to the substance use field (e.g. Bickel *et al.* 1998; Vuchinich 1997), including the contributions to this book. Behavioural economics is a system of specific concepts that applies the general principles of relativism and molarity to understanding the use of psychoactive substances. In general, the value of substance use, and therefore the extent to which it is preferred, is viewed as a function of the benefit/cost ratio of substance consumption in relation to the benefit/cost ratios of other available activities.

Effects of Constraints on Access to the Substance

One type of behavioural economic research has focused on substance use as a function of constraints on access to the substance, especially price (summarized in Bickel *et al.* 1998; Vuchinich 1997). (It may be important to emphasize here that "price" is conceptualized quite broadly, so that it includes monetary expenditures but also a variety of negative

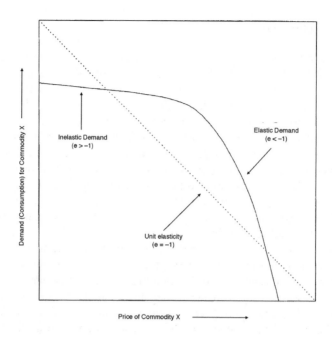

Figure 1: Demand for hypothetical Commodity X as a function of its own price (solid line). Own-price elasticity of demand is defined as the ratio of proportional changes in consumption of X to proportional changes in the price of X. The dotted line shows unit elasticity, in which consumption decreases by the same proportion as price increases. The demand curve for X shows the typical mixed elasticity, with relatively inelastic demand at low prices and relatively elastic demand at high prices.

consequences that may result from substance use.) Early research demonstrated that substance consumption varies inversely with cost (e.g. Griffiths *et al.* 1980; Ornstein 1980), and behavioural economic concepts and research have organized and expanded upon these relations through the analysis of demand curves. Demand is the amount of a commodity that is purchased, and is the primary dependent variable in microeconomics (Kagel *et al.* 1995). A demand curve plots the inverse relation between consumption of a commodity and its price. This is shown by the solid line in Figure 1, which is a demand curve for hypothetical commodity X. Own-price elasticity of demand, which is the ratio of proportional changes in consumption to proportional changes in price (cf. Hursh 1993), quantifies how consumption changes as price changes. The dotted line in Figure 1 shows "unit elasticity," which describes demand decreasing by the same proportion that price increases. Demand elasticities fall along a continuum from inelastic demand, which shows little or no changes in consumption as price changes (the left part of the demand curve in Figure 1), to elastic demand, which shows substantial changes in consumption as price changes (the right part of the demand curve in Figure 1). Demand for a particular commodity typically shows mixed elasticity across a range of price changes, being more inelastic at low prices and more elastic at high prices, as with the solid line in Figure 1.

Behavioural economic research on substance use has demonstrated the utility of such demand curve analyses. Bickel *et al.* (1990, 1993), and DeGrandpre *et al.* (1993) re-analysed data from numerous drug self-administration experiments (including cocaine, codeine, *d*-amphetamine, ethanol, ketamine, methohexital, morphine, pentobarbital, phencyclidine, and procaine) by using demand curves. They found that the demand curves revealed the typical mixed elasticity for all drugs studied, with demand being inelastic at lower prices and elastic at higher prices (see Figure 1). Similar relations were found when data from 17 studies of human cigarette smoking were reanalysed (DeGrandpre *et al.* 1992), and in an experiment with human cigarette smokers that explicitly employed a demand curve analysis (Bickel *et al.* 1991). This same inverse relation between substance consumption and price has also been observed in the natural environment for alcoholic beverages (e.g. Leung & Phelps 1993), cigarettes (e.g. Chaloupka 1991), and illicit drugs (e.g. Chaloupka *et al.* 1999; Saffer & Chaloupka 1999). Research on substance use as a function of cost has consistently found a quantifiable inverse relation (Bickel *et al.* 1993; DeGrandpre & Bickel 1996) that generalizes across species, substances, normal and clinical populations, and laboratory and natural environments. Such findings indicate that the consumption of abused substances can be usefully described with the same analytic tools that apply to all commodities.

Effects of Constraints on Access to Alternative Activities

The relativism inherent in behavioural economics implies that the value of substance use will depend on the more general context of what other activities are also available for engagement and on the variability in their benefit/cost ratios. This more general context is a key issue in substance use research, because strong preferences for substances arise in natural environments that presumably contain opportunities to engage in a variety of other activities. In general, this perspective suggests that substance use will vary inversely with the benefit/cost ratios of other activities, and a number of laboratory studies with animal and human participants have demonstrated this qualitative relationship with a variety of substances (Bickel *et al.* 1995; Carroll *et al.* 1991; Chutuape *et al.* 1994; Comer *et al.* 1997; Hatsukami *et al.* 1994; Nader & Woolverton 1991; Samson & Lindberg 1984; Vuchinich & Tucker 1983).

Behavioural economic concepts concerning substitutability relations between commodities (e.g. Green & Freed 1993) can quantify how drug demand interacts with the availability of and demand for other reinforcers. Substitutability relations categorize and quantify how demand for one commodity changes with price-induced changes in demand for another commodity. This is represented in Figure 2, which shows two possible ways that demand for (hypothetical) commodity Y may change as a function of the price of commodity X. Demand for substitutable commodities varies inversely, and demand for complementary commodities varies directly. If commodities X and Y are available for consumption, demand for X would be reduced if its price were increased (not shown in Figure 2). If demand for Y increased when demand for X decreased (solid line in Figure 2), even though the price of Y was unchanged, Y would be a substitute for X. If, under the same circumstances, demand for Y decreased when demand for X decreased (dotted line in Figure 2), Y would be a complement of X. Cross-price elasticity of demand, defined as the ratio of proportional changes in consumption of one commodity to proportional changes in

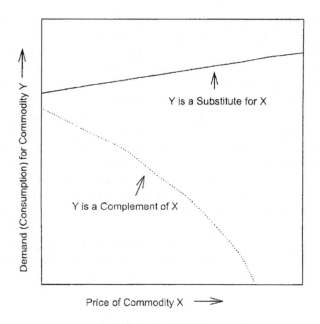

Figure 2: Demand for hypothetical Commodity Y as a function of the price of Commodity X. Cross-price elasticity of demand is defined as the ratio of proportional changes in consumption of Y to proportional changes in the price of X. Positive cross-price elasticity (solid line) indicates that Y is a substitute for X (consumption of Y increases as consumption of X decreases). Negative cross-price elasticity (dotted line) indicates that Y is a complement of X (consumption of Y decreases as consumption of X decreases).

the price of another commodity, quantifies these relations across commodities (cf. Hursh 1993). Positive and negative cross-price elasticities indicate economic substitutes and complements, respectively. Common examples of economic substitutes and complements include, respectively, coffee and tea, and soup and crackers.

Bickel *et al.* (1995) evaluated the utility of the cross-price elasticity concept in a re-analysis of 16 drug self-administration studies that permitted the determination of substitutability relations between drug consumption (including caffeine, nicotine, cocaine, etonitazene, ethanol, heroin, methadone, morphine, pentobarbital, and phencyclidine) and alternative drug and non-drug reinforcers (e.g. food, sucrose, water). Demand for the drugs entered into relations with other reinforcers at all points along the substitutability continuum. Thus, behavioural economic concepts concerning substitutability relations are useful for describing how demand for drugs interacts with demand for other commodities.

Variability in the benefit/cost ratios of activities other than substance use presumably also is important in understanding variability in substance abuse in the natural environment. Vuchinich & Tucker (1996b) applied this reasoning to an analysis of relapse episodes in a clinical sample of alcohol abusers after treatment. They found that relapses occurred more often when the reward structure in the recovering individuals' environments transitioned from more to less alternative rewards being available. Decreasing substance abuse and maintaining the change (i.e. recovery) can be conceptualized as involving the reverse process wherein the reward structure transitions from less to more alternative rewards being available. Such relationships between the maintenance of recovery and increased access to valued non-drinking rewards were found in both treated and untreated problem drinkers who had abstained continuously for several years (Tucker *et al.* 1994, 1995).

Hyperbolic Temporal Discounting: Back to the Matching Law

Although the outcomes of our choice alternatives are sometimes immediately available, much of the time the outcomes of our choices do not occur right away. That is, behaviour is allocated to current activities that produce outcomes occurring sooner or later in the future. Such choice situations are especially important for understanding substance use and addiction, because individuals presumably are repeatedly choosing between an immediately available but relatively small reward (substance consumption) and engaging in activities that will produce delayed but more valuable rewards in various life-health areas (e.g. positive intimate, family, or social relations; vocational or academic success). Access to the more valuable but delayed rewards is facilitated by foregoing the less valuable but sooner reward; conversely, engaging the smaller sooner rewards risks reduced access to the larger later reward (cf. Vuchinich & Tucker 1996b). Research derived from the matching law has made significant contributions to the analysis of such choices.

Equations (2) and (3) showed that relative behavioural allocation is directly proportional to the relative amount of reinforcement and inversely proportional to the relative delay of reinforcement, respectively. Variability in these two dimensions of reinforcement can be combined multiplicatively (e.g. Rachlin & Green 1972), as in Equation (5).

$$\frac{B_1}{B_2} = \frac{A_1}{A_2} \times \frac{D_2}{D_1} \tag{5}$$

Equation (5) describes choice in situations involving different amounts of reinforcement that are available after different delays. If the smaller reinforcer is available relatively sooner and the larger reinforcer is available relatively later, then choice in this situation can be described as either impulsive or self-controlled. Choice of the smaller, sooner reinforcer (SSR) is labelled impulsive, and choice of the larger later reinforcer (LLR) is labelled as self-controlled (cf. Ainslie 1975; Rachlin 1974). The version of the matching law in Equation (5) states that preference will be directly proportional to amount of reinforcement and inversely proportional to delay of reinforcement. The critical importance of this form of the matching law for understanding impulsiveness and self-control choice is the manner in which the value of rewards is predicted to vary as a function of delay. As articulated below, the matching law predicts that preference between the two reinforcers will depend on the temporal distance from them at which behavioural allocation occurs. At some choice points the individual will be impulsive and at other choice points the individual will be self-controlled, even though nothing differs between the choice points except for the temporal distance from reinforcement. Also as discussed below, this predicted *preference reversal* is in sharp contrast to more traditional views of changes in reward value over time (see also Ainslie, Chapter 2, this volume).

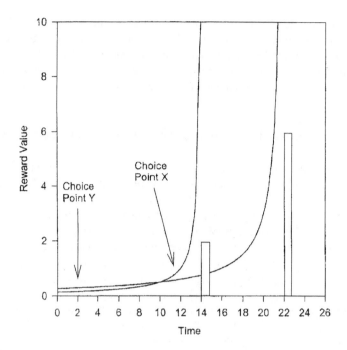

Figure 3: Intertemporal choice between two seconds of food available at time 14 and 6 seconds of food available at time 22. Value curves to the left of the rewards were drawn from Equation (6). See text for explanation.

Temporal Discounting

These choice dynamics are best described with a hypothetical but concrete example from the animal laboratory (e.g. Rachlin & Green 1972). Say alternative one (the LLR) is six seconds of food ($A_1 = 6$) and alternative two (the SSR) is two seconds of food ($A_2 = 2$), and that the LLR is available 8 seconds after the SSR. These relations are shown in Figure 3, with time along the abscissa, reward value along the ordinate, and the rewards represented as vertical boxes at the times they are available. In Figure 3, the two-second food reward (A_2) is available at time 14, and the 6-second food reward (A_1) is available at time 22. As derived from Equation (5), the value of any delayed reinforcer at a particular point in time is given by the A/D fraction, as shown in Equation (6).

$$v_i = \frac{A_i}{D_i} \qquad (6)$$

In Equation (6), v_i is the present value of a reward of amount A_i that is available after a delay of D_i. In Figure 3, the curves to the left of the rewards trace the respective A/D fractions for the SSR and LLR as delay changes; thus, these curves represent the value of the rewards during the times before they are available. This change in reward value as a function of delay is termed temporal discounting, because the present value of a delayed reward is discounted below what its value will be at the time it is received in the future. Equation (6) is one form of a temporal discounting function, because it describes how reward value changes with delay.

In Equation (5), the B_1/B_2 ratio measures whether the subject prefers alternative one or alternative two: a behaviour ratio greater than unity (1.0) indicates a preference for alternative A_1, while a behaviour ratio less than unity indicates a preference for alternative A_2. At Choice Point X at time 12 in Figure 3, the LLR is delayed by 10 seconds ($A_1 = 6$, $D_1 = 10$) and the SSR is delayed by two seconds ($A_2 = 2$, $D_2 = 2$). Inserting these amount and delay values into Equation (5) yields a B_1/B_2 ratio of 0.60, indicating a preference for alternative two, the SSR (impulsiveness). At Choice Point X, the absolute values (from Equation (6)) of alternative one and alternative two would be 0.600 and 1.000, respectively. But preference is predicted to change if we further delay both rewards by 10 seconds, so that choice occurs at a greater temporal distance from both rewards. This is shown as Choice Point Y at time 2 in Figure 3. Now alternative one is 6 seconds of food delayed by 20 seconds ($A_1 = 6$, $D_1 = 20$), and alternative two is two seconds of food delayed by 12 seconds ($A_2 = 2$, $D_2 = 12$). Inserting these modified amounts and delay values into Equation (5) yields a B_1/B_2 ratio of 1.80, indicating a preference for alternative one, the LLR (self-control). At Choice Point Y, the absolute values of alternative one and alternative two (from Equation (6)) would be 0.300 and 0.167, respectively. Thus, the values of both rewards are less at Choice Point Y than at Choice Point X, because of temporal discounting, and the shape of the discount function inherent in the matching law predicts that preference between the rewards will reverse simply with the passage of time. For example, someone offered a choice between 1 candy bar at 1:00 PM seven days from now and two candy bars at 1:00 PM eight days from now probably would prefer the two candy bars delayed by eight days. However, at 12:55 PM on the 7th day, if the same person were offered a choice between one candy bar in 5 minutes and two candy bars in 24 hours and 5 minutes, their preference may have reversed and they would choose the more immediate 1 candy bar.

Before discussing some of the implications of this type of temporal discounting function, we need to mention two important problems that arose with measuring the value of a delayed reinforcer with the simple A/D fraction in Equation (6), as predicted by the strict matching law (Rachlin & Laibson 1997). First, D would be zero for an immediate reinforcer, so its value would be infinite (or undefined) at the moment it is received. This is reflected in Figure 3 by the dramatic increase in the value curves when receipt of the rewards is imminent (i.e. shortly before times 14 and 22). This implies that any immediate reinforcer, no matter how small, would be preferred to any delayed reinforcer, no matter how large and no matter how brief the delay. Second, employing the simple A/D fraction in Equation (6) to describe how reward value changes as delay changes implies that all individuals will discount delayed reinforcement to the same degree. Thus, Equation (6) has no way to describe individual differences among subjects in the degree of temporal discounting. Neither of these implications of Equation (6) accords well with common sense or with laboratory or casual observation.

Mazur (1987) addressed these two issues in an extensive, parametric study of temporal changes in the value of delayed reinforcement. His data provided strong support for the temporal discounting function shown in Equation (7).

$$v_i = \frac{A_i}{1 + kD_i} \tag{7}$$

In Equation (7), v_i, A_i, and D_i represent the present value of a delayed reward, the amount of a delayed reward, and the delay of the reward, respectively. The k parameter in Equation (7) is a constant that is proportional to the degree of temporal discounting, with higher and lower k values describing greater and lesser degrees of discounting, respectively. By the inclusion of 1 and k in the denominator of Equation (7), this equation effectively dealt with the two problems with the simple A/D fraction. First, with 1 in the denominator of Equation (7), the value of a reinforcer never exceeds its amount, even when it is immediately available (i.e. if $D_i = 0$, then $v_i = A_i$). Second, variability in the k parameter allows for greater or lesser degrees of temporal discounting, which can incorporate differences between individuals in how much they value delayed rewards. This discount function derived from the matching law is in the form of a hyperbola, hence it is termed hyperbolic temporal discounting.

Hyperbolic temporal discounting was a significant departure from previous notions regarding how the value of delayed outcomes changed over time. Dating back to Samuelson's (1937) discounted utility model of intertemporal choice, both economics and psychology had been dominated by an exponential discounting function, as in Equation (8).

$$v_i = A_i\, e^{-kD_i} \tag{8}$$

In Equation (8), v_i, A_i, k, and D_i are the same as in Equation (7), and e is the base of the natural logarithms. The key difference between exponential and hyperbolic temporal discounting is that the rate of discounting is constant at all delays in the former but varies with delay in the latter. That is, with an exponential discounting function, equal increments in delay produce constant proportional decrements in reward value. With a hyperbolic discounting function, in contrast, equal increments in delay produce larger decrements in reward value at short delays than at long delays.

These relationships are displayed in Figure 4, which shows an intertemporal choice between an SSR that is available at time 6 and an LLR that is available at time 10. The top and bottom panels in Figure 4 show reward value curves drawn according to the hyperbolic discounting function in Equation (7) and the exponential discounting function in Equation (8), respectively. With exponential discounting, in the bottom panel, each unit of time along the abscissa is related to constant proportional changes in the value of the rewards. That is, the proportional changes in reward value between times 1 and 3 is the same as that between times 3 and 5. Thus, preference between the SSR and the LLR remains constant over time. Given the value of k used in the bottom panel of Figure 4, this individual would prefer the LLR regardless of the point of choice along the abscissa (a high enough k value would produce a constant preference for the SSR). On the other hand, with hyperbolic discounting, in the top panel, the rate of discounting is inversely related to the temporal distance from reward, so units of time along the abscissa close to reward availability are related to greater changes in reward value than are time units farther away from reward availability. That is, reward value changes by a smaller proportion between times 1 and 3 than it does between times 3 and 5. Thus, preference between an SSR and an LLR will change, with the point of preference reversal depending on the value of k and the temporal distance from reward at which the choice is made.

Temporal Discounting, Substance Use, and Addiction

Considerable empirical evidence now exists with both animal and human participants that temporal discounting of reward value is better described by the hyperbolic discounting

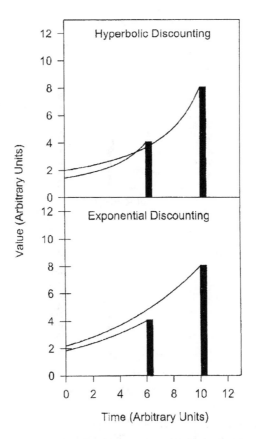

Figure 4: Both panels show an intertemporal choice between a smaller and larger reward available at time 6 and time 10, respectively. The upper and lower panels show hyperbolic (from Equation (7)) and exponential (from Equation (8)) discount functions, respectively.

function than by the exponential function (reviewed by Kirby [1997] and by Lowenstein & Prelec [1992]). Ainslie (e.g. 1975, 1992), Rachlin (e.g. 1974, 2000a), and others (e.g. Lowenstein & Prelec 1992) have written extensively on the general implications of hyperbolic discounting for understanding impulsiveness and the development of self-control. These intertemporal choice dynamics obviously are important for our understanding of addiction. In Figure 4, the SSR and LLR are analogous to an alcohol or drug consumption episode and a more valuable but delayed non-drinking or non-drug activity, respectively. The choice dynamics that result from hyperbolic discounting are consistent with two general and important aspects of substance use and addiction patterns. First, even when reward availability does not change, individuals will display ambivalence in that their preference for substance use will vary over time depending on the temporal distance to the availability of the substance and the alternative activity. The LLRs will be preferred before the point where the reward value curves cross, and substance use will be preferred after that point. But, once the person exits the situation involving imminent substance availability, preference will revert back to the LLRs, and the individual may regret the

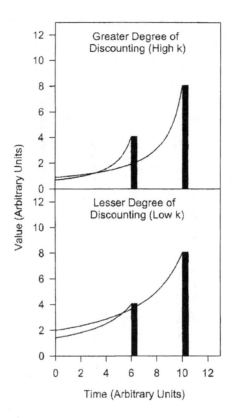

Figure 5: Both panels show an intertemporal choice between a smaller and larger reward available at time 6 and time 10, respectively. The upper and lower panels show greater and lesser degrees of hyperbolic temporal discounting, respectively.

substance use episode. Such ambivalence is a key feature of addiction (e.g. Miller 1998; Orford 2001). Second, the LLRs that enter into these intertemporal choice dynamics with substance use will likely differ across individuals and across time for the same individual (Vuchinich & Tucker 1996a, b). Such variability is consistent with the diversity of life health problems associated with addiction in populations of problem alcohol and drug users (e.g. Maisto & McCollam 1980).

This perspective also makes a straightforward prediction regarding differences in the degree of temporal discounting between problem substance users and normal populations. This prediction is displayed graphically in Figure 5, which again shows an intertemporal choice between an SSR that is available at time 6 and an LLR that is available at time 10. The reward value curves in both panels of Figure 5 were drawn using the hyperbolic function in Equation (7), with the top and bottom panels showing the curves for relatively high and relatively low values of k, respectively. The higher k used in the top panel produces steeper value curves than the lower k used in the bottom panel. Preference between the SSR and LLR reverses with the passage of time in both panels, with higher and lower discounting producing sooner and later preference shifts, respectively. As suggested by Figure 5, an individual with a high degree of temporal discounting (top panel) would spend more time preferring the SSR (i.e. substance use) than an individual with a low degree of discounting (bottom panel). This leads to the prediction that *k* values would be larger among substance abusers compared to normal individuals. This prediction has been supported in several recent studies of temporal discounting that compared normal individuals with problem drinkers (Vuchinich & Simpson 1998), heroin addicts (Bretteville-Jensen 1999; Kirby *et al.* 1999; Madden *et al.* 1997; Petry *et al.* 1998), smokers (Bickel *et al.* 1999; Mitchell 1999), and compulsive gamblers (Petry & Casarella 1999).

Four Theories of Addiction

The temporal inconsistencies in preference caused by hyperbolic temporal discounting are an important element in explaining addiction from the choice perspective. Hyperbolic discounting alone, however, is widely regarded as an insufficient explanation (Herrnstein & Prelec 1992; Monterosso & Ainslie 1999; Rachlin 1997). Thus, the implications of hyperbolic discounting have been further developed, and other choice dynamics have been proposed to explain the apparently self-defeating behaviour pattern of addiction. In this section, we sketch four theories of addiction that have been developed within the choice perspective: (1) a theory of addiction based on implications of hyperbolic discounting (e.g. Ainslie 1992, 2001), (2) the melioration theory of addiction (Herrnstein & Prelec 1992; Heyman 1996), (3) the relative theory of addiction (Rachlin 1997, 2000b), and (4) the theory of rational addiction (Becker & Murphy 1988). Hyperbolic discounting, melioration, and relative addiction theory originated in the psychological literature, while rational addiction theory originated in the economic literature. (The four theories are also discussed by Skog, Chapter 6, this volume.)

Before sketching the theories, we will mention two important commonalities and two important distinctions among them. The first commonality is that long-term behavioural allocation patterns of consumption of the addictive substance and engaging in other activities are the focus of each theory. Thus, these theories are molar, as opposed to molecular, explanations of addiction. The melioration, relative and rational theories seek the causes of addiction in the dynamics of temporally extended patterns of behavioural allocation to substance use and other activities, rather than in some sort of internal cognitive or neurophysiological mechanism (cf. Rachlin 1997). Ainslie's theory too is concerned with extended patterns of behaviour but, unlike the other theories, he proposes internal processes representing "will" and "the self" to account for these patterns.

The second commonality, applying to the melioration, relative and rational theories, is the notion that consumption of addictive commodities during one time period reduces the utility derived in later time periods from the addictive substance and from engaging in other activities. In general, utility is defined as the benefit derived from engaging in an activity. Because of tolerance, consumption of the addictive commodity in one time period reduces utility of the same level of consumption in future periods. Because addictive commodity consumption disrupts the ability to engage effectively in alternative activities, consumption of the former in one time period reduces the utility derived from the latter in later time periods. Thus, each theory proposes a sort of intertemporal dependency between consumption and utility in different time periods that is critical in accounting for addiction.

The melioration, relative, and rational addiction theories employ some sort of utility maximization process, but an important distinction among these three theories is the manner in which utility maximization is proposed to govern the behavioural allocation process. Distinguishing between local utility and global utility is critical: local utility is the benefit derived from engaging in an activity during the time of that engagement, while global utility is the sum of the local utilities of multiple activities over a more extended time period. The melioration, relative, and rational addiction theories maintain that excessive consumption results from the maximization of local utility, the maximization of global utility from two particular activities, and the maximization of global utility from all activities, respectively.

In the context of the matching law discussed earlier (i.e. Equation (1)), the local utility of alternative one is a function of the rate of R_1 while engaging in B_1, and the local utility of alternative two is a function of the rate of R_2 while engaging in B_2. Global utility is a function of the sum of R_1 and R_2 over the length of the session. The original matching law in Equation (1) is an empirical generalization subject to at least two theoretical interpretations, one based on maximization of global utility (Rachlin *et al.* 1988) and one based on maximization of local utility, termed melioration (e.g. Heyman & Herrnstein 1986). Regarding melioration, rearranging the terms of Equation (1) yields Equation (9).

$$\frac{B_1}{R_1} = \frac{B_2}{R_2} \tag{9}$$

This equation shows that, at the stable equilibrium point of matching, the benefit/cost ratios of the two response alternatives are equal. Regardless of the actual size of the fractions in Equation (1), Equation (9) shows that, at the matching point, the ratio of reinforcement (utility) gained to behavioural output is the same across the response alternatives. This fact about matching led Herrnstein (1982) to propose that a choice rule that directly compared the benefit/cost ratios of the response alternatives was the process that produced matching, and he termed this process melioration.

Melioration holds that behaviour is allocated regardless of global utility and completely according to local utility. Thus, the two response alternatives are kept separate, their local utilities are compared, and behaviour is always allocated to the alternative with the highest local utility. So, while an animal is engaging in B_1 and collecting R_1, at some point the rate of R_1 will fall below the local rate of collecting R_2 by engaging in B_2. At that point the animal will switch over to alternative two, and remain there until the local rate of collecting R_2 while engaging in B_2 falls below the local rate of R_1, at which point it will switch back to alternative one. This process over a temporally extended interval of comparing rates of local utility and engaging in the alternative that produces the highest rate of local utility produces matching.

Maximization of global utility is a theoretical interpretation of the matching relation different from melioration, and is based on the common assumption of utility maximization in consumer demand theory in economics (Rachlin *et al.* 1976). According to this view, behaviour is allocated across the response alternatives according to the response distribution (i.e. rates of B_1 and B_2) that maximizes global utility ($R_1 + R_2$), rather than according to the response distribution that equalizes the rates of local utility (i.e. melioration). Melioration views the organism as continuously choosing between B_1 and B_2 according to which alternative yields the highest local utility (R_1 or R_2). Maximization, on the other hand, views the organism as continuously choosing between different combinations or packages of B_1 and B_2 according to which combination yields the highest global utility ($R_1 + R_2$). According to maximization, behavioural allocation is sensitive to global utility, with future utility appropriately discounted, and insensitive to local utility (except insofar as it contributes to overall utility). Despite a concerted effort, to date it has not been possible to devise a critical empirical test between the melioration and maximization accounts of matching (Heyman & Herrnstein 1986; Rachlin *et al.* 1988). Thus, both remain viable theoretical interpretations of matching and both provide a framework for considering addiction.

A second important distinction among the theories is that Ainslie's, Rachlin's and Herrnstein & Prelec's theories assume a hyperbolic discounting function, whereas Becker & Murphy's rational addiction theory presupposes exponential discounting. The implications of this distinction were covered in the previous section.

Ainslie's Theory of Addiction

It should first be noted that George Ainslie's theory of addiction is less formally stated than others to be considered in this book. As already made clear, the theory begins with the notion of hyperbolic discounting (see Ainslie 1975; Ainslie & Haslam 1992a; Ainslie & Monterosso, Chapter 2, this volume) but the implications of this idea are explored far more widely than in the explanation of addiction to psychoactive substances and embrace a range of behaviours in which the issue of impulsiveness and impulse control is central, including obsessive-compulsive neurosis (Ainslie 1975), dissociative disorders (Ainslie 1999), bulimia, itches, physical pain, flaws of character (Ainslie & Haslam 1992b) and, indeed, many aspects of everyday human experience. Ainslie has rarely devoted an essay solely to substance addictions (an exception being Ainslie [2000]) but common addictions are typically used as examples to which the phenomenon of temporary reversals of preference due to hyperbolic discounting has maximum relevance, thereby offering accounts of the hallmark characteristics of the addict's behaviour and experience — resolution, temptation, ambivalence, vacillation, indulgence and regret. Thus, Ainslie's work may be said to contain an implicit theory of addiction in the sense that addiction is a paradigm case representing a part of the range of self-defeating behaviours he wishes to account for. The most complete coverage of Ainslie's ideas, far more wide-ranging than can be even suggested in this short introduction, will be found in two books (Ainslie 1992, 2001), both of which contain extended discussions of addiction.

Hyperbolic discounting can explain impulsive choices and thus the addict's repeated surrender to temptation despite earlier resolutions to quit or curtail substance use, but it does not explain how such impulsiveness can ever be avoided — how, in other words, addicts and the rest of humankind at various times resist temptation and exercise self-control. More precisely, why is the LLR ever preferred to the SSR even when the SSR is imminent? Ainslie (e.g. Ainslie & Haslam 1992b) describes four kinds of tactics used for this purpose.

Extrapsychic mechanisms   The most obvious method is by a device known as "precommitment," meaning the deliberate engineering of the physical or social environment so that the impulsive choice becomes impossible or much more difficult to make. This device was first noted by the economist Strotz (1956) and is exemplified by the myth of Ulysses and the Sirens (see Elster 1984, 2000). An obvious example from the addictions field is the voluntary ingestion of the drug disulfiram, which a dependent problem drinker knows will make her feel very ill if she consumes alcohol. Similarly, the sociologist Howard Becker (1960) described "side-bets" in which a person stakes something valuable (e.g. money, social standing) on her ability to maintain a decision in the face of temptation. Early experiments (Ainslie 1974; Rachlin & Green 1972) showed that even pigeons can learn to make responses that restrict their future possible choices by making an SSR unavailable, suggesting that what is learned here is not merely a product of higher mental processes or human culture. Several methods developed by behaviour therapists in the 1970s can be included in this category of self-control devices (see, e.g. Thoresen & Mahoney 1974).

Control of attention   This refers to restrictions on the processing of information about the SSR. It is similar in some ways to the Freudian concept of repression, although originating obviously from a very different theoretical base. From Ainslie's viewpoint, the avoidance of information, unlike in repression, can be conscious as well as unconscious. Ways in which attentional mechanisms were used by children in "delay of gratification" experiments were described by Walter Mischel and his colleagues in the 1960s (e.g. Mischel & Ebbeson 1970).

Preparation of emotion   This describes attempts to inhibit emotional responses associated with the SSR or even to augment emotions that are incompatible with the appetite for it. In the case of addictions, it mainly applies to the cognitive control of "craving" responses, something again appealed to in cognitive-behavioural models of addiction therapy (see, e.g. Beck *et al.* 1993). At the same time, parallels with various Freudian defence mechanisms are again obvious. Ainslie & Haslam (1992b) concede that the distinction between efforts at self-control in this category and those under "control of attention" is sometimes difficult to make.

Personal rules   This is by far the most important category of methods of self-control described by Ainslie and the one that is used to create a major extension to theory. This eventuates in Ainslie's account of the concept most frequently used by individuals who have recovered unaided from addictive disorders when asked how they achieved it — "willpower."

The fundamental case of temporary reversals of preference due to hyperbolic discounting involves a single pair of smaller sooner and larger later rewards, but it must be expected that identical or very similar choice conflicts will recur many times in the future. It can easily be shown that, if hyperbolically discounted rewards from an extended series of similar choices are summed over time, there comes a point when the aggregate rewards from the LLRs exceed those from the SSRs, even when the first SSR is closely approached (see Ainslie & Monterosso, Chapter 2, this volume, Figure 2A). Thus, to avoid a reversal of preference a person can "bunch" a whole series of choices together in anticipation of the higher aggregate reward obtainable from preferring the LLRs. She does this by adopting "personal rules" that dictate the choice to be made in a whole class of conflict situations involving the need to delay gratification. These personal rules correspond to the idea of "principles" or "universal rules" of behaviour that have been recommended as a means of achieving will-power by philosophers down the ages and were discussed by leading 19th century psychologists (see Ainslie 1975: 483–485).

By analogy with the public side-bets described by Becker (1960) (see above), the person is seen as committing himself to a course of action by making "private side-bets," a form of personal rule-making in which his current choice serves as the best predictor of what his future choices will be. If he succeeds in resisting the SSR and wins the bet, his expectation of future reward is proportionately strengthened and his ability to overcome similar temptations in the future is enhanced; if he fails, he forfeits his bet and loses whatever elements of his view of himself had been staked, with a decreased expectation of being able to resist the SSRs of the same kind in future. In the latter instance, the consequences of failure are reminiscent of those of the "abstinence violation effect" described by Marlatt & Gordon (1985). More generally, Ainslie's discussion of private side-bets and their effects invites comparison with Bandura's (1977) concept of "self-efficacy" as the most important factor determining whether efforts at behaviour change will be successful.

Ainslie then proposes that, rather than being characterized by rational and consistent preferences as conventionally assumed, the "self" is in fact made up of conflicting prefer-ences for a variety of rewards that, because of hyperbolic discounting, achieve dominance over each other at different points in time. The appetite for and motivation to acquire each reward, together with their associated mental processes, are described as an "interest" in that reward and the interaction between these competing interests is portrayed as an internal economic market-place — hence "picoeconomics," the study of economic forces *within* the person (Ainslie 1992). In particular, the interests of a present self compete strategically with those of an anticipated future self that may attempt to subvert them. This battle may be complicated by the existence of mid-range interests against which short- and long-range interests combine.

So how are relatively stable choices ever made in this intrapsychic free-for-all of successive motivational states attached to short-range, mid-range and long-range interests? Ainslie here borrows concepts used to analyse interpersonal or international conflict (e.g. Schelling 1960) and applies them to the intrapersonal bargaining situation. In particular, he uses the model of repeated instances of the prisoner's dilemma game, in which players must choose between cooperative and non-cooperative options, to represent a bargaining process involving successive motivational states (see Ainslie 1992: 155–162, 2001: 90–94). This intricate and subtle arena of competing personal rules and complex intrapersonal bargaining strategies leaves plenty of room for the evasions, distortions and other forms of self-deception well-recognized in the addict's behaviour, as well as in ordinary human conduct, and these are deduced by Ainslie from his theory (see Ainslie 1992, 2000, 2001).

It should finally be pointed out that, despite their obvious relevance to the modification of addictive behaviours, Ainslie also warns of the dangers of the self-control devices he describes (see, e.g. Ainslie 1999). These dangers and the many other facets of Ainslie's rich and varied body of work should be consulted in the original sources.

The Melioration Theory of Addiction

The melioration theory of addiction (Herrnstein & Prelec 1992; Heyman 1996) holds that the maximization of local utility derived from substance use and from other activities can lead to addiction. In this theory, all non-substance use activities are considered together as one choice option, so the individual is allocating behaviour to substance use or non-substance use activities. These choice options are mutually exclusive and exhaustive. The local utility of substance use is the benefit derived during substance consumption, and the local utility of non-substance use activities is the utility derived while engaged in them. Global utility is the sum of the local utilities of substance use and non-substance use activities. According to melioration theory, the individual's behavioural allocation is insensitive to global utility and completely sensitive to the comparison of local utilities.

As noted above, a key element of the melioration theory of addiction is that substance use lowers the utility derived from such use and from non-substance use activities. This process is depicted graphically in Figure 6 (Figures 6–8 in this section are similar to figures in Rachlin [1997]). In Figure 6, utility is along the ordinate, and the relative allocation of behaviour to substance use and non-substance use activities is along the abscissa. Movement to the right along the abscissa signifies relatively more behaviour being allocated to substance use and less to other activities, the process of addiction, and conversely for

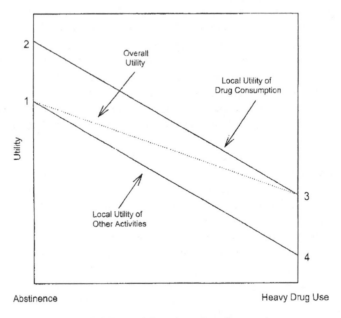

Figure 6: Processes in the melioration theory of addiction. Utility of substance use and other activities are shown as a function of the relative behavioural allocation to substance use and other activities.

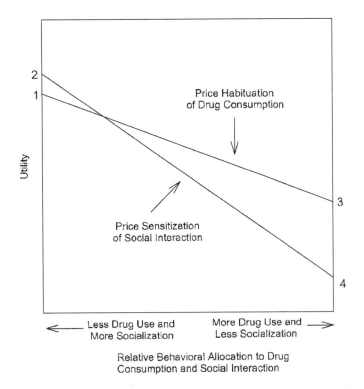

Figure 7: Processes in the relative theory of addiction. Utility of substance use and social interaction are shown as a function of relative behavioural allocation to substance use and social interaction.

movement to the left. The local utility of substance use, the local utility of other activities, and global utility are signified by lines 2–3, 1–4, and 1–3, respectively. Melioration maintains that behaviour is allocated according to which choice option provides the highest local utility. As seen in Figure 6, even though both local utilities and global utility are being reduced by substance use, the individual continues to use the substance. Increasing levels of addictive commodity consumption, movement to the right along the abscissa of Figure 6, reduce both local and global utility, but the melioration process continues to drive addictive consumption because the local utility of that consumption remains higher than the local utility of not consuming. Although the process of melioration has considerable empirical support in basic laboratory experiments (Heyman & Herrnstein 1986; Rachlin & Laibson 1997), there is no direct evidence in addiction studies that favours it over other theories of addiction (but see Heyman's Chapter 4, this volume).

Theoretically, the process of recovery from addiction may involve a "restructuring" of how the choice alternatives are perceived (cf. Heyman 1996; Rachlin 1997). So far in this exposition, only events during the substance use episode are included in the computation of local utility derived from substance use. For example, the utility derived from an evening of heavy drinking is kept separate from the next morning's hangover. If, however, the temporal

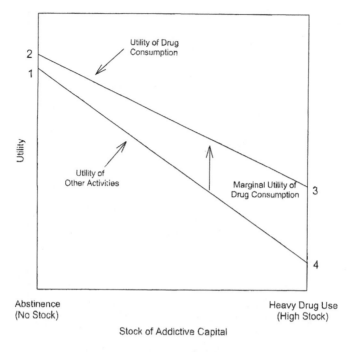

Figure 8: Processes in the theory of rational addiction. Utility of substance use and other activities are shown as a function of the stock of addictive capital.

boundary of what constitutes local utility is expanded, it may alter the computation of local utility so that the value of a substance use episode is changed. In this example, if local utility is expanded to include the time spent drinking plus the hangover, and not just the drinking, this may reduce the utility derived from drinking and therefore lower its value. To our knowledge, there are no data available that can address whether or not such a process occurs in recovery from addiction.

Rachlin's Relative Theory of Addiction

Rachlin's (1997, 2000b) relative theory of addiction is based on maximization of global utility derived from two activities, substance use and social interaction. A basic assumption of relative addiction theory is that substances of abuse (e.g. alcohol, nicotine, cocaine) are mutually substitutable with social interaction (see Figure 2). Because demand for economic substitutes varies inversely, increased demand for the addictive substance is associated with decreased demand for social interaction, and decreased demand for the addictive substance is associated with increased demand for social interaction. Relative addiction theory proposes a process whereby patterns of consumption over time modify the benefit/cost ratios of addictive consumption and social interaction that can account for the excessive consumption of addiction.

Two key processes of relative addiction theory are price habituation and price sensitization, which refer to changes over time in the benefit/cost ratios of activities as more or less of them are engaged in. With price-habituated commodities, there is a negative relation between consumption and the benefit/cost ratio. The more a price-habituated commodity is consumed, the less benefit is derived from a given unit of behavioural allocation (e.g. tolerance to alcohol). With price-sensitized commodities, on the other hand, there is a positive relation between consumption and the benefit/cost ratio. The more a price-sensitized commodity is consumed, the more benefit is derived from a given unit of behavioural allocation (e.g. enjoyment derived from interacting with a friend). According to relative addiction theory, addictive substances are price-habituated and social interaction is price-sensitized. Because addictive substances and social interaction are mutual substitutes, maximization of utility from the two commodities will lead to the one with the highest benefit/cost ratio being consumed.

The central choice dynamic of relative addiction theory is the rate of price habituation of the addictive substance in relation to the rate of price sensitization of social interaction. This process is depicted graphically in Figure 7. In the figure, utility is along the ordinate, and the relative allocation of behaviour to substance use and social interaction is along the abscissa. Movement to the right along the abscissa signifies relatively more behaviour being allocated to substance use and less to social interaction, the process of addiction, and conversely for movement to the left. The utility derived from a given unit of behavioural allocation to substance use and to social interaction are signified by lines 1–3 and 2–4, respectively. The price habituation and price sensitization of substance use and social interaction, respectively, are shown with lines sloping down to the right. Movement to the right and left raises and lowers the price of both commodities, respectively. According to relative addiction theory, the individual will maximize the utility derived from these two commodities by consuming the one with the highest benefit/cost ratio.

As an example, assume over a period of time an individual's behaviour is at a stable allocation pattern of drinking and social interaction at the point of intersection of lines 1–3 and 2–4 in Figure 7. This behavioural allocation pattern involves relatively more social interaction and less substance use. However, an event (e.g. marital separation) then occurs that makes social interaction more expensive or more difficult to obtain (cf. Vuchinich & Tucker 1996a, b), which reduces the behavioural allocation to social interaction. Because drinking and social interaction are mutually substitutable, after the event the individual begins to drink more to make up for less social interaction (movement to the right along the abscissa in Figure 7). Because of the price habituation and price sensitization of drinking and social interaction, respectively, drinking more and socializing less will decrease the benefit/cost ratios of both drinking and socializing. A critical aspect of relative addiction theory is that if the rate of price sensitization of social interaction is higher than the rate of price habituation of the addictive substance (relative price sensitization), then the benefit/cost ratio of the addictive commodity will be greater than the benefit/cost ratio of social interaction. This is shown in Figure 7 with the steeper slope of line 2–4 (social interaction) than of line 1–3 (substance use). Movement along the abscissa to the right of the point of intersection results in relatively more utility being derived from substance use than from social interaction. Because the two commodities are mutually substitutable, the addictive commodity is always preferred, thus leading to the runaway consumption characteristic of addiction.

It is important to note that the relative rates of price sensitization and price habituation are critical in this theory. If the rate of price habituation of the addictive substance were higher than the rate of price sensitization of social interaction (relative price habituation), at some point the benefit/cost ratio of addictive substance consumption would fall below the benefit/cost ratio of social interaction. This would be represented in Figure 7 if line 1–3 were steeper than line 2–4. At that point the individual would begin to socialize more and drink less, and therefore move to the left along the abscissa. Rachlin (1997, 2000b) reviewed some evidence that cigarette smoking and social interaction reveal some features that are compatible with the assumptions of relative addiction theory. Beyond this, however, little direct evidence exists in addiction studies that favours relative addiction theory over others (see Melberg, Chapter 11, this volume).

Given its focus on the benefit/cost ratios of substance consumption and social interaction, relative addiction theory would look to these variables as being important in the recovery from addiction. Events that produced a large enough increase in the price of addictive substance consumption and/or a large enough decrease in the price of social interaction could tip the balance of the cost/benefit ratios so that an addicted individual would curtail or quit their consumption. There are no data available to determine if such a process is important in addiction recovery.

The Theory of Rational Addiction

The theory of rational addiction (Becker & Murphy 1988) has become a dominant force in the relevant economic literature. It is based on the common economists' assumption that the allocation of limited resources to available commodities is governed by a choice process that maximizes some lifetime utility function, given the discounting of future utilities and a constrained budget. The "rational" in rational addiction theory primarily means that individuals are proposed to take into account the future effects of current consumption when making decisions about current consumption. The incorporation of future effects on current consumption was a significant step beyond earlier ("myopic") economic models of addiction (e.g. Pollack 1970) in which only past consumption was thought to affect present consumption.

Like melioration theory, rational addiction theory groups all non-substance use activities into one category, and the individual is seen as allocating behaviour to substance use or some other activity (without specifying the other activity). Like both melioration and relative addiction theory, rational addiction theory assumes that past (and present) substance use lowers the present (and future) utility derived from a given level of substance use, and that addictive commodity consumption lowers the utility derived from other activities. An important distinction is made between total and marginal utility derived from a given level of commodity consumption. Total utility is the benefit derived from a given level of consumption during a given time period; marginal utility is the contribution to total utility made by consumption of the next unit of a commodity. For example, if one ate three peaches in a day, the marginal utility of the third peach would be that amount of utility added to total utility by its consumption. In general, marginal utility diminishes as more of a commodity is consumed (e.g. the third peach adds less marginal utility to total utility than the second peach).

The theory of rational addiction models the effect of past (and present) consumption on present (and future) consumption and utility through the accumulation of stock of consumption capital. This "addictive stock" is analogous to the relative behavioural allocations to substance use and other activities in melioration and relative addiction theory (i.e. the abscissas in Figures 6 and 7). Addictive stock increases with consumption and depreciates at a rate that varies across individuals and commodities. Stock accumulation (a consumption rate higher than the depreciation rate) lowers total utility derived from substance use and other activities, but raises the marginal utility of consumption of the addictive good. The latter feature, termed adjacent complementarity, is a key feature of rational addiction, in that it proposes that substance use in adjacent time periods is complementary (see Figure 2). That is, more or less consumption in one time period will produce more or less consumption in adjacent time periods, respectively. The price of the addictive good, degree of adjacent complementarity, rate of stock depreciation, and degree of temporal discounting are key aspects of the theory that determine whether addiction will occur (Becker & Murphy 1988).

These relations are depicted graphically in Figure 8. In the figure, utility is along the ordinate, and the stock of addictive capital is along the abscissa. A rate of substance consumption greater or less than the rate of stock depreciation would move the individual to the right or to the left along the abscissa, respectively. The utility derived from a given level of substance use and from engagement in other activities are signified by lines 2–3 and 1–4, respectively. The marginal utility of an instance of substance use is represented by the distance between line 1–4 and line 2–3 (adjacent complementarity). As substance use occurs and stock accumulates, the individual moves to the right along the abscissa. Such movement reduces the total utility derived from substance use and other activities, but raises the marginal utility of each instance of substance use. This increase in marginal utility leads to more substance use and further movement along the abscissa, the process of addiction.

Becker & Murphy's full model of addiction is somewhat more complex than described above. In particular, the function relating addictive stock to present consumption shows two points of equilibrium, at one of which the addict is trapped in a steady state of high consumption. Another crucial feature of the model is the rate of discounting that determines whether or not consumption will increase and addiction progress. Rational addiction theory as formally set out by Becker & Murphy (1988) may be difficult for the non-economist to follow but Skog (1999) has provided a useful exposition of the theory in non-mathematical terms, together with critical comments. Rational addiction theory is also summarized by Bretteville-Jensen (Chapter 10, this volume).

Empirical evaluations of rational addiction theory, which have consisted primarily of demand equations that regress past, current, and future prices, and past and future consumption, onto current consumption, have met with considerable success in studies involving the consumption of alcohol (e.g. Grossman *et al.* 1998), cigarettes (e.g. Chaloupka 1991), and cocaine (e.g. Grossman & Chaloupka 1998; see also Chaloupka *et al.*, Chapter 3, this volume). While this empirical focus on price-consumption relations has generally yielded positive results, other critical elements of rational addiction theory remain unevaluated. Variability in consumption due to the degree of adjacent complementarity and the rate of stock depreciation has not been studied, and the discounting-consumption relation has received meager empirical attention in the economic literature (e.g. Bretteville-Jensen 1999; Chaloupka 1991; Chapter 10, this volume). Moreover, as discussed earlier, behavioural economic research on the discounting-consumption relation has supported a type of a hyperbolic discount function (hyperbolic) inconsistent with the exponential function currently included in rational addiction theory. Rational addiction theorists have been much more concerned with understanding the occurrence of addiction and the effects of price on consumption than with understanding recovery from addiction. Their focus on the effects of price on consumption indicates that price increases would lead to consumption reductions or termination in some individuals, although the logic of this suggestion has been disputed (Neri & Heather 1995). Also, the occurrence of positive life events can lower the level of stock of consumption capital, which would lower the marginal utility of addictive consumption and therefore would reduce consumption.

Summary

Molecular analyses dominate contemporary scientific thinking in substance abuse and addiction. Theory and research on substance abuse guided by molecular approaches are inherently reductive and have produced the current focus on cognitive and neurophysiological mechanisms as the controlling variables of excessive consumption (cf. Heather 1998; Vuchinich 1995). Of course, this scientific activity obviously is critical, has made major advances, and its past, present, and future contributions cannot be gainsaid. But such molecular, reductive explanations of addiction are only part of the story, so to speak, because they naturally lead to an understanding of forces that act from inside the individual at the time of drug or alcohol consumption. Another and indispensable part of the story will involve an understanding of forces that act from outside the individual over a time-frame much broader than particular consumption episodes, such as intimate, family, and social relationships, and the structure and function of community, cultural, and societal practices and institutions (Vuchinich & Tucker 1996b). Developing an understanding of how excessive consumption fits into the behaviour patterns generated by these outside forces, at a molar level of analysis, will be a major advance in the field and likely will lead to more effective clinical, public health, and public policy interventions. The contributions to this book are efforts in the development of such an understanding.

References

Ainslie, G. (1974). Impulse control in pigeons. *Journal of the Experimental Analysis of Behavior, 21,* 485–489.
Ainslie, G. (1975). Specious reward: A behavioral theory of impulsiveness and self-control. *Psychological Bulletin, 82,* 463–496.
Ainslie, G. (1992). *Picoeconomics: The strategic interaction of successive motivational states within the person.* Cambridge, UK: Cambridge University Press.
Ainslie, G. (1999). The dangers of willpower. In: J. Elster, & O.-J. Skog (Eds), *Getting hooked: Rationality and addiction* (pp. 65–92). Cambridge: Cambridge University Press.

Ainslie, G. (2000). A research-based theory of addictive motivation. *Law and Philosophy*, *19*, 77–115.

Ainslie, G. (2001). *Breakdown of will*. Cambridge: Cambridge University Press.

Ainslie, G., & Haslam, N. (1992a). Hyperbolic discounting. In: G. Loewenstein, & J. Elster (Eds), *Choice over time* (pp. 57–92). New York: Russell Sage Foundation.

Ainslie, G., & Haslam, N. (1992b). Self-control. In: G. Loewenstein, & J. Elster (Eds), *Choice over time* (pp. 177–212). New York: Russell Sage Foundation.

Allison, J. (1979). Demand economics and experimental psychology. *Behavioral Science*, *24*, 403–415.

Bandura, A. (1977). Self-efficacy: Toward a unifying theory of behavioral change. *Psychological Review*, *84*, 191–215.

Baum, W. M. (1973). The correlation based law of effect. *Journal of the Experimental Analysis of Behavior*, *20*, 137–153.

Beck, A. T., Wright, F. D., Newman, C. F., & Liese, B. S. (1993). *Cognitive therapy of substance abuse*. New York: Guilford.

Becker, H. S. (1960). Notes on the concept of commitment. *American Journal of Sociology*, *66*, 32–40.

Becker, G. S., & Murphy, K. M. (1988). A theory of rational addiction. *Journal of Political Economy*, *96*, 675–700.

Bickel, W. K., DeGrandpre, R. J., & Higgins, S. T. (1993). Behavioral economics: A novel experimental approach to the study of drug dependence. *Drug and Alcohol Dependence*, *33*, 173–192.

Bickel, W. K., DeGrandpre, R. J., & Higgins, S. T. (1995). The behavioral economics of concurrent drug reinforcers: A review and reanalysis of drug self-administration research. *Psychopharmacology*, *118*, 250–259.

Bickel, W. K., DeGrandpre, R. J., Higgins, S. T., & Hughes, J. R. (1990). Behavioral economics of drug self-administration: I. Functional equivalence of response requirement and drug dose. *Life Sciences*, *47*, 1501–1510.

Bickel, W. K., DeGrandpre, R. J., Hughes, J. R., & Higgins, S. T. (1991). Behavioral economics of drug self-administration: II. A unit-price analysis of cigarette smoking. *Journal of the Experimental Analysis of Behavior*, *55*, 145–154.

Bickel, W. K., Madden, G. J., & Petry, N. M. (1998). The price of change: The behavioral economics of drug dependence. *Behavior Therapy*, *29*, 545–565.

Bickel, W. K., Odum, A. L., & Madden, G. J. (1999). Impulsivity and cigarette smoking: Delay discounting in current, never, and ex-smokers. *Psychopharmacology*, *146*, 447–454.

Bretteville-Jensen, A. L. (1999). Addiction and discounting. *Journal of Health Economics*, *18*, 393–408.

Carroll, M. E., Carmona, G. G., & May, S. A. (1991). Modifying drug-reinforced behavior by altering the economic conditions of the drug and the non-drug reinforcer. *Journal of the Experimental Analysis of Behavior*, *56*, 361–376.

Catania, A. C. (1963). Concurrent performances: A baseline for the study of reinforcement magnitude. *Journal of the Experimental Analysis of Behavior*, *6*, 299–300.

Chaloupka, F. J. (1991). Rational addictive behavior and cigarette smoking. *Journal of Political Economy*, *99*, 722–742.

Chaloupka, F. J., Grossman, M., & Tauras, J. A. (1999). The demand for cocaine and marijuana by youth. In: F. J. Chaloupka, W. K. Bickel, M. Grossman, & H. Saffer (Eds), *The economic analysis of substance use and abuse: An integration of econometric and behavioral economic perspectives* (pp. 133–156). Chicago: University of Chicago Press.

Chung, S.-H., & Herrnstein, R. J. (1967). Choice and delay of reinforcement. *Journal of the Experimental Analysis of Behavior*, *10*, 67–74.

Chutuape, M. A. D., Mitchell, S. H., & de Wit, H. (1994). Ethanol preloads increase ethanol preference under concurrent random-ration schedules in social drinkers. *Experimental and Clinical Psychopharmacology, 2,* 310–318.

Comer, S. D., Collins, E. D., & Fischman, M. W. (1997). Choice between money and intranasal heroin in morphine-maintained humans. *Behavioral Pharmacology, 8,* 677–690.

DeGrandpre, R. J., & Bickel, W. K. (1996). Drug dependence as consumer demand. In: L. Green, & J. H. Kagel (Eds), *Advances in behavioral economics: Substance use and abuse* (Vol. 3, pp. 1–36). Norwood, NJ: Ablex.

DeGrandpre, R. J., Bickel, W. K., Hughes, J. R., & Higgins, S. T. (1992). Behavioral economics of drug self-administration: III. A reanalysis of the nicotine regulation hypothesis. *Psychopharmacology, 108,* 1–10.

DeGrandpre, R. J., Bickel, W. K., Hughes, J. R., Layng, M. P., & Badger, G. (1993). Unit price as a useful metric in analyzing effects of reinforcer magnitude. *Journal of the Experimental Analysis of Behavior, 60,* 641–666.

Elsmore, T. F., Fletcher, D. V., Conrad, D. G., & Sodetz, F. J. (1980). Reduction in heroin intake in baboons by an economic constraint. *Pharmacology Biochemistry & Behavior, 13,* 729–731.

Elster, J. (1984). *Ulysses and the Sirens: Studies in rationality and irrationality.* Cambridge: Cambridge University Press.

Elster, J. (2000). *Ulysses unbound: Studies in rationality, precommitment and constraints.* Cambridge: Cambridge University Press.

Grace, R. (1994). A contextual model of concurrent-chains choice. *Journal of the Experimental Analysis of Behavior, 61,* 113–129.

Green, L., & Freed, D. E. (1993). The substitutability of reinforcers. *Journal of the Experimental Analysis of Behavior, 60,* 141–158.

Green, L., & Kagel, J. H. (Eds) (1987). *Advances in behavioral economics* (Vol. 1). Norwood, NJ: Ablex.

Griffiths, R. R., Bigelow, G. E., & Henningfield, J. E. (1980). Similarities in human and animal drug-taking behavior. In: N. K. Mello (Ed.), *Advances in substance abuse: Behavioral and biological research* (Vol. 1, pp. 1–90). Greenwich, CT: JAI Press.

Grossman, M., & Chaloupka, F. J. (1998). The demand for cocaine by young adults: A rational addiction approach. *Journal of Health Economics, 17,* 427–474.

Grossman, M., Chaloupka, F. J., & Sirtalan, I. (1998). An empirical analysis of alcohol addiction: Results from the monitoring the future panels. *Economic Inquiry, 36,* 39–48.

Hatsukami, D. K., Thompson, T. N., Pentel, P. R., & Carroll, M. E. (1994). Self-administration of smoked cocaine. *Experimental and Clinical Psychopharmacology, 2,* 115–125.

Heather, N. (1998). A conceptual framework for explaining drug addiction. *Journal of Psychopharmacology, 12,* 3–7.

Herrnstein, R. J. (1961). Relative and absolute strength of response as a function of frequency of reinforcement. *Journal of the Experimental Analysis of Behavior, 4,* 267–272.

Herrnstein, R. J. (1969). Method and theory in the study of avoidance. *Psychological Review, 76,* 46–69.

Herrnstein, R. J. (1970). On the law of effect. *Journal of the Experimental Analysis of Behavior, 13,* 243–266.

Herrnstein, R. J. (1982). Melioration as behavioral dynamism. In: M. L. Commons, R. J. Herrnstein, & H. Rachlin (Eds), *Quantitative analyses of behavior: Matching and maximizing accounts* (Vol. II, pp. 433–458). Cambridge, MA: Ballinger Publishing.

Herrnstein, R. J., & Prelec, D. (1992). A theory of addiction. In: G. Loewenstein, & J. Elster (Eds), *Choice over time* (pp. 331–360). New York: Russell Sage Foundation.

Heyman, G. M. (1996). Resolving the contradictions of addiction. *Behavioral and Brain Sciences*, *19*, 561–610.

Heyman, G. M., & Herrnstein, R. J. (1986). More on concurrent ratio-interval schedules: A replication and review. *Journal of the Experimental Analysis of Behavior*, *46*, 331–351.

Hursh, S. R. (1980). Economic concepts for the analysis of behavior. *Journal of the Experimental Analysis of Behavior*, *34*, 219–238.

Hursh, S. R. (1993). Behavioral economics of drug self-administration: An introduction. *Drug and Alcohol Dependence*, *33*, 165–172.

Kagel, J. H., Battalio, R. C., & Green, L. (1995). *Economic choice theory: An experimental analysis of animal behavior*. New York: Cambridge University Press.

Kirby, K. N. (1997). Bidding on the future: Evidence against normative discounting of delayed rewards. *Journal of Experimental Psychology: General*, *126*, 54–70.

Kirby, K. N., Petry, N. M., & Bickel, W. K. (1999). Heroin addicts have higher discount rates for delayed rewards than non-drug-using controls. *Journal of Experimental Psychology: General*, *128*, 78–87.

Lacey, H. M., & Rachlin, H. (1978). Behavior, cognition, and theories of choice. *Behaviorism*, *6*, 177–202.

Leung, S.-F., & Phelps, C. E. (1993). "My kingdom for a drink . . .?" A review of the estimates of the price sensitivity of demand for alcoholic beverages. In: M. E. Hilton, & G. Bloss (Eds), *Economics and the prevention of alcohol-related problems* (pp. 1–31). Rockville, MD: National Institute on Alcohol Abuse and Alcoholism Research Monograph No. 25. NIH Pub. No. 93-3513.

Lowenstein, G. F., & Prelec, D. (1992). Anomalies in intertemporal choice: Evidence and an interpretation. *The Quarterly Journal of Economics*, *107*, 573–597.

Madden, G. J., Petry, N. M., Badger, G. J., & Bickel, W. K. (1997). Impulsive and self-control choices in opioid-dependent patients and non-drug-using-control participants. *Experimental and Clinical Psychopharmacology*, *5*, 256–263.

Maisto, S. A., & McCollam, J. B. (1980). The use of multiple measures of life health to assess alcohol treatment outcome: A review and critique. In: L. C. Sobell, M. B. Sobell, & E. Ward (Eds), *Evaluating alcohol and drug abuse treatment effectiveness* (pp. 15–76). New York: Pergamon.

Marlatt, G. A., & Gordon, J. R. (1985). *Relapse prevention: Maintenance strategies in the treatment of addictive behaviors*. New York: Guilford.

Mazur, J. (1987). An adjusting procedure for studying delayed reinforcement. In: M. Commons, J. Mazur, J. A. Nevin, & H. Rachlin (Eds), *Quantitative analysis of behavior: The effect of delay and of intervening events on reinforcement value* (Vol. 5). Hillsdale, NJ: Lawrence Erlbaum Associates.

Mazur, J. E. (2001). Hyperbolic value addition and general models of animal choice. *Psychological Review*, *108*, 96–112.

McDowell, J. J. (1988). Matching theory in natural human environments. *The Behavior Analyst*, *11*, 95–109.

Miller, W. R. (1998). Enhancing motivation for change. In: W. R. Miller, & N. Heather (Eds), *Treating addictive behaviors* (2nd ed., pp. 121–132). New York: Plenum Press.

Mischel, W., & Ebbeson, E. B. (1970). Attention in delay of gratification. *Journal of Personality & Social Psychology*, *16*, 329–337.

Mitchell, S. H. (1999). Measures of impulsivity in cigarette smoker and non-smokers. *Psychopharmacology*, *146*, 455–464.

Monterosso, J., & Ainslie, G. (1999). Beyond discounting: Possible experimental models of impulse control. *Psychopharmacology*, *146*, 339–347.

Nader, M. A., & Woolverton, W. L. (1991). Effects of increasing the magnitude of an alternative reinforcer on drug choice in a discrete-trials choice procedure. *Psychopharmacology*, *105*, 169–174.

Neri, F., & Heather, N. (1995). Heroin control policy under the theory of rational addiction. *Addiction Research, 3*, 81–91.

Orford, J. (2001). *Excessive appetites* (2nd ed.). Chichester, UK: Wiley.

Petry, N. M., Bickel, W. K., & Arnett, M. (1998). Shortened time horizons and insensitivity to future consequences in heroin addicts. *Addiction, 93*, 729–738.

Petry, N. M., & Casarella, T. (1999). Excessive discounting of delayed rewards in substance abusers with gambling problems. *Drug and Alcohol Dependence, 56*, 25–32.

Pollack, R. A. (1970). Habit formation and dynamic demand functions. *Journal of Political Economy, 78*, 745–763.

Ornstein, S. I. (1980). Control of alcohol consumption through price increases. *Journal of Studies on Alcohol, 41*, 807–818.

Rachlin, H. (1974). Self-control. *Behaviorism, 2*, 94–107.

Rachlin, H. (1987). Animal choice and human choice. In: L. Green, & J. Kagel (Eds), *Advances in behavioral economics* (Vol. 1, pp. 48–64). Norwood, NJ: Ablex Publishing Corp.

Rachlin, H. (1997). Four teleological theories of addiction. *Psychonomic Bulletin and Review, 4*, 462–473.

Rachlin, H. (2000a). *The science of self-control*. Cambridge, MA: Harvard University Press.

Rachlin, H. (2000b). The lonely addict. In: W. K. Bickel, & R. E. Vuchinich (Eds), *Reframing health behavior change with behavioral economics* (pp. 145–166). Mahwah, NJ: Lawrence Erlbaum Associates.

Rachlin, H., & Green, L. (1972). Commitment, choice, and self-control. *Journal of the Experimental Analysis of Behavior, 17*, 15–22.

Rachlin, H., Green, L., Kagel, J., & Battalio, R. (1976). Economic demand theory and psychological studies of choice. In: G. Bower (Ed.), *The psychology of learning and motivation* (pp. 129–154). New York: Academic Press.

Rachlin, H., Green, L., & Tormey, B. (1988). Is there a decisive test between matching and maximizing? *Journal of the Experimental Analysis of Behavior, 50*, 113–123.

Rachlin, H., & Laibson, D. I. (1997). *The matching law: Papers in psychology and economics by Richard Herrnstein*. Cambridge, MA: Harvard University Press.

Robinson, T. E., & Berridge, K. C. (1993). The neural basis of drug craving: An incentive-sensitization theory of addiction. *Brain Research Reviews, 18*, 247–291.

Saffer, H., & Chaloupka, F. J. (1999). Demographic differentials in the demand for alcohol and illicit drugs. In: F. J. Chaloupka, W. K. Bickel, M. Grossman, & H. Saffer (Eds), *The economic analysis of substance use and abuse: An integration of econometric and behavioral economic perspectives* (pp. 187–212). Chicago: University of Chicago Press.

Samson, H. H., & Lindberg, K. (1984). Comparison of sucrose-sucrose to sucrose-ethanol concurrent responding in the rat: Reinforcement schedule and fluid concentration effects. *Pharmacology Biochemistry & Behavior, 20*, 973–977.

Samuelson, P. (1937). A note on the measurement of utility. *Review of Economic Studies, 4*, 155–161.

Schelling, T. C. (1960). *The strategy of conflict*. Cambridge, MA: Harvard University.

Skog, O.-J. (1999). Rationality, irrationality and addiction: Notes on Becker and Murphy's theory of addiction. In: J. Elster, & O.-J. Skog (Eds), *Getting hooked: Rationality and addiction* (pp. 173–207). Cambridge: Cambridge University Press.

Staddon, J. E. R. (1973). On the notion of cause, with applications to behaviorism. *Behaviorism, 1*, 25–64.

Staddon, J. E. R. (Ed.) (1980). *Limits to action: The allocation of individual behavior*. New York: Academic Press.

Strotz, R. H. (1956). Myopia and inconsistency in dynamic utility maximization. *Review of Economic Studies, 23*, 165–180.

Thoresen, C. E., & Mahoney, M. J. (1974). *Behavioral self-control*. New York: Holt, Rinehart & Winston.

Tucker, J. A., Vuchinich, R. E., & Gladsjo, J. A. (1994). Environmental events surrounding natural recovery from alcohol-related problems. *Journal of Studies on Alcohol, 55*, 401–411.

Tucker, J. A., Vuchinich, R. E., & Pukish, M. A. (1995). Molar environmental contexts surrounding recovery from alcohol problems by treated and untreated problem drinkers. *Experimental and Clinical Psychopharmacology, 3*, 195–204.

Vuchinich, R. E. (1982). Have behavioral theories of alcohol abuse focused too much on alcohol consumption? *Bulletin of the Society of Psychologists in Substance Abuse, 1*, 151–154.

Vuchinich, R. E. (1995). Alcohol abuse as molar choice: An update of a 1982 proposal. *Psychology of Addictive Behaviors, 9*, 223–235.

Vuchinich, R. E. (1997). Behavioral economics of drug consumption. In: B. A. Johnson, & J. D. Roache (Eds), *Drug addiction and its treatment: Nexus of neuroscience and behavior* (pp. 73–90). Philadelphia: Lippincott-Raven.

Vuchinich, R. E., & Simpson, C. A. (1998). Hyperbolic temporal discounting in social drinkers and problem drinkers. *Experimental and Clinical Psychopharmacology, 6*, 292–305.

Vuchinich, R. E., & Tucker, J. A. (1983). Behavioral theories of choice as a framework for studying drinking behavior. *Journal of Abnormal Psychology, 92*, 408–416.

Vuchinich, R. E., & Tucker, J. A. (1996a). The molar context of alcohol abuse. In: L. Green, & J. Kagel (Eds), *Advances in behavioral economics: Substance use and abuse* (Vol. 3, pp. 133–162). Norwood, NJ: Ablex Press.

Vuchinich, R. E., & Tucker, J. A. (1996b). Alcoholic relapse, life events, and behavioral theories of choice: A prospective analysis. *Experimental and Clinical Psychopharmacology, 4*, 19–28.

Part I

Views from Four Theories of Addiction

Chapter 2

Hyperbolic Discounting as a Factor in Addiction: A Critical Analysis

George Ainslie and John Monterosso

Rational choice theory (RCT) is the conventional decision-making model in not only economics and behavioral psychology, but fields ranging from philosophy to law (see Korobkin & Ulen 2000). RCT holds that utility is the selective factor for all choice — all behavior that is not reflexive — and thus that all choice must maximize expected utility. Psychology also looks at the process by which utility is realized, which it refers to as reinforcement or reward. We will talk of RCT as the theory that all choice maximizes expected reward.

There is now an enormous catalog of behavior patterns that violate RCT (Kahneman *et al.* 1982; Loewenstein & Elster 1992; Thaler 1991). The greatest contradiction to this theory in terms of sheer amount of motivation involved is inconsistent preference, usually manifested as temporary preference for options that are inordinately costly or harmful in the long run. Such options range from the extreme intertemporal ambivalence seen in alcoholism and drug abuse to more ordinary phenomena such as overeating, credit card debt, overconsumption of passive entertainment, and other bad habits too widespread to be diagnosed as pathological (e.g. Offer 1998).

Hyperbolic Discounting Supplies a Mechanism for Temporary Preference

Parametric research has revealed a fundamental property of reward that has some obvious bearing on the phenomenon of temporary preference, and hence on the clinical problems of addiction in particular: It has long been known that the value of an expected reward diminishes with delay. The (relatively) new finding is that this temporal discounting does not occur at a fixed rate per unit of time, but rather in proportion to overall delay; the longer the delay that precedes a reward, the less the reward is further devalued with additional delay. Mathematically, this is represented by temporal discount functions with delay in the denominator (Baum & Rachlin 1969; Grace 1996; Mazur 1984; Myerson & Green 1995).

Choice, Behavioural Economics and Addiction
© 2003 Published by Elsevier Ltd.
ISBN: 0-08-044056-8

Mazur's formula is simplest:

$$V = \frac{A}{1 + kD} \tag{1}$$

where V is value, A is the undiscounted reward value, D is delay, and k is a constant describing the individual subject's degree of impatience. Functions in this class are referred to as *hyperbolic*, as contrasted with *exponential* functions, which model temporal discounting as occurring at a fixed rate over time.

The implications of hyperbolic discounting clearly bear on phenomenon of temporary preference. A subject who discounts expected rewards hyperbolically is apt to choose imminent but inferior alternatives that she would pass up if she chose at a distance. Choosing $80 to be received in one year over $100 to be received in 13 months would be absurd. But if the choice is between receiving the same $80 immediately versus $100 in one month, the immediate alternative may be attractive. This pattern of preference (which Loewenstein & Prelec [1992] refer to as "the common difference effect") has been demonstrated in humans (Bohm 1994; Kirby & Herrnstein 1995), rats (Deluty 1978), and pigeons (Ainslie & Herrnstein 1981; Mazur 2001). Systematic preference reversals of this type (Figure 1) would not occur for an exponential discounter; given a fixed rate of discounting per unit of time, the more compelling of a set of alternatives does not change based on temporal distance to the option set. Thus, hyperbolic discounting supplies a promising mechanism for temporary preference.

Temporal Discount Rate Can be Used as an Individual Difference Measure

Hyperbolic discounting provides a framework for understanding the cycles of resolution, indulgence and regret that are the sin qua non of addiction. However, fruitful application of the temporal discounting perspective to the field of addiction requires moving beyond the generalities of hyperbolic discounting. In particular, practical application requires an individual difference variable that will relate to variability in clinically relevant measures like vulnerability (who becomes addicted), severity (who has the better prognosis), treatment matching (who will benefit from a particular type of treatment), or perhaps efficacy of

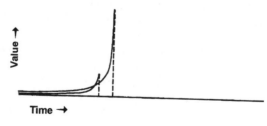

Time →

Figure 1: Hyperbolic discount curves from two rewards of different sizes available at different times (vertical dashed lines). The smaller-earlier reward is temporarily valued higher (preferred) for a period just before it's available, as shown by the portion of its curve that projects above that from the later-larger reward.

treatments (which psychotherapy or pharmacotherapy is most effective). The natural place to turn for an individual difference measure is the steepness of individuals' discounting.[1] If problematic drug use is the choice of an immediate but transient reward at the expense of delayed but more substantial reward, then individual differences in the steepness with which the future is discounted ought to relate to the problem of addiction.

Methodologies for Assessing Rate of Discounting in Humans

A variety of paradigms have been used to quantify steepness of temporal discounting in humans. The rewards used include, points (Forzano & Logue 1994), health outcomes (Chapman 1996, 2000; Chapman *et al.* 2001; van der Pol & Cairns 2001), hypothetical drug or alcohol (Bickel *et al.* 1999; Madden *et al.* 1997 1999; Petry 2001), hypothetical money with context (e.g. "you just won some amount at a casino") (Bohm 1994; Chapman 1996; Chesson & Viscusi 2000; Thaler 1981), hypothetical money without context (Ainslie & Haendel 1983; Fuchs 1982; Madden *et al.* 1997), actual money (Ainslie & Haendel 1983; Crean *et al.* 2000; Kirby & Herrnstein 1995; Richards *et al.* 1999; Wallace 1979),[2] consumer goods (Kirby & Herrnstein 1995), food (Forzano & Logue 1994; Mischel & Grusec 1967; Mischel *et al.*, 1969); and juice (Forzano & Logue 1992). Less frequently, choices among punishments have been used, including shocks (Cook & Barnes 1964; Hare 1966a; Mischel *et al.* 1969) and aversive noise (Navarick 1982). In terms of the procedures used, some studies have used choices among a fixed set of alternatives (Ainslie & Haendel 1983; Kirby *et al.* 1999; Kirby & Marakovic 1996; Monterosso *et al.* 2001; van der Pol & Cairns 2001), some have used a titration procedure with choice stimuli generated so as to narrow in on the subject's level of discounting (Crean *et al.* 2000; Kirby & Herrnstein 1995; Madden *et al.* 1997; Richards *et al.* 1999), while others have required subjects to generate indifference amounts rather than to make choices (Cairns, 2000; Chapman 1996).

Since delay discounting is offered as an operational definition for impulsive choice (Ainslie 1975, 1992; Mowrer & Ullman 1945), it is useful to consider it in relation to more traditional self-report measures of impulsivity. Overall, correlations between temporal discount rate and impulsivity measured by self-report have been modest (Kirby *et al.* 1999; Madden *et al.* 1997; Mitchell 1999; Richards *et al.* 1999; Vuchinich & Simpson 1998). However, it should be noted that dozens of impulsivity scales and sub-scales have been created to measure impulsivity, and the intercorrelations among them are modest as well, suggesting different underlying conceptions of the construct (Corulla 1987; Parker *et al.* 1993).

Application of Temporal Discount-Rate Assessment to Addiction

The most expedient way to make empirical contact between temporal discount rates and the phenomenon of addiction is to compare the discount rates of addicted and non-addicted populations. In particular, it has been hypothesized that addicted populations may be more myopic (have higher k values) than non-addicted populations (Ainslie 1975; Bickel *et al.* 1999; Madden *et al.* 1997; Vuchinich & Tucker 1988). Across a range of addicted populations, the evidence has been consistent with this hypothesis. Using hypothetical money, a heterogeneous group of substance-dependent subjects discounted more steeply than controls (Ainslie & Haendel 1983); heavy social drinkers and problem drinkers both discounted delayed rewards more steeply than did light drinkers (Vuchinich & Simpson 1998); smokers discounted the future more steeply than non-smokers (Bickel *et al.* 1999; Cairns & van der Pol 2000; Fuchs 1982); and opioid-dependent patients discounted money more steeply than controls (Bretteville-Jensen 1999; Madden *et al.* 1997, 1999). Similar results were obtained using actual monetary rewards. Compared to controls, heroin-dependent subjects chose more immediate nickels over tokens exchangeable for dimes in 10 days (Wallace 1979), regular smokers discounted money more steeply than did a population who had never smoked (Mitchell 1999), and heroin-dependent subjects had steeper discount functions than demographically matched (age, gender and education) controls (Kirby *et al.* 1999). Also of interest, Odum *et al.* (2000) found that heroin addicts who shared needles discounted money more steeply than heroin addicts who did not.[3]

Some Limitations on Drug vs. Non-drug Group Comparisons of Discount Rate

Steeper discounting among addicted populations does not necessarily imply that steep temporal discounting is a causal factor in addiction. First, addicted and non-addicted populations are self-selected, and so are liable to differ in myriad ways other than their drug use. Several studies have taken efforts to match drug and control samples on characteristics such as IQ, age, race, and income (Kirby *et al.* 1999; Madden *et al.* 1997). However, even the most conscientious attempts to match samples cannot eliminate the problem of self-selection. Firstly, matching samples on a dimension in which the respective populations differ systematically produces undermatching because of regression to the mean (Kahneman 1965). However, this is only a small problem, and can be compensated for. A more vexing problems is that of systematic *unmatching* (Meehl 1970). Causal inference requires controlling for nuisance variables — those which may affect both the hypothesized causal antecedent and the *explanandum*. If we hypothesize that temporal myopia is a causal factor in addiction, then we might want to control for, say, religion (though we know of no such study that did). Rates of drug dependence are lower among people who identify themselves as religious. Furthermore, as one would expect given differing proscriptions, differences in rates of dependence exist across religious affiliations (Anthony *et al.* 1994). It is entirely possible that religiosity might also be related to choices made on a delay discounting experiment. For instance, more religious people may overall demonstrate shallower (we suspect) temporal discounting. And so, if we wanted to gain support for our hypothesis that steep discounting is a causal factor in addiction, we might want to match our sample on identified religion. This way, if we did see a relationship between group membership (addict vs. control) and discount rate, we could rule out the possibility that it is merely a byproduct of religiosity's relation to both drug use and delay discounting.

The problem, however, is that Kahneman's (1965) point regarding undermatching aside, is that while religiosity may be a causal contributor to addiction, it is certainly not the only causal contributor to addiction. And those unconsidered variables (and there is no way to exhaust that list) will have been systematically unmatched as a result of the care taken to match religiosity.

...for any but the most trivial and "unpsychological" examples of input variable X [addiction], the naturalistic self-selection of the organism for treatments or levels of X [addiction] must itself be determined. Hence the result of holding constant an identified nuisance variable Z [religiosity] will, in general, be to systematically unmatch pair members with respect to some unidentified nuisance variable (Meehl 1970: 376–377, brackets added).

As an illustration, suppose low parental love is one of the countless other causal factors in addiction. What can we say, in terms of parental love, about a religious person who, despite religion's protective effects, becomes addicted? Or about a non-religious person who, despite the absence of this protective factor, does *not* have problems with addiction? On average, the former will be less loved than is typical, and the latter more loved. And so, by artificially matching our groups on religious affiliation, we have unmatched on parental love, and thus have a new variable to worry about as far as a potential basis for a spurious relationship between delay discounting and group membership.

Furthermore, there are demand characteristics to worry about (Orne 1962). From the standpoint of the drug dependent subject, she is very likely participating in a study in which she sees her drug problems as, to the experimenter, her primary identity. Such a subject, aware she is in the lab *as an addict*, may even conceive the experimenter's hypothesis with respect to the presentation of delay of gratification choices. Indeed, subjects in our experiments have indicated as much. And she may, in general, be inclined to give the experimenter what he wants.

Finally, even if discount rate could be shown to be causally linked to drug use, it is unclear from the cohort-comparisons reported in which direction the causal arrow points. It is possible, for example, that the effects of chronic drug use on the brain (Kosten 1998; London *et al.* 1990; Volkow *et al.* 1988, 1991) might affect performance on delay discounting tasks, as has been shown in other decision-making procedures (Grant *et al.* 2000; Rogers *et al.* 1999). Or, perhaps the life-style of the addict might dispose her to emphasize immediate attainment of reward. Of course, the possibility that drug use, or being a drug addict, may lead to steeper discounting does not preclude that the causal arrow points in the other direction as well, but it weakens the ability to infer such a connection from group differences.

All said, the existence of consistent steeper discounting among addicted populations supports but does not prove the hypothesis that individual differences in temporal discount rate, as measured by existing procedures, have anything to do with addictive behavior.

Hyperbolic Discounting Alone is Not Enough

There is considerable doubt whether the psychological processes underlying [intertemporal choice] actually draw on a personal discount function... Decision makers appear to have as many discount rates as choice situations into which they can be placed. Moreover, different measures of discount rates are either uncorrelated, or are correlated weakly or idiosyncratically (Roelofsma & Read 2000: 171–172).

While hyperbolic discounting has consistently provided a better account of intertemporal choice than has exponential discounting, the story has been far from simple. Over the past fifteen years, researchers have demonstrated patterns of choice that seem anomalous even from the framework of hyperbolic discounting (for reviews, see Loewenstein & Prelec 1992; Loewenstein & Thaler 1989; Roelofsma 1996). Some of these patterns are of particular interest to behavioral economic researchers in the field of addiction. We will address the following problems with the hyperbolic discounting hypothesis, and suggest how they might be solved within the hyperbolic discounting framework:

(1) Discount slopes in humans are variable and unstable;
    (a) *Steepness of discounting varies enormously across qualitatively different rewards*;
    (b) *Steepness of discounting is not even well correlated across modalities of reward within an individual*;
    (c) *Discounting measures have only modest reliability.*
(2) Humans' discounting is shallower for larger rewards;
(3) Addictive behaviors often do not depend on the proximity of temptation;
(4) People may come to feel imprisoned by their self-control, while a hyperbolic shape seems to predict that avoiding temporary preferences will always increase long-range reward;
(5) Some discount rates in humans appear to be negative — that is, delayed rewards may be valued more than immediate ones;
(6) The most prudent rewards often lose their rewarding power, even after periods of non-occurrence when appetite should be fresh.

Discount Slopes in Humans Are Variable and Unstable

Steepness of Discounting Varies Enormously across Qualitatively Different Rewards

Some rewards are regularly discounted more steeply than other rewards. Indeed, Navarick suggested the possibility that different rewards might be ranked "according to their potential for producing effects of delay of reinforcement" (Navarick 1986: 354). In general, when points or money are used, discounting is relatively modest. In fact, with points or money, researchers have sometimes failed to show any discounting on the time-scale of minutes — the duration of a typical experiment (Logue *et al.* 1986, 1990). Plotting the discount function with money (at least large quantities of money) requires a more extended time scale, and thus favors a procedure where subjects do not respond to contingencies experienced during an experiment, but only to questions they are presented with (e.g. Would you rather $500 tomorrow, or $1,000 in 1 year?) In an experiment in which subjects expressed preferences for hypothetical amounts of money to be received in the future, adults discounted $10,000 by only about half over 10 years (Green *et al.* 1997).

In contrast, studies using other rewards have found steep discounting. Navarick (1982) found subjects on average preferred five seconds of silence followed by 75 seconds of aversive noise over 75 seconds of aversive noise followed by 20 seconds of silence (Navarick 2001). Similarly, with a positive reward — access to slides of famous people — subjects chose ten seconds of reward followed by 70 seconds of time-out over 40 seconds of time-out followed by 40 seconds of reward slightly more than half the time (Navarick 1986). With juice as reward, Forzano & Logue (1992) found subjects to be, on average, indifferent between an immediate three seconds access to juice and six seconds access delayed by 39 seconds. In each of these cases, the value of a reinforcer was diminished by half or more in an amount of time on the order of a minute. This represents a difference of six to seven orders of magnitude when compared to discounting of large hypothetical monetary quantities.

While the above discrepancies are based on comparisons across studies, variability in steepness of discounting across qualitatively different rewards has also been demonstrated within the same study. Of special interest to the field of addiction, recent studies have reported that heroin-dependent subjects discounted hypothetical heroin more steeply than hypothetical money (the median k parameter was 19 times as high in one study and 15 times as high in the second, better controlled study) (Madden *et al.* 1997, 1999). Comparison between smokers discounting for cigarettes vs. money yielded a qualitatively similar result, though the magnitude of the difference was much smaller; discounting for cigarettes, again in terms of median k, was approximately 17% higher than for money (Bickel *et al.* 1999). Results of a fourth study suggest that active alcoholics, abstinent alcoholics, and controls all discounted alcohol more steeply than money (Petry 2001). However, this study did not control for magnitude of the qualitatively different rewards, and so is difficult to interpret (see next section). It is worth noting that money, the most common reward in discounting experiments – may be ill suited for them since the consummatory period is unspecified. An immediate windfall, particularly for a well-to-do subject, may not change near, or even distant, future consumption.

Steepness of Discounting Is Not Well Correlated across Modalities of Reward Even within an Individual

All the studies of which we are aware that sought to relate steepness of discounting to drug use have used monetary rewards, or else monetary rewards and a second reward (hypothetical drug). Implicit in this design is the expectation that discounting is not modality specific — that a steep discounter of monetary rewards will be a steep discounter also when different rewards (such as those most relevant to their addiction) are at stake. However, research assessing the generality of individual discount rates across modalities has been rather discouraging. In a careful comparison of outcomes related to health outcomes and outcomes related to monetary outcomes, Chapman (1996) found little relation between subjects' discounting in one domain and the other ($r = 0.11$). Furthermore, a principal component factor analysis of the monetary and health items she used suggested a clear two-factor solution which neatly separated monetary and health dimensions. A more recent study again found only a modest relationship between discount rates in the modalities of money and health ($r = 0.24$) (Chapman *et al.* 2001). Furthermore, discount rates in this study were virtually unrelated to subsequent real-life choices hypothesized to relate to delay discounting — getting a flu vaccination and contributing to a retirement fund. More encouragingly, the data reported in Madden *et al.* (1999) allow the correlation to be computed between discounting of hypothetical heroin and hypothetical money. By our calculation, after logarithmic transformation, the correlation is 0.69. Nevertheless, there appears to be, at least in some instances, considerable modality specificity to temporal discount rates.

Discounting Measures Have Only Modest Reliability

The value of any individual difference measure is subject first to the limits of its reliability. Are measures of individual temporal discounting reliable? Is a steep discounter on Monday a steep discounter on Friday? Given that methods for assessing individual discounting vary widely, there is no single answer to the question. One study that presented cocaine-dependent subjects with a fixed set of questions about hypothetical money reported split-half reliability (that is, within session) of 0.79 (Monterosso *et al.* 2001). Also using hypothetical money, another study found the test-retest reliability (after one week) to be an encouraging 0.84 (Simpson & Vuchinich 2000). Less encouragingly, using vignettes in the domains of health and money, test-retest reliability after a one year interval was only 0.26 in the domain of health and 0.39 in the domain of money (Chapman *et al.* 2001). The higher rate of test-retest reliability in the domain of money as opposed to health is consistent with other studies reported by Chapman and colleagues (Chapman 1996; Chapman & Elstein 1995). Unpublished data reported by Chapman and colleagues suggest that the low rates of reliability they found were likely to be due to the long test-related interval rather than the type of measurement procedure used; with similar health and financial vignettes but only a two-week interval, test-retest reliability was a more respectable 0.73.

Suggestion: Human Subjects' Responses Have Been Modified by Impulse Controls

Apparent discounting in human subjects is much more variable than in non-human animals. In human experiments in which the standard delay discounting procedure is used, subjects at the 10th percentile in discount rate may differ from those at the 90th percentile by a factor variously found to be 200 (Monterosso *et al.* 2001), 250 (Richards *et al.* 1999) and 600 (Madden *et al.* 1999). In animal experiments this factor has been just seven for both pigeons (Mazur 2000) and rats (Ainslie & Monterosso 2003). Much of this difference is probably attributable to differences in the modalities of reward commonly used in humans and animals. Most human studies have used amounts of money over long time delays, arguably apt to be judged by some subjects as calling for prudence. The rewards in the animal studies were food. When Forzano & Logue (1992) studied students' preferences for juice, the 90th percentile was only 13 times the tenth. This suggests that when rewards call for a gut reaction, discounting is relatively similar among subjects; when rewards lend themselves to higher order process like planning and calculation, differences in subjects' backgrounds come much more into play.

Dependence on such higher order processes may also account for the variability of discounting within subjects. We know of no comparisons between modalities of reward in individual animals, but we have measured the test-retest reliability of discount rate in rats to be 0.81 over ten weeks, a very long time for these animals (Ainslie & Monterosso 2003).

Humans' Discounting Is Shallower for Larger Rewards

Within the same class of rewards, human subjects discount less steeply when the rewards are larger or more valued. Given the choice of $5 today or $10 in one year, many people would be inclined to take the immediate $5. If, however, a sufficient number of 0s are added to each of those amounts, the number of people willing to wait for the "later-larger" money rises dramatically. Far fewer people would choose $50,000 today over $100,000 in one year. Thus, the devaluation that occurs appears to be inversely related to the magnitude of the reward. This intuition has been confirmed in lab experiments with monetary outcomes (Benzion *et al.* 1989; Green *et al.* 1997; Thaler 1981), as well as for outcomes in the domain of health (Chapman 1996; Chapman & Elstein 1995). By the same token, in experiments using primary rewards (food and juice), both children (Mischel & Ebbesen 1970) and adults (Forzano & Logue 1992) made more self-controlled choices when the reward was especially valued.

Thus, human subjects discount less when more is at stake. Significantly, shallower discounting with larger amounts occurs only in humans. In animal experiments the reverse has been found. Wogar *et al.* (1993) found that the amount of additional time hungry rats were willing to wait in order to double their pay-off of food was greater when the choice was between one and two pellets than it was when the choice was between three and six pellets. This contrast suggests that the shallower discounting seen with large amounts in humans does not reflect a basic property of the discounting process. People's greater patience when larger rewards are at stake must have a more complex cause; as with the great variability in human discount rates the elicitation of self-control is a leading possibility.

Hyperbolic Discounting Motivates Self-Control

There have been many opinions about how people achieve self-control. The simplest would be that people learn to modify the steepness of their discount curves directly. Certainly reductions in apparent impatience are observed, but the hypothesis that the basic discount curve changes faces one probably fatal difficulty: If organisms can directly change the steepness of their discount functions, they will always be motivated to discount the future as little as possible, since the current effectiveness of a given delayed reward is greatest when there is least discounting. Given a choice, they should always choose to make delayed rewards be worth as much as possible. To learn to discount the future less, that is, to value the future more, would be to learn to coin reward.

The literature of cognitive psychology often implies that people can learn to ignore reward, or at least to distance themselves from its effect, and make decisions according to reason instead. However, this approach treats reason as a force separate from motivation, an imponderable factor that makes a systematic analysis of choice virtually impossible (see critique in Ainslie 1996). Hyperbolic curves suggest a less mysterious possibility: foresight provides leverage that the attenuated motives at a distance from expected outcomes, "the still voice of reason," can manipulate to constrain future passions. These curves predict several self-control mechanisms.

Since a person's preference among a fixed set of alternatives can vary predictably as a function of the passage of time, it follows that one of the obstacles she may face in trying to attain her current preferences is the expected preferences of her future selves. The dieter who has just finished bingeing has both a current clear preference for moderate consumption in the future, and an equally clear expectation that her own future self may pose a threat to this current preference. She may thus be expected to behave strategically towards the competitive interests of her future self — that is, to try to *commit* to her current interests. Ainslie (1975, 1992, 2001) has identified four several distinct commitment tactics, three that must be chosen in advance and one that can be invoked concurrently with temptation. To the extent that a subject in an experiment has learned such mechanisms, they might influence her valuation of delayed outcomes. Thus, variability of individual discount rates might relate less to differences in basic discounting than to differences in self-control style or sophistication. Furthermore, the different ways that a subject applies such tactics across modalities of reward could well cause differences in her apparent discounting of these modalities.

Extrapsychic devices   The most direct method of commitment is to arrange for some external control or influence. A current preference for eating in moderation can be secured by undergoing gastric bypass surgery or, less permanently, by checking into a "fat farm." Buying only healthy food at the supermarket does not guarantee that you will not go on a late-night junk food binge, but it adds the disincentive of having to go to a store when the urge strikes. David Laibson (1997) has suggested that a need for this kind of commitment accounts for people's otherwise unaccountable preference for relatively illiquid investments. Extrapsychic commitment has been demonstrated even in pigeons (Ainslie 1974; Green & Rachlin 1996), though only in a situation where the commitment method was highly salient; presumably people are far more creative at finding external factors that may have a committing effect. For instance, proclaiming to your friends that you will never eat meat again does not eliminate it as an option, but it adds a new cost — that of losing face. Reputation may be a major vehicle of commitment (Becker 1960).

Control of attention   Another method to guard against future changes of preference is by the control of attention. Someone struggling to maintain fidelity to a spouse may not allow herself to notice the flirtations of an attractive third party. Attending to such information may foreseeably lead to the likelihood of creating preferences in opposition to current preferences. Attention control can occur as either deliberate avoidance of information or an avoidance that is not itself acknowledged. The latter case is the repression that Freud at one time held to be the cornerstone of all defensive processes (Freud 1814/1956: 16). The repressing individual avoids unwanted thoughts, feelings or behaviors by not attending to the psychically loaded information. Aside from the distortions that Freud noted, its disadvantage is a loss of information that may be needed for other decisions.

Control of emotions   Emotions such as fear, anger and sexual arousal can, up to a point, be vicious circles. After the emotion has gotten underway, there is a lower threshold for further emotional activity of the same kind, until some satiation point is reached. If a person expects an emotion to make currently unpreferred reward dominant, she may commit herself not to choose the reward through early inhibition of that emotion. There have been some experimental demonstrations of this tactic. For instance, Walter Mischel and colleagues found that, while children below around six were poor at self-control, many older children were able to resist the temptation of an immediately available marshmallow in favor of a more preferred reward. Those that succeeded in avoiding the impulsive preference reversal often used emotion control in the form of thinking about the immediately available marshmallow in a "cool" way, or by imagining it to be undesirable (Mischel & Moore 1980; Mischel & Mischel 1983). However, emotion-forestalling devices tend to distort rather than normalize motivation, and may make people emotionally unresponsive, as in alexithymia (Nemiah 1977). At the moment, there seems to be no way to analyze them using animal models.

Prior Commitment Is Not Enough

Tactics that commit choice in advance are admittedly not conspicuous in subjects' evaluations of experimental rewards. They are sometimes evident in addicts' efforts to avoid temptation, so we have summarized them briefly. However, although these commitment devices are recognizable, they are also marginal. We mostly do not need to bind ourselves by some physical device, or contract, or even reputation, to keep our intentions steady. It is certainly good advice for an addict to avoid the haunts where her substance is readily available; but most people who have given up a bad habit do not depend on keeping temptation at a distance or out of sight. People who have given up smoking, for instance, often say that they "just did it" one day. They are said to have used *willpower*. If they relapse, they are more apt to attribute it to an exceptional circumstance — the pressure of an exam, a resentment of meddlesome advice givers — than to the imminent availability of a cigarette. Rationalization, not proximity, is the most notorious threat to willpower.

Western culture has long been familiar with commitment that does not entail keeping a distance from temptation. Writers since antiquity have related self-control to choosing according to principle, that is, choosing in categories containing a number of expectable choices rather than just the choice at hand. Aristotle said that incontinence (akrasia) was the result of choosing according to "particulars" instead of "universals" (Aristotle 1984: *Nichomachean Ethics* Chapter 1147a pp. 24–28); Kant said that the highest kind of decision making involved making all choices as if they defined universal rules (the "categorical imperative"; Kant 1793/1960: 15–49); the Victorian psychologist Sully said that will consists of uniting "particular actions... under a common rule" so that "they are viewed as members of a class of actions subserving one comprehensive end" (Sully 1884: 663). This strategy lets people resist temptation "with both alternatives steadily held in view" (James 1890: 534). In recent years behavioral psychologists have followed this approach to decrease pigeons' preference for smaller-earlier rewards — Heyman & Tanz (1995) by giving them extra reward for choosing according to "overall" rather than "local" maxima, Siegel & Rachlin (1996) by making choice depend on only every 31st peck, thus arguably creating a "molar" rather than "molecular" choice pattern.

The fundamental insight is that you increase your self-control by choosing according to category rather than on a case-by-case basis (e.g. a preference for being a non-smoker, even as you prefer this particular cigarette). But just such an effect is predicted by hyperbolic discount curves. Although hyperbolae spike up sharply in the period just before a reward is due and are thus exquisitely sensitive to short delays, their tails become not only more level, but also higher than the tails of exponential curves at long delays. The relatively high tails of hyperbolic curves imply a potential for great increases in value if series of expected future rewards are added together — and there is good evidence that the discounted values of series of rewards are additive (Mazur 1997). Exponential curves keep declining relentlessly at a constant proportion of their remaining height for every unit of time that passes. Hyperbolic curves level off more. The greater height of their tails means that curves from series of alternative rewards, if bundled together, will favor the larger-later rewards increasingly as the series lengthens (Figure 2a). Exponential curves do not predict increased tolerance for delay with summation of series of choices (Figure 2b).

Experiments with both human and rodent subjects confirm a greater tolerance for delay with bundled rewards. Kirby & Guastello (2001) gave college students choices between

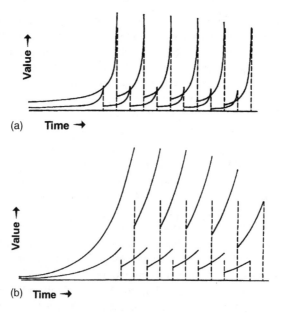

Figure 2: (a) Summed hyperbolic curves from a series of larger-later rewards and a series of smaller-earlier alternatives (vertical dashed lines). Each curve depicts the summed dis- counted values of all future (more to the right) rewards in the series. As the series gets longer and the summed curves peak higher above the current rewards, the initial period of temporary preference for the series of smaller rewards shrinks to zero. (Compare the top of the first short vertical dashed line with that of the last vertical dashed lines). The curves from the final (right-hand) pair of rewards are the same as in Figure 1. (b) Summed exponential curves from the same series of paired alternative rewards (vertical dashed lines). Summing increases their heights as the series get longer (more to the left), but does not change their *relative* heights. (This would also be true if the curves were so steep that the smaller, earlier rewards were preferred; but in that case summing would add little to their total height, anyway, because the tails of exponential curves are so low.)

smaller and earlier rewards and larger but more delayed alternatives, both with money and food. In one condition, the choice was made five times, each time separated by a week. In another condition, the choice was made between the two alternatives up front and for all five weeks at once. As predicted from the summation of hyperbolically discounted rewards, preference for the later larger alternative was increased in the condition in which a series of choices was bundled together (Kirby & Guastello 2001). We recently demonstrated the same phenomenon in rats. Eight rats were run through two conditions of a procedure designed to determine how much immediate sugar water was equal in value to a delayed standard reward of 150 ml after a three second interval. In one condition of the procedure, choices were made on a trial-by-trial basis, while in another condition, every choice determined the reward that would be delivered for three consecutive trials. As predicted by hyperbolic discounting, tolerance for delay was greater for all subjects in the bundled condition (Ainslie & Monterosso 2003).

But a piece of the puzzle is still missing: if a person is a population of reward-seeking processes, what could make this throng choose according to principle? We suggest that it is the same thing that determines trust among nations, or among business people in areas not regulated by law: hard experience of the relevant bargaining contingencies. If a person has no awareness of a relationship among her decisions, then the life of any long-range plan will be short. Before it reaches its goal an incompatible plan will become more attractive at some point. A child who wants friends may have too many urges to be selfish. Someone who wants to lose weight may encounter too many tempting foods. An imminent payoff for an individual act of selfishness or particular snack is apt to be worth the little damage it does to friendships or the minor weight gain. It would probably not be worth losing all expectation of friendship or slimness, but such huge outcomes are rarely at stake in individual choices. As long as she attends only to the contingencies of each individual decision, a person stays riddled with impulses. There is no incentive to plan, because plans are usually rendered idle by the experience of reversing preferences.

However, an astute person — or someone who borrows the astuteness of her culture — is aware that her preferences are volatile. The best way she has to predict what she will do in the face of a future temptation is to see what she does with a similar temptation in the present. The act of selfishness predicts further selfishness and the eventual loss of friendship with all but the most long-suffering people. The snack predicts future snacks and inevitable weight gain. However, insofar as she is responsive to this rough insight about self-prediction, she will move toward choosing according to principle. Her current choices will become test cases, choices about selfishness and eating which this elementary insight will bundle together in her expectations to form series. When she chooses to be selfish, she chooses an expectation of future selfishness as well, and when she overeats the act bodes more overeating. She looks principled, but what literally happens is that her successive selves form a repeated prisoner's dilemma relationship, which they come to solve in the same way as tacit interpersonal bargainers do; each expects future selves to perceive the current choice as a precedent for cooperation or defection, and this expectation adds to those incentives that depend on that choice alone.[4]

Our hypothesis is that the will is an intertemporal bargaining situation, dependent for its force on a person's recursive evaluations of the prospects for her own behavior. Such an internally fed back process is probably impossible to study with controlled experiments.

However, given its formal similarity to the repeated prisoner's dilemma, we have tried to use an interpersonal prisoner's dilemma as a model (Monterosso *et al.* 2002). Subjects played long strings of sequential prisoners dilemmas. When stable cooperation or stable defection spontaneously occurred, false feedback was given to subjects indicating to them that their counterpart had broken the trend. A large asymmetry was observed, with false defection doing far more damage to mutual cooperation than false cooperation repaired mutual defection. While original levels of mutual defection were restored after a single "recovery" move, cooperation rates were incompletely restored after even eight rounds of recovery moves following a single defection. While this may not confirm the usefulness of the interpersonal analog to intrapsychic bargaining, it is certainly consistent with the lore on self-control (e.g. "every gain on the wrong side undoes the effect of many conquests on the right; Bain 1886: 440).

It is also instructive that an intertemporal bargaining model fits descriptions of will over the centuries better than other published theories of will, and solves thought experiments that have otherwise seemed paradoxical in the philosophy of mind (see Ainslie 2001: 117–140 for discussion of Kavka's problem and Newcomb's problem, as well as the venerable argument over freedom of will). Thought experiments may prove to be a particularly useful way of isolating the active ingredient of subtle incentives like the value of precedents. Consider a smoker who is trying to quit, but who craves a cigarette. Suppose that the choice at hand — to smoke the cigarette or not — is explicitly disconnected from future similar choices by specifying what those choices were destined to be. For example, suppose a trustworthy angel tells her that she is destined to smoke a pack a day from tomorrow on. Given this certainty, she would have no incentive to turn down the desired cigarette — it would seem pointless. What if the destiny revealed was instead that she was never to smoke again after today? Here, too, there seems to be little incentive to turn down the cigarette — it would be harmless. Fixing future smoking choices in either direction evidently makes smoking the dominant current choice. Only if future smoking is in doubt does a current abstention seem worth the effort. But its importance cannot come from any physical consequences for future choices; hence the conclusion that it matters as a precedent. Indeed when Kirby & Guastello (2001) merely suggested to student subjects that the subjects' current choices might serve as predictions of their future choices, preference for larger-later alternatives increased, although not as much as when the experimenters bundled the choices directly.

Thus, subjects in amount-versus-delay experiments who seems to have markedly shallower discount curves for a particular reward, as compared with other kinds of reward or other subjects, may actually have been evaluating this reward as a member of a broader category. Such evaluation will have made her choice predict, and thus depend on, future rewards that may overshadow the reward literally at stake. She will then seem more patient with this reward than with other kinds, and more patient than younger or otherwise less skilled subjects for whom the reward at hand dominates the choice.

Addictive Choices Do Not Depend on the Proximity of Temptation

As hyperbolic mechanisms for addictive choices get proposed, they are often criticized for seeming to force the choice into a Ulysses-and-the-Sirens mold. Clinicians are well aware that the precipitant for a relapse is not always, or even usually, a sudden coming into close proximity with a tempting opportunity. Rather lapses are apt to follow a significant event, good or bad, in the person's day, and be explained by the person herself with a more-or-less plausible rationalization.

But although this pattern would not be seen in a naive subject trying to control temptation by prior commitment, it is exactly what we would expect in someone struggling to use the willpower mechanism we have just described. In principle, personal rules make it possible for a person never to prefer small early alternatives at the expense of the series of larger later ones. She may be able to keep temptations close at hand without succumbing to them. However, although she may always prefer a series of larger later rewards to the series of small early ones, she would most rather have a small reward now *and* expect the larger ones later. The danger is no longer one of the poorer reward coming so close that she will suddenly choose it, but of her finding a credible distinction between this choice and the other members of the series that form the stake of her private side bet. Proximity is still a contributor to her temptation, of course, but the deciding factor is no longer whether a prior commitment is too weak but whether a tentative loophole currently looks to her like she could get away with it. The person will not experience this situation as the exotic voyage past some Siren or other, but as a simultaneous struggle between two ways of conceiving a choice. Her rules have enabled her to live in close proximity to her temptations, but while she is there the struggle will be continuous rather than episodic. Lapses will occur through loopholes, variously clever and inept, rather than through a global shift of preference in favor of the forbidden activity. A person is apt to express preference for the course of action required by her rule even as she is evading it, as Sjoberg & Johnson (1978) found in their study of smoking lapses.

Among other things, intertemporal bargaining allows people to establish personal rules for valuation of money and other important goods. A person who works in finance will surely be forced to rule that she will calculate value according to exponential curves, for instance, or she will lose out to competitors who do. However, the shallower she makes this artificial curve, the more she risks that at some point her expected reward from obeying this curve will not be enough to overcome spikes of temptation, which are still governed by her underlying hyperbola. Ruling that she should not discount future goods at all would be still harder, and thus riskier.

It seems to be possible to shield rules against imminent temptation by defining them so that investment decisions are not weighed against your strongest temptations. As Shefrin & Thaler (1988) have pointed out, people assign their wealth to different "mental accounts" such as current income, current assets, and future income. These accounts seem to represent personal rules for how readily the money they govern may be used to satisfy immediate wants. In effect, the person draws boundaries where she thinks they will never demand so great an act of abstention that she will prefer to abandon them by spending money from the asset account ("breaking into capital"), or borrowing against future income. We believe that people are apt to have a fourth account to the left of Shefrin and Thaler's three: a category for comparatively small windfalls like gifts or prizes, or money earned under exceptional circumstances like the pay as experimental subjects. Money in this category is beyond the protection of rules, as Thaler (1990) reports noticing personally when it was suggested to him that he spend $300 in football winnings evenly over his expected lifetime. Only in this account are the person's valuations of single choices apt to be governed by the hyperbolic formula for single cases.

People May Come to Feel Imprisoned by Their Self-Control, While a Hyperbolic Shape Seems to Predict that Avoiding Temporary Preferences Will Always Increase Long-Range Reward

Intertemporal bargaining is still not a complete solution. Until Victorian times philosophers regarded willpower as an unmixed blessing. It was Kierkegaard who first pointed out that it could become a prison (May 1958). His heirs, the existentialists, continue to identify an "idealistic orientation" which, although it inhibits the pursuit of transient pleasure, makes a person "inauthentic" (Kobasa & Maddi 1983). The most obvious side-effect of an iron will is compulsiveness, arguably also a plague that grows proportionally as a society gets more sophisticated at self-control. Most psychotherapy deals with problems concerning overcontrol, described for instance by psychoanalysts as a punitive superego, by cognitive therapists as overgeneralization and magnification, and by gestalt therapists as dependence on cognitive maps (many summarized in Corsini 1984), rather than the simple inability to give up an impulse.

The intertemporal bargaining hypothesis predicts just such a potential for personal rules to grow pathologically. Reliance on this bargaining causes a decision to be worth as much or more as a precedent than it is in its own right. This does not necessarily imply that it is the wrong decision. On the contrary, you would think from the logic of summing discount curves that judging choices in whole categories rather than by themselves would have to improve your overall rate of reward (Figure 2a). Cooperation in a repetitive prisoner's dilemma would have to serve the players' long range interests, or else they would abandon it. How, then, can this cooperation ever become a prison?

The likeliest answer is that in everyday life a person can discern many possible principles in a given situation; and the way of grouping choices that finally inspires intertemporal cooperation need not be the most productive, because of the selective effect of distinctness: personal rules operate most effectively on distinct, countable goals. Thus, to a person who is afraid of her spontaneous wishes, a rule to maximize foreseeable wealth or to never spend money unnecessarily will be more reassuring than the assortment of softer rules and social incentives by which people usually arrange to control their spending. Likewise, a person who is chronically afraid that she will get too angry, will make or adopt narrow rules for conduct rather than relying on vague rules like putting herself in the other person's shoes. In such cases the person often knows that she is impairing her long range effectiveness, but cannot give up the guarantee that explicit rules supply.

So cooperation among successive motivational states does not necessarily bring the most reward in the long run. The mechanics of policing this cooperation may produce the intrapsychic equivalent of regimentation, which will increase your efficiency at reward-getting in the categories you have defined, but reduce your sensitivity to less well-marked kinds of reward. Even short of frank compulsiveness, the systemization that lets rules recruit motivation most effectively may undermine our longest range interests.

The attempt to optimize our prospects with personal rules confronts us with the paradox of definition — that to define a concept is to alter it, in this case toward something more formalized. If you conclude that you should maximize money, you become a miser; if you rule that you should minimize your vulnerability to emotional influence, you will develop the numbing insensitivity that clinicians have named alexithymia (Nemiah 1977); if you conclude that you should minimize risk, you become obsessively careful; and so forth. The logic of rules may come to so overshadow your responsiveness to current experience that your behavior becomes formal and inefficient. A miser's strict rules for thrift make her too rigid to optimize her chances in a competitive market, and even a daring financier undermines the productiveness of her capital if she rules that she must maximize each year's profit (Malekzadeh & Nahavandi 1987). Similarly, strict autonomy means shielding yourself against exploitation by others' ability to invoke your passions; but alexithymics cannot use the richest strategy available for maximizing emotional reward, the cultivation of human relationships (Ainslie 1995). Likewise, avoidance of danger at any cost is poor risk management.

In this way people who depend on willpower for impulse control are in danger of being coerced by logic that does not serve what they themselves regard as their best interests. Concrete rules dominate subtle intuitions; and even though you have a sense that you will regret having sold out to them, you face the immediate danger of succumbing to short-range urges like addictions if you do not. If you have not learned ways of categorizing long-range rewards that permit them to dominate systematic series of mid-range rewards, your mid-range interests will make you compulsive.

The proneness of intertemporal bargainers to fall into compulsions may explain some hitherto perplexing characteristics of addictive behavior. The robustness of suboptimal rules may sometimes let addictions serve long range interests. Better to be fat, you might think, than anorectic. Your will may become so confining that a pattern of regular lapses actually makes you better off in the long run. The lore of addictionology often attributes bingeing to a patient's inhibitedness in the rest of her life; her general overcontrol is said to set up periodic episodes of breaking loose. The model of intertemporal bargaining predicted by hyperbolic discount curves provides a specific rationale for this pattern: Rules that eliminate any large source of emotional reward will create a proportional motive for you to bypass or break those rules. If those rules have, in William James' phrase, "grown too narrow for the actual case" (James 1990/1896), even your long range interest will lie in partially escaping from them. Thus, personal rules that serve compulsion range interests can create alliances between long and short range interests. The person's occasional binge comes to serve as a corrective to the comparative sterility of such rules, a means of providing richer experiences than these rules allow while its transient nature still limits the damage it does. The longest range interest of an alcoholic who is too rigid when sober may be to tacitly foster the cycle of drunkenness and sobriety, rather than be continuously imprisoned by her rules.

Alcoholics are sometimes described who become nicer, or more genuinely creative, or more fully human when drunk. Furthermore, some addicts plan binges in advance. Such people may believe that their binges are undesirable — indeed, "rationality" will almost certainly dictate such a belief — but the therapists they hire find them mysteriously unresponsive to treatment. The patient who arranges for drinking several days in advance — who goes off the disulfiram that commits her to sickness if she drinks, for instance, or who brings bottles to her rehabilitation program for later use — cannot simply be yielding to a short range impulse. This is behavioral evidence that she experiences a rational plan like giving up drinking as a compulsion which, even at a distance, appears to need hedging, although she may be unable to report any such thing.

This phenomenon suggests why a simplistic policy of "the more willpower, the better" contradicts the experience of many addicts. To them, more willpower means less of the human qualities they value most in themselves. They are able to listen to reason only when reason, represented by personal rules, stops starving their own longest range prospects for emotional reward.

Some Discount Rates in Humans Appear to Be Negative — That is, Delayed Rewards May Be Valued More than Immediate Ones

A finding that might seem to strike at the heart of an internal marketplace model of choice is a preference for *more* delayed goods and *less* delayed punishments. It is not difficult to find human self-reports of preferences that seem to reflect such negative discounting in people. Subjects say that they would rather have $1,000,000 tomorrow, rather than immediately (Rachlin *et al.* 2000), and most individuals would prefer that a kiss with the movie star they find most attractive be delayed rather than immediate (Loewenstein 1987). Elster and Loewenstein call such reverse discounting "savoring": the process of "deriving positive utility from anticipation of desirable events" (Elster & Loewenstein 1992: 224). A related observation is that, when deciding on a sequence of rewards of various magnitudes, subjects generally prefer ascending order rather than the descending order predicted by a positive temporal discounting. One study had subjects imagine that they had won a prize of three free meals at three different restaurants: one mediocre, one quite good, and one world-class. The dinners were to be scheduled to occur on the first of the month over each of the next three months, with the only choice being their order. The modal response is to choose the sequence of ascending value (Loewenstein & Prelec 1993). Except in cases where there is a strong expectation that outcomes will generally descend (such as health across one's lifetime; Chapman 2000), people typically prefer to save the best for last.

As the Victorian economist Jevons said, "There is little doubt that, in minds of much intelligence and foresight, the greatest force of feeling and motive is what arises from the anticipation of the future" (Jevons 1871: 40, quoted by Elster & Loewenstein 1992: 223). The reason for savoring is clearly to increase pleasure. Utility theory has had little to say about the relationships of external events to the experience of pleasure, but there is at least some popular recognition that managing pleasure can be a matter of managing appetite. Our culture warns us not to eat dessert first or read ahead in a novel; indeed it often recommends "working up" an appetite. It has not told us why such practices should make a difference. However, the phenomenon of hyperbolic discounting suggests a hypothesis not only about savoring but about appetite generally. This is the a broader problem of premature satiation, discussion of which will suggest a rationale for savoring.

The Most Constant Rewards Often Lose their Rewarding Power, Even After Periods of Non-Occurrence when Appetite should Be Fresh

Rationality turns out to be less a matter of comparing the sizes of goods than of avoiding seductive derailments. The will, looked at as an intertemporal bargaining strategy, has costs of its own that detract from its value in achieving rationality. It is also limited in scope; purely mental processes options like paying attention and recalling memories, for instance, are probably chosen too quickly to be evaluated as precedents, and thus cannot be well controlled by will. This is a particularly serious limitation in a wealthy society, where physical needs are satisfied readily and most effort goes into pursuing various kinds of emotional satisfaction. The problem that hyperbolic discounting creates here is premature satiation; the solutions people find are apt to be even more costly, and seemingly irrational, than the compulsiveness that comes with willpower.

Hyperbolic discounting can be expected to attenuate many kinds of emotional satisfaction, according to the following logic:

- Rewards that are freely available will be limited by how much appetite you have for them, which often depends on deferring consumption of them;
- Hyperbolic discounting makes you innately impatient to increase your rate of consuming a reward, which often moves you to satiate your appetite for it prematurely (Figure 3a and b);
- You can pace your consumption of physical rewards through personal rules, but this will not work for rewards, like the emotions, that depend only on attention.
- To the extent that you cannot keep your attention from anticipating a familiar sequence of events, this familiarity alone will dissipate your appetite. The only protection from anticipation is for the events to be surprising;
- Premature satiation therefore weeds out emotions not cued by events that are adequately surprising.

The impatience for knowledge that is so adaptive in hostile environments spoils the enjoyment of sustained success, as emotion researcher Sylvan Tomkins noted:

> The paradox is that it is just those achievements which are most solid, which work best, and which continue to work that excite and reward us least. The price of skill is the loss of the experience of value — and of the zest for living (Tomkins 1978: 212).

In the absence of some factor that refreshes available appetite, ethologist Konrad Lorenz said:

> The normal rhythm of eating with enjoyment after having become really hungry, the enjoyment of any consummation after having strenuously striven for it, the joy in achieving success after toiling for it in near-despair — in short, the whole glorious amplitude of the waves of human emotions, all that makes

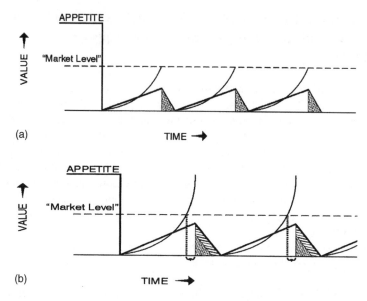

Figure 3: (a) Cycles of growing reward potential (rising straight lines) and actual consumption (gray areas) leading to satiety. Consumption begins when discounted value of expected consumption reaches the competitive market level. Hyperbolic discount curves of the total value of each act of consumption decline with delay from its anticipated onset (right to left as delay increases). (b) Increased reward (stripes) resulting from increased appetite when there is an obligatory delay in the moment of starting consumption from the moment of choice ("{" brackets); the choice to consume occurs when the discounted value of the delayed consumption reaches the market level.

> life worth living — is dampened down to a scarcely perceptible oscillation between scarcely perceptible tiny displeasures and pleasures. The result is an immeasurable boredom. [This is because] . . . the mechanisms equilibrating pleasure and displeasure are thrown off balance because civilized man lacks obstacles which force him to accept a healthy amount of painful, toilsome displeasure (Lorenz 1970: 355–357, brackets added).

Failure of appetite is familiar enough, but without hyperbolic discounting to explain why people don't accept that "healthy amount of painful, toilsome displeasure" it has not made motivational sense. Premature satiation emerges as a pervasive impulse that is increasingly important as a society gets efficient at satisfying appetites. Where willpower can be effective, as in the timing of consuming externally supplied goods, we would expect people to develop personal rules for cultivating appetite. In effect: "save the best for last," "don't take vacation days until you must use them or lose them," "don't consume something until you start to get diminishing returns from anticipation." The need to defend appetites from premature satiation explains the savoring that human subjects so often manifest, an apparent reversal of discounting that is actually a response to discounting. Where willpower cannot be effective, as when the goods are entirely emotional and appetite can be spoiled by mere anticipation, we are apt to see people adopt even subtler strategies that peg their emotions to surprises — gambling in its many, often subtle, forms — consideration of which is beyond the scope of this paper (see Ainslie 2001: 161–197).

Converse to the problem of premature satiation is the problem of dread, the tendency of anticipated pains to have more impact than imminent pains with the same dimensions. The majority of normal human subjects choose an immediate shock over an equally intense delayed shock[5] (Cook & Barnes 1964; Hare 1966a), and this tendency is most apparent when larger shocks are used (Hare 1966b). Similarly, negative discount rates in the domain of hypothetical losses have been observed in at least a portion of subjects (Chapman 1996; Chapman *et al.* 2001; Loewenstein 1987; van der Pol & Cairns 2001). Presumably, a week's postponement of a colonoscopy leaves us with both the pain of the procedure, plus the additional aversiveness of seven days of dread. Humans' preference for immediate aversive outcomes over less immediate ones has no documented analog in the Skinner box; like savoring, it seems to require a capacity for self-control. The phenomenon being controlled — the urge to rehearse the anticipated pain despite resulting distress in the present — is no more likely to respond to willpower than is premature satiation of anticipated emotional pleasure. The only discipline possible for the will is to hasten the cause of the distress and thus "get it over with."

Conclusions

Delay has a profound effect on the value of expected reward. In animal subjects the form of this effect is a highly reliable hyperbola. However, it is unlikely that the discount rates derived from human experiments similarly reveal the underlying relationship between delay and value. Mechanisms of self-control, in particular that by which choices take on heightened relevance as perceived precedents, can change the contingencies in unreported ways. The fact that discount rates in standard human experiments are so much lower than in animal experiments that it is a prima facie reason to suspect interposed cultural and cognitive layers of processing. The negative discount rates found in humans but not lower animals using some rewards and aversive experiences, and humans' reported preferences for ascending rewards when choosing a series, also point toward interposed control processes. In any case, the low correlation between discount rates across domains, noted earlier, indicates that delay experiments provide a highly imperfect measure of a person's general delay sensitivity.

Accordingly some authors are pessimistic about the existence of an underlying innate discount function. Indeed there is a movement to give up on the idea of constructing a general model of intertemporal choice. Roelofsma and Read write:

> The study of intertemporal choice is currently undergoing a change in emphasis, as has already occurred in the study of decision making under risk and uncertainty. Rather than searching for the holy grail of a single utility function, researchers now take the more pragmatic view that preferences are constructed based on the circumstances of their expression (Roelofsma & Read 2000: 172).

But this pessimism is premature. Although experiments elicit human behaviors toward delayed reward that are as variable as those in real life, there is good reason to believe that much of this variability results from exactly those strategic responses that are predicted by hyperbolic discounting. There are now good data supporting the intertemporal bargaining model of will, which transforms the task of impulse control from one of prior commitment to one of dealing with potential rationalizations. Furthermore, predicted problems with the use of will match clinical problems that are actually observed, including addicts' frequent rejection of binding commitments to sobriety. And the possibility of strongly motivated premature satiation of appetite provides what we believe to be the first explicit motivational theory for both the decline of emotional reward with familiarity and human countermeasures like savoring and gambling.

This is to argue that the preference patterns that have been described as anomalies for a theory of hyperbolic discounting are actually consistent with, and even predictive of, the implications of this theory. Hyperbolic curves cannot be substituted simply for exponential curves in an otherwise unchanged theory of maximizing expected utility. Hyperbolae imply temporary preferences that demand strategic responses, which with experience will weave a fabric of incentives much like that which interpersonal bargaining games have woven in societies. The addictions we deal with as therapists are embedded in this kind of incentive structure, and confront us with corresponding subtleties.

Notes

1. Most typically in behavioral economic experiments, the best fit discount parameter k (from Equation (1) or some variant) is used as the measure of individual discount rate. Myerson and colleagues have recently argued that area under the discount curve makes for a less theoretically loaded measure (Myerson et al. 2001).

2. To save money, some experimental procedures use probabilistically real money. Subjects may be given their selected preference for just one trial, chosen randomly after the experiment (Crean et al. 2000; Richards et al. 1999).

3. At least one study reported that smokers had *lower* temporal discount rates (Chesson & Viscusi 2000). This study used complex stimuli, requiring subjects to both choose and provide indifference amounts between some amount of money delivered at a set time and another amount of money that would be delivered at one of two possible times, according to some specified probability. The study yielded several findings that are counter to other reported studies — lower temporal discounting in (1) smokers; (2) lower income subjects; (3) younger subjects; and (4) subjects with the most education.

4. The terms of the prisoner's dilemma must be modified slightly to deal with the fact that future selves cannot retaliate strategically against past selves (see Ainslie 2001: 90–94).

5. Interestingly, subjects with Antisocial Personality Disorder, relative to normals, had a greater preference to choose more delayed shock (Hare 1966a).

References

Ainslie, G. (1974). Impulse control in pigeons. *Journal of the Experimental Analysis of Behavior*, *21*(3), 485–489.

Ainslie, G. (1975). Specious reward: A behavioral theory of impulsiveness and impulse control. *Psychological Bulletin*, *82*, 463–496.

Ainslie, G. (1992). *Picoeconomics: The strategic interaction of successive motivational states within the person.* New York, NY: Cambridge University Press.

Ainslie, G. (1995). A utility-maximizing mechanism for vicarious reward: Comments on Julian Simons "Interpersonal allocation continuous with intertemporal allocation". *Rationality and Society, 7*, 393–403.

Ainslie, G. (1996). Studying self-regulation the hard way. *Psychological Inquiry, 7*, 16–20.

Ainslie, G. (2001). *Breakdown of will.* New York: Cambridge University Press.

Ainslie, G., & Haendel, V. (1983). The motives of the will. In: E. Gottheil, K. Druley, T. Skodola, & H. Waxman (Eds), *Etiology aspects of alcohol and drug abuse.* Springfield: Charles C. Thomas.

Ainslie, G., & Herrnstein, R. J. (1981). Preference reversal and delayed reinforcement. *Animal Learning & Behavior, 9*(4), 476–482.

Ainslie, G., & Monterosso, J. (2003). Building blocks of self-control: Increased tolerance for delay with bundled rewards. *Journal of the Experimental Analysis of Behavior, 79*(1), 37–48.

Anthony, J., Warner, L., & Kessler, R. (1994). Comparative epidemiology of dependence on tobacco, alcohol, controlled substances, and inhalants: Basic findings from the National Comorbidity Survey. *Experimental and Clinical Psychopharmacology, 2*, 244–268.

Aristotle (1984). *The complete works of Aristotle.* Princeton: Princeton University Press.

Bain, A. (1859/1886). *The emotions and the will.* New York: Appleton.

Baum, W., & Rachlin, H. (1969). Choice as time allocation. *Journal of the Experimental Analysis of Behavior, 12*, 861–874.

Becker, H. S. (1960). Notes on the concept of commitment. *American Journal of Sociology, 66*, 32–40.

Benzion, U., Rapoport, A., & Yagil, J. (1989). Discount rates inferred from decisions: An experimental study. *Management Science, 35*, 270–284.

Bickel, W., Odum, A., & Madden, G. (1999). Impulsivity and cigarette smoking: Delay discounting in current, never, and ex-smokers. *Psychopharmacology, 146*, 447–454.

Bohm, P. (1994). Time preference and preference reversal among experienced subjects: The effects of real payments. *Economic Journal, 104*(427), 1370–1378.

Bretteville-Jensen, A. L. (1999). Addiction and discounting. *Journal of Health Economics, 18*(4), 393–407.

Cairns, J., & van der Pol, M. (2000). Valuing future private and social benefits: The discounted utility model vs. hyperbolic discounting models. *Journal of Economic Psychology, 21*(2), 191–205.

Chapman, G. B. (1996). Temporal discounting and utility for health and money. *Journal of Experimental Psychology: Learning, Memory, & Cognition, 22*(3), 771–791.

Chapman, G. B. (2000). Preferences for improving and declining sequences of health outcomes. *Journal of Behavioral Decision Making, 13*(2), 203–218.

Chapman, G. B., Brewer, N. T. *et al.* (2001). Value for the future and preventive health behavior. *Journal of Experimental Psychology: Applied, 7*(3), 235–250.

Chapman, G., & Elstein, A. (1995). Valuing the future: Temporal discounting of health and money. *Medical Decision Making, 15*, 373–386.

Chesson, H., & Viscusi, W. K. (2000). The heterogeneity of time-risk tradeoffs. *Journal of Behavioral Decision Making, 13*(2), 251–258.

Cook, J., & Barnes, L. (1964). Choice of delay of inevitable shock. *Journal of Abnormal & Social Psychology, 68*(6), 669–672.

Corsini, R. J. (1984). *Current psychotherapies* (3rd ed.). Itasca, IL: Peacock.

Corulla, W. J. (1987). A psychometric investigation of the Sensation Seeking Scale Form V and its relation to the 1.7 Impulsiveness questionnaire. *Personality and Individual Differences, 8*, 651–658.

Crean, J. P., de Wit, H., & Richards, J. B. (2000). Reward discounting as a measure of impulsive behavior in a psychiatric outpatient population. *Experimental and Clinical Psychopharmacology, 8*(2), 155–162.

Deluty, M. (1978). Self-control and impulsiveness involving aversive events. *Behavior Analysis Letters, 3*, 213–219.

Elster, J., & Loewenstein, G. (1992). Utility from memory and anticipation. In: G. Lowenstein, & J. Elster (Eds), *Choice over time* (pp. 213–234). New York: Russell Sage Foundation.

Forzano, L. B., & Logue, A. W. (1992). Predictors of adult humans' self-control and impulsiveness for food reinforcers. *Appetite, 19*(1), 33–47.

Forzano, L. B., & Logue, A. W. (1994). Self-control in adult humans: Comparison of qualitatively different reinforcers. *Learning and Motivation, 25*(1), 65–82.

Freud, S. (1914/1956). On the history of the psychoanalytic movement. In: J. Strachey, & A. Freud (Eds), *The standard edition of the complete psychological works of Sigmund Freud* (Vol. 14). London: Hogarth.

Fuchs, V. R. (1982). *Time preferences and health: An exploratory study.* E. A. of Health.

Grace, R. (1996). Choice between fixed and variable delays to reinforcement in the adjusting-delay procedure and concurrent chains. *Journal of Experimental Psychology: Animal Processes, 22*, 362–383.

Grant, S., Contoreggi, C., & London, E. D. (2000). Drug abusers show impaired performance in a laboratory test of decision making. *Neuropsychologia, 38*(8), 1180–1187.

Green, L., Myerson, J., & McFadden, E. (1997). Rate of temporal discounting decreases with amount of reward. *Memory and Cognition, 25*(5), 715–723.

Green, L., & Rachlin, H. (1996). Commitment using punishment. *Journal of the Experimental Analysis of Behavior, 65*(3), 593–601.

Hare, R. D. (1966a). Preference for delay of shock as a function of its intensity and probability. *Psychonomic Science, 5*(10), 393–394.

Hare, R. D. (1966b). Psychopathy and choice of immediate vs. delayed punishment. *Journal of Abnormal Psychology, 71*(1), 25–29.

Heyman, G. M., & Tanz, L. (1995). How to teach a pigeon to maximize overall reinforcement rate. *Journal of the Experimental Analysis of Behavior, 64*, 277–297.

James, W. (1890). *The principles of psychology.* New York.

James, W. (1990/1896). The moral philosopher and the moral life. In: *The will to believe and other essays.* Magnolia, MA: Peter Smit.

Jevons, W. (1871). *The theory of political economy.* London: Macmillan.

Kahneman, D. (1965). Control of spurious association and the reliability of the controlled variable. *Psychological Bulletin, 64*(5), 326–329.

Kahneman, D., Slovic, P., & Tversk, A. (Eds) (1982). *Judgment under uncertainty: Heuristics and biases.* New York: Cambridge University Press.

Kant, I. (1793/1960). *Religion within the limits of reason alone.* New York: Harper and Row.

Kirby, K. N., & Guastello, B. (2001). Making choices in anticipation of similar future choices can increase self-control. *Journal of Experimental Psychology: Applied, 7*(2), 154–164.

Kirby, K. N., & Herrnstein, R. J. (1995). Preference reversals due to myopic discounting of delayed reward. *Psychological Science, 6*(2), 83–89.

Kirby, K. N., & Marakovic, N. N. (1996). Delay-discounting probabilistic rewards: Rates decrease as amounts increase. *Psychonomic Bulletin and Review, 3*(1), 100–104.

Kirby, K. N., Petry, N. M., & Bickel, W. K. (1999). Heroin addicts have higher discount rates for delayed rewards than non-drug-using controls. *Journal of Experimental Psychology: General, 128*(1), 78–87.

Kobasa, S. C., & Maddi, S. R. (1983). Existential personality theory. In: R. J. Corsini, & A. J. Marsella (Eds), *Personality theories, research and assessment.* Itasca, IL: Peacock Publishers.

Korobkin, R. B., & Ulen, T. S. (2000). Law and behavioral science: Removing the rationality assumption from law and economics. *California Law Review, 88*, 1051–1144.

Kosten, T. R. (1998). Pharmacotherapy of cerebral ischemia in cocaine dependence. *Drug Alcohol Depend, 49*(2), 133–144.

Laibson, D. (1997). Golden eggs and hyperbolic discounting. *Quarterly Journal of Economics, 62*, 443–479.

Loewenstein, G. (1987). Anticipation and the valuation of delayed consumption. *Economic Journal, 97*(387), 666–684.

Loewenstein, G., & Elster, J. (Eds) (1992). *Choice over time.* New York: Russell Sage Foundation.

Loewenstein, G., & Prelec, D. (1992). Anomalies in intertemporal choice: Evidence and interpretation. *Quarterly Journal of Economics, 107*, 573–597.

Loewenstein, G., & Prelec, D. (1993). Preferences for sequences of outcomes. *Psychological Review, 100*(1), 91–108.

Loewenstein, G., & Thaler, R. (1989). Intertemporal choice. *Journal of Economic Perspectives, 3*, 181–193.

Logue, A. W., King, G. R., Chavarro, A., & Volpe, J. S. (1990). Matching and maximizing in a self-control paradigm using human subjects. *Learning and Motivation, 21*(3), 340–368.

Logue, A. W., Pena-Correal, T. E., Rodriguez, M. L., & Kabela, E. (1986). Self-control in adult humans: Variation in positive reinforcer amount and delay. *Journal of the Experimental Analysis of Behavior, 46*(2), 159–173.

London, E. D., Cascella, N. G., Wong, D. F., Phillips, R. L., Dannals, R. F., Links, J. M., Herning, R., Grayson, R., Jaffe, J. H., & Wagner, H. N. (1990). Cocaine-induced reduction of glucose utilization in human brain: A study using positron emission tomography. *Archives of General Psychiatry, 47*(6), 567–574.

Lorenz, K. (1970). The enmity between generations and its probable ethological causes. *Psychoanalytic Review, 57*, 333–377.

Madden, G. J., Bickel, W. K., & Jacobs, E. A. (1999). Discounting of delayed rewards in opioid-dependent outpatients: Exponential or hyperbolic discounting functions? *Experimental and Clinical Psychopharmacology, 7*(3), 284–293.

Madden, G. J., Petry, N. M., Badger, G. L., & Bickel, W. K. (1997). Impulsive and self-control choices in opioid-dependent patients and non-drug-using control participants: Drug and monetary rewards. *Experimental and Clinical Psychopharmacology, 5*(3), 256–262.

Malekzadeh, A. R., & Nahavandi, A. (1987). Merger mania: Who wins? Who loses? *Journal of Business Strategy, 8*, 76–79.

May, R. (1958). The origins and existential movement in psychology. In: E. A. May, & H. F. Ellenberger (Eds), *Existence: A new dimension in psychiatry and psychology* (pp. 3–36). New York: Basic Books.

Mazur, J. E. (1984). Tests of an equivalence rule for fixed and variable reinforcer delays. *Journal of Experimental Psychology: Animal Behavior Processes, 10*(4), 426–436.

Mazur, J. E. (1997). Choice, delay, probability, and conditioned reinforcement. *Animal Learning and Behavior, 25*, 131–147.

Mazur, J. E. (2000). Tradeoffs among delay, rate, and amount of reinforcement. *Behavioral Processes, 49*(1), 1–10.

Mazur, J. E. (2001). Hyperbolic value addition and general models of animal choice. *Psychological Review, 108*, 96–112.

Meehl, P. E. (1970). Nuisance variables and the ex post facto design. In: M. Radner, & S. Winokur (Eds), *Analysis of theories and methods of physics and osychology* (Vol. 4, p. 402). Minneapolis: University of Minnesota Press.

Mischel, W., & Ebbesen, E. B. (1970). Attention in delay of gratification. *Journal of Personality and Social Psychology, 16*(2), 329–337.

Mischel, W., & Grusec, J. (1967). Waiting for rewards and punishments: Effects of time and probability on choice. *Journal of Personality and Social Psychology, 5*(1), 24–31.

Mischel, W., Grusec, J., & Master, J. C. (1969). Effects of expected delay time on the subjective value of rewards and punishments. *Journal of Personality and Social Psychology, 11*(4), 363–373.

Mischel, H., & Mischel, W. (1983). The development of children's knowledge of self-control strategies. *Child Development, 54*, 603–619.

Mischel, W., & Moore, B. (1980). The role of ideation in voluntary delay for symbolically-presented rewards. *Cognitive Therapy and Research, 4*, 211–221.

Mitchell, S. (1999). Measures of impulsivity in cigarette smokers and non-smokers. *Psychopharmacology, 146*, 455–464.

Monterosso, J., Ainslie, G., Toppi-Mullen, P., & Gault, B. (2002). The fragility of cooperation: An empirical study employing false-feedback in a sequential iterated prisoner's dilemma. *Journal of Economic Psychology, 23*, 437–448.

Monterosso, J., Ehrman, R., Napier, K., O'Brien, C., & Childress, A. (2001). Three decision-making tasks in cocaine-dependent patients: Do they measure the same construct? *Addiction, 96*(12), 1825–1837.

Mowrer, O. H., & Ullman, A. D. (1945). Time as a determinant in integrative learning. *Psychological Review, 52*, 61–90.

Myerson, J., & Green, L. (1995). Discounting of delayed rewards: Models of individual choice. *Journal of the Experimental Analysis of Behavior, 64*, 263–276.

Myerson, J., Green, L., & Warusawith, M. (2001). Area under the curve as a measure of discounting. *Journal of the Experimental Analysis of Behavior, 76*(2), 235–243.

Navarick, D. (1982). Negative reinforcement and choice in humans. *Learning and Motivation, 13*, 361–377.

Navarick, D. J. (1986). Human impulsivity and choice: A challenge to traditional operant methodology. *Psychological Record, 36*(3), 343–356.

Navarick, D. J. (2001). Control of impulsive choice through biasing instructions. *Psychological Record, 51*(4), 549–560.

Nemiah, J. C. (1977). Alexithymia: Theoretical considerations. *Psychotherapy and Psychosomatics, 28*, 199–206.

Odum, A. L., Madden, G. J., Badger, G. J., & Bickel, W. K. (2000). Needle sharing in opioid-dependent outpatients: Psychological processes underlying risk. *Drug and Alcohol Dependence, 60*(3), 259–266.

Offer, A. (1998). Epidemics of abundance: Overeating and slimming in the USA and Britain since the 1950s. Discussion Papers in Economic and Social History 25.

Orne, M. T. (1962). On the social psychology of the psychological experiment: With particular reference to demand characteristics and their implications. *American Psychologist, 17*(10), 776–783.

Parker, J. D. A., Bagby, R. M., & Webster, C. (1993). Domains of the impulsivity construct: A factor analytic investigation. *Personality and Individual Differences, 15*, 267–274.

Petry, N. M. (2001). Delay discounting of money and alcohol in actively using alcoholics, currently abstinent alcoholics, and controls. *Psychopharmacology, 154*(3), 243–250.

Rachlin, H., Brown, J., & Cross, D. (2000). Discounting in judgments of delay and probability. *Journal of Behavioral Decision Making, 13*(2), 145–159.

Richards, J. B., Zhang, L., Mitchell, S., & de Wit, H. (1999). Delay or probability discounting in a model of impulsive behavior: Effect of alcohol. *Journal of the Experimental Analysis of Behavior, 71*(2), 121–143.

Roelofsma, P. H. M. P. (1996). Modeling intertemporal choices: An anomaly approach. *Acta Psychologica, 93*, 5–22.

Roelofsma, P. H. M. P., & Read, D. (2000). Intransitive intertemporal choice. *Journal of Behavioral Decision Making, 13*(2), 161–177.

Rogers, R. D., Everitt, B. J., Baldacchino, A., Blackshaw, A. J., Swainson, R., Wynne, K., Baker, N. B., Hunter, J., Carthy, T., Booker, E., London, M., Deakin, J. F., Sahakian, B. J., & Robbins, T. W. (1999). Dissociable deficits in the decision-making cognition of chronic amphetamine abusers, opiate abusers, patients with focal damage to prefrontal cortex, and tryptophan-depleted normal volunteers: Evidence for monoaminergic mechanisms. *Neuropsychopharmacology, 20*(4), 322–339.

Shefrin, H. M., & Thaler, R. H. (1988). The behavioral life-cycle hypothesis. *Economic Inquiry, 26*, 609–643.

Siegel, E., & Rachlin, H. (1996). Soft commitment: Self-control achieved by response persistence. *Journal of the Experimental Analysis of Behavior, 64*, 117–128.

Simpson, C. A., & Vuchinich, R. E. (2000). Reliability of a measure of temporal discounting. *Psychological Record, 50*(1), 3–16.

Sjoberg, L., & Johnson, T. (1978). Trying to give up smoking: A study of volitional breakdowns. *Addictive Behaviors, 3*, 149–167.

Sully, J. (1884). *Outlines of psychology*. New York: Appleton.

Thaler, R. (1981). Some empirical evidence on dynamic inconsistency. *Economic Letters, 8*, 201–207.

Thaler, R. (1990). Anomalies: Saving, fungibility, and mental accounts. *Journal of Economic Perspectives, 4*, 193–205.

Thaler, R. (1991). *Quasi rational economics*. New York: Russell Sage.

Tomkins, S. S. (1978). Script theory: Differential magnification of affects. *Nebraska Symposium on Motivation, 26*, 201–236.

van der Pol, M., & Cairns, J. (2001). Estimating time preferences for health using discrete choice experiments. *Social Science and Medicine, 52*(9), 1459–1470.

Volkow, N. D., Fowler, J. S., Wolf, A. P., Hitzemann, R., Dewey, S., Bendriem, B., Alpert, R., & Hoff, A. (1991). Changes in brain glucose metabolism in cocaine dependence and withdrawal [see comments]. *The American Journal of Psychiatry, 148*(5), 621–626.

Volkow, N. D., Mullani, N., Gould, K. L., Adler, S., & Krajewski, K. (1988). Cerebral blood flow in chronic cocaine users: A study with positron emission tomography. *The British Journal of Psychiatry, 152*, 641–648.

Vuchinich, R. E., & Simpson, C. A. (1998). Hyperbolic temporal discounting in social drinkers and problem drinkers. *Experimental and Clinical Psychopharmacology, 6*(3), 292–305.

Vuchinich, R. E., & Tucker, J. A. (1988). Contributions from behavioral theories of choice to an analysis of alcohol abuse. *Journal of Abnormal Psychology, 97*(2), 181–195.

Wallace, C. (1979). The effects of delayed rewards, social pressure, and frustration on the response of opiate addicts. *NIDA Monograph Series, 25*, 6–25.

Wogar, M. A., Bradshaw, C. M., & Szabadi, E. (1993). Effect of lesions of the ascending 5-hydroxytryptaminergic pathways on choice between delayed reinforcers. *Psychopharmacology, 111*(2), 239–243.

Comments on Ainslie and Monterosso

William R. Miller

As a psychologist who studies ambivalence, I must confess to experiencing some as I reviewed this very rational paper and others presented at this conference. On the one hand, I find it fascinating to view behavior through lenses from other disciplines, to see how they may be useful in resolving puzzles of human nature. Economic models such as those being discussed here seem to be promising in this regard. On the other hand, I find myself dissatisfied with such mechanistic models of behavior, which seem in their economy to be missing something fundamental about human nature. Reliable rat and pigeon principles tend to break down somewhere in the human cortex. My remarks will therefore steer a course about halfway between hyperbolic adulation and outright discounting.

The Promise of Economic Models

Clearly approach-avoidance conflict is fundamental to the phenomenon of addiction, and economists surely have much to teach us about factors that attract or deter people to spend their time and money in particular ways. One of the entrapping elements of single or double approach-avoidance conflict is that the gradient of reward changes with proximity. When being torn between two lovers, as the person draws closer to one of them, that lover's flaws become more apparent while the allure of the other increases. Even with one relationship, absence can make the heart grow fonder, whereas prolonged proximity may throw cold water on the fire. The concept of hyperbolic discounting is one component of this conflict paradigm, suggesting that with proximity, allure can increase dramatically, perhaps irresistibly, much as magnets are drawn to each other once they come within critical range. Proximity superheats utility. Yet at the same time there are processes at work by which distance may also *enhance* utility. Abstinence can make the heart grow fonder. The abstainer savors thinking about a drink, and any attempts *not* to think about it paradoxically enhance the obsession. Being conflicted is a common, even defining characteristic of addictive behavior (Miller & Rollnick 2002).

As Drs Ainslie & Monterosso recognize, such an economic model of human behavior must consider a daunting complexity of variables that affect the steepness of discounting. The devaluing of delayed reward varies in part as a trait (e.g. delay of gratification is a characteristic that is under-represented among people with substance use disorders), but it also varies within the individual across time and rewards. The utility gradient for any particular reward is affected by experience, satiety, and the other reinforcers with which it is competing. For dependent people, the utility of the next dose can increase with each dose. The use of "extrapsychic" devices such as disulfiram or naltrexone can affect utility gradients, but so do higher cognitive processes of valuing. I often cite David Premack's example of a smoker who:

> dates his quitting [smoking] from a day on which he had gone to pick up his children at the city library. A thunderstorm greeted him as he arrived there; and at the same time a search of his pockets disclosed a familiar problem: he was out of cigarettes. Glancing back at the library, he caught a glimpse of his children stepping out in the rain, but he continued around the corner, certain that he could find a parking space, rush in, buy the cigarettes, and be back before the children got seriously wet. The view of himself as a father who would 'actually leave the kids in the rain while he ran after cigarettes' was . . . humiliating, and he quit smoking (Premack 1970: 115).

Reward value fell dramatically as smoking suddenly took on new meaning. Nothing else had changed. The man had learned no new coping skills. No actual contingencies were altered. No reconditioning occurred. There was no reduction in his nicotine dependence level. Yet in the twinkling of an eye he became a non-smoker.

The Limitations of Economic Models

To some extent, the math can work in economic models. What troubles me about them, and indeed about most of the models of behavior within my own discipline of psychology, is the extent to which they construe the human person as a closed system, operating by rational and lawful principles with, perhaps, a small error term for random chaos. To turn a phrase from Ainslie and Monterosso, reductionism is a plague that grows proportionally as our society gets more sophisticated at controlling human behavior. We come to experience and conceptualize ourselves as powerless victims of mechanism, and thereby enter into a self-fulfilling prophecy (Fromm 1941).

Some years ago the eminent learning theorist, Frank Logan, gave the keynote address to the International Conference on Treatment of Addictive Behaviors. He offered a brilliant and encyclopedic review of research on animal self-administration of alcohol (including one ill-advised study of the effects of intoxication in elephants). He concluded that one needs nothing more than animal learning models to explain how people get trapped in addiction, but that there is no adequate animal model of recovery (Logan 1993). Animal learning principles describe the dilemma but not its resolution. To understand how people escape from addiction — be it in treatment, in Alcoholics Anonymous, or in the natural course of life events — one must turn to that which is uniquely human, to the higher-order processes of the human mind.

This brings us to the phenomena of agency, of the capacity for higher-order override of our animal nature (Howard 1986). It is the "you" noun in sentences where the verb's object is your self, your behavior, your appetite, your attention. It is the "self" in "self-control." With increased interest in and research on the automaticity of behavior

(Bargh & Ferguson 2000), human agency is sometimes dismissed as metaphoric, even though it is utterly self-evident to human beings (including most behavioral scientists) and in courts of law. To leave agency out of the equation when studying addictive behavior is like trying to understand traffic patterns or road rage by scrutinizing the automobile.

I also have several problems with the dominant model of *homo economicus* as a rational self-interested maximizer. First of these is the rather dubious assumption that human beings are rational, an assumption easily belied by spending a few hours in a psychotherapy clinic or a psychology department faculty meeting. Second is the dismal assumption that human beings are driven only, or even primarily by self-interest, which is but one vector in the cross-culturally consistent structure of values (Schwartz 1992). Third, as pointed out by Ainslie & Monterosso, is the fact that humans are not particularly efficient maximizers, at least when the criterion is self-interest.

Chief among human failings when it comes to efficient maximization of personal gain is the annoying tendency to guide one's behavior in accordance with higher-order principles that are little compromised by current contingencies. Rule-governed behavior is sometimes castigated by radical behaviorists as insufficiently responsive to extant contingencies. In other contexts there is a different term for governing one's behavior by higher-order principles that are minimally responsive to fluctuating material contingencies. It is called *character*.

I have long been interested in the phenomenon of "living as if," that is, behaving as though reality were different than its current state (Miller 1985). This is not a particularly good idea when dealing with physical laws; living as if one can fly will not help a jumper to do so. When it comes to complex social contingencies, however, living as if has a way of altering reality. This is the genius of Gandhi and Martin Luther King, the magic of *My Fair Lady* and *The Man of La Mancha*, and the wisdom behind the A.A. aphorism, "Fake it till you make it."

Empirical studies of change, including some unexpected findings in my own work, also offer ample reason to question mechanistic models (Miller 2000). It was the puzzle of how brief interventions could possibly work so well that led me to motivational interviewing. How is it that sitting with a listener for a single session can trigger change in addictive behaviors that have persisted for years despite substantial aversive consequences? My psycholinguist colleague, Paul Amrhein, has been analyzing client language in motivational interviewing, and now has persuasive evidence that the active ingredient is a change in client *commitment*. No actual contingencies have changed, but clients leave the session voicing stronger need, ability, and intention to change, and the pattern of their commitment language predicts their subsequent substance use (see Amrhein *et al.* in press). In sum, they have done the same thing that self-changers report when asked how they did it: they *decided*.

We have also been studying the phenomenon of *quantum change*: sudden, dramatic, and seemingly permanent transformations of the Ebenezer Scrooge variety (Miller & C'de Baca 2001). Decades later, quantum changers still remember their experience quite vividly, and speak of having passed through a one-way door. This is what happened to Bill Wilson, co-founder of A.A. (Kurtz 1979), and it is much more common than one might guess. For people previously struggling with addictions, a common report is of a sudden and permanent loss of desire to drink, of craving to use. In essence, within a span of minutes or hours, the person's *identity* changed from addict to abstainer. It is not merely behavior change, they tell us. Unlike many who struggle with addictive behaviors, quantum changers may have no real concern about impending relapse. They also have little or no sense of having done it themselves, of coming to a conclusion or exerting will power, of maximizing self-interest. They were changed suddenly, utterly, permanently, and remain puzzled as to how it happened. This was a topic of considerable interest to William James (1902).

Finally, there are the puzzling findings of treatment outcome research in the addiction field. Why is it that the same treatment, when delivered by different therapists, has dramatically different outcomes (Najavits & Weiss 1994)? Why is it that therapist empathy is such a potent determinant of client outcomes (Miller 2000)? Why is it that the dose of treatment received, when studied in controlled trials, is largely unrelated to behavioral outcomes, while the voluntary length of stay in treatment is a reasonably good prognostic sign? Why is it that the teaching of behavioral coping skills has one of the strongest track records in addiction treatment research, yet outcomes appear to be unrelated to whether or not clients actually learn the target skills? (Morgenstern & Longabaugh 2000). And why is it, if people are rational maximizers of self-interest, that behavioral outcomes are so spectacularly unresponsive to education about consequences or confrontation with reality? (Miller & Wilbourne 2002).

I don't claim to have the answers to these questions, and I am always interested in models that may help us to account for more of the variance in change. I look forward to savoring the remaining papers and asking myself two questions: whether these economic models are something more than another metaphor to describe addictive behavior, and what such models might teach us about addiction that we didn't already know.

References

Amrhein, P. C., Miller, W. R., Yahne, C. E., Palmer, M., & Fulcher, L. (in press). Client commitment language during motivational interviewing predicts drug use outcomes. *Journal of Consulting and Clinical Psychology.*

Bargh, J. A., & Ferguson, M. J. (2000). Beyond behaviorism: On the automaticity of higher mental processes. *Psychological Bulletin, 126*, 925–945.

Fromm, E. (1941). *Escape from freedom.* New York: Avon Books.

Howard, G. S. (1986). *Dare we develop a human science?* Notre Dame, IN: Academic Publications.

James, W. (1902). *The varieties of religious experience: A study in human nature.* Cambridge, MA: Harvard University Press.

Kurtz, E. (1979). *Not God: A history of Alcoholics Anonymous.* Center City, Minnesota: Hazelden.

Logan, F. A. (1993). Animal learning and motivation and addictive drugs. *Psychological Reports, 73*, 291–306.

Miller, W. R. (1985). *Living as if.* Philadelphia: Westminster Press.

Miller, W. R. (2000). Rediscovering fire: Small interventions, large effects. *Psychology of Addictive Behaviors, 14*, 6–18.

Miller, W. R., & C'de Baca, J. (2001). *Quantum change: When epiphanies and sudden insights transform ordinary lives.* New York: Guilford Press.

Miller, W. R., & Rollnick, S. (2002). *Motivational interviewing: Preparing people for change* (2nd ed.). New York: Guilford Press.

Miller, W. R., & Wilbourne, P. L. (2002). Mesa Grande: A methodological analysis of clinical trials of treatments for alcohol use disorders. *Addiction, 97,* 265–277.

Morgenstern, J., & Longabaugh, R. (2000). Cognitive-behavioral treatment for alcohol dependence: A review of evidence for its hypothesized mechanisms of action. *Addiction, 95,* 1475–1490.

Najavits, L. M., & Weiss, R. D. (1994). Variations in therapist effectiveness in the treatment of patients with substance use disorders: An empirical review. *Addiction, 89,* 679–688.

Premack, D. (1970). Mechanisms of self-control. In: W. A. Hunt (Ed.), *Learning mechanisms in smoking* (pp. 107–123). Chicago: Aldine.

Schwartz, S. H. (1992). Universals in the content and structure of values: Theoretical advances and empirical tests in 20 countries. *Advances in Experimental Social Psychology, 25,* 1–65.

Reply to Miller

George Ainslie and John Monterosso

We agree with most of Dr. Miller's points: being conflicted is a defining characteristic of addictive behavior; people are not "powerless victims of mechanism"; escape from addiction depends on the higher order processes of the human mind; human beings are often not rational and often not driven by self-interest, which in any case is not the same thing as rationality; their behavior sometimes changes in quantum leaps; the progress of psychotherapy is not proportional to the ostensible determinants of this progress; and (incidentally) Frank Logan, GA's first teacher in psychology when both were at Yale, was a brilliant researcher and theorist.

We do not share Dr. Miller's pessimism about reconciling the higher mental processes with reductionism. True, there is a well-entrenched dichotomy between "animal learning principles" and "higher-order processes"; but the "higher-order override of our animal nature" may not be so much a matter of rising above our animal nature as of riding it, as someone might ride a horse — a figure used by both Freud and the great neurologist Paul McLean. That is, we may have to go where our horse wants to go, and the skill of riding may be that of getting our horse to want to go where we do. Of course, the rider, the "you noun," might conceivably have a separate, non-animal nature, and might dwell in a black box that is impenetrable to science and understandable only empathically. However, the finding of seemingly basic hyperbolic discounting suggests a more parsimonious model, one in which the rider grows organically from the horse. This model does not belittle the role of higher-order, autonomous agency. On the contrary, it argues against the possibility of either predicting human choice from a knowledge of external options or of controlling this choice by manipulating these options.

The key lies in understanding the person, not as a passive consumer in a market economy, but as a market economy in her own right — a population of partially conflicting interests in a limited-warfare relationship with one another (Schelling 1960: 53–80), which make decisions somewhat with a view to influencing each other. We argue that, just as economics came to understand more complex financial transactions when it used game theory to analyze them strategically (Smith 1992), a strategic approach can let psychology combine "animal learning principles" to describe how a very intelligent horse can come to generate a rider. That the rider never replaces the horse, but only brokers its incentives, is fated by the relentless motivational pressure from hyperbolic discount curves.

The distinguishing features of the rider are foresight and the flexibility to see its current choices as predictive of future ones. The mechanism of will that we presented here meets Dr. Miller's test of being "uniquely human" — GA tried and failed to find evidence that pigeons which improved their delay tolerance were using their current choices as cues predicting long range reward (unpublished data). In this model the will is not controlled by external incentives (what we take as Dr. Miller's "closed system") with "a small error term for random chaos." Rather, it is chaotic in the technical sense (Ayers 1997): its choices are fed back recursively, so that their implications for future choice may be the greatest determinant of which ones will be final. If decisions were randomly chaotic, they would be experienced as "more like epileptic seizures than free responsible choices" (Kane 1989: 231). However, in the recursive kind of chaos caused by intertemporal bargaining, a person's choice is sensitively dependent on her own interpretation of that choice itself, which, we argue, should engender a feeling of owning the choice (see Ainslie 2001: 129–134).

Such sensitive dependence will sometimes lead to the quantum change that Dr. Miller describes: a chance juxtaposition on a rainy day that reveals smoking as a dangerously coercive motive suddenly makes the act a more damaging precedent, that is, one which imperils a greater stake; given this interpretation, the father's subsequent act of smoking would damage his will proportionately more, by the abstinence violation effect (e.g. Marlatt & Gordon 1980). The will is not, then, a "powerless victim of mechanism," except in the general sense that all phenomena have causes. And it is certainly not a mere metaphor.

The premature satiation hypothesis that we described in the last part of the present paper suggests fixes for Dr. Miller's remaining two problems with maximizing mechanisms: elementary strategic thinking will lead a person to empathize with others, and to construct beliefs beyond the objective evidence for them. This reasoning is developed in Ainslie (1995, 2001: 161–197), and is only sketched here:

Maximal satisfaction from otherwise freely available emotional rewards depends on their deferral and the consequent build-up of appetite for them. Hyperbolic discount curves create a relentless urge to harvest these rewards prematurely. Therefore, unless people peg their emotions to occasions that are both optimally *un*responsive to their current wishes and optimally surprising, their emotional lives will have the highly satiated quality of daydreams. That is, we have to keep our appetites fresh by gambling. The richest source of external occasions to gamble on is the apparent experience of other people, creating an incentive to "put ourselves in their shoes." Emotions that we generate by the occasion of other people's emotions avoid the drawback of arbitrary control and thus stay fresh. Here is a mechanism for vicarious experience as a primary good, rather than some kind of ploy; whether a theorist wants to call the pursuit of this good "self-interest" is a matter of taste.

By similar logic, performing tasks efficiently often means getting done too soon for optimal emotional arousal. Merely conveying facts to a patient about substance abuse, for instance, need not entail any emotional engagement. Where therapeutic change depends on this engagement, the patient, and probably the therapist, must believe in the importance of a longer, indirect task that keeps them appropriately occupied while empathy develops. This, we suspect, accounts for the profusion of comparably effective schools of psychotherapy that each claim exclusive validity, and that succeed even when their supposed mechanisms are disproven.

We agree with Dr. Miller that the most effective psychotherapy depends on the therapist's empathic engagement with, rather than technical understanding of, the addict or other patient. Still, advancing the science of motivational conflict can only help therapists understand the incentives their patients face. Conventional motivational theory gets in the way of understanding, not because it is reductionistic, but because it is wrong: A person cannot act rationally without commitments; the will is very real but not an organ; its use brings pathologies of its own, which may make someone sometimes prefer an addiction; and risk per se, including the risk of vicarious experience, is a basic necessity for emotional satisfaction. Without a recognition of such properties, person's choices may seem irrational or even perverse when they are actually complex strategic moves.

References

Ainslie, G. (1995). A utility-maximizing mechanism for vicarious reward: Comments on Julian Simon's "Interpersonal allocation continuous with intertemporal allocation". *Rationality and Society, 7*, 393–403.

Ainslie, G. (2001). *Breakdown of will*. New York: Cambridge University Press.

Ayers, S. (1997). The application of chaos theory to psychology. *Theory and Psychology, 7*, 373–398.

Kane, R. (1989). Two kinds of incompatibilism. *Philosophy and Phenomenological Research, 50*, 220–254.

Marlatt, G. A., & Gordon, J. R. (1980). Determinants of relapse: Implications for the maintenance of behavior change. In: P. O. Davidson, & S. M. Davidson (Eds), *Behavioral medicine: Changing health lifestyles* (pp. 410–452). Elmsford, NY: Pergamon.

Schelling, T. C. (1960). *The strategy of conflict*. Cambridge, MS: Harvard University Press.

Smith, V. (1992). Game theory and experimental economics: Beginnings and early influences. In: E. R. Weintraub (Ed.), *Toward a history of game theory*. Durham, NC: Duke University.

Chapter 3

Evolving Models of Addictive Behavior: From Neoclassical to Behavioral Economics

Frank J. Chaloupka, Sherry Emery and Lan Liang

Introduction

Although there has been a market for cigarettes and other addictive substances virtually since these substances were discovered, it is only relatively recently that economists have begun to characterize the demand for addictive products. According to neo-classical economic models, rational consumers maximize their utility (happiness or well-being) through their market transactions. Many researchers, however, once viewed cigarette smoking and other addictive behaviors as irrational and therefore unsuitable for conventional economic analysis (Elster 1979; Schelling 1984b; Winston 1980). If demand for cigarettes were not "rational" in this neo-classical framework, it would therefore violate the basic laws of economics, including perhaps the most fundamental law, that embodied in the downward-sloping demand curve. As the now-substantial body of economic research demonstrates, however, the demand for cigarettes clearly responds to changes in prices and other factors, as found in applications of both traditional models of demand and more recent studies that explicitly account for the addictive nature of smoking.

Conceptually, economists use a relatively broad definition of price that includes not only the monetary price of purchasing a product, but also the time and other costs associated with using the product. Restrictions on smoking in public places and private work-sites, for example, impose additional costs on smokers by forcing them to go outdoors to smoke, raising the time and discomfort associated with smoking, or by imposing fines for smoking in restricted areas. Similarly, limits on youth access to tobacco may raise the time and potential legal costs associated with smoking by minors, while new information on the health consequences of tobacco use can raise the perceived long-term costs of smoking.

In addition to price, a variety of other factors can affect demand for cigarettes and other tobacco products. For example, nearly all econometric studies of cigarette demand use a variety of factors to control for tastes, including gender, race, education, marital status, employment status, and religiosity. In addition, factors such as income, advertising and other promotional activities have been shown to influence demand for cigarettes and other

Choice, Behavioural Economics and Addiction
© 2003 Published by Elsevier Ltd.
ISBN: 0-08-044056-8

tobacco products. These factors may also be related to the likelihood of addiction, and thus affect demand for cigarettes in multiple ways.

This paper begins with a review of conventional studies of the impact of money price on cigarette demand. This is followed by a discussion of economic models of addiction and their applications to cigarette demand. Implications for the effects of price on cigarette demand from the relatively new field of behavioral economics are then reviewed.

Conventional Economic Analyses of Individual Level Smoking Data

A relatively small but growing number of cigarette demand studies have used data on individuals taken from large-scale surveys to examine the relationship between cigarette prices and demand for cigarettes, or cigarette consumption. Among the earliest of the cigarette demand studies employing individual-level data were those conducted by Lewit and his colleagues (Lewit & Coate 1982; Lewit *et al.* 1981). These studies estimated an overall price elasticity of demand for cigarettes of approximately −0.40. In other words, Lewit and his colleagues showed that demand for cigarettes fell by approximately 4% when cigarette prices increased by 10%. In studies, like the Lewit studies, which use individual level data on smoking behavior, overall price elasticity of demand for cigarettes can be broken down into two components: participation elasticity, or the extent to which price influences the decision to be a smoker; and conditional demand elasticity: the extent to which price influences the amount smoked (number of cigarettes) among smokers. Slightly over half of the decrease in demand shown in the Lewit studies could be accounted for by reductions in the number of smokers, or participation elasticity. The remaining decline could be attributed to reductions in the amount smoked by the remaining smokers, or conditional elasticity of demand. Several subsequent studies using individual level data have approximated Lewit and colleagues' results (e.g. Hu *et al.* 1995a), producing a general consensus among economists that the overall price elasticity of demand for cigarettes among adults is approximately −0.40 (NCI 1993).

Several studies have investigated the relationship between age and responsiveness to cigarette prices, and found an inverse relationship between (the absolute value of) price elasticity and age (Chaloupka & Grossman 1996; Chaloupka & Wechsler 1997; Evans & Huang 1998; Farrelly & Bray 1998; Grossman *et al.* 1983; Lewit & Coate 1982; Lewit *et al.* 1981, 1997; Tauras & Chaloupka 1998). Estimates of youth price elasticity of demand for cigarettes from these studies were as much as two to three times larger than adult elasticities. At the same time, however, several studies have failed to find a statistically significant estimate for the price elasticity of demand for cigarettes among youth (DeCicca *et al.* 1998a; Douglas 1998; Douglas & Hariharan 1994; Wasserman *et al.* 1991).

In general, researchers examining the effects of price on smoking participation using individual-level data from cross-sectional surveys have assumed that much of the price effect estimated for youth smoking participation reflects the impact of price on smoking initiation, while the estimate for adults is largely capturing the effects of price on smoking cessation. A few recent studies have attempted to directly examine the impact of cigarette prices on smoking initiation among youth, producing mixed results (DeCicca *et al.* 1998a; Dee & Evans 1998). Emery and her colleagues (2001) differentiated between experimenters (youth who had smoked less than 100 cigarettes in their lifetime) and established smokers (youth who had smoked at least 100 cigarettes and had smoked in the past 30 days), finding statistically insignificant price elasticities among experimenters. Their models estimated a total price elasticity of −1.7 among current smokers, which is quite comparable with many other previous studies. For established smokers, their models estimated a total price elasticity of −2.24, with a conditional demand elasticity of −0.68. These results suggest that cigarette prices may not be an important factor in youth's experimentation with (or initiation to) cigarettes, but may play an important role in deterring progression to established smoking and may moderate the amount smoked among those who become established smokers. Thus, while no clear consensus currently exists for the estimates of adolescent price elasticity of demand for cigarettes, the weight of the evidence suggests that youth are significantly more sensitive to cigarette price changes than are adults.

Lewit *et al.* (1981) offered two hypotheses why youth should be more price sensitive than adults, at least in the short run. First, given the addictive nature of smoking, long-term adult smokers are likely to adjust less quickly to changes in price than youth who have been smoking for a relatively short time, if at all. In addition, peer behavior is likely to be much more influential for youth, multiplying the effects of price on youth smoking. That is, an increase in cigarette price directly reduces youth smoking and then again indirectly reduces it through its impact on peer smoking. Grossman & Chaloupka (1997) offered two additional potential explanations. First, the fraction of disposable income a young smoker spends on cigarettes is likely to exceed that spent by an adult smoker. Second, compared to adults, youth are more likely to be present-oriented — to discount the future more heavily than adults. In the context of an economic model of addictive behavior (discussed below), Becker *et al.* (1991) predicted that changes in money price will have a greater impact on individuals with higher discount rates since they give less weight to the future consequences of addictive consumption.

In addition to age, several studies have examined the relationship between gender, race, and responsiveness to cigarette prices. Chaloupka & Pacula (1998b) concluded that young men and young blacks were more responsive to price than young women and young whites. Similarly, Farrelly and his colleagues estimated that blacks were about twice as responsive as whites to cigarette prices, while Hispanics were even more price sensitive. In addition, they found that men were more price sensitive than women. Finally, they estimated that individuals with family incomes below the sample median were about 70% more responsive to price than those with higher family incomes. The higher elasticity estimates for minorities may reflect demographic patterns of smoking behavior and therefore conform to the hypotheses about the relationship between addictiveness and price responsiveness postulated in the context of youth smoking behavior. Historically, at a population level, Blacks and Latinos have smoked less than Whites (Haynes *et al.* 1990; Navarro 1996; Palinkas *et al.* 1993; Perez-Stable *et al.* 1993). Thus, it is conceivable that, similar to youth, they are less addicted and therefore potentially more able to change their smoking behavior in response to cigarette price changes. The higher elasticities found among men and lower income smokers are more difficult to explain.

Evans & Farrelly (1998) recently examined a phenomenon not previously studied by economists: the compensating behavior by smokers in response to tax and price changes. They found consistent evidence that, although smokers reduced daily cigarette consumption in response to higher taxes, they also compensated for that reduced number of cigarettes in several ways. In particular, smokers in high-tax states consumed longer cigarettes and those that are higher in tar and nicotine, with young adult smokers most likely to engage in this compensating behavior. As a result, they argued that the perceived health benefits associated with higher cigarette taxes are likely to be somewhat overstated. Given this compensating behavior, Evans and Farrelly suggested that if cigarette taxes are to be used to reduce the health consequences of smoking, then taxes based on tar and nicotine content would be appropriate, an idea first suggested by Harris (1980).

In summary, conventional studies of the demand for cigarettes have shown that, despite the addictiveness of the nicotine in cigarettes, demand for cigarettes behaves much like demand for other goods, falling when prices rise. The conventional models of demand found, however, that different types of individuals respond differently to changes in cigarette prices. One plausible explanation for these differences is variations across groups in the extent to which they are addicted to cigarettes. These studies suggest a relationship between addiction levels and the demand function.

Addiction Models and Cigarette Demand

The first discussion by an economist of the effects of addiction on demand can be found in Marshall's (1920) *Principles of Economics*, where he observed that:

> Whether a commodity conforms to the law of diminishing or increasing return, the increase in consumption arising from a fall in price is gradual; and, further, habits which have once grown up around the use of a commodity while its price is low are not so quickly abandoned when its price rises again (Appendix H, Section 3: 807).

As Phlips (1983) noted, Marshall's statement clearly introduced the three basic dimensions of addiction (U.S. Department of Health and Human Services 1988) of gradual adaptation (tolerance), irreversibility (withdrawal), and positive effects of habits (reinforcement) that are used in many of the more recent formal models of addictive behavior. Until recently, however, economists have either ignored the addictive nature of goods such as cigarettes when estimating demand or have assumed that behaviors such as smoking were irrational and could not be analyzed in the rational, constrained utility maximizing framework of economics.

Many of the most recent studies of cigarette demand explicitly address the addictive nature of cigarette smoking. Economic models of addiction can be divided into three basic groups: imperfectly rational models of addictive behavior, models of myopic addictive behavior, and models of rational addictive behavior.

Imperfectly Rational Addiction Models

Elster (1979), McKenzie (1979), Winston (1980), and Schelling (1978, 1980, 1984a, b) best exemplify the economic models of imperfectly rational addictive behavior. These models generally assume stable but inconsistent short-run and long-run preferences. This is seen, for example, in Schelling's (1978: 290) description of a smoker trying to "kick the habit":

> Everybody behaves like two people, one who wants clean lungs and long life and another who adores tobacco . . .. The two are in a continual contest for control; the "straight" one often in command most of the time, but the wayward one needing only to get occasional control to spoil the other's best laid plan.

Thus, the farsighted personality may enroll in a smoking cessation program, only to be undone by the shortsighted personality's relapse in a weak moment. Winston (1980) formally modeled this behavior and described how this contest between personalities leads to the evolution of what he called "anti-markets," which he defined as firms or institutions that individuals will pay to help them stop consuming.

Strotz (1956) was the first to develop a formal model of such behavior, describing the constrained utility maximization process as one in which an individual chooses a future consumption path that maximizes current utility, but later in life changes this plan "even though his original expectations of future desires and means of consumption are verified" (165). This inconsistency between current and future preferences only arises when a non-exponential discount function is used.[1] Strotz went on to suggest that rational persons will recognize this inconsistency and plan accordingly, by pre-committing their future behavior or by modifying consumption plans to be consistent with future preferences when unable to pre-commit. Pollak (1968) went one step further, arguing that an individual may behave naively even when using an exponential discount function. Thaler & Shefrin (1981) described the problem similarly, referring to an individual at any point in time as both a "farsighted planner and a myopic doer" (392), with the two in continual conflict. While these models present interesting discussions of some aspects of addictive behavior, they have not been applied empirically to cigarette smoking or other addictions.

Myopic Addiction Models

The naive behavior described in some of the imperfectly rational models of addiction is the basis for many of the myopic models of addictive behavior. As Pollak (1975) observed, behavior is naive in the sense that an individual recognizes the dependence of current addictive consumption decisions on past consumption, but then ignores the impact of current and past choices on future consumption decisions when making current choices. Many of these models treat preferences as endogenous, allowing tastes to change over time in response to past consumption (El-Safty 1976a, b; Gorman 1967; Hammond 1976a, b; Pollak 1970, 1976, 1978; von Weizsäcker 1971).

These models are similar in spirit to those in which tastes change in response to factors other than past consumption, including advertising (Dixit & Norman 1978; Galbraith 1958, 1972) and prices (Pollak 1977). Others allow past consumption to affect current consumption through an accumulated stock of past consumption (e.g. Houthakker & Taylor, 1966, 1970).

These models are comparable to those of the demand for durable consumer goods that use a stock adjustment process (e.g. Chow's [1960] model of the demand for automobiles, and Garcia dos Santos' [1972] analysis of the demands for household durables.) As Phlips (1983) noted, however, the distinction between models with endogenous tastes and those with stable preferences within a household production framework is purely semantic, since the underlying mathematics of the two are the same.

The earliest theoretical models of demand in the context of myopic addiction can be traced to the irreversible demand models (Duesenberry 1949; Farrell 1952; Haavelmo 1944; Modigliani 1949). Farrell, for example, described an irreversible demand function as one in which current demand depends on all past price and income combinations. As a result, price and income elasticities are constant, but may differ for increases and decreases in price and income. Farrell tested this model empirically, using U.K. data on the demands for tobacco and beer from 1870 through 1938, in a model that included not only current price and income, but also price, income, and consumption in the prior year. In general, his estimates were inconclusive, although he did find limited evidence of habit formation for tobacco use.

The notion of asymmetric responses to price and income reappeared in Scitovsky (1976) and was applied to cigarette demand by Young (1983) and Pekurinen (1989), using data from the U.S. and Finland, respectively. Both found that smoking was almost twice as responsive to price reductions as it was to price increases, which they interpreted as evidence of addiction.

Most empirical applications of myopic models of addiction are based on the pioneering work by Houthakker & Taylor (1966, 1970), which formally introduced the dependence of current consumption on past consumption by modeling current demand as a function of a "stock of habits" representing the depreciated sum of all past consumption. Houthakker & Taylor estimated demand functions for a variety of goods, including cigarettes, using annual aggregates for the U.S. and several western European countries. Their estimates provided considerable support for their hypothesis of habit formation in demand for almost all of the non-durable consumer goods, including cigarettes, they examined.

Mullahy (1985) took a similar approach in his empirical examination of cigarette demand using individual level data from the 1979 National Health Interview Survey. In his model, the stock of past cigarette consumption has a negative impact on the production of commodities such as health and the satisfaction received from current smoking. Mullahy found strong support for the hypothesis that cigarette smoking is an addictive behavior, as shown by the positive and significant estimates he obtained for the addictive stock in both the smoking participation and conditional demand equations. His estimates for price are quite similar to those obtained by Lewit & Coate (1982), with the overall price elasticity of demand centered on -0.47. In addition, Mullahy estimated that men were more price responsive than women (total price elasticities of -0.56 and -0.39, respectively). Finally, using an interaction between the addictive stock and price, Mullahy concluded that more-addicted smokers (defined as those with a larger addictive stock) were less responsive to price than their less-addicted counterparts. Other approaches to estimating myopic demand models have similarly concluded that cigarette smoking is an addictive behavior and that price has a significant impact on cigarette demand (e.g. Baltagi & Levin 1986; Jones 1994).

Rational Addiction Models

Several researchers have modeled addiction as a rational behavior. In this context, rationality simply implies that individuals incorporate the interdependence between past, current, and future consumption into their utility maximization process. This is in contrast to the assumption, implicit in myopic models of addictive behavior, that future implications are ignored when making current decisions. In other words, myopic behavior implies an infinite discounting of the future, while rational behavior implies that future implications are considered, while not ruling out a relatively high discount rate. Several of the rational addiction models, including those of Lluch (1974), Spinnewyn (1981), and Boyer (1983), assume that tastes are endogenous. These models build on the significant contributions of Ryder & Heal (1963), Boyer (1978), and others in the optimal growth literature who have developed endogenous taste models with rational behavior. Spinnewyn (1981) and Phlips & Spinnewyn (1982) argued that incorporating rational decision making into models of habit formation results in models that are "formally equivalent to models without habit formation" (Spinnewyn 1981: 92). Thus, they argue, assuming rationality only leads to unnecessary complications.

This assertion was challenged by Pashardes (1986) who derived demand equations for a rational consumer in which current consumption is determined by past consumption and current preferences with full knowledge about the impact of current decisions on the future costs of consumption. Pashardes found considerable empirical evidence to support the hypothesis of rational behavior in general, as well as evidence that cigarette smoking is an addictive behavior. Finally, he noted that expectations concerning the future price and other costs of consumption played an important role in consumer behavior.

Becker & Murphy (1988) similarly rejected the notion that myopic behavior is empirically indistinguishable from rational behavior in their theory of rational addiction. They assumed that individuals consistently maximize utility over their life cycle, taking into account the future consequences of their choices. In their model, utility at any point in time depends on current addictive consumption, current non-addictive consumption, and the stock of past addictive consumption. Tolerance is incorporated by assuming that the marginal utility of the addictive stock is negative. Reinforcement is modeled by assuming that an increase in the addictive stock raises the marginal utility of current addictive consumption. Finally withdrawal is captured since total utility falls with the cessation of addictive consumption.

Becker & Murphy (1988) and Becker *et al.* (1991) developed several hypotheses from this basic model. First, addictive consumption displays "adjacent complementarity"; that is, due to reinforcement, the quantities of the addictive good consumed in different time periods are complements. As a result, current consumption of an addictive good is inversely related not only to the current price of the good, but also to all past and future prices. Consequently, the long-run effect of a permanent change in price will exceed the short-run effect.[2] Moreover, in the Becker and Murphy model, the ratio of the long-run to short-run price effect rises as the degree of addiction rises. In addition, they predict that the effect of an anticipated price change will be greater than the impact of a comparable unanticipated price change, while a permanent price change will have a larger impact on demand than a temporary price change. Finally, price responsiveness varies with time preference: addicts with higher discount rates will be relatively more responsive to changes in money price than those with lower discount rates. The opposite will be true with respect to the effects of information concerning the future consequences of addictive consumption. Thus, the model suggests that younger, less educated, and lower income persons will be relatively more responsive to current changes in the money price of cigarettes, while older, more educated, and higher income persons will be relatively more responsive to new information on the health consequences of cigarette smoking and future price changes.[3]

Strong adjacent complementarity, reflecting strong addiction, can lead to unstable steady states in the Becker and Murphy model. This is a key feature of their rational addiction theory, helping to explain the binge behavior and "cold turkey" quit behavior observed among addicts. Furthermore, these unstable steady states imply that there will be a bimodal distribution of consumption, again something that is observed for many addictive goods. In addition, Becker and Murphy's model implies that temporary events, including price reductions, peer pressure, or stressful events, can lead to permanent addictions.

Chaloupka (1988, 1990, 1991, 1992) used data from the Second National Health and Nutrition Examination Survey conducted in the late 1970s in the first empirical application of the rational addiction model. He found consistent evidence that cigarette smoking was an addictive behavior and that smokers did not behave myopically. Chaloupka's (1991) estimates of the long-run price elasticity of demand fell in the range from −0.27 to −0.48, larger than the elasticities obtained from conventional demand equations using the same data. In addition to estimating the rational addiction demand equations for the full sample, Chaloupka also explored the implications of the Becker and Murphy model with respect to the rate of time preference by estimating comparable demand equations for subsamples based on age and educational attainment. Chaloupka's (1991) estimates were generally consistent with the hypothesis that less educated or younger persons behave more myopically than their more educated or older counterparts. In addition, less educated persons were more price responsive, with long-run price elasticities ranging from −0.57 to −0.62, than were more educated persons, who were generally unresponsive to price. Chaloupka (1990) also estimated separate demand equations for subsamples based on gender, concluding that men behaved more myopically and were relatively more responsive to price (long-run price elasticity centered on −0.60) than women (statistically insignificant effect of price on demand).

Similar findings were obtained by Becker et al. (1994) using aggregate, state-level sales data for the U.S. over the period from 1955 through 1985. They found clear evidence that smoking was addictive, as well as evidence of non-myopic, although not fully rational, behavior.[4] Estimates from other studies employing U.S. data (Keeler et al. 1993; Sung et al. 1994) and data from other countries, including Finland (Pekurinen 1991) and Australia (Bardsley & Olekalns 1998) are generally consistent with the hypothesis of rational addiction. In contrast, Duffy (1996a), Cameron (1997), and Conniffe (1995), using annual time-series data for the U.K., Greece, and Ireland, respectively, found little support for the rational addiction model. These latter studies, however, are generally limited by the relatively small number of observations available for their analyses, and by the use of several highly correlated regressors.

Douglas (1998) used hazard models to examine the determinants of smoking initiation and cessation in the context of the Becker & Murphy (1988) rational addiction model. In contrast to his finding that price does not significantly affect the hazard of smoking initiation, Douglas concluded that increases in price significantly increase the likelihood (hazard) of smoking cessation. He estimated a price elasticity for the duration of the smoking habit of -1.07 with respect to future price, consistent with the hypothesis of rational addiction; paradoxically, past and current prices were not found to have a statistically significant effect on cessation. Similarly, his parametric and non-parametric results imply that the hazard of smoking cessation has a positive duration dependence, a finding Douglas suggested is consistent with rational addiction in that the rational smoker will discount future health costs less as they become more imminent.

Critiques of the Rational Addiction Model

While the rational addiction model has gained acceptance among some economists, many object to several assumptions of the model. Perhaps the most criticized aspect of the model is the assumption of perfect foresight. As Winston (1980: 302) explained, in the context of the Stigler & Becker (1977) model:

> [T]he addict looks strange because he sits down at period $j = 0$, surveys future income, production technologies, investment/addiction functions, and consumption preferences over his lifetime to period T, maximizes the discounted value of his expected utility, and decides to be an alcoholic. That's the way he will get the greatest satisfaction out of life. Alcoholics are alcoholics because they want to be alcoholics, ex ante, with full knowledge of its consequences.

Similarly, Akerlof (1991) noted that individuals who become addicted in the rational addiction model do not regret their past decisions, given that they are assumed to have been fully aware of the consequences of their consumption of a potentially addictive good when making those decisions.

A recent theoretical paper by Orphanides & Zervos (1995) addressed this and other perceived inconsistencies of the rational addiction model that arise largely from the assumption of perfect foresight. In particular, the authors introduced uncertainty into the model by assuming that inexperienced users are not fully aware of the potential harm associated with consuming an addictive substance. Thus, it is possible to explain the regret often observed in addicted individuals, but which cannot be accommodated in the Becker & Murphy models. Orphanides & Zervos describe a model where not every individual is susceptible to addiction. Thus, there is a probabilistic calculation involved with the consumption of an addictive good: the consumer gambles that they are not among the group susceptible to addiction. An individual's knowledge about their probability of addiction comes from the observed effects of that good on others, as well as through his or her own experimentation with that good. More specifically, they assume that the harmful effects (including addiction) of consuming a potentially addictive good are not the same for all individuals, that each individual possesses a subjective understanding of his or her potential to become addicted, and that this subjective belief is updated via a Bayesian learning process as the individual consumes the addictive good. Thus, an individual who underestimates his or her potential for addiction and experiments with an addictive substance can end up becoming addicted. Rather than the "happy addicts" implied by the rational addiction model (Winston 1980), these addicts will regret becoming addicted. As Orphanides & Zervos noted, the incorporation of subjective beliefs into the rational addiction model helps explain youthful experimentation, the importance of peer influences, and other commonly observed facets of addiction.

More recently, in a model focusing on cigarette smoking, Suranovic *et al.* (1999) also reconsidered the Becker & Murphy (1988) model of rational addiction. As described above, adjacent complementarity is a key feature of the rational addiction model. Suranovic *et al.* noted, however, that one implication of adjacent complementarity is that efforts to reduce current consumption will lead to reductions in utility. These "quitting costs" are an important feature of their model and help explain the seeming inconsistency between smokers' stated wishes to quit smoking and their continued cigarette consumption. In addition, they help explain why smokers engage in various behavior modification treatments, such as the use of the nicotine patch, which help make quitting easier.

A second point of departure from the Becker & Murphy model concerns the timing of the consequences of smoking, which Suranovic *et al.* assume are concentrated at the end of a smoker's life. In addition, rather than assuming that individuals choose a lifetime consumption path that maximizes the present value of their lifetime utility, Suranovic *et al.* assume "boundedly rational" behavior, implying that individuals choose current consumption only. As a result, their model suggests that aging is enough to induce cessation among some smokers. As in the Becker & Murphy model, their model implies that quitting "cold-turkey" is likely in the case of a strong addiction (one where quitting costs rise rapidly for small reductions in consumption). However, in contrast to Becker & Murphy, Suranovic *et al.* predicted gradual reductions in consumption progressing to quitting in the case of relatively weak addictions. Interestingly, some newly emerging epidemiologic evidence supports this prediction (Farkas 1998).

In addition, as Becker & Mulligan (1997) describe, addiction and time preference may be related. As discussed above, the Becker & Murphy (1988) model of rational addiction implied that people who discount the future more heavily were more likely to become addicted (and hence less price responsive, but addicted individuals are more price responsive in the long run than are less addicted individuals). In their theoretical discussion on the determination of time preference, Becker & Mulligan suggest that addictive consumption, by raising current utility at the expense of future utility, can make even rational persons behave more myopically.

Finally, Showalter (1998), in his analysis of the behavior of firms producing an addictive good, suggests an alternative interpretation for the finding in most empirical applications of the rational addiction model that future consumption has a significant impact on current consumption. Rather than resulting from rational behavior on the part of consumers, Showalter shows that the same finding could result from myopic behavior by consumers coupled with rational behavior by firms. In his empirical applications of this model, Showalter finds that the rational and myopic demand models produce similar predictions, but that neither does well in predicting actual behavior, a finding he attributes to the difficulties of accurately forecasting prices.

Behavioral Economic Analyses of Cigarette Demand

Behavioral economics involves the application of the principles of consumer demand theory to experimental psychology (Hursh & Bauman 1987), and offers another set of tools and hypotheses for understanding some of the contradictions and conundrums that persist in the economics of addictive behavior. Over the past decade, there have been numerous behavioral economic analyses of a variety of addictive behaviors, including cigarette smoking (Bickel & DeGrandpre 1996). These studies examine the impact of price and other factors on the self-administration of a number of addictive substances by humans as well as a variety of non-human species in a laboratory setting. Price, in this context, is defined as the response or effort required to receive one dose of a drug (Bickel *et al.* 1993). As in standard economic analyses, an increase in price is expected to lead to a reduction in the quantity of drug demanded. One advantage of this experimental approach for the analysis of cigarette demand, both in general and as it relates to policy debates specifically, is that it allows researchers to study the effects on demand of changes in cigarette prices that are many times larger than the price differences that are observed in the cross-sectional or time-series data that have been used in the econometric studies of demand. One limitation of the approach, however, is that these methods are generally applicable only to dependent individuals. For example, for ethical reasons (and others), they cannot be used to address issues related to the effect of price on smoking initiation.

In a series of papers, Bickel, DeGrandpre, and their colleagues have reported the results of research on cigarette smoking conducted in their behavioral economics laboratory (Bickel & DeGrandpre 1996; Bickel *et al.* 1991, 1995; Bickel & Madden 1998; DeGrandpre & Bickel 1995; DeGrandpre *et al.* 1992, 1994). These experiments typically involved individuals aged 18 and older who smoked a pack or more of cigarettes per day, and who participated in between two and five three-hour experimental sessions per week.[5] Price, in these experiments, was defined as the number of complete pulls and resets of a plunger required to receive a preset number of puffs on a cigarette. For example, 50 pulls on the plunger may be required to obtain two puffs on a cigarette. Puffs were monitored by a puff-volume sensor so that each subject receives essentially the same dose per puff (Bickel & Madden 1998).

A wide range of prices was used in these experiments. In some, respondents were also presented with an opportunity to earn money for pulls on the plunger that could then be spent on cigarettes. As in the econometric studies described above, the behavioral economic analyses have consistently found an inverse relationship between cigarette smoking and price. Estimates of the price elasticity of demand obtained from these studies were surprisingly consistent with those obtained from econometric studies. For example, Bickel *et al.* (1995) estimated a mean price elasticity of demand of -0.56 for five subjects in an experiment in which price ranged from 12 to 1600 pulls per puff. A particularly interesting finding from the behavioral economics research was that the price elasticity of demand rises as price rises. For example, DeGrandpre & Bickel (1995) estimated a mean price elasticity of -1.58 for prices ranging from 400 to 4500 pulls per puff. These findings appear to be generalizable not only across drugs but also across species (Bickel *et al.* 1990).

Theoretical Advances in the Behavioral Economics of Smoking

In addition to the empirical work conducted in laboratory settings, in recent years a growing body of theoretical work has evolved out of explorations of the application of psychological theories to economic models of addictive behavior in general and cigarette smoking in particular. Such models evolved to explain seemingly irrational behavior exhibited by individuals with self-control problems, both in their dynamic decisions with respect to consumption and their approaches to addressing these self-control problems.

In this context, a person is characterized as having a self-control problem if their long-term utility is diminished by decisions or actions taken to maximize utility in the short run. For example, in the long run, a smoker may want to quit smoking. Thus, having a cigarette today diminishes their long run utility at the same time that it also maximizes their current utility. In order to reach their long run goal, a smoker may impose rules on themselves or create other structures that appear to constrain current utility, but help them to maximize long run utility. These self-control mechanisms can appear to be irrational from an economic perspective unless viewed as means to address the contradictions represented by self-control problems.

As described above, Thaler & Shefrin (1981) explained such behavior by characterizing the individual as embodying two agents, the planner and the do-er. The planner has one set of preferences that apply to future behavior: for example, to save money in the future or to quit smoking. The do-er, however, has another set of preferences that apply only to current behavior: for example to spend money or to smoke. In order to prevent the do-er from diminishing the long-run utility of the planner, the individual adopts commitment devices, such as savings plans or enrollment in a costly smoking cessation treatment rather than quitting cold-turkey. In the case of an integrated individual, where there is no distinction between the planner and the do-er, such commitment devices would appear irrational from an economic perspective. However, the inter-temporal variability in preferences means that integration does not occur without commitment devices, and therefore these devices begin to make sense.

Laibson (1997) describes a model that can account for the conflict between today's preferences and future preferences, which was characterized as a self-control problem by earlier economists. Laibson explains these intertemporal inconsistencies as a function of a hyperbolic discount structure. This idea differs from the traditional economics and rational addiction models, which allow for changing tastes over time but apply a constant discount rate to decisions about current and future consumption made by one individual. These traditional models reflect the assumption of an exponential discount function over time. A hyperbolic discount rate implies that an individual is relatively impatient in the short run, but will apply a lower discount rate to decisions made in the future. However, when the future arrives, these decisions become subject to the short-run high discount rate. This model explains how an individual can plan to make more difficult decisions, like quitting smoking, in the future, but when the future becomes the present will pursue a strategy of more immediate gratification.

Ainslie (1992) describes a discount function that is a modification of the hyperbolic discount function, and which allows for willpower or personal rules (Ainslie 1992). Thus, an individual may still value future abstention over future consumption, only to have these values reverse as the future becomes the present. The key distinction, however, is that in the present an individual can take into account more than the current period as they are considering present consumption. If the discounted values of later decisions are evaluated at the same time as the individual is considering whether to consume or abstain in the present, it is possible that the sum of current and future discounted consumption events is less than the value of the sum of current and future discounted abstention. In such a scenario, an individual will choose to abstain in the current period even though current consumption, taken alone, is clearly superior. In this framework, Ainslie shows that any temptation may be resisted if an individual with a hyperbolic discount function takes into account enough future time periods. Individuals may differ in their ability or inclination to consider future time periods when making current consumption choices, but have the potential to make consistent choices — to abstain in the present if future abstention is valued higher than future consumption even if current consumption is valued higher than current abstention. The ability to make consistent choices depends on the individual's willpower, or length of time horizon they take into account.

Finally, O'Donoghue & Rabin (1999, 2000) have developed further modifications of the hyperbolic discounting function to describe individuals' self-control problems and variations across individuals in their methods of managing self-control problems. In this framework, individuals can be described as either sophisticated or naïve with respect to their self-control problem. Much like Ainslie's characterization of willpower, when making decisions about consumption of an addictive good, a sophisticated individual in O'Donoghue & Rabin's models will foresee their self-control problems and take them into account in their current decisions. Thus, a sophisticate will correctly predict that they may have self-control problems in the future, and adjust their current consumption decisions accordingly. In contrast, the naïf will not foresee their future self-control problems, and thus cannot appropriately adjust their current behavior to take the future into account.

The behavioral implications of sophistication and naiveté depend on the type of activity being considered: whether there are immediate costs or immediate rewards. In cases where there are immediate costs and delayed rewards, sophisticated individuals have a clear advantage over naives. For example, when considering quitting smoking, a naïf will procrastinate and as a result will continue to smoke in future periods. The result is analogous to simple hyperbolic discounting, whereas the future period becomes the present, the procrastinator will pursue the immediate gratification of indulging rather than abstaining as planned. In contrast, a sophisticate may procrastinate (smoke now, but plan to quit in the future), but will not procrastinate when the future costs become too high. This case is similar to Ainslie's characterization of willpower, where the sophisticate will take into account future utilities when considering the utility of indulging (smoking) in the present.

In O'Donoghue & Rabin's framework, however, when the consumption involves an immediate reward and delayed costs, the outcomes differ slightly. Again, it is useful to consider the case of quitting smoking. This time, there is an immediate reward and delayed costs in continuing to smoke, rather than the immediate cost and delayed reward of quitting. In this scenario, the naïf will again continue to smoke because they fail to foresee the later costs and will indulge in the present. The sophisticate, on the other hand, will foresee the later costs, but correctly predict that they will have self-control problems in the future — in this case, they will likely relapse. As a result, the sophisticate will view quitting in the present as a lost cause, since they foresee relapse in the future, and therefore will not quit in the present.

Conclusions: The Relationship Between Rational Addiction and Behavioral Economics Models of Addiction, and Next Steps

In sum, the recent theoretical developments in the behavioral economics of addiction in general and smoking in particular provide a framework for considering behavior that the traditional economics and rational addiction models do not fully address. These rational addiction models, however, represented important advances in our understanding of addictive behaviors. Indeed, in order to understand addiction, economists needed to address the issue of whether addiction behavior could be characterized as rational. Early models of addiction characterized smokers' preferences as generally stable, but imperfectly rational (Baltagi & Levin 1986; Jones 1994; Mullahy 1985; Pekurinen 1989; Pollak 1975; Young 1983). In these models, addiction was explained by inconsistencies between smokers' short-run and long-run preferences, whereby smokers wanted to quit in the long run but were driven by their short term preference to have a cigarette now. These ideas are echoed in Thaler & Shefrin's (1981) characterization of the "planner" and the "do-er." Formal modeling of imperfect rationality required a non-exponential discount function, which foreshadowed Laibson's notion of a hyperbolic discount curve.

Early models of addiction characterized demand for addictive products, like cigarettes, as myopic. In other words, demand depended on past and perhaps current levels of consumption but ignored future preferences. By incorporating future expectations about prices and consumption levels into the myopic model, the idea of rational addiction evolved. Becker & Murphy (1988) described a model of rational addiction that allowed for three key attributes of addiction: tolerance, reinforcement, and withdrawal. This rational addiction model, however, presumed perfect foresight of the future; critics noted that such a model did not allow for an addict's regret. Under rational addiction, therefore, an addict essentially chooses to be an addict ex ante.

Addicts' regret was addressed with the introduction of the idea that consumers of an addictive product recognize that addiction is not a certainty (Orphanides & Zervos 1995). Thus, consumers must subjectively judge the probability that they will experience the harmful effects of the addictive product, based on their observations of others' experiences as well as their own experiences with that or similar products. If this judgment of these probabilities, or gamble, is wrong, the consumer can become a regretful addict. This model helped explain youthful experimentation that evolves into addiction. Suranovic *et al.* (1999) advanced the theory of rational addiction by describing that one implication of the complementary relationship between current, past and future consumption is that efforts to reduce current consumption will lead to reductions in future utility. These "quitting costs" thus explain the addict's regret: the seeming inconsistency between smokers' stated wishes to quit smoking and their continued cigarette consumption. The behavioral economics approach described by O'Donoghue & Rabin (1999) applies a slightly different perspective to this phenomenon, by dividing individuals into those who are sophisticated and can correctly predict how they will behave in the future, and those who are naïve and fail to do so.

While there is substantial overlap between the rational addiction and behavioral economics models of individuals' demand for addictive products, in many cases behavioral economics models promise to explain complexities in addictive behavior that the rational addiction models have not fully addressed. In large part, however, the theoretical explanations of behavioral economics largely remain to be confirmed empirically, and also raise several additional important empirical questions. For example, is the hyperbolic discount function a generalizable model, or is there a segment of the population that applies the traditional exponential discount function, and its assumptions about intertemporal consistency, to decisions about the consumption of addictive goods? Similarly, even considering only hyperbolic discounters, how does this population vary in the degree to which it takes into account future time horizons? To what extent are individuals in the population sophisticated or naïve, and how does this vary across age groups or educational levels? Since these models and the questions they raise involve behavior and choices over time, detailed longitudinal data from a broad population are necessary to address these empirical considerations.

Notes

1. Vuchinich & Simpson (1998) provided an interesting application of this idea to the demand for alcoholic beverages, comparing behavior under hyperbolic vs. exponential discounting.
2. Myopic addiction models also predict that the long run price elasticity of demand will be larger than the short run elasticity.
3. See Chaloupka (1988, 1990, 1992) or Becker *et al.* (1994) for a more formal discussion of these price effects.
4. The authors concluded that there was insufficient information in the data to accurately estimate the discount rate, but that their estimates were clearly inconsistent with myopic behavior.
5. For a discussion of a number of other requirements for the participants and more detail on the features of these experiments, see Bickel & Madden (1998).

References

Ainslie, G. (1992). *Picoeconomics: The strategic interaction of successive motivational states within the person.* Cambridge: Cambridge University Press.

Akerlof, G. A. (1991). Procrastination and obedience. *American Economic Review, 81,* 1–19.

Becker, G. S., Grossman, M., & Murphy, K. M. (1991). Rational addiction and the effect of price on consumption. *American Economic Review, 81,* 237–241.

Becker, G. S., Grossman, M., & Murphy, K. M. (1994). An empirical analysis of cigarette addiction. *American Economic Review, 84*(3), 396–418.

Becker, G. S., & Mulligan, C. B. (1997). The endogenous determination of time preference. *Quarterly Journal of Economics, 112*(3), 729–758.

Becker, G. S., & Murphy, K. M. (1988). A theory of rational addiction. *Journal of Political Economy, 96*(4), 675–700.

Bickel, W. K., & DeGrandpre, R. J. (1996). Modeling drug abuse policy in the behavioral economics laboratory. In: L. Green, & J. H. Kagel (Eds), *Advances in behavioral economics. Volume 3: Substance use and abuse.* Norwood, NJ: Ablex Publishing Corporation.

Bickel, W. K., DeGrandpre, R. J., & Higgins, S. T. (1993). Behavioral economics: A novel experimental approach to the study of drug dependence. *Drug and Alcohol Dependence, 33*(2), 173–192.

Bickel, W. K., DeGrandpre, R. J., Higgins, S. T., & Hughes, J. R. (1990). Behavioral economics of drug self-administration. I. Functional equivalence of response requirement and drug dose. *Life Science, 47*, 1501–1510.

Bickel, W. K., DeGrandpre, R. J., Higgins, S. T., Hughes, J. R., & Badger, G. (1995). Effects of simulated employment and recreation on cigarette smoking: A behavioral economic analysis. *Experimental and Clinical Psychopharmacology, 3*, 467–476.

Bickel, W. K., DeGrandpre, R. J., Hughes, J. R., & Higgins, S. T. (1991). Behavioral economics of drug self-administration. II. A unit-price analysis of cigarette smoking. *Journal of the Experimental Analysis of Behavior, 55*(2), 145–154.

Bickel, W. K., & Madden, G. J. (1998). *The behavioral economics of smoking.* National Bureau of Economic Research Working Paper No. 6444.

Boyer, M. (1983). Rational demand and expenditures patterns under habit formation. *Journal of Economic Theory, 31*, 27–53.

Cameron, S. (1997). Are Greek smokers rational addicts? *Applied Economics Letters, 4*(7), 401–402.

Chaloupka, F. J. (1988). *An economic analysis of addictive behavior: The case of cigarette smoking* [dissertation]. New York: City University of New York Graduate School.

Chaloupka, F. J. (1990). Men, women, and addiction: The case of cigarette smoking. National Bureau of Economic Research Working Paper No. 3267.

Chaloupka, F. J. (1991). Rational addictive behavior and cigarette smoking. *Journal of Political Economy, 99*(4), 722–742.

Chaloupka, F. J. (1992). Clean indoor air laws, addiction, and cigarette smoking. *Applied Economics, 24*(2), 193–205.

Chaloupka, F. J., & Grossman, M. (1996). Price, tobacco control policies and youth smoking. National Bureau of Economic Research Working Paper No. 5740.

Chaloupka, F. J., & Pacula, R. L. (1998b). An examination of gender and race differences in youth smoking responsiveness to price and tobacco control policies. National Bureau of Economic Research Working Paper No. 6541.

Chaloupka, F. J., & Wechsler, H. (1997). Price, tobacco control policies and smoking among young adults. *Journal of Health Economics, 16*(3), 359–373.

DeCicca, P., Kenkel, D., & Mathios, A. (1998). Putting out the fires: Will higher cigarette taxes reduce youth smoking? Presented at the Annual Meetings of the American Economic Association.

Dee, T. S., & Evans, W. N. (1998). A comment on DeCicca, Kenkel, and Mathios. Working Paper. School of Economics, Georgia Institute of Technology.

DeGrandpre, R. J., & Bickel, W. K. (1995). Human drug self-administration in a medium of exchange. *Experimental and Clinical Psychopharmacology, 3*, 349–357.

DeGrandpre, R. J., Bickel, W. K., Higgins, S. T., & Hughes, J. R. (1994). A behavioral economic analysis of concurrently available money and cigarettes. *Journal of the Experimental Analysis of Behavior, 61*(2), 191–201.

DeGrandpre, R. J., Bickel, W. K., Hughes, J. R., & Higgins, S. T. (1992). Behavioral economics of drug self-administration. III. A reanalysis of the nicotine regulation hypothesis. *Psychopharmacology, 108*(1–2), 1–10.

Douglas, S. (1998). The duration of the smoking habit. *Economic Inquiry, 36*(1), 49–64.

Douglas, S., & Hariharan, G. (1994). The hazard of starting smoking: Estimates from a split population duration model. *Journal of Health Economics, 13*(2), 213–230.

Duesenberry, J. S. (1949). *Income, saving, and the theory of consumer behavior.* Cambridge, MA: Harvard University Press.

El-Safty, A. E. (1976a). Adaptive behavior, demand, and preferences. *Journal of Economic Theory,* *13*, 298–318.

El-Safty, A. E. (1976b). Adaptive behavior and the existence of Weizsäcker's long-run indifference curves. *Journal of Economic Theory, 13*, 319–328.

Elster, J. (1979). *Ulysses and the sirens: Studies in rationality and irrationality.* Cambridge: Cambridge University Press.

Evans, W. N., & Farrelly, M. C. (1998). The compensating behavior of smokers: Taxes, tar, and nicotine. *RAND Journal of Economics, 29*(3), 578–595.

Evans, W. N., & Huang, L. X. (1998). Cigarette taxes and teen smoking: New evidence from panels of repeated cross-sections. Working paper. Department of Economics, University of Maryland.

Farkas, A. J. (1998). *When does cigarette fading increase the likelihood of future cessation?* Cancer Prevention and Control Program, Cancer Center. La Jolla, CA: University of California, San Diego (May).

Farrell, M. J. (1952). Irreversible demand functions. *Econometrica, 20*, 171–186.

Farrelly, M. C., & Bray, J. W. (1998). Office on Smoking and Health. Response to increases in cigarette prices by race/ethnicity, income, and age groups — United States 1976–1993. *Morbidity and Mortality Weekly Report, 47*(29), 605–609.

Gorman, W. M. (1967). Tastes, habits, and choices. *International Economic Review, 8*, 218–222.

Grossman, M., & Chaloupka, F. J. (1997). Cigarette taxes: The straw to break the camel's back. *Public Health Reports, 112*(4), 290–297.

Grossman, M., Coate, D., Lewit, E. M., & Shakotko, R. A. (1983). *Economic and other factors in youth smoking.* Washington: National Science Foundation.

Haavelmo, T. (1944). The probability approach in econometrics. *Econometrica, 12*, 96–124.

Hammond, P. J. (1976a). Changing tastes and coherent dynamic choice. *Review of Economic Studies, 43*, 159–173.

Hammond, P. J. (1976b). Endogenous tastes and stable long-run choice. *Journal of Economic Theory, 13*, 329–340.

Harris, J. E. (1980). Taxing tar and nicotine. *American Economic Review, 70*(3), 300–311.

Haynes, S. G., Harvey, C., Montes, H., Nickens, H., & Cohen, B. H., VII (1990). Patterns of cigarette smoking among Hispanics in the United States: Results from HHANES 1982–1984. *American Journal of Public Health, 80*(Supplement), 47–53.

Houthakker, H. S., & Taylor, L. D. (1970). *Consumer demand in the United States 1929–1970: Analyses and projections* (2nd ed.). Cambridge, MA: Harvard University Press.

Hu, T.-W., Ren, Q.-F., Keeler, T. E., & Bartlett, J. (1995). The demand for cigarettes in California and behavioural risk factors. *Health Economics, 4*(1), 7–14.

Hursh, S. R., & Bauman, R. A. (1987). The behavioral analysis of demand. In: L. Green, & J. H. Kagel (Eds), *Advances in behavioral economics* (Vol. 1, pp. 117–165). Norwood, NJ: Ablex Publishing Corporation.

Jones, A. M. (1994). Health, addiction, social interaction and the decision to quit smoking. *Journal of Health Economics, 13*, 93–110.

Keeler, T. E., Hu, T.-W., Barnett, P. G., & Manning, W. G. (1993). Taxation, regulation and addiction: A demand function for cigarettes based on time-series evidence. *Journal of Health Economics, 12*(1), 1–18.

Lewit, E. M., & Coate, D. (1982). The potential for using excise taxes to reduce smoking. *Journal of Health Economics, 1*(2), 121–145.

Lewit, E. M., Coate, D., & Grossman, M. (1981). The effects of government regulation on teenage smoking. *Journal of Law and Economics, 24*(3), 545–569.

Lewit, E. M., Hyland, A., Kerrebrock, N., & Cummings, K. M. (1997). Price, public policy and smoking in young people. *Tobacco Control, 6*(S2), 17–24.

Marshall, A. (1920). *Principles of economics* (8th ed.). London: Macmillan.

McKenzie, R. B. (1979). The non-rational domain and the limits of economic analysis. *Southern Economic Journal, 46*(1), 145–157.

Modigliani, F. (1949). Fluctuations in the savings-income ratio: A problem in economic forecasting. In: *Studies in income and wealth* (Vol. 11, pp. 371–443). New York: National Bureau of Economic Research.

Mullahy, J. (1985). *Cigarette smoking: Habits, health concerns, and heterogeneous unobservables in a micro-econometric analysis of consumer demand* [dissertation]. Charlottesville, VA: University of Virginia.

Navarro, A. M. (1996). Cigarette smoking among adult Latinos: The California Tobacco Baseline Survey. *Annals of Behavioral Medicine, 18*(4), 238–245.

O'Donoghue, T., & Rabin, M. (1999). Doing it now or later. *American Economic Review, 89*, 103–124.

O'Donoghue, T., & Rabin, M. (2000). The economics of immediate gratification. *Journal of Behavioral Decision Making, 13*, 133–250.

Orphanides, A., & Zervos, D. (1995). Rational addiction with learning and regret. *Journal of Political Economy, 103*, 739–758.

Palinkas, L. A., Pierce, J. P., Rosbrook, B., Pickwell, S., Johnson, M., & Bal, D. G. (1993). Cigarette smoking behavior and beliefs of Hispanics in California. *American Journal of Preventive Medicine, 9*(6), 331–337.

Pashardes, P. (1986). Myopic and forward looking behavior in a dynamic demand system. *International Economic Review, 27*, 387–397.

Perez-Stable, E. J., Marin, B. V., & Marin, G. A. (1993). Comprehensive smoking cessation program for the San Francisco Bay Area Latino community: Programa Latino Para Dejar de Fumar. *Am J Health Promot, 7*(6), 430–442, 475.

Phlips, L., & Spinnewyn, F. (1982). Rationality vs. myopia in dynamic demand systems. In: R. L. Basman, & G. F. Rhodes Jr. (Eds), *Advances in econometrics* (Vol. 1, pp. 3–33). Greenwich, CT: JAI Press.

Pollak, R. A. (1968). Consistent planning. *Review of Economic Studies, 35*, 201–208.

Pollak, R. A. (1970). Habit formation and dynamic demand functions. *Journal of Political Economy, 78*, 745–763.

Pollak, R. A. (1975). The intertemporal cost of living index. *Annals of Economic and Social Measurement, 4*, 179–195.

Pollak, R. A. (1976). Habit formation and long-run utility functions. *Journal of Economic Theory, 13*, 272–297.

Pollak, R. A. (1977). Price dependent preferences. *American Economic Review, 67*, 64–75.

Pollak, R. A. (1978). Endogenous tastes in demand and welfare analysis. *American Economic Review, 68*, 374–379.

Ryder, H. E., & Heal, G. M. (1963). Optimal growth with intertemporally dependent preferences. *Review of Economic Studies, 40*, 1–31.

Schelling, T. C. (1978). Egonomics, or the art of self-management. *American Economic Review, 68*, 290–294.

Schelling, T. C. (1980). The intimate contest for self-command. *The Public Interest, 60*, 94–113.

Schelling, T. C. (1984a). *Choice and consequence.* Cambridge, MA: Harvard University Press.

Schelling, T. C. (1984b). Self-command in practice, in policy, and in a theory of rational choice. *American Economic Review, 74*, 1–11.

Showalter, M. H. (1998). Firm behavior in a market with addiction: The case of cigarettes. Working Paper. Department of Economics, Brigham Young University.

Spinnewyn, F. (1981). Rational habit formation. *European Economic Review, 15*, 91–109.

Stigler, G., & Becker, G. S. (1977). De gustibus non est disputandum. *American Economic Review*, *67*, 76–90.

Strotz, R. H. (1956). Myopia and inconsistency in dynamic utility maximization. *Review of Economic Studies*, *23*, 165–180.

Sung, H.-Y., Hu, T.-W., & Keeler, T. E. (1994). Cigarette taxation and demand: An empirical model. *Contemporary Economic Policy*, *12*(3), 91–100.

Suranovic, S. M., Goldfarb, R. S., & Leonard, T. C. (1999). An economic theory of cigarette addiction. *Journal of Health Economics*, *18*, 1–29.

Thaler, R., & Shefrin, H. M. (1981). An economic theory of self control. *Journal of Political Economy*, *89*, 392–406.

von Weizsäcker, C. C. (1971). Notes on endogenous change of tastes. *Journal of Economic Theory*, *3*, 345–372.

Vuchinich, R. E., & Simpson, C. A. (1998). Delayed reward discounting in alcohol abuse. National Bureau of Economic Research Working Paper No. 6410.

Wasserman, J., Manning, W. G., Newhouse, J. P., & Winkler, J. D. (1991). The effects of excise taxes and regulations on cigarette smoking. *Journal of Health Economics*, *10*(1), 43–64.

Winston, G. C. (1980). Addiction and backsliding: A theory of compulsive consumption. *Journal of Economic Behavior and Organization*, *1*(4), 295–324.

Comments on Chaloupka, Emery, and Liang

Robert MacCoun

Frank Chaloupka has made major contributions to the empirical study of addictive drug use, and he and his colleagues provide a valuable review of the growing economic literature on addiction. Their paper documents recent movement away from the strict "rational addiction" framework of Gary Becker and his colleagues, in the direction of models that correspond more closely to recent psychological theorizing about addiction. This is a shift in orientation as well as content. The newer theories tend to start with the behavior of addicts and try to model it; Becker and colleagues started with a model (rational choice) and tried to make it behave like an addict.

By focusing my brief comments on Becker's rational addiction theory (RAT), I necessarily exaggerate the differences between economics and psychology regarding addiction, because Becker's model is economics' least psychological statement. Elsewhere, Peter Reuter and I described RAT as "an intellectual *tour de force* of unknown relevance to the phenomenon of real-world addiction" (MacCoun & Reuter 2001: 64). Here, writing without my economist co-author, I am inclined to be less equivocal. There are good reasons to believe that RAT is wrong as a model of the addiction process. But at the same time, I think it is a mistake to dismiss its contribution to drug policy analysis.

RAT as a Process Model of Addict Choice

I will not rehearse the cogent points about RAT made in other papers in this volume (or in Skog's (1999a, b) sophisticated and fair-minded assessments). But in brief, there is now a wealth of evidence suggesting that important aspects of RAT are almost certainly wrong. First and foremost, in dozens of direct empirical tests, temporal discounting — by addicts, non-addicted people, and animals — is better described by hyperbolic discounting than by exponential discounting (see, e.g. Ainslie & Monterosso Chapter 1, Rachlin Chapter 4, Skog Chapter 5, Cardinal *et al.* Chapter 6, Bickel and Johnson Chapter 8, Mitchell Chapter 11, this volume).[1] Exponential discounting implies, as Chaloupka and colleagues put it, "that individuals consistently maximize utility over their life cycle." Hyperbolic discounting implies preference reversals over time.

Moreover, it is not at all clear that people — be they pension managers or heroin addicts — have anything like a coherent "lifetime utility function." The notion is contradicted by much theory and evidence in cognitive psychology (see Kahneman & Tversky's 2000 edited collection), behavioral finance (e.g. Benartzi & Thaler 1995), and behavioral economics

(Rabin 2000; Rabin & Thaler 2001) showing a disconnect between our assessments of isolated, moment-by-moment choices and the way we might assess aggregated, lifetime utility — if we actually did so.

For example, Rabin (2000) has shown that the degree of concavity necessary to describe risk attitudes in low stake situations generates preposterous predictions for high stake choices. Rabin & Thaler (2001: 225) argue that "the correct conclusion for economists to draw, both from thought experiments and from actual data, is that people do not display a consistent coefficient of relative risk aversion, so it is a waste of time to try to measure it." In fairness, this body of work does not examine drug addicts, but everything we know about addicts suggest less planning, not more, than recent studies find in college students and financial investors.

Price Matters

If I and others are correct that RAT is wrong as a process model of addict choice, then what are we to make of the moderate empirical success of the theory in econometric tests? RAT's greatest empirical success, and its most important contribution, is the notion that addicts are sensitive to current drug prices. For the rationality debate, this is more molehill than mountain. Responsiveness to price is about as minimal a requirement for rationality as one could ask for. Pigeons are price-sensitive in the psychology laboratory; most animals are price-sensitive in ethological studies of foraging behavior in the wild.

But for policy analysis, addict sensitivity to prices is enormously useful information. For a long time, many of us had unthinkingly accepted the idea that addicts were so chemically enslaved that they'd obtain their daily dose at almost any cost. If addicts are indifferent to price, then any intervention that drives up the price of a drug will have unintended deleterious consequences — addicts will divert more of their income from the support of their household and dependents; they may commit more income-generating crime; and illegal drug traffickers or licit tobacco companies will earn more profits at the expense of public health.

Chaloupka and colleagues cite evidence that smokers engage in compensatory behavioral responses to tax and price increases, which would imply that "the perceived health benefits associated with higher cigarette taxes are likely to be somewhat overstated." (For further evidence, see MacCoun & Reuter 2001, Chapter 15; Stratton *et al.* 2001.) Of course, a corollary is that these compensatory responses imply that estimates of price elasticity of demand probably overstate smokers' willingness to reduce their habit in the face of rising prices. At least initially, smokers can reduce the quantity of tobacco they purchase without reducing the quantity of tars and nicotines they consume, by inhaling deeper, holding the smoke in longer, or switching to brands with more tars or less efficient filters.

The behavioral economics literature suggests that there may be better ways to model addiction than the RAT account, but Becker and his colleagues surely deserve credit for establishing price as an important variable in a literature previously dominated by classical conditioning cues, faulty parenting, peer pressure, and other variables less amenable to aggregate measurement and forecasting.

Back to the Future

Accepting that current prices matter is quite different from accepting that *future* prices matter. Chaloupka, Emery, and Laing review evidence that future prices are associated with current tobacco consumption, and following Becker and colleagues, they interpret this as an indication that users form rational expectations and incorporate those expectations into their current choices. I do not contest the notion that addicts, like non-addicts, sometimes consider the future consequences of their actions. As a father of two young children, I am quite preoccupied with college tuition levels two decades from now. Because it clearly affects my concerns about how to pay for their education, rather than my decision about whether to pay for it, there's a temptation to say, "Well, of course, but that's your child's education, not your cigarette (coffee, cocaine, etc.) habit." But, of course, that response begs the question that we are asking: Just how important is the addict's habit to the addict?

Economists who believe in rational expectations need to shoulder more of the burden of proof here. Our understanding of hyperbolic discounting and temporal myopia, as well as a rich ethnographic literature on addict behavior, make it hard to swallow the idea that future price changes play anything but a trivial role in addicts' current choices.

If addicts aren't considering future prices, why are future prices associated with current use? Future prices might be an econometric proxy for unobserved concurrent rational expectations about the future. But they might also be a proxy for a host of other concurrent factors that are correlated with future prices.[2] Tobacco prices can increase because of rising agricultural and other business costs. But they can also rise because of increases in tobacco taxes.[3] It takes tremendous political mobilization to raise "sin" taxes in the face of powerful industry opposition (see MacCoun & Reuter 2001, Chapter 8). How can we be sure it is the anticipated price rise, rather than the impassioned anti-smoking campaigns, that is producing reductions in current consumption? One could make a similar argument at a smaller scale about price increases due to rising tort litigation expenses.

So if future prices are associated with current consumption, the burden would seem to lie with RAT theorists to do more to show that this indicates a rational expectation effect. On the dependent measure side, one would like to see direct measures of perceived expectations about cigarette prices, and statistical evidence that such expectations mediate the "effect" of future prices on current consumption.[4] On the independent variable side, one might test the differential "effects" of future tax increases vs. non-tax price increases, and the effects of tax initiatives vs. non-tax anti-smoking campaigns. One could operationalize anti-tobacco campaigns using advertising budgets, minutes of radio and TV airtime, newspaper column inches, and so on. Supplementing U.S. data with evidence from other nations might provide more variance in tax levels and price trends.

Tobacco is Different

Chaloupka and his colleagues have published important studies of illicit drug use, but their review indicates that most of the econometric work on addiction has focused on tobacco. From a public health standpoint, this focus makes great sense, as tobacco's health harms swamp those of the other drugs. And from a methodological standpoint, there's no question that tobacco data are far richer and more reliable than data on illicit drug use. Still, the heavy focus on tobacco does create some inferential problems.

On the demand side, tobacco differs from other addictive drugs in many ways. It is less intoxicating and more easily integrated into daily activities than other drugs (at least outside the U.S.!). Until recently, the costs it imposed on others were not seen as a significant factor, so anti-smoking stigma is far less developed than, say, anti-heroin stigma. And nicotine is probably more dependency-promoting than many drugs, a fact that probably strengthens the case that Becker, Chaloupka and others are making about rationality; if nicotine is more addictive than other drugs and tobacco addicts appear rational, there is an *a fortiori* case that other addicts might be rational too.

On the supply side, the fact that tobacco is legal makes the case for generalization more daunting. Tobacco can be readily purchased in many different locations (no network or dealer contacts needed). Tobacco prices are surely lower than they would be in an illicit market. Tobacco users are far less likely to be criminally active than, say, heroin addicts, who often commit crimes to raise money for their habit, and who by definition are willing to break the law. We know far less about the case for rational addiction involving illegal drugs, and the data (especially on prices) are far noisier (Manski *et al.* 2001).

From a policy perspective, the fact that tobacco is legal means that it can be advertised and promoted, and it can be regulated and taxed. Regulation creates a host of policy levers unavailable to the prohibitionist (MacCoun *et al.* 1996). Because taxes and other price controls are possible, the rational addiction formulation has clear policy relevance. But the policy implications for a prohibition regime are far murkier. If correct, RAT encourages us to drive up drug prices, since that should reduce consumption with little increase in income-generating crime. But our only mechanisms for doing so are the various forms of supply reduction: interdiction, source-country controls, aggressive enforcement against street dealers. And there are serious questions about whether these efforts actually reduce illicit drug supplies to any significant degree, and whether the benefits outweigh the collateral damage (see Caulkins & MacCoun in press; Manski *et al.* 2001; Reuter *et al.* 1988).

Notes

1. In their paper, Chaloupka and colleagues describe Laibson's model as hyperbolic, and Ainslie's model as quasi-hyperbolic. In fact, it is the other way around. Laibson's model comes closer to a step function; it is more tractable but fails to capture some empirical subtleties of discounting behavior.

2. One possibility is that price increases are a response to current prevalence, though I think at least some analyses rule this out.

3. Over the period 1985–2000, average real tobacco prices (excluding tobacco taxes) have risen 100%, while average combined state and federal tobacco taxes have risen 56%. (Rosalie Pacula, Senior Economist at RAND, personal communication on 30 January 2003.)

4. Specifically, current consumption should be correlated more strongly with expected future prices than with actual future prices, because expected prices are the intermediate causal link and because if prices diverge from expectations, it is the expectations that should drive choices. See Baron & Kenny (1986).

References

Baron, R. M., & Kenny, D. A. (1986). The moderator-mediator variable distinction in social psychological research: Conceptual, strategic, and statistical considerations. *Journal of Personality & Social Psychology, 51,* 1173–1182.

Benartzi, S., & Thaler, R. H. (1995). Myopic loss aversion and the equity premium puzzle. *Quarterly Journal of Economics, 110,* 73–92.

Caulkins, J., & MacCoun, R. J. (in press). Limited rationality and the limits of supply reduction. *Journal of Drug Issues.*

Kahneman, D., & Tversky, A. (Eds) (2000). *Choices, values, and frames.* Cambridge, UK: Cambridge University Press.

MacCoun, R., & Reuter, P. (2001). *Drug war heresies: Learning from other vices, times, and places.* New York: Cambridge University Press.

MacCoun, R., Reuter, P., & Schelling, T. (1996). Assessing alternative drug control regimes. *Journal of Policy Analysis and Management, 15,* 1–23.

Manski, C., Pepper, J., & Petrie, C. (2001). *Informing America's policy on illegal drugs: What we don't know keeps hurting us.* Washington, DC: National Academy of Sciences.

Rabin, M. (2000). Risk aversion and expected-utility theory: A calibration theorem. *Econometrica, 68,* 1281–1292.

Rabin, M., & Thaler, R. (2001). Risk aversion. *Journal of Economic Perspectives, 15,* 219–232.

Reuter, P., Crawford, G., & Cave, J. (1988). *Sealing the borders: The effects of increased military participation in drug interdiction.* Santa Monica, CA: RAND.

Skog, O. J. (1999a). Rationality, irrationality, and addiction — Notes on Becker and Murphy's theory of addiction. In: J. Elster, & O. J. Skog (Eds), *Getting hooked: Rationality and addiction* (pp. 173–207). Cambridge, U.K.: Cambridge University Press.

Skog, O. J. (1999b). Hyperbolic discounting, willpower, and addiction. In: J. Elster (Ed.), *Addiction: Entries and exits* (pp. 151–168).

Stratton, K., Shetty, P., Wallace, R., & Bondurant, S. (Eds) (2001). *Clearing the smoke: Assessing the science base for tobacco harm reduction.* Institute of Medicine, National Academy Press.

Chapter 4

Consumption Dependent Changes in Reward Value: A Framework for Understanding Addiction

Gene M. Heyman

Introduction

The title of this conference, *Choice, Behavioural Economics, and Addiction*, and the content of the papers suggest that addiction entails voluntary drug use. Although all of the speakers seem to share this assumption, it is at odds with how many outside of the boundaries of this conference talk and think about addiction. Addiction is widely understood as a destructive form of drug use, and in accordance with this understanding the standard definition of addiction, as documented by the dictionary, is "compulsive" drug use, where "compulsive" is defined as driven by an "irresistible" force (see, e.g. Oxford English Dictionary, 3rd ed.; American Heritage Dictionary, 3rd ed.). In support of "common sense," it is not obvious that individuals would repeatedly take drugs voluntarily if the drug effects were seriously self-injurious, and, according to standard usage, an act cannot be both "voluntary" and "compulsive." Hence, the idea that guides this conference, that drug use in addicts is voluntary, requires some explanation.

But these discrepancies could be ignored if it were just a matter of "scientific" vs. "everyday" word usage. However, many scientists also define addiction as compulsive drug use (e.g. Koob 2000; Volkow & Fowler 2000). From these articles, it is not clear if the term "compulsive" has simply become a synonym for "strong preference." However, at least some leading experts accept the standard definition of "compulsion" as "irresistible." For example, in the journal *Science*, Alan Leshner, the recent director of the National Institute on Drug Abuse, wrote that addiction begins as voluntary drug use but then becomes involuntary and should be considered a chronic illness, like diabetes or hypertension (Leshner 1997). Jellinek (1952), who championed the disease model of alcoholism more than 50 years ago, made similar arguments about alcoholics. His ideas have become widely accepted by journalists, clinicians, and at least some scientists. For example, media reports on problem drinking usually contain the catch-phrase, "the disease of alcoholism," and editorials in the scientific journal *Alcoholism: Clinical and Experimental Research* promote the view that alcoholism is a disease (which implies involuntary or irresistible drinking (e.g. Erickson 1998)). Thus, the issue of whether it is legitimate to assume, as have the conferees, that addiction entails voluntary drug use needs to be addressed. Indeed in this paper this question takes precedence in regard to order of presentation.

The second section introduces a choice-based analysis of addiction. The analysis builds on a paper by Herrnstein & Prelec (1992). This paper introduced a simple but fundamental distinction regarding whether the behavior to be explained is a single choice leading to a particular outcome or a series (distribution) of choices leading to a disposition or state. In the arena of eating, an example of the former is the decision to have, say, a Chinese meal or an Italian meal, whereas an example of the latter is an extended diet resulting in weight loss. The distinction, as will be shown, leads to a proof that in repeated choice situations an individual can choose the lowest overall reinforcement rate (e.g. Heyman & Herrnstein 1986). Or put another way, from the idea of distributed choice, it is possible to derive addiction.

The second section ends with a description of an experiment based on the distributed choice theory of addiction (Heyman & Dunn 2002). The study compared drug users and non-drug users in series of two-choice tests. One choice was better from the perspective of the current trial, whereas the other choice was better from the perspective of two or more consecutive trials. This dilemma, it is argued, is analogous to the problem facing an addict who is trying to quit using drugs. The subjects in the study varied in regards to their history of illicit drug use, and this difference turned out to be correlated with performance in the experimental procedure. As the history of illicit drug use increased, a tendency to treat the experimental procedure as a simple, non-repeating, one-choice situation increased.

The third, and last, section of this paper evaluates the generality of the idea that consumption-based changes in reward value yield choice dilemmas. This section is based on the elementary observation that, since consumption dependent changes in reward value are common (e.g. satiation and tolerance), then choice dilemmas of the sort that face the addict (and the subjects in the experimental procedure) must be common. The section ends with a brief discussion of why drug-related choice dilemmas are more difficult than the choice dilemmas that attend conventional rewards, like food or sex.

An Overview of Addiction: Compulsion or Ambivalence?

The goals of this section are to provide a checklist of the behaviors that a model of addiction should predict and to answer the question of whether drug consumption in those who meet the criteria for addiction is compulsive or voluntary. The empirical material includes the American Psychiatric Association's definition of addiction, estimates of the time course and recovery rates for addiction, and psychosocial correlates of recovery. The criterion for determining whether drug consumption is voluntary will be the degree to which it is influenced by the factors that influence decision making. These factors include new information, insights, values, incentives, and rewards. For example, when an individual can be persuaded to behave in some specified way by such interventions as new information, new personal values, legal sanctions, or, more generally, by rewards and punishments, then that behavior is, according to this argument, voluntary. In contrast, when a behavior persists more or less at the same rate regardless of these same factors, then that behavior is deemed to be involuntary.

The distinction can be captured by a thought experiment. Imagine what would be involved in trying to persuade someone not to wink and not to blink. Although the topographies are roughly similar, it is quite plausible that rather modest social sanctions, such as a frown or simply turning away, would discourage further winks, whereas plausibility similarly suggests that a blink, say in response to a blast of air directed to the eye, could not be dissuaded by any amount of money or training. Of course, drug use is not as simple, topographically, as is the exercise of the eye, and with the greater topographic complexity come three problems. First, complex acts like the maintenance of an addiction will entail voluntary and involuntary elements. For example, hedonic motives, such as the desire to feel better or calmer, likely reflect states that vary widely as a function of innate differences. Second, the degree to which an act can be influenced by contingencies must vary along dimensions that have yet to be established. For example, it is possible that behaviors that are less susceptible to environmental contingencies come with their own built-in, virtually immediate rewards (e.g. sexual behaviors). Third, it may often be difficult to distinguish the influence of a contingency and the influence of a change in disposition. For example, someone who lowers their body temperature by means of a swim in ice-cold water has not really *learned* to lower their body temperature — rather they have learned to place themselves in a situation that elicits a change in body temperature.

Although each of these points deserves attention, we need not wait for further research to come to a conclusion about the influence of ideas, values, and consequences on drug use. As is shown next, there is little question that a wide range of rather ordinary persuasive influences can significantly modify the level of drug use in addicts (individuals who meet the criteria for "substance dependence").

It may also be useful to point out what do not count as criteria for the distinction between voluntary and involuntary behavior. I am not asking whether addictive drugs change the brain. Of course they do, but this does not discriminate addictive drug use from any experience that alters behavior. Similarly, the question is not whether there is a biological predisposition for addiction. Most likely there is a biological predisposition for most if not all voluntary behaviors. People are born with musical, athletic, and intellectual talents that help guide their careers, just as some are born with a predisposition for alcoholism (e.g. Cloninger 1987; Pickens *et al.* 1991). Put somewhat differently, that drug use is voluntary does not preclude biologically-oriented addiction research. Indeed, according to the approach advocated here, the difference between voluntary and involuntary behavior is at root biological: the neural bases of voluntary behavior are more susceptible to the influence of contingencies and learning, whereas the neural bases of involuntary behaviors are less susceptible to these factors.

Thus, the question to ask is: "does drug consumption in addicts systematically vary as a function of its consequences?" Can new information, values, laws, and incentives bring drug use to a halt in someone who meets the criteria for addiction? And, conversely, does drug consumption persist when the consequences, as framed by the user, favor persistence? If the answers to these questions are "yes" then, according to the persuasion criterion, addiction is a case of voluntary drug consumption.

The American Psychiatric Association Criteria for Drug Dependence ·

The American Psychiatric Association publishes a diagnostic manual for identifying psychiatric disorders (e.g. APA 1994). One of the purposes of the text is to provide clinicians and researchers with reliable criteria for identifying psychiatric disorders (see, e.g. Spitzer *et al.* 1979). For "substance dependence," the APA term for addiction, the reliability ratings are consistently among the highest of any psychiatric disorder. Sometimes overall agreement levels reach above 95% using conventional concordance measures (e.g. Helzer *et al.* 1985). Consequently, the APA criteria have become widely accepted as the defining characteristics for drug use problems and, as such, they also make a good starting point for any review of the nature of addiction.

According to the manual, the "essential feature" of *substance dependence*:

> is a cluster of cognitive, behavioral, and physiological symptoms indicating that the individual continues use of the substance despite significant substance-related problems. There is a pattern of repeated self-administration that usually results in tolerance, withdrawal, and compulsive drug-taking behavior (176).

Following this general statement is an account of the criteria for identifying *tolerance*, *withdrawal*, and *compulsive* and a list of seven signs or symptoms. As neither tolerance nor withdrawal are necessary or sufficient, the pivotal term is "compulsive." The manual identifies compulsive drug use in the following way:

> The individual may take the substance in larger amounts or over a longer period than was originally intended (e.g. continuing to drink until severely intoxicated despite having set a limit of only one drink) . . . Often there have been unsuccessful efforts to decrease or discontinue use . . . The individual may spend a great deal of time obtaining the substance, using the substance, or recovering from its effects . . . Despite recognizing the contributing role of the substance to a psychological or physical problem (e.g. severe depressive symptoms or damage to organ systems), the person continues to use the substance. The key issue in evaluating this criterion is not the existence of the problem, but rather the individual's failure to abstain from using the substance despite having evidence of the difficulty it is causing (178–179).

The seven signs and symptoms come with the rule that if three occur within a 12-month period then the individual meets the criteria for substance dependence. The list includes items from the above passage and tolerance and withdrawal (APA 1994: 181).

Compulsion or Changes in Preference?

As a diagnostic tool for researchers and clinicians the APA account has proven itself many times over (Robins & Regier 1991; Warner *et al.* 1995). However, when it comes to defining "compulsive," the manual uses behavioral criteria that do not require the dictionary definition of "irresistible" or involuntary. For instance, the manual states that to drink more than was initially intended is a sign of compulsion. Yet, it is an everyday experience that our predictions about our future voluntary acts — such as how much we will work, watch television, or talk on the phone — are consistently and repeatedly wrong. Once engaged in an activity, it is commonplace to find that it is more interesting or satisfying than we thought it would be. However, this does not mean that we would not have stopped had the incentives changed. Similarly, there is a non-compulsive interpretation of relapse. If a currently abstinent ex-drug user enters a setting in which his or her drug of choice is readily available, then the context for the decision to indulge or abstain may shrink from what is good overall to what is good for the next few moments. Since one cigarette does not cause cancer and one shot of heroin does not condemn the user to a "junkie life style," a person can quite correctly reason that "since it's just for one last time," the drug is the best choice. However, a series of "one-last times" turns into a relapse. In this example, the process includes reason, a shortsighted time horizon, and incentives. There is nothing compulsive in deciding that, as measured over the next few moments, the drug is better than not having the drug. In sum, the APA's approach to defining "compulsion" deviates from the dictionary account, and it is ambiguous in that the behavioral examples are open to a decision analysis as well as the conventional "compulsive" interpretation.

More on the Nature of Addiction: Supplementing the APA Account

The argument so far is intuitive. We can imagine that the APA symptoms reflect an ambivalent attitude toward drug use, but we can also imagine that they are the signs of a compulsion. The correlates of recovery provide the decisive data, but first it would be useful to say something about recovery itself. Is it common, and if so, how long does addiction usually last?

On the Duration of Addiction: General Population Surveys Show that Most Addicts Recover

The introduction to many scientific papers on addiction includes the phrase: "addiction is a chronic relapsing disorder," or words to that effect. Although these papers usually do not attempt to support this assertion with reference to the clinical literature, the claim that addiction is typically a chronic disorder has empirical support. Addicts in treatment often continue to use drugs (e.g. Condelli *et al.* 1991; Kidorf & Stitzer 1993) and, following treatment, relapse is more common than long-term abstinence (e.g. Hunt *et al.* 1971; Wasserman *et al.* 1998). Thus, on the basis of the clinical literature, the claim that addiction is a "relapsing disorder" or even a "relapsing disease" is plausible.

However, in the most extensive survey of psychiatric disorders among the general public, most people who met the criteria for addiction to an illicit drug did not seek treatment (Anthony & Helzer 1991). This is significant because when the population of addicts is expanded to include those who did not seek treatment — and hence is more representative — recovery not relapse is the rule. For example, in the most recent, large, national survey of psychiatric disorders that selected subjects independently of whether they sought treatment, addiction had the highest recovery rate of any psychiatric disorder (Warner *et al.* 1995) Approximately 76% of those who met the criteria for dependence on an illicit drug at some point in their life, no longer did so. It might be argued that the methods of these large, national surveys are too crude to provide reliable or valid results. But, small-scale intensive ethnographies of heroin and cocaine users that selected subjects on criteria other than clinic attendance lead to the conclusion that for most people addiction is a limited disorder, often ending in their early 30s (e.g. Biernacki 1986; Robins 1993; Robins & Murphy 1967; Waldorf *et al.* 1991). (Interestingly, the national surveys indicate that duration of heavy use for the two legal addicting drugs, alcohol and tobacco, persists longer than does heavy use of the illicit addictive drugs (e.g. Helzer *et al.* 1991).)

According to the evidence, recovery from addiction is common, expert opinion notwithstanding. Consequently, it is reasonable to ask about the correlates of recovery. Do they include the factors that influence voluntary behavior? Or will they support the view that addiction is a form of compulsive behavior, on the order of, say, compulsive hand washing, or the "involuntary" movements and vocalizations that identify Tourette's syndrome?

The Correlates of Recovery: Ideas, Incentives, and Values

One of the distinctive characteristics of voluntary action is that it is highly susceptible to the influence of ideas, especially when the ideas are backed by larger social trends. For example, over the last twenty years or so, the concept of "natural food" has altered the eating and shopping habits of millions of people. Do similar trends apply to drug consumption among addicts?

Most regular smokers meet the criteria for "cigarette addiction," and according to a recent text, many experts in addiction count cigarette smoking as one of the most addictive forms of drug consumption (e.g. Gahlinger 2001). Smoking is legal and despite recent prohibitions, it probably remains the most public addiction. People smoke at or near work, at home, in bars, at parties, at the beach, and according to the ads, even while on horseback. Smoking is part of the culture. Thus, if addicted smokers are actually voluntary smokers, they should be influenced by new ideas about smoking, especially when these ideas are reinforced by other cultural trends. As is demonstrated next, the history of smoking shows the predicted pattern.

With the invention of a cigarette-making machine in the late 19th century, cigarette smoking gradually spread, first among men and then among women. By about 1955, more than 60% of American males and more than 30% of American females were regular smokers (e.g. Giovino *et al.* 1995). But since 1964, the trend has reversed. Over half of those who were ever regular smokers have quit, and currently less than a quarter of the U.S. adult population smokes (e.g. Smith & Fiore 1999). The turning point was the publication of the Surgeon General's Report on the health risks of smoking (USDHHS 1964). The report's fundamental message was that smoking increased the likelihood of a variety of life-threatening illnesses, including cancer. This information was not new, as claims that smoking jeopardized health date as far back as 1604 (King James I, *A Counterblaste to Tobacco*). Rather what was new was the credibility of the data. There were 387 pages of graphs, tables, and statistics, and a supporting cast of scientists that numbered in the hundreds. For anyone who took science seriously, it was difficult to dismiss the possibility that smoking markedly increased the chances of serious illness.

If drug use in addicts is subject to the influence of ideas and values, then the Surgeon General's Report should have led to a decrease in smoking among regular smokers, especially among those who had been trained to respect research and new information. The accompanying graph (Figure 1) tests this idea (USDH&HS 1990, 1994). On the *x*-axis is the year, starting with the year after the Surgeon General's Report. On the *y*-axis is the proportion of smokers who have quit as a function of education level. The steeper the slope, the greater is the change in the probability that a smoker has quit. Since 1964 the overall proportion of smokers who have become ex-smokers has greatly increased. But, as predicted, cessation has increased faster for those who are more educated, and, as a result, educational achievement has become an increasingly stronger predictor of who smokes.

Incentives Decrease Drug Use in Addicts

In the laboratory, the study of voluntary behavior has largely been the study of the influence of rewards and punishment on responding (e.g. Mazur 2002; Skinner 1953). Thus, if drug consumption among addicts is voluntary, it should be susceptible to the influences of reward and punishment. Under a variety of conditions, money and various tangible rewards have reduced or eliminated drug use in smokers (Stitzer *et al.* 1986), cocaine addicts (Higgins *et al.* 1994), and alcoholics (e.g. Bigelow & Liebson 1972). In one of the more realistic studies, severe alcoholics were given a free drink and then offered incentives for not taking a second drink (Cohen *et al.* 1971). The procedure was highly effective at inducing a bout of heavy drinking. For example, the larger the priming drink, the more likely a binge. However, for every priming dose there was an incentive that would promote self-control. With a drink in hand and one under the belt, money persuaded "out of control" drinkers to contain themselves. (However, it may still be the case that under non-laboratory conditions, most serious drinkers are better off as teetotalers than as social drinkers.)

Values and Recovery from Addiction

Autobiographical accounts of recovery often tell of a pivotal emotional experience that sets in motion a chain of events that leads to recovery (e.g. Waldorf 1983). An interesting and overlooked source of these stories is an article published in 1983 by Jorquez. One of the interviewees is Wendy. She places the first steps of her recovery to a solitary sunset and a powerful urge to become a responsible person. She writes that:

> One evening . . . I climbed on this rock, and just sat there alone waiting for the sunset . . . Then I snapped . . . "What am I doing? God did not put me here on earth to be using heroin!" For the first time I felt guilty about being a user. I began to have these powerful feelings for my parents to be proud of me again. And I thought about my son and my responsibilities to him. I stayed clean for about two weeks that time (Jorquez 1983: 353).

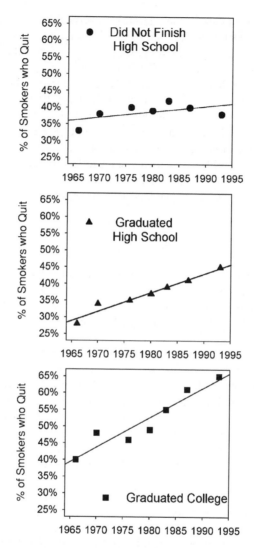

Figure 1: The information in this graph was obtained from the 1990 Surgeon General's Report (U.S. Department of Health & Human Services 1990) and the *Morbidity and Mortality Weekly Review* (U.S. Department of Health & Human Services 1994). These results were initially gathered as part of the NHIS survey on smoking. Ever smoking was defined as smoking 100 or more cigarettes. Quitting was determined by the question "Do you currently smoke?" Although, there was no attempt to validate the respondents' answers, experts in smoking epidemiology believe that the results of this survey are valid. Internal consistency in the data support this belief.

Over a two-year period Wendy gradually moved from heavy drug use to abstinence and had not used drugs for about two years at the time the article was published. For the entire sample in this study the average time since last use was about 6.5 years. An ethnography that used systematic interview methods supports Wendy's version of recovery (Waldorf 1983). In a population of 100 recovered heroin addicts, the most frequently cited reason for the transition from heavy heroin consumption to abstinence was an event that led to feelings of regret about addiction or the junkie lifestyle.

Summary: On the Correlation Between Behavior and Word Usage

This review reveals that new information, incentives, and values can markedly reduce the level of drug consumption in individuals who were daily drug users and who would meet the APA criteria for addiction (for a more complete account of this literature, see Heyman 2001). This point becomes important by contrast. New scientific insights, monetary pay-offs, and religious beliefs have so far proven to have little or no influence on disorders such as schizophrenia and Tourette's syndrome. Thus, by the "persuasion" criterion, addiction entails voluntary drug use and Tourette's syndrome entails involuntary ticking. (Of course, as indicated earlier, not all contingencies will reduce drug use, and, conversely, not all contingencies will have no effect on Tourette ticking.) In support of this distinction and general approach, everyday language conforms to this analysis. Although voluntary behavior is defined in terms of the exercise of the "will," the legal system excuses just those acts that are least susceptible to contingencies: accidents, acts committed by the immature, and acts committed by the insane. Consequently to apply the label "compulsive" to addiction is to ignore: (1) much of what is known about drug use; (2) much of what is known about non-drug related psychiatric disorders; and (3) everyday experience as embodied in language.

Distributed Choice and Addiction

In a paper on the nature of choice, Herrnstein & Prelec (1992) introduced an elementary yet illuminating classification scheme. They pointed out that some choices are distinct and unitary, whereas other choices are aggregates of "many smaller decisions, distributed over a period of time." In the first case, the decision has a relatively well-bounded endpoint; in the second case, a series of decisions establishes a disposition or state. For example, at a particular time and place, a consumer can buy an exercise machine. But to be physically fit, the consumer will have to repeatedly decide to use the exercise machine. The purchase requires but one decisive choice. In contrast, fitness reflects many choices, no one of which is decisive. Herrnstein and Prelec aptly called the second case "distributed choice." Its relevance to this paper is that addiction is an instance of distributed choice. One Friday night binge does not turn a social drinker into an alcoholic. Similarly, for the alcoholic, one weekend of sobriety does not turn him or her into a teetotaler. Rather, alcoholism and abstinence (or controlled drinking) are states that reflect the cumulative effects of many small decisions, and, as with fitness, no one decision is decisive.

The Implications of Distributed Choice and their Application to Addiction

The distinction between distributed and unitary choice is a byproduct of the ideas and experimental results associated with Herrnstein's matching law (Herrnstein 1970, 1990), especially the research that focused on the relationship between matching (defined below) and the economic theory that individuals make choices so as to maximize overall reward or utility. Scores of papers have been written on this issue (see Herrnstein 1990; Heyman 1982; Rachlin *et al.* 1988; Vaughan 1981), but the key ideas as they apply to addiction can be captured in a few paragraphs and a simple graph. (As distributed choice is a quantitative concept, it falls along a continuum with unitary choices. This issue has not been analyzed or investigated and is ignored in this paper.)

Distributed Choice and Consumption Dependent Changes in Value

When a good or activity is chosen or consumed repeatedly, there is the opportunity for its value to change as a function of how often it has been chosen or consumed. For instance, one of the properties of the substances and activities that maintain appetitive behavior (including addictive drugs) is that they either decrease (tolerance) or increase (sensitization) in value as they are consumed. Moreover, with addictive drugs, there are also consumption dependent changes in the value of competing non-drug activities. These interactions are both direct and indirect. Intoxication and withdrawal directly follow drug use and interfere with many conventional activities, thereby undermining their value. Social stigma and legal difficulties are less direct costs that also decrease the value of competing activities. For example, an arrest record decreases employment opportunities, and this, in turn, may increase the likelihood of drug use.

Consumption Dependent Changes in Value Create Ambiguous Environments

Consumption dependent changes in reward value are familiar. We all know about satiation, tolerance, and sensitization. But this familiarity has not led to an appreciation of the implications of these processes for theories of choice and more generally for the understanding of addiction and other self-destructive appetites. The key implication is ambiguity. In situations in which there are consumption dependent changes in reward value there is the strong likelihood that there will be two or more competing reward contingencies. For each contingency, a different response strategy maximizes reward. Thus, assuming reward maximization, consumption dependent changes in reward value create choice dilemmas, or, put slightly differently, they render the environment ambiguous as to which action is "best." An example is given in Figure 2. It shows the reward contingencies for several simple distributed choice experiments, including the one presented in this paper (see also Rachlin & Siegel 1994).

In both panels, the *x*-axis depicts the number of choices out of the last ten that were for option *A*, and the *y*-axis represents the reward value (or utility) associated with each choice. However, for the left and right panels, the domains for calculating value differ. In the left

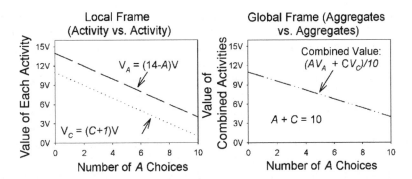

Figure 2: A simple distributed choice "experiment." On the x-axis is the number of choices for alternative A in the most recent 10 trials. On the y-axis in the left panel are the local reward rates. On the y-axis in the right panel is the overall rate of reinforcement, counting rewards from alternative A and alternative B. Note that the best choice in the left panel is A, whereas the best choice in the right panel is B. However, as described in the text, the reward functions in the left and right panels are the same. The different outcomes are due to different ways of framing the choices.

panel, reward value is calculated in terms of each activity taken separately. For example, the input for the value of activity A is restricted to behavior at A and similarly for activity C: $V_A = (14 - A)V$ and $V_C = (C + 1)V$. This seems a natural enough way to compare the value of competing activities. However, it is not the only possible way to approach the problem.

In the right panel, reward value is calculated in terms of each of the possible combinations of activities. That is, instead of comparing activity A to activity C, the right panel compares aggregates whose elements are A and C. For example, the y-axis shows the values of an aggregate of 4 As plus 6 Cs vs. an aggregate of 6 As and 4 Cs. This way of displaying the choices reflects the implicit, but usually overlooked, fact that from a distance two competing entities can be seen as elements of a combination, and if the relative frequencies of the elements change, then the characteristics of the overarching combinations change. Consequently, the domain for the y-axis entails all 11 possible combinations and is referred to as the "global" reward (or utility) rate. Put another way, the decision as to which option to choose in the left panel requires simply checking the height of each option at the moment of choice, whereas the decision as to which option to choose in the right panel requires checking the heights of all possible combinations of options yet encountered: $(V_{A+B} = (AV_A + CV_C)10)$.

The difference in the frame of reference turns out to be important. For example, given the choice rule "Always choose the best alternative," the two ways of organizing the choices yield exactly opposite courses of action. From the perspective of local reward rates, the value of activity A, V_A, is always larger than the value of the competing activity, V_C. Hence an individual with this frame of reference will always choose activity A. But A-choices drive down the future value of both options (A and C), and a series of 10 A choices will drive both local reward rates to their lowest possible level. Nevertheless, if the choice is framed in terms of the local rates, the predicted equilibrium point is exclusive preference for activity A. This is what the logic of "doing what is best" demands.

In the right panel the negative sloping diagonal line traces out the value of the eleven possible combinations of drug and non-drug choices. For example, the *y*-value that corresponds to the leftmost point on the *x*-axis gives the value of 0 *A*s and 10 *C*s, whereas the *y*-value that corresponds to the rightmost point on the *x*-axis, gives the value of 10 *A*s and 0 *C*s. Choice distributions with more *C*-activity choices are associated with higher global reward rates. Thus, from a global perspective, *C* choices should increase, reaching the limit of 10 *C* choices in a row. This is just the opposite of what the local frame of reference predicts. Also note that if choice is under the control of global reward rates, logic says choose the *C* activity even though the *A* activity provides a larger reward on the current trial (which is the frame of reference for local reward rates). For both panels of the graph, the mathematical functions relating value to choice are the same (e.g. $V_A = (14 - A)V$ and $V_C = (C + 1)V$, where $A + C = 10$), and the choice rule is the same: "Choose the option with the highest value." The difference is in how the options are framed.

The message of this example is that consumption dependent changes in reward value create situations in which there are conflicting behavioral outcomes as a function of how reward contingencies are framed. One implication of this point is that the contingencies of reward, the bedrock of behavioral analysis, are ambiguous. This observation will be returned to at the end of this paper.

But perhaps this conflict is only theoretical. If individuals steadfastly adhered to a local or global perspective, the ambiguities of alternative reward functions would remain latent and not a real problem. For instance, in economics textbooks, the universal assumption is that choices are framed in terms of the global reward (utility) rates. The textbook graphs invariably show consumers choosing between "market baskets" that each contain different combinations of the same sets of goods (e.g. Frank 1991; Nicholson 1985; Samuelson 1970). These graphs correspond to the right panel of Figure 2, and economics texts and papers do not discuss the possibility of alternative ways of framing choices. Like economists, psychologists have generally ignored the problem that reward contingencies are inherently ambiguous. Texts on learning and motivation assume one reward contingency per situation. And even Herrnstein & Prelec (1992) graphed reward functions in ways that hid the full extent of the potential dilemma. They always plot the local and global functions along the same *x*-axis. For example, imagine the two panels of Figure 2 collapsed along a single *x*-axis. This is misleading and does not seem sensible as each function applies to a different domain, as described earlier.

Implicit in the practices of economists and experimental psychologists is the assumption that frame of reference is static. Accordingly, the ambiguity demonstrated by Figure 2 is a theoretical but not a real problem. However, two rather elementary observations suggest that economists and psychologists are leading their students astray. First, everyday experience suggests that when individuals step back to analyze choice situations, they often adopt a global perspective. A good example of this is the analysis of choice in economics, as just described. In the texts consumers choose between aggregates of goods, called "market baskets." But, in laboratory studies of behavior that provide choices with direct consequences, the local framework predicts the pattern of choices. This generalization rests on logic and observation.

The logical implication of control by local reward rates is that choice proportions will approximate reward proportions. (See, for example, a paper by Herrnstein (1990) for a proof of this statement.) This equality of choice and reward proportions is known as the "matching law," and literature reviews show that matching is the expected outcome in most laboratory experiments (e.g. Herrnstein 1990; Williams 1988). Moreover, matching occurs for all species yet tested (including humans) and for a wide array of laboratory and non-laboratory environments. In other words, it is highly likely that those who assume a global framework when donning their analytical hats switch to a local framework when facing actual choices. Or, put yet another way, the frame of reference for decision-making is dynamic and situation-dependent. This conclusion, as is shown next, leads to an account of individual differences in susceptibility to the addictive properties of drugs.

Distributive Choice and Addiction

The left side of Figure 2 describes Herrnstein & Prelec's (1992) primrose path theory of addiction. Let A stand for an addictive drug and let C stand for competing non-drug activities, and assume that the subject is governed by the local rates of reward (as experiments suggest is usually the case). For example, imagine that the left panel represents the reward contingencies for a heroin addict. The downward slopes reflect the observations that heroin use reduces its own value (e.g. tolerance) and also the value of competing conventional activities (e.g. the impact of intoxication on professional responsibilities). However, since the local reward rate for heroin never falls below that of the conventional competition, heroin has the higher reward value and is invariably chosen — the primrose path to addiction.

However, this is just half the story. Addiction also entails attempts to curtail drug use and periods, perhaps brief, of abstinence. The motivation for abstinence follows immediately from the right panel. If the heroin addict frames his or her choices in terms of the combined benefits and costs (e.g. the heroin addict life-style vs. a conventional life-style), the graph says that the preferred course of action is non-drug activity. Thus, the two panels of Figure 2 generate an addictive pattern of heroin use — periods of heavy use followed by abstinence, followed by periods of heavy use, etc. Also notice that the global framework sets the criterion for determining whether behavior is excessive. For instance, from the perspective of the global framework, heroin use is excessive because it persists yet lowers overall reward rates. In contrast, from the local framework, there is no level of heroin consumption that is excessive.

Conditions that Influence the Frame of Reference

According to this analysis, whether drug consumption persists or desists depends on the factors that establish the frame of reference. Restricting the discussion to laboratory studies, there are but three experiments that explicitly tested conditions that might influence whether choice was guided by the local or global reward values. Two experiments varied stimulus conditions, one with humans and the other with pigeons. In the human study, the temporal pattern of the inter-trial intervals influenced whether choices proceeded according to a local or global framework. When trials were presented in clusters of three, global choices increased (Kudadjie-Gyamfi & Rachlin 1996; Rachlin & Siegel 1994). When there was no discernible overarching temporal pattern, local choices persisted. In the experiment with pigeons, the introduction of a stimulus (a light) increased the frequency of global choices (Heyman & Tanz 1995). When the pigeons responded so as to maximize reward, from the perspective of the global strategy, a light went on. The pigeons learned to respond so as to keep this light on. But in sessions in which the light was not available, the subjects responded according to the local rates of reward (as predicted by the matching law). The third study addressed drug use and frame of reference directly (Heyman & Dunn 2002). It tested the hypothesis that individual differences in decision making help explain individual differences in illicit drug use. It will be described in some detail, as it provides a test of the distributed choice approach to addiction.

An Experimental Test of the Hypothesis that Individual Differences in a Laboratory Distributed Choice Procedure Predicts Differences in Drug Use

Most people who experiment with illicit drugs do not go on to become regular users (Anthony & Helzer 1991; SAMHSA 2001), and recall that among those who do become regular users, there is wide variation in the duration of the disorder (see Section 1 of this paper and Heyman 2001). Epidemiological research shows that these differences are correlated with a variety of factors, including employment history, education level, the percentage of fat in the diet, the likelihood of using car seat belts, exercise patterns, divorce rate, delinquency, and the absence of additional psychiatric disorders (e.g. Abood & Conway 1994; Anthony & Helzer 1991; Hersch & Viscusi 1998; Robins & Murphy 1967). These correlates suggest a general and enduring approach to distributed choice problems. For instance, the likelihood of a car accident on any particular drive (say, going to the super market) is vanishingly small. Hence, from a local perspective, it is reasonable to suppose that the comfort of not wearing a seat belt has more value than wearing one (counting the effort of putting them on as a cost). However, from a global perspective, seat belts save lives. Thus, the correlation between seat belt wearing and not smoking (Hersch & Viscusi 1998) suggests the possibility of a general disposition for a more local or more global frame of reference. The experiment, described next, evaluated this line of thought. It tested whether individual differences in a laboratory distributed choice task predicted differences in illicit drug use.

The purpose of the experiment (Heyman & Dunn 2002) was to test whether performance in a simple, computer-based distributed choice game predicted drug use history. The game was played on a laptop computer. There were two choices. One button was the best choice from the perspective of the current trial (the local solution) and the other button was the best choice from the perspective of two or more trials (the global solution). As in the contingencies outlined in Figure 2, the button that was the best local solution decreased future benefits for both options and led to a lower overall rate of reward. In contrast, the button that corresponded to the global solution increased future benefits and led to a higher overall rate of reward. Also, as in Figure 2, the changes in reward value were a linear function of previous choices. However, the averaging window was not ten responses but just two. This is the smallest possible temporal horizon for a distributed choice problem.

The details of the contingency included the following relations. Each choice had two programmed consequences: it earned a nickel and it determined the length of the delay until the next choice trial. Longer delays meant longer waits or dead time until the next choice trial, and since the session lasted a fixed period (five minutes), longer wait times also meant lower rates of reward. Thus, at each trial the local solution produced the shortest wait time on the current trial, but increased the wait times for both alternatives on the next trial. In contrast, the global solution produced the longest wait time for the current trial, but reduced wait times on the next trial. These wait times were not especially long, for example the longest was 14 seconds. However, they were noticeable, and in pilot tests subjects stated that they did not like to wait for the next trial to start.

Over the course of the experimental session, subjects played five different distributed choice games. In each game, the absolute inter-trial wait times were varied so that differences between the local and global solutions would vary. We did this to test the prediction that preference for the local solution would increase as the immediate advantage of the local solution increased. For example, in one game a switch from the global to the local solution always reduced the current wait time by 3.0 seconds, whereas in another game the decrease was twice as large, 6.0 seconds. If subjects preferred shorter wait times (as expected) then preference for the local solution should be greater in the 6.0-second game. Other features of the procedure included a battery of cognitive tests and questionnaires regarding drug use and social-economic status.

Subjects were selected with the goal of producing a wide range of drug use histories. Illicit drug users were recruited from the North Charles Center for the Addictions and McLean Hospital's Alcohol and Drug Abuse Treatment Unit. The North Charles clinic provides counseling services and methadone for individuals who are dependent on opiates (usually heroin). The McLean drug treatment clinic is primarily a non-residential day program that provides counseling and daily drug screening. For the McLean patients, the primary drug of abuse was usually cocaine. Control subjects were recruited by newspaper ads from neighborhoods near the methadone and McLean clinics. The majority of control and drug clinic subjects were white and had graduated high school.

The basic finding was that there was a correlation between drug use history and performance in the distributed choice game. Drug clinic subjects were more likely to favor the local solution and control subjects were more likely to favor the global solution.break Figure 3 shows these results on a game-by-game basis.

Details of the graph reveal that differences between clinic subjects and controls did not emerge straight off, but took time to develop. That is, they were a function of experience with the procedure. We also found that quantitative differences in the games made a difference. In games in which the immediate advantage of the local solution was larger, subjects were more likely to choose the local solution (e.g. Game 4), and in games in which the immediate advantage of the local solution was smaller, subjects were more likely to choose the global solution (e.g. Game 3).

Were the Differences in Game Performance Related to Differences in Drug History or the Correlates of Drug History?

The two groups differed in terms of several important demographic characteristics. Drug clinic subjects left school earlier, had lower incomes, and lower IQs (101 and 114,

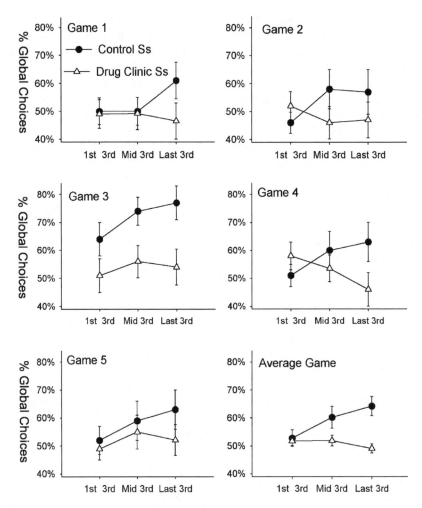

Figure 3: A summary of the distributed choice experiment (Heyman & Dunn 2002). On the *x*-axis session trials are divided into three consecutive blocks. Each block was composed of about 13–15 trials. On the *y*-axis is the percentage of global choices for each block of trials. The control subjects, filled circles, generally made more global choices than the drug clinic subjects (open triangles). In each of the five games, differences between control and drug clinic subjects emerged as a function of exposure to the game. The games differed in terms of the magnitude of the advantage of switching from the global to the local (see Heyman & Dunn 2002).

respectively). We used analysis of covariance to analytically control for education and IQ differences. The results showed that group differences in game performance did not depend on group differences in IQ or educational achievement. In other words, although there were group differences in academic achievement and its correlates, these differences were not strongly correlated with performance in the distributed choice task. On the other hand, the correlations among the psychosocial variables, e.g. IQ, education, and income, were robust and significant. That is, the sample was not too small to detect robust correlates of IQ and education.

The experiment was based on the idea that differences in how individuals approached a laboratory distributed choice problem would be correlated with their history of illicit drug use. The assumptions leading to this hypothesis were that drug use is an example of a distributed choice dilemma, and that there are enduring individual differences in how people approach distributed choice problems. The experimental results supported the assumptions and hypothesis.

Limitations of the Experiment

This experiment is the first attempt to determine whether individual differences in distributed choice are related to individual differences in drug use. Consequently, the generality of the results are unexplored and confounding factors remain unanalyzed. Some of the issues that require attention include the following.

The drug clinic subjects had been using heroin and/or cocaine for an average of about 10 years. But as noted in the review of the addiction literature, there is much individual variation in the duration of addiction. Thus, it is possible that a bias toward local solutions in the computer game does not distinguish addicts from non-addicts, but instead distinguishes long-term drug users from the rest of the population, including those individuals who were addicted for a few years and then quit. Second, the drug users were recruited from treatment centers. Bob Schuster (personal communication, March 2002) suggested that treatment seeking might reflect a global perspective. Possibly, then, long-term drug users who were not in treatment might show even greater preferences for the local solution than the clinic subjects who participated in this study. In other words, the current results may underestimate the range of performances that would have been obtained had we tested a population of drug users who did not seek treatment. Third, the differences in performance may reflect a correlate of drug use, but not drug use itself. For example, drug users who seek treatment are about twice as likely to be afflicted with additional psychiatric disorders than drug users who do not seek treatment (e.g. Regier *et al.* 1990). Thus, preference for local solutions could be causally linked to psychiatric distress rather than to addiction. Finally, it is not known if preference for the local solution among illicit drug users is a consequence of drug use or reflects qualities that preceded and perhaps abetted long-term drug use. In sum, the experimental results point to new and interesting questions, which, if answered, would markedly increase our understanding of drug use and of decision-making.

A Graphic Test of the Claim that Competing Local and Global Equilibriums are a General Problem for Appetitive Behavior

According to the discussion that introduced the experiment, motivated behavior typically involves consumption or choice dependent changes in reward value and thus motivated behavior typically entails the possibility of two or more ideal choice strategies, depending on the frame of reference. This next section of the paper explores this claim by means of graphs. In two graphs there are consumption dependent changes in reward value, and, for comparison, there is a graph in which reward value remains constant, independently of changes in consumption levels.

The three pairs of graphs show the predicted behavioral outcomes for the local and global frame of reference for three conditions. For the top and middle pair, the local rate of reward for alternative A, which is meant to represent an addictive-substance, decreases as a function of consumption (e.g. tolerance). In the bottom panel, both local reward rates are constant and unaffected by consumption. As before, the choice rule for the left panels is "select the local rate of reward that is best," whereas, the choice rule for the right panels is "select the distribution of activities that is best."

In the top panel, the reward value of A decreases rapidly as a function of consumption and then replenishes rapidly while the subject is engaged in behavior B. The mathematics are based on an analysis of a commonly used reward schedule (the variable-interval, Heyman 1979, 1982; Heyman & Luce 1979), but here it is assumed that reward value changes as a function of internal processes, such as satiation, tolerance, and deprivation. For example, during consumption bouts, satiation and tolerance lead to a decrease in reward value, and then when consumption comes to a halt, deprivation sets in, thereby driving reward value back to an initial asymptotic level.

Given these dynamics and the rate constants for the changes in value, the local rate perspective in the top pair of panels predicts a strong preference for the addictive substance (A *choices* $= 76\%$), whereas the global rate perspective predicts an equilibrium point with an equally strong preference for the non-addictive substance (B *choices* $= 77\%$). For someone whose preferences were controlled by the global framework, any preference for A in excess of 23% is excessive. Hence, a person under the control of the local contingencies is consuming the addictive substance at about three times the rate that they should. Conversely, from the perspective of the local framework, someone stuck in the global framework is favoring the smaller reward over the larger reward.

In the middle panel, the local and global equilibrium points differ but not by as much as in the top panel. The predicted outcomes are a 24% preference for the addictive substance when the frame of reference is local, and a 7% preference for the addictive substance when the frame of reference is global. The local and global solutions are closer together because the addictive substance replenishes and habituates more slowly (relative to the addictive substance in the top panel).

In the bottom panel, the local and global perspectives predict the same outcome so that ambiguity is not possible. Here, though, there are no consumption dependent changes in reward value.

The graphs suggest several new generalizations for cases in which there are consumption dependent decreases in reward value. (1) When the origins and slopes of the reward functions differ, the local and global equilibrium points will differ. In these cases, the local equilibrium will involve overindulgence in the appetite that has the higher initial value (at a consumption level of zero). (2) The magnitude of the difference between the local and global equilibriums varies systematically as a function of quantitative differences in the competing reward functions. (3) When the rates of tolerance are the same for both options,

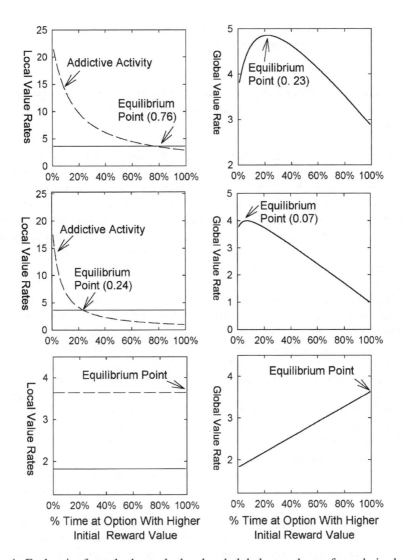

Figure 4: Each pair of panels shows the local and global reward rates for a choice between two alternatives. For the addictive activity, reward value decreased as a function of consumption, and replenished as a function of time spent in the competing activity. The rates of decline and replenishment mimic those associated with the reward dynamics of variable interval schedules (see, Heyman 1982 for the equations), but in this graph the curves identify tolerance and the loss of tolerance. In the top panel the rates of tolerance and loss of tolerance are three times greater than in the middle panel. In the bottom panel consumption does not alter reward rate and consequently the local and global frame of reference lead to the same pattern of choices: exclusive preference for the non-drug activity.

as in Figure 2, the relationship between the initial values will determine the relationship between the local and global equilibrium points.

If Consumption Dependent Changes in Reward Value Set the Stage for Addiction, Then Why are Some Substances Much More Likely to Become the Focus of an Addiction Than Others?

Although consumption dependent changes in reward value accompany virtually all appetitive activities, appetitive problems are much more likely with drugs than with other substances and activities. This outcome follows from the graphs. For instance, appetitive goals that reinforce a local perspective or that are accompanied by an especially large difference between the local equilibrium point and the global equilibrium point will be more problematic. Drugs that are recognized as addictive meet these conditions. Intoxication and other drug effects enhance the local perspective or create a more extreme local equilibrium. Some of the key observations that support these conclusions include the following points.

By definition, intoxication entails a state in which normal mental faculties are compromised. This should decrease the likelihood of a more global, encompassing perspective. In contrast, other rewards, even somewhat problematic ones, such as food, do not alter judgment. Various drug effects undermine conventional activities. For instance, intoxication and withdrawal interfere with many conventional responsibilities, thus making the heavy drug user less susceptible to the rewarding effects of conventional activities. This produces the downward sloping reward functions of Figures 2 and 4, and the greater the downward slope of the competing reward function, the greater the preference for the addictive activity, all else being equal. In contrast, many conventional goals increase the reward value of competing activities. For instance, success in one's profession often leads to outcomes, such as committee assignments and invitations to give talks that compete with professional achievement. Somewhat similarly, the satiating mechanisms associated with drug use are relatively weak in comparison to those associated with primary conventional rewards. Food makes you full and exercise tired. In contrast, there are no similar direct satiating mechanisms for most addictive drugs. To be sure, one can get full on alcohol, but with distilled drinks it is possible to become extremely intoxicated well before one is bloated on drink. Parallel contrasts between addictive drugs and conventional activities extend to withdrawal, and indirect effects such as stigma. However, without going into details, it should be clear that many of the behavioral effects of addictive drugs reinforce the choice dilemma that is posed by consumption dependent changes in reward value. Of course, for each drug the story will be somewhat different (e.g. cigarettes are addictive but not intoxicating), and a more complete account will include these details.

A Brief Evaluation of Other Choice Theories of Addiction

At this conference, presenters have focused on four choice models of addiction: hyperbolic discounting (Ainslie 1975; Rachlin & Green 1972), the Becker–Murphy economic analysis

(1990), Rachlin's substitution theory (1997), and Herrnstein & Prelec's primrose path theory (1992). Although these four approaches have rather different histories and focus on different aspects of behavior, they can be compared in terms of how well they correspond to the APA account of addiction presented at the beginning of this paper.

The hyperbolic model can explain impulsivity and ambivalence (e.g. Ainslie 1975). However, it does not have terms for representing consumption dependent changes in value. Consequently, it is really more appropriate for modeling one-shot, non-repeating choices, whereas, as emphasized in this paper, addiction entails a series of choices. Ainslie has dealt with this by considering the implications of a series of delayed choices, which he represents as a series of overlapping hyperbolic discount curves. However, in Ainslie's graphs reward value does not change as a function of consumption. This may be realistic for some goals but not for those involving drugs.

Becker & Murphy's "reward model" and Rachlin's substitution model share a number of common properties and will be discussed together. The equations explicitly represent consumption dependent changes in value. However, they assume that for each environment there is but one reward function. Consequently, these models entail no criterion for defining excessive consumption, and similarly there is no formal way of representing ambivalence and relapse. These are not really models of addiction. Rather, they are equations that generate extreme but unambivalent preferences. For example, an individual who behaved according to the rules of Rachlin's substitution theory or Becker & Murphy's rational choice model has no reason (within the boundaries of the model) to regret their behavior. In contrast, a person who comes under the control of global contingencies will regret choices made according to a local frame of reference.

This paper is an elaboration of Herrnstein & Prelec's distinction between unitary and distributed choices and their primrose path theory of addiction (the left panel of Figure 2). The ideas emphasized here, such as consumption-dependent changes in reward value, competing value functions, an ambiguous environment, frame of reference, and local and global choice equilibriums are concepts that have their basis in the distinction between unitary and distributed choices. However, these ideas are at best a framework for understanding addiction. They provide a general approach for understanding addiction. What is needed next is integration at the conceptual level with other theories that have sought to explain the persistence of drug use despite aversive consequences (e.g. Koob & LeMoal 2000; Robinson & Berridge 1993), and a more detailed account of how the specific inputs to drug use, such as cravings, intoxication, and changes in brain function, influence the decision to use or forgo drugs. Some of these inputs affect the relative value of the drug (e.g. craving) and others may affect decision-making itself (see, e.g. Grant *et al.* 2000; Volkow *et al.* 1991).

Common Misunderstandings of Choice-Based Analyses of Addiction

Choice-based accounts of addiction are easily misunderstood. The common criticisms are that they "amount to blaming the victim," "they ignore biology," and they are "contradicted by the success of pharmacological treatments." Although these criticisms reflect important and influential ideas about the nature of behavior and the ethics of treatment, they will only be touched on briefly in this paper.

Choice in a Deterministic World

If choice is part of the natural world, then the rationale for helping individuals make better choices must be similar to the rationale for ameliorating any natural process, as, say, when we search for a cure for cancer. In both cases, the goal is to help create a better world and to make a difference. However, there are differences, and in general the politics of correcting voluntary behavior will likely prove to be more complicated than the politics of non-voluntary disorders. For instance, it is often not clear as to which institutions are responsible for problems that involve choice. In the case of criminal acts there has been a long-standing debate as to whether criminals and society would be better served by rehabilitation or by punishment. A similar debate attends drug use. It is not clear whether punishment should play a role in "drug treatment," or whether the stigma that is associated with voluntary disorders plays a useful or harmful role. For instance, it is often overlooked that ex-addicts often point out that the desire to lead a more productive life that their parents and/or children could take pride in led them to quit using drugs (e.g. Jorquez 1983; Waldorf 1983).

A corollary of the idea that drug use in addicts is subject to the influence of its consequences is that in principle there exist circumstances such that quitting is not possible. For example, consider individuals with the following characteristics: (1) they can imagine that sobriety would help create a better overall life-style; but (2) they have no conventional alternatives that provide as much reward value in the short term as does drug intoxication; and (3) they have no techniques for escaping the local reward rates. Under these conditions, drug use persists — voluntarily but inescapably. However, this imagined situation might have no real life counterpart. Even heavy drug users are not intoxicated all the time, leaving a temporal window for strategies that will counter the influence of the drug. For instance, during periods of sobriety, the heroin addict or alcoholic can make arrangements that prevent contact with the drug (for other examples of these strategies, see Ainslie 1975).

The Emphasis on Choice Denies the Importance of Biology

The idea that drug use among those who are addicted is a matter of choice is often understood as a denial of the biological bases of addiction. However, if psychological processes are seen as a product of evolutionary processes, then there is no conflict. Put most generally, the difference between voluntary and involuntary behavior is in the "wiring." The biology of voluntary behavior allows for the influence of experience, and, in particular, it allows reward contingencies to shape behavior. In contrast, the biology of involuntary behavior does not permit the direct influence of reward contingencies. Thus, the question is not whether drugs alter the brain, but whether they alter the brain in ways that leave drug use immune to the influence of incentives, new information, and the various factors that normally influence choice. The review of the correlates of recovery presented in Section 1 of this paper shows that the answer to this question is "no."

Although a wide array of findings support the view that drug addicts remain voluntary drug users, even after decades of drug use (see, e.g. Jorquez 1983), the literature, including the experiment presented in this paper, shows that there are biases in decision making associated with drug use. Several researchers have presented data that suggest that these biases are associated with the functioning of the prefrontal cortex (e.g. Everitt *et al.* 2001; Grant *et al.* 2000), and it is plausible that addictive drugs, especially stimulants, undermine the functioning of brain regions important in the cognitive functions that contribute to decision making (Volkow *et al.* 1991). Thus, the toxic effects of addictive drugs may promote further drug use by undermining cognition in ways that promote the control of local reward functions.

Psychopharmacological Correlates of Recovery

Clinical research shows that pharmacological treatments have increased the likelihood of successful and long-lasting abstinence in some heroin addicts and smokers (e.g. Dole & Nyswander 1967; Fiore *et al.* 1994). This is not discrepant with the conclusion that those who meet the criterion for addiction actually choose to continue to use drugs and could be persuaded to stop. Indeed, as the distinction between voluntary and involuntary behavior is fundamentally a matter of biology, voluntary behavior must be as subject to pharmacological manipulations as is involuntary behavior. In support of this point, a common property of successful biological treatments for addiction is that they directly or indirectly reduce the reward value of the drug. For example, methadone blocks the rush that accompanies heroin injections and nicotine replacement techniques (e.g. the patch) indirectly decrease the reward value of cigarettes by attenuating withdrawal symptoms. Given the relativity of reward, these treatments can be described as pharmacological methods for increasing the relative reward value of competing non-drug activities, which is the strategy employed in the successful incentive-based drug treatment programs (e.g. Higgins *et al.* 1994). In other words, clinicians have two general methods for altering the addict's preferences: behavioral and pharmacological.

The Future and Limits of Strictly Behavioral Accounts

The experimental results demonstrate that individual differences in decision making are correlated with individual differences in drug use. These differences reflect educational influences, basic cognitive processes, and the biological mechanisms that mediate cognition. These observations imply that at least some of the variance in decision-making is correlated with cognitive factors that are beyond the scrutiny of behavioral methods and with biological factors that are well beyond the influence of reward contingencies. That is, a strictly behavioral account of addiction is necessarily incomplete. What will be needed are techniques that can uncover individual differences in cognitive functioning and individual differences in the biology of voluntary behavior. Put another way, we now have a reasonable outline of the contingencies that apply to drug use, and it is time to make similar progress in the understanding of the factors that determine which contingencies come to control individual behavior. In particular, it would be especially useful and especially interesting to better understand why under similar circumstances some individuals excessively consume drugs, as predicted by the local reward rates, and others eschew or moderately consume drugs, as predicted by the global reward rates.

Acknowledgments

I would like to thank Drs. Ben Williams and Jerry Zuriff for their helpful comments on an earlier version of this paper. I am also grateful for the cooperation and help of Patrick Griswold and the helpful staff of the North Charles Institute on the Addictions and Dr. Roger Weiss, Bill Lopez and the helpful staff of the Alcohol and Drug Abuse Treatment Program at McLean Hospital. The research was supported by a grant (R21 DA11954) from the National Institute on Drug Abuse.

References

Abood, D. A., & Conway, T. L. (1994). Smoking status, body composition, exercise, and diet among Navy men. *Health Values, 18*, 51–62.

Ainslie, G. (1975). Specious reward: A behavioral theory of impulsiveness and control. *Psychological Bulletin, 82*, 463–496.

American Psychiatric Association (1994). *Diagnostic and statistical manual of mental disorders* (4th ed., DSM-IV). Washington, DC: Author.

Anthony, J. C., & Helzer, J. E. (1991). Syndromes of drug abuse and dependence. In: L. N. Robins, & D. A. Regier (Eds), *Psychiatric disorders in America* (pp. 116–154). New York: Free Press.

Becker, G. S., & Murphy, K. M. (1990). A theory of rational addiction. *Journal of Political Economy, 96*, 675–700.

Biernacki, P. (1986). *Pathways from heroin addiction: Recovery without treatment*. Philadelphia: Temple University Press.

Bigelow, B., & Liebson, I. (1972). Cost factors controlling alcoholic drinking. *Psychological Record, 22*, 305–314.

Cloninger, C. R. (1987). Neurogenetic adaptive mechanisms in alcoholism. *Science, 236*, 410–416.

Cohen, M., Liebson, I., Faillace, L., & Speers, W. (1971). Alcoholism: Controlled drinking and incentives for abstinence. *Psychological Reports, 28*, 575–580.

Condelli, W. S., Fairbank, J. A., Dennis, M. L., & Rachal, J. V. (1991). Cocaine use by clients in methadone treatment programs: Significance, scope and behavioral interventions. *Journal of Substance Abuse Treatment, 8*, 203–212.

Dole, V., & Nyswander, M. (1967). Heroin addiction — A metabolic disease. *Archives of Internal Medicine, 120*, 19–24.

Erickson, C. K. (1998). Voices of the afflicted. *Alcoholism: Clinical and Experimental Research, 22*, 1483–1484.

Everitt, B. J., Dickinson, A., & Robbins, T. W. (2001). The neuropsychological basis of addictive behaviour. *Brain Research Reviews, 36*, 129–138.

Fiore, M. C., Stevens, S. S., Jorenby, D. E., & Baker, T. B. (1994). The effectiveness of the nicotine patch for smoking cessation. *Journal of the Medical Association of America, 271*, 1940–1947.

Frank, R. H. (1991). *Microeconomics and behavior*. New York: McGraw-Hill.

Gahlinger, P. M. (2001). *Illegal drugs: A Sagebrush medical guide*. Salt Lake City: Sagebrush Press.

Giovino, G. A., Henningfield, J. E., Tomar, S. L., Escobedo, L. G., & Slade, J. (1995). Epidemiology of tobacco use and dependence. *Epidemiologic Reviews, 17*, 48–65.

Grant, S., Contoreggi, C., & London, E. D. (2000). Drug abusers show impaired performance in a laboratory test of decision making. *Neuropsychology, 38*, 1180–1187.

Helzer, J. E., Burnam, A., & McEvoy, L. T. (1991) Alcohol abuse and dependence. In: L. N. Robins, & D. A. Regier (Eds), *Psychiatric disorders in America* (pp. 81–115). New York: Free Press.

Helzer, J. E., Robins, L. N., McEvoy, L. T., Spitzagel, E. L., Stolzmanm, R. K., Farmer, A., & Brockington, I. F. (1985). A comparison of clinical and diagnostic interview schedule diagnoses. *Archives of General Psychiatry, 42,* 657–666.

Herrnstein, R. J. (1970). On the law of effect. *Journal of the Experimental Analysis of Behavior, 13,* 243–266.

Herrnstein, R. J. (1990). Behavior, reinforcement, and utility. *Psychological Science, 1,* 217–224.

Herrnstein, R. J., & Prelec, D. (1992). A theory of addiction. In: G. Loewenstein, & J. Elster (Eds), *Choice over time* (pp. 331–360). New York: Russell Sage Foundation.

Hersch, J., & Viscusi, W. K. (1998). Smoking and other risky behaviors. *Journal of Drug Issues, 28,* 645–661.

Heyman, G. M. (1979). Matching and maximizing in concurrent schedules. *Psychological Review, 86,* 495–500.

Heyman, G. M. (1982). Is time allocation elicited behavior? In: M. Commons, R. Herrnstein, & H. Rachlin (Eds), *Quantitative analyses of behavior, Vol. 2: Matching and maximizing accounts* (pp. 459–490). Cambridge, MA: Ballinger Press.

Heyman, G. M. (2001). Is addiction a chronic, relapsing disease? Relapse rates, estimates of duration, and a theory of addiction. In: P. Heymann, & W. Brownsberger (Eds), *Drug addiction and drug policy* (pp. 81–117). Harvard University Press.

Heyman, G. M., & Dunn, B. (2002). Decision biases and persistent illicit drug use: An experimental study of distributed choice in drug clinic patients. *Drug and Alcohol Dependence, 67,* 192–203.

Heyman, G. M., & Herrnstein, R. J. (1986). More on concurrent interval ratio schedules. *Journal of the Experimental Analysis of Behavior, 46,* 331–351.

Heyman, G. M., & Luce, R. D. (1979). Operant matching is not a logical consequence of reinforcement rate maximization. *Animal Learning and Behavior, 7,* 133–140.

Heyman, G. M., & Tanz, L. E. (1995). How to teach a pigeon to maximize overall reinforcement rate. *Journal of the Experimental Analysis of Behavior, 64,* 277–297.

Higgins, S., Budney, A., Bickel, W., Foerg, F., Donham, R., & Badger, G. (1994). Incentives improved outcome in outpatient behavioral treatment of cocaine dependence. *Archives of General Psychiatry, 51,* 568–576.

Hunt, W. A., Barnett, L., & Branch, L. (1971). Relapse rates in addiction programs. *Journal of Clinical Psychology, 27,* 455–456.

Jellinek, E. M. (1952). Phases of alcohol addiction. *Quarterly Journal of Studies on Alcohol, 13,* 673–684.

Jorquez, J. (1983). The retirement phase of heroin using careers. *Journal of Drug Issues, 13,* 343–365.

Kidorf, M., & Stitzer, M. L. (1993). Descriptive analysis of cocaine use of methadone patients. *Drug and Alcohol Dependence, 32,* 267–275.

Koob, G. F. (2000). Neurobiology of addiction: Toward the development of new therapies. *Annals of the New York Academy of Sciences, 909,* 170–185.

Koob, G. F., & LeMoal, M. (2000). Drug addiction, dysregulation of reward, and allostasis. *Neuropsychopharmacology, 24,* 99–129.

Kudadjie-Gyamfi, E., & Rachlin, H. (1996). Temporal patterning in choice among delayed outcomes. *Organizational Behavior and Human Decision Processes, 65,* 61–67.

Leshner, A. I. (1997). Addiction is a brain disease, and it matters. *Science, 278,* 45–47.

Mazur, J. E. (2002). *Learning and behavior.* Saddle River, NJ: Prentice-Hall.

Nicholson, W. (1985). *Microeconomic theory* (3rd ed.). Chicago: Dryden Press.

Pickens, R. W., Svikis, D. S., McGue, M., Lykken, D. T., Heston, L. L., & Clayton, P. (1991). Heterogeneity in the inheritance of alcoholism. *Archives of General Psychiatry, 48,* 19–28.

Rachlin, H. (1997). Four teleological theories of addiction. *Psychonomic Bulletin and Review, 4,* 462–473.

Rachlin, H., & Green, L. (1972). Commitment, choice, and self-control. *Journal of the Experimental Analysis of Behavior, 17,* 15–22.

Rachlin, H., Green, L., & Tormey, B. (1988). Is there a decisive test between matching and maximizing? *Journal of the Experimental Analysis of Behavior, 50,* 113–123.

Rachlin, H., & Siegel, E. (1994). Temporal patterning in probabilistic choice. *Organizational Behavior and Human Decision Processing, 59,* 161–176.

Regier, D. A., Farmer, M. E., Rae, D. S., Locke, B. Z., Keith, S. J., Judd, L. L., & Goodwin, F. K. (1990). Comorbidity of mental disorders with alcohol and other drug abuse. *Journal of the American Medical Association, 264,* 2511–2518.

Robins, L. N. (1993). Vietnam veterans' rapid recovery from heroin addiction: A fluke or normal expectation? *Archives of General Psychiatry, 188,* 1041–1054.

Robins, L. N., & Murphy, G. (1967). Drug use in a normal population of young Negro men. *American Journal of Public Health, 57,* 1580–1596.

Robins, L. N., & Regier, D. (1991). *Psychiatric disorders in America.* New York: Free Press.

Robinson, T. E., & Berridge, K. C. (1993). The neural basis of drug craving: An incentive-sensitization theory of addiction. *Brain Research Reviews, 18,* 247–291.

Samuelson, P. A. (1970). *Economics* (7th ed.). New York: McGraw-Hill.

Skinner, B. F. (1953). *Science and human behavior.* New York: Macmillan.

Smith, S. S., & Fiore, M. C. (1999). The epidemiology of tobacco use, dependence, and cessation in the United States. *Primary Care, 26,* 433–461.

Spitzer, R., Forman, J., & Nee, J. (1979). DSM-III field trial: I. Initial interrater diagnostic reliability. *American Journal of Psychiatry, 136,* 815–817.

Stitzer, M. L., Rand, C. S., Bigelow, G. E., & Mead, A. M. (1986). Contingent payment procedures for smoking reduction and cessation. *Journal of Applied Behavioral Analysis, 19,* 197–202.

Substance Abuse and Mental Health Services Administration (2001). *Summary of findings from the 2000 National household survey on drug abuse.* Rockville, MD: Office of Applied Studies.

U.S. Department of Health & Human Services (1964). *Smoking and health. Report of the advisory committee to the Surgeon General.* U.S. Department of Health, Education, and Welfare, Public Health Service. Center for Disease Control. PHS Publication No. 1103.

U.S. Department of Health & Human Services (1990). *The health benefits of smoking cessation, a report of the Surgeon General.* U.S. Department of Health and Human Services, Public Health Service, Centers for Disease Control, Center for Chronic Disease Prevention an Health Promotion, Office of Smoking an Health. DHHS Publication No. (CDC) 90–8416.

U.S. Department of Health & Human Services (1994). Cigarette smoking among adults CUS 1993. *Morbidity and Mortality Weekly Review, 43,* 925–930.

Vaughan, W. (1981). Melioration, matching, and maximization. *Journal of the Experimental Analysis of Behavior, 36,* 141–149.

Volkow, N. D., & Fowler, J. S. (2000). Addiction, a disease of compulsion and drive: Involvement of the orbitofrontal cortex. *Cerebral Cortex, 10,* 318–325.

Volkow, N. D., Fowler, J. S., Wolf, A. P., Hitzemann, R. *et al.* (1991). Changes in brain glucose metabolism in cocaine dependence and withdrawal. *American Journal of Psychiatry, 148,* 621–626.

Waldorf, D. (1983). Natural recovery from opiate addiction: Some social-psychological processes of untreated recovery. *Journal of Drug Issues, 13,* 239–279.

Waldorf, D., Reinarman, C., & Murphy, S. (1991). *Cocaine changes.* Philadelphia: Temple University Press.

Warner, L., Kessler, R. C., Hughes, M., Anthony, J. C., & Nelson, C. B. (1995). Prevalence and correlates of drug use and dependence in the United States. *Archives of General Psychiatry, 52,* 219–229.

Wasserman, D. A., Weinstein, M. G., Havassy, B. E., & Hall, S. M. (1998). Factors associated with lapses to heroin use during methadone maintenance. *Drug and Alcohol Dependence, 52,* 183–192.

Williams, B. A. (1988). Reinforcement, choice, and response strength. In: R. C. Atkinson, R. J. Herrnstein, G. Lindzey, & R. D. Luce (Eds), *Stevens' handbook of experimental psychology* (2nd ed., Vol. 2, pp. 167–244). New York: Wiley.

Comments on Heyman

Suzanne H. Mitchell

Heyman's paper examines the idea that, while one of the hallmarks of drug addiction is that drug consumption is viewed as compulsive rather than voluntary, drug consumption can still be examined as the outcome of a choice between consuming and engaging in some other behavior. Heyman argues, in his paper, that the two ideas (compulsive and voluntary behavior) can be reconciled in distributed models of choice if certain individual difference factors are considered. In this commentary, I have chosen to focus on whether individuals show variations in the characteristics that are key to Heyman's model.

Identifying individual differences associated with drug addiction is important for two reasons. First, if the differences predate the drug addiction, they may be useful to identify individuals who are vulnerable to developing addiction. Second, if the differences arise due to the drug use, they may inform us about the neuroadaptations underlying chronic drug use, and/or provide guidance about the most appropriate treatment. Already research has revealed that there are numerous individual difference variables that appear related to drug use and abuse, that range from the sociological (e.g. family living arrangements: Thomas & Hsiu 1993) to the psychological (e.g. personality: Geist & Herrmann 1990) to the biological (e.g. levels of 5-HIAAA in cerebrospinal fluid in non-human primates are negatively associated with alcohol consumption: Higley & Bennett 1999). However, studies with human participants should be looked on somewhat skeptically because the majority are cross-sectional designs that involve comparing drug users and either never-users or ex-users. In many studies these groups are not equivalent on all relevant dimensions, as was the case in the Heyman & Dunn (2002) study described by Heyman, which can dilute the confidence that should be placed in their conclusions without additional, confirmatory evidence.

Individual Differences in Frame of Reference

The individual difference variable focused on in Heyman's paper is decision-making, and specifically whether individuals use a "local" or a "global" solution to a decision-making problem. This distinction between local and global solutions rests on the "frame of reference" that is thought to be used when making decisions. It is theoretically unclear whether frame of reference models should be viewed as event-based or time-based, although studies could be devised to examine this issue. Taking a time-based perspective, a local frame of reference implies that the time horizon of the individual is very narrow, such that only the most immediate consequences of the choice are given weight. A global frame of reference implies that the time horizon of the individual is very broad, such that consequences/precursor events remote from the decision are factored into the values of the choice options being evaluated. As far as I can understand, this idea of frame of reference/time horizon does not specify a priori whether the individual is integrating information about future consequences (in which case it is essentially identical to the concept of delay discounting) or the individual is integrating information about the impact of past events, or both.

In Heyman's paper, the source of discrepancies in decision making between drug users and control participants is hypothesized to lie in the frame of reference in which decisions are made. However, the precise mechanism by which frame of reference impacts decision making is unspecified. As pointed out elsewhere in this volume [Cardinal *et al.* Chapter 6], a number of processes can be hypothesized to be involved when an individual compares alternatives that differ on several dimensions (e.g. amount of reward and delay to its receipt, or in Heyman's distributed choice task, the amount of reward and the length of the wait time). At a very simple level, the basic process(es) by which the dimensions of each choice solution are perceived may be distorted so the long-term advantages of the global solution are no longer apparent. Or the processes required to "weight" the dimensions of each solution may be disrupted or additional factors may influence the weighting processes in the drug use group compared with the control group, e.g. a need for immediate income. Alternatively, the comparison process itself may be compromised, e.g. if a decision is made without sufficient time elapsing for the evaluative processes to be completed. A single measure of decision making, such as percentage choice of one solution over another, only looks at the final outcome of these processes. While examining percentage choice is a desirable first step in understanding individual differences in decision making associated with drug use, it is only a first step. Only multiple measures that examine various facets of the decision can illuminate what differs in the decision-making process between control and drug using populations. Understanding which process or processes are disrupted is probably more important than attributing the effects to frame of reference.

Heyman combines the idea that drug users and non-users differ in their frame of reference when choosing between courses of action with the Primrose Path model of Addiction (Herrnstein & Prelec 1992). This model proposes that addictions develop because of the contingencies relating drug use and non-drug use. Clear, though simplified descriptions of the original model are given in Rachlin (1997, 2000); these descriptions will not be repeated here. It should be noted however that the Primrose Path Model focuses on the frequency with which an individual has performed certain behaviors in the past, e.g. the frequency of drinking in the last 10 days, say. In combining the frame of reference idea with the Primrose Path Model, Heyman implies that the frame of reference idea involves the narrowness of focus on past events rather than the future, as in temporal discounting analyses.

The Distributed Choice Task

Heyman is to be commended on devising a task in which participants make choices between options that vary in ways consistent with the Primrose Path model. The most salient characteristic of the Primrose Path model is that the value of undesirable activities, such as drug use, is always higher than the value of desirable activities, such as abstinence.

In Heyman's distributed choice task the undesirable activity is selecting the local solution, whereas the desirable activity is selecting the global solution. The current value of the local choice is presumably higher because the number of ticks expended is lower, though both options deliver the same size reinforcer (5 cents). A second characteristic of the Primrose Path model is that repeated choice of the undesirable activity is associated with decreases in the value of that activity and the desirable activity, whereas repeated choice of the desirable activity is associated with increases in the value of that activity and the undesirable activity. Thus, in Heyman's task, selection of the local solution results in increases in the wait time that must be endured to earn whichever option is selected next, the local or the global solution. In contrast, selection of the global solution results in decreases in wait time that must be endured to earn whichever option is selected next. Mathematically it can be shown that the only way to maximize the amount of money earned in this task is to select the global solution every time. The idea is that both the opiate users and controls are exposed to these same programmed contingencies. However, the narrower frame of reference for the opiate users should result in those individuals being somehow insensitive to the long-term or overall changes in the contingencies and so their behavior is only governed by the immediate contingencies. To state the situation in a different way, it is as if the drug users view the contingencies through a pinhole, whereas controls view the contingencies using a wide-angle lens.

As noted earlier, Heyman has done a good job of putting together a task to capture and operationalize features of the Primrose Path model. Although perhaps a focus on that model is not critical, rather the task could be viewed primarily as a decision-making problem because the Primrose Path model itself has several problematic features. The model implies that the experienced drug users and controls experience the same contingencies linking drug use frequency with subjective value. Given the physiological processes of tolerance and sensitization, this assumption seems unlikely to be met. Indeed, Heyman himself has suggested ways in which drug use changes the contingencies (Heyman 1996). Further, it is not entirely clear how we can measure the subjective value of the desirable and undesirable activities (i.e. the drug-using vs. drug-free lifestyle) practically, making it difficult to refute the model. Finally, the implications of several features are unclear, e.g. the gradient at which subjective value declines as a function of increased choice of the undesirable, drug-using activity, the magnitude of the difference in the subjective value for the drug-using over the drug-free lifestyle.

The data presented by Heyman indicate that control subjects tended to select the global solution more than opiate users, who appeared to choose between the two solutions on a random basis. This difference in response strategy appeared to become pronounced as participants experienced the alterations in the contingencies as a consequence of their choices. Further, the smaller the relative advantage of the local solution, the more control subjects picked the global solution. Heyman interprets these data as indicating that control subjects *do* have a more global frame of reference than the opiate users, as hypothesized; that is, they take into account how their past choices impacted their current state.

A Temporal Discounting Analysis of the Distributed Choice Task

I would like to present a complementary analysis of the Heyman & Dunn (2002) data in terms of hyperbolic temporal discounting. Heyman discusses this model briefly and notes that a problem with this model is that it contains no consideration of the effects of repeated consumption on the value of rewards, as one would need to fully specify the value of a drug to an individual. This is indeed lacking from the model. However, the same lack is evident in the distributed choice model. In that model, the level and the gradient of the straight line relating drug choices to value (see Heyman: Figure 2) has been hypothesized to be related to repeated consumption (Heyman 1996). However, no method has yet been determined to specify either the level or the gradient of the function. Thus, the lack of a factor to account for the effects of repeated consumption in the hyperbolic discounting model does not seem like sufficient reason to dismiss the model. Consequently, in the following analysis, the subjective value of the global and local solutions was found by applying the hyperbolic discounting equation (Mazur 1987):

$$V = \frac{M}{1 + kX}$$

V represents the subjective value of the solution, M represents the objective value of the reward (i.e. 5 cents), k is a fitted parameter indexing the rate of discounting (opiate users = 0.220 and controls = 0.027, based on data presented in Madden *et al.* 1997), and X is the length of the delay to the next trial. Once calculated, the subjective value of the global solution can be subtracted from that of the local solution to assess the magnitude of the local solution advantage. For example, in the 75% game for 0 local solution choices in the last 2 choices, the value of the local solution is 4.10 and the global solution is 2.66 (to 2 decimal places), so the local solution advantage is 1.44 (see Figure 1 for the 75% game subjective values for opiate users and controls). Table 1 summarizes the magnitude of the local advantage for the opiate users and the controls. As can be clearly seen from

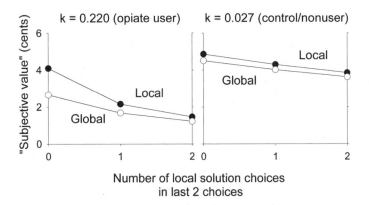

Figure 1: The subjective value of the local and global solutions in the discrete choice task for opiate users and for control participants. Subjective value was calculated using a hyperbolic function (Mazur 1987). *K* values used in the equation were taken from Madden *et al.* (1997). Note: abscissae are number of *local* solution choices in last two choices, not global solution choices as in Heyman's paper, to correspond more closely with the more commonly-used depictions of the Primrose Path model.

Table 1: The difference between the subjective value (in cents) of the local and global solutions for each type of game in the distributed choice task, i.e. the size of the local solution advantage.

Game	Number of Local Solution Choices		
	0	**1**	**2**
75% game			
Opiate user	1.44	0.48	0.24
Control	0.36	0.28	0.23
60% game			
Opiate user	1.09	0.41	0.21
Control	0.34	0.27	0.22
2-tick game			
Opiate user	1.09	0.34	0.17
Control	0.24	0.19	0.15
4-tick game			
Opiate user	1.32	0.51	0.27
Control	0.44	0.35	0.28
43% game			
Opiate user	0.69	0.30	0.17
Control	0.31	0.25	0.20

Figure 1 and Table 1, the size of the local solution advantage is substantially larger for opiate users than for controls; this is especially true when there have been 0 local solution choices. Perhaps this is why opiate users selected the local solution relatively more and the global solution relatively less than controls (Heyman: Figure 3). Thus, the pattern of subjective values based on temporal discounting values is very different for the two groups, and can be used to explain why opiate users selected the local solution relatively more than the controls.

One final idea that I would like to return to is the idea of temporal discounting vs. sensitivity to prior event contingencies. Numerous experiments in humans have demonstrated that individuals discount future consequences. However, it is unclear to me whether the focus on the present implied by temporal discounting also involves discounting past event/consequences. Are individuals who discount the future also the ones who discount the past? Are they the ones least likely to learn from past mistakes, especially as those past mistakes recede into the more distant past? Such information would have several policy implications with respect to drug abuse treatment and punishment for drug-related offenses, but is as yet an unexplored area.

References

Geist, C. R., & Herrmann, S. M. (1990). A comparison of the psychological characteristics of smokers, ex-smokers, and non-smokers. *Journal of Clinical Psychology, 46*, 102–105.

Herrnstein, R. J., & Prelec, D. (1992). A theory of addiction. In: G. Loewenstein, & J. Elster (Eds), *Choice over time* (pp. 331–360). New York, NY: Russell Sage Foundation.

Heyman, G. M. (1996). Resolving the contradictions of addiction. *Behavioural and Brain Sciences, 19*, 561–574.

Higley, J. D., & Bennett, A. J. (1999). Central nervous system serotonin and personality as variables contributing to excessive alcohol consumption in non-human primates. *Alcohol and Alcoholism, 34*, 402–418.

Madden, G. J., Petry, N. M., Badger, G. J., & Bickel, W. K. (1997). Impulsive and self-control choices in opioid-dependent patients and non-drug-using control participants: Drug and monetary rewards. *Experimental and Clinical Psychopharmacology, 5*, 256–262.

Mazur, J. E. (1987). An adjusting procedure for studying delayed reinforcement. In: M. J. Commons, J. E. Mazur, J. A. Nevin, & H. Rachlin (Eds), *The effect of delay and of intervening events on reinforcement value: Vol. 5. Quantitative analysis of behavior series* (pp. 55–73). Hillsdale, NJ: Lawrence Erlbaum.

Rachlin, H. (1997). Four teleological theories of addiction. *Psychological Bulletin and Review, 4*, 462–473.

Rachlin, H. (2000). *The science of self-control*. Cambridge, MA: Harvard University.

Thomas, B. S., & Hsiu, L. T. (1993). The role of selected risk factors in predicting adolescent drug use and its adverse consequences. *International Journal of the Addictions, 28*, 1549–1563.

Chapter 5

Economic Concepts in the Behavioral Study of Addiction

Howard Rachlin

Introduction

The application of economic theory to the study and understanding of addiction has been a great success — as the present conference makes clear. And you should never argue with success. I therefore hasten to say that economic theory is the most powerful tool we have in our efforts to understand and to develop treatment for addiction. But for that very reason economic theory needs to be very carefully applied.

Consider the correspondence between price and operant response. For example, the price of a pack of cigarettes in our human money economy and the number of bar presses a rat is required to make in a Skinner box to obtain a pellet of food (on a fixed ratio schedule) have corresponding effects on consumption. This correspondence enables us to obtain demand curves in the animal laboratory and to measure demand elasticity (Hursh & Winger 1995). In my own work, I have frequently treated operant response requirements as if they were equivalent to prices and even gone further, treating a fixed sum of responses on two levers as if it were a "budget" that could be "spent" on various "packages of goods" obtainable by distribution of responding across the levers (Rachlin *et al.* 1976). Moreover, in developing what I have called Relative Addiction Theory (Rachlin 1977), I have relied on the concept of demand elasticity which in turn relies on the concept of money price.

I believe that these sorts of analyses are highly useful. Nevertheless, usefulness in one context may blind us to the many differences between price and response requirement in other contexts. One purpose of the present article is to examine the points where the analogy breaks down as well as the points where it holds.

Price in Animal Models of Human Consumption

Economic theory in its most fundamental form applies to trade — the exchange of goods. The most primitive economy is a barter economy in which goods are traded for each other

Choice, Behavioural Economics and Addiction
© 2003 Published by Elsevier Ltd.
ISBN: 0-08-044056-8

without money prices. Suppose Jack has ten apples and no oranges, and someone were to come along and ask him, "How many of your apples would you trade for one orange?" Because he has plenty of apples but no oranges, Jack might well be willing to trade as much as three or four apples for an orange. Let us say that Jack trades three of his apples for the orange; he is just as happy with his new package of seven apples and one orange as he was with ten apples and no oranges. The reason why Jack is willing to trade at all is that, while apples and oranges may be about equally valuable, they are imperfectly substitutable for each other. Jack prefers to have a *mixture* of apples and oranges than to have all of one kind of fruit. Thus, he is willing to have less total fruit (eight pieces rather than ten) if he can have a *mixture* rather than all of one kind.

Now, after this first trade, he is asked how many of his remaining apples he is willing to trade for a second orange. Since he already has one orange (he already has a mixture) he would be less willing to part with his apples. So, this time, he would trade, let us say, only two apples for the second orange. This leaves him with only seven pieces of fruit, five apples plus two oranges; but he is just as happy as he was before. As Jack keeps trading apples for oranges, and gains more of a mixture, he becomes less and less willing to part with his diminishing stock of apples. At some point he begins to demand several oranges for each of the (now scarce) apples he surrenders. Finally, let us assume, he ends up with 17 oranges and no apples. Figure 1a shows Jack's package of apples and oranges after each of these hypothetical trades. Since they are, by hypothesis, even trades (assuming transitivity of indifference), the line connecting them is an indifference contour. Jack values ten apples (one end of the line) equally to 17 oranges (the other end) and equally to all points in between. If Jack had started with eleven apples, another indifference contour could have been constructed above this one; if he had started with nine apples, another indifference contour could have been constructed below it. The shapes of the indifference contours so constructed depend critically on the degree of substitutability between the commodities being traded. The more substitutable the commodities are, the flatter the indifference contours will be; the less substitutable the commodities are, the more bent the indifference contours will be. (Indifference contours for completely substitutable commodities would not bend at all; they would be straight lines.) The contours for oranges vs. grapefruits would be flatter than those for oranges vs. apples; the contours for oranges vs. bread would be steeper (more bent) than those for oranges vs. apples. That is, oranges and grapefruits are typically *substitutes* while oranges and bread are *complements*.

Figure 1b shows the same (hypothetical) data as in Figure 1a plotted, inversely, in terms of apples spent rather than apples kept, for each orange obtained. In making these successive trades between apples and oranges, Jack is essentially paying for oranges with his apples. Figure 1b shows that the more oranges Jack has, the less he is willing to pay for the next one. This is nothing but an instance of diminishing marginal utility in a universe containing only oranges and apples. In trades within this universe, the price of oranges is calculated in terms of number of apples given up while the price of apples would be calculated in terms of oranges given up. *In a barter economy the concept of price has meaning only in terms of the particular goods being traded for one another.* Price, in a barter economy, thus depends not only on the relative value of the goods but on their degree of mutual substitutability. If elasticity of demand for oranges were to be inferred from functions like those of Figure 1b, elasticity of demand for oranges would be higher if apples were being traded for oranges

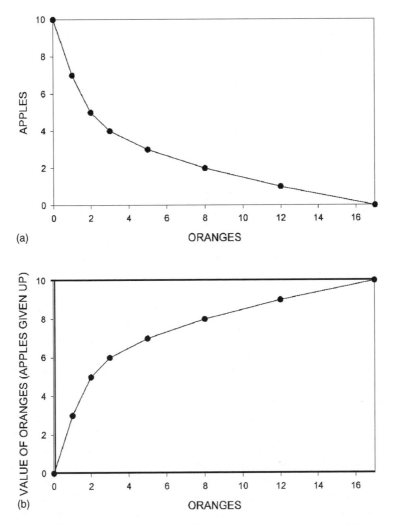

Figure 1: (a) Hypothetical trades between apples and oranges. (b) Value of oranges in terms of apples given up.

and lower if bread were being traded for oranges. In a simple barter economy, elasticity of demand is not a fixed characteristic of a commodity.

Now, suppose the barter universe consisted of numerous goods, not just apples and oranges. In order to maximize the value of all the goods he had, each trader would attempt to trade some of the goods he had lots of for some of the goods that he had little of. One of the useful things a money economy does is to provide a single commodity substitutable for almost all others; money is *fungible*. When a person buys something with money, he is essentially trading whatever he *could* have bought with that money for what he does buy with it. Money is obviously a very handy thing to have in an economy. In a money economy, elasticity of demand for any given commodity would have a fixed meaning; the money being traded for it represents degree of substitutability between that good and all other goods that money can buy.

But a rat in a Skinner box does not have money. The economy of a rat in a Skinner box is more like a barter economy than like a money economy. You could say that a rat pressing a lever for food on a ratio schedule is trading leisure (the inverse of response rate) for food. The more leisure it gives up (the faster it presses the lever), the more food it gets in return. Oppositely, the price of the food is leisure given up. But, in a barter economy, this price will depend not only on the relative values of leisure and food for a hungry rat but also on the degree of substitutability between leisure and food. Thus, *the measured elasticity of the demand for food, or any other reinforcer, where price is determined by number of lever presses, will depend on the degree of substitutability between leisure and that reinforcer*. Since leisure is a negatively defined commodity — what the rat does when it is not responding — degree of substitutability between leisure and the reinforcer, hence measured elasticity of demand, will depend not only on the characteristics of the reinforcer, but also on what activities other than lever pressing are available to the rat in the Skinner box. This in turn will depend not only on force requirements and the like but also on the dimensions of the Skinner box and the availability of water, or a running wheel, or wood shavings, or another rat, and so forth. In a barter economy, such as that of a rat in a Skinner box, elasticity of demand has no fixed meaning. It would be possible, nevertheless, to compare the elasticity of one reinforcer to that of another reinforcer determined under the same conditions, but it is not possible to generalize from one condition to another (let alone from rats to humans) or to say anything absolute about demand elasticity for any given commodity.

The concept of price has no place, except metaphorically, in the economic analysis of the behavior of rats in Skinner boxes. Analysis of such behavior in terms of price elasticity is actually just an analysis of the substitutability of leisure — whatever activities are available in the Skinner box other than the operant response — for the particular reinforcer being used. What this means for the study of addiction is that by focusing on price and elasticity of demand we have been, at best, concentrating on only one substitute for addiction — leisure. Translated into the real world of human addiction, a focus on the money price of the addictive commodity translates into a focus on the substitution for the addictive activity of *purchasable* activities (activities other than the addictive activity that can be bought); reductions in the addictive activity would then allow more money to be spent on those substitutes. But in the real world of human addiction there may be many substitutes for addictive activity that cannot be immediately bought with the money saved from reductions of the addictive activity. *If you stop smoking, for example, you cannot go out and buy social support with the money you used to spend on cigarettes*. Yet, in the case of the individual addict, availability of substitutes such as social support may be easier to control than the money price of the addictive commodity. In other words, it may be easier to *release* constraints on substitutes for the addictive activity than to *impose* constraints on the addictive activity itself. Green & Fisher (2000) cite numerous instances of the manipulation of behavior both in the animal laboratory and in the real world by the manipulation of the availability of substitutes.

Behavior as a Good

Another fundamental difference between human economies and rats in a Skinner box is ability to own property in human economies and the lack of this ability in a Skinner box. Consequently, the focus of economic theory has been on the allocation of resources among goods where "goods" are seen as property. The "consumer" in economic terms is really a buyer. Once a product is bought the economist loses interest in the buyer; the economist is interested in whether the shopper buys the steak, not whether she eats it. Actual consumption of the goods is largely irrelevant for the economist. In the example of Jack trading apples for oranges, the economist sees the apples and oranges as packages of goods owned by Jack to be consumed only after the trading is over. On the other hand, the focus of most operant studies has been on the allocation of *behavior* among various available activities. The rat in the Skinner box can *eat* a food pellet but it cannot usually *have* the pellet, let alone trade it for anything else. Studies of token reinforcement with non-humans are an exception (see Foster *et al.* 2001; Widholm *et al.* 2001 for recent examples). But, as opposed to token studies with humans, animal token studies have just begun to be examined from an economic viewpoint and have not yet been applied to problems of addiction.

A more internally consistent application of economic theory to individual behavior is obtained when we focus on allocation of time among activities rather than allocation of money among purchases. The various studies reported in Staddon's (1980) "Limits to Action" essentially took this approach. The organism was seen as allocating its time among various activities. Consistent with Premack's (1965) conception of reinforcement, all activities, including bar pressing or key pecking as well as wheel running, eating or drinking, were considered to be consummatory activities. Consistent with economic "revealed preference theory" (Samuelson 1973), utility functions maximized by particular allocations under one set of constraints were used, together with the assumption of utility maximization, to predict allocations under other constraints.

Such economic analyses make use of the concept of price only to define constraints, not to draw inferences about elasticity. For example, an hour-long session with a rat pressing a lever for food under an FR 60 schedule may be divided into so many minutes of lever pressing, so many minutes of leisure and so many minutes of eating, adding up to 60 (assuming eating time is counted as session time). The ratio schedule sets a ratio between time spent eating and time spent lever pressing (Rachlin 1978) that constrains the rat to only certain combinations of the three activities. From the combinations chosen under two or three different ratio schedules, a set of utility functions may be derived from which behavior with other schedules may be predicted. Figure 2 diagrams this sort of analysis.

Figure 2a depicts a three-dimensional space defined by three axes — time spent eating, time spent lever pressing, and leisure. Each point in the space represents an allocation of time among the three activities. The triangle connecting the 1-hour points on the three axes represents the constraint that all three activities must fit into a 1-hour session. Each corner of the triangle represents an allocation of the whole hour to the one activity at that corner. Points on the edges of the triangle represent allocations of the hour to two activities; points within the triangle represent non-zero allocations of the hour among all three activities.

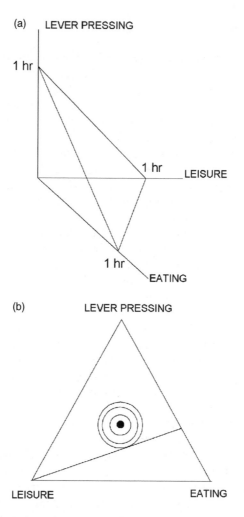

Figure 2: (a) One hour divided among eating lever pressing and leisure. (b) Maximization of value given fixed ratio between time spent eating and lever pressing.

Figure 2b shows the same triangle viewed head on. The line going up to the right from the lower left (leisure) corner represents a fixed ratio between eating and lever pressing such as would be imposed by a ratio schedule (with the assumption that each response takes a fixed amount of time). Performance on the ratio schedule is represented by a point on the line. The schedule imposes a fixed ratio between eating and lever pressing. The rat is essentially choosing among points on the line. The point (arbitrarily set) in the middle of the triangle represents the rat's ideal allocation between the three activities. If the rat's actual allocation among the three activities were as close as it could come to this ideal allocation, given the constraints of the ratio schedule, it would chose the point tangent to one of the circles. The circle represents a conceivable utility function with the variables being time spent eating, lever pressing, and neither (leisure), with utility maximized given the constraints imposed by the ratio schedule.

Although the utility function of Figure 2 is represented as a series of concentric circles there is no a priori reason that the form has to be circular; it could be any shape. In actual practice, a series of various schedules would be imposed. By observation of the allocations chosen, the shape of the utility function could be inferred. Once the utility function were known, the allocation that maximized utility for any new reinforcement schedule could be calculated; hence, according to revealed preference theory, the response rate could be predicted. Rachlin & Burkhard (1978) carried out such an analysis with children playing with toys under various constraints and Rachlin (1978) also applied the analysis to predict pigeons' pecking rate under various ratio and interval single-key and concurrent reinforcement schedules.

Economic theorists such as Becker (1996) have translated economic terms into behavioral terms but psychologists, in employing such terms, must be careful to use them in their behavioral rather than in their original economic context.

One example of such translation from economic to behavioral language is in the concept of "stock" (Becker & Murphy 1988). That concept makes use of the fact that present consumption may influence the value of future consumption. For example, another way of saying that a person habituates (builds up tolerance) to an addictive substance is to say that present consumption reduces the unit value of future consumption of that substance. On the other hand, if a person becomes sensitized to an addictive substance (or must learn by experience how to use that substance in order to derive utility from it), we could say that present consumption increases the unit value of future consumption.

As consumption proceeds the consumer may be said to be building up stock in the commodity consumed; as time passes without consumption, stock dissipates. The unit value of any given activity would thus vary with amount of stock possessed, decreasing with amount of stock in the case of habituation and increasing with amount of stock in the case of sensitization. In a traditional money economy your stock of property would be stored in a bank, a warehouse, or your home; the quality and quantity of that property in turn could affect your current decisions. In a time allocation situation, where the concept of property has no meaning, your current decisions may be conceived as being affected by the state of your nervous system in the form of "stock" from prior consumption.

In the case of habituation it is as if present consumption were substitutable for future consumption: drinking a Coke now might well decrease the value of drinking a Pepsi five minutes from now; in the case of sensitization it is as if present consumption were complementary to future consumption: drinking a coke now might well increase the value of eating a pretzel five minutes from now.[1]

The fact that future value may be affected by present consumption underlies Herrnstein & Prelec's (1992) behavioral, "primrose path" theory of addiction as well as Becker & Murphy's (1988) economic, "rational" theory of addiction. In Herrnstein and Prelec's theory, addictive behavior (such as consumption of alcohol beyond a certain rate) reduces the value, not only of future addictive behavior (future alcohol consumption) but also the value of all other possible activities. As addiction proceeds, all possible activities are together reduced in value. Thus, the addict, as addiction proceeds, becomes less and less happy regardless of what he chooses to do. Yet, up to a point, the value of the addictive activity

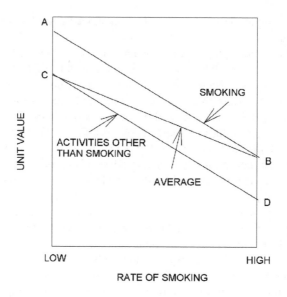

Figure 3: The "primrose path" to smoking.

remains higher than the value of all possible alternatives. Assuming that the addict always chooses the highest valued of all currently available alternatives regardless of the effect of the current choice on future value (called "melioration"), the addictive activity would always be chosen.

Figure 3 diagrams how the primrose path might work in a particular case, let us say, smoking (the example is highly simplified). It is assumed that smoking is the kind of addiction where tolerance builds up with each cigarette smoked and dissipates with time not smoking. In Becker and Murphy's terms, increases of stock decrease unit value of the addictive activity. (The horizontal axis could be labeled "stock.") The faster the rate of smoking, the lower the value of each cigarette smoked. This is shown by the negative slope of line A–B, indicating unit value of smoking (each cigarette) as a function of rate of smoking. Line C–D indicates that increased smoking rate, over an extended period, also reduces the future value of other activities as well as smoking. Health and social approval deteriorate, for example, decreasing in turn the ability to exercise, the enjoyment of entertainment, the taste of food, etc. Note that the unit value of smoking is always higher than the unit value of not smoking regardless of smoking rate. Thus, a meliorator (one who chooses the highest valued current activity regardless of its effect on future value), starting at point C as a non-smoker, will always choose to smoke and move steadily to point B. And will stay at point B. However, at point B, the unit value of both smoking and non-smoking is lower than it was initially, at point C. According to this model, then, the course of addiction takes the addict from a condition (at point C) where performing the addictive activity would be a positive reinforcer (an increase in value from point C to point A) to a condition (at point B) where performing the addictive activity is a negative reinforcer (it prevents a decrease in value from point B to point D).[2]

Relative Addiction

I have proposed an economic-psychological theory of substitution in addiction, an extension of Herrnstein & Prelec's (1992) primrose path theory described above, called "relative addiction" (Rachlin 1997, 2000). Relative addiction theory originally relied on the distinction between negative and positive addictions made by the economists, Stigler & Becker (1977). Positive and negative addictions were initially distinguished in terms of differing demand elasticities. Let us first consider negative and positive addictions in isolation.

Negative addictions were said to result from *inelastic* demand combined with build-up of tolerance: negative addiction occurs as consumption of the addictive substance causes the unit t-value of future consumption to *decrease* (tolerance) which, in turn, requires more consumption so as to make up for the decrease in unit value. For example, the more alcohol you drink, the lower you will value each future drink. As a drink's unit value decreases (while its actual money price remains constant) its effective price must increase. But since your demand for the value you get from drinking is *inelastic*, you must drink more and more to keep total value at the desired level, regardless of price. Drinking more decreases unit value (and increases effective price) even further, requiring you to consume even more and so on, until you are drinking all the time. Most activities that we usually call addictions (alcohol, cocaine, cigarettes, etc.) are negative addictions. These activities attain their maximum unit value within a very short period but, after that, as they are repeated at a high rate, unit value decreases; drinking a quart of whisky, for example, may have the same effect on the alcoholic as drinking a glass of whiskey does on the social drinker. The heroin addict, it has been said, is always chasing after (and never achieving) that first high. High rates of the addictive activity occur because, although the unit value of the addictive activity is steadily decreasing, it is nevertheless still higher than the unit value of *available* substitutes. Long periods of abstinence from a negative addiction tend to increase unit value as habituation dissipates and thus increase demand for the negatively addicted activity. One reason why addicts seek treatment, perhaps not sufficiently acknowledged by the addiction treatment community, is not to give up the addiction completely but rather to impose a period of abstinence upon themselves so as to increase unit value when they resume the addictive activity.

Positive addictions work in exactly the opposite manner. Positive addictions result from *elastic* demand combined with an *increase* in unit value as consumption proceeds: consumption of the addictive substance *reduces* its effective price which, because of *elastic* demand, causes increased consumption; increased consumption in turn reduces the effective price still more and so on again causing runaway consumption. A positive addiction is one where high value is not attainable initially. We have to learn or become sensitized to positively addicted activities. Examples would be listening to classical music, reading novels, exercising, doing crossword puzzles, collecting stamps. Cooperative social interaction, leading to social support, is another such activity. Although social support is freely available to most infants, a child has to learn the social skills necessary to derive social support as an adult — and the learning process is a long one (Ainsworth & Bowlby 1991).

Positive addictions, because they depend on elastic demand, are much less stable than negative addictions. If a negative addiction is interrupted by external factors, such as loss of income or unavailability of the addictive commodity, its unit value goes up, effective price goes down and demand remains high. If income rises or the addictive commodity again becomes available, addiction resumes. However, if a positive addiction is interrupted, unit value goes down and effective price goes up, perhaps to its originally high value, as consumption remains at low or zero levels. Thus, a person who had developed a habit of reading or writing poetry or listening to or playing classical music as a teenager, and then abandons these pursuits as an adult (devoting time to college studies or career), and then tries to take them up again after retirement, will find that they have lost their value. The same is true for social activity: a long period of abstinence causes us to lose our taste for socialization; we have to learn all over again how to work and play with others.

It was argued at the beginning of this article, however, that the economic concepts of price and elasticity, underlying negative and positive addictions, are inappropriate in a psychological analysis of addiction. Is there a way to express positive and negative addictions without these concepts?

The concepts of price and elasticity were initially necessary in order to explain negative and positive addictions separately from each other — negative addictions vs. everything else and positive addictions vs. everything else. But when we consider negative addictions and positive addictions as mutual substitutes — negative addictions vs. positive addictions — price and elasticity drop out of the equation and instead we need to consider only degree of substitutability of the positive addiction for the negative addiction.

How does relative addiction work without the concepts of elasticity and price? First, we have to assume that there exists a negative addiction and a positive addiction that are mutually substitutable. At present, the potential addict is engaging in the positively addictive activity at a high rate and in the negatively addictive activity at a low rate. (These initial rates may not be due to any self-control process but to extrinsic reinforcement and punishment imposed by parents, school, society in general.) Suppose further that the initial value of the negatively addictive activity is high but choice of that activity will reduce its future value and that the initial value of the positively addictive activity is low but choice of that activity will increase its future value. As an example, consider alcoholic drinking to be the negative addiction, and social interaction (and support) to be the positive addiction.[3]

A young man currently has strong social ties to family and school, and drinks only moderately if at all. But, let us suppose, he either joins a fraternity where drinking is common or begins to go out with a woman who drinks. (Or, he just loses the social support he previously had — by the death of a parent or a spouse, for example.) Now the *extrinsic* social forces that originally punished heavy drinking and reinforced moderation are replaced by other extrinsic forces that do the opposite. So he begins to drink. The value of drinking beyond a moderate amount is initially high and is initially, *extrinsically*, socially supported. At this point socializing and drinking may be complements rather than substitutes. However, as rate of drinking increases beyond a moderate amount, several things happen: tolerance builds up so that more and more drinking is required to achieve the same effect; social reinforcement begins to diminish as his drinking has a direct negative effect on his social skills; he begins to substitute drinking for social activity; finally (just as athletes and musicians lose their edge without practice) the reduction of his rate of social activity diminishes his social skills, hence social reinforcement per unit of social activity. Although increased drinking decreases the unit value of each drink, this may be compensated for by further increases of drinking. However, the value of social activity decreases doubly; first, drinking above a certain point directly decreases social acceptance and social reinforcement; second, as drinking begins to substitute for social activity, the decreased rate of social activity further decreases its unit value. Thus, while the direct effect of drinking on the future value of drinking is negative, the effect of drinking on the future value of social activity may be even more negative, being both direct and indirect.

In this explanation of relative addiction the concept of substitutability itself substitutes for the concepts of price, elasticity, and demand. But the basic underlying principle is the same as before — the effect of present choices on the value of future alternatives. The real-world consequence of such a theory is the focus, in treatment, on the substitution of positive addictions for negative addictions rather than on increasing the price of the addictive activity. The theory suggests that such substitution is not an indirect method to be used perhaps because it is kinder to the addict or politically correct, but rather because it is the most efficient and enduring method of controlling addiction. This is not to say, of course, that other methods, including manipulation of stimulus control, drug treatments, and even punishment of the addictive activity, do not work or should not be tried. Nevertheless, because it is direct, substitution of positive addictions for negative addictions has a better chance, I believe, of resisting relapse and, even in cases where relapse does occur, of being reinstituted.

Reinforcement and Utility Maximization

The identification of reinforcement with utility maximization is a perfect case, it may seem, of inappropriate adoption of economic terms into behavioral psychology. Reinforcement, as the term has been used in Skinnerian behaviorism (Skinner 1938), refers either to an immediate discrete consequence of a discrete operant act or to the immediate value of some equally discrete delayed consequence of the act. It is easy to explain, in terms of reinforcement, why a person might lack self-control — a second dessert, for me at least, is an immediate reinforcer — but it is difficult to explain why we are all not addicts — what reinforces self-control? My discrete act of pushing away that second dessert is never reinforced by a discrete consequence — even a delayed one. If I push my dessert away this evening I will not wake up three weeks from now a healthier and happier person. Where is the larger later reward for that act?

On the other hand, utility maximization, as economists typically understand the term, easily explains why a person does not choose addictive activities — it is part of their rational plan to maximize happiness over their lifetimes. But utility maximization has a hard time explaining why people *do* become addicts. Economic explanations of addiction such as that of Becker & Murphy (1988) are couched in the language of rationality (they speak of "rational addiction"); they hence have been rejected as absurd by economists (various personal communications) and psychologists alike (for example, Herrnstein & Prelec 1992).

I believe that such rejection is mistaken and that, despite their apparent incompatibility, reinforcement and utility maximization actually are two ways of talking about the very same behavior. The basic problem in reconciling the two is in the economist's assumption — sometimes verbalized, sometimes just assumed — that utility maximization per se is an internal process ("conscious" and/or "rational") and that the *behavior* of utility maximization is only a result of that process. Once the assumption of internality is abandoned, once reinforcement and utility maximization are seen as methods in the analysis of the behavior of whole organisms, their correspondence becomes clear. The Becker–Murphy model of addiction may then be seen not as implying that anyone sits down at the beginning of life and plans, in his mind, to become an addict, and then slavishly follows that predetermined plan, but as an attempt by economists to explain addiction in terms of utility maximization — corresponding to the attempts of many psychologists to explain addiction in terms of reinforcement. The remainder of this paper consists of an argument for this correspondence.

I would like to begin with a description of a self-control experiment, performed in my laboratory several years ago, and then — with this experiment on the table, so to speak — try to explain its relevance to the issue of utility maximization. The experiment was done with pigeons as subjects and is actually a *demonstration* rather than an experiment. It makes what is really a semantic point — that the behavioral psychologist's language of "reinforcement" and "punishment" and the economist's language of "maximization of utility" are mutually translatable descriptions of the very same behavior. *Neither the behaviorist's language nor that of the economist requires the concept of conscious rationality. But both languages require the concept of sensitivity to environmental contingencies.* Because non-human animals do not seem, on the face of it, to possess conscious rationality, and do seem to be sensitive to environmental contingencies, the correspondence of the economist's and behavioral psychologist's language may most easily be seen in the behavior of non-human animals.

Patterning in Self-Control: Soft Commitment (Siegel & Rachlin 1995)

Let me begin with some facts about pigeon choice that we know from many prior experiments (for example, Rachlin & Green 1972). A pigeon is first deprived of food until it is at 80% of its weight when allowed to eat freely; thus, the pigeon is very hungry. Then the pigeon is trained to peck a lit button (much like an elevator button) to obtain food from a hopper. Then the pigeon is offered a choice between two buttons to peck, a green button and a red button — as illustrated in Figure 4a. A single peck on the green button leads to an immediate reward of 2 seconds of access to food; a single peck on the red button leads to a 4-second blackout (a delay) followed by a reward of 4 seconds of access to food. I will call the reward following a peck on the green button the smaller-sooner reward, or SS; I will call the reward following a peck on the red button the larger-later reward, or LL.

When offered such a choice, pigeons invariably choose SS (as shown by the thick arrow in Figure 4). In other words, hungry pigeons are impulsive — their time discount functions are very steep. They prefer a small amount of food delivered immediately to twice as much delayed by only four seconds.

Figure 4b shows what happens when a delay of 10 seconds is added to both alternatives, so that after pecking the green button the pigeon has to wait 10 seconds before obtaining

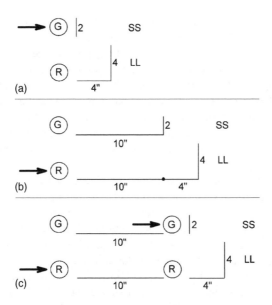

Figure 4: Choices between a smaller-sooner (SS) and larger-later (LL) reward with various additional delays. Preference is shown by heavy arrow.

SS and, after pecking the red button, the pigeon has to wait 14 seconds before obtaining LL. The pigeon, like humans in corresponding situations, reverses its preference and now chooses the larger, more delayed reward. Such a preference reversal cannot be explained by exponential (or "rational") delay discounting but it can be explained in terms of hyperbolic discount functions, which cross somewhere between zero and ten seconds of added delay.

Figure 4c shows what happens if the pigeon is given an initial choice as in Figure 4b, but is allowed to choose again after 10 seconds have elapsed. The pigeon initially chooses LL, as before, but then, given the opportunity, reverses its choice and obtains the smaller reward.

Finally, in the crucial part of the experiment, shown in Figure 5, the SS and LL rewards are made dependent, not on an extra 10 seconds of waiting but on 30 extra pecks on either button followed by a 31st peck on either button leading to its corresponding reward. However, while the pigeon is pecking, both buttons are continuously lit; any peck on either button counts

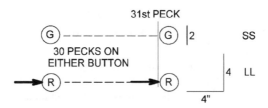

Figure 5: Soft commitment. Pigeon's preference does not reverse if it means disrupting pattern.

toward the total. Which reward the pigeon actually obtains depends only on which button it pecks on the 31st peck. The first 30 pecks are essentially what an economist would call "sunk costs." The pigeon can reverse its choice at any point in the sequence.

Given what we know its preferences to be, the pigeon should begin to peck on the button leading to the larger reward and then switch as SS comes closer. The pigeons do begin to peck on the button leading to the larger reward but, regardless of their current preferences, they usually continue to peck the button leading to LL (the red button) and obtain the larger reward. It is as if the pigeons' two supposed irrationalities — their preference reversal over time and their weighting of "sunk costs" cancel each other out and result in rational choice after all — obtaining the larger reward.

To the behaviorist, this experiment indicates that pigeons have a built-in mechanism that commits them to a pattern of behavior once it is begun. The pattern of pecking generated by the 31-peck requirement (fixed-ratio schedule) is indeed rigid. Even when we provide a signal (a 1-second pause during which both buttons change color to white) that clearly indicates when the next peck on either button will produce the reward, pigeons generally continue to peck the red button and obtain the larger reward.

With the 31-peck requirement the pigeon is choosing not between the smaller-sooner and the larger-later rewards alone but between two extended behavioral patterns: 31 pecks plus a smaller reward vs. 31 pecks plus a 4-second delay plus a larger reward. These two rigid fixed-ratio patterns have a coherence of their own (interruption is intrinsically punishing) and can be chosen as *wholes*.

In other experiments, human subjects play prisoner's-dilemma-like games against a computer playing tit-for-tat (for example, Kudadjie-Gyamfi & Rachlin 1996). Against tit-for-tat, choice of the smaller current alternative ("cooperation") is reinforced in the long run by the computer's cooperation in turn. Thus, cooperation against tit-for-tat is the same as self-control. In this experiment, we have found significantly more cooperation when trials are patterned (. . . choice-outcome, choice-outcome, choice-outcome . . . 30 seconds . . . choice-outcome, choice-outcome, choice-outcome . . .) than when they are evenly spaced (choice-outcome . . . 10 seconds . . . choice-outcome . . . 10 seconds . . . choice-outcome . . . 10 seconds . . .).

In the case of the pigeons, the patterning was their own rigid response to the fixed-ratio reinforcement schedule. In the case of humans, patterning was imposed by the experiment itself. What is common between the results of the pigeon and human experiments is that, in both cases, patterning of behavior increased choice of the higher overall reward at the expense of the higher immediate reward. That is, patterning increased self-control.

Cognitive Psychology and Behavioral Psychology

Now I would like to take a step back and discuss cognitive and behavioral psychology. Figure 6 shows, in a general way, how behavioral and cognitive theorists conceptualize choice behavior. The thick vertical line represents the boundary between the person and the world. To the right of the thick line is an example of a cognitive organization of behavior; to the left, a behavioral organization. The four heavy horizontal arrows represent the independent and dependent variables of both cognitive and behavioral

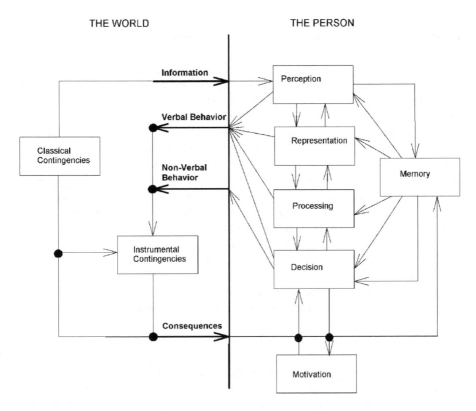

Figure 6: Cognitive and behavioral approaches to the explanation of behavior.

experiments — events in the world affecting the person and behavior of the person observable in the world. The upper arrow heading from the world into the person represents information — signals relevant to important events in the world. The upper arrow going to the left is verbal behavior — what the person says and writes. The lower arrow going to the left is non-verbal behavior — the actual choices that a person makes. The lower arrow going to the right indicates consequences — or outcomes — of choices.

The elements of cognitive theory (in highly simplistic and abstract form, not intended to reflect any particular theory) are the internal mechanisms that mediate between the arrows going in and the arrows going out. Information, in the form of instructions and experimental displays, is first perceived, then represented and processed, and a decision is made on the basis of it. All of these processes are influenced by memory. In addition, processes may be altered by motives (or visceral factors). The workings of some or all of these mechanisms are (in some cognitive theories) accessible to introspection and expressible by verbal behavior. When a decision is made, that decision is expressed in verbal or non-verbal behavior or some combination of the two. Finally, the outcome of the decision ("consequences") is retained in memory and may affect future operation of any component of the decision mechanism.

The simplistic model of Figure 6 does not indicate any of the quite complex and elaborate sub-mechanisms (neural networks or parallel processing) that may operate within or across the boxes in the figure. There is some dispute within cognitive psychology about which if any internal mechanisms contain sub-mechanisms that work on logical principles and where if anywhere in the process principles of optimality apply. Moreover, strictly speaking, a purely cognitive theory is silent about the physiological instantiation (the hardware) corresponding to the flow of information (the software) represented in the figure. The workings of the boxes labeled perception, representation, memory, and so forth, and their interaction as an information processing system, is what cognitive theories are all about.

What goes on to the right of the heavy vertical line of Figure 6 is unquestionably interesting and important. No behaviorist can deny that. But the behaviorist is fundamentally interested, not in the principles underlying internal mechanisms, but in the principles underlying the prediction and control of behavior. The cognitivist and the behaviorist both want, ultimately, to explain current behavior — to answer the question, Why is this person acting in this way? But their explanations of current behavior refer to different events. The cognitivist, in explaining current actions, refers to current events inside the organism; the behaviorist, in explaining current actions, refers to past actions and past environmental events and to the relations over time between those events and actions. The behavioral equivalent to a cognitive mechanism is a contingency but *a contingency has no meaning at an instant of time*.

No behaviorist, not even a teleological behaviorist like me, denies that there are mechanisms inside the person mediating between the incoming and outgoing arrows of Figure 6. The organism is not empty. But, just as the cognitive psychologist may be interested fundamentally in the internal software and only secondarily, if at all, in the particular underlying hardware (the particular brain physiology), so the behaviorist is interested fundamentally in the relations *in the environment* between the four arrows of Figure 6 and only secondarily, if at all, in the mechanisms (software or hardware) that mediate between the ingoing and outgoing arrows.

Skinnerian Behaviorism

Skinnerian analysis proceeds as follows. There is some behavior in which you are interested (say, addiction). First you look for a single stimulus in the environment that reliably causes that behavior. I think we can all agree that there is no such single environmental cause of addiction; if there were, we could cure addiction by just eliminating its stimulus. Failing to find a stimulus, Skinnerian analysis bids you to look for a *reinforcer*, to ask, what are the consequences of any given bit of behavior?

For example, Rudy Vuchinich asked me to come here today and speak. And here I am. Presumably this is voluntary behavior. You could ask, *how* am I doing it, tracing a chain of internal events from the e-mail entering my eyes and the phone call entering my ears, engaging my cognitive system, and this behavior (my standing here and talking) finally emerged. Or, you could ask, what are the reinforcers (and punishers)? This would involve an examination of the consequences of my behavior as they affect me — a chance to be the center of attention, for a while, of a distinguished group of psychologists and economists, to perhaps influence them, to improve my own research due to feedback from you. You would have to look for similar behavior by me in the past and similar consequences. These, Skinner says, are the true causes of my present behavior. *I have no privileged access to my own motives.* I may have better access to my own behavior and its consequences than you have (because I'm always there when I'm behaving), and that's an advantage for me. But you have an objective view that I do not have, and that's an advantage for you. (The behavior therapist aims to work with this advantage.[4])

So what's wrong with this method of analyzing behavior? The problem is that, just as it is not possible to find an external stimulus as the cause of behavior in almost all interesting cases, so it is not possible to find an external reinforcer in many interesting cases. For example, although you can easily discover the reinforcers for my talk here today, you will not be able to find a reinforcer for this particular sentence. Yet, according to Skinner, every individual act (each sentence, each word) must have its individual immediate reinforcer — either a primary reinforcer (like a pellet of food) or a secondary reinforcer (like the sound of the food hopper in a Skinner box). It is often impossible to trace every individual act of a rat or pigeon (let alone a human being) to its eventual reinforcement. Similarly, as many ingenious experiments by cognitive psychologists have shown, it is not possible for the economist to trace every person's every act to maximization of utility.

As I previously indicated, this problem becomes apparent in research on self-control. On the one hand, it is easy to explain *failures* of self-control in terms of immediate reinforcement. If I have a second or third cocktail at a party, the reinforcers of my behavior — the cocktails themselves — are easy to spot. But what if the waiter tries to hand me a cocktail and I refuse? What reinforces that act? What reinforces *successes* in self-control? I refuse the cocktail and exactly nothing happens. The usual tactic of the behavior analyst at this point is to postulate some sort of inner reinforcement — my satisfaction. I covertly pat myself on the back. But to postulate such an internal mechanism is to engage in cognitive analysis rather than behavioral analysis (as I have defined it). Cognitive psychologists are much better at postulating internal mechanisms than behaviorists are — they are trained for it — and the behaviorist begins to look overly simplistic. This is the problem with Skinnerian behaviorism, a problem pointed out many times.

Teleological Behaviorism (Rachlin 1994, 2000)

Teleological behaviorism, on the other hand, confronted with a clearly voluntary act (like refusing a cocktail), for which there is no apparent external reinforcement, looks, not into the organism, but into the past and future for patterns of behavior. According to teleological behaviorism, the question of why I am speaking right now cannot be broken up into the question of why I am speaking this sentence, why I am speaking the next sentence, and so forth. Rather, you have to look at why I am giving this talk as a whole — the extrinsic social reinforcers I mentioned previously as well as the intrinsic value of the activity itself. If I had to decide whether to utter each sentence individually I'd be tongue-tied — since there is no reinforcement for each sentence individually. Similarly, in the area of self-control, there is no reinforcement for each act of cocktail refusal, cigarette refusal, heroin refusal. It is sometimes said that the reinforcement for such acts is delayed. But, as I said, if I refuse a single cocktail tonight, I will not wake up three weeks from today, suddenly a healthier, happier person. A single act of self-control is not reinforced — *now or ever*. Reinforcement is to be found not in individual acts but in the value (the utility, if you will) of a pattern of acts strung out over time. This value may be extrinsic to the pattern — like social approval — or intrinsic in the pattern itself.[5]

To put it more formally, there is a long activity lasting T time units and a short activity lasting t time units, where $T = Nt$. A problem of self-control arises when the two inequalities stated at the top of Figure 7 are satisfied. The symbol V stands for value. In other words, a problem of self-control arises when the value of a longer activity is greater than that of an equal duration of repetitions of a shorter activity and the value of the shorter activity is greater than that of an equal fraction of the longer activity.[6]

For example, suppose you were driving from New York to California. You like both classical and popular music. So you take along 10 classical and 10 pop CD's to play on your car CD player for the trip. Let us assume that the order of your preference (illustrated in Figure 7) is as follows:

$$T/t = N$$

$$A: \ V_T > N^*V_t$$

$$B: \ V_t > V_{T/N}$$

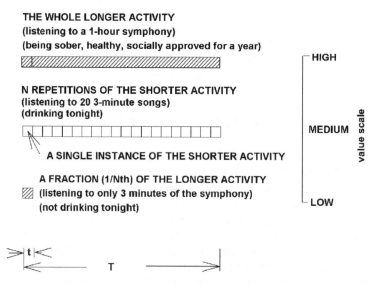

THE WHOLE LONGER ACTIVITY
(listening to a 1-hour symphony)
(being sober, healthy, socially approved for a year)

N REPETITIONS OF THE SHORTER ACTIVITY
(listening to 20 3-minute songs)
(drinking tonight)

A SINGLE INSTANCE OF THE SHORTER ACTIVITY

A FRACTION (1/Nth) OF THE LONGER ACTIVITY
(listening to only 3 minutes of the symphony)
(not drinking tonight)

HIGH

MEDIUM

LOW

value scale

Figure 7: How the relative values of behavioral patterns may conflict with the relative values of the components of the patterns.

(1) listening to a whole one-hour symphony;
(2) listening to a three-minute popular song;
(3) listening to three minutes of the symphony.

The problem is of course that in order to listen to the whole symphony (No. 1 on your list) you've got to listen to the first three minutes of the symphony (No. 3 on your list). So the immediate choice is always between No. 3 and No. 2 (the popular song). If you always do what you immediately prefer, you're likely to reach California without ever having heard the symphony. Of course, you could listen to just one popular song and then the symphony but after listening to the song you'd be in the same position that you were in the first place. The value of the symphony, as the gestalt psychologists never tired of pointing out, lies not in the sum of the values of its parts — even the sum of the delay-discounted values of its parts; it lies in the symphony as a whole. You can see this by imagining how you would feel if a symphony CD were defective and the last three minutes were missing. You would not consider that you had 57/60th worth of enjoyment from the CD. Most likely the whole experience would be ruined even though you had already listened to, and supposedly enjoyed, 57 minutes of the symphony.

The same considerations apply in most examples of human self-control — the choice between studying and not studying, between reading a novel and watching a TV program, between being sober and having a drink. The alcoholic does not chose to be an alcoholic. He prefers not to be one. His preference ordering is:

(1) not being an alcoholic;
(2) drinking tonight;
(3) not drinking tonight.

He just chooses to drink tonight, and tonight, and tonight — and ends up as an alcoholic without ever having chosen to be one.

The cognitive psychologist naturally sees self-control in terms of internal mechanisms; the teleological behaviorist sees self-control as more or less valuable behavioral patterns, reinforced in different behavioral contexts *as whole patterns*. This difference between the behavioral and cognitive approaches is not just a semantic issue. It determines where you should look — into the person, or into the person's past (the person's reinforcement history, in Skinner's terms) — to discover the causes of a person's behavior. Obviously both paths need to be pursued, both are valuable. But the economist's means of behavioral control are the same as those of the behaviorist — in modifying environmental contingencies rather than in trying to manipulate internal mechanisms.

But, you may ask, what about cases where reinforcement and punishment seem not to work? The teleological behaviorist's answer to that question is that *reinforcement is not a mechanism that can work or fail to work. Rather, the concept of reinforcement (like its cousin, the concept of utility maximization) is an approach to understanding behavior*. If a behaviorist cannot explain a person's voluntary behavior in terms of reinforcement and punishment, it is the *behaviorist's* fault, not the person's fault. Similarly, if the economist finds that people fail to maximize utility, the economist has not correctly determined where utility lies or has not properly evaluated the prevailing constraints. The question we should ask is not, "Is utility maximized?" But, assuming that utility is maximized, the question for psychology and economics alike should be, "What are the dimensions of utility in this context?" and "What is the best way to measure them?"

What do these considerations mean for relative addiction theory, a theory that relies on the effect of present choice on future value? One way to preserve the theory is to focus not on future value directly but *first* on the effect of present choice on the coherency of behavioral patterning — that is, the effect of present choice on the construction and preservation of behavioral rules — and only *then* on the value and substitutability of patterns. The initial individual acts of self-control, like the initial individual notes of a symphony, have value only provisionally. If they are not followed up by completion of the pattern they lose this provisional value — they are wasted. Thus, current acts of self-control affect the value not only of *future* alternatives, they may also affect the value of *past* alternatives.

When the recovering alcoholic takes a drink, he decreases not only the future value of drinking but also the value of his *past* socialization; the value of that past socialization depended on its follow-through in the present. Failing that follow-through those past social activities lose their value (which they held only provisionally). Another way of saying this is that, unlike drinking, social activities attain their high value, and serve as an effective substitute for drinking, only when they occur in a long-term pattern. Organization of behavior into such patterns, as I understand it, has been all along the focus of the work of George Ainslie, Gene Heyman, and myself. And, there is much still to be done.

Notes

1. Becker & Murphy (1988) call the latter phenomenon, "adjacent complementarity."
2. Of course, this is a great oversimplification. Lines A–B and C–D need not be parallel or even straight. See Herrnstein & Prelec (1992) and Rachlin (2000) for discussion of more complex cases.
3. Social interaction, as an activity, is necessary (although perhaps not sufficient) for social support. Studies of cooperative behavior in games such as the prisoner's dilemma show that cooperation with others is sensitive to the probability of social reinforcement and punishment (Baker & Rachlin 2001). Thus, social support (social reinforcement) depends on social interaction (cooperation) and vice-versa.
4. The point of the recent play, Copenhagen, as I understood it, was exactly that. Heisenberg's motives for visiting Bohr during WWII were as much of a mystery to Heisenberg himself as they were to Bohr — and to the audience.
5. In dealing with individual human behavior, the behaviorist calculates reinforcement value in terms of consummatory behavior rather than in terms of the goods being bought. Value — or utility for that matter — for an individual is primarily in eating the apple and only secondarily in having the apple.
6. By an "activity" I mean an instance of a class of activities defined functionally (an "operant," in Skinner's (1938) terms.) Thus, eating a large steak for dinner and eating a pint of ice cream that night while watching TV would be two instances of the same activity — overeating.

References

Ainsworth, M. D. S., & Bowlby, J. (1991). An ethological approach to personality development. *American Psychologist, 46*, 333–341.
Baker, F., & Rachlin, H. (2001). Probability of reciprocation in prisoner's dilemma games. *Journal of Behavioral Decision Making, 14*, 51–67.

Becker, G. S. (1996). *Accounting for tastes*. Cambridge, MA: Harvard University Press.

Becker, G., & Murphy, K. M. (1988). A theory of rational addiction. *Journal of Political Economy*, *96*, 675–700.

Foster, T. A., Hackenberg, T. D., & Vaidya, M. (2001). Second-order schedules of token reinforcement with pigeons: Effects of fixed- and variable-ratio exchange schedules. *Journal of the Experimental Analysis of Behavior*, *76*, 159–178.

Green, L., & Fisher, E. B. (2000). Economic substitutability: Some implications for health behavior. In: W. K. Bickel, & R. E. Vuchinich (Eds), *Reframing health behavior change with behavioral economics* (pp. 115–144). Mahwah, NJ: Erlbaum.

Herrnstein, R. J., & Prelec, D. (1992). A theory of addiction. In: G. Loewenstein, & J. Elster (Eds), *Choice over time* (pp. 331–361). New York: Russell Sage Press.

Hursh, S. R., & Winger, G. (1995). Normalized demand curves for drugs and other reinforcers. *Journal of the Experimental Analysis of Behavior*, *64*, 373–384.

Kudadjie-Gyamfi, E., & Rachlin, H. (1996). Temporal patterning in choice among delayed outcomes. *Organizational Behavior and Human Decision Processes*, *65*, 61–67.

Premack, D. (1965). Reinforcement theory. In: D. Levine (Ed.), *Nebraska symposium on motivation: 1965* (pp. 123–179). Lincoln: University of Nebraska Press.

Rachlin, H. (1978). A molar theory of reinforcement schedules. *Journal of the Experimental Analysis of Behavior*, *30*, 345–360.

Rachlin, H. (1994). *Behavior and mind*. New York: Oxford University Press.

Rachlin, H. (1997). Four teleological theories of addiction. *Psychonomic Bulletin & Review*, *4*, 462–473.

Rachlin, H. (2000). *The science of self-control*. Cambridge, MA: Harvard University Press.

Rachlin, H., & Burkhard, B. (1978). The temporal triangle: Substitution in instrumental conditioning. *Psychological Review*, *85*, 22–48.

Rachlin, H., & Green, L. (1972). Commitment, choice and self-control. *Journal of the Experimental Analysis of Behavior*, *17*, 15–22.

Rachlin, H., Green, L., Kagel, J. H., & Battalio, R. C. (1976). Economic demand theory and psychological studies of choice. In: G. Bower (Ed.), *The psychology of learning and motivation* (Vol. 10). New York: Academic Press.

Samuelson, P. A. (1973). *Economics: An introductory analysis* (9th ed.). New York: McGraw-Hill.

Siegel, E., & Rachlin, H. (1995). Soft commitment: Self-control as achieved by response persistence. *Journal of the Experimental Analysis of Behavior*, *64*, 117–128.

Skinner, B. F. (1938). *The behavior of organisms*. New York: Appleton-Century-Crofts.

Staddon, J. E. R. (Ed.) (1980). *Limits to action: The allocation of individual behavior*. New York: Academic Press.

Stigler, G. J., & Becker, G. S. (1977). De gustibus non est disputandum. *American Economic Review*, *67*, 76–90.

Widholm, J. J., Silberberg, A., Hursh, S. R., Imam, A., & Warren-Boulton, F. R. (2001). Stock optimizing in choice when a token deposit is the operant. *Journal of the Experimental Analysis of Behavior*, *76*, 245–264.

Comments on Rachlin

Rudy E. Vuchinich

I'm not going to comment on the technical aspects of Howard Rachlin's paper, which would be beyond my expertise anyway. Instead, I want to discuss some more general and difficult issues in our field, and then comment on how Rachlin's work has and will continue to help us deal with them. The two general aspects of this work I will come back to are: (1) the "externality" and "molarity" of teleological behaviorism; and (2) the focus of the theory of relative addiction on a (more or less) specific activity other than substance use, social interaction.

"Addiction" is a Metaphor for Excessive Consumption

I want to start by taking a few minutes to discuss the history of the term "addiction," which is a very powerful word used to talk about excessive consumption. The term "addiction" derives from the Latin word "addictus," which meant "assigned by decree, made over, bound to another, hence attached by restraint or obligation" (MacAndrew 1988: 164). So how did a word that meant "obligation" come to be used in reference to "excessive consumption?" Apparently "addiction" entered the vocabulary of excessive consumption via early 17th century British clergy, who "had long been in the habit of labeling excessive drinkers as 'addicted' . . . and had additionally described habitual drunkenness as a 'disease' in its own right" (Warner 1994: 689). A term initiated by some British preachers is now in widespread use in the culture at large and in the scientific community. "Addiction" has been used in reference to heavy alcohol consumption for almost 400 years. During the 20th century, opiate and other drug use have become addictions, with tobacco or nicotine probably being the most recent addiction.

So, are there any problems with this? Maybe no problems, maybe a lot of problems, depending on how we interpret the meaning of the term addiction — that is, depending on how the term addiction guides our behavior as scientists and professionals in addressing excessive consumption. Languages evolve in part through metaphorical extension, where a term for one thing is used to describe another thing because of some apparent similarity between them (Jaynes 1976). This happens all the time in descriptions of behavior patterns, in both normal and scientific language, so it is a perfectly normal process. But if the metaphorical roots of the new description get lost, which they almost always do, then the term can produce some mischief.

Theodore Sarbin wrote a paper in 1968 entitled "Ontology recapitulates philology: the mythic nature of anxiety" (Sarbin 1968), which many of you psychologists probably have read. The paper was about how potentially useful descriptions of behavior may lose their utility because of changes in their meaning. He argued that when the metaphorical character of a term becomes "opaque," that is, no longer widely recognized, the term readily becomes reified, internalized, and attributed causal significance. So, in normal and scientific language, a descriptive metaphor for overt behavior eventually becomes an internal force that causes the behavior. This can create problems in dealing effectively with the behavior, because then one is attempting to deal with an internal cause of the behavior when what one actually has is the behavior pattern itself. This is a problem because the real causes of the behavior therefore remain unidentified.

So, I guess there are two questions: (1) whether or not this process has occurred with the term addiction; and (2) if so, is this something we should worry about? I think the answer to the first question is a definite "Yes." Those clergy in the early 1600s apparently saw similarities between the behavior of heavy drinkers and the behavior of one who is obligated to do something. So, they used the term addiction metaphorically to describe devotion to drinking. I doubt the clergy believed that drinkers drank because they were obligated or addicted. They probably only meant that they were drinking as if obligated to do so, that is, as if addicted. Over all these years, however, the term addiction has gone from being a metaphorical description of devotion to an activity, to being an internal entity whose existence is revealed by that devotion, to, finally, being the internal cause of that devotion. I think there is little doubt this has happened, certainly in the lay community and in much of the scientific community as well. When I teach about substance abuse and students talk about someone's addiction, I like to ask them, "Well, exactly where is that person's addiction?" Most of them readily locate the addiction in the brain, and the few who are unwilling to do that have no qualms about locating it in some sort of conceptual nervous system.

So, yes, the addiction metaphor has been reified, internalized, and attributed causal significance. Now the second question, is this something we should worry about? I think the answer here also is a "Yes." Addiction is a metaphor for excessive consumption, but changes in its meaning over the years have led to too much time being spent looking for the internal addiction and too little time spent looking for the contextual determinants of excessive consumption. Redressing this imbalance is one of the great strengths of the behavioral economics of substance abuse. That is, the behavioral economics of substance abuse would have us focus directly on those contextual determinants.

Characterizing the Environment

A broad view of the scientific study of excessive consumption goes back well before the 20th century. In that history, serious concern about the importance of the person's interaction with the environment is a relatively recent innovation. It really got started in a big way with Conger's (1956) tension reduction theory of alcoholism, which was based on Hull's (1952) learning theory, and with early extensions of Skinner's (1938) system into applied behavior analysis (e.g. Mello 1972). This was major progress, but these views provided relatively narrow conceptions of the environment. The learning theory approach got developed by behavior therapists in the 1960s and 1970s, but they relapsed into the cognitive behavioral movement in the 1970s and 1980s. This moved their attention away from the environment and towards cognition at the time of excessive consumption.

The Skinnerians stayed focused on the outside world, but that focus was on the local environment, on things that are happening at the time of the excessive consumption.

Then along came the behavioral economics of substance abuse in the 1980s and 1990s, with its emphasis on patterns of excessive consumption over time in relation to patterns of access to other activities over time. Now, I think, we have a scientific conceptual framework that will allow us to develop a more effective understanding of how excessive consumption develops, how it is maintained, and what we can do to prevent it or to change it. One critical reason I believe this about behavioral economics is that it demands that the person's interaction with the environment over time be the crux of the analysis.

How this area develops in the future is anybody's guess, but for now we have four sets of ideas that are providing most of the guidance: hyperbolic temporal discounting, and the melioration, rational, and relative theories of addiction. Whether one of these theories, or some combination of them, or a new theory provides the best guidance will be decided by future work. But for now I'm left with looking at what some of the relative advantages and disadvantages might be in two particular areas.

First, I think the history of the term "addiction" has some valuable lessons, perhaps most importantly to beware of the internalization of our behavioral observations and descriptions. Maybe, as I'll suggest in a moment, we should just do away with "addiction," altogether and conceive a new metaphor for excessive consumption. In the meantime, how well will melioration, relative, and rational addiction help us to avoid the internalizing tendencies in our language? Here I think Rachlin's (1992) teleological behaviorism has an advantage, since it explicitly conceives of psychological terms as referring to molar behavior-environment relations.

Second, I've always felt that a fundamental aspect of the behavioral economic perspective is that it leads us to pay attention to behavior patterns other than excessive consumption (Vuchinich & Tucker 1988). (The first thing I wrote in this literature was titled "Have behavioral theories of alcohol abuse focused too much on alcohol consumption?" [Vuchinich 1982].) That is, what is the more general behavioral and environmental context into which the pattern of excessive consumption fits? How well will current theories in this area lead us in addressing this general issue? That is, how well will questions raised by these theories focus our attention explicitly on overt patterns of non-substance use activities over time? Both melioration and rational addiction create a two-option behavioral allocation scenario, with the choice being between substance use and something else. By grouping all non-substance use activities into one category, however, those activities and their supporting environments remain nebulous and ambiguous. This ambiguity on one side of the choice may make it easy to relapse back into focusing on the other side of the choice, the substance use itself. Again I think Rachlin's relative addiction has an advantage by explicitly focusing on a particular non-substance use activity, social interaction. It may turn out that social interaction is itself too broad or that it is not the most important nonsubstance use activity, but at least it seems like a good place to start.

A New Metaphor for Excessive Consumption?

I want to wrap this up with a quote by Harry Levine from a great 1978 paper on the history of addiction.

[T]here is the beginning of what I would call a "postaddiction" model of drug and alcohol problems emerging[.] A new formulation of drug and alcohol problems does not look primarily at the interaction between individual and drug, but at the relationship between individual and society. [excessive consumption], therefore, is not simply defined as an issue of individual control and responsibility, but can be seen as a social and structural process (Levine 1978: 166).

If we are in a "post-addiction" world, than perhaps we need to drop the addiction metaphor for excessive consumption and coin a new metaphor. How about an economic metaphor, in which excessive consumption is seen as contextually driven resource allocation, rather than as internally driven compulsion, as in the addiction metaphor? Going further, maybe we should label this new metaphor "substitution." So, if someone is consuming excessively, we no longer say they are behaving as if obligated (addicted) to consume. Instead we say they are behaving as if substituting the consumption for something else. If Rachlin is on the right track, then maybe this wouldn't be a metaphor at all. Maybe this would be a literal description of what is actually going on.

References

Conger, J. J. (1956). Alcoholism: Theory, problem, and challenge. II. Reinforcement theory and the dynamics of alcoholism. *Quarterly Journal of Studies on Alcohol, 17*, 296–305.

Hull, C. L. (1952). *A behavior system.* New Haven, CT: Yale University Press.

Jaynes, J. (1976). *The origin of consciousness in the breakdown of the bicameral mind.* Boston: Houghton Miffiin.

Levine, H. G. (1978). The discovery of addiction: Changing conceptions of habitual drunkenness in America. *Journal of Studies on Alcohol, 39*, 143–174.

MacAndrew, C. (1988). On the possibility of an addiction-free mode of being. In: S. Peele (Ed.), *Visions of addiction: Major contemporary perspectives on addiction and alcoholism* (pp. 163–182). Lexington, MA: Lexington Books.

Mello, N. K. (1972). Behavioral studies of alcoholism. In: B. Kissin, & H. Begleiter (Eds), *The biology of alcoholism* (Vol. 2, pp. 219–291). New York: Plenum Press.

Rachlin, H. (1992). Teleological behaviorism. *American Psychologist, 47*, 1371–1382.

Sarbin, T. R. (1968). Ontology recapitulates philology: The mythic nature of anxiety. *American Psychologist, 23*, 411–418.

Skinner, B. F. (1938). *The behavior of organisms: An experimental analysis.* Englewood Cliffs, NJ: Prentice-Hall.

Vuchinich, R. E. (1982). Have behavioral theories of alcohol abuse focused too much on alcohol consumption? *Bulletin of the Society of Psychologists in Substance Abuse, 1*, 151–154.

Vuchinich, R. E., & Tucker, J. A. (1988). Contributions from behavioral theories of choice to an analysis of alcohol abuse. *Journal of Abnormal Psychology, 97*, 181–195.

Warner, J. (1994). "Resolv'd to drink no more": Addiction as a preindustrial construct. *Journal of Studies on Alcohol, 55*, 685–691.

Part II

Other Perspectives on Addiction

Chapter 6

Addiction: Definitions and Mechanisms

Ole-Jørgen Skog

Introduction

Addictive behaviours pose two major challenges: firstly, the practical problem of preventing and reducing the sufferings of the addicts themselves and of third parties; secondly, the theoretical problem of understanding the paradox of voluntary self-destructive behaviour. Why do people voluntarily engage in activities that they know may seriously hurt them in the long run; why do they start, why do they persist, and why do they relapse?

One fairly obvious response to the second puzzle is that the claim is misguided and that addictive behaviours are *not* voluntary. According to this view the addict has lost his capacity for deliberate choice, at least in relation to the drug or activity he or she is addicted to. This view has long historical roots, but also modern adherents. For instance, Donald Goodwin has claimed that: "The elaborate definition of alcohol dependence proposed by the American Psychiatric Association can be collapsed more or less to a single sentence: Alcoholism involves a compulsion to drink, causing damage to self and others" (Goodwin 1991: 599). Likewise, Mark Keller has claimed that: ". . . an alcoholic cannot consistently choose whether he shall drink or not. There comes an occasion when he is powerless, when he cannot help drinking. For that is the essence or nature of a drug addiction" (Keller 1972: 162).

During the last few decades, this conception has been seriously challenged. Firstly, evidence has accumulated that addicts are in fact able to choose and that these choices are strongly influenced by environmental restraints and opportunities (Heather & Robertson 1981; Marlatt *et al.* 1973; Mello & og Mendelson 1965, 1966, 1972; Pattison *et al.* 1977). Secondly, the argument offered by the advocates of the no-choice interpretation is typically due to a conceptual mistake (cf. Watson 1999). Quite often, it is based on the observation that addicts claim that they do not wish to perform a certain act, but still they do at some later stage. However, this is not a compulsion; it is just an example of dynamic inconsistency. In advance, the agent intended to abstain, but at the time of acting he has changed his mind. He may be ambivalent, having good reasons for abstaining, but obviously even stronger reasons for indulging (cf. Skog 2000).

Choice, Behavioural Economics and Addiction
© 2003 Published by Elsevier Ltd.
ISBN: 0-08-044056-8

As new developments in neuroscience accumulate, we may expect a revitalization of disease conceptions. Undoubtedly, more or less permanent effects of drugs on the brains of addicts will be identified and understood in increasing detail in the years to come. One can even imagine that addictions may be diagnosed with reasonable precision some time in the future, solely on the basis of neurological examinations.

However, even if this should come true, it does not mean that addicts are unable to choose. Everything we do, think and feel has a neurobiological substrate. From a scientific point of view, all mental activity must be understood as corresponding to neurological activity in the brain.[1] Hence, a close correspondence between the mental and the physical must be presumed, although we do not yet have a good understanding of how the mental is generated by physical processes (and perhaps never will). Still, there is no reason to doubt that the mental is generated that way. It is obviously true that when a person learns to ride a bicycle, there will occur some permanent changes in the cyclist's brain. Some day these changes may be understood in great detail. And when I decided to go to university, there were also permanent changes in my brain — and more changes as time went by, and I learned more.

The point I wish to make is simply that being able to identify the neurological substrate of addiction does not make it a disease, any more than the identification of the neurological substrate of learning to ride a bicycle makes cycling a disease — or involuntary. The fact that all chemical addictions seem to involve some of the same structures, notably in nucleus accumbens (Gardner & David 1999) is, of course, interesting, and *may* suggest that the basic neurological mechanisms underlying these conditions are closely related. It may even suggest that the corresponding mental mechanisms are closely related, although this does not necessarily follow. But it does not suggest that the agent is unable to choose.

A distinction is often made between physical and psychological dependence.[2] From the point of view I have just outlined, this distinction can be misleading, as psychological dependence will always have a physical substrate in form of neuro-adaptions or sensitizations of one sort or another. The only meaningful statement one can make is that certain addictions are accompanied by this or that neuro-adaption (e.g. withdrawal or tolerance), while others are not. Compared to all other neuro-adaptions that underlie addictions, withdrawal and tolerance stand out mainly in one respect: they have been known for a long time, since they are not very difficult to observe by a third party. Other neuro-adaptions may be of a more subtle and complex nature, and they are not as easily observed. I feel quite confident that the phenomena referred to as psychological dependence do in fact correspond to subtle physical phenomena (other than withdrawal and tolerance).

Denying that addicts are unable to choose does not necessarily mean that we should refrain from calling addiction a disease. The concept of disease is mainly a social concept — a flag saying that the person in question has certain rights, including the right to treatment and care (if these are available). From the point of view of social policy, there can be good reasons for calling addiction a disease. However, the defining trait of this disease is not an inability to choose, but the existence of excessive appetites of a certain type. Nothing would prevent us from saying that an excessive (as judged by the agent, society, or both) appetite that causes severe motivational conflict is a disease. With a disease concept construed like this, the diagnosis would make it possible to understand the agent's actions, and to offer him help and assistance to curtail his appetite, but without taking away his moral responsibility for his own actions.

Tying the disease concept to appetites rather than to actions is reasonable also for the following reason: while an agent deliberately chooses how to act on the basis of his appetites, values, and opportunities, the appetites and values themselves are not chosen. According to standard theory, a rational person cannot manipulate his own appetite at will (cf. Elster 1984).

If I like writing, I cannot simply decide that I don't like it; I can only decide not to write, possibly at the cost of great frustration. Therefore, excessive appetites and high blood pressure have at least two things in common: they will not go away simply by an act of will, but both may be controlled if the agent tries hard and acts appropriately.

In the following pages I shall discuss addictions, using a mentalistic (as opposed to a physicalistic) language. I shall assume that addicts are able to choose, and consequently that they are not helpless spectators of their own body's movements. From this perspective, the phenomenon at hand must be understood as excessive appetites (cf. Orford 1985) — appetites that can be so strong that they are very difficult (but not impossible) to resist. These strong motives may be difficult to understand for a person who has never experienced anything of the sort. As Walt Whitman puts it: "None know — none can know, but they who have felt it — the burning, withering thirst for drink, which habit forms in the appetite of the wretched victim of intoxication" (Whitman [1842] 1929: 148).

I shall continue as follows. First I discuss how the concept of addiction could be defined from a mental point of view. My point of departure will be the definition offered in the Diagnostic and Statistical Manual of the American Psychiatric Association (DSM-IV) and Nick Heather's recent analysis (Heather 1998). Next follows a discussion of three recent choice theories of addiction. Firstly, Gary Becker's theory of addiction as rational choice (Becker 1992; Becker & Murphy 1988), secondly George Ainslie's divided-self theory (Ainslie 1994, 1999, 2001), and lastly Richard Herrnstein and Drazen Prelec's primrose path theory (Herrnstein & Prelec 1992), and Howard Rachlin's extension of the latter into a theory of the lonely addict (Rachlin 2000).

Defining Addiction: The Issue of Factual and Counterfactual Definitions

Dependence is obviously something that comes in degrees (Edwards 1982). Any cut-off would necessarily be more or less arbitrary. However, it is convenient to have a label for those who are severely addicted, provided we do not forget that this is really a continuous concept. I will use the words "addiction" and "dependence" interchangeably, as a short-hand for "at the high end of the spectrum."

DSM-IV (1994) lists seven criteria and suggests that dependence is present when three or more have occurred within the last 12 months. The criteria are: (1) tolerance; (2) withdrawal; (3) often consuming more than was intended; (4) persistent desire or unsuccessful efforts to cut down; (5) spending a great deal of time with drug-related activities; (6) giving up important social, occupational, or recreational activities; (7) continuing consumption despite physical or psychological harm.

Heather (1998) argues, convincingly, to the effect that item 4 on the list is a *sine qua non*. If this criterion is not fulfilled, he proposes to call it a state of neuro-adaption. However, Heather goes one step further, and claims that the "essence of addiction is not so much *difficulty* in refraining as a demonstrated *failure* to have refrained from it despite having attempted to do so." He also claims that "where a behaviour does not involve an attempt to refrain from it, there is no need for a concept of addiction" (Heather 1998: 4).

Failure to refrain can obviously be an important *diagnostic* criterion for addiction; if a person has struggled long and hard to overcome a destructive consumption habit, he is probably addicted. However, the reverse is not necessarily true, and to say that a person is not addicted unless he or she struggled and failed is problematic. For instance, a person who does not wish to quit consuming drug X under the prevailing circumstances, and who makes no attempt, could both find it difficult to refrain and experience repeated failures if the situation had been different. Imagine the same person in two different contexts. In context A, his spouse (reluctantly) accepts his excessive X-ing, users are not stigmatized, and it does not destroy the family economy. He is not struggling to get out of his habit. Then the context changes to B: users are stigmatized, prices go up to such an extent that he no longer can deal with his economic obligations, and his wife threatens to leave him. He will now struggle to end his abuse. The person is the same, only the socio-economic context has changed. Does it make sense to say that this person was addicted under B but not under A?

Of course, addiction can be defined as the definer thinks fit. But it may nevertheless be considered inconvenient to exclude certain phenomena that upon inspection turns out to be closely related to what one consider addiction proper. The possibility mentioned above suggests that the definition needs a counterfactual supplement. Hence, the definition should say that a person is addicted "if the person has demonstrated failure to refrain, despite having attempted to do so, or who would have demonstrated such failures under different environmental conditions."

As an example, consider a long-term heavy smoker back in the 1950s. He had no solid evidence that his habit was harmful. He had a strong appetite for nicotine, but no very good reason for abstaining, and was consequently a happy smoker. However, according to Heather, there is no such thing as a "happy addict," and it follows from this view that he is not addicted. A few years later, the same person has become convinced that tobacco is in fact harmful, and he is strongly motivated to quit. However, despite numerous attempts, he has not succeeded. Now he *is* addicted, according to the same view. The smoker's appetite for nicotine may not have changed during this short period. The main difference between the two states is simply that he has obtained information that generated a strong motive that initially was not there. According to the counterfactual definition he was addicted on both occasions.

The reverse case offers a second example: a man has for a long time struggled hard (partly due to pressure from his wife) to quit his heavy drinking, but has experienced numerous relapses. He is obviously addicted according to both definitions. Then his family finally leaves him, his life is in ruins, and his motivation for quitting disappears. He continues to drink heavily without any further attempts to quit. According to the logic of Heather's definition he should no longer be considered an addict.

A third example: a person suddenly realizes that a lot of bad things that have happened to him are caused by his heavy consumption of drug X. This gives him a substantial motive for quitting. He makes one serious attempt to quit, fails dramatically, and never makes another wholehearted attempt. For instance, he may realize that he is insufficiently motivated by the future gains in life-quality, and that the gains do not match the temporary set-back he will have to tolerate, say, due to withdrawal etc. He is not, literally speaking, a happy addict, but feels that, all things considered, he is *less unhappy* when he continues rather than discontinues his consumption. According to Heather's definition, this person is not addicted.

In the latter case the motivation generated is not sufficient to generate an ongoing struggle. The person knows that he should not consume X because it is bad for him, but the motivational force of the risk is insufficient. However, one could easily imagine that, at a certain stage, another serious consequence of drug X becomes evident — one that can be avoided by quitting. Now the motivation for quitting becomes strong enough and the person starts his struggle to curtail the habit. According to Heather's definition, this individual has now become addicted. According to the counterfactual definition he was addicted even before the last stage.

There is obviously a difference between the types of addition captured by Heather's factual definition and the types captured by the counterfactual supplement. Hence, we need labels to signify the distinction. Following Orford (1985), we could call the former type *dissonant* addicts, while the latter type are *consonant* addicts. The consonant addict is a "willing" addict under the prevailing circumstances, though not necessarily a happy addict. In fact, he or she may be quite unhappy, but finds life less intolerable with the drug than without the drug. It should be added, however, that dissonance comes in degrees, and the dichotomy is just a short-hand (see below).

Regarding consonant addicts, Ainslie (1999: 85) has argued that "addiction in this sense is an ordinary taste; such a taste would not puzzle us if it did not typically lead to a stage in which the person recognized his error but could not escape — in other words, to enslavement." However, all the persons exemplified above may in fact feel a strong enslavement. The 1950 smoker probably knew that abstention was very unpleasant, and he may have realized that it would be extremely difficult ("impossible") for him to quit. The divorced heavy drinker of the second example may feel even more enslaved, as he has resigned from making further attempts. And the consumer of drug X may, even at the first stage, have a strong feeling of enslavement, as he has very good reasons (strong motives) for discontinuing his habit. Hence, he is suffering from *akrasia*, or weakness of the will — not in the sense of dynamic inconsistency, but in the sense of a simultaneous inconsistency. He has a desire to quit, but not the willpower needed to quit (i.e. his motivation is insufficient).[3] I submit that this phenomenon of having great difficulty in abstaining from a certain activity, in spite of having very good reasons for abstention, is no less puzzling than the dynamic inconsistencies produced by hyperbolic discounting (see below), and that consonant addiction is not just "an ordinary taste."

Heather's argument for his definition might be that, unless we can observe that the individual has struggled to end his habit, we have no grounds for distinguishing this behaviour from any other behaviour — i.e. for separating addictive behaviour from ordinary habits: How do we know that a person is addicted if he has not attempted to quit, and failed? This is an epistemic, rather than an ontological argument. It concerns the methodological problem of demonstrating that something belongs to the concept's extension. My response would be that we have good reasons for including the counterfactual supplement. First, we avoid the problematic situation that people belong to, or do not belong to, the category "addicted," depending on more or less trivial environmental changes. Second, the fact that it may not always be easily determined on the basis of naturalistic observation that a person is an (consonant) addict is not an argument against defining the concept counterfactually. This is a practical problem, which only means that we may find it difficult to formulate a definite diagnosis in certain cases.

From a scientific point of view, the important issue is whether or not a counterfactual definition can be *operationalised*. Obviously it can, but it requires that we test the consonant addict, e.g. by manipulating his environment, letting continued consumption have unpleasant consequences. Although this may prove difficult from a practical (or ethical) point of view in certain cases, it is not a problem in principle. The situation is parallel for many somatic disorders; it may be difficult to decide from naturalistic observation if a person is suffering from a certain somatic disease or not. In order to reach a definitive diagnosis, laboratory tests are very often necessary (i.e. manipulation[4]), or one may perhaps have to wait until the disease has developed into some more definitive stage.

Several of the no-struggle cases I have described above are ambivalent about their own consumption, and have strong (but not strong enough) reasons for changing their own behaviour. But they feel enslaved. Others, like the 1950s smokers before they realized the consequences, may feel they have no good reasons for quitting. Therefore, they are not ambivalent. They may or may not feel enslaved, depending on whether or not they have been forced by the circumstances to abstain for a while. All of these cases would be counted as addicted under the counterfactual definition.

In particular, a person who has been drinking regularly and heavily for many years, who has never experienced problems he has attributed to drinking, and who lives in a culture where his drinking goes unnoticed may not know that he would experience large problems if he discontinued his habit. He does not feel enslaved and has no motive for changing his life style. He is still addicted according to the counterfactual definition, provided he would experience great difficulties in a situation that required him to stop or cut back. In this case, Ainslie's argument that this is simply an ordinary appetite might be more to the point. However, I would still argue that there is a difference between this case and an ordinary appetite. I may have a strong appetite for collecting antiques, I may spend a lot of time and money on this, even to such an extent that other people find my preoccupation with antiques rather absurd. However, if I had no problem reducing this activity if the circumstances demanded it, I would have a strong appetite, but no addiction. Addiction is not just a strong appetite — it is a strong appetite that continues to have a very strong impact on the agent's behaviour, even if the circumstances give him (according to his own evaluation) very good reasons for cutting back.

In Figure 1, a schematic classification of different types of addiction (according to the counterfactual definition) is reproduced. Firstly, a person may or may not have experienced that it is in fact difficult for him or her to live without his addictive substance. Those who have not will not actually feel enslaved, although they are (naïve addicts). Secondly, those who feel enslaved due to such experiences may or may not have good subjective reasons for curtailing their habit. Those who have not reckon that life with the drug is better than life without and feel that there are no good reasons for stopping (e.g. the 1950 smoker); they are "happy" addicts, or at least "less unhappy" addicts. Thirdly, those who have strong motives for cutting back are obviously ambivalent, and may or may not have tried and failed at some stage of the consumption career. If they have not, their motivation is clearly

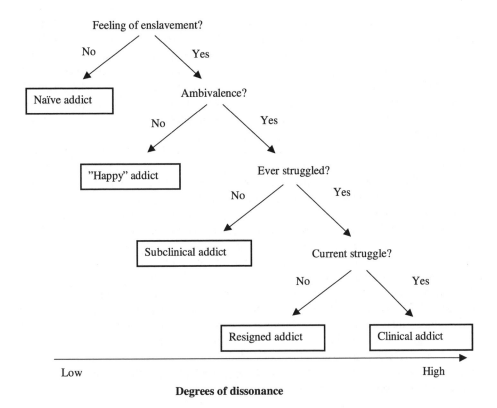

Figure 1: Classification scheme for cases fulfilling the counterfactual definition of addiction.

insufficient, probably because their consumption level is high but not extremely high, and negative consequences are present but not very strong. These cases are probably seldom encountered in treatment units, and might be called sub-clinical addicts. Lastly, those who have struggled in the past may still be struggling, or they may have resigned (at least for the time being). Those who are still struggling are probably those most frequently encountered in treatment units, and could be called clinical addicts.

These five types differ in terms of degree of dissonance. The naïve addict is the true consonant addict, while the "happy" addict probably feels only a light dissonance, if any at all. At the other extreme, the clinical addict is probably experiencing the highest level of dissonance between his values and actions.

Of all these types, only the clinical addicts qualify for Heather's definition. Since he obviously will not deny the reality of the other states described, the discussion boils down to semantics: should "resigned addicts" etc. be called addicts or something else, e.g. varying degrees of neuro-adaption. Generally, one can call things whatever one likes. From the point of view of treatment, the Heather-type of addict is obviously the most important one: they are easily diagnosed, and they are open to treatment. However, from the more general perspective of understanding addictive phenomena, and in particular understanding the processes leading to the clinical state and beyond (the resigned addict), it is useful to have a wider conceptual net. The other types are in the addiction therapist's backyard, and it would be unwise to ignore them. A lot of them may ultimately come into the clinic.[5]

Still, it should be added that in one respect, the Heather-type serves as a benchmark for all the other types. The counterfactual supplement stipulates that all these other types would be transformed into clinical addicts if the circumstances changed so that the agent's motivation for curtailing his or her habit was strong enough.

Some cases might fit the DSM-IV definition without fulfilling the counterfactual definition. For instance, the agent may have developed tolerance, could be spending a great deal of time with drug-related activities, and have given up important social and recreational activities, thus fulfilling criteria 1, 5 and 6. However, if the circumstances should change, he may simply cut back. This person simply has a strong appetite, and there is no enslavement. I would find it more reasonable to call this person a heavy consumer or a problem consumer, and reserve the concept of addiction for more severe cases.

In principle, one could also imagine an agent who would not respond at all to changes that in most other agents would induce a struggle to curtail the habit. He may in effect be willing to tolerate even quite substantial pains. According to the counterfactual definition, this agent is not addicted, although our intuition might strongly suggest that he is even more addicted than most. However, if this type exists at all, he might better be conceived as a truly compulsive consumer, rather than an "ordinary" addict.

Given these conceptual clarifications, we shall now turn to the analysis of the mechanisms governing the addict's choice. Are these choices rational or irrational, and in the latter case, where does rationality break down?

Rational Addiction

The most heroic of the choice theories of addiction has been suggested by Gary Becker (Becker 1992; Becker & Murphy 1988; Becker *et al.* 1992). Becker takes the full step, and suggests that the addict is not only choosing to do what he does, but even that he is fully rational. Becker's addicts are fully informed about the consequences and risks, they take the future into consideration, and are doing what is best for them given their own preferences and the prevailing circumstances. Moreover, these agents are assumed to have consistent preferences, which excludes dynamic inconsistency and implies exponential time discounting.

Addictive drugs are supposed to have the following properties. Firstly, they are attractive, so that the consumer prefers consumption to abstention. Secondly, present consumption has negative consequences for the consumer's future level of well-being. For instance, this could be due to tolerance, which means that the consumer will obtain less pleasure from a given quantity and therefore needs more of the drug in order to obtain the same level of pleasure. However, the implication is wider than this. Becker's assumption implies that all consumption alternatives (including abstention) will give the consumer less pleasure in the future if he chooses to consume now. Consequently, there is a future "punishment" for consumption, whatever the agent chooses to do in the future. Besides tolerance, delayed harmful effects could support this mechanism. However, the agent can to some extent (but not fully) compensate for this unpleasant, delayed effect by continued consumption in the future. This is the third property of addictive drugs, and Becker links this to reinforcement. Other possible mechanisms underlying this property could be relief from withdrawal and, more generally, any suppression of unpleasant side effects (including bad conscience). The rational consumer is supposed to be fully informed about these properties.

According to this theory, the agent ends up in a state of addiction because he discounts future consequences heavily, and is therefore insufficiently motivated by future problems. The theory implies two different types of "rational addicts" (cf. Skog 1999), and two ways into addiction. The first type is very myopic, and will be on a slippery slope where he chooses what is best at the present state, ignoring that the long-term effect is deterioration (even according to his own criteria) of his life quality. If given a new start in life, but with the same preferences and the same lack of interest in the future, he would repeat his consumption career all over again.

The second type is only moderately myopic. If fully informed about his own disposition, the negative future consequences would be sufficient to prevent him from starting a heavy consumption career. However, if he lacks complete information, he would take a calculated risk and could end up in a state of addiction (Orphanides & Zervos 1995). And once he is there, he would prefer to continue as an addict. Once trapped, he has no motive for quitting, since he always does what he thinks best, all things considered. Only environmental changes (e.g. increased costs of continued abuse) could induce a motive for quitting. Under the latter circumstances he would simply quit — there would be no struggle and no relapses.[6] However, if this addict was given a new start, but now with the information he lacked originally, he would *not* end up at the high consumption level.

The main problem with "rational addiction" is that this is *not* an addiction, neither in Heather's sense nor in the counterfactual sense. The rational addict is not suffering from akrasia. There is no ambivalence, no struggle and no repeated relapses, and neither can these phenomena be induced by manipulation of his environment. In short, the so-called "rational addict" is simply a heavy consumer who does what he does because he likes it. The closest one can get to something resembling addiction in this theory is the latter of the two types. This "addict" does not wish to quit (his own utility calculation does not "allow" him to quit) once he has entered the high-consumption mode. But he would not have entered it if he had known what he now knows. However, being rational, he knows that he cannot undo his past, and this being what it is, he thinks it best to continue consuming heavily (cf. Skog 1999). In short, a rational person who wishes to quit will quit — and if he does not quit, this is because he does not want to. At best, the theory of "rational addiction" is a theory of strong appetites that the agent has no real motive to change. It describes what we called above heavy or problem consumers who are not addicted.

In order to explain addiction we need to go beyond the rigid framework of standard rational choice theory. In his Nobel lecture, Becker came close to admitting this. Commenting on his rational addiction theory, he stated that: "My work may have sometimes assumed too much rationality, but I believe it has been an antidote to the extensive research that does not credit people with enough rationality" (Becker 1996: 155–156). Becker's last remark is undoubtedly well-founded. However, we do not have to choose between too much or too little. Nothing could prevent us from constructing theories that are based on realistic assumptions about the deliberations and choices people make. Such theories may not be quite as parsimonious as Becker's theory, but they may come closer to the truth.

It should be added that it is possible to revise the theory of "rational addiction," so as to allow for akrasia. This could either be obtained by allowing an agent's preferences (pro and con motives) to fluctuate over time, and/or by allowing the agent's time discounting to fluctuate over time. Neither of these revisions need violate the assumption of rationality, but they would provoke Becker's aversion to unstable preferences (Becker 1976). I have analysed the latter case in some detail (Skog 1997). This alteration introduces temporary preferences and generates the same strategic battles within the person as Ainslie describe for hyperbolic discounters (see below). The effect of the first amendment would be similar.

Temporary Preferences and Hyperbolic Discounting

The clinical addict's struggle to curtail his habit is characterized by intermittent periods of abstention or moderate consumption, followed by periods of relapse to the old pattern of abuse. Clearly, this state is not one with a fixed balance between the agent's pro and con motives. The balance fluctuates over time, and sometimes abstention motives have the upper hand, while consumption motives are dominant in other periods.

An interpretation of this pattern has been suggested by Ainslie (1975, 1994). He claims that people (and animals) are hard-wired to discount the future hyperbolically, as opposed to the exponential discounting assumed in standard utility theory (including neo-classical economic theory). While exponential discounting implies that people never give in to temptations, hyperbolic discounting implies the opposite. Typically, in the choice between a smaller but sooner reward A and a larger but delayed reward B, the exponential discounter would consistently prefer one or the other, and would not change his mind as the actual time of choice comes closer. A hyperbolic discounter would behave differently (cf. Figure 2, left-hand diagram). Well in advance of the moment of choice (which is t_1), the agent might find it best to wait for the larger, delayed reward B (his valuation curve for B is higher than the one for A). However, shortly before the moment of choice the curves intersect, and during the interval t_0 to t_1 he thinks that A is the best alternative. In effect, he tends to give in to temptation. Hyperbolic discounting therefore predicts temporary preferences.

The same mechanism applies when the agent is choosing between abstention and consumption, where consumption is followed by a delayed, unpleasant side-effect (Figure 2, right-hand diagram). Prior to t_0 the agent thinks that the unpleasant side-effect B is larger than the pleasure of consuming A. However, when the reward A is very close, i.e. during the time interval t_0 to t_1, his valuation is reversed. During this phase he is discounting the future side-effects so much that they do not match up with the instantaneous reward A, and the temptation becomes "irresistible." Hyperbolic discounting does in effect predict relapse.

Hyperbolic discounting is predicted by Herrnstein's matching law (Herrnstein 1961). Experimental evidence, both with animals and humans, confirms that hyperbolic discounting is the normal state of affairs (Mazur 1987). In particular, Vuchinich & Simpson (1998) have demonstrated that, in the case of heavy social drinkers and problem drinkers, a hyperbolic function describes temporal discounting more accurately than an exponential function.

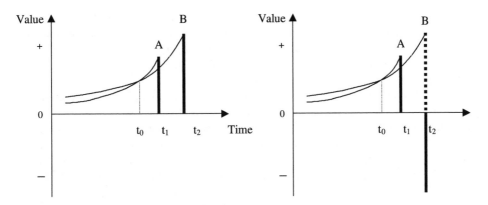

Figure 2: Hyperbolic discounting of future rewards. The curves describe the subjective, discounted values of the rewards at different points in time. *Left*: A is an early, small reward, while B is a delayed, larger reward. The agent must choose between them. *Right*: A is an early reward, followed by a delayed punishment B, which is larger than A.
(The broken bar is a mirror image of B, inserted for the ease of comparison.)

An agent who is struggling to overcome his addiction is in effect engaged in a battle between his own long-term and short-term motives. At a distance, he is firmly determined not to consume the drug again, but when the opportunity is near, he changes his mind. Ainslie (1994) describes four strategies the agent may use in order to overcome temptations. The agent could obtain self-control by setting up a causal mechanism that will prevent him from choosing A at t_0 (self-binding, or the Ulysses strategy).[7] Soft strategies include trying to divert his own attention away from the temptation (attention control), or the preparation of emotions — either negative emotions towards A, or positive emotions towards B.

Lastly, the agent could use a bundling strategy, or personal rules. The agent realizes that he will be faced with many similar choices (e.g. many drinks or cigarettes) in the future, and that he will have no reason to believe that he will be able to resist the temptation in the future if he is unable to resist this time. This changes his mental book-keeping from many single events into one series of identical choices, where the alternatives are "always A" and "always B." Ainslie (1994) demonstrates that this change may be sufficient to motivate the agent to overcome the temptation and to wait for the big, delayed reward.

Whether or not these strategies will work in real life depends, among other things, on the person's willpower — i.e. his ability to be motivated by distant choices of the same kind. The problem with personal rules is that an agent who sees "always abstain" as better than "always indulge," typically will find "indulge now and abstain in the future" the best option. His long-term motivation is therefore constantly threatened by short-term motives, and he is tempted to define the imminent choice as an exception to his personal rule — "I can smoke today — but just today — since this is my birthday," "...since we have friends to dinner," etc. Consequently, personal rules do not offer a once-and-for-all cure for addiction, and relapses are to be expected.

Temporary preferences are at the core of Ainslie's theory of self-control and willpower, and Ainslie attributes temporary preferences to hyperbolic discounting. However, although many cases of temporary preferences may be due to hyperbolic discounting, this may not be the only mechanism. On the contrary, I shall argue that many cases of temporary preferences must be explained by something else.

Ainslie's argument, and the experimental evidence mentioned, makes reference to situations where the time distances are outside the agent's personal control. Not only is the extra delay of the large reward B (compared to the small reward A) outside the agent's control, even the agent's location on the time axis is outside his control. Although certain choices — in particular economic choices — do in fact have the structure outlined in Figure 2, with strict environmental confinements (e.g. a bank or an employer) defining the agent's location on the time axis, this is *not* so in relation to many personal choices. In these cases, it is up to the agent himself to decide if the next event A is now, in ten minutes, in one hour, tomorrow, or whenever. And if he makes the decision now that the next event is in five hours, there is nothing to prevent him from deciding ten minutes later that it is now. Hence, the temporal structure of personal decision problems is often not well defined.

Therefore, in the context of decision problems that are not temporally well defined, if the agent on some occasions feels that is best to abstain, while making the reverse judgement on other occasions, the explanation for the difference cannot be closeness to the time of choice. Other factors must explain the difference. An obvious explanation would be all kinds of fluctuations in the person's motivations. These fluctuations could be due to identifiable environmental stimuli or cues, or they could be related to the agent's physical, cognitive or emotional state. Certain cues — external or internal — may trigger the appetite for drugs, while other cues may trigger the appetite for abstention. Sometimes the first could be dominant, at other times the latter. Furthermore, people's patience or rate of time discounting probably tends to vary over time. In certain periods the agent may be strongly motivated by the future, while in other periods he could be more short-sighted (cf. Skog 1997). Even these variations could depend on both external stimuli and internal state.

When the agent's appetite for drugs is small compared to the motives for abstention, it is easy to decide — and to hold on to this decision — that the next event is remote. When the appetite is strong, the agent may be strongly motivated to decide that the next event is imminent. Consequently, under these circumstances, it is the appetite that determines the time distance, and not vice versa.

Fluctuations caused by internal or external cues, either in the pro or con appetites, or in the rate of time discounting, would give rise to temporary preferences. And when the agent has experienced his own preference reversals a sufficiently large number of times, he will end up in the same strategic battles as Ainslie describes. The only difference is that the temporary preferences are caused by fluctuations in preferences, rather than hyperbolic discounting.

The fact that many personal choices lack a well-defined temporal structure does *not* in effect imply that Ainslie's theory of self-control and personal rules is invalidated. The essential starting point for this part of Ainslie's theory is temporary preferences, and it does not matter very much for the theory if these are products of hyperbolic discounting or something else.

Melioration and Relative Addiction

As opposed to the theory of rational addiction, melioration theory (Herrnstein & Prelec 1992) and the special case of melioration called relative addiction theory (Rachlin 2000) are concerned with persons who are less than fully rational. These theories describe agents who are not motivated by the long-term future consequences of their present actions. They ignore the fact that their current choices have consequences for their own future well-being.

As is also the case in Becker's theory, these theories explicitly assume that consumption of addictive drugs both reduces the future value of consumption and the future value of alternatives to consumption. As opposed to Becker's theory, however, each consumption choice is guided only by the present in melioration theory. In the case of addictive drugs the agent obtains more pleasure from the drug than from alternatives to drugs. Consequently, even these theories describe the addiction process as a slippery slope or "primrose path" where each consumption act is preferred, and where the agent fails to realize that the sum of these acts brings about a lowering of future welfare. Hence, addiction is seen as the result of a series of myopic choices.

While Becker's theory describes a perfect maximizer who happens to attribute low value to the future, melioration theories describe agents who use heuristic rules and approximations when they deliberate. These heuristics work well enough in most real-life situations, but not in relation to certain consumption goods, such as addictive substances. This is due to the addictive substances' peculiar combination of good short-term and bad long-term effects.

These theories do in effect explain the catastrophic outcome as a result of a heuristic that fails under special circumstances, i.e. a cold mechanism. However, there are warm mechanisms to consider as well, and these may be of no less importance. In particular, the failure to acknowledge the negative long-term effects could be due to another type of akrasia, namely motivated belief formation (Elster 1999a). The good reasons for abstaining or restraining current consumption (namely present or future problems) can be clouded or even completely distorted by wishful thinking ("it happens to others, but not to me," "it isn't all that dangerous," "the problems I face have nothing to do with my consumption of drugs," etc.). Moreover, the positive effects of consumption may be systematically overestimated. The agent is in effect unable to hold on to rational, well-grounded beliefs about his own situation, being dragged into irrational beliefs by his own strong appetite. For instance, it is well documented that gamblers are frequently the victims of irrational beliefs (Waagenaar 1988).

When the agent ultimately realizes that the deterioration of his life is due to his abuse, he may try to curtail his consumption. According to Rachlin (2000), this might be possible on the condition that the addict succeeds in extending his time horizon. The mechanism Rachlin has in mind has some similarity to Ainslie's personal rules, although the formalism and the underlying assumptions are different.

The basic idea is this. If the agent continues consumption, his well-being will continue to be at a low level, or it may deteriorate even further. If he stops consuming, his life will become even worse for a while, but will then gradually improve. If the agent sees this he will realize that, overall, he is better off abstaining than consuming. Hence, switching from myopic evaluation of singular events to long-term evaluation of behavioural patterns can bring about a change in behaviour. Whether or not the agent will actually stop consuming is dependent on the length of his time horizon, i.e. the motivational power of future improvements.

In consequence, Rachlin brings in discounting of the future through the back-door. The length of the time-horizon plays the same role in this theory as the bundling horizon (i.e. the number of future choices the agent is motivated by) in Ainslie's theory. However, the underlying mechanisms are different in the two theories. In Ainslie's theory, the agent sees his current choice as a precedent for future choices. Exactly how the switch from singular events to patterns takes place in Rachlin's theory is less clear, but the assumption appears to be that the agent sees a pattern and is motivated by this pattern thereafter. This leaves later relapse unexplained, since Rachlin does not outline any mechanisms explaining how the horizon can be shortened again.

Herrnstein & Prelec's melioration theory compares the utility of consumption with the alternatives to consumption, whatever they may be. Rachlin (2000) explicitly assumes that the alternative is socializing, and his theory is in effect a special case of Herrnstein & Prelec's. Rachlin hypothesizes that drug consumption and socializing are substitutable and competing alternatives, and consequently that more of one automatically means less of the other, and vice versa.

The claim that excessive consumption of addictive drugs may lead to deterioration of social ties is undoubtedly a reasonable one. However, Rachlin's claim goes much beyond this. In order to construct a primrose path he has to assume: (1) that the consumer locally prefers drug consumption to socializing; (2) that increased consumption implies less socializing (and vice versa); and (3) that increased consumption reduces both the value of drugs and socializing (and vice versa). The evidence for all these claims is not convincing.

For instance, one could easily imagine that socially isolated individuals visit public drinking places *because* they offer an opportunity for socializing. In that case, drinking comes with social contact, and the two activities would be positively correlated rather than mutually exclusive alternatives (i.e. negatively correlated). Second, some individuals develop an alcohol problem because they are well integrated into a wet culture or sub-culture, rather than because they are isolated. Then, drinking is not a substitute for social contact, it is a product of social contact. For instance, it is well known that the prevalence of heavy drinking is much higher in high consumption cultures than in low consumption cultures (Skog 1985). The standard explanation for this is a social interaction mechanism, implying that the risk for developing a drinking problem is higher when a person is integrated into a wet culture (Skog 1985). Third, a lot of socially isolated individuals drink less than the average, and the empirical relationship between social isolation and drinking is u-shaped (Leifman *et al.* 1993; Skog 1980). Hence, in a lot of cases, social isolation seems to produce less drinking, rather than more drinking. Fourth, there is no evidence to support the idea that reduced consumption by itself will lead to more socializing, as the theory predicts. If this were true, the way out of addiction would be much easier. The very fact that many addict's loneliness does *not* decrease significantly during abstention is probably the reason why lonely addicts relapse so quickly (Skog 1990; Vuchinich & Tucker 1996). While drugs may be a kind of substitute for social contact in certain cases, the reverse need not be true.[8]

In conclusion, the relationship between drug consumption and social contact is complex and multi-faceted. It cannot be made to fit the strict rules required in order to produce a primrose path. Therefore, Rachlin's attempt to specify the alternative to consumption of addictive drugs is too narrow. The facts that social isolation may sometimes be an important causal factor for drug abuse, and that isolation may be an important by-product of abuse, as well as an important obstacle to recovery, is no proof for this part of Rachlin's theory.

Summary and Conclusion

Although the theories under consideration are quite different in several respects, they have one thing in common: They all put time discounting into focus, and conceive the addict as a person who is living in the present, being insufficiently motivated by the future.

Melioration theory explains entry into addiction as a primrose path, where the agent is seeking immediate pleasure, not being sufficiently motivated by the gradual deterioration that follows from heavy drug consumption. The entry mechanism is the same in Becker's theory, although this is mainly a theory of heavy consumption, rather than addiction proper. The basic idea is plausible, and has been confirmed in a few empirical studies. Vuchinich & Simpson (1998) verified that problem drinkers and heavy social drinkers discount the future more heavily than light drinkers, and Bretteville-Jensen (1999) has demonstrated that active injectors of heroin and amphetamine have a higher discount rate than those who have never used these substances.

Melioration theory explains recovery as a result of "restructuring," where the agent "sees" a larger pattern and thus becomes more motivated by the future. The agent "realizes" that abstention will lead to future improvements that offset a temporary setback, say, due to withdrawal. The underlying mechanism could be insight, although Rachlin fails to give a plausible account of how the agent suddenly becomes more motivated by the future. Furthermore, the theory in its present form does not offer a convincing explanation of relapse. According to the theory's logic, this could be due to a shortening of the time horizon, but no causal mechanism to this effect has been proposed.

Ainslie's general theory of motivation is more concerned with processes underlying relapse and the struggle to get out of addiction, and less with entry into addiction. Time discounting plays a double role in Ainslie's theory. Firstly, the motivational power of future consequences is governed by hard-wired hyperbolic discounting, which results in temporary preferences. Secondly, temporary preferences generate regrets, which gives rise to a cognitive overlay of personal rules in relation to bundles of similar choices in the future. The longer into the future the agent sees, the stronger the motivation for resisting temptations. Success depends on the agent's ability to see the imminent choice as a precedent for future choices. I have argued that, since many personal decision problems are not temporally well defined, the first mechanism may not always be relevant, but this need not invalidate the second mechanism.

Time discounting is not the whole story, however. A full-fledged action theory of addiction also needs to address other mechanisms and other issues. Firstly, information processing and belief formation obviously play an important role in human agency in general, and in relation to addictive behaviours in particular. Secondly, the agent's preferences and priorities are not fixed entities, but change in response to internal states and external stimuli. Thirdly, the role of external stimuli also extends to the socio-cultural embeddedness of individual choice.

Concerning the first issue, it seems clear that even individuals who are not discounting the future heavily may run a substantial risk if they seriously and systematically underestimate their own personal risk. This bias may be due to another flaw in people's characters, namely wishful thinking, and the closely-related phenomenon of denial. It is well known that beliefs and expectations strongly influence how people experience the immediate effect of drugs (Goldman *et al.* 1987; MacAndrew & Edgerton 1969). However, the way people's beliefs about long-term effects of addictive drugs are formed is less well known. Studies of gambling suggest that different types of irrational belief-formation may play an important role (cf. Elster 1999b; Waagenaar 1988).

Regarding the second issue, I have argued that temporary preferences could result from all kinds of fluctuations in the agent's pro and con motives, as well as in his rate of time discounting (Skog 1997). Hyperbolic discounting is probably not the most important mechanism. Any kind of fluctuation could be fed into Ainslie's theory of willpower. Moreover, fluctuations could also help the primrose path theory to explain relapse. A sudden growth in appetite could undermine recovery, and so could a sudden strike of myopia. From an empirical point of view, we need to study instabilities in people's preferences more systematically. We need to know more about how large and how frequent these fluctuations are and what triggers them.

At the more general level, environmental factors shape people's preferences and beliefs, and they represent constraints on people's choices. Environmental factors thus determine who (and how many) will develop an addiction. For instance, in relation to alcohol, it is well documented that the availability of the substance has an impact on aggregate consumption, as well as on the prevalence of heavy consumption and problem rates (Edwards *et al.* 1994). Secondly, drug taking behaviour is typically conformist behaviour: The likelihood that any given individual will engage in this sort of behaviour and the extent to which he is doing so very much depends on what other individuals are doing.[9] Hence, a theory of addiction should not restrict itself to the agent's level of socializing, as Rachlin's theory does; it also need to take into consideration who the agent is socializing with, and in particular the drug-taking habits of these individuals. Just as loneliness under certain circumstances may foster addiction, so may strong integration into a heavy consuming sub-culture.

Notes

1. This is not a reductionistic thesis, since I do not claim that we could replace all mentalistic concepts, such as values, preferences, feelings, motivations and intentions, with a purely physicalistic terminology.

2. Edwards *et al.* (1982) prefer the term neuro-adaption instead of physical dependence.

3. A realistic version of simultaneous inconsistency could be the following. The agent has good and "noble" reasons for abstaining, but stronger and less "noble" (in his own hierarchy) reasons for indulging. He may feel that indulgence is morally wrong, say by inflicting harm on significant others, and he may wish that he did not have the appetite (a secondary preference for abstention), but still he gives in to his "lower," selfish motives.

4. Certain allergies offer an example: the clinician needs to provoke the patient's body in order to reach a definitive diagnosis. In a similar manner the clinical alcoholism therapist may have to provoke the client's appetite for alcohol and his motives for abstention in order to determine the true nature of his condition.

5. I cannot resist the temptation of adding that Heather's definition also makes life too easy for the therapist. If the therapist cannot help the patient to curtail his habit, he can simply advise him to stop trying. If the patient follows this advice, he would no longer be addicted.

6. Only additional environmental changes, unforeseen by the agent, could bring him back into a heavy consumption state.

7. The agent may sometimes obtain the same effect simply by promising himself that he will invest in such mechanisms if he should give in to short-term temptations in the future (cf. Skog 1997).

8. This u-shaped relationship does in fact follow from the social interaction mechanism (Skog 1980), and is explained by informal social control. The weakly integrated are less controlled by their peers, and will therefore tend to spread out along the consumption scale to a larger extent (i.e. larger variance) than the strongly integrated. Hence, the weakly integrated will dominate at both ends of the distribution, while the strongly integrated will dominate at intermediate consumption levels.

9. See Skog (1980) for a review of the literature regarding alcohol consumption.

References

Ainslie, G. (1975). Specious rewards. A behavioral theory of impulsiveness and impulse control. *Psychological Bulletin, 82*, 463–496.

Ainslie, G. (1994). *Picoeconomics*. Cambridge, Cambridge University Press.

Ainslie, G. (1999). The dangers of willpower. In: J. Elster, & O.-J. Skog (Eds), *Getting hooked: Rationality and addiction* (pp. 65–92). Cambridge University Press.

Ainslie, G. (2001). *Breakdown of will*. Cambridge, Cambridge University Press.

Becker, G. (1976). *The economic approach to human behavior*. Chicago, University of Chicago Press.

Becker, G. S. (1992). Habits, addictions, and traditions. *Kyklos, 45*, 327–346.

Becker, G. (1996). *Accounting for tastes*. Cambridge, MA: Harvard University Press.

Becker, G. S., Grossman, M., & Murphy, K. M. (1992). Rational addiction and the effect of price on consumption. In: G. Loewenstein, & J. Elster (Eds), *Choice over time* (pp. 361–370). NY: Russell Sage Foundation.

Becker, G. S., & Murphy, K. M. (1988). A theory of rational addiction. *Journal of Political Economy, 96*, 675–700.

Bretteville-Jensen, A. L. (1999). Addiction and discounting. *Journal of Health Economics, 18*, 393–407.

Diagnostic and Statistical Manual of Mental Disorders (4th ed.). (1994). Washington, DC: American Psychiatric Association.

Edwards, G. (1982). *The treatment of drinking problems*. NY: McGraw-Hill.

Edwards, G., Anderson, P., Babor, T., Casswell, S., Ferrence, R., Giesbrecht, N., Godfrey, C., Holder, H., Lemmens, P., Mäkelä, K., Midanik, L., Norström, T., Österberg, E., Romelsjö, A., Room, R., Simpura, J., & Skog, O.-J. (1994). *Alcohol policy and the public good*. Oxford University Press.

Edwards, G., Arif, A., & Hodgson, R. (1982). Nomenclature and classification of drug- and alcohol-related problems: A shortened version of a WHO Memorandum. *British Journal of Addiction, 77*, 3–20.

Elster, J. (1984). *Ulysses and the sirens* (Rev. ed.). Cambridge: Cambridge University Press.

Elster, J. (1999a). *Strong feelings*. Cambridge, MA: Harvard University Press.

Elster, J. (1999b). Gambling and addiction. In: J. Elster, & O.-J. Skog (Eds), *Getting hooked: Rationality and addiction* (pp. 208–234). Cambridge: Cambridge University Press.

Gardner, E. L., & David, J. (1999). The neurobiology of chemical addiction. In: J. Elster, & O.-J. Skog (Eds), *Getting hooked: Rationality and addiction* (pp. 93–136). Cambridge University Press.

Goldman, M. S., Brown, S. A., & Chritiansen, B. A. (1987). Expectancy theory: Thinking about drinking. In: H. T. Blane, & K. E. Leonard (Eds), *Psychological theories of drinking and alcoholism*. NY: Guilford.

Goodwin, D. W. (1991). The etiology of alcoholism. In: D. J. Pittman, & H. R. White (Eds), *Society, culture, and drinking patterns re-examined* (pp. 598–608). New Brunswick, NJ: Rutgers Center of Alcohol Studies.

Heather, N. (1998). A conceptual framework for explaining drug addiction. *Journal of Psychopharmacology, 12*, 3–7.

Heather, N., & Robertson, I. (1981). *Controlled drinking*. London: Methuen.

Herrnstein, R. J. (1961). Relative and absolute strengths of response as a function of frequency of reinforcement. *Journal of Experimental Analysis of Behavior, 4*, 267–272.

Herrnstein, R. J., & Prelec, D. (1992). A theory of addiction. In: G. Loewenstein, & J. Elster (Eds), *Choice over time* (pp. 331–360). NY: Russell Sage Foundation.

Keller, M. (1972). On the loss-of-control phenomenon in alcoholism. *British Journal of Addiction, 67*, 153–166.

Leifman, H., Kühlhorn, E., Allebeck, P., Andreasson, S., & Romelsjö, A. (1993). Antecedents and covariates to a sober lifestyle and its consequences. *Social Science and Medicine, 41*, 113–121.

MacAndrew & Edgerton (1969). *Drunken comportment*. Chicago: Aldine Publishing Company.

Marlatt, G. A., Demming, B., & Reid, J. B. (1973). Loss of control drinking in alcoholics: An experimental analogue. *Journal of Abnormal Psychology, 81*, 233–241.

Mazur, J. E. (1987). An adjusting procedure for studying delayed reinforcement. In: M. L. Commons, J. E. Mazur, J. A. Nevin, & H. Rachlin (Eds), *Quantitative analysis of behavior V: The effect of delay and of intervening events on reinforcement value* (pp. 55–73). Hillsdale, NJ: Erlbaum.

Mello, N. K., & og Mendelson, J. H. (1965). Operant analysis of drinking patterns of chronic alcoholics. *Nature, 206*, 43–46.

Mello, N. K., & og Mendelson, J. H. (1966). Experimental analysis of drinking behavior of chronic alcoholics. *Annals of New York Academy of Sciences, 133*, 828–845.

Mello, N. K., & og Mendelson, J. H. (1972). Drinking pattern during work contingent and non-contingent alcohol acquisition. *Psychosomatic Medicine, 34*, 139–164.

Orford, J. (1985). *Excessive appetites: A psychological view of addiction*. Chichester: Wiley.

Orphanides, A., & Zervos, D. (1995). Rational addiction with learning and regret. *Journal of Political Economy, 103*, 739–758.

Pattison, E. M., Sobell, M. B., & Sobell, L. C. (1977). *Emerging concepts of alcohol dependence*. New York: Springer.

Rachlin, H. (2000). *The science of self-control*. Cambridge, MA: Harvard University Press.

Skog, O. J. (1980). Social interaction and the distribution of alcohol consumption. *Journal of Drug Issues, 10*, 71–92.

Skog, O. J. (1985). The collectivity of drinking cultures. A theory of the distribution of alcohol consumption. *British Journal of Addiction, 80*, 83–99.

Skog, O.-J. (1990). Alcohol in a social network perspective: Implications for epidemiology. *Alcologia, 2*, 13–21.

Skog, O.-J. (1997). The strength of weak will. *Rationality and Society, 9*, 245–271.

Skog, O.-J. (1999). Rationality, irrationality, and addiction — Notes on Becker & Murphy's theory of addiction. In: J. Elster, & O.-J. Skog (Eds), *Getting hooked: Rationality and addiction* (pp. 173–207). Cambridge: Cambridge University Press.

Skog, O.-J. (2000). Addict's choice. *Addiction, 95*, 1309–1314.

Vuchinich, R. E., & Simpson, C. A. (1998). Hyperbolic temporal discounting in social drinkers and problem drinkers. *Experimental and Clinical Psychopharmacology, 6*, 292–305.

Vuchinich, R. E., & Tucker, J. (1996). Alcohol relapse, life events and behavioral theories of choice: A prospective analysis. *Experimental and Clinical Psychopharmacology, 4*, 19–28.

Waagenaar, W. A. (1988). *Paradoxes of gambling behavior*. London: Lawrence Erlbaum.

Watson, G. (1999). Disordered appetites: Addiction, compulsion, and dependence. In: J. Elster (Ed.), *Addiction: Entries and exits* (pp. 3–28). Russell Sage Foundation.

Whitman, W. ([1842] 1929). *Franklin Evans or the inebriate*. NY: Random House.

Comments on Skog

Nick Heather

I am very pleased to have this opportunity to comment on Ole-Jørgen Skog's paper because it was Ole-Jørgen who first introduced me to the ideas under consideration here at a conference in Rotterdam in 1992. He told me about the writings of George Ainslie, Jon Elster, Donald Davidson and some others and I began to follow up these leads. As a clinical psychologist by training, most of my career had been devoted to research on the outcome of treatment for alcohol problems and other substance use disorders but I had always retained a theoretical interest in my subject. More particularly, I had always been convinced that, to arrive at a satisfactory explanation of addiction, it would be necessary to go to the heart of the problem by studying such things as failure of self-control, temptation and "weakness of will." Imagine my excitement, then, to discover the existence of a large and vibrant body of work that was devoted to these very concepts. So I will always be grateful to Ole-Jørgen for showing me this path.

Defining Addiction

Skog devotes the first part of his paper mainly to a critique of a definition of drug addiction I offered in an article a few years ago as "a demonstrated failure to have refrained from (substance use) despite having attempted to do so" (Heather 1998: 4). I shall confine my comments here to this portion of his paper.

Note immediately that this is not merely a pedantic disagreement since it has led to an interesting typology of "addiction" shown in Skog's Figure 1. It is true, though, that a response to his critique could easily descend into semantics and I shall therefore try to identify differences between us with empirical consequences. Skog also states that the definition was made for purely methodological purposes; this is partly true but I maintain that it mostly serves a heuristic purpose, as I hope to demonstrate.

The etymology of addiction derives from the slave markets of ancient Rome where it was used to describe the fate of a slave who had been purchased and "addicted" to (i.e. "made over to" or "bound to") a new owner. In later times, it became used to refer to something that one was obligated to do, such as repaying a bank loan or doing conscripted military service (Vuchinich 1999). These etymological and historical examples do not in themselves prove that my definition is useful but they do show that the concept of addiction has always denoted a form of enslavement or, at least, a restriction of freedom to act. This is what I take to be the essence of addictive behaviour and experience and a starting point for any attempt to explain what we know as addiction.

But there is no need to press this point here since Skog accepts, in his counterfactual definition, that the presence of some form of enslavement is necessary for a meaningful definition of addiction, his only point of departure being that the evidence for this enslavement can be potential as well as actual; it should embrace not only those who have demonstrated a failure to refrain despite having tried but also those who would have demonstrated such a failure under different environmental conditions. In considering the merits of this proposal it will be convenient to focus on Skog's typology of addiction in his Figure 1.

The "naive addict," exemplified by the 1950s smoker who is blissfully unaware of the health risks of her habit, causes no difficulty for my definition. Skog tells us that these persons "will not feel enslaved, although they are" (p. 162). What are we to make of this? What other basis could there be for attributing a feeling of enslavement to someone, and ruling out the possibility that they are acting entirely willingly, except a statement from the person to that effect? And what other reason could a person have for describing herself as enslaved except that she had tried to break free (i.e. cease or curtail the behaviour) and had not been able to?

As for the claim that the naive addict would be unable to break free if circumstances changed, the question remains, and has not been satisfactorily answered by Skog, how could we ever be sure about this at the time. If our smoker, having later become aware than smoking was endangering her health, tried to quit and failed, then Skog would take this as evidence that she had previously been addicted. But if she were able to quit without difficulty, then he must say that she cannot previously have been addicted. The circularity of this position is obvious.

All we know, or can reasonably assume, about the condition of the "naive addict" is that it involves a state of neuro-adaptation to the drug in question. My argument is precisely that neuro-adaptation is not a sufficient condition for failure to refrain from drug use to occur (see Heather 1998). This is shown by reports of hospital patients who have received large quantities of opioid drugs as analgesics but have no difficulty in refraining from use following discharge from hospital (Lindesmith 1968; Zinberg 1984). It is also shown, even more certainly, by the familiar occurrence of a longstanding heavy smoker or drinker quitting heavy use, with little apparent difficulty, on the first occasion of trying. For these reasons and others, as Edwards, Arif & Hodgson (1982) convincingly argued, addiction should be seen in behavioural and not in neurophysiological terms.[1] I submit that Skog, in common with many others in the addictions field, continues to confuse the concepts of neuroadaptation and addictive behaviour.

Skog attempts to avoid the inherent circularity of his argument by imagining ways in which the counterfactual definition could be operationalised — by, for example, a laboratory test carried out before the person had attempted to change the behaviour. The most obvious example of what Skog has in mind would be provided by the cue reactivity paradigm (Drummond *et al.* 1995), in which drug users are presented with stimuli frequently associated in the past with drug consumption while physiological reactivity and subjective reports of craving are measured. Procedures of this kind have some power to predict outcome of treatment and therefore of the ability to desist from drug-taking (Drobes *et al.* 2001). However, what is thought to be measured here is the strength of a learned association between specific stimuli and drug reinforcement, which itself depends on learning history and the underlying level of neuro-adaptation to the substance. We know, again, that a high level of desire for a drug is not a sufficient condition for addiction, in the sense that I wish to define it, to occur (Heather 1998). It is unlikely in principle that we could ever find a test that would reliably predict how difficult a "naive addict" would find it to change behaviour when he eventually got round to trying.[2]

Incidentally, as should by now be clear, I completely agree with Skog that a strong appetite for a substance or activity is not a sufficient ground for calling something an addiction.[3] Indeed, his example of the devoted antique collector who would find no difficulty in cutting back his interest if circumstances changed is exactly the kind of case I would cite to support my own argument. I note however that, earlier in his paper, Skog points to an excessive appetite as the defining trait of a disease of addiction. Leaving aside the possibility of any inconsistency in these views, the key question here is, who is to say what is excessive. Other people, or society in general, may judge an appetite to be excessive that the agent regards merely as a strong but legitimate preference. If it is the agent who judges an appetite to be excessive, this must surely mean that the appetite is regarded as unwanted; if it is unwanted, there must by definition be a problem of self-control.

This leads on to consideration of Skog's next category, the "happy addict" — who, it turns out, is not all that happy! This person is said to acknowledge a feeling of enslavement to his habit but is not ambivalent about it and has never tried to change it. One problem here is that it is difficult to imagine how one could feel enslaved by a habit but not ambivalent about it — unless, of course, one wholeheartedly enjoyed the feeling of being enslaved. Whether or not this is possible is, I suppose, a moot point. In any event, the same arguments as applied to the "naive addict" also apply here; if someone has never tried to change their behaviour, how can we be sure that they are not merely indulging a strong preference that it would be invidious to label as an addiction?

Perhaps the greatest difficulty for my definition is presented by Skog's "subclinical addict." This is someone who has a sense of enslavement and is ambivalent about the behaviour but who has never struggled to change it. The key feature of this person, for present purposes, is that: "... he is suffering from akrasia or weakness of will, not in the sense of dynamic inconsistency but of simultaneous inconsistency. He has the desire to quit but not the willpower needed to quit (i.e. his motivation is insufficient)" (p. 161). This, says Skog, is no less puzzling than the dynamic inconsistencies produced by hyperbolic discounting and shows that consonant addiction is not just "an ordinary taste."

This appears a strong argument since it seems, at first sight, perverse to refuse to call this person addicted. However, there may be an empirical issue here: do so-called consonant addicts experience the simultaneous inconsistency of which Skog speaks? An alternative view might be that these people experience a sense of regret and guilt after each ingestion yet nevertheless continue to consume. They can therefore be seen as showing dynamic inconsistency without this guilt leading to a firm avowal or pledge to change behaviour and without the inconsistency ever leading to a sustained effort to change the behaviour. When they do indulge the habit, the moment of indulgence is not characterized by a sense of conflict but by an albeit reluctant commitment to taking X, a feeling something like, "to hell with it, despite knowing that it isn't good for me in the long run, I am going to X again." An investigation of this issue might, admittedly, become rather scholastic. However, I note that Skog himself describes his consonant addicts as "willing" consumers of X, presumably at the point of ingestion. And in a footnote he suggests they may be characterized as giving in to "lower," selfish motives for indulging in X. Both characterizations suggest temporal rather than simultaneous inconsistency.

But whether or not the inconsistency is temporal or simultaneous, this case still causes problems for my definition because there has been no observable failure to refrain. If I wish to include this case in my definition, as I think I must, it means that the definition should be expanded to cover instances where someone complains that their behaviour is to some extent out of their control. This impairment to self-control is implied by introspective reports of guilt or regret after ingestion but could be operationally defined (or even quantified — see Heather *et al.* 1993) by verbal behaviour relating specifically to self-control. So the definition becomes: "(addiction is shown by) a demonstrated failure to have refrained from a behaviour despite having attempted to do so or a complaint by the person that the behaviour is out of his or her control." Of course, the two parts of the definition could amount to pretty much the same thing, the only difference being the duration and strength of a commitment to change. In other words, a feeling of guilt or regret implies at least a desire to change without this desire resulting in an attempt to do so that is sustained noticeably longer than the habitual periodicity of the behaviour. Conversely, a demonstrated failure to have refrained despite trying is equivalent to a palpable failure of self-control.

What of the "resigned addict"? An example of this is the man described by Skog who has made one serious attempt to quit consuming drug X, failed dramatically and never wholeheartedly tried again. This is because "he is less unhappy when he continues rather than discontinues his consumption" (p. 161). A similar case is the man who has struggled for a long time to quit but, having lost his family, considers his life in ruins and cannot find the motivation to try again.[4] I could defend my definition by recalling that it uses the past tense; both examples have tried to quit in the past and have failed, so both might be termed addicts under the definition.

The proper response to these examples, however, is to say that I am less concerned to classify persons as "addicts" or "not addicts" than to classify behaviour as showing or not showing addiction. This kind of distinction may be difficult to maintain consistently but it is always useful to remind ourselves that what we should be trying to account for is a class of behaviour that applies across a wide range of substances and activities, rather than a class of persons whose past or present inability to control their substance use may be the only thing they have in common. Thus, I am obliged to say that the examples Skog gives describe individuals who have shown addictive behaviour in the past but who no longer do so, albeit because they have given up trying to change the behaviour in question. The same logic applies to people who are no longer trying to change their behaviour because they have already succeeded in changing it — for example, to former heavy drinkers who have eventually become long-term total abstainers. The views of Alcoholics Anonymous notwithstanding, it makes little sense to call such persons "addicted" even though, if they did ever return to drinking, they would show evidence of a rapid reinstatement of tolerance and withdrawal (Edwards & Gross 1976) and once more experience difficulty in refraining from heavy use.

All this does, though, necessitate a further modification to my definition, this time to clarify the period of time to which it refers. Thus, the definition should be: "(addiction is shown by) a demonstrated failure to refrain from a behaviour despite attempts to do so or a complaint by the person that the behaviour is out of his or her control."

This leaves only the "clinical addict." According to Skog, this person has feelings of enslavement and ambivalence, and has struggled in the past to change behaviour and continues to do so. This type clearly fits my definition, with the rider that I would also now include what Skog calls the "subclinical addict." The crucial disagreement with Skog, though, is that I wish to restrict the term addiction to individuals falling into this category or, rather, I wish to confine the term addictive behaviour to descriptions of the behaviour of individuals fitting the definition. As suggested earlier, I do this mainly on heuristic grounds — that it directs the attention of those of us wishing to make sense of what is commonly called addiction to its most essential characteristic, the feature of addiction that has puzzled us down the centuries, and that represents the only reason why a special term like addiction has evolved and continues to be necessary.

As to what I would call the other types Skog delineates, the term "excessive user" suffices to cover them all. In this use, "excessive" would be defined by some objective criteria, such as levels or patterns of alcohol consumption shown by epidemiological evidence to be associated with harmful consequences or increased risk of such consequences. Alternatively, one could follow Edwards *et al.* (1982) and speak of "hazardous" or "harmful" use of a substance or practice of an activity. However, at the risk of repetition, unless there is an ongoing struggle to escape enslavement to a behaviour, I suggest that, for scientific purposes, the attribution of addiction is withheld.

Notes

1. Edwards *et al.* were concerned to define dependence, not addiction, but, like Skog, for the purposes of this argument I regard these terms as synonymous.
2. I accept that it would be permissible to say, on the basis of laboratory tests or any other relevant information, that someone would probably be addicted if they ever tried to cut down or quit.
3. A similar view is expressed by Orford (2001: 260) in his book, Excessive Appetites.
4. Apart from the number of quit attempts, these two cases are identical for our purposes. They are also similar to the person Skog cannot resist imagining whom the therapist has advised to stop trying to curtail his habit.

References

Drobes, D. J., Saladin, M. E., & Tiffany, S. T. (2001). Classical conditioning mechanisms in alcohol dependence. In: N. Heather, T. J. Peters, & T. Stockwell (Eds), *International handbook of alcohol dependence and problems* (pp. 281–288). Chichester, UK: Wiley.

Drummond, D. C., Tiffany, S. T., Glautier, S., & Remington, B. (1995). *Addictive behavior: Cue exposure theory and practice.* Chichester, UK: Wiley.

Edwards, G., Arif, A., & Hodgson, R. (1982). Nomenclature and classification of drug- and alcohol-related problems: A shortened version of a WHO Memorandum. *British Journal of Addiction, 77,* 3–20.

Edwards, G., & Gross, M. M. (1976). Alcohol dependence: Provisional description of a clinical syndrome. *British Medical Journal, 281,* 1058–1061.

Heather, N. (1998). A conceptual framework for explaining drug addiction. *Journal of Psychopharmacology, 12,* 3–7.

Heather, N., Tebbutt, J. S., Mattick, R. P., & Zamir, R. (1993). Development of a scale for measuring impaired control over alcohol consumption: A preliminary report. *Journal of Studies on Alcohol, 54*, 700–709.

Lindesmith, A. R. (1968). *Addiction and opiates*. Chicago: Aldine.

Orford, J. (2001). *Excessive appetites* (2nd ed.). Chichester, UK: Wiley.

Vuchinich, R. E. (1999). Behavioral economics as a framework for organizing the expanded range of substance abuse interventions. In: J. A. Tucker, D. M. Donovan, & G. A. Marlatt (Eds), *Changing addictive behavior: Bridging clinical and public health strategies* (pp. 191–218). New York: Guilford Press.

Zinberg, N. E. (1984). *Drug, set and setting: The basis for controlled intoxicant use*. New Haven, CT: Yale University Press.

Reply to Heather

Ole-Jørgen Skog

There is an important conceptual distinction between states and events. Getting married is an event, bringing about the state of being married. States are sometimes important when we wish to explain events: a car crashed (an event) because the driver was intoxicated (a state).

Addiction can be conceptualised both as a state and as events. The disagreement between Nick Heather and myself seems to be that while Heather wishes to define addictive events, I try to define addictive states, as well as events. As Heather puts it, he is "less concerned to classify persons as 'addicts' or 'not addicts' than to classify behaviour as showing or not showing addiction" (p. 179). Behaviour is an event. To say that a person is in the state of being addicted is to classify this person as an addict.

The naïve and "happy" addicts in my typology do not display addictive behaviour (ambivalence and struggle). For this reason, they are not classified as addicts in Heather's scheme. However, they are in an addictive *state* according to my definition, and would therefore be expected to display addictive behaviour, if provoked by environmental change.

I am surprised to see that Heather insists that my position is circular. Consider again the 1950 smoker. When he became aware of the fact that he was endangering his health, he attempted to quit. If he failed, I would say that he was in fact addicted, even before the attempt. If he were able to quit without difficulty, I would say that he was probably not in an addictive state prior to the attempt. There is no circularity here. To take a parallel example: A person is allergic to a chemical X if he displays allergic reactions when exposed to X. However, if a person has never been exposed to X, we would not know that he is allergic or not to this chemical. The best way to find out is to expose him to X. If an allergic reaction was observed, we would conclude that he was in the state of "being allergic to X" even before we made the test. It seems to me that Heather's misguided claim derives from his preoccupation with events, and lack of interest in states. One can be allergic (a state) without ever displaying allergic symptoms (events).

The same epistemological problem pops up in yet another guise. For instance, a person can be in the state of being enslaved without knowing it, i.e. without feeling the symptoms of enslavement. The naïve addict is an example. For instance, in Paris during World War II, some heavy drinkers without serious complications may suddenly have realized that they were actually enslaved when rationing forced them to reduce their intake to only one litre of wine per week (or less than 20 g ethanol per day). Or consider the naïve 1950 smoker who has never been without tobacco. If, while being at a deserted place, far from other people, he suddenly realizes that he has lost his tobacco, he may for the first time realize that he is in fact strongly enslaved.

Chapter 7

Choosing Delayed Rewards: Perspectives from Learning Theory, Neurochemistry, and Neuroanatomy

Rudolf N. Cardinal, Trevor W. Robbins and Barry J. Everitt

Introduction

Delayed reinforcement is of interest from two theoretical perspectives. Firstly, how do animals succeed in bridging delays to reinforcement at all? Natural reinforcers always follow the action that obtained them by a delay, even if it is short. Thus, to control the world successfully, animals must be able to use delayed reinforcement. In some species, the delay to reinforcement may be very long indeed; humans routinely make decisions on the basis of outcomes that are decades away.

Secondly, individuals differ in their ability to choose delayed rewards. Impulsive choice is exemplified by the tendency of an individual to choose a reward that is small or poor, but is available immediately, in preference to a larger reward that is only obtainable after a period of time (Ainslie 1975). Impulsive choice may reflect reduced efficacy of delayed reinforcement. It has been considered a normal human characteristic (Aristotle 350 BC, 1925), but impulsive choice contributes to deleterious states such as drug addiction (Bickel *et al.* 1999; Evenden 1999a; Heyman 1996; Mitchell 1999; Poulos *et al.* 1995) and has been suggested to underlie a number of other clinical disorders, including attention-deficit/hyperactivity disorder (ADHD) (Sagvolden *et al.* 1998; Sagvolden & Sergeant 1998). Why are some individuals impulsive in their choices?

In this paper, as a background to these questions, modern theories of animal learning (specifically, Pavlovian and instrumental conditioning) will first be summarized. These theories are based on studies showing that multiple dissociable psychological processes contribute to rats' actions. The potential ways in which delayed reinforcement can affect instrumental *learning* will be considered. Theories of instrumental *choice* will then be briefly reviewed, examining their applicability to choice between delayed reinforcers and their relevance to neuropsychological studies. Interventional studies will be reviewed that examine the role of selected neurochemical systems (the serotonin and dopamine neuromodulator systems) and neuroanatomical regions (the nucleus accumbens core, anterior cingulate cortex, medial prefrontal cortex, and orbitofrontal cortex) in rats' ability to choose delayed rewards. Finally, the applications of these studies to addiction and other disorders of impulsivity will be considered.

The Rat Responds for Rewards Based on Multiple Representations of Reinforcer Value

In addition to innate, unlearned behaviour, rats may acquire new behavioural responses through Pavlovian conditioning, in which the experimenter arranges a contingency between stimuli in the world by presenting those stimuli independently of the animal's behaviour (Pavlov 1927). Similarly, rats exhibit goal-directed behaviour learned through instrumental conditioning, in which the experimenter arranges a contingency between the animal's behaviour and a reinforcing outcome (Thorndike 1911). When considering subjects choosing between delayed rewards, it is natural to think of instrumental conditioning as the underlying psychological process. However, instrumental conditioning is not a unitary phenomenon. Apparently simple goal-directed responding depends on multiple representations within the brain (Dickinson 1994; Dickinson & Balleine 1994). Additionally, under certain circumstances, such behaviour can cease to be goal-directed and become habitual (Adams 1982; Dickinson 1994), and Pavlovian conditioning can have a direct influence on instrumental responding. Indeed, it is apparent that many psychological processes contribute to learning and performance of instrumental behaviour (summarized here but reviewed thoroughly by Dickinson (1994), Dickinson & Balleine (1994), Cardinal *et al.* (2002)); thus, complex tasks such as choosing between delayed rewards may depend on a number of these processes.

Specifically, rats can learn the *instrumental contingency* between an action such as lever-pressing and an outcome (such as food). This knowledge is represented in declarative fashion in the brain (Dickinson 1994). To produce goal-directed action, this knowledge interacts with another declarative representation, that of the *instrumental incentive value* of the food, in order to determine whether the rat does or does not perform the action. If the rat knows that lever-pressing produces food and values the food highly, it is likely to press the lever. Surprisingly, there is a second system that assigns a value to foodstuffs — the food's *affective* or *hedonic value*. Through direct experience, the hedonic value is "written into" the instrumental incentive value governing goal-directed action (a process termed incentive learning: Dickinson 1994; Dickinson & Balleine 1994). There are circumstances in which these two values can differ (see Dickinson 1994; Dickinson & Balleine 1994; Cardinal *et al.* 2002).

Although rats possess declarative knowledge of the consequences of their actions, they also possess a procedural, stimulus–response "habit" system; this system is less flexible (for example, it contains no explicit knowledge of the reinforcer, so the probability of performing the habitual action does not change immediately if the value of the reinforcer is altered). Over-training is a typical way in which a goal-directed response becomes habitual (see Adams 1982; Dickinson 1985, 1994; Dickinson *et al.* 1983, 1995).

Finally, Pavlovian conditioned stimuli (CSs) can modulate instrumental performance directly (Dickinson 1994; Dickinson & Balleine 1994), an effect termed

Pavlovian–instrumental transfer (PIT). For example, a Pavlovian CS that predicts the arrival of sucrose solution will enhance instrumental lever-pressing for sucrose (Estes 1948; Lovibond 1983); this, at least in part, represents *conditioned motivation* (see Cardinal *et al.* 2002). The ability of a Pavlovian CS to affect instrumental performance depends upon the relevance of the unconditioned stimulus (US) to the animal's motivational state at the time; therefore, a neural system must exist to judge the current value (or salience) of the US when the CS is presented. This value has been dissociated both from the instrumental incentive value and the hedonic value of foodstuffs (Dickinson 1986; Dickinson & Dawson 1987a, b; Dickinson *et al.* 2000; see Cardinal *et al.* 2002). As emphasized by Gjelsvik (Chapter 7, this volume), cue-induced motivation (PIT) may have great significance for addiction (with potential roles in acquisition, maintenance, and cue-induced relapse; see, e.g. Gawin 1991; O'Brien *et al.* 1998; Tiffany & Drobes 1990) as it represents a mechanism by which uncontrolled (non-contingent) stimuli can radically affect goal-directed responding.

Thus, an ostensibly simple behaviour — lever-pressing in rats — is influenced by many dissociable psychological processes. Understanding of these processes is by no means complete. For example, it is not clear how conditioned reinforcement (in which neutral stimuli paired with primary reward gain affective or motivational value such that animals will work for them: see Mackintosh 1974; Williams 1991, 1994a; Williams & Dunn 1991) relates to the valuation processes described above. Conditioned reinforcers might act in several ways (for example, by gaining instrumental incentive value and also affecting behaviour via PIT). Thus, the fact that multiple psychological processes contribute to a behaviour such as lever-pressing must be borne in mind when considering a complex phenomenon such as responding for delayed reinforcement.

Mechanisms by Which Delayed Reinforcement Can Affect Instrumental Learning

Early theorists considered the fundamental problem of delayed reinforcement: how a response can be strengthened by reinforcement that follows it. Hull (1932) postulated that the strength of a stimulus–response (S–R) association is inversely related to the delay between the response and the reinforcement, assuming a logarithmic relationship. Indeed, instrumental learning has repeatedly been shown to be a decreasing function of the delay (e.g. Dickinson *et al.* 1992; Lattal & Gleeson 1990). Interestingly, in several early studies, the delay was bridged by distinctive cues or environments; the cue that precedes eventual reward has the potential to become a secondary or conditioned reinforcer, making the "underlying" response–reinforcement delay gradient function unclear. The importance of this effect was first shown by Grice (1948), who trained rats on a visual discrimination task with delayed reinforcement. The rats were given a choice between a white and a black alley; both led to a grey goal box, but only one (reached from the white alley) contained food. A delay to reinforcement was added by inserting two grey alleys of variable length. Grice found that learning was noticeably impaired by as short a delay as 0.5 s, and severely impaired by 5 s, a deficit that could be ameliorated by having more discriminable goal boxes or by forcing the rats to make discriminable motor responses in the black and white start alleys. Grice argued that learning under conditions of delayed reward was due to immediate secondary (conditioned) reinforcement, based on traces of visual or proprioceptive stimuli. Clearly, if the "primary" delay gradient is a meaningful concept, it is steep; the distinction becomes one of whether the delay gradient applies to direct reinforcement of responses (Hull) or to stimulus–reward association (Grice).

Killeen & Fetterman (1988), in contrast, suggest that the very idea of a "delay gradient" is misleading. In their model, reinforcement always strengthens the responses that the animal is presently making, and never acts "backwards in time" to strengthen past responses. The observed "gradient" arises from the fact that the animal has a finite probability of leaving the behavioural state it was in when it responded. If reinforcement follows immediately, there is a high probability of strengthening the response that caused reinforcement, but the longer the reinforcer is delayed, the greater the chance that the animal has moved to another state, in which case a different response will be reinforced. This point has also been made by Spence (1956), Mowrer (1960), and Revusky & Garcia (1970); see also Mackintosh (1974: 155–159).

When considering choice between reinforcers when one is delayed, one reason for the failure of a subject to choose the delayed reinforcer may therefore be that a response–reinforcer, stimulus–reinforcer, or stimulus–response association is weaker for the delayed alternative. Additionally, if the delay is bridged by a stimulus acting as a conditioned reinforcer, then neural interventions known to increase the power of conditioned reinforcers should improve subjects' ability to choose the delayed reward.

Delayed Reinforcement in Choice

Utility Theory as an Approach to Normal and Pathological Choice in Animals

To analyse choice involving delayed reinforcement, it is natural to attempt to quantify the value of reinforcers to the subject, and utility theory is a way of analysing choice that has explicitly or implicitly underlain many studies using delayed reinforcement. Formal utility theory is based on six axioms defining attributes of preference that perfectly rational agents should possess (von Neumann & Morgenstern 1947, reviewed by Russell & Norvig 1995). A full statement of these axioms is beyond the scope of this paper, but one, for example, is *transitivity*: if an agent prefers A to B and B to C, then it must prefer A to C. (If the agent violated this principle, preferring $A > B > C > A$, and initially possesses A, then an observer could offer the agent C in exchange for A plus a small monetary payment; similarly B for C and A for B, after which the agent ends up in its original state but with less money, which — assuming money is desirable — is irrational.) Given that an agent obeys the axioms of utility theory, then there must exist a *utility function* U that assigns a real number to every outcome O such that $U(O_1) > U(O_2)$ if O_1 is preferred to O_2, and $U(O_1) = U(O_2)$ if the agent is indifferent between the two outcomes.

Goal-directed action requires that the agent assigns value (goal status) to outcome states, but also that it knows the consequences of its actions. To allow for the fact that actions may not always have totally predictable consequences, the agent's knowledge about the causal nature of the world may be represented in the form $p(action \rightarrow outcome_n | evidence)$ denoting the probability, given the available evidence, that *action* causes $outcome_n$. The *expected utility* of an action is therefore given by $EU(action|evidence) = \sum_n p(action \rightarrow outcome_n|evidence) \times U(outcome_n)$. Rational decision making follows if the agent selects the action with the maximum expected utility (the MEU principle). The theory specifies neither the utility functions themselves — anything can be valued — nor the way that the decision is arrived at, which may be explicit or implicit.

However, this decision-making approach suffers from two particular deficiencies. Firstly, computing the expected utilities takes finite time. In real-world situations it may often be better to make an imperfect decision quickly than *eventually* to make what *would* have been the perfect decision — a difficult problem (Russell & Norvig 1995). Secondly, the MEU principle implies that in identical situations the same action will always be taken (it is a "pure" strategy). Once again, this may not be a wise real-world strategy. Game theory (von Neumann & Morgenstern 1947) has shown that there are many situations involving choice under uncertainty when the optimal strategy is to assign probabilities to making different choices but to let the actual decision be governed by chance (a "mixed" strategy), and how randomness is used by animals in decision making is poorly understood (see Mérö 1998).

Within the framework of utility theory, there are two ways to produce "pathological" decision making, such as that contributing to drug addiction. One is to alter the utility functions. For example, assigning a higher utility to poverty than wealth would cause a perfectly rational agent to give its money away; if gambling had intrinsic utility then an agent might gamble despite the financial loss. While the underlying choice remains rational, the agent's preferences generate abnormal behaviour. Indeed, some investigators see it as axiomatic that animals make rational or optimal decisions (see Williams 1994b: 91–94), so that the experimenter's job is to discover the value system of the subject. The other possibility, considered less often, is that utilities are computed normally but the decision-making process itself fails. Indeed, normal humans are not "normative": they systematically deviate from the axioms of decision theory (Heckerman *et al.* 1992; Kahneman *et al.* 1982; see also Chase *et al.* 1998). The distinction is difficult. As an illustration, consider a smoker who desires to abstain but then lights a cigarette. Are we to consider the decision flawed or the actual utility of smoking higher than he first thought? If "optimality can be considered axiomatic" (Williams 1994b: 94), the latter is the case, but such a theory cannot distinguish between the act of our relapsing smoker and one who has no wish to give up. Nevertheless, this distinction seems important; if so, a more reductionist approach is required to the way the brain reaches decisions.

Choice Within the Brain: "Top–Down" and "Bottom–Up" Approaches

To choose between two goals that differ in nature, such as food vs. money, they must be compared on a single dimension. Utility functions achieve this by converting multifactorial alternatives to real numbers. Neurally, a similar process is logically unavoidable — if at no earlier stage of processing, incompatible behaviours must compete for access to motor output structures (although there is no a priori reason why the neural comparison process should be simple or linear).

There is a long history of behavioural research into the computation of reward utility and consequent behavioural strategy (reviewed by Williams 1994b), including the utility of artificial reinforcers (see Shizgal 1997). Initial attempts involved the calculation of reinforcement efficacy by establishing the relationship between response rate and the frequency and amount of reinforcement; however, such studies soon established that this relationship was not simple (see Williams 1994b: 82–83). For example, response rates are affected by whether a ratio or an interval schedule of reinforcement is used, even when the reinforcement rate is identical (Dawson & Dickinson 1990). Similarly, the mechanisms governing motor aspects of responding are neurally dissociable from motivational mechanisms (see e.g. Robbins & Everitt 1992).

Another approach has been to relate reinforcement efficacy to *choice* behaviour. This literature grew following the discovery by Herrnstein (1961, 1970) of the "matching law". Herrnstein (1961) trained pigeons to respond on two concurrent variable interval (VI) schedules, and varied the relative availability of reinforcement on the two schedules while holding the overall reinforcement rate constant. He observed that the proportion of the total behaviour allocated to each response key approximately matched the proportion of reinforcers allocated to that key. This defines the matching law: $R_1/(R_1 + R_2) = r_1/(r_1 + r_2)$ where R represents the behavioural response rate for each alternative, and r the reinforcement. Herrnstein (1970) extended this relationship to take account of more than two alternatives, particularly including "unmeasured" activities the animal may engage in, and derived a "general principle of response output" (Herrnstein 1970: 256): $R_1 = kr_1/(r_1 + r_e)$, where R_1 is the rate of the response being measured, r_1 is the quantity of reinforcement for that response, r_e is the reinforcement for all other responses, and k is a parameter determining the maximum response rate. Although there are situations where the matching law is not useful — in particular, ratio schedules, where the distribution of reinforcement necessarily *follows* the distribution of responding — a vast literature has sought to define the effects of varying parameters of reinforcement (such as rate, probability, delay, and magnitude) based on this work (see de Villiers & Herrnstein 1976).

This approach has not been without problems. In many circumstances, subjects have been found to "overmatch" (exhibit relative preferences that are exaggerated relative to the predictions of the matching law) or "undermatch" (exhibit reduced preferences), requiring further development of the mathematical models (Baum 1974, 1979), though it has been argued that this is a circular approach (Rachlin 1971). Maximum response rates (k) have been shown to vary with the kind of reinforcement used (Belke 1998), violating an assumption of Herrnstein's law. Nevertheless, the matching law and its extensions do a good job of describing the relationship between reinforcement rate and behaviour on concurrent VI and concurrent-chain schedules (Williams 1994b).

The matching law described a molar property of behaviour — that is, the overall distribution of a large number of responses. As responses are made on a moment-to-moment basis, the question arises of what "molecular" choice process operates to produce matching at a molar level. Suggestions vary from "momentary maximizing" theory, which suggests that subjects choose (in all-or-none fashion) the response with the highest instantaneous reinforcement probability, to the idea that matching is the underlying choice rule (Mackintosh 1974: 192–195; Williams 1994b).

All these theories have a common theme: it is assumed that some value is computed for each alternative behaviour, and a decision rule allocates behaviour according to the relative distribution of values. In order to produce a single value for each alternative, different reinforcement parameters (rate, magnitude, delay, and probability) converge on a single dimension (Baum & Rachlin 1969). Often, the effects of these different parameters are assumed to be calculated independently (Ho *et al.* 1999; Killeen 1972; Rachlin *et al.* 1991). Though some investigators have supported the latter assumption (Mazur 1987, 1997), others, using different techniques, have found that the effects of reinforcer delay and magnitude are not independent (Ito 1985; White & Pipe 1987). In either case, the assumption that all choice alternatives are reduced to a single value and then compared in order to select the option with the greatest value corresponds directly to a form of utility theory, as described above.

Utility theory can fail to characterize human decision making (Kahneman *et al.* 1982), just as similar approaches have not fully characterized choice in other animals (Williams 1994b: 105). Perhaps more success can be achieved by considering the multiple psychological systems that have been discovered to contribute to instrumental performance. Rather than being fundamental, rationality (and the MEU principle) may represent an ideal that is approximated by a set of heuristic psychological processes implemented in the brain. In this framework, behaviour and choice are seen as the asymptotic sum of contributions from cognitive goal-directed systems, habitual responding and other motivational influences (e.g. Dickinson 1994). As discussed above, rats possess *at least* two representations of the value of foodstuffs (Dickinson & Balleine 1994), namely hedonic value and the incentive value governing instrumental responding; Pavlovian incentive value is probably a third (see above). A "bottom–up" analysis of the neuropsychological mechanisms by which these multiple motivational systems calculate the value of environmental events and interact with each other may prove more productive than the "top–down" approach. To take a hypothetical example, suppose that stimulus–response habits obey the matching law, but that cognitive, voluntary decisions can override habits in some circumstances and have a different value system. It may be that acknowledging the existence of these two systems, and determining when each operates, will more rapidly lead to an accurate description of choice behaviour than attempting to model choice with a single, but highly complicated, value system.

Temporal Discounting and Impulsive Choice

Given these caveats, studies of impulsive choice have produced some highly consistent results regarding the effects of delayed reinforcement in well-defined choice paradigms. In a typical experimental situation, a subject chooses between an immediate, small reward or a large, delayed reward; the time discounting function quantifies the effect of the delay on preference. Kacelnik (1997) points out that economic models of choice tend to be based on exponential time discounting functions. If it is assumed that delayed reward is preferred less because there is a constant probability of losing the reward per unit of waiting time, or that there is a constant "interest rate" for the reward obtained immediately (and that the subject's behaviour is attuned to this fact, i.e. that choice is normative), then exponential models emerge: if a delayed reward of magnitude A is chosen and there is a probability p of loss in every unit of time waited, the perceived value V of the delayed reward should be $V = A(1 - p)^T = A\,e^{-kT}$ where $k = -\ln(1 - p)$.

However, the exponential model has been emphatically rejected by experimental work with humans and other animals. The literature on human cognitive decisions will not be considered here. The rat literature contains several demonstrations (many based on the adjusting-delay task of Mazur 1987), using natural reinforcers and intracranial self-stimulation (Grice 1948; Mazur 1987; Mazur *et al.* 1987; Richards *et al.* 1997), that time discounting is described well by a *hyperbolic* discount function (Figure 1A) or a very similar power law (Grace 1996); see Kacelnik (1997) for a discussion of why hyperbolic discounting may be in some sense optimal. One interesting prediction from this function is that preference between a large and a small reward should be observed to reverse depending on the time that the choice is made (Figure 1B), and such preference reversal is a reliable experimental finding (for references see Bradshaw & Szabadi 1992).

At present, the neuropsychological system responsible for hyperbolic discounting is unknown — such discounting might, for example, result from poor knowledge of the action–outcome contingency at long delays, from weak stimulus–response habits, or from reduced utility of delayed rewards in the context of perfect contingency knowledge. Neuropsychological research along these lines is a young field. However, consideration of the neural basis of Pavlovian and instrumental conditioning in animals has led to the identification of several brain regions and neurotransmitter systems that may contribute to choice, reinforcement and value assessment (reviewed by Cardinal *et al.* 2002). Given the

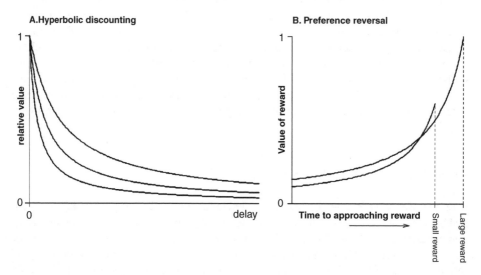

Figure 1: (A) Hyperbolic discounting, governed by the equation *Value = magnitude/* $(1 + K \times delay)$. Large values of *K* give the steepest curve. (B) Preference reversal. Given a choice between an early reward of value 0.6 and a later reward of value 1, hyperbolic discounting predicts that the larger reward will be chosen if the choice is made far in advance (towards the left of the graph). However, as time advances, there comes a time just before delivery of the small reward when preference reverses and the small reward is chosen.
Figure adapted from Ainslie (1975).

importance of impulsive choice in addiction (Bickel *et al.* 1999; Evenden 1999a; Heyman 1996; Mitchell 1999; Poulos *et al.* 1995) and ADHD (Sagvolden *et al.* 1998; Sagvolden & Sergeant 1998), a number of groups have studied the effects on impulsive choice of manipulating neurochemical and neuroanatomical systems implicated in addiction and ADHD; these studies will be reviewed next.

Neurochemical Studies of Impulsive Choice

Serotonin (5-HT)

Abnormalities of the utility function for delayed reinforcement have been suggested to occur following neurochemical manipulations. The suggestion that serotonin is involved in impulse control follows from the twin observations that drugs that suppress 5-HT function appear to reduce behavioural inhibition, making animals more impulsive in a "motor" sense (Evenden 1999b; Soubrié 1986), and that low levels of serotonin metabolites in cerebrospinal fluid are associated with impulsive aggression and violence in humans (Åsberg *et al.* 1976; Brown & Linnoila 1990; Linnoila *et al.* 1983, 1993) and risk-taking behaviour in monkeys (Mehlman *et al.* 1994; see also Evenden 1998). In the sphere of delayed reinforcement, forebrain serotonin depletion, which leads to "impulsive choice" in a variety of paradigms (Bizot *et al.* 1999; Richards & Seiden 1995; Wogar *et al.* 1993b), has been suggested to reflect a modification of the temporal discounting function (Ho *et al.* 1999; Wogar *et al.* 1993b). Specifically, 5-HT depletion is suggested to steepen the function, such that delayed rewards lose their capacity to motivate or reinforce behaviour. The 5-HT-depleted animal becomes hypersensitive to delays (or hyposensitive to delayed reward). As delayed rewards have unusually low utility, the animal consistently chooses small, immediate rewards over large, delayed rewards, a characteristic of impulsivity (Ainslie 1975). Conversely, increasing serotonin function with the 5-HT indirect agonist fenfluramine decreases impulsivity (Poulos *et al.* 1996).

Dopamine (DA)

Much of the interest in the relationship between dopamine and impulsivity comes from the discovery that amphetamine and similar psychostimulants are an effective therapy for ADHD (Bradley 1937). Though these drugs have many actions, they are powerful releasers of dopamine from storage vesicles in the terminals of dopaminergic neurons, and prevent dopamine re-uptake from the synaptic cleft, potentiating its action (for references see Feldman *et al.* 1997: 293/552/558). Sagvolden & Sergeant have proposed that many features of ADHD, including preference for immediate reinforcement and hyperactivity on simple reinforcement schedules due to short inter-response times, are due to an abnormally short and steep delay gradient, and that this is due to a hypofunctional dopamine system (Sagvolden *et al.* 1998). Indeed, they go on to suggest nucleus accumbens (Acb) DA as the specific culprit (Sagvolden *et al.* 1998; Sagvolden & Sergeant 1998). Acb DA has long been implicated in aspects of responding for reinforcement, though its role is not yet fully understood (see Cardinal *et al.* 2002).

Many of the inferences regarding the neural abnormalities in children with ADHD have in fact been drawn from studies of the spontaneously hypertensive rat (SHR), an inbred strain of rat that serves as an animal model of ADHD (Sagvolden 2000; Sagvolden *et al.* 1992, 1993; Wultz *et al.* 1990). This rat exhibits pervasive hyperactivity and attention problems that resemble ADHD, is abnormally sensitive to immediate reinforcement in the sense that it exhibits a steeper "scallop" of responding on fixed-interval (FI) schedules (Sagvolden *et al.* 1992), and is impulsive on measures of "execution impulsivity" (Evenden & Meyerson 1999).

Examination of the brains of SHRs supports the assertion that they have an abnormality of dopamine systems. Depolarization- and psychostimulant-induced dopamine release in nucleus accumbens brain slices is altered in the SHR compared to Wistar Kyoto progenitor control rats in a complex pattern that has been attributed to hypofunction of the mesolimbic dopamine system projecting to the Acb (de Villiers *et al.* 1995; Russell *et al.* 1998, 2000), though abnormalities have also been found in dopamine release in slices of dorsal striatum and prefrontal cortex (Russell *et al.* 1995). Within the Acb, differences in gene expression and dopamine receptor density have been observed in both the core and shell subregions (Carey *et al.* 1998; Papa *et al.* 1996, 1998).

Impulsive choice has been suggested to reflect an alteration in reinforcement processes, namely that delayed reinforcers have lost their effectiveness, and has been suggested to underlie attention-deficit/hyperactivity disorder (ADHD) (Sagvolden *et al.* 1998; Sagvolden & Sergeant 1998). ADHD is amenable to treatment with psychomotor stimulant drugs (Bradley 1937; Solanto 1998), suggesting that they might promote the choice of delayed rewards. However, in laboratory models of impulsive choice, the effects of acute administration of psychostimulants have varied: some studies have found that they promote choice of delayed reinforcers (Richards *et al.* 1999; Sagvolden *et al.* 1992; Wade *et al.* 2000), while others have found the opposite effect (Charrier & Thiébot 1996; Evenden & Ryan 1996), and it has been shown that the same psychostimulant can have opposite effects in different tasks designed to measure impulsivity (Richards *et al.* 1997).

Intriguingly, in studies of delayed reinforcement, it has been demonstrated that signalled delays generally maintain higher rates of free-operant responding than unsignalled delays (see Lattal 1987 for a review), and signals present during the delay to reinforcement can have an important role in discrete-trials choice (Mazur 1997). A signal or cue that is associated selectively with a reinforcing outcome may become a conditioned reinforcer, and conditioned reinforcement can affect choice behaviour (Williams & Dunn 1991). Since amphetamine-like drugs potentiate the effects of conditioned reinforcers (Hill 1970; Robbins 1976, 1978; Robbins *et al.* 1983), Cardinal *et al.* (2000) tested the hypothesis that amphetamine promotes the choice of signalled delayed reinforcement by potentiating conditioned reinforcing properties of the cue. Rats were given regular discrete-trial choices between an immediate small reinforcer and a delayed large reinforcer. For one group of rats, illumination of a stimulus light during the delay provided a signal that was unambiguously associated with the large reinforcer (termed the Cue condition; Figure 2). This design is commonly used to establish stimuli as conditioned reinforcers in delay-of-reinforcement experiments (for reviews see Mazur 1997; Williams 1994a). In the No Cue condition, rats awaited and collected the reinforcers in darkness, with no signal present during the delay. Given that the effect of amphetamine on performance of this task in the absence

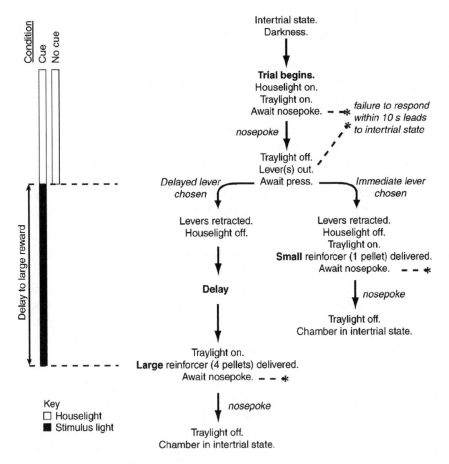

Figure 2: Delayed reinforcement choice task (Cardinal *et al.* 2000, 2001), based on Evenden & Ryan (1996). The figure shows the format of a single trial; trials began at 100-s intervals. Sessions lasted 100 min and consisted of 5 blocks, each comprising two trials on which only one lever was presented (one trial for each lever, in randomized order) followed by ten choice trials. The delay to the large reinforcer was varied systematically across the session: delays for each block were 0, 10, 20, 40, and 60 s, respectively. In the Cue condition, a stimulus light was illuminated during the delay to the large reinforcer; this was absent in the No Cue condition.

of differential cues was to increase preference for the small immediate reward (reduced tolerance of delay, Evenden & Ryan 1996), the addition of a conditioned reinforcer would be expected to reduce or reverse this effect. To prevent rats accumulating more food overall by choosing the immediate reward frequently, the time between successive trials was held constant (see Sonuga-Barke *et al.* 1998); thus, choice of the small immediate reinforcer was always suboptimal.

Cardinal *et al.* (2000) found that the effects of amphetamine depended on the effects of the cue, decreasing preference for the large, delayed reinforcer in the No Cue condition, but increasing it in the Cue condition. This finding is consistent with Evenden & Ryan (1996), who used a task equivalent to the No Cue condition of Cardinal *et al.* (2000) and found that amphetamine reduced preference for the delayed reward. It is also consistent with results obtained using an adjusting-amount procedure (Richards *et al.* 1997) in which a tone was sounded for the duration of the delay, analogous to the Cue condition of Cardinal *et al.* (2000); in this task, amphetamine and the amphetamine analogue, methamphetamine increase preference for the larger, delayed reward (Richards *et al.* 1997, 1999; Wade *et al.* 2000). The results of Cardinal *et al.* (2000) therefore support the idea that "delay discounting" of the efficacy of future rewards is not a unitary process (Ainslie 1975), but rather that the observed phenomenon of discounting arises from several underlying processes of which conditioned reinforcement is one.

Neuroanatomical Studies of Impulsive Choice

In contrast to the literature on the neurochemistry of impulsivity, little is known of the neuroanatomical basis of impulsive choice. However, three lines of evidence have suggested the nucleus accumbens (Acb) and its cortical afferents, including the anterior cingulate and medial prefrontal cortices (ACC, mPFC), as candidate structures that may be involved in regulating choice between alternative reinforcers.

First, these structures have been firmly implicated in reinforcement processes. The Acb, once suggested to mediate the reinforcing efficacy of natural and artificial rewards (see Koob 1992 and also Wise 1981, 1982, 1985, 1994), is now thought not to be necessary for this, but instead to be a key site for the motivational impact of impending rewards (reviewed by Cardinal *et al.* 2002; Everitt *et al.* 1999; Parkinson *et al.* 2000; Robbins & Everitt 1996; Salamone *et al.* 1997). Many of its afferents have also been shown to be involved in reward-related learning, including the ACC (Bussey *et al.* 1997; Bussey *et al.* 1997; Parkinson *et al.* 2000) and mPFC (e.g. Balleine & Dickinson 1998; Bechara *et al.* 1999; Richardson & Gratton 1998; Tzschentke 2000).

Second, these regions are important recipients of dopaminergic and serotonergic afferents (Fallon & Loughlin 1995; Halliday *et al.* 1995), and pharmacological manipulations of dopamine and serotonin systems have been shown to affect impulsive choice in rats, as described above.

Third, abnormalities of these regions have been detected in humans with ADHD, and in animal models of ADHD. Abnormal functioning of prefrontal cortical regions, including medial prefrontal and anterior cingulate cortex, has been observed in ADHD patients (Bush *et al.* 1999; Ernst *et al.* 1998; Rubia *et al.* 1999). In the spontaneously hypertensive rat (SHR), differences in dopamine receptor density and gene expression have been observed within the core and shell regions of the Acb (Carey *et al.* 1998; Papa *et al.* 1996, 1998; Sadile 2000). Abnormalities of dopamine release have been detected in the Acb (de Villiers *et al.* 1995; Russell 2000; Russell *et al.* 1998) and prefrontal cortex (Russell *et al.* 1995), in addition to possible dysfunction in the dorsal striatum and amygdala (Papa *et al.* 2000; Russell *et al.* 1995).

Role of the Nucleus Accumbens (Acb)

Using the task described earlier (Figure 2), with no cues present during the delay to avoid the potential confound of conditioned reinforcement, Cardinal *et al.* (2001) examined the effects of excitotoxic lesions of the nucleus accumbens core (AcbC; Figure 3) on rats' ability to choose a delayed reward. Subjects were trained pre-operatively and assigned to matched groups before being tested post-operatively, to avoid any possible effects of the lesion on learning of the task.

AcbC-lesioned subjects exhibited a persistent and profound deficit in subjects' ability to choose a delayed reward, making impulsive choices (Figure 4). This was not due to an inflexible bias away from the lever producing the delayed reinforcer; AcbC-lesioned rats still chose the large reinforcer more frequently at zero delay than at other delays, and removal of the delays resulted in a rapid and significant increase

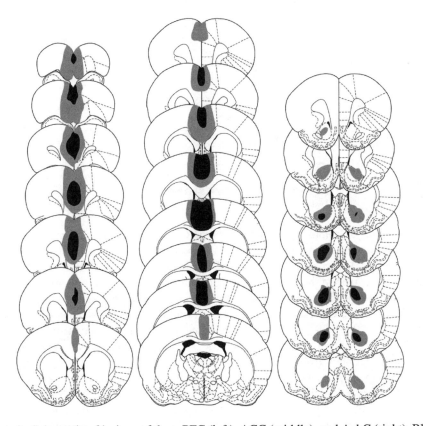

Figure 3: Schematic of lesions of the mPFC (left), ACC (middle), and AcbC (right). Black shading indicates the extent of neuronal loss common to all subjects; grey indicates the area lesioned in at least one subject. Coronal sections are +4.7 through +1.7 mm (mPFC), +2.7 mm through −1.3 mm (ACC), and +2.7 through +0.48 mm (AcbC) relative to bregma. Outlines are taken from Paxinos & Watson (1998).

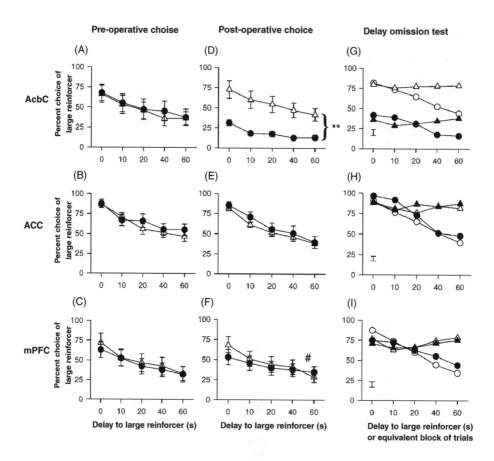

Figure 4: Effect of lesions of the AcbC (top), ACC (middle), or mPFC (bottom) on choice of delayed reward (•, lesioned group; △, corresponding sham group; error bars, standard error of the mean). The "no cue" condition (see Figure 2) was used throughout. A–C show the pattern of choice in the last 3 sessions preceding surgery; corresponding sham/lesion groups were matched for performance. Subjects' preference for the large reinforcer declined with delay, as is typical for trained subjects performing this task (Evenden & Ryan 1996; Cardinal *et al.* 2000). D–F illustrate choice in the first seven post-operative sessions. The AcbC-lesioned group was markedly impaired (**$p < 0.01$), choosing the delayed reinforcer significantly less often than shams at every delay, including zero. However, both groups still exhibited a within-session shift in preference. ACC lesions had no effect on choice. The mPFC-lesioned subjects exhibited a "flatter" within-session preference shift than shams ([#]$p < 0.05$, group (delay interaction). G–I illustrate the effects of omitting all delays in alternating sessions (•/○, lesioned/sham groups with delays; ▲/△, lesioned/sham groups without delays; error bars, standard error of the difference for the three-way interaction). All groups remained sensitive to the contingencies. Delay removal increased both the sham- and AcbC-lesioned groups' preference for the larger reward; ACC- and mPFC-lesioned rats were also as sensitive to removal of the delays as shams. Reprinted with permission from Cardinal *et al.* (2001). Copyright (2001) American Association for the Advancement of Science.

in the rats' preference for the large reinforcer. Thus, the pattern of choice reflected a reduced preference for the large reinforcer when it was delayed, suggesting that delays reduced the effectiveness or value of reinforcers much more in AcbC-lesioned rats than in controls.

In the initial set of post-operative testing sessions, the AcbC-lesioned rats preferred the small reinforcer even at zero delay, avoiding the large reinforcer. This paradoxical finding probably reflects an induced bias away from the lever providing delayed reinforcement (Cardinal *et al.* 2000; Evenden & Ryan 1996). However, the majority of AcbC-lesioned subjects (6/10) showed a consistent preference for the large reinforcer after prolonged training without delays (Figure 5A). This did not overcome the tendency to avoid the lever previously associated with delayed reinforcement in all lesioned subjects; given that the pre-operative performance of the same animals was equal to that of controls, it is possible that the post-operative experience of delayed reinforcement may have been aversive for AcbC-lesioned rats (or at least, much less preferable than immediate small reinforcement), inducing them to avoid that lever permanently. However, even when sham and AcbC-lesioned subjects were selected who showed near-exclusive preference for the large reinforcer in the absence of delays (Figure 5E), reintroduction of delays caused a dramatic and selective fall in

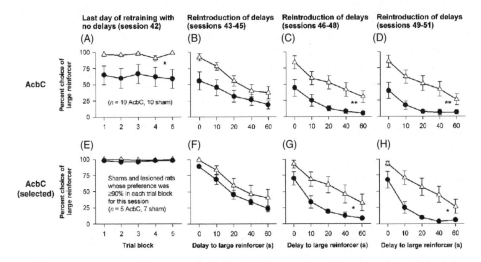

Figure 5: A illustrates the preference of AcbC-lesioned rats following extended training in the absence of any delays (a further six sessions after completion of other behavioural tests; ●, AcbC-lesioned group; △, shams; error bars, standard error of the mean). B–D show performance over consecutive blocks of sessions upon the reintroduction of delays ($^*p < 0.05$, $^{**}p < 0.01$, difference from shams). Panels E–H show data from the same sessions as A–D, but only include data from those rats selected for $\geq 90\%$ preference for the large reinforcer in every trial block on the last day of training with no delays. The sham and lesioned groups were therefore matched in E. F–H show that despite this matching, preference for the large reinforcer in the AcbC group collapsed upon reintroduction of the delays. As these data exhibit significant heterogeneity of variance, the highly conservative correction of Box (1954) was applied (see Howell 1997: 322, 457, 464); $^*p < 0.05$ for the corrected between-group difference.

preference for the large, delayed reinforcer in the AcbC-lesioned group (accompanied by a decline in preference at zero delay, Figure 5F–H, which represents generalization of their avoidance of the delayed reinforcer from trial blocks on which delays were present to the first trial block). In summary, these results show that AcbC-lesioned rats are hypersensitive to the effects of delaying reinforcement even when they are clearly able to discriminate the two reinforcers.

The task used by Cardinal *et al.* (2001) does not determine whether AcbC-lesioned rats exhibit altered sensitivity to reinforcer *magnitude* or *delay*. Either abnormality might produce impulsive choice (see Ho *et al.* 1999). However, in this study, the AcbC group did discriminate between the large and the small reinforcer, consistent with the observation that the expectancy of reward magnitude continues to have normal effects upon rats' reaction time following excitotoxic Acb lesions (Brown & Bowman 1995). A large proportion of the AcbC group showed a preference, sometimes absolute, for the large reward when prolonged training was given with no delays, and 5/10 AcbC-lesioned rats met a very stringent criterion of preference for the large reward under these conditions (Figure 5E). These same rats were exquisitely sensitive to delays, preferring the large reinforcer much less than similarly-selected shams when it was delayed.

It is possible that the AcbC group discriminated between the reinforcer magnitudes, but to a lesser extent than normal rats. In this scenario, AcbC-lesioned rats exhibit impulsive choice because the perceived value of the large reinforcer is abnormally low, and insufficient to overcome the normal effects of delay discounting. Models such as the multiplicative hyperbolic discounting model of Ho *et al.* (1999) have been derived based on behavioural techniques allowing magnitude and delay discounting parameters to be determined independently. Unfortunately, the behavioural technique used by Cardinal *et al.* (2001) cannot be analysed using this model. For example, sham subjects' preferences approached 100% choice of the large reinforcer at zero delays (Figure 5A), whereas in the model of Ho *et al.* (1999) relative preference between a 1-pellet and a 4-pellet reinforcer cannot exceed 80%. The behavioural result comes as no surprise, for it is the well-known phenomenon of maximization on discrete-trial schedules (see Mackintosh 1974: 190–195), but it implies that behaviour in this task cannot be quantified according to the hyperbolic discounting model.

Thus, the task used by Cardinal *et al.* (2001) does not allow the two explanations of impulsive choice (variations in sensitivity to reinforcer magnitude or delay) to be distinguished conclusively. While this may be possible in delay-of-reinforcement choice tasks using indifference-point methodology (Ho *et al.* 1999), there is an alternative. Relative preference for two reinforcers is often inferred from the distribution of responses on concurrent VI schedules of reinforcement (discussed earlier), which, while complex to interpret when delayed reinforcement is used, are simpler to interpret with immediate reinforcement. Such a schedule could be used to assess whether or not AcbC-lesioned rats exhibited relative indifference ("undermatching" compared to shams) between the reinforcers used by Cardinal *et al.* (2001). This would provide evidence for reduced reinforcer magnitude discrimination following AcbC lesions, or for an abnormality of the matching process itself, while normal performance (or overmatching) would make this explanation less likely and therefore support the view that AcbC lesions produce a steeper delay-of-reinforcement gradient. As yet, published data do not allow this question to be answered.

Finally, an explanation in terms of temporal perception might also be offered for the effects of AcbC lesions. The basal ganglia have been suggested to be a component of an "internal clock", based on the effects of dopaminergic manipulations on timing tasks (see Gibbon *et al.* 1997). Similarly, forebrain serotonin depletion, which affects Acb among many other structures, impairs timing ability (Al-Zahrani *et al.* 1997; Morrissey *et al.* 1993, 1994; Wogar *et al.* 1993a), though these impairments sometimes reflect enhanced behavioural switching rather than a true timing deficit (Al-Ruwaitea *et al.* 1997a; Al-Zahrani *et al.* 1996; Ho *et al.* 1995); see Al-Ruwaitea *et al.* (1997b) for a review. Applying the distinctions of Killeen & Fetterman (1988) to the task of Cardinal *et al.* (2001) (Figure 2), a lesion that increased the speed of an "internal clock" might affect choice prospectively (i.e. the lesioned subject perceives itself to be at a later time-point in the session than it actually is, hastening the within-session shift towards the lever producing immediate reinforcement), or might affect *retrospective* choice (i.e. the lesioned subject experiences a given delay as longer than it remembered, causing a decrease in its preference for the lever producing delayed reinforcement). Again, there is at present no evidence to address the question of whether excitotoxic AcbC lesions affect behavioural timing.

At the least, the findings of Cardinal *et al.* (2001) show that the Acb contributes significantly to animals' ability to choose a delayed reward. If further experiments show that it does so specifically by maintaining the value of a reinforcer over a delay, a new avenue of inquiry into Acb function might open up. It has previously been shown in primates that neuronal activity related to the expectation of reward across a delay can be found in the ventral striatum (Schultz *et al.* 1992, 1995, 1998, 2000); such activity is a candidate representation of the goals of activity (Schultz *et al.* 2000). Additionally, striatal neurons may respond to past events, maintaining a form of memory that might assist the association of past acts with reinforcement (Schultz *et al.* 1995). These findings represent important data on the forms of information that the AcbC may use to promote actions leading to delayed rewards, and a future challenge will be to discover the manner in which these neural signals influence overt behaviour, and the psychological processes they govern. Given the involvement of the Acb in aversive motivation (see Parkinson *et al.* 1999; Salamone 1994), it will also be important to determine whether lesions of Acb induce impulsive choice in an aversive context, impairing the ability to choose a small immediate penalty in preference to a large delayed penalty.

Role of the Anterior Cingulate Cortex (ACC)

Cardinal *et al.* (2001) found that excitotoxic lesions of the ACC (Figure 3) had no effect on choice in the same task, establishing that the ACC is not required for rats to choose a delayed reinforcer (Figure 4). Moreover, ACC-lesioned rats remained equally sensitive to unexpected removal of the delays in this task (Figure 4), suggesting that their choices were no more inflexible or "habitual" than those of shams. This finding stands in apparent contrast to previous reports of motor impulsivity or disinhibited responding in ACC-lesioned rats. For example, such rats have been found to over-respond to unrewarded stimuli (Bussey *et al.* 1997; Parkinson *et al.* 2000), and to respond prematurely in situations where they are required to wait (Muir *et al.* 1996). However, such a dissociation is not in itself unexpected, as motor impulsivity and impulsive choice have been dissociated before ("execution" and "outcome" impulsivity; Evenden 1999b). Thus, these results suggest that despite findings of ACC abnormalities in disorders of impulsivity (e.g. Bush *et al.* 1999), ACC dysfunction is not an important contributor to impulsive choice.

Role of the Medial Prefrontal Cortex (mPFC)

In the task used by Cardinal *et al.* (2001), lesions of the mPFC "flattened" the within-session shift from the large to the small reward; the mean preference for the large reward was *below* that of shams at zero delay, but *above* that of shams at the maximum delay (Figure 4F). There is no obvious explanation for this effect within theories of choice of delayed reinforcement; it seems clear that the mPFC lesion resulted in some form of insensitivity to the contingencies or stimuli present in the task.

Given that Balleine & Dickinson (1998) demonstrated that lesions encompassing the prelimbic cortex impaired rats' sensitivity to instrumental contingencies, it might be that a failure of contingency perception was responsible for the performance of mPFC-lesioned rats in the present task. However, these rats were just as sensitive as controls to the unexpected removal of all delays; their responding was not inflexible, as might have been expected according to this account.

A more plausible interpretation is that mPFC lesions disrupted the control over behaviour by the passage of time in each session. There is strong evidence that normal rats learn a session-wide temporal discrimination in this task, and that this temporal discriminative stimulus comes to control responding — in particular the tendency to shift from the large to the small reward as the session progresses (Cardinal *et al.* 2000). Disruption of such temporal stimulus control might be expected to produce a flattening of the within-session shift of the kind seen. Indeed, aspirative lesions of the mPFC have previously been shown to induce a general deficit in timing ability in rats (Dietrich & Allen 1998); lesioned subjects showed a temporal discrimination function that was less steep than normal in the peak procedure, an operant task that assesses the ability to time a discriminative stimulus (Catania 1970; Roberts 1981).

Role of the Orbitofrontal Cortex (OFC)

Finally, Mobini *et al.* (2002) have recently studied the effects of lesions encompassing the OFC on a task very similar to those of Evenden & Ryan (1996) and Cardinal *et al.* (2001). The OFC is a prefrontal cortical region strongly implicated in the assessment of reward value that projects to the AcbC (see Cardinal *et al.* 2002). Intriguingly, OFC lesions induced impulsive choice in a manner very similar to AcbC lesions (and, as for AcbC lesions, it is not known whether the impulsive choice was as a result of altered sensitivity to reinforcer magnitude or delay; see above). Although the lesions of Mobini *et al.* (2002) damaged the prelimbic cortex in addition to the OFC, their hypothesis that OFC damage was responsible for the behavioural effect is strengthened by the finding of Cardinal *et al.* (2001) that mPFC lesions encompassing the prelimbic cortex did not induce impulsive choice.

Conclusions

Theories of Learning and Choice with Delayed Reward

Two broad approaches to choice behaviour will be summarized, and a synthesis offered.

Model 1: Informed choice. According to this model, subjects make prospective choices between alternatives based on full knowledge of the response–outcome contingencies and of the value of each outcome. These choices represent goal-directed actions. Subjects' sensitivity to delay in choice tasks is therefore a consequence of temporal discounting of the perceived (prospective) value of the delayed reward.

This model is necessarily applicable only to fully-trained subjects — subjects who have learned the instrumental contingencies. It may be particularly applicable when humans are offered explicit hypothetical choices: "would you prefer $800 now, or $1000 in a year?" (Myerson & Green 1995; Rachlin *et al.* 1991). As the contingencies cannot be offered "pre-packaged" to experimental animals through language, such subjects must be trained through direct experience of the rewards in the experimental situation. This introduces the complication that delays to reinforcement can affect operant and discrimination learning, so care is typically taken by experimenters to ensure subjects are "well trained". Slow acquisition of delay sensitivity must be attributed to difficulties in learning the instrumental contingencies across a delay and/or learning the appropriate incentive value of delayed reward through experience of waiting. In tasks where the delay is systematically and predictably varied (e.g. Evenden & Ryan 1996; Cardinal *et al.* 2000), learning may also be slowed by the requirement to learn discriminative stimuli predicting the delay contingency currently in force. Thus, this model is inherently an incomplete description of the effects of delayed reinforcement, as it does not deal with the effects of delays on learning.

Model 2: Differential associative response strength. According to an extreme form of this model, based on simple S–R theory (Grindley 1932; Guthrie 1935; Hull 1943; Thorndike 1911), rats' choice behaviour reflects differential reinforcement of stimulus–response habits. The change in associative strength is some function of reward magnitude multiplied by the time-discounted "trace strength" of the preceding response. Choice is determined by a process of competition between the available responses (e.g. the principles of matching: de Villiers & Herrnstein 1976; Herrnstein 1970). Choice is therefore "retrospective" in a sense, as preference for a particular alternative depends upon prior experience of that alternative, and time discounting reflects the decay of the traces available to be associated with reward. A similar model, after Grice (1948), may be constructed in which animals respond for immediate conditioned reinforcement (by goal-directed behaviour or S–R habit) and the acquisition of associations between a chain of stimuli and eventual reward accounts for the observed phenomenon of temporal discounting, by similar mechanisms.

The S–R view accounts for some of the theoretical appeal of exponential temporal discounting models. In exponential decay, at any one moment in time the trace strength of a response follows directly from the trace strength at the previous instant (if x_t is the trace strength at time t and A is the starting value, then $x_t = A\,e^{-kt}$ and $x_{t+1} = e^{-k}x_t$). In contrast, in the hyperbolic discounting model and all others in which preference reversal occurs, the strength of the trace at any one moment cannot be calculated in such a manner: information about the absolute time since the response must be available. (This is clearly illustrated by the preference reversal graphs in Figure 1B; if two such decay curves cross, then an observer travelling along one curve cannot know at the crossover point whether its own curve is the recent, rapidly-decaying trace, or the older, slowly-decaying trace, without further information — namely the time since the response, or its starting strength.) This process does not model "mnemonic decay" in any clear way. Thus, the empirical observation of *hyperbolic* discounting specifies the information that must be available to the subject at any one moment in time; in the context of "retrospective" choice, this constrains the possible underlying psychological mechanisms, and there is no obvious candidate within the S–R model.

Furthermore, while S–R models can account for effects of delays on learning as well as choice, they do not take into account the fact that goal-directed actions contribute to choice in rats (Dickinson 1994) and would clearly not provide a satisfactory account of human choice (cf. Ainslie 1975; Myerson & Green 1995; Rachlin *et al.* 1991).

Model 3: Composite. A multifactorial model is therefore suggested, based on that of Dickinson (1994). The "response strength" of any behaviour is governed by: (1) goal-directed action (Dickinson & Balleine 1994), in which knowledge of the instrumental contingency combines with the incentive value of the expected outcome; (2) stimulus–response habits, which gain strength slowly with the number of reinforcers presented (Dickinson *et al.* 1995); and (3) Pavlovian–instrumental transfer, mediated by the Pavlovian association between contextual, discriminative, or other conditioned stimuli and the outcome of the instrumental action. Ordinarily, behaviour conforming to the matching law and to hyperbolic temporal discounting is seen as a product of these processes. Delayed reinforcement may act: (a) to impair learning of the instrumental contingency (Dickinson *et al.* 1992); (b) to reduce the incentive value of the delayed reward, as speculated by many models; (c) to reduce the reinforcement of stimulus–response habits; and (d) to reduce the Pavlovian association between stimuli present at the moment of action and the ultimate reinforcer.

This model, though qualitative, makes several predictions. Firstly, manipulations of components of this composite behaviour should affect choice. For example, manipulations of the association between cues immediately consequent on choice and the outcome (e.g. the presence or absence of a cue bridging the delay) should affect choice independently of the actual delay to reinforcement, a prediction not made by Kacelnik's (1997) normative model of hyperbolic discounting, but one that has experimental support (Cardinal *et al.* 2000; Mazur 1997). Secondly, pharmacological and neural manipulations known to dissociate these processes should also be capable of affecting choice (Cardinal *et al.* 2000).

This model is obviously compatible with mathematical models of temporal discounting, but interprets the discount function as the sum of the contributions of several processes operating in any one situation. Similar composite models have been offered before (a casual example is Pinker 1997: 395–396), though with a different decomposition of the processes contributing to choice (compare, for example, distinct contributions of conditioned and primary reinforcement to response strength: Killeen & Fetterman 1988: 287–289). One interesting challenge may be to establish what processes contribute most significantly to choice of a reinforcer at different delays. Consider an obvious hypothesis: instrumental incentive value in the rat depends upon declarative knowledge, as discussed above, and in this way is analogous to human hypothetical choices. Thus, it may be that when reward is extremely delayed (as in some human experiments), only instrumental incentive value is important (as delay $d \rightarrow \infty$, total value $V \rightarrow V_{\text{instrumental}}$). When a dieting human calmly decides to abstain from chocolate cake and the dessert trolley is then pushed under his nose, it would not be expected from the rat literature (see Cardinal *et al.* 2002) that the instrumental incentive value of chocolate cake suddenly changes — after all, the subject's underlying motivational state of hunger (or lack of it) has not altered. However, alternative, possibly Pavlovian motivational processes may create an extra boost to the value of the cake (observed as a tendency to choose the cake), as the cake is now immediately available (as $d \rightarrow 0$, $V_{\text{cake-other}}$ increases dramatically). The net value function ($V_{\text{cake}} = V_{\text{cake-instrumental}} + V_{\text{cake-other}}$, vs. $V_{\text{weight loss}}$) could then exhibit preference reversal, leading our diner to succumb and choose the immediate reinforcer. This illustrates but one possible scenario. Nevertheless, if different processes do contribute at different delays, there would be important implications for our understanding of individual differences in impulsive choice.

Neural Basis of Choosing Delayed Reinforcers

As described above, there is now direct evidence that the Acb is involved in the pathogenesis of impulsive choice: the integrity of the Acb is critical for animals to tolerate delays to appetitive reinforcement (Cardinal *et al.* 2001). In addition to providing neuroanatomical insight into the normal process through which delayed reinforcement affects behaviour, this finding suggests a mechanism by which Acb dysfunction may contribute to addiction, ADHD, and other impulse control disorders.

As lesions of the ACC and mPFC, two afferents to the AcbC, did not impair rats' capacity to choose a delayed reward (Cardinal *et al.* 2001), it remains to be established which afferents to the AcbC contribute to its ability to promote the choice of delayed rewards, and through what efferent pathways it does this. Obvious afferent structures that may provide specific information concerning reinforcer value to the Acb are the basolateral amygdala and the OFC, both implicated in the assessment of reward value (see Cardinal *et al.* 2002). The OFC may also be an important efferent target of information travelling through the Acb, as this "limbic loop" of the basal ganglia projects back (through the ventral pallidum) to medial OFC (Alexander *et al.* 1986). In support of the conjecture that an OFC–AcbC circuit may play an important role in animals' ability to choose a delayed reinforcer (Cardinal *et al.* 2001), Mobini *et al.* (2002) recently found that OFC lesions induce impulsive choice in rats in a manner very similar to AcbC lesions. If this hypothesis is correct, then a "disconnection" lesion (a lesion of the OFC in one hemisphere and the AcbC in the other) should impair subjects' ability to choose delayed reinforcement. In addition, it remains to be seen whether the nucleus accumbens shell (AcbSh) also plays a role in the choice of delayed rewards. This is another interesting target of investigation, given the abnormalities of dopamine receptor function detected in the AcbSh of the SHR (Carey *et al.* 1998; Papa *et al.* 1996, 1998; Sadile 2000).

Finally, the limbic corticostriatal circuit of which the Acb is a part may not be the only system involved in delayed reinforcement. In principle, any structure that represents future reinforcers across a delay may contribute to their choice, and exert conditioned reinforcing effects on current behaviour, while any structure that maintains a "memory trace" of responses across a delay may support the reinforcement of those responses. The ventral striatum and OFC exhibit such activity (Schultz *et al.* 1995, 1998, 2000), but so do other structures including the dorsal striatum (e.g. Schultz *et al.* 1995), implicated in the reinforcement of stimulus–response habits (Mishkin *et al.* 1984; Packard & McGaugh 1996; Parkinson *et al.* 2000; Robbins & Everitt 1992; White 1997).

Application to Addiction and Other Disorders of Impulsivity

The observation that AcbC damage can induce impulsive choice has implications for the understanding of ADHD and drug addiction, two clinical disorders in which impulsive choice is a factor.

AcbC-lesioned animals exhibited two signs of ADHD (APA 1994; Sagvolden & Sergeant 1998): locomotor hyperactivity and impulsive choice. However, such animals do not exhibit attentional deficits: neither 6-OHDA-induced dopamine depletion of the Acb (Cole & Robbins 1989) nor excitotoxic lesions of the AcbC (Christakou, Robbins, & Everitt, unpublished data) affect accuracy in tests of visuospatial attentional function. Thus, AcbC-lesioned rats may represent an animal model of the hyperactive–impulsive subtype of ADHD (APA 1994). Interventional neuroanatomical studies of impulsive choice are clearly important for the understanding of the pathogenesis of ADHD, for they allow a causal role to be established between dysfunction of a brain region and impulsive choice. Damage to two other structures observed to be abnormal in ADHD — the ACC and mPFC — did not induce impulsive choice; abnormalities of structure or function observed in these regions in ADHD brains may therefore be responsible for other features of the disorder (such as motoric disinhibition), or these regions may have altered as a consequence of a disease process beginning elsewhere. A clearer understanding of the neurochemical and neuroanatomical basis of the symptoms and signs of ADHD may lead to more effective therapy.

The same considerations apply to drug addiction, in which impulsive choice plays a prominent role in maintaining the selection of drugs of abuse in favour of other, longer-term rewards. Furthermore, if the suggestion that Pavlovian (cue-induced) motivational processes contribute to preference reversal effects and to addiction is correct (see above and Gjelsvik, Chapter 7, this volume), then the role of the AcbC is doubly important (see Cardinal *et al.* 2002), for PIT requires the AcbC (Hall *et al.* 2001); noncontingent CSs elevate AcbC DA levels (Bassareo & DiChiara 1999; Ito *et al.* 2000), DA antagonists block PIT (Dickinson *et al.* 2000), and enhancement of Acb DA function boosts PIT (Wyvell & Berridge 2000). The process of addiction is complicated further by the ability of drugs of abuse (including opiates, ethanol, and psychostimulants) to produce chronic neuroadaptations in brain regions including the Acb (see Koob *et al.* 1998). Addictive drugs may be unique among reinforcers in producing sensitization, the phenomenon by which repeated drug administration leads to an enhanced response to the drug (Altman *et al.* 1996; Kalivas *et al.* 1998; Robinson & Berridge 1993); psychostimulant sensitization enhances the sensitivity of the Acb to DA stimulation (Cador *et al.* 1995), and enhances PIT subsequently (Wyvell & Berridge 2001); chronic methamphetamine has also been shown to increase impulsive choice (Richards *et al.* 1999). One mechanism contributing to addiction may therefore be the ability of drugs of abuse to induce damage or dysfunction in the AcbC, further promoting subsequent impulsive choice and future drug-taking.

Acknowledgements

This work was supported by a Wellcome Trust Programme Grant and conducted within the MRC Co-operative for Brain, Behaviour and Neuropsychiatry. RNC was in receipt of a research studentship from the U.K. Medical Research Council and a James Baird award from the University of Cambridge School of Clinical Medicine.

References

Adams, C. D. (1982). Variations in the sensitivity of instrumental responding to reinforcer devaluation. *Quarterly Journal of Experimental Psychology, Section B – Comparative and Physiological Psychology, 34*, 77–98.

Ainslie, G. (1975). Specious reward: A behavioral theory of impulsiveness and impulse control. *Psychological Bulletin, 82*, 463–496.

Alexander, G. E., DeLong, M. R., & Strick, P. L. (1986). Parallel organization of functionally segregated circuits linking basal ganglia and cortex. *Annual Review of Neuroscience, 9*, 357–381.

Al-Ruwaitea, A. S., Al-Zahrani, S. S., Ho, M. Y., Bradshaw, C. M., & Szabadi, E. (1997a). Effect of central 5-hydroxytryptamine depletion on performance in the "time-left" procedure: Further evidence for a role of the 5-hydroxytryptaminergic pathways in behavioral "switching". *Psychopharmacology, 134*, 179–186.

Al-Ruwaitea, A. S. A., Al-Zahrani, S. S. A., Ho, M. Y., Bradshaw, C. M., & Szabadi, E. (1997b). 5-Hydroxytryptamine and interval timing. In: C. M. Bradshaw, & E. Szabadi (Eds), *Time and behavior: Psychological and neurobehavioral analyses* (pp. 517–570). Amsterdam: Elsevier.

Altman, J., Everitt, B. J., Glautier, S. *et al.* (1996). The biological, social and clinical bases of drug addiction: Commentary and debate. *Psychopharmacology, 125*, 285–345.

Al-Zahrani, S. S. A., Ho, M. Y., Al-Ruwaitea, A. S. A., Bradshaw, C. M., & Szabadi, E. (1997). Effect of destruction of the 5-hydroxytryptaminergic pathways on temporal memory: Quantitative analysis with a delayed interval bisection task. *Psychopharmacology, 129*, 48–55.

Al-Zahrani, S. S., Ho, M. Y., Velazquez Martinez, D. N., Lopez Cabrera, M., Bradshaw, C. M., & Szabadi, E. (1996). Effect of destruction of the 5-hydroxytryptaminergic pathways on behavioral timing and "switching" in a free-operant psychophysical procedure. *Psychopharmacology, 127*, 346–352.

APA (1994). *Diagnostic and statistical manual of mental disorders, Version IV (DSM-IV)*. Washington, DC: American Psychiatric Association.

Aristotle (350 BC/1925). *Nicomachean ethics*. W. D. Ross (Trans.). Oxford: Clarendon Press.

Åsberg, M., Träskman, L., & Thorén, P. (1976). 5-HIAA in the cerebrospinal fluid: A biochemical suicide predictor. *Archives of General Psychiatry, 33*, 1193–1197.

Balleine, B. W., & Dickinson, A. (1998). Goal-directed instrumental action: Contingency and incentive learning and their cortical substrates. *Neuropharmacology, 37*, 407–419.

Bassareo, V., & DiChiara, G. (1999). Differential responsiveness of dopamine transmission to food-stimuli in nucleus accumbens shell/core compartments. *Neuroscience, 89*, 637–641.

Baum, W. M. (1974). On two types of deviation from the matching law: Bias and undermatching. *Journal of the Experimental Analysis of Behavior, 22*, 231–242.

Baum, W. M. (1979). Matching, undermatching, and overmatching in studies of choice. *Journal of the Experimental Analysis of Behavior, 32*, 269–281.

Baum, W. M., & Rachlin, H. C. (1969). Choice as time allocation. *Journal of the Experimental Analysis of Behavior, 12*, 861–874.

Bechara, A., Damasio, H., Damasio, A. R., & Lee, G. P. (1999). Different contributions of the human amygdala and ventromedial prefrontal cortex to decision-making. *Journal of Neuroscience, 19*, 5473–5481.

Belke, T. W. (1998). Qualitatively different reinforcers and parameters of Herrnstein's (1970) response-strength equation. *Animal Learning and Behavior, 26*, 235–242.

Bickel, W. K., Odum, A. L., & Madden, G. J. (1999). Impulsivity and cigarette smoking: Delay discounting in current, never, and ex-smokers. *Psychopharmacology, 146*, 447–454.

Bizot, J., Le Bihan, C., Puech, A. J., Hamon, M., & Thiébot, M. (1999). Serotonin and tolerance to delay of reward in rats. *Psychopharmacology, 146*, 400–412.

Box, G. E. P. (1954). Some theorems on quadratic forms applied in the study of analysis of variance problems: I. Effect of inequality of variance in the one-way classification. *Annals of Mathematical Statistics, 25*, 290–302.

Bradley, C. (1937). The behavior of children receiving Benzedrine. *American Journal of Psychiatry, 94*, 577–585.

Bradshaw, C. M., & Szabadi, E. (1992). Choice between delayed reinforcers in a discrete-trials schedule — the effect of deprivation level. *Quarterly Journal of Experimental Psychology, Section B — Comparative and Physiological Psychology, 44B*, 1–16.

Brown, V. J., & Bowman, E. M. (1995). Discriminative cues indicating reward magnitude continue to determine reaction time of rats following lesions of the nucleus accumbens. *European Journal of Neuroscience, 7*, 2479–2485.

Brown, G. L., & Linnoila, M. (1990). CSF serotonin metabolite (5HIAA) studies in depression, impulsivity and violence. *Journal of Clinical Psychiatry, 51*(Suppl. 4), 31–41.

Bush, G., Frazier, J. A., Rauch, S. L. *et al.* (1999). Anterior cingulate cortex dysfunction in attention-deficit/hyperactivity disorder revealed by fMRI and the Counting Stroop. *Biological Psychiatry, 45*, 1542–1552.

Bussey, T. J., Everitt, B. J., & Robbins, T. W. (1997). Dissociable effects of cingulate and medial frontal cortex lesions on stimulus-reward learning using a novel Pavlovian autoshaping procedure for the rat: Implications for the neurobiology of emotion. *Behavioral Neuroscience, 111*, 908–919.

Bussey, T. J., Muir, J. L., Everitt, B. J., & Robbins, T. W. (1997). Triple dissociation of anterior cingulate, posterior cingulate, and medial frontal cortices on visual discrimination tasks using a touchscreen testing procedure for the rat. *Behavioral Neuroscience, 111*, 920–936.

Cador, M., Bjijou, Y., & Stinus, L. (1995). Evidence of a complete independence of the neurobiological substrates for the induction and expression of behavioral sensitization to amphetamine. *Neuroscience, 65*, 385–395.

Cardinal, R. N., Parkinson, J. A., Hall, J., & Everitt, B. J. (2002). Emotion and motivation: The role of the amygdala, ventral striatum, and prefrontal cortex. *Neuroscience and Biobehavioral Reviews, 26*, 321–352.

Cardinal, R. N., Pennicott, D. R., Sugathapala, C. L., Robbins, T. W., & Everitt, B. J. (2001). Impulsive choice induced in rats by lesions of the nucleus accumbens core. *Science, 292*, 2499–2501.

Cardinal, R. N., Robbins, T. W., & Everitt, B. J. (2000). The effects of d-amphetamine, chlordiazepoxide, alpha-flupenthixol and behavioral manipulations on choice of signalled and unsignalled delayed reinforcement in rats. *Psychopharmacology, 152,* 362–375.

Carey, M. P., Diewald, L. M., Esposito, F. J. *et al.* (1998). Differential distribution, affinity and plasticity of dopamine D-1 and D-2 receptors in the target sites of the mesolimbic system in an animal model of ADHD. *Behavioral Brain Research, 94,* 173–185.

Catania, A. C. (1970). Reinforcement schedules and psychophysical judgment: A study of some temporal properties of behavior. In: W. N. Schoenfeld (Ed.), *The theory of reinforcement schedules* (pp. 1–42). New York: Appleton-Century-Crofts.

Charrier, D., & Thiébot, M. H. (1996). Effects of psychotropic drugs on rat responding in an operant paradigm involving choice between delayed reinforcers. *Pharmacology, Biochemistry and Behavior, 54,* 149–157.

Chase, V. M., Hertwig, R., & Gigerenzer, G. (1998). Visions of rationality. *Trends in Cognitive Sciences, 2,* 206–214.

Cole, B. J., & Robbins, T. W. (1989). Effects of 6-hydroxydopamine lesions of the nucleus accumbens septi on performance of a 5-choice serial reaction time task in rats: Implications for theories of selective attention and arousal. *Behavioral Brain Research, 33,* 165–179.

Dawson, G. R., & Dickinson, A. (1990). Performance on ratio and interval schedules with matched reinforcement rates. *Quarterly Journal of Experimental Psychology, Section B – Comparative and Physiological Psychology, 42,* 225–239.

de Villiers, P. A., & Herrnstein, R. J. (1976). Toward a law of response strength. *Psychological Bulletin, 83,* 1131–1153.

de Villiers, A. S., Russell, V. A., Sagvolden, T., Searson, A., Jaffer, A., & Taljaard, J. J. (1995). Alpha 2-adrenoceptor mediated inhibition of [3H]dopamine release from nucleus accumbens slices and monoamine levels in a rat model for attention-deficit hyperactivity disorder. *Neurochemical Research, 20,* 427–433.

Dickinson, A. (1985). Actions and habits — the development of behavioral autonomy. *Philosophical Transactions of the Royal Society of London, Series B — Biological Sciences, 308,* 67–78.

Dickinson, A. (1986). Re-examination of the role of the instrumental contingency in the sodium-appetite irrelevant incentive effect. *Quarterly Journal of Experimental Psychology, Section B — Comparative and Physiological Psychology, 38,* 161–172.

Dickinson, A. (1994). Instrumental conditioning. In: N. J. Mackintosh (Ed.), *Animal learning and cognition* (pp. 45–79). San Diego: Academic Press.

Dickinson, A., & Balleine, B. (1994). Motivational control of goal-directed action. *Animal Learning and Behavior, 22,* 1–18.

Dickinson, A., Balleine, B., Watt, A., Gonzalez, F., & Boakes, R. A. (1995). Motivational control after extended instrumental training. *Animal Learning and Behavior, 23,* 197–206.

Dickinson, A., & Dawson, G. R. (1987a). Pavlovian processes in the motivational control of instrumental performance. *Quarterly Journal of Experimental Psychology, Section B — Comparative and Physiological Psychology, 39,* 201–213.

Dickinson, A., & Dawson, G. R. (1987b). The role of the instrumental contingency in the motivational control of performance. *Quarterly Journal of Experimental Psychology, Section B — Comparative and Physiological Psychology, 39,* 77–93.

Dickinson, A., Nicholas, D. J., & Adams, C. D. (1983). The effect of the instrumental training contingency on susceptibility to reinforcer devaluation. *Quarterly Journal of Experimental Psychology, Section B — Comparative and Physiological Psychology, 35,* 35–51.

Dickinson, A., Smith, J., & Mirenowicz, J. (2000). Dissociation of Pavlovian and instrumental incentive learning under dopamine antagonists. *Behavioral Neuroscience, 114,* 468–483.

Dickinson, A., Watt, A., & Griffiths, W. J. H. (1992). Free-operant acquisition with delayed reinforcement. *Quarterly Journal of Experimental Psychology, Section B — Comparative and Physiological Psychology, 45*, 241–258.

Dietrich, A., & Allen, J. D. (1998). Functional dissociation of the prefrontal cortex and the hippocampus in timing behavior. *Behavioral Neuroscience, 112*, 1043–1047.

Ernst, M., Zametkin, A. J., Matochik, J. A., Jons, P. H., & Cohen, R. M. (1998). DOPA decarboxylase activity in attention deficit hyperactivity disorder adults. A [fluorine-18] fluorodopa positron emission tomographic study. *Journal of Neuroscience, 18*, 5901–5907.

Estes, W. K. (1948). Discriminative conditioning. II. Effects of a Pavlovian conditioned stimulus upon a subsequently established operant response. *Journal of Experimental Psychology, 38*, 173–177.

Evenden, J. L. (1998). Serotonergic and steroidal influences on impulsive behavior in rats. *Comprehensive Summaries of Uppsala Dissertations from the Faculty of Medicine, 764*.

Evenden, J. L. (1999a). Impulsivity: A discussion of clinical and experimental findings. *Journal of Psychopharmacology, 13*, 180–192.

Evenden, J. L. (1999b). Varieties of impulsivity. *Psychopharmacology, 146*, 348–361.

Evenden, J. L., & Meyerson, B. (1999). The behavior of spontaneously hypertensive and Wistar Kyoto rats under a paced fixed consecutive number schedule of reinforcement. *Pharmacology, Biochemistry and Behavior, 63*, 71–82.

Evenden, J. L., & Ryan, C. N. (1996). The pharmacology of impulsive behavior in rats: The effects of drugs on response choice with varying delays of reinforcement. *Psychopharmacology, 128*, 161–170.

Everitt, B. J., Parkinson, J. A., Olmstead, M. C., Arroyo, M., Robledo, P., & Robbins, T. W. (1999). Associative processes in addiction and reward: The role of amygdala–ventral striatal subsystems. *Annals of the New York Academy of Sciences, 877*, 412–438.

Fallon, J. H., & Loughlin, S. E. (1995). Substantia nigra. In: G. Paxinos (Ed.), *The rat nervous system* (pp. 215–237). London: Academic Press.

Feldman, R. S., Meyer, J. S., & Quenzer, L. F. (1997). *Principles of neuropsychopharmacology.* Sunderland, MA: Sinauer.

Gawin, F. H. (1991). Cocaine addiction: Psychology and neurophysiology. *Science, 251*, 1580–1586.

Gibbon, J., Malapani, C., Dale, C. L., & Gallistel, C. (1997). Toward a neurobiology of temporal cognition: Advances and challenges. *Current Opinion in Neurobiology, 7*, 170–184.

Grace, R. C. (1996). Choice between fixed and variable delays to reinforcement in the adjusting-delay procedure and concurrent chains. *Journal of Experimental Psychology: Animal Behavior Processes, 22*, 362–383.

Grice, G. R. (1948). The relation of secondary reinforcement to delayed reward in visual discrimination learning. *Journal of Experimental Psychology, 38*, 1–16.

Grindley, G. C. (1932). The formation of a simple habit in guinea pigs. *British Journal of Psychology, 23*, 127–147.

Guthrie, E. R. (1935). *The psychology of learning.* New York: Harper.

Hall, J., Parkinson, J. A., Connor, T. M., Dickinson, A., & Everitt, B. J. (2001). Involvement of the central nucleus of the amygdala and nucleus accumbens core in mediating Pavlovian influences on instrumental behavior. *European Journal of Neuroscience, 13*, 1984–1992.

Halliday, G., Harding, A., & Paxinos, G. (1995). Serotonin and tachykinin systems. In: G. Paxinos (Ed.), *The rat nervous system* (pp. 929–974). London: Academic Press.

Heckerman, D. E., Horvitz, E. J., & Nathwani, B. N. (1992). Toward normative expert systems: Part I. The Pathfinder project. *Methods of Information in Medicine, 31*, 90–105.

Herrnstein, R. J. (1961). Relative and absolute strength of responses as a function of frequency of reinforcement. *Journal of the Experimental Analysis of Behavior, 4*, 267–272.

Herrnstein, R. J. (1970). On the law of effect. *Journal of the Experimental Analysis of Behavior, 13,* 243–266.

Heyman, G. M. (1996). Resolving the contradictions of addiction. *Behavioral and Brain Sciences, 19,* 561–610.

Hill, R. T. (1970). Facilitation of conditioned reinforcement as a mechanism of psychomotor stimulation. In: E. Costa, & S. Garattini (Eds), *International symposium on amphetamines and related compounds* (pp. 781–795). New York: Raven Press.

Ho, M. Y., Al-Zahrani, S. S., Velazquez Martinez, D. N., Lopez Cabrera, M., Bradshaw, C. M., & Szabadi, E. (1995). The role of the ascending 5-hydroxytryptaminergic pathways in timing behavior: Further observations with the interval bisection task. *Psychopharmacology, 120,* 213–219.

Ho, M., Mobini, S., Chiang, T., Bradshaw, C. M., & Szabadi, E. (1999). Theory and method in the quantitative analysis of "impulsive choice" behavior: Implications for psychopharmacology. *Psychopharmacology, 146,* 362–372.

Howell, D. C. (1997). *Statistical methods for psychology* (4th ed.). Belmont, CA: Wadsworth.

Hull, C. L. (1932). The goal gradient hypothesis and maze learning. *Psychological Review, 39,* 25–43.

Hull, C. L. (1943). *Principles of behavior.* New York: Appleton-Century-Crofts.

Ito, M. (1985). Choice and amount of reinforcement in rats. *Learning and Motivation, 16,* 95–108.

Ito, R., Dalley, J. W., Howes, S. R., Robbins, T. W., & Everitt, B. J. (2000). Dissociation in conditioned dopamine release in the nucleus accumbens core and shell in response to cocaine cues and during cocaine-seeking behavior in rats. *Journal of Neuroscience, 20,* 7489–7495.

Kacelnik, A. (1997). Normative and descriptive models of decision making: Time discounting and risk sensitivity. *Characterizing human psychological adaptations* (Ciba Foundation Symposium 208), 51–70. Chichester: Wiley.

Kahneman, D., Slovic, P., & Tversky, A. (Eds) (1982). *Judgement under uncertainty: Heuristics and biases.* New York: Cambridge University Press.

Kalivas, P. W., Pierce, R. C., Cornish, J., & Sorg, B. A. (1998). A role for sensitization in craving and relapse in cocaine addiction. *Journal of Psychopharmacology, 12,* 49–53.

Killeen, P. R. (1972). The matching law. *Journal of the Experimental Analysis of Behavior, 17,* 489–495.

Killeen, P. R., & Fetterman, J. G. (1988). A behavioral theory of timing. *Psychological Review, 95,* 274–295.

Koob, G. F. (1992). Dopamine, addiction and reward. *Seminars in the Neurosciences, 4,* 139–148.

Koob, G. F., Sanna, P. P., & Bloom, F. E. (1998). Neuroscience of addiction. *Neuron, 21,* 467–476.

Lattal, K. A. (1987). Considerations in the experimental analysis of reinforcement delay. In: M. L. Commons, J. E. Mazur, J. A. Nevin, & H. Rachlin (Eds), *Quantitative analyses of behavior: V. The effect of delay and of intervening events on reinforcement value* (pp. 107–123). Hillsdale, NJ: Lawrence Erlbaum.

Lattal, K. A., & Gleeson, S. (1990). Response acquisition with delayed reinforcement. *Journal of Experimental Psychology: Animal Behavior Processes, 16,* 27–39.

Linnoila, M., Virkkunen, M., George, T., & Higley, D. (1993). Impulse control disorders. *International Clinical Psychopharmacology, 8*(Suppl. 1), 53–56.

Linnoila, M., Virkkunen, M., Scheinin, M., Nuutila, A., Rimon, R., & Goodwin, F. K. (1983). Low cerebrospinal fluid 5-hydroxyindoleacetic acid concentration differentiates impulsive from non-impulsive violent behavior. *Life Sciences, 33,* 2609–2614.

Lovibond, P. F. (1983). Facilitation of instrumental behavior by a Pavlovian appetitive conditioned stimulus. *Journal of Experimental Psychology: Animal Behavior Processes, 9,* 225–247.

Mackintosh, N. J. (1974). *The psychology of animal learning.* London: Academic Press.

Mazur, J. E. (1987). An adjusting procedure for studying delayed reinforcement. In: M. L. Commons, J. E. Mazur, J. A. Nevin, & H. Rachlin (Eds), *Quantitative analyses of behavior: V. The effect of delay and of intervening events on reinforcement value* (pp. 55–73). Hillsdale, NJ: Lawrence Erlbaum.

Mazur, J. E. (1997). Choice, delay, probability, and conditioned reinforcement. *Animal Learning and Behavior, 25*, 131–147.

Mazur, J. E., Stellar, J. R., & Waraczynski, M. (1987). Self-control choice with electrical stimulation of the brain as a reinforcer. *Behavioral Processes, 15*, 143–153.

Mehlman, P. T., Higley, J. D., Faucher, I. *et al.* (1994). Low CSF 5-HIAA concentrations and severe aggression and impaired impulse control in nonhuman primates. *American Journal of Psychiatry, 151*, 1485–1491.

Mérö, L. (1998). *Moral calculations: Game theory, logic, and human frailty.* New York: Springer-Verlag.

Mishkin, M., Malamut, B., & Bachevalier, J. (1984). Memories and habits: Two neural systems. In: G. Lynch, J. L. McGaugh, & N. M. Weinberger (Eds), *Neurobiology of learning and memory* (pp. 65–77). New York: Guildford Press.

Mitchell, S. H. (1999). Measures of impulsivity in cigarette smokers and non-smokers. *Psychopharmacology, 146*, 455–464.

Mobini, S., Body, S., Ho, M. Y. *et al.* (2002). Effects of lesions of the orbitofrontal cortex on sensitivity to delayed and probabilistic reinforcement. *Psychopharmacology, 160*, 290–298.

Morrissey, G., Ho, M. Y., Wogar, M. A., Bradshaw, C. M., & Szabadi, E. (1994). Effect of lesions of the ascending 5-hydroxytryptaminergic pathways on timing behavior investigated with the fixed-interval peak procedure. *Psychopharmacology, 114*, 463–468.

Morrissey, G., Wogar, M. A., Bradshaw, C. M., & Szabadi, E. (1993). Effect of lesions of the ascending 5-hydroxytryptaminergic pathways on timing behavior investigated with an interval bisection task. *Psychopharmacology, 112*, 80–85.

Mowrer, O. H. (1960). *Learning theory and behavior.* New York: Wiley.

Muir, J. L., Everitt, B. J., & Robbins, T. W. (1996). The cerebral cortex of the rat and visual attentional function: Dissociable effects of mediofrontal, cingulate, anterior dorsolateral, and parietal cortex lesions on a five-choice serial reaction time task. *Cerebral Cortex, 6*, 470–481.

Myerson, J., & Green, L. (1995). Discounting of delayed rewards: Models of individual choice. *Journal of the Experimental Analysis of Behavior, 64*, 263–276.

O'Brien, C. P., Childress, A. R., Ehrman, R., & Robbins, S. J. (1998). Conditioning factors in drug abuse: Can they explain compulsion? *Journal of Psychopharmacology, 12*, 15–22.

Packard, M. G., & McGaugh, J. L. (1996). Inactivation of hippocampus or caudate nucleus with lidocaine differentially affects expression of place and response learning. *Neurobiology of Learning and Memory, 65*, 65–72.

Papa, M., Sagvolden, T., Sergeant, J. A., & Sadile, A. G. (1996). Reduced CaMKII-positive neurones in the accumbens shell of an animal model of attention-deficit hyperactivity disorder. *Neuroreport, 7*, 3017–3020.

Papa, M., Sellitti, S., & Sadile, A. G. (2000). Remodeling of neural networks in the anterior forebrain of an animal model of hyperactivity and attention deficits as monitored by molecular imaging probes. *Neuroscience and Biobehavioral Reviews, 24*, 149–156.

Papa, M., Sergeant, J. A., & Sadile, A. G. (1998). Reduced transduction mechanisms in the anterior accumbal interface of an animal model of attention-deficit hyperactivity disorder. *Behavioral Brain Research, 94*, 187–195.

Parkinson, J. A., Cardinal, R. N., & Everitt, B. J. (2000). Limbic cortical-ventral striatal systems underlying appetitive conditioning. *Progress in Brain Research, 126*, 263–285.

Parkinson, J. A., Robbins, T. W., & Everitt, B. J. (1999). Selective excitotoxic lesions of the nucleus accumbens core and shell differentially affect aversive Pavlovian conditioning to discrete and contextual cues. *Psychobiology, 27*, 256–266.

Parkinson, J. A., Willoughby, P. J., Robbins, T. W., & Everitt, B. J. (2000). Disconnection of the anterior cingulate cortex and nucleus accumbens core impairs Pavlovian approach behavior: Further evidence for limbic cortical–ventral striatopallidal systems. *Behavioral Neuroscience, 114*, 42–63.

Pavlov, I. P. (1927). *Conditioned reflexes*. Oxford: Oxford University Press.

Paxinos, G., & Watson, C. (1998). *The rat brain in stereotaxic coordinates* (4th ed.). Academic Press.

Pinker, S. (1997). *How the mind works*. London: Allen Lane — Penguin Press.

Poulos, C. X., Le, A. D., & Parker, J. L. (1995). Impulsivity predicts individual susceptibility to high levels of alcohol self-administration. *Behavioral Pharmacology, 6*, 810–814.

Poulos, C. X., Parker, J. L., & Le, A. D. (1996). Dexfenfluramine and 8-OH-DPAT modulate impulsivity in a delay-of-reward paradigm: Implications for a correspondence with alcohol consumption. *Behavioral Pharmacology, 7*, 395–399.

Rachlin, H. (1971). On the tautology of the matching law. *Journal of the Experimental Analysis of Behavior, 15*, 249–251.

Rachlin, H., Raineri, A., & Cross, D. (1991). Subjective probability and delay. *Journal of the Experimental Analysis of Behavior, 55*, 233–244.

Revusky, S., & Garcia, J. (1970). Learned associations over long delays. In: G. H. Bower (Ed.), *The psychology of learning and motivation* (Vol. 4, pp. 1–84). New York: Academic Press.

Richards, J. B., Chock, M. A., Carlson, B., de Wit, H., & Seiden, L. (1997). Comparison of two models of impulsive behavior in rats: Effects of amphetamine and haloperidol. *Society for Neuroscience Abstracts, 23*, 2406.

Richards, J. B., Mitchell, S. H., de Wit, H., & Seiden, L. S. (1997). Determination of discount functions in rats with an adjusting-amount procedure. *Journal of the Experimental Analysis of Behavior, 67*, 353–366.

Richards, J. B., Sabol, K. E., & de Wit, H. (1999). Effects of methamphetamine on the adjusting amount procedure, a model of impulsive behavior in rats. *Psychopharmacology, 146*, 432–439.

Richards, J. B., & Seiden, L. S. (1995). Serotonin depletion increases impulsive behavior in rats. *Society for Neuroscience Abstracts, 21*, 1693.

Richardson, N. R., & Gratton, A. (1998). Changes in medial prefrontal cortical dopamine levels associated with response-contingent food reward: An electrochemical study in rat. *Journal of Neuroscience, 18*, 9130–9138.

Robbins, T. W. (1976). Relationship between reward-enhancing and stereotypical effects of psychomotor stimulant drugs. *Nature, 264*, 57–59.

Robbins, T. W. (1978). The acquisition of responding with conditioned reinforcement: Effects of pipradrol, methylphenidate, d-amphetamine, and nomifensine. *Psychopharmacology, 58*, 79–87.

Robbins, T. W., & Everitt, B. J. (1992). Functions of dopamine in the dorsal and ventral striatum. *Seminars in the Neurosciences, 4*, 119–127.

Robbins, T. W., & Everitt, B. J. (1996). Neurobehavioral mechanisms of reward and motivation. *Current Opinion in Neurobiology, 6*, 228–236.

Robbins, T. W., Watson, B. A., Gaskin, M., & Ennis, C. (1983). Contrasting interactions of pipradrol, d-amphetamine, cocaine, cocaine analogues, apomorphine and other drugs with conditioned reinforcement. *Psychopharmacology, 80*, 113–119.

Roberts, S. (1981). Isolation of an internal clock. *Journal of Experimental Psychology: Animal Behavior Processes, 7*, 242–268.

Robinson, T. E., & Berridge, K. C. (1993). The neural basis of drug craving: An incentive-sensitization theory of addiction. *Brain Research Reviews, 18*, 247–291.

Rubia, K., Overmeyer, S., Taylor, E. *et al.* (1999). Hypofrontality in attention deficit hyperactivity disorder during higher-order motor control: A study with functional MRI. *American Journal of Psychiatry, 156*, 891–896.

Russell, V. A. (2000). The nucleus accumbens motor-limbic interface of the spontaneously hypertensive rat as studied in vitro by the superfusion slice technique. *Neuroscience and Biobehavioral Reviews, 24*, 133–136.

Russell, V., Devilliers, A., Sagvolden, T., Lamm, M., & Taljaard, J. (1995). Altered dopaminergic function in the prefrontal cortex, nucleus accumbens and caudate-putamen of an animal model of attention-deficit hyperactivity disorder — the spontaneously hypertensive rat. *Brain Research, 676*, 343–351.

Russell, V., de Villiers, A., Sagvolden, T., Lamm, M., & Taljaard, J. (1998). Differences between electrically-, ritalin- and d-amphetamine-stimulated release of [H-3]dopamine from brain slices suggest impaired vesicular storage of dopamine in an animal model of attention-deficit hyperactivity disorder. *Behavioral Brain Research, 94*, 163–171.

Russell, S. J., & Norvig, P. N. (1995). *Artificial intelligence: A modern approach.* Upper Saddle River, NJ: Prentice-Hall.

Sadile, A. G. (2000). Multiple evidence of a segmental defect in the anterior forebrain of an animal model of hyperactivity and attention deficit. *Neuroscience and Biobehavioral Reviews, 24*, 161–169.

Sagvolden, T. (2000). Behavioral validation of the spontaneously hypertensive rat (SHR) as an animal model of attention-deficit/hyperactivity disorder (AD/HD). *Neuroscience and Biobehavioral Reviews, 24*, 31–39.

Sagvolden, T., Aase, H., Zeiner, P., & Berger, D. (1998). Altered reinforcement mechanisms in attention-deficit/hyperactivity disorder. *Behavioral Brain Research, 94*, 61–71.

Sagvolden, T., Metzger, M. A., Schiorbeck, H. K., Rugland, A. L., Spinnangr, I., & Sagvolden, G. (1992). The spontaneously hypertensive rat (SHR) as an animal model of childhood hyperactivity (ADHD): Changed reactivity to reinforcers and to psychomotor stimulants. *Behavioral and Neural Biology, 58*, 103–112.

Sagvolden, T., Pettersen, M. B., & Larsen, M. C. (1993). Spontaneously hypertensive rats (SHR) as a putative animal model of childhood hyperkinesis: SHR behavior compared to four other rat strains. *Physiology and Behavior, 54*, 1047–1055.

Sagvolden, T., & Sergeant, J. A. (1998). Attention deficit/hyperactivity disorder — from brain dysfunctions to behavior. *Behavioral Brain Research, 94*, 1–10.

Salamone, J. D. (1994). The involvement of nucleus accumbens dopamine in appetitive and aversive motivation. *Behavioral Brain Research, 61*, 117–133.

Salamone, J. D., Cousins, M. S., & Snyder, B. J. (1997). Behavioral functions of nucleus accumbens dopamine: Empirical and conceptual problems with the anhedonia hypothesis. *Neuroscience and Biobehavioral Reviews, 21*, 341–359.

Schultz, W., Apicella, P., Romo, R., & Scarnati, E. (1995). Context-dependent activity in primate striatum reflecting past and future behavioral events. In: J. C. Houk, J. L. Davis, & D. G. Beiser (Eds), *Models of information processing in the basal ganglia* (pp. 11–27). Cambridge, MA/London: MIT Press.

Schultz, W., Apicella, P., Scarnati, E., & Ljungberg, T. (1992). Neuronal activity in monkey ventral striatum related to the expectation of reward. *Journal of Neuroscience, 12*, 4595–4610.

Schultz, W., Tremblay, L., & Hollerman, J. R. (1998). Reward prediction in primate basal ganglia and frontal cortex. *Neuropharmacology, 37*, 421–429.

Schultz, W., Tremblay, W., & Hollerman, J. R. (2000). Reward processing in primate orbitofrontal cortex and basal ganglia. *Cerebral Cortex, 10*, 272–283.

Shizgal, P. (1997). Neural basis of utility estimation. *Current Opinion in Neurobiology, 7*, 198–208.

Solanto, M. V. (1998). Neuropsychopharmacological mechanisms of stimulant drug action in attention-deficit hyperactivity disorder: A review and integration. *Behavioral Brain Research, 94*, 127–152.

Sonuga-Barke, E. J. S., Saxton, T., & Hall, M. (1998). The role of interval underestimation in hyperactive children's failure to suppress responses over time. *Behavioral Brain Research, 94,* 45–50.

Soubrié, P. (1986). Reconciling the role of central serotonin neurons in human and animal behavior. *Behavioral and Brain Sciences, 9,* 319–335.

Spence, K. W. (1956). *Behavior theory and conditioning.* Englewood Cliffs, NJ: Prentice-Hall.

Thorndike, E. L. (1911). *Animal intelligence: Experimental studies.* New York: Macmillan.

Tiffany, S. T., & Drobes, D. J. (1990). Imagery and smoking urges: The manipulation of affective content. *Addictive Behaviors, 15,* 531–539.

Tzschentke, T. M. (2000). The medial prefrontal cortex as a part of the brain reward system. *Amino Acids, 19,* 211–219.

von Neumann, J., & Morgenstern, O. (1947). *Theory of games and economic behavior.* Princeton, NJ: Princeton University Press.

Wade, T. R., de Wit, H., & Richards, J. B. (2000). Effects of dopaminergic drugs on delayed reward as a measure of impulsive behavior in rats. *Psychopharmacology, 150,* 90–101.

White, N. M. (1997). Mnemonic functions of the basal ganglia. *Current Opinion in Neurobiology, 7,* 164–169.

White, K. G., & Pipe, M. E. (1987). Sensitivity to reinforcer duration in a self-control procedure. *Journal of the Experimental Analysis of Behavior, 48,* 235–250.

Williams, B. A. (1991). Marking and bridging vs. conditioned reinforcement. *Animal Learning and Behavior, 19,* 264–269.

Williams, B. A. (1994a). Conditioned reinforcement: Neglected or outmoded explanatory construct? *Psychonomic Bulletin and Review, 1,* 457–475.

Williams, B. A. (1994b). Reinforcement and choice. In: N. J. Mackintosh (Ed.), *Animal learning and cognition* (pp. 81–108). Academic Press.

Williams, B. A., & Dunn, R. (1991). Preference for conditioned reinforcement. *Journal of the Experimental Analysis of Behavior, 55,* 37–46.

Wise, R. A. (1981). Brain dopamine and reward. In: S. J. Cooper (Ed.), *Theory in psychopharmacology* (Vol. 1, pp. 103–122). London: Academic Press.

Wise, R. A. (1982). Neuroleptics and operant behavior: The anhedonia hypothesis. *Behavioral and Brain Sciences, 5,* 39–87.

Wise, R. A. (1985). The anhedonia hypothesis: Mark III. *Behavioral and Brain Sciences, 8,* 178–186.

Wise, R. A. (1994). A brief history of the anhedonia hypothesis. In: C. R. Legg, & D. Booth (Eds), *Appetite: Neural and behavioral bases* (pp. 243–263). New York: Oxford University Press.

Wogar, M. A., Bradshaw, C. M., & Szabadi, E. (1993a). Does the effect of central 5-hydroxytryptamine depletion on timing depend on motivational change? *Psychopharmacology, 112,* 86–92.

Wogar, M. A., Bradshaw, C. M., & Szabadi, E. (1993b). Effect of lesions of the ascending 5-hydroxytryptaminergic pathways on choice between delayed reinforcers. *Psychopharmacology, 111,* 239–243.

Wultz, B., Sagvolden, T., Moser, E. I., & Moser, M. B. (1990). The spontaneously hypertensive rat as an animal model of attention-deficit hyperactivity disorder: Effects of methylphenidate on exploratory behavior. *Behavioral and Neural Biology, 53,* 88–102.

Wyvell, C. L., & Berridge, K. C. (2000). Intra-accumbens amphetamine increases the conditioned incentive salience of sucrose reward: Enhancement of reward "wanting" without enhanced "liking" or response reinforcement. *Journal of Neuroscience, 20,* 8122–8130.

Wyvell, C. L., & Berridge, K. C. (2001). Incentive sensitization by previous amphetamine exposure: Increased cue-triggered "wanting" for sucrose reward. *Journal of Neuroscience, 21,* 7831–7840.

Comments on Cardinal, Robbins, and Everitt

Warren K. Bickel

The paper by Cardinal, Robbins, & Everitt and the work that it summarizes is very impressive and outstanding. I am a student of their research and I learn from it. Thus, my comments must be acknowledged as some fine points of disagreement regarding a body of work that I largely laud and appreciate. Indeed, one of my comments may be appropriately considered using their work as a foil to address a larger issue that is relevant to all of us involved in the behavioural economics of drug dependence.

Modulation vs. Separable Process

A central point of the Cardinal paper is that drug dependence is a complexly determined phenomenon that is composed of multiple, disassociable, interacting processes. I agree! Accepting this point suggests that the task of the scientist involved in this field is to identify these different processes, how they interact and self-reinforce, and assemble them into this complex phenomenon that we refer to as drug dependence. However, key to this task is to distinguish between behavioural processes that modulate another ongoing process and those processes that independently contribute to the manifestation of drug dependence (Bickel & Johnson 2003).

This constitutes a point where I disagree with Cardinal *et al.* In their paper, they describe a study that they recently published (Cardinal *et al.* 2000). In that study, they examine the preference for a large-delayed reward over a smaller-sooner reward at a variety of delays under a variety of conditions. Specifically, they examined the effects of *d*-amphetamine (0.0, 0.3, 1.0, and 1.6 mg/kg) on baseline under conditions when the later larger reward was and was not signaled. Under the non-signaled condition, amphetamine reduced preference for the larger later reinforcer at the 1.0 and 1.6 mg/kg doses and had no effect at the 0.3 mg/kg doses. Under the signaled condition, they found that amphetamine increased preference for the larger later reinforcer at 0.3 mg/kg dose and had no effect at other doses. Examination of the figures associated with the study shows the same functional relationship between delay and selection of the later-larger reward independent of drug or the presence or absence of a signal; namely, that preference for the larger-later reward monotonically decreased as delay increases. In the paper, Cardinal *et al.* state that this these data support the idea "that 'delay discounting' of the efficacy of future rewards is not a unitary process, but rather that the observed phenomenon of discounting arises from several underlying processes of which conditioned reinforcement is one".

Showing that a functional relationship retains its general shape but shifts under a variety of manipulations indicates that various manipulations may modulate an effect, but fails to prove that the functional relationship is composed in part by that other process such as conditioned reinforcement. If conditioned reinforcement as evidenced by the signaled condition was an underlying process that determined delay discounting, then the presence or absence of that event should not merely shift, but rather fundamentally alter that functional relationship. Although delay discounting may be shown to be composed of several other phenomena, it is more likely to be shown at another level of analysis. In my view, shifting a functional relationship while retaining its integrity is not sufficient to make such claims.

Substitution

Cardinal and colleagues discuss the research in the context of the matching law and, indeed, the matching law is a fundamental point of departure for several papers at this conference. What I would like to do is address one assumption of the matching law and its implications for developing an understanding of the drug dependence.

An assumption of the matching law in general and in relation to the field of drug dependence in particular is that drugs of dependence and all pro-social activities (e.g. employment, health, family, and friends) are perfectly substitutable. This raises the larger issue: do reinforcers only act as perfect substitutes? The empirical answer to that question is no. Indeed, what is clearly and empirically established is that substitution is just one of several types of interactions.

These interactions have been fully described in behavioural economics. According to behavioural economics, reinforcers can interact in one of three ways that form a continuum (Bickel *et al.* 1995; Madden 2000). At one end of the continuum, reinforcers can interact as a substitute. For example, as the price of watching a movie in a theatre increases and its consumption decreases, there may be a corresponding increase in consumption of video rentals, even though the price of video rentals remained unchanged. Movies and video rentals are considered substitutes. At the other end of the continuum, reinforcers can interact as complements. For example, as the price of soup increases and its consumption decreases, there may be a corresponding decrease in the consumption of soup crackers, even though their price remains unchanged. Soup and soup crackers are considered complements. In between these two extremes is independence. For example, increases in the price of watching a movie in a theatre has no effect on the consumption of soup crackers. Watching a movie and soup crackers would be considered independent of one another.

Not only does behavioural economics provide a conceptual schema to categorize the interactions among reinforcers; they also provide a metric to measure these interactions. Specifically, this metric is cross-price elasticity. Cross-price elasticity is the proportional change in consumption of a reinforcer whose price remains constant as a function of the proportional change in price of another reinforcer. Positive values of cross-price elasticity are indicative of substitutes, negative values are indicative of complements and values near zero are indicative of independence among reinforcers.

In order to examine the relevance of these concepts to drug reinforcers, we reanalyzed data from 16 studies that employed two reinforcers where at least one was a drug, and under conditions where the price of one reinforcer was held constant and the other was increased (Bickel *et al.* 1995). These studies examined a variety of different drugs (e.g. alcohol, cigarettes, methadone, and PCP) in a variety of species (e.g. humans, monkeys, and rats). We found clear and unmistakable evidence of each type of interaction and evidence for the continuum of interaction. We have also successfully empirically demonstrated the relevance of these concepts for categorizing different types of poly-drug abuse in heroin dependent individuals (Petry & Bickel 1999).

These findings demonstrating different types of reinforcer interactions provide an empirical challenge for the matching law that all reinforcers are substitutes. Moreover, when complements are examined in procedures similar to those typically employed to study the matching law, results will be obtained that appropriately would be considered anti-matching (Hursh 1980).

Recognition of the differing ways that reinforcers can interact suggests that we need to complicate our laboratory procedures so that we are not examining choice among differing amounts of the same reinforcer. This will entail conducting studies that are more challenging and will result in a broader array of data that may, in turn, require our theories to be revised. Complicating our experiments, I believe, will give us greater insights into drug dependence and permit us to better understand the behavioural processes that compose it.

Acknowledgment

These comments were supported by NIDA grants R37 DA06526 and1 R01 DA11692.

References

Bickel, W. K., DeGrandpre, R. J., & Higgins, S. T. (1995). The behavioral economics of concurrent drug reinforcers: A review and reanalysis of drug self-administration research. *Psychopharmacology*, *118*, 250–259.

Bickel, W. K., & Johnson, M. W. (2003). Delay discounting: A fundamental behavioral process in drug dependence. In: G. Lowenstein, D. Read, & R. Baumeister (Eds), *Time and decision: Economic and psychological perspectives on intertemporal choice*. New York, NY: Russell Sage.

Cardinal, R. N., Robbins, T. W., & Everitt, B. J. (2000). The effects of *d*-amphetamine, chlordiazepoxide, alpha-flupenthixol and behavioral manipulations on choice of signalled and unsignalled delayed reinforcement in rats. *Psychopharmacology*, *152*, 362–375.

Hursh, S. R. (1980). Economics concepts for the analysis of behavior. *Journal of the Experimental Analysis of Behavior*, *34*, 219–238.

Madden, G. J. (2000). A behavioral economics primer. In: W. K. Bickel, & R. E. Vuchinich (Eds), *Reframing health behavior change with behavioral economics* (pp. 3–26). New Jersey: Lawrence Erlbaum Associates.

Petry, N. M., & Bickel, W. K. (1999). A behavioral economic analysis of polydrug abuse in heroin addicts. In: F. J. Chaloupka, M. Grossman, W. K. Bickel, & H. Shaffer (Eds), *The economic analysis of substance use and abuse: An integration of economic and behavioral economic research* (pp. 213–238). Chicago, IL: University of Chicago Press.

Reply to Bickel

Rudolf N. Cardinal, Trevor W. Robbins and Barry J. Everitt

We thank Bickel for his kind comments on our article. We agree with him that identifying and characterizing the multiple processes contributing to choice is of fundamental importance to the understanding of disorders of choice such as impulsivity and drug addiction. Bickel makes the important point that one must also consider the interaction between reinforcers, as illustrated by the economic concept of cross-price elasticity, when considering choice involving multiple reinforcers, as is typical of real-world addiction.

Bickel comments on the theoretical implications of our finding that signals acting during a delay to reinforcement (putatively acting as conditioned reinforcers) interact with and alter the effects of psychostimulant drug administration. We commented in our paper that this was a piece of evidence supporting the view that multiple processes contribute to the macroscopic phenomenon of delay discounting — the manner in which preference for a reward declines as it is progressively delayed. Bickel's point is that the presence of a putative conditioned reinforcer in our study (Cardinal *et al.* 2000) altered the effects of a psychostimulant drug on choice involving delayed reinforcement, but did not "fundamentally alter (the) functional relationship" between delay and choice.

It is clear that a subject's tendency to choose a particular delayed reinforcer depends not only upon the delay, but also upon the presence or absence of a signal during that delay (and that, if administered, psychostimulants also affect choice, and can interact with the delay and with any signal present). The delay and the signal both contribute to observable behaviour. Thus, we feel it is accurate to assert that this is an example of observed behaviour — described as discounting — depending upon the effects of at least two processes.

Bickel is quite right to point out that it has not been established that conditioned reinforcement is responsible for part of the effects of the delay itself, and our study did not do so; as delays unmistakably affect choice even when they are unsignalled, the effects of signals present during the delay must be to some degree separable from the effects of the delay itself. Nor has it been clearly established whether signals present during the delay have effects that interact linearly with those of the delay, or interact nonlinearly. (We presume the latter is what Bickel refers to when he speaks of a "fundamental alteration" in the relationship between delay and choice.)

However, we feel that an overemphasis on the idea that "delays" and "cues" are themselves represented by neural processes may be misleading. Instead, they are clearly variables that affect several processes. It has never been proven that the effects of a delay are computed by a single neural process, providing a value that may be combined with other values (of reward magnitude, probability, etc.) to allow the reinforcer with the highest value to be selected in standard utility-theory fashion, as the term "delay discounting" may itself suggest. On the other hand, it has been shown, independently of experiments involving delayed reinforcement, that animals are influenced by several clearly separable processes when working for reinforcement (reviewed by Cardinal *et al.* 2002). These include the instrumental contingency between actions and outcomes, the instrumental incentive value of the reinforcer (most closely analogous to "value" as conceptualized by traditional utility theorists), cue-induced Pavlovian motivational processes, habits, and so forth. Some of these processes have been proven to be affected by delays to reinforcement. For example, delays impair instrumental action–outcome contingency learning (Dickinson *et al.* 1992), and very probably reduce the incentive value of delayed rewards. Therefore, as there is excellent evidence that the selection of non-delayed reinforcers is governed by multiple processes, and delays can affect at least some of these processes, we feel the analysis of choice among delayed reinforcers should take account of these multiple processes from the outset.

References

Cardinal, R. N., Parkinson, J. A., Hall, J., & Everitt, B. J. (2002). Emotion and motivation: The role of the amygdala, ventral striatum, and prefrontal cortex. *Neuroscience and Biobehavioral Reviews, 26*, 321–352.

Cardinal, R. N., Robbins, T. W., & Everitt, B. J. (2000). The effects of *d*-amphetamine, chlordiazepoxide, alpha-flupenthixol and behavioral manipulations on choice of signalled and unsignalled delayed reinforcement in rats. *Psychopharmacology, 152*, 362–375.

Dickinson, A., Watt, A., & Griffiths, W. J. H. (1992). Free-operant acquisition with delayed reinforcement. *Quarterly Journal of Experimental Psychology, Section B — Comparative and Physiological Psychology, 45*, 241–258.

Chapter 8

Reason and Addiction

Olav Gjelsvik

Introduction

Some addicts are unwilling addicts. They seem to engage in voluntary, self-destructive addictive behaviour they do not want (in a sense that needs specification) to engage in. There might even be a history of failed, desperate attempts at quitting and great despair.

This paper aims to focus on the unwillingness of unwilling addicts. Since they are unwilling, that seems an important starting point for therapy in these cases. Therapy in the case of a willing addict will be different. An important aspect of this starting point is that unwilling addicts seem to have good reason to be unwilling. In this sense their unwillingness seems to be an expression of their rationality. My basic claim in this paper is that, in order to account for this potential aspect of addiction in humans, we seem to need a richer notion of normativity and rationality than that provided by the explanatory notions of rationality employed by decision theorists. I shall end this paper by giving an outline of a richer and more substantive normative framework in which one might delineate addiction. I believe we can do this while preserving the explanatory insights of decision theoretic approaches to addiction. I concentrate on norms about the discounting of future well-being, and on issues around irrational desires and motivational states. I also argue that the explanatory decision theoretic approaches base themselves on auxiliary hypotheses about rationality, and these hypotheses need independent testing.

Addiction is extremely complex. I shall start with an overview of some aspects of this complexity, and then give deeper illustrations of just two points. In the second part of the paper, I discuss Becker/Murphy's and Ainslie's approaches to addiction. In the third part, I outline my own framework for thinking about reason and addiction. I stress that this will be a framework, not a theory.

The Complexity of Addiction

One aspect is the many different approaches to what is thought of as one phenomenon. Addiction is approached both from brain biology, employing a neurophysiological language, and from decision science, employing an intentional and normative language, and conceptions of rationality. There are many puzzles about the relationship between these approaches, ranging from issues around the age-old mind-body problem, issues around weak will, and issues around the relationship between the various special sciences.

Another aspect is this: the intentional and normative language of belief and desire is always an employment of conceptions of rationality, and this brings with it a whole range of issues about reason, rationality, and choice. Among these issues is whether or to what extent addictive behaviour can be seen as compatible with choice. In the neighbourhood of this issue there are other issues which relate to philosophical topics. Is the addict's freedom of will impaired in some way or other by the loss of control which seems to characterize the addicted state? Is the responsibility of the addict impaired with regard to her continued consumption? Remember that intentional agency is not sufficient for responsibility; many intentional agents are not responsible, even if they have the ability to choose. Consider a three-year-old child — obviously a chooser, but not a responsible agent in anything but a causal sense.

A yet further complication is the fact that addiction has several characteristic stages or phases; among them are: becoming addicted; being addicted; trying to quit (and, sometimes, succeeding); and relapse. It seems entirely reasonable to demand that an adequate theory of addiction should be able to handle all these possible stages, and get the relationships between them rightly understood. Becoming addicted is a process, and we need a theory which explains why it occurs, and why sometimes it is not completed. Being addicted is a state, and one needs both to characterize this state, and relate this characterization to ways into it and out of it. (This need is basic even if there is just a gradual change from not being addicted to being addicted.) Trying to quit does not always occur, just as the process of becoming addicted is not always completed. Still, attempts at quitting occur, more frequently for some addictions than for others, and we need to understand how their occurrence is possible, and understand what happens when they succeed or fail. (Thomas Schelling has given us wonderful examples of addicts who voluntarily submit themselves to extortion to escape their own addiction. (See Schelling (1984), essays 4 and 5, and Schelling (1999a, b).) It is also a clear characteristic that all ex-addicts are prone to relapse, and this tendency should be accounted for. An approach to addiction which is in conflict with the fact that relapse often occurs cannot be an adequate approach to addiction.

Things are made even more complicated by the need to address anew the relationship between biology, decision science and contested rationality issues for each of the significant possible stages in addiction. And when we address the relationship between biology and decision science for each of these stages, we might do that in many different ways. One important way is to ask whether and to what extent there is important causal knowledge we would miss by sticking to, for instance, the biological perspective and a neurophysiological description of the processes. This way of asking stresses the fundamental importance of causal knowledge for explanation: the point of explanation is to provide causal knowledge. Our question asks whether there is causal knowledge to be had in addition to the knowledge provided by the biological approach. Such knowledge would, of course, be of great relevance for therapy. If there is no such knowledge to be had, a decision theoretic approach to addiction would be of no significance.

Illustration of First Complexity: Becoming Addicted

When becoming addicted there is a gradual change in the reward system in the brain. We might, for simplicity, think of it as a change in the mesolimbic system, a change which has different characteristics for different chemical addictions, but which also has a common element in the change in the potential for dopamine uptake in nucleus accumbens. This process can be described in detail relative to intake of the chemical substance in question, and relative to this intake the change can be well explained by brain biology. (For details, see Gardner 1999; Gardner & David 1999; Goldstein 1994; Rolls 1999, especially Chapter 6.)

An interesting question is the contrastive question of why the intake continues rather than stops, or perhaps, why the consumption of the substance(s) in question continues and increases. Causal knowledge of why the intake continues can, or so it seems, be captured by different descriptions; one at the level of a biological understanding of the reward system of the brain, and another at the level of choice: the beliefs and desires of the agent. Is one level better than the other, and to be preferred? It might also be, however, that the explanation of why the intake continues is not the same as the explanation of why the consumption continues. This is because the intake might continue even if there is no question of choice, and pure compulsion. The consumption of the substance, we might say, continues only as long as this is the better choice among the relevant alternatives. In the case of pure compulsion this framework of relevant alternatives no longer makes sense, while the biological perspective makes perfect sense; these alternatives and how they are balanced have no role in the biological explanation of the continuation of the intake. When we rightly rule out such compulsion, and see the behaviour as the result of choice, this approach must be grounded in facts about the agent.

The decision approaches therefore share something: they aim to capture special and interesting types of causal stories, and thereby provide causal knowledge the biological approach cannot provide. Decision approaches open up for social input. They open for intentionally characterized input in general. Imagine a consumer who is facing a choice about consuming an addictive substance. She believes there are some good and some bad consequences from consumption, but is not sure about how bad, and is about to consume. At this moment she is presented with newly-won knowledge to the effect that this addictive substance has some very bad effects. This new knowledge would make a difference for our imagined consumer. The new knowledge would change the way she evaluates the alternatives, and in many cases consumption would stop. Then it would make a behavioural difference. In those cases the stopping would be a causal result of being fed the new knowledge. This is an intentional causal path — a causal story. Knowledge of this causal story is not available to biology, but may be very important for us.

We can also easily imagine a different case where this consumer is already quite hooked when she receives this same new information. There are scenarios where she tries but is unable to quit, but still generates an overwhelming desire to quit, and is frustrated and angry with herself for being unable to quit. This addict would be trapped — we might in plain language say that reason cannot control her behaviour; her behaviour is controlled by some force which she might think of as alien to herself. We now have two different scenarios where this new knowledge makes a causal difference: the first case where the result is a difference in behavioural output, the other case where the result is a difference in attitudes towards her own continued consumption. Both these possible causal roles of this knowledge are situated in intentional descriptions.

It is natural to think that some biologically describable fact is relevant and does indeed contribute in its particular way to the explanation of why the causal role of this knowledge is different in the two cases. That is very important. Still, we can have perfectly valid intentional causal knowledge without knowing that biological fact, and our use of our intentional causal knowledge will in many ways be independent of even potential knowledge of that biological fact. It is also perfectly possible that the causal role of this new knowledge is different for two addicts with exactly the same changes in their mesolimbic system.

Illustration of the Second Complexity: Basic Issues in Rationality and Time-Discounting

If one were to address the issue, concerning the case above, of whether the choice of continued consumption is a rational choice, one would need to engage in the issue of what rational choice is. There are very different conceptions of what it is to be irrational, or "against reason," within philosophy. We have, among other things, to inquire into the source of reasons for acting some way or desiring something. Reasons for caring and acting might either be seen as provided by desires (i.e. by motivational states) or by facts about what is good or worth achieving. We might call these approaches the desire-based and the value-based approaches to reasons for acting. These are very different ways of looking at reasons, and they both run through the history of philosophy.

A desire-based view on reasons is either plain or ideal. The plain view says that we have a reason to do something just in case it might fulfill one of our present desires. In the ideal view the point is that we would have such a reason-giving desire if we knew all the facts and went through an ideal process of deliberation. Still, the basic fact about a desire-based view is that reasons are provided by motivational facts. This model can be called voluntaristic.

A value-based view holds that reasons are provided by the facts, and not by how we happen to be motivated. Motivational facts are not themselves reason-giving, but are instead seen as our (more or less rational) responses to what reasons the facts provide. The fact that we have a certain desire may, of course, indirectly give us a reason to satisfy that desire, but that is only because of the fact that the satisfaction of the desire gives us pleasure or well-being. If, however, the desire in question gives us no such fulfillment, then we have no (normative) reason to satisfy that desire. A value-based approach to reason would think of actions towards the satisfaction of such a desire as irrational, even if we were strongly motivated to satisfy it. Such motivation is irrational.

Decision-science/economics is, of course, completely dominated by a desire-based or voluntaristic approach to reasons. Recently this science, dominated by rational choice explanations, has extended its possible explananda. In order to explain more types of behaviour, traditional conceptions of rationality are being replaced by thinner, less normative and, in one sense, more subjective conceptions of rationality. The case of consistency-requirements, through time and at a point in time, is an interesting example. In the past, economics tended to see all discounting of future well-being as irrational. Recently, many have seen such discounting as rational as long as there were no dynamic inconsistencies. Some writers have moved towards allowing dynamic inconsistencies to be rational, as long as there is consistency at each point in time. But if one's approach to reason is entirely desire-based, there is a real question about why one should stop here; people are as a matter of fact not consistent at each moment in time, and there is a question about the source for the (rational?) demand for consistency. (For an excellent overview of this development see Frederick *et al.* 2002).

In philosophy there is, I would say, the opposite development to that of decision science; there is a reaction against the consequences of a desire-based approach to reason, and a reaction against collapsing the normative notion of rationality into a purely explanatory notion. The value-based view on reason is becoming more widespread, especially as advocated by T. M. Scanlon at Harvard or John Broome and Derek Parfit in Oxford (see, e.g. Broome 1999; Parfit 1997: 98–130; Scanlon 1987, 1998).

Broome's and Parfit's conceptions of rationality are thick, substantive, normative, and make objectivity claims. It should be noted that explanation of behaviour can be exactly similar on such a value-based view as on a desire-based view, since behaviour is explained by how we are in fact motivated, by our motivating reasons, not by what reasons we have. (We must not identify the reasons there are with the motivating reasons.) We may, however, know that we have reason to be motivated differently from the way we are motivated. On the value-based approach, the motivations which explain behaviour will themselves be divided naturally into rational and irrational motivations.

This very distinction between a value-based and a desire-based approach to reason can be observed in the case of discounting of value in time. Here we must tread carefully for another reason as well. In standard economic theory, one discounts the value of future goods, i.e. a future table may be worth less than a present identical table. Such discounting is just right for the fertile economies we live in. (John Broome discusses in great detail the relationship between discounting of goods and discounting of well-being in his "Discounting the future" [Broome 1992, 1999].) Another question concerns the discounting of future well-being. We should pay less now for a future wine-bottle in a fertile economy than for a present wine-bottle, but the well-being or enjoyment we get out of consuming one such wine-bottle should perhaps not be discounted. Discounting of the value of future goods and discounting of the value of future well-being therefore work differently. Philosophers are routinely concerned with the latter, and economists are routinely concerned with the former. Classical economists have been much concerned with the relationship between these issues (see Lowenstein 1992).

The mechanism that characterizes many decision-based approaches to addiction is precisely a discounting of future value. This discounting must be discounting of the value of future well-being, not the discounting of the value of future goods. For the rest of this paper, discounting is discounting of future well-being. On Parfit's view on rationality, it is irrational to discount future well-being, and if such discounting is a necessary characteristic of a decision-science account of addiction, then someone cannot become addicted by successive rational choices. Scanlon has a more moderate view on irrationality, and a less substantive view on rationality, and holds that as long as a person evaluatively believes her present discounting of future well-being to be right, we should not call such a discounter irrational. On Scanlon's view a person could become addicted by choices which (in this appropriate sense) are rational. And it is indeed natural to think that it is not irrational to act on present desires even if those desires are based on false beliefs; desires are rational when they are the right responses to what we believe (including evaluative beliefs).

We see that we here encounter a deep difference which turns on what desires ought to be subjected to rationality considerations, on whether desires in many areas are rational when they are the right responses to either what is good or to what is believed to be good. The standard economic approach is to treat desires just like tastes. In particular: is heavy discounting of the future just like a strong preference for vanilla ice cream, and just another preference? Jon Elster raises this question, and his answer is in a way "yes." He says: "If we want to explain behaviour on the assumption that people make the most out of what they have, the idea is exactly right" (Elster 1999a, b: 146). Elster's argument states explicitly that it is the explanation of behaviour we need the notion of rationality for. If that is so, then there are no rationality issues beyond the motivational and explanatory issues, even if there might be issues of reason and reasonableness beyond the explanatory issues. Against this I suggest a wider notion of rationality, connected with the notion of reason, but possibly with Scanlon's modification in place; one is not irrational in one's motivations when these are endorsed by one's evaluative beliefs.

If we take that (moderate) line, there need be no disagreement with Elster about how potential addicts are motivated, and therefore no disagreement about how we explain the development of an addiction: People maximize utility as they subjectively see things at each moment of choice, and make the most of it relative to how they are motivated. The remaining question is why we should think that the motivating and/or explanatory reasons in this case are rational. If the agent believes that strong discounting is wrong, but still discounts strongly, then there seems to be something irrational in the motivational states of this agent, even if the agent maximizes utility relative to all motivating reasons at each moment of choice. If, on the other hand, the agent believes that she ought to discount to the exact degree that she does discount, there is no internal conflict, and no subjective irrationality. Scanlon (and I) would then say that the agent is not irrational. Still, the agent might hold a false or unreasonable evaluative belief about discounting. Really extreme discounting, no concern for the future at all, nevertheless appears irrational to most of us.

In any case, a preference for discounting future well-being seems different from a preference for vanilla or strawberry ice cream, and we normally do not even hold evaluative beliefs about the rightness or wrongness of the latter. And if presented with some visually and otherwise extremely attractive strawberry ice cream, it would not be irrational to change to preferring strawberry ice cream. However, Elster writes, about the temporal case: "I am inclined to say, nevertheless, that any viscerally induced and behaviourally manifested disregard for the future is a sign of irrationality, regardless of the exact mechanism by which the effect is produced" (Elster 1999a, b: 147). My challenge to Elster would be for him to spell out the following: How can discounting of the future both be a taste not subjected to rationality considerations, while it is also the case that a viscerally induced change in time preferences is irrational? (Viscerally induced changes in a taste are not irrational!) Elster also needs to explain why only a viscerally produced change towards disregarding the future is irrational, while the opposite viscerally produced change towards disregarding the present is not.

It seems to me that he cannot have it both ways, and that his (to my mind) correct view on the change of time preference has to be backed by a view different from his on the general issue of the rationality of time-discounting. I believe a different view here would imply that motivational facts do not determine the rationality of time-preference, but that things are the other way around; facts about the good or our evaluational judgement determine the rationality of motivations for options at different temporal locations. Then we move towards Parfit's view. I have earlier argued that only a modest discounting of future value is compatible with exhibiting the type of rational self-governance that is required for responsibility (see Gjelsvik 1999a, b). That partially explains why we should not treat children or mentally handicapped people as morally and legally responsible, and that fact is fully recognized in the legal systems of most countries.

Two Theories of Addiction

I have stated above that minimally, an intentionally-based theory of addiction must somehow capture the ambiguity of the unwilling addicts who consume the addictive substance but hate the fact that they do so. Such a theory must, it seems to me, provide a way in which the unwillingness to consume is the voice of reason in the conflict with the desire to consume. Only if that is so can we rationally regret our earlier choices, rationally direct anger towards ourselves, etc. That is typically what we do, and typically what, for instance, a smoker who is unsuccessfully trying to quit experiences. Of course, this requirement may be contested in various ways, but to me it seems quite clear that we need to get this ambiguity of the addict right in order to fully justify the value of an intentional approach to addiction. This type of ambiguity is not fully represented in the biological approach, but that is as it should be, that is part of what provides a need for something in addition to a biological approach.

I now want to turn to some major examples of rational choice approaches to addiction in order to see whether they can be seen as opening up properly for a satisfactory representation of this ambiguity and the unwillingness of the unwilling addict — a recognizable and well-known character in real life, ripe for various types of therapies and treatments. I shall look at two such theories, Becker's & Murphy's (1988), and Ainslie's (1992a, b). I apologize for not giving a more complete survey at this point; it seems to me, at least, that these two approaches are very interesting, that a discussion of them has great value even if there are other approaches, and that a complete overview will get out of hand.

"Rational" Addiction — Becker and Murphy

Let me first turn to Becker & Murphy's (1988) theory of rational addiction. I do this not because I think they give a full view of the state of addicts, but because they present a plausible structure for a part of an addict's beliefs and desires when in the addicted state. Remember also that I believe we ought to move towards Parfit's view on rationality. Beliefs about the rightness and wrongness of discounting could be a possible source of ambiguity, a source not recognized in Becker's and Murphy's paper.

Becker & Murphy's theory, simply put, is this. (My presentation of the Becker/Murphy view is much indebted to Ole-Jørgen Skog's [1999a] discussion of it.)

Consider a consumer good G with two basic properties:

(a) The higher the consumption of G is in the past, the smaller the welfare (value/utility) which can be obtained from the consumption of a given number of units in the present. (This can been thought of as tolerance, but can perhaps also be seen as delayed harmful effects of past consumption.)

(b) The higher the consumption of G is in the past, the larger the gain by consuming one more unit in the present. (The mechanism can be thought of as relief from withdrawal symptoms, or perhaps related to the fact that as a result of sensitization towards a drug one seems to want it more.)

Consider facing a choice about consuming a good with these properties. The combination of properties is such that a rational consumer of the good G faces a dilemma about how to weigh the short-term effects of consuming the good against the long-term effects of consuming the good. Simply put, present high consumption will lead to future high consumption with a lower over-all welfare level. One has to weigh this future negative effect against the present benefits. How much one discounts value over time will determine one's consumption level. If one does not discount future value very much, one might settle for no or a modest consumption, whereas if one discounts future value substantially, the balance will tip in favour of high consumption.

Becker & Murphy (1988) exhibit an addict as a "rational" consumer of a good G with these properties. When an addict, the person finds herself in a state of high consumption of G and with a considerably lower overall welfare level than she would have had in a state of low consumption of G. One point to note here is that the fact that addictive substances have these ascribed properties needs full and detailed backing and support from the biological level. It is, however, quite plausible that there is some such support. There is, in fact, a basic need for all decision-theoretically-based theories of addiction to represent the well-being or utility-related properties of the addictive substance in a way that can be fully backed and explained by the biological knowledge we have available. Becker & Murphy here seems to have got something right both in methodology and as a matter of fact: The representation of the properties of the addictive substance is there and seems reasonable for the time being.

Addiction of the type of an unwilling or trapped addict, however, cannot come about if all choices are made with full information about all future consequences of one's choices, and with a stable exponential discount factor. Becker & Murphy suggest in a footnote that the discount factor might vary; perhaps one cares less about the future during a period, for example, in which one is depressed. Ole-Jørgen Skog (1999a) has treated this possibility very instructively. By allowing for variations in the exponential discount factor, we can say: there are scenarios where this basic model entails that a consumer who discounts the future a lot will start consuming G, and consume permanently at a very high level, in spite of a reduction in the longer run in the overall welfare level. The cause of the continued high consumption is the rise in marginal utility of G, given the high past consumption. This is a willing addict, who cares little about the future, for whom it is rational to start consuming a lot, even with perfect foresight of the effects. There is an intermediate level of discounting of future value where a rational consumer with perfect foresight will not start to consume G in large quantities. Even if he will not start such consumption from scratch, he will not stop consuming at a high level if the past consumption level is high enough. These people, if attuned to high consumption, are "unwillingly" big consumers when they discount future value less. They realise that they are worse off than they would have been had they not started high consumption. They would have chosen to consume only small quantities if they had started out with the discount factor they now have. Rational consumers who discount future value fairly little will not start to consume much of G. People who discount future value very little might also be able to reduce a high level of consumption if they find themselves there, as long as the long-term reduction in welfare matters more to them than the short-term gain (for instance, in relief from withdrawal symptoms).

One group of interest in this theory of addiction is the intermediate group, the group of consumers who will not start high consumption, but who are unable to reduce consumption if they have consumed much in the recent past. A further increase in the discount-factor might lead to drastic reductions in consumption. Such an increase would in fact free one from the addiction. I repeat that a rational agent who discounts less than those of this intermediate group, and also those of this intermediate group with perfect foresight and a stable discount rate, cannot be trapped in the envisaged way.

The vital explanatory factor here is therefore the addict's actual discount factor (in conjunction with the properties of the addictive substance). The crucial explanatory factor has to be different at different times if we are to have any chance of accounting for unwilling addicts. (The auxiliary hypotheses about variable discount-factors would, of course, need independent empirical backing.)

Now, the question I want to discuss is the question of whether the "entrapped" Becker-type addict could really, rationally try to quit and fail during a period with a stable discount factor and, relatedly, the issue of the sense in which the Becker addict is unwilling. The answer to the question of whether such a Becker addict could rationally try to quit and fail seems to be no. If such an addict were to try to quit (rationally try), the discount-factor must have increased to the point where it is rational not to consume. If the discount-factor stays at that level, quitting would not only be rational, it would be easy. Such an account of quitting goes against much of what we know about trying to quit. The theory would then fail because it cannot account for the stages of addiction, in this case the third stage.

Simultaneously we (at least I) hold the view that trying to quit is often the rational thing to do. It is hard but rational. (Note the conflict with the purely explanatory notion of rationality when I put it like that.) The Becker picture captures none of this.

This Becker-type addict is able to judge that (relative to his present discount factor) he would have been better off today if he had a different past from the one he has. But his past choices were always rational relative to the tastes he had then. Assume that there are no rationality consideration about tastes. If that is so, this person has no reason for regretting anything. Can this judgement that she would have been better off had she had different tastes in the past really result in a deeply felt desire to quit? Since the preferences are given, it is clear that this cannot result in a change of preferences or different action. It therefore cannot result in rational regret, rational anger at oneself, etc. Of course, there may be irrational regrets, but that is not the interesting issue; they are not the voice of reason. As long as we assume this person to be rational, the evaluational judgement can therefore at most result in a wish or a fancy to the effect that she were a different person with a different past from the one she has, since then she would enjoy her present tastes better. Wishes of that kind come cheap. A desire to quit which leads to actual attempts at quitting is something very different from a desire that we never started. The unwillingness of the strongly unwilling addict does sometimes lead to attempts at quitting, attempts which might be desperate. This is what seems to be given.

On the present assumptions, Becker & Murphy's addict did nothing in her past she needs to regret; all her choices were rational by the standards she had when she made them. Orphanides & Zervos (1995) describe rational choice under uncertainty as a way into addiction. However, in that case there is also nothing to regret (even if they claim otherwise), since all choices are rational choices under uncertainty when made. The regret they describe is (at best) irrational regret. We all know that we do not choose our preferences, that preferences might be partly determined by our past choices, and that we might, when we learn new things, wish our preferences to be different from what they are even when they are the result of rational choices. The presence of such a wish is not what we are looking for to ground the unwillingness of an unwilling addict. We need minimally an unwillingness which is manifested in a desire to quit which sometimes leads to rational action and attempts towards quitting. I claim we need more than that: we need a rationally-based unwillingness to continue the addictive consumption which is there even when we do continue, and related rational regrets and sometimes self-directed rational anger.

My conclusion is therefore that the Becker-type theory will not do. It has nevertheless taught us all a lesson about representing the utility-related properties of an addictive substance, and all workers in this area should pay attention to the need for representing also biological findings in the decision-theoretic framework. But this rational addict is very far from the addicts we meet, and Becker and Murphy have to introduce externally caused changes in the discount factor in order to get anything remotely like the unwillingness of the unwilling addict. This might seem ad hoc in itself. Still, the unwillingness they can get in does not amount to much, and not to what we want. The ambiguity they get in is strictly related to the ambiguity caused by externally caused changes in the discount factor.

Hyperbolic Discounting of Value and Addiction — Ainslie

George Ainslie's work on addiction uses hyperbolic discounting of value as the basic explanatory mechanism. Our state of nature, according to Ainslie (1992a, b), is to fail to have consistent preferences through time. The latter is the exception rather than the rule. Still, at the end of the day, a human adult seems to control her or his impulsiveness. The former exception is now the rule. We need an account of how this comes about when the basic picture is that dynamic inconsistencies make up the state of nature. Achieving consistency, or achieving it in the right type of way, we can see as achieving willpower, i.e. the ability to resist temptations. This may not be all there is to willpower, but it is part of it.

This provides a very interesting picture of the way into an addiction, and one great thing it does is to bring ambiguity and temporary preference into the heart of the explanatory structure. (This can, however, also be done in different ways — see, for instance, O'Donoghue & Rabin 1999.) There are, however two problems here at the very start. One has recently been pointed out with great force by Ole-Jørgen Skog in discussions in Oslo and also in his paper at this conference (see Chapter 5), and that is that Ainslie's theory seems to presuppose an externally-given temporal structure for occasions of consumption choice. On the whole, that is not how it is in addiction — it is very much up to us to determine this temporal structure.

Ainslie's elegant treatment of the problem of going to bed at 11 at night vs. staying up for two more hours and be exhausted the next day is very convincing, and so is his treatment of being offered an addictive substance at a particular time every day. But this is not how it normally is. If there is no externally-given temporal structure for the decision problems in addiction, the situation we face is much more messy. Another problem is raised by Michael Bratman's (1995) criticism of Ainslie's account of the rationality of bundling/bunching of choices. In respect for this, I shall not assume that bunching is rational.

Let us push these problems aside for the moment and focus on another — the lesson from Becker. Theories of addiction within the hyperbolic framework need, in my judgement, to account for the change which occurs when one enters the state of being addicted. It is natural and plausible to see, as Becker does, the continued consumption of the addictive drug as bringing about changes in one's perception of utilities, and herein might lie a clue for how to represent this important change. The change into being addicted must be directly related to the utility-related properties of the addictive substances, and these properties need to be given a basis in the biological story.

There are ways of dealing with these theoretical needs, and I have suggested one way in an earlier paper (Gjelsvik 1999a, b). My approach then involved representing the addictive substance in the decision-theoretic framework as having properties roughly similar to those it has on Becker's view. For simplicity, that discussion introduces a finite time-perspective and a finite number of occasions of consumption the subject actually takes into consideration, and ignores issues about backward induction. Everything else remains the same as in Ainslie's discussion. As the past contains more and more drinking, and we then add up the sums of discounted future consumption (in my example there were 30 such occasions), we soon reach a point where the preference *Never Drink > Always Drink* is no longer stable, even if it is when we start our drinking behaviour. ("Never Drink" is the summed discounted value of never drinking on these 30 occasions, while "Always Drink" is summed discounted value of always drinking on the next 30 occasions.) At this point in time (when the preference is no longer stable), the preference is still there most of the time, but for a brief period of time, namely at the time of consumption choice, there is the preference *Always Drink > Never Drink*. This period is much briefer than the period when *Drink* is preferred to *Abstain*. ("Drink" is the discounted value of drinking on the coming occasion, while "Abstain" is the corresponding value of abstaining on the coming occasion.) Still, this change in the representation of bundled choice, which occurs as a result of past consumption, implies that, with the new perception of the utilities, bunching/bundling of choices (not raising the issue of whether bunching is rational or not) will not in itself be sufficient to overcome the temptation. In this case, one needs to employ additional precommitment techniques to succeed in resisting the temptation at the point in time when consumption would be rational if one did not employ these additional techniques. The thought then is that this is the point when one enters the state of being addicted. (For a thorough discussion of important aspects of such changes in the perception of utilities, see Skog 1999b.)

To represent the change that occurs when the potential addict has become addicted in this way has various advantages. It is well suited as a representation of why abstaining now (in the addicted state) is much more difficult than it used to be when there was little drinking in the past; it also makes the explanation of relapse much easier.

The question that is my focus, however, is whether we have the right sort of basis for seeing an unwilling addict as unwilling. At each moment of choice the Ainsliean agent chooses what he sees as best at that moment. I assume also that the agent is rational in the sense that, if there is a known precommitment technique which it is rational to use at a moment in time, then using that technique will be chosen at that moment in time.

The person knows that he in fact lives out the strategy *Always Drink* even if she most of the time prefers *Never Drink*, and she might wish that that was indeed different. Still, by assumption, the person does what is rational by her own standards at each moment of choice. If the person could reflectively establish a way in which the interest *Never Drink* was the favoured expression of herself or of her rational self, then there would be a sense in which the rational self was frustrated when the person realizes the strategy *Always Drink*. But as long as discounting is just a taste, and any taste is just as rational as any other, such a strategy seems unavailable. As long as the person makes the most out of each choice, why should there be such a thing as regret or shame? Would not regret then be an irrational reaction we should just fight and get rid of?

Note that the Ainsliean hyperbolic framework might explain well the situation of an addict described by Schelling — an addict who by rational choice subjected herself to extortion to escape the addiction (see again Schelling 1999a, b). I am, I remind you, assuming that the addict we are considering is a rational addict who would go for such an option if it were available. An addict who goes for all precommitments there are that are not too expensive has no reason for rationally regretting anything, and no real reason, no rational ground, for being frustrated in her addiction. Self-blame would be appropriate if there were available options, and she failed to pursue them. On these assumptions we make, there is no reason for regretting the addictive behaviour there is, and there is no reason for being an unwilling addict. If there is a desire to quit which persists after repeated failures at quitting, this desire is not expressive of one's rationality or reason — one has in fact done what one could to make the best out of things. Yet apparently rational regrets and rational self-directed anger seem to flourish among the unwilling addicts I know, and this reminds me of myself when I tried to quit smoking.

My conclusion is that the hyperbolic discounting approach to addiction succeeds greatly on some points where the Becker account fails, namely in giving a central place for motivational ambiguity, and in accounting for attempts at quitting. Still, there seems to be something missing. What I find missing in the approach is a general reason for regretting the addiction. One might try to locate such a reason in the general preference for *Never Drink* over *Always Drink*. If the price we have to pay to account for the state of being addicted is that we let such a general preference be changed into a preference we have most of the time and not all the time, and no longer at the moment of choice, then that resource for a grounding of the general desire to quit is no longer available in a strong or clean form. In the end this may not really matter all that much, however. As long as each choice is a fully rational choice by the standards set by the approach, there is no such good reason for regretting the addiction anyway. Similarly, a person in a prisoner's dilemma has no reason for regretting pursuing the rational choice, even if another outcome is better for oneself and indeed for both players. These better choices are simply not available for rational beings, that is determined by the pay-off structure, and the wish for them is nothing but a wish for the world to be a different place from the place it is.

The general preference for *Never Drink* over *Always Drink*, therefore, cannot supply what we seem to need — a rational basis for being genuinely dissatisfied with ourselves. The ambiguity generated by the hyperbolic form of the discounting does great things in explaining what we do, but will not do for this.

The challenge was to find some other way of accounting for the state of being addicted which was compatible with a general view of the addict as a potential unwilling addict, in a way in which the unwillingness could be rational, based on something like rational regret, and where the frustrated desire to quit could be seen as expressive of reason and rationality even when frustrated. I conclude that neither of the two theories we have looked at is able to provide that fully, even if they have great strengths.

A Different Approach

This is our situation: Becker & Murphy's theory had one important feature, and that was the way it represented the utility-related properties of addictive substances and activities. This representation was a reasonable match with much biological knowledge, and must be interpreted as causal consequences for future well-being of continued consumption of the substance or of continuation of the activity. Ainslie's approach had the great virtue of bringing motivational ambiguity into the heart of the approach, and Ainslie has done us all a great service in showing how far one can go towards a general theory of human motivation from this starting point, where his theory of bunching of choices, or personal rules, is fascinating, even if it is contested whether bunching can be seen as rational from game-theoretic considerations. Ainslie's approach should, however, try to integrate Becker's good point above in his hyperbolic approach (as is done by O'Donoghue & Rabin 1999).

I claim these two theoretical approaches cannot account for the unwillingness of the unwilling addict. I also claim that it is important for all intentionalist approaches to addiction to capture this in order to make contact with starting points for therapy. Notice how the first point relates to the slimming or thinning of the normative concept of reason or rationality these theorists undertake when they: (a) see the rational as accounted for by the motivational — with what explains intentional behaviour —; and (b) then move away from standard normative conceptions of rationality in order to get more and more realistic about how people as a matter of fact are motivated. I claim we can perfectly well explain intentional behaviour in their (Becker's or Ainslie's) decision-theoretic framework without thinking of their respective representations of choice as exhaustive of what we think of as reason and rationality. I claim that there is a lot more to reason than actual motivation at a time. I have for instance claimed in an earlier paper that the normally developed human being in our society is responsive to norms which both rule out temporary preference (dynamic inconsistencies) and heavy discounting of value in the case of future well-being, even if our responsiveness may fall short of what it ought to be (see Gjelsvik 1999a, b). I tend to think of the status of these rules or axioms as somewhat like the status of consistency norms as they are given in von Neumann & Morgenstern's axiomatization of the norms of rational choice (see Neumann & Morgenstern 1944). Furthermore, I claim, while there are reasons for discounting the value of future goods, there are no reasons for discounting the value of future well-being. Alternatively, we could also think of the norms about discounting of well-being as norms with a normative role parallel to that of norms constraining risk-seeking or risk-aversion. When attitudes to risk become extreme, they also become normatively open to criticism.

I now want to outline an alternative framework for thinking about addiction, where my value-based conception of reason is put to work. This will come in two parts. The first part deals with failures to live by norms we accept as right and binding in general. Breaking such norms is in that case irrational. The second addresses the need for looking at the rationality of desire in order to get an account of the unwillingness of the unwilling addict, and to make connections with therapy.

Breaking Norms and Irrationality

There are systematic tendencies of the human mind to break logical norms, norms about statistical reasoning, etc. An overview of some of this (especially the case of statistical reasoning) was given some time ago by Nisbett & Ross (1980) (or, e.g. Stich 1990).) The case of logic is, for instance, discussed by Stich (1990), Johnson-Laird (1983) and among many others. We all assert acceptance of the logical norms in question when asked about them, still we break them, and there are systematic tendencies in our ways of breaking the logical laws. These difficulties on our part should not and do not, at least not as I see things, influence our conception of logical validity in the least. We can conceptualize these tendencies as our having difficulties with special types of salience; we are systematically prone to go for what is salient in certain situations rather than for what is logically right and valid. There might be evolutionary explanations of such tendencies, but even so they should not in any way at all influence what we hold as normatively right.

Discounting the value of future well-being can naturally be thought of as just an instance of a similar thing: Temporal closeness is a type of salience, and we have a tendency to go for what is salient and relatively speaking overvalue that, which is just the same thing as discounting the value of what is not salient. As a result we get at least some form of exponential discounting of future well-being. But salience might explain preference reversals as well. When asked whether we prefer $100 in a year or $150 in two years, neither option is really salient, and our answer may be determined by the norms we accept about discounting of future value. If, however, we are asked about $100 *now* or $150 in a year, then the $100 *is* very salient, and we go for that option. Taken in conjunction with the result above, this can be thought of as a temporal change of preference. We can, however, conceptualize this change in different ways. We can think of it as confirming that we are hyperbolic discounters. We can also think that this shows that we at bottom exponential discounters are also very prone to be over-influenced by striking salience — here as in many other parallel contexts. O'Donoghue & Rabin's (1999) representation of temporal change of preference (based on work by Laibson and others) seems to me to fit extremely well with this latter way of looking at it (Laibson 1994).

Note how the latter interpretation of temporal inconsistency sees the influence of salience as influence upon us to break norms we actually accept, just as we often break norms about logical or statistical reasoning we accept. Ainslie's view on temporal inconsistency is different; he does not see it as irrational as such, but rather like the human condition. If we stick to the former interpretation of temporal inconsistencies, we can see hyperbolic discounting as a tool we can use to describe irrational tendencies in us, tendencies which explain preference-shift behaviour. The fact that they explain intentional behaviour should not, however, lead us to identify rationality with them; similar tendencies explain behaviour in which we systematically make logical and statistical errors.

Very many of Ainslie's insights can be preserved within the framework which I am now suggesting, the framework that sees the conceptual terrain as at bottom quite different from the way he sees this terrain. The conceptual terrain is, I suggest, that we rational human beings exhibit strong trends towards irrationalities in all our internalizations of norms we accept as correct. Furthermore I hold that developing responsiveness towards these true and correct norms, towards reason, is very much a matter of mastering and conquering the irrational influences of salience. In the case of acquiring motivational rationality, we typically fall short of realizing in behaviour the norms and values we accept and embrace theoretically if presented with them. This is only to be expected, it is in fact more naturally to be expected in the case of motivational norms than in any other part of rationality.

This conceptual approach can therefore employ hyperbolic discounting as an explanatory tool to explain irrational intentional behaviour, a pragmatically employed tool that at bottom is a reflection of our bias towards the salient option. This does mean that we do not see hyperbolic discounting as a neutral taste; it is in itself subject to considerations about acceptability or correctness. If there is little discounting or little temporal inconsistency, we can see the case as normal, as almost rational. People will themselves express the norms they accept when asked about choices where no option is salient, and they may then embrace norms which rule their own temporary preference change or heavy discounting as wrong. Since they have this (albeit limited) responsiveness towards these right or true norms, they have a rational basis for being genuinely dissatisfied with themselves when they discount and are moved by what is salient. In the addicted state, when they are addicted to a substance with the Becker-type properties, we see that their norms normally would imply that they should stop consuming this substance in order to be rational — the consequences for well-being of consuming these substances are precisely such that someone who did not discount future well-being at all would not be rationally moved to consume them. We have then, in these cases, a rational basis for these addicts' unwillingness.

I share Ainslie's commitment to temporary preference as an enormously important explanatory tool, even if I suggest that we conceptualize it differently from the way he does. Most of his explanatory insights can carry over to my position. One such feature concerns personal rules or bunching/bundling of choices. My approach, which sees no discounting of future well-being as the normatively right, has no difficulty in seeing the adoption of a personal rule as a tool to promote the interest of the correct norms. It is a tool for reducing the power of salience, and it is rational to adopt such strategies (if you can) as long as salience has power over you, and the norms you accept need help to win through in practice. Of course, there is much fragility here, and great motivational difficulties in installing such a tool; the actual preference structure, induced by salience, makes it the best rule to consume now and abstain later. People who have a less than normally solid internalization of the norms against discounting of well-being may often try to live by personal rules in order to avoid giving in to salience. Since personal rules will be more fragile than a strong internalization of norms against discounting (because personal rules base themselves on the pay-off structures induced by salience, but try to include many pay-offs instead of just one, and the best is exception now, then follow the rule), people who rely heavily on personal rules will be more disposed to develop addictions than people with strong norms against discounting. But some people with weak norms against discounting may not even employ personal rules, and they will be even more at risk for addiction than similar people who employ personal rules. Ainsliean insights can be preserved in my different conceptual framework.

Since we think of the conceptual structure as that of salience invading our norm-informed and norm-run behaviour, and hyperbolic discounting as a pragmatically available tool to explain behaviour, then the extent to which we have the relevant decision-situation (i.e. face an externally given temporal structure) will also determine the usefulness of this tool. If there is no externally given temporal structure to speak of in the central cases of addiction, then that is not a theoretical problem for me, but the practical problem that the tool I am using is not easily applicable. I may have, however, access to other tools that do not depend on external temporal structures. Situational cues are typically both salient and powerful. We might therefore still be perfectly able to explain the behaviour which is of exactly this sort — giving in to salience — even if the explanations might typically be more easily available after the fact (the act), since the ability to predict might be much reduced if we have no knowledge of contexts and the occurrence of salient cues. We do, however, often know things about contexts and situational cues. That is a great help in those cases. Whether we do know such things does not matter conceptually, as long as there is no conceptual connection between prediction and explanation anyway, and explanation is much more important for us than prediction.

There is another side to this, and that is that the enormous importance of cues through all stages of addiction, but especially the latter stages (quitting and relapse). Unexpected exposure to various things raises the salience of options, something which can justly be seen as craving. Giving in to such craving when you know or believe you should not because of the future possible consequences of doing so can, on my approach, be directly represented in the conceptual structure as an instance of salience-induced preference reversal. (Your precommitment technique repertoire is weakened since you quit some time ago. I discuss this in Gjelsvik 1999a, b.) I think it is important that approaches to addiction put cues and cravings at center stage, and somehow give them a direct role in our explanatory theorizing — that seems to me to be what biologists are telling us. As long as we employ the intentional vocabulary, the sensitivity to perceived context is vitally important, and such insight should be preserved. The advantage for intentional causal understanding, i.e. a full intentional understanding of the unwilling addict, far outweighs any losses. The repercussions for therapy seem rich and rewarding.

My aim in this section has so far been to provide a general framework which allows us, and also some of the addicts, to see the motivations which explain and cause addictive behaviour as irrational. I achieve this by moving the notion of rationality away from behaviour and its explanation and situating rationality in a richer context. In particular, I have introduced norms about discounting, the acceptance of which would make much behaviour wrong or irrational. I have also stressed the general theoretical need for taking biological knowledge seriously, and the need for representing the utility-related properties of addictive substances in ways which do biological knowledge justice. At the same time I have introduced a value-based view of reason, a much thicker or fatter notion of normativity which as a result introduces rationality issues around the rationality of the desires that explain behaviour, including motivational attitudes towards discounting. Such norms allow seeing discounting of the value of future well-being as irrational, and hyperbolic discounting as irrational. I believe this irrationality of the motivations that determine our addictive behaviour can be seen (even if only dimly seen) by addicts themselves, and that this might be part of what grounds the intuition that the unwillingness of the unwilling addict expresses the voice of reason. I have also suggested that tendencies towards discounting of the value of future well-being (or utility, but not future goods) should be seen as an instance of a failure to fully master salience.

Irrational Desires for Addictive Substances

There might be reasons for going even further here, and employing the resources of a value-based approach to reason in assessing our desires themselves. One biopsychological, neuro-based approach to addictive craving by Robinson & Berridge (1993) suggests that the craving developed by addicts can be characterized as extremely strong "wantings," which are such that satisfaction of these "wantings" is associated with very little pleasure or "liking"; the latter can be (almost) zero. I have not pursued this approach since, to my knowledge, it is not (yet) a widely accepted view. If it were, it might have interesting implications. In particular, it might have the implication that the desires that lead to and explain addictive behaviour are desires that, according to a value-based approach to reason, we have no good reason to fulfill. We only have reason to satisfy a desire when that satisfaction brings something of worth with it — be it pleasure, well-being or whatever. If there is nothing of worth in fulfilling a desire, then that desire is an irrational desire. This can be known by a person with such a desire, and such a person can see the irrationality of being motivated by this same desire. My value-based approach to reason sees the desire-based view as depending for its plausibility on the general feature that we normally desire what is worth desiring. Since that is normally so, most of our desires are normally rational. The case of Robinson and Berridge's view is interesting for me because it brings out the point that a desire for an addictive substance is not in any way worth fulfilling — there is only wanting, and no liking. If the drug addiction itself creates desires rightly describable as irrational, and internally seen as irrational by the addict, that would turn things around. The unwillingness of the unwilling addict might have another and completely different rational basis here.

One way of looking at the utility-related properties of addictive substances in Becker's representation is indeed that consumption of these substances lead to a mismatch between how much one wants to consume the substance and what one gets out of consuming it. If rational desires are the desires worth fulfilling, we might say that consumption of addictive substances leads to the development of more and more irrational desires for consuming the substance. A precondition for knowingly consuming such substances at all, with the properties given to them by Becker, is precisely that one is subject to another unreasonableness or potential irrationality, namely the irrationality of discounting of future value we exhibit when we go against our evaluative beliefs about discounting. If we see things like this, then addiction is a state where our behaviour is not irrationally caused (by the mechanism of discounting), but caused by desires that are themselves irrational. We can put it like this: an irrational meta-preference (discounting of future well-being) makes it possible to be moved by these irrational desires. This perspective on the interplay of irrationalities is only made available by the value-based approach to reason.

At this point, it might be useful to remind ourselves of the criteria for substance dependence listed by the American Psychiatric Association (see, e.g.: 181). There are seven criteria, and a person is said to be dependent when she satisfies three of these within a 12-month period. The two first criteria are tolerance and withdrawal. Criterion 3 invokes the notion of intention, and states that the substance is often taken in larger amounts than intended. The fourth criterion is a persistent desire to cut down, the fifth that one spends too much time and effort to obtain the substance, the sixth that important social or recreational activities are given up or reduced, and the seventh that substance use is continued despite knowledge of having a problem that is likely to be caused or exacerbated by the substance.

My point in bringing in these criteria is, of course, that so many of them are normative criteria where the normativity seems given by a value-based approach to reason. "Knowledge of a problem" is straightforwardly normative by the notion of a problem. The statement that "important social or recreational activities are given up" is at bottom a straightforwardly normative statement about the relative value of those activities for a good human life. That too much time is spent to obtain the substance is really the same type of normative statement. The psychiatric criteria are therefore couched in an intentional language, and also in a normative view on how much time it is worth spending obtaining such a substance, how much social or recreational activities it is worth giving up in a human life and so on. The normative view expressed by the diagnostic criteria is precisely the normative view that the fulfillment of the desire for the addictive substance in question is in no way worth the cost of obtaining this substance. This can be true in different ways: by the fact that one spends too much time and effort obtaining the substance, by the fact that one gives up activities important for human life, etc. At bottom these psychiatric diagnoses are given in a value-based normative frame. A human being who is not motivated by desires worth fulfilling is not just mentally ill, this human being is also most likely suffering from a biological change in the mesolimbic system and in nucleus accumbens. The normative point has priority, though, for seeing this as a psychiatric disorder.

There are further issues here than the need for a thick normative conception to make the right connection with therapy. I also believe that my approach makes immediate contact with many other issues in the neighbourhood of addiction, in particular issues about responsibility for one's addictive behaviour. Responsibility requires normative insights and responsivness to substantive norms that cannot be captured by the thin rational choice conception of rationality. If it could, we could just as well ascribe responsibility to children. The normative equipment required for responsibility is much more substantive than that of availability of simple rational choice explanations. It involves the absence of the irrationalities characteristic of addiction.

Conclusion

As a conclusion I think this is important: The fundamental choice in addiction theory is between studying addiction from a strictly biological point of view and studying addiction within an intentional framework. There are many concerns here, and there is always a question about the usefulness of bringing in the intentional framework. I think the latter question should be seen as involving the question about whether to bring in a thick or thin intentional framework. This is because I think we should aim wider than just explaining addictive behaviour; we should try to understand addiction itself, and to do that we need a wide intentional human context in which we see things on the basis of our biological knowledge. It is the thicker and normative intentional framework which provides a coherent unity to the phenomenon of addiction, a unity that exists through all the stages of addiction, and it does that in such a way that connections with other issues, for instance the important connections with therapy and also legal issues, can be raised in a meaningful way. This framework we can and should adopt without losing any explanatory insights, and indeed this framework gives us the possibility of gaining new explanatory insights; we can, perhaps, explain the self-directed negative reactions of addicts. With this thicker framework in place, we see the need for independent empirical studies of all auxiliary hypotheses about the intentional factors whose presence are vital in intentional explanations of addiction, in particular empirical studies of what evaluative beliefs people hold about how they ought to be motivated and how those beliefs relate to how they in fact are motivated. Such studies can learn a lot from existing research into people's views about how we ought to reason in logic and statistics, in contrast to how we, as a matter of fact, do reason. The methodological issues are challenging and fascinating, and range far beyond the decision sciences.

Acknowledgments

In my thinking about addiction I am much indebted to Jon Elster's addiction group, in particular to Jon Elster, Ole-Jørgen Skog and George Ainslie. Without Jon Elster I would not have done any work in this field at all, at least nothing like the present work. This paper has also received penetrating written comments from Ole-Jørgen Skog, and a wonderful discussion by George Ainslie at the meeting in Birmingham. I thank all three. I am also very grateful to Rudy Vuchinich and Nick Heather for organizing the event in Birmingham; without their initiative and stimulating encouragement I would never have got around to writing this paper.

References

Ainslie, G. (1992a). *Picoeconomics*. Cambridge.
Ainslie, G. (1992b). Hyberbolic discounting (with Nick Haslam). In: G. Loewenstein, & J. Elster (Eds), *Choice over time*. Russell Sage Foundation.
Becker, G. S., & Murphy, K. M. (1988). A theory of rational addiction. *Journal of Political Economy*, *96*, 675–700.
Bratman, M. (1995). Planning and temptation. In: May, Friedman, & Clarke (Eds), *Minds and morals* (pp. 293–310). Cambridge: Bradford Books, MIT Press.
Broome (1999). *Ethics out of economics*. Oxford: Oxford University Press.
Elster, J. (Ed.) (1999a). *Addiction, entries and exits*. Russell Sage.
Elster, J. (1999b). *Strong feelings*. Cambridge: Bradford Books, MIT Press.

Frederick, S., Loewenstein, G., & O'Donoghue, T. (2002). Time discounting and time preference: A critical review. *Journal of Economic Literature, XL*(June), 401–531.

Gardner, E. L. (1999). The neurobiology and genetics of addiction: Implications of the "reward deficiency syndrome" for theraputic strategies in chemical dependency. In: J. Elster (Ed.), *Addiction, entries and exits* (pp. 57–119). New York: Russell Sage.

Gardner, E. L., & David, J. (1999). The neurobiology of chemical addiction. In: J. Elster, & O.-J. Skog (Eds), *Getting hooked* (pp. 93–136). Cambridge: Cambridge University Press.

Gjelsvik, O. (1999a). Freedom and the will and addiction. In: J. Elster (Ed.), *Addiction, entries and exits* (pp. 29–54). New York: Russell Sage.

Gjelsvik, O. (1999b). Addiction, weakness of will, and relapse. In: J. Elster, & O.-J. Skog (Eds), *Getting hooked.* Cambridge: Cambridge University Press.

Goldstein, A. (1994). *Addiction.* New York: Freeman.

Johnson-Laird, P. (1983). *Mental models.* Cambrdige, MA: Harvard University Press.

Laibson, D. (1994). *Essays in hyberbolic discounting.* Ph.D. Dissertation, MIT.

Lowenstein, G. (1992). The fall and rise of psychological explanations in the economics of intertemporal choice. In: G. Loewenstein, & J. Elster (Eds), *Choice over time* (pp. 3–34). New York: Russell Sage.

Nisbett, R., & Ross, L. (1980). *Human inference: Strategies and shortcomings of social judgement.* Englewood Cliffs, NJ: Prentice-Hall.

Neumannn, J. von, & Morgenstern, O. (1944). *Theory of games and economic behavior* (2nd ed.). Princeton: Princeton University Press.

O'Donoghue, T., & Rabin, M. (1999). Addiction and self-control. In: J. Elster (Ed.), *Addiction* (pp. 169–206). New York: Russell Sage.

Orphanides, A., & Zervos, D. (1995). Rational addiction with learning and regret. *Journal of Political Economy, 103*, 739–758.

Parfit, D. (1997). Reason and motivation. *Proceedings of the Aristotelian Society* (Supplementary Volume), 98–130.

Robinson, T. E., & Berridge, K. (1993). The neural basis of drug-craving: And incentive-sensitization theory of addiction. *Brain Research Reviews, 18*, 247–291.

Rolls, E. T. (1999). *The brain and emotion.* Oxford: Oxford University Press.

Scanlon, T. (1987). The significance of choice. Tanner lectures on human values, held in Brasenose College, Oxford 1986, published in *Tanner Lectures on Human Values, 8.* Cambridge: Cambridge University Press.

Scanlon, T. (1998). *What we owe to each other.* Cambridge, MA: Harvard University Press.

Schelling, T. (1999a). *Choice and Consequence.* Cambridge, MA: Harvard University Press.

Schelling, T. (1999b). Epilogue: Rationally coping with lapses from rationality. In: J. Elster, & O.-J. Skog (Eds), *Getting hooked.* Cambridge: Cambridge University Press.

Skog, O.-J. (1999a). Rationality, irrationality, and addiction — notes on Becker & Murphy's theory of addiction. In: J. Elster, & O.-J. Skog (Eds), *Getting hooked.* Cambridge: Cambridge University Press.

Skog, O.-J. (1999b). Hyperbolic discounting, willpower and addiction. In: J. Elster (Ed.), *Addiction, entries and exits* (pp. 151–168). New York: Russell Sage.

Stich, S. (1990). *The fragmentation of reason.* Cambridge, MA: MIT Press.

Comments on Gjelsvik

George Ainslie

I'm glad to have a philosopher at the conference, Olav Gjelsvik especially. We've worked together for many years at Jon Elster's conferences. I think of myself as a philosopher. The point of my work with motivation has been to get back to what I regard as basic philosophical questions about the nature of higher mental processes. I couldn't agree more that we "need a richer notion of rationality than that provided by the explanatory notions of rationality employed by decision theorists." Rationality is like a Chinese puzzle, easy to fit together except for a single remaining piece, but maddeningly difficult to solve completely. Professor Gjelsvik has an excellent understanding of the flaws in current theories, including mine as I have presented it. He has shown clearly that you can't describe an unwilling addict with the exponential curves used by Becker & Murphy (1988). He has asked me tough questions as well. I hope I've answered a couple of them. I think his objections are based on my not having explained my work well enough in earlier presentations.

One objection is that, without an externally given temporal structure, hyperbolic discount curves are limited in what they can explain: many impulses are continuously at hand and not given at certain time by the environment. I hope I have shown that by adopting the strategy of bundling choices into categories people convert what is essentially a temporal binding-yourself-as-you-sail-past-the-Sirens type of process to a simultaneous judging-whether-this-case-fits-a-rule. An impulse then prevails, not because of the proximity of an external lure, but because you have found an excuse or a rationalization. Thus, the temporal objection shouldn't tell against the hyperbolic explanation for impulses, but this may not have been clear in earlier presentations.

Secondly, the repeated prisoner's dilemma as originally formulated can't describe intertemporal bargaining because later selves can't retaliate against earlier ones, as shown by Bratman (1987, 1995a, b, 1998) in the works Gjelsvik cites. However, I think the demonstration of the modified prisoner's dilemma that we just enacted here shows how there can be a rational intertemporal form.[1] A person deciding whether to choose the dime for everyone vs. the dollar for herself alone is not doing anything irrational as she estimates what her behavior is apt to do to the choices of the remaining players.

Gjelsvik raises two larger questions about which I'd like to make the rest of my comments. These involve the possible inadequacies of a marketplace-based model of rationality. One is that there may be a need for some kind of ego that stands outside of the marketplace and only sometimes consults it:

> A value-based view [as opposed to a desire-based or marketplace view]
> holds that reasons are provided [by] the facts, and not by how we happen to

be motivated. Motivational facts are not themselves reason giving, but are instead seen as our (more or less) rational responses to what reasons the facts provide. The fact that we have a certain desire may, of course, indirectly give us a reason to satisfy that desire, but that is only because the satisfaction of the desire gives us pleasure or well-being.

This reservation about relying upon a marketplace model of choice is shared by much of cognitive psychology. However, it ignores the need for a common dimension along which the reasons provided by facts must compete for being selected — a dimension that could be called rewardingness. Many philosophers from the time of Spinoza have said that value comes from emotional experience — that reason ultimately serves the passions. I argue that what Gjelsvik is calling value-based facts are really experiences seen at a distance, where some of the heat of the moment is taken out of them, and not a separate kind of motive altogether.

This is not to dismiss his objection. It is hard to describe a satisfactory interface between what we take as our human, subtle, internally fed-back motives and the gross machinery of reward. Howard Rachlin said earlier that the self could be modeled by a block of wood floating in a stream; but in order to get a fully workable marketplace model you've got to equip the block of wood with some kind of response capability, and this capability can't use extra force. The model that the ego has larger forces around it and is steering among them is familiar — a canoe steering through rapids, for instance — but that model still invokes a separate kind of force, the small but autonomous strength of the canoeist. What we need to do for a really integrated theory, one that does without the separate ego standing outside of the marketplace, is to derive the logic of the canoeist or the block of wood from the properties of the rushing water itself, in some way transforming this physical inanimate force into the kind of subtlety that we experience as our own will in decision making. That is a tough challenge, but I think it's doable. I'm not going to attempt it here, but I'm glad that Gjelsvik has pointed out the problem (see Ainslie 2001: 129–134).

Secondly, Gjelsvik raises the problem that perhaps some impulses are not from temporal discounting, but from what he's calling salience. Salience might include things that are overvalued because they're close, but also things that are overvalued for other reasons. The two main suggestions about such salience in the recent literature are the findings of Kahneman and his collaborators, who look for areas where we have illusions about causality (e.g. Kahneman & Tversky 1984) and the "visceral reward" that Loewenstein (1999) writes about which seems sometimes to override intention. The Kahneman illusions are simply mistakes; if people in this kind of situation are told the actual properties of their tasks they will often change their choices. In cases where they don't change they seem to be getting additional value that was not counted in the analysis of their behavior. Gamblers, for instance, may know that the odds are against them, but gambling has a value in providing surprise and thus combatting premature satiation, as I argued yesterday (see Chapter 1, this volume).

But beyond the cognitive illusion objection, there is Loewenstein's visceral reward, an objection that is more robust. There really does seem to be a kind of experience that is positively fed back once it starts, and I've written about this as the mechanism of emotion control — potentially a committing tactic but also a possible source of temporary preferences (Ainslie 2001: 77–78). The question is whether it can explain

Conditioned Appetite

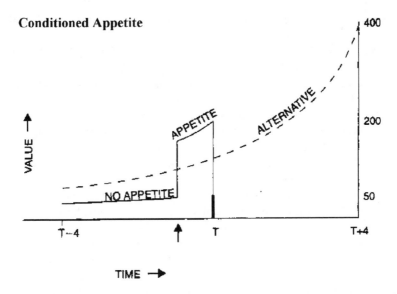

Figure 1: In the conditioning — or salience — model of appetite a conditioned cue at the upward arrow raises the value of an earlier reward at time T from the shorter bar (in bold) to the taller bar. Its exponential discount curve is thus moved above that for the later-larger reward. But without amnesia for the cue and reward, a predictable sequence of appetite followed by reward should develop a curve from the higher bar all the way back, leading, "rationally," to consistent preference for the smaller reward on the basis of its earlier occurrence.

temporary preferences on a basis other than the hyperbolic discounting of the rewards it entails.

Picture the standard amount-vs.-delay situation (Figure 1) — a dessert at time T, say, made salient by the appearance of the dessert cart at the upward arrow. The rewards of abstaining are summarized as a point reward at $T + 4$. You generate a "conditioned" appetite at the arrow, which makes the (exponentially) discounted value of the dessert rise above that of abstaining. This would seem to be a change of preference, without resorting to hyperbolic curves. The problem is that if the sequence of appetite and dessert is predictable, the discount curve should come to be based on this from the beginning, and, if exponential, should *always* stay above the curve from abstention. This would describe rational behavior, even rational addiction. But not unwilling addiction.

However, Loewenstein says that you can't really learn the value of a visceral reward in such a way that you can take it into account before your appetite is aroused. He cites accounts of subjects dealing mostly with aversive experiences, who are unable to report remembering the painfulness of painful experiences. The trouble is that there are many other examples of people remembering such experiences quite well. Animals are very efficient at it (Herrnstein 1969); people, and I suppose animals, sometimes become hypermnemonic, so that the awfulness of experience is not only present but grows larger than it was. Memory for visceral experiences is quite variable. You can't rest an entire theory on the fact that people sometimes cannot remember the emotional quality of an urge.

I would try to solve this problem by making two additional assumptions. The first is that emotions themselves, including appetites, are behaviors. This requires somewhat more explanation than I've got time for right now, but I argue in my books and in an article about Lowenstein's (1999) paper (Ainslie 1992: 39–48; 1999) that conditioning itself is not a robust explanation for the kind of phenomenon we call conditioned. Conditioning is a way of shaping a certain kind of motivated behavior. This behavior is experienced as a different kind from voluntary behavior because it occurs too rapidly or too indistinctly to be tested by personal rules — the lack that can sometimes be corrected by biofeedback (Basmajian 1989); but it is reward-dependent.

The second assumption, based on anecdotal experience, is that we do not always have direct sensory information about our potential appetites, but must try out whether "that would taste good" or "I'd be likely to panic" by what used to be called vicarious trial and error. We imagine the activity and assess our emotional reaction to it. But trying it out also starts the process of having the appetite, which is rewarding in its own right. In Figure 2, a person at time *T*-4 prefers abstention and might be well be advised to avoid trying out her appetite; but she might get away with entertaining some appetite and inhibiting it before it drives the value of the dessert too high. People tend to play this hit-and-run game with

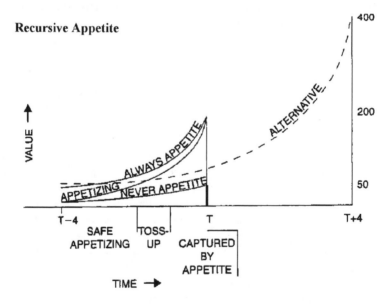

Figure 2: Assuming that discount curves are hyperbolic and appetite is shaped by reward like any other behavior, generating appetite ("appetizing") will increase reward but may cause a shift in preference to the smaller-earlier reward. An individual at *T* − 4 might thus be motivated to inhibit her appetite, but might also try to get some additional reward by appetizing and stopping before the point of preference change — a risky behavior from the viewpoint of her long range interest.

appetites, trying to enjoy them without getting to the point where their curves cross and they get captured by the impulse they are playing with. Sometimes they win and sometimes they lose. If they *never* lose — if they always resist the temptation — the cue stops being an occasion for appetite, ironically spoiling the game.

There's some experimental work by Roger Meyer who had actual heroin addicts taking heroin in the program out at the University of Connecticut. He showed that even though the addicts were in the same environment all the time, they would only get craving on the days when the heroin was available. In other words, the appetite seemed to actually be preparation for consuming the reward. If you never consume the reward, the appetite doesn't come. In a way, it's like having a pet. In a multiple model of self as a population of reward-dependent processes, pets are a good example. If you always feed a pet at a certain time, he will stop begging for food at other times. If you once feed him some other time you have great difficulty getting him to stop begging at that time again. Trying is cheap, but getting fed is a great reward, so the pet — or appetite — does it a lot. If you never take a dessert from the cart, I would be fairly sure that the cart stops occasioning your appetite. I would argue that you have to be susceptible to the idea that you might get the dessert from the dessert cart in order for the appetite to beg for dessert when it appears.

Audience Question: If You Never Ate, You'll Never Get Hungry? Is That What You're Saying?

At least to some extent that's true. There is an early twentieth century study of a group of starving people who reported that when they had lost hope of getting food they lost their subjective hunger (Carlson 1916). Of course, they still had drive. If food had appeared they'd have gotten hungry fast, but in the absence of the prospect of food and the extinction of the possible cues for food, they stopped generating hunger. So yes, that happens, but you have to be very consistent in never gratifying a desire before you stop the craving. This is more evidence that emotion and appetite are ultimately reward-dependent behavior and not a reflex activity.

The point of this somewhat sketchy argument is that hyperbolic discounting should be able to account for the full range of addictive phenomena. By the same token, I think the salience model is not up to the job. Salience as Gjelsvik presents it is an amalgam of the cognitive error theory — honoring desire over values, and consequently developing a "taste" for discounting the future steeply — and visceral reward theory — having our fancy captured by a situational cue, much as Loewenstein describes. The concept suffers from the same limitations as these components: value divorced from desire has no selective principle accessible to further study, but represents an irreduceable *elan vital* with no constraints. Just look at the problems raised by the uncoerced choice of a taste for discounting: were it not for discounting, the distant future would be as valuable as the present, and a child could enjoy Christmas all year as if it were tomorrow. Who wouldn't decide to do this? Of all things, discounting has to be a factor that's imposed on us, not something we can pick by a cognition. Regarding the second component, insofar as preference-reversing visceral arousal does not depend on proximity, it depends on conditioning-cum-amnesia, a dubious mechanism as I have just argued.

Irrationality is a particularly complex form of Chinese puzzle, with the additional complication that we may not know for sure when we have solved it. If we do ever know, it will be because Professor Gjelsvik and a few like-minded analysts have bored deep enough to ask the tough questions that are needed to reveal hidden assumptions. I'm grateful to him once more for this service.

Note

1. In an earlier discussion session the audience participated in an imaginary game show: I announced that I would go along every row, starting at the front, and give each member of the audience a chance to say "cooperate" or "defect." Each time someone said "cooperate" I awarded a (imaginary) dime to her and to everyone else in the audience. Each time someone said "defect" I awarded a dollar (also imaginary) only to her. I asked that they play this game solely to maximize their individual total income, without worrying about friendship, politeness, the common good, etc. I said that I would stop at an unpredictable point after at least twenty players had played, at which time each member could collect her earnings. After some play I discussed how, like successive motivational states within a person, each successive player had a direct interest in the behavior of each subsequent player; and she had to guess their future choices somewhat by noticing the choices already made. Realizing that her move would be the most salient of these choices right after she had made it, she had an incentive to forego a sure dollar, but only if she thought that this choice was be both necessary and sufficient to make later players do likewise.

References

Ainslie, G. (1992). *Picoeconomics: The strategic interaction of successive motivational states within the person.* Cambridge, UK: Cambridge University Press.

Ainslie, G. (1999). The intuitive explanation of passionate mistakes, and why its not adequate. In: J. Elster (Ed.), *Addiction: Entries and exits* (pp. 209–238). New York: Sage.

Ainslie, G. (2001). *Breakdown of will.* New York: Cambridge University Press.

Basmajian, J. V. (1989). *Biofeedback: Principles and practice for clinicians* (3rd ed.). Baltimore: Williams & Wilkins.

Becker, G. S., & Murphy, K. M. (1988). A theory of rational addiction. *Journal of Political Economy, 96,* 675–700.

Bratman, M. (1987). *Intentions, plans and practical reason.* Cambridge, MA: Harvard University Press.

Bratman, M. (1995a). Planning and temptation. In: May, Friedman, & Clarke (Eds), *Minds and morals* (pp. 293–310). Cambridge: Bradford Books, MIT Press.

Bratman, M. (1995b). Reflection, planning and temporally extended agency. *The Philosophical Review, 109,* 35–61.

Bratman, M. (1998). *Two faces of intention.* Cambridge: Cambridge University Press.

Carlson, A. J. (1916) The relation of hunger to appetite. *The control of hunger in health and disease.* Chicago, IL: University of Chicago Press.

Herrnstein, R. J. (1969). Method and theory in the study of avoidance. *Psychological Review, 76,* 49–69.

Kahneman, D., & Tversky, A. (1984). Choices, values, and frames. *American Psychologist, 39,* 350–431.

Loewenstein, G. F. (1999). A visceral account of addiction. In: J. Elster, & O.-J. Skog (Eds), *Getting hooked: Rationality and addiction.* Cambridge, UK: Cambridge University Press.

Reply to Ainslie

Olav Gjelsvik

George Ainslie has made wonderful contributions towards the understanding of human motivation in general and addictive behaviour in particular. In fact he is one of very few present thinkers who really have a system for understanding and explaining human behaviour. In the case of addiction, his system is applied to provide a significant theory of addiction. It is a great pleasure indeed to have his comments, especially for someone like me who neither has a philosophical system nor a full theory of addiction. I shall comment on our differences, both generally and on the two issues he focuses on.

A General Remark on Our Differences

Thinking about his comments, I find it helpful to point out that they are generated from the point of view of his system. There are deep differences between his way of thinking and mine, and they are strikingly brought out by his remark that philosophers from Spinoza onwards have held that "reason ultimately serves the passions." Ainslie does indeed endorse this view on reason — that is a fundamental aspect of his system. This is again clearly brought out by his metaphor of the canoeist in the rapid stream. What we really need, says Ainslie, is to "describe the logic of the canoeist or the block of wood from the properties of the rushing water itself, in some way transforming this physical inanimate force into the kind of subtlety that we experience as our own will in decision making." This is a bottom–up strategy for understanding rationality; it is a programme for building a satisfactory theory from the flow of different motivations through time. In order to succeed, there are strict constraints on what materials to build with.

My philosophical view is very different; I hold that Ainslie's view that reason ultimately serves the passions, a view which is normally called Hume's view, is a wrong view. Reason is for me a normative concept, and as such it is not, and cannot be, a servant of the passions. Reason is irreducible as other normative concepts also are. We might say that reason is a servant of the objective good or well-being in general, but that remark must then be understood within the context of the irreducibility of reason and normativity. I think we need this normative concept of reason to make room in the right way for agency in our picture of the world and to understand fully our own reactive attitudes towards our own human motivation. With this irreducible normative conception of reason in place, we can see that growing up and maturing as a person is normatively speaking a process which modifies our motivations in the direction prescribed by reason.

Two Concrete Disagreements: The Market-Place and Salience

When this is said at a general level, we might identify some of our disagreements about the two big issues Ainslie focuses on. The first concerns what he calls the marketplace-based model of rationality. This issue is seen by me as the issue of whether he is actually able to build a satisfactory model of rationality from the type of building materials he recognizes. It might, I believe, be shared ground between us that people convert what is essentially a temporal binding-yourself-as-you-sail-past-the-Sirens type of process to a process of judging-whether-this-case-fits-a-rule. The question I raise is whether Ainslie is fully entitled to describe the latter as rational, whether that can really be achieved without "animating" the "inanimate" force. I thought inter-temporal bargaining, and only that, was supposed to do this job in Ainslie's system. It worries me that Ainslie seems to resort to descriptions of what we actually do, and describes what we do as rational, as he also does in his description of the experiment he carried out at this meeting. We need to see clearly how, by using bargaining theory or something else, he earns the right to his description of judging-whether-this-case-fits-a-rule as rational. We need that in order to see clearly how the particular rationality in question arises out of the "inanimate" "rationality" he starts out from. If that cannot be achieved, then that fact might be taken to provide grounds for holding that we should not engage in Ainslie's "reductive" project. That would be my way of taking it.

The second large issue is about salience. Salience for me is *the psychological standing out of an object* — normally, but not necessarily, caused by closeness, temporal or spatial. Salience often causes a motivation different from the motivation you ought to have (normatively speaking). As a result we choose and act irrationally; even if the act is free and "rational" relative to how we are in fact motivated, we are no longer rationally motivated (normatively speaking) because of the causal influence of the salient object. Ainslie thinks this conception of salience leads to severe problems, and he dislikes my view of temporal discounting as a normatively wrong motivation caused in this way by temporal salience. He comments that "were it not for discounting, the distant future would be as valuable as the present, and a child could enjoy Christmas all year as if it were tomorrow."

I fail to see to see exactly what is wrong with my view. My view is that value and worth is provided by facts. In the case of Christmas, there is the actual value of the well-being Christmas brings, which should not, normatively speaking, be discounted. If presented with a choice between that well-being and some smaller well-being closer in time, we should choose Christmas. This is a normative view, and Ainslie can of course disagree with it. His comment about the child seems to me to bring in the issue of anticipation. I think that raises other issues. We are temporal beings able to enjoy pleasures of both looking forward to/anticipating and remembering; that is part of the psychological make-up of many of us. Children seem to be very good at enjoying looking forward to things, maybe to the extent that it counteracts their strong discounting tendencies in some cases. For us a bit older, it is good to be able to enjoy memories when there is little to look forward to. The pleasure of anticipating x typically increases as we move closer to x in time. The value of the pleasure of anticipating or looking forward to Christmas will therefore (with the pleasure) to some extent depend on how far off Christmas is. These phenomena are open to empirical investigation, and I make no normative claims whatsoever about whether and to what extent we should look forward to things. If Christmas is a long way off, however, and that is a fact, there is no way a minimally rational "child could enjoy Christmas all year as if it were tomorrow."

From where I stand the advantage gained by my view is not only normative. Another advantage is that we can explain and understand the acts and especially the later self-directed attitudes of the child who is "tricked" by the question, "Will you have this chocolate bar now and no Christmas presents, or abstain from this chocolate now and have Christmas presents instead?" But since I have dealt with that in my paper in this volume, and also in the papers of mine referred to in that paper, I shall not go further into the issue.

Chapter 9

Junk Time: Pathological Behavior as the Interaction of Evolutionary and Cultural Forces

Warren K. Bickel and Matthew W. Johnson

Introduction

> A junky runs on *junk time*. When his junk is cut off, the clock runs down and stops. All he can do is hang on and wait for non-junk time to start (William Burroughs 1953: 87, emphasis added).

Junk time, a phrase taken from the above quote by William Burroughs, will be used here to refer to the extreme devaluing or discounting of future events by individuals who are drug dependent. We use this term because the time orientation of drug dependent individuals appears to be very different from those who are not dependent. For example, in a recent report from our group, we asked heroin dependent individuals and matched controls to complete the following story. The story started: "After awakening, Bill began to think about his future. In general, he expected to . . .." The datum of interest was not the story, but rather the time-frame involved. On average, heroin-dependent individuals referred to a future of nine days, while matched controls referred to a future of 4.7 years (Petry *et al.* 1998). Our contention is that the profound difference in time orientation observed in this study is important in understanding drug dependence. More specifically, we will argue that such extreme temporal discounting both contributes to, and is affected by the development of, drug dependence.

To understand the time orientation of the drug dependent and its relation to the development of drug dependence, we will apply a relatively novel strategy to the study of drug dependence. Traditionally, the study of drug dependence explores the proximate causes of drug dependence. Proximate causes are the answer to "how" questions, and address the mechanisms that produce the behavior of interest. Addressing proximate causes has certainly been effective and has generated a wealth of knowledge. Among the important knowledge generated by addressing proximate causes is the observation that drug dependence results from the interaction of the drug with regions of the brain that are evolutionarily quite old (Nestler & Landsman 2001). These regions, such as the limbic system, regulate an organism's response to reinforcers such as food, drink, sex, and social interaction. Indeed, Nestler & Landsman (2001: 834) state, "the loss of control that addicts show with respect to drug seeking and taking may relate to the ability of drugs of abuse to commandeer these natural reward circuits and disrupt an individual's motivation and drive for normal reinforcers."

Informed by the results of these proximate investigations into the process of drug dependence, we seek to apply a complementary and novel tactic that may identify processes that are important in the genesis of drug dependence and serve as new targets for mechanistic study. The aim of this tactic is to identify the ultimate causes of behavior and use that knowledge in proximate studies. Ultimate causes refer to "why" questions and they try to identify the evolutionary pressures that would result in the behavior of interest. Looking for ultimate causes as they relate to drug dependence, although not unprecedented, may not appear germane at first glance, because most drugs were not widely available when the regions of the brain associated with drug dependence evolved. Thus, consistent with the notion that brain systems may be commandeered (Nestler & Landsman 2001), processes selected originally to deal with other reinforcers, such as food, may come to function with a new reinforcer, namely drugs.

The utilization of an evolved feature for a new function has been termed "exaptation" (Gould 1991; Gould & Vrba 1982). Identifying exaptations requires characterizing the evolved feature, its original functions, and the environmental pressures that may have resulted in its evolution, as well as evidence that the same evolved mechanism has become involved in a new function. In order to explore whether temporal discounting is an important aspect of drug dependence that has been exapted from other functions, we will employ concepts from three distinct, but overlapping fields: namely, evolutionary psychology, human behavioral ecology (life history theory) and behavioral economics.

Evolutionary psychology endeavors to identify psychological mechanisms that underlie human behavior and the evolutionary forces that shaped these mechanisms. More specifically, evolutionary psychology assumes that these mechanisms of behavior (also referred to as modules) evolved to address specific past environmental circumstances that exerted consistent selective pressures. Also, a tenet of this approach is that these mechanisms are not general processes, but tend to be directed to specific adaptive problems.

Human behavioral ecology is concerned with examining the link between ecological conditions and adaptive behavior. A fundamental assumption of this approach is that a trade-off must occur between components of fitness because of limited resources of the organism and environment. For example, under more severe developmental conditions, trade-offs may occur favoring survival over growth. Not surprisingly, human behavioral ecology frames the study of adaptive behavior in terms of decision rules. Therefore, advocates of this approach "tend to focus on explaining behavioral variation as adaptive responses to environmental variation: They assume that this adaptive variation (facultative behavior, phenotypic response) is governed by evolved mechanisms that instantiate the relevant conditional strategy or decision rule" (Smith 2000: 30).

Consequently, humans can rapidly shift phenotype and, therefore, are likely to be well adapted to contemporary environments. Many of these trade-offs occur along a dimension of current vs. future allocation of resources. For example, an organism may produce a large number of offspring now, or may delay offspring production and focus resources toward current survival. This decision may be influenced by current conditions, such as the ability of the current environment to support a large number of offspring.

Behavioral economics is "the study of the allocation of behavior within a system of constraint" (Bickel *et al.* 1995: 258) and examines conditions that influence the consumption of commodities. One important concept of significance in understanding drug dependence is the temporal discounting of reinforcers. Temporal discounting refers to the observation that the value of a delayed reinforcer is discounted (reduced in value or considered to be worth less) compared to the value of an immediate reinforcer. Indeed, to the extent that most individuals would prefer a reinforcer now rather than later, the discounting of delayed reinforcers is intuitive (Kirby 1997). Behavioral economics assumes that temporal discounting occurs whenever a reinforcer is delayed.

In this paper, we will use concepts from these different approaches to argue that discounting is an evolved psychological mechanism that has been exapted in the process of drug dependence. To make that argument will require that we first explore some general features of temporal discounting, including evidence that it is an evolutionary endowment, that discounting has a developmental course, and that it can be influenced by our culture. After addressing these issues, we will consider the role of discounting in drug dependence. To address this, we will examine whether drug dependents discount delayed reinforcers more than other individuals, what aspects of drug dependence may be influenced by temporal discounting and, finally, what the effects are of therapeutic interventions on discounting of delayed reinforcers. Collectively, this exploration into discounting and its relationship with drug dependence will describe a process that may be integral to drug dependence and, in so doing, begin to situate drug dependence in the complex interactions of ontogeny and phylogeny.

General Features of Discounting

Temporal Discounting as an Evolved Psychological Mechanism

We argue that temporal discounting is an evolved psychological mechanism. Important issues to be addressed in the evolutionary analysis of psychological mechanisms are: (1) identification of selective pressures that were present in the evolutionary past that are responsible for the selection of the mechanism; (2) a description of the psychological mechanism selected by these pressures; and (3) the manner in which the mechanism is currently expressed in present times and its interaction with today's culture (Cosmides *et al.* 1992). Here, we address the first two concerns. The third matter will be discussed in more detail in the section on culture below.

To address the first issue, we must identify environmental pressures that could have produced a preference for immediate reinforcers. For this task, we must look to past environments that drove the selection of our present biology, because complex systems are unlikely to have developed in the relatively recent time since the beginning of agriculture and civilization (Buss 1999; Cosmides *et al.* 1992). What was pre-agricultural life like for humans? Until about 13,000 years ago (i.e. 99% of its past), the human lineage survived as hunter-gatherers (Lee & Devore 1968). This way of life consisted of gathering wild plants and hunting wild animals (Diamond 1997). Our hunter-gatherer past is important because the adaptation of dietary systems is thought to have a strong influence over the forms of other systems. Indeed, most animals spend more waking hours in the acquisition of food than in any other activity (Tooby & DeVore 1987: 234).

Hunting and gathering are opportunistic activities, for a wild animal must be pursued immediately, and nutritive plant products must be consumed when these items are noticed because of environmental uncertainty. Competitors, accident, disease, and generally unreliable food sources make delaying consumption a very risky enterprise. Thus, procurement efforts were best directed toward immediately available resources, as delaying consumption would jeopardize future availability (Bickel & Marsch 2001). Those individuals who exhibited inflated preference for delayed reinforcers would have been at a survival disadvantage, ultimately resulting in relatively few descendents. Importantly, these factors that engendered temporal discounting in hunter-gatherer humans are present in the environments of non-human animals as well. These animals also benefit from the immediate consumption of reinforcers, and are potentially impaired by delayed consumption (Bickel & Marsch 2001). Therefore if temporal discounting is an evolved psychological mechanism, we should observe it in other species of animals. Evidence for this will be discussed below.

Much work has been done which serves to address the second issue, describing the mechanism in detail. Temporal discounting has been extensively investigated in both human and non-human animals. Mazur (1987) conducted an experiment that demonstrated that the hyperbolic function expressed in Eq. (1) accurately describes the devaluation of reinforcers over time in pigeons. In this experiment, pigeons were presented with two choice alternatives. A peck on one key led to two seconds of access to grain (the small reinforcer) after a set delay, and a peck on another key led to six seconds of access to grain (the larger reinforcer) after a delay that adjusted between trials. Two consecutive pecks on the smaller reinforcer key decreased delay to the larger reinforcer by one second. Two consecutive pecks on the larger reinforcer key increased the delay to the larger reinforcer by one second. The pigeons' choices eventually stabilized around an indifference point, where a particular value of the adjusting delay to the larger reinforcer was equally preferred to the set (shorter) delay to the smaller reinforcer. Indifference points were determined at various set values for the delay to the smaller reinforcer, ranging between zero and 20 seconds. By finding indifference points at these various set delays to the smaller reinforcer, temporal discounting was fully described across time, and this allowed for testing of the shape of the discounting functions. Results indicated that the hyperbolic decay model expressed in Eq. (1) more accurately described the data than the exponential model expressed in Eq. (2). In both equations, V_p is the present value of the reward, V is the undiscounted value of the reward (i.e. value when presented immediately), D is the delay from the choice until the receipt of the reward, and k is a free parameter. In Eq. (2), e is Euler's number. The superiority of the hyperbolic decay model has also been demonstrated in animal work with rats serving as subjects (Mazur *et al.* 1987; Richards *et al.* 1997).

$$V_p = \frac{V}{1 + kD} \tag{1}$$

$$V_p = V e^{-kD} \tag{2}$$

The implications for this finding are profound. Normative economic theory has defined Eq. (2) as rational (e.g. Lancaster 1963; Meyer 1976). It describes an independence of discounting rate and delay. In other words, for every unit of increased delay, value decreases by a constant proportion. In contrast, Eq. (1) describes an initially large drop in value, followed by decreases in value that are proportionally smaller with each additional unit of delay. The hyperbolic model describes a markedly impulsive style of discounting, because it readily predicts preference reversals over time even when assuming that both reinforcers are discounted at the same rate. For example, when offered a choice between a smaller sooner reinforcer and a larger later reinforcer, a subject may choose the smaller sooner alternative. However, by adding an equal delay to both alternatives, subjects may switch to the larger later reinforcer (Green *et al.* 1994a, b).

Researchers have also successfully used similar procedures to understand temporal discounting in humans. These experiments typically offer the research participant a series of discrete choices between two amounts of money, holding the delay of the larger later reward fixed while varying the magnitude of a smaller immediate reward in order to determine each indifference point. These indifference points are then used to construct discounting functions analogous to those in the animal literature (Rachlin *et al.* 1991). Although there are a number of differences between temporal discounting experiments done with non-human animals and humans, including reinforcers studied and time frames involved, the hyperbolic model has consistently prevailed over the exponential model in both non-humans and humans (Green *et al.* 1981; Green *et al.* 1994a, b; Green *et al.* 1996, 1997; Green & Myerson 1993; Kirby 1997; Kirby & Marakovi 1996). Although there are vast differences in the k discount rate parameter (humans having a rate several orders of magnitude smaller than pigeons and rats), the hyperbolic shape of the function is shared across species, suggesting common descent or convergent evolution due to similar environmental pressures. Common descent of the trait would suggest that temporal discounting might be an extremely ancient psychological mechanism, given the deep time suggested by a common ancestor of pigeons and humans. Figure 1 illustrates the qualitatively fixed nature of discounting as observed across humans, rats, and pigeons. This qualitative similarity is consistent with the uncertain environments shared by non-human animals and humanity's hunter-gatherer ancestors.

Temporal discounting appears to be consistent with the notion of an evolved psychological mechanism; however, one aspect of discounting may call into question its role as an evolved mechanism. Several authors have noted that, in order to be appropriately classified as an evolved mechanism, a trait must have performed a specific task that solved specific adaptive problems better than alternative traits did in the evolutionary past (Buss 1999; Smith 2000; Symons 1992). General notions such as "learning" or "fitness maximizing" are rejected as adapted mechanisms due to a failure to meet this criterion (Symons 1992). Hyperbolic temporal discounting, however, may violate this criterion because it appears to be independent of reinforcer type. The same form is observed in humans discounting money (e.g. Rachlin *et al.* 1991), humans discounting their drug of dependence (Madden *et al.* 1997), and in non-human animals discounting food (e.g. Mazur 1987; Mazur *et al.* 1987). This pervasiveness across reinforcer types might be viewed as a violation of the task-specificity criterion for adapted mechanisms, and may suggest that, in the case of reinforcers absent during the evolutionary past such as money and drugs, temporal discounting in humans functions as an exaptation, rather than an adaptation.

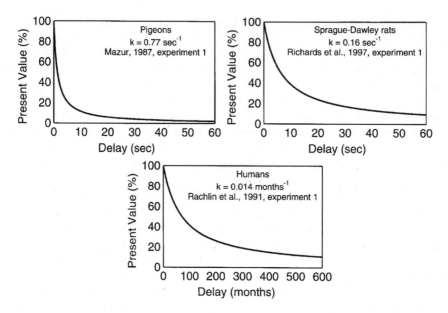

Figure 1: Temporal discounting curves from experimental group data in three different species. Although discounting rate differed drastically, the hyperbolic decay model
(Eq. (1)), accounted for a high degree of variance in all three studies.

Another possible objection to our argument arises from our assertion that the temporal discounting observed in human and non-human animal research reflects the same
underlying process. Because human experiments ask participants to make prospective
judgments about future rewards, these experiments might be qualitatively different than
non-human animal experiments, in which subjects actually experience delay within the
experiment. In other words, in the non-human animal experiments, animals are actually
exposed to the delay-reinforcer magnitude combinations in the titration process, while
humans are presented with hypothetical questions or are promised real rewards, but
these are only delivered after the experiment is complete (e.g. Johnson & Bickel 2002).
One possible interpretation is that humans are making decisions based on the results
of higher order cognitive processes (i.e. consciously decided), resulting in a qualitatively different discounting process than that employed by the animals in non-human
animal experiments.

In order to address this concern and argue that both human and non-human discounting
research involve the same underlying behavioral process, we propose that three factors
be evaluated. First, we suggest that adaptive pressures driving the two situations be
considered. As suggested earlier in this paper, both non-human animals and ancestral
human hunter-gatherers were faced with adaptive challenges of resource acquisition that
made temporal discounting beneficial. Second, we suggest that similarities in empirical data
be considered. As mentioned earlier, extensive research in both humans and non-humans
suggests that the hyperbolic decay model expressed in Eq. (1) accurately describes the data

in both situations. Importantly, in humans this model consistently outperforms Eq. (2), an equation economists had long thought to describe intertemporal choice because of its "rationality." If human prospective decision making fundamentally involves more sophisticated decision processes, how odd that our temporal discounting more closely resembles the pattern observed in non-humans, as opposed to this more "rational" model. Thirdly, we suggest that evidence for the biological substrates in the two situations be examined. The neurotransmitter serotonin appears to play an important role in impulsivity for both humans and non-human animals. Rats given drugs that increase serotonin function, such as fenfluramine, increase their preference for larger delayed reinforcers relative to smaller sooner reinforcers (Poulos *et al.* 1996). Additionally, drugs that decrease serotonin function increase preference for smaller sooner reinforcers relative to larger delayed ones (Bizot *et al.* 1999). Consistent with animals studies of intertemporal choice, fenfluramine has also been shown to decreased impulsive responding in adult human males with conduct disorder in a choice procedure similar to the studies conducted in our laboratory (Cherek & Lane 2000). In addition, low serotonin function has been shown to play a role in human impulsive behaviors such as suicide (Mann & Arango 1999). Taken together, these lines of evidence suggest that a similar biological substrate underlies impulsive decision making in both humans and non-humans.

Developmental Course of Discounting

In the prior section, uncertainty was identified as an important selective pressure that would favor greater temporal discounting among species. Uncertainty may also play a role at various points in the life history of individuals. Indeed, uncertainty may loom largest during childhood and adolescence. Childhood and adolescence, in particular, are portions of the life cycle that may be associated with greater uncertainty and perhaps, as we outline below, this is an important factor contributing to the widely held view that the young live today as if tomorrow will never come. Also, implicit in such a widely held notion that the young experience more uncertainty and are "reckless" as a result is the complementary notion that older individuals tend to experience more certainty and therefore may consider the future more. Collectively, these two complementary notions suggest that discounting may have a developmental course.

To address the evolutionary forces that would select such developmental changes, we need to recognize and differentiate the type of developmental activities or work necessary to leave descendents or to be reproductively fit (Chisholm 1999). Specifically, to leave descendents requires survival, preparation for reproduction (including growth, development, maturation), and reproduction. Reproduction can be further subdivided into the production of offspring and their rearing. These are the developmental tasks that any organism must successfully complete to meet the criterion of reproductive fitness. Completing these tasks might be relatively easy in an environment where food and potential reproductive partners abound. However, such an Eden rarely exists and scarcity is, more often than not, the rule. Thus, to complete these developmental tasks in the face of scarcity and uncertainty requires the organism to engage in a variety of trade-offs, such as survival vs. reproduction, growth vs. reproduction, and quantity vs. quality of offspring. Thus, not surprisingly, we would expect "natural selection to favor mechanisms or algorithms for selecting between or making decisions about alternative ways to allocate resources" (Chisholm 1999: 41).

Many of these trade-offs occur along a dimension of current vs. future allocation of resources. For example, producing a large number of offspring instead of focusing resources on a smaller number of offspring might be an effective decision in environments characterized by considerable uncertainty such as mortality by disease, homicide, or other environmental hazards. By having a large number of offspring, one increases the odds that at least one or more offspring will survive these uncontrollable hazards. Also, by immediately producing these offspring, there is a chance that some will survive even if the parent dies relatively early in the development of offspring. On the other hand, in environments characterized by stability, a more successful strategy might be to produce relatively few offspring and focus resources on them, so that each is maximally prepared for survival. In this case, instead of placing more resources into immediate quantity of reproduction, the organism can ensure the transmission of its genetics by continued allocation of resources to the future quality of offspring development. This scenario also introduces the first major source of uncertainty in childhood; that is, the degree of parental investment (Chisholm 1999). The degree of parental investment is not guaranteed for any one particular offspring. Therefore, offspring are best served by immediately utilizing resources offered by the parent. During the vast periods of time that humans were hunter-gatherers, those children who chose immediate over delayed consumption in the face of uncertain parental investment may have been better equipped to survive and eventually reproduce.

During adolescence and after puberty, there may be intense competition among males for the acquisition of resources. This acquisition of resources may lead to better development and enhance attractiveness to potential mates. Such competitiveness may lead to aggression among the youth and lead potentially to homicide. This evolutionary source of competitiveness among males has been suggested as a factor in the largely invariant age related pattern in crime and homicide. More specifically, starting between ages 10 and 12 homicides and other crimes increase dramatically among youth. The percentage of youth participating in these activities peaks around age 18 to 22 and then begins to decline. Also, this competitiveness among males may suggest a reason for the gender differences in crime, drug abuse, and other behavioral problems (Hirschi & Gottfredson 1983; Wilson & Daly 1985).

Also, in our contemporary society, the ability to predict what one's life may be like in the next 10 years is considerably harder among adolescents than among adults. This relative lack of certainty may also promote discounting and, similarly, the relatively greater predictability of the future by adults may lead to less discounting. Collectively, this characterization of uncertainty during the life cycle suggests that discounting should have a developmental course with greater discounting early in life and relatively less discounting later in life.

Only a few studies permit a test of this hypothesis of age-related differences in discounting. The most comprehensive of these is a study by Green *et al.* (1994a, b). That study compared the discounting of hypothetical monetary rewards ($100 to $10 000) among children (mean age of 12.1 years), young adults (mean age of 20.3 years), and older adults (mean age of 67.9 years). Figure 2 presents the results from this study and shows that children discounted the most, older adults discounted the least, and the young adults' discounting was intermediate between them. The hyperbolic function (Eq. (1))

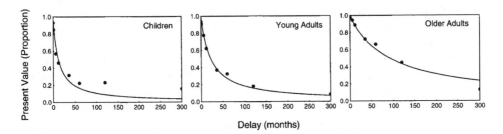

Figure 2: Discounting curves for children, young adults, and older adults (Green *et al.* 1994a, b). Discount rate decreased with age.

well described the data for all three groups. Support for these results is found when across study comparisons of time preference (discounting) are made between college students (Horowitz 1991; Thaler 1981) and adults nearing retirement (Kotlikoff *et al.* 1982). An interesting question that remains is whether these age-related changes are largely biological (developing nervous system) in nature or are perhaps culturally derived. Both processes are likely involved and in the next section we will consider the issue of culture in greater detail.

Cultural Influences on Discounting

In the section on the evolutionary basis of temporal discounting, humans and non-humans were shown to share the same hyperbolic discounting function, demonstrating cross-species generality and supporting our view of discounting as an evolved psychological mechanism. Differences between human and non-human temporal discounting, however, were also noted; namely, humans generally discount future events less so than non-humans. Explaining the cross-species discontinuity in the degree of discounting suggests at least two possibilities (Bickel & Marsch 2000). One possibility is that the relatively limited discounting observed in humans results from the unique genetic endowment of humans that evolved at some time since the human lineage separated from non-humans. An alternative possibility is that humans like non-humans were temporally myopic in the beginning of their phylogenetic history, but humans, as a result of their ability to cumulatively acquire knowledge across generations, learned to have longer temporal views. Such changes were likely in response to environmental changes that were eventually incorporated into cultural practices. From this perspective, temporal discounting could be related to the process of socialization in our culture and suggests that our biology can accommodate either limited or considerable temporal discounting. This point suggests that discounting may be qualitatively fixed (hyperbolic in form) and quantitatively flexible (degree of discounting). Of course, these two possible sources (genetically or culturally based) of the limited temporal discounting of humans may represent extremes along a continuum, with the answer lying in between.

Nonetheless, our view is that the development of an extended temporal horizon is largely learned from our culture and, therefore, our culture may constrict or expand considerations of the future, over time, depending upon the prevailing contingencies (quantitatively flexible). These changes in temporal horizon, once incorporated into the culture, may then influence successive generations. In reviewing evidence in support of this argument, we will briefly review several important developments in human history that led to the adoption of different time horizons (see Bickel & Marsch 2000 for a more detailed review).

As we noted earlier, humans have an extensive history as hunter-gatherers that likely supported a relatively short temporal horizon. Actions in this mode are opportunistic responses to the circumstances that present themselves. All this changed 13,000 years ago, when a new technology, agriculture, developed that changed the economic activity of humans from an event-based to a time-based mode. With the advent of agriculture, concerns moved from seeking food or obtaining food when it was available to planning for tomorrow by planting seeds today. Agriculture eliminated the social system based on roving bands of humans and permitted permanent settlements with larger numbers of individuals. Larger populations were possible because farmers and herders could feed 10 to 100 more individuals per acre of land than from hunting and gathering (Diamond 1997). These permanent settlements are what later permitted the development of specialized skills, governments, technology, and other advances of civilization.

The next important epoch in the development of temporal discounting in humans resulted from the transition from temporal views evidenced in antiquity to the ones introduced by the Judeo-Christian heritage. Circular views of time were widespread in antiquity. The Egyptians, for example, regarded time as a succession of recurring phases (circa 1500 BC) where the world was essentially static and unchanging. Such a temporal view is evident in their approach to chronology. Time was marked by the years of a pharaoh's reign. Time was restarted with each new pharaoh (Whitrow 1989). Although in ancient Greece a greater number of views were evident, a circular view of time was prevalent. Indeed, from 500 BC forward, there was generally little belief in the progress of the future. In this regard, Whitrow (1989: 46) noted, "the typical Greek tended to be backward looking, since the future appeared to him to be the domain of total uncertainty, his only guide to it being delusive expectation." Similarly, Imperial Rome was primarily focused on the past and the present, and not the future.

This view of time largely changed with the advent and popularization of Judeo-Christian beliefs. The Jews believed in a linear concept of time and that the future gradually revealed God's purpose (Whitrow 1989). This view was continued and elaborated by Christianity. Christians believed that individuals can be changed, saved, and, in the future, enter the kingdom of God. With its attention to the future, Christianity ushered in what serves as our contemporary view of time. Specifically, a central notion of Christianity was that one worked today for the future.

The most recent event that changed temporal perspective is the contemporary culture of consumerism and leisure. Prior to the industrialization of America (circa 1870), and particularly in agricultural and artisan settings, leisure was seamlessly woven into the fabric of life. As O'Malley (1996: 257) noted, "Preindustrial societies enjoyed less of a distinction between 'work' and 'rest' . . . they intermingled constantly in the course of living. A wise and diligent farmer, finishing one task, went straight to work on another, and even at rest, the farmer remained a farmer; there was relatively little sense of 'time off.' " Prior to the late 1800s, individuals purchased fewer leisure goods and services, and often made their own music and toys (Butsch 1990). During this time, Victorian culture was a strong force in American society. Victorian ideals "taught people to work hard, to postpone gratification, to repress themselves sexually, and to improve themselves and to be sober, conscientious and even compulsive" (Howe 1976: 17) — indeed, to have extended temporal horizons.

Industrialization produced a profound change by dramatically separating leisure from work, particularly with the advent of factory work. A growing number of wage earners enjoyed a new kind of free time, and with that free time the commercialization of leisure began (Rosenzweig 1983). Among the innovations that filled leisure time were movies, phonographs, and saloons. Indeed, such leisure, with its immediately available commodities, may have shortened temporal horizons, and this change was evidenced in our monetary budgets. The proportion of income that was spent on items other than food, clothing and shelter increased from 10 to 25% from 1875 to the 1930s in working class families. By the 1980s, 40% of income was allocated to "goods intensive" recreation (Horowitz 1985). Not surprisingly, recent longitudinal studies of rates of saving confirm that there has been a major and apparently permanent decline in saving in modern times in 23 western countries that comprise 60% of the world's output (Maital & Maital 1994). A decrease in savings is certainly suggestive of a shortened temporal horizon. Collectively, these changes lead to a replacement of a restrictive culture with one characterized by increased permissiveness and self-indulgence. Thus, sanctions against impulsive behavior or short temporal horizons were dramatically lessened in this new permissive culture. These trends certainly carry through to contemporary times with an ever-increasing array of immediately available food and recreational items.

Next we consider an additional factor in modern society that may promote a myopic temporal perspective that is manifested in the form of "deviant," shortsighted behavior. In so doing, we will discuss how environments that have considerable economic deterioration and destabilization are associated with a high prevalence of environmental risk and uncertainty. These environments are also associated with considerable criminal, drug use, and other shortsighted behaviors. In discussing the "culture of poverty," we are not suggesting that economic poverty per se causes shortsighted behavior (e.g. drug use or criminal behavior). Rather, as Lewis (1966) suggests, the culture of poverty represents a culture of instability, criminality, violence, and deprivation — indeed, a culture that fails to promote consideration of the future consequences of behavior.

Environments characterized by economic deterioration and destabilization, in which the future outcomes of one's behavior are typically characterized by risk and uncertainty, may select for shortsighted behavior. In many inner-city environments, where community instability and decay (e.g. poverty and violence) are endemic (e.g. Greene 1996), considering one's future may seem a fruitless endeavor for individuals who may not expect to experience the future. In such a situation, the most adaptive strategy may be to consider exclusively the immediate consequences of a behavior (Strathman *et al.* 1994). Indeed, a variety of studies have demonstrated that behaviors leading to unpredictable future outcomes may be replaced by behaviors that result in more immediate predictable outcomes (e.g. Christensen *et al.* 1988; King & Logue 1992; Navarick 1987). In general, individuals living in an environment permeated by unpredictability and risk may engage in more present-oriented rather than future-oriented behavior. In contrast, individuals living in a more predictable environment may be more future-oriented and engage in less risky behavior (Hill *et al.* 1997).

Indeed, the prevalence of substance abuse, criminal and many other types of risk behavior is highest in urban and low SES residential environments (e.g. Crum *et al.* 1996; Harrell & Peterson 1992). For example, in a meta-analysis of predictors of homicide, resource deprivation or poverty has been shown to be the strongest predictor of high homicide rates (Land *et al.* 1990). Furthermore, a strong correlation (r correlation $= 0.88$) has been reported between the average life expectancy of individuals in an urban environment and their neighborhood homicide rates, with those individuals with the shortest life expectancy also living in places where homicide rates are highest (Wilson & Daly 1997). In addition, teenage pregnancy is highest among those in low SES, urban environments where individuals also experience poorer and more uncertain health, as well as higher age-specific mortality rates, than individuals in non-urban or higher SES contexts (Geronimus 1987, 1996).

Importantly, four studies measured temporal discounting or some reasonable proxy measure (e.g. impulsivity) as a function of SES and neighborhood variables. O'Rand & Ellis (1974) measured time perspective as a function of social class. Specifically, they examined time perspective in two samples of adolescents of comparable age who came from differing backgrounds. The two groups came from a lower-class and a middle-class background. The results reveal that lower-class youth had a more restricted temporal view than youth from the middle-class, that upwardly mobile lower-class youth have incorporated some features of the temporal perspective evidenced by the middle-class youth, and that temporal perspective influenced success in performance roles. The second study by Lawrance (1991) used econometric methods to measure temporal perspective and found temporal discounting to be negatively related to income and educational level. One possible interpretation of the data is that high temporal discounting may reduce investment in education, which, in turn, has a negative impact on income. The third study examined the interaction of impulsivity and neighborhood context on juvenile criminal offending (Lynam *et al.* 2000). Results indicated that impulsivity interacted with neighborhood context to influence juvenile offending. Specifically, impulsivity placed juvenile boys at great risk for offending in the poorest neighborhoods, while impulsivity posed little risk for offending in better neighborhoods. A fourth study (Green *et al.* 1996) showed that low-income older adults temporally discounted money to a greater extent than high-income older adults.

Collectively, the account provided in this section shows that temporal discounting is flexible and can either be increased or decreased depending upon the cultural conditions. Indeed, the history of humans with respect to temporal perspective may be conceptualized as an inverted U-shaped function, where first considerable discounting was evidenced followed by a lesser degree of discounting, and most recently by greater discounting. This account is consistent with human behavioral ecology that suggests that differing "strategies" will be employed under differing environmental consequences.

Temporal Discounting and Drug Dependence

Is Temporal Discounting Involved in Drug Dependence?

Several published studies have investigated the link between temporal discounting and drug dependence (Bickel & Marsch 2001). The majority of these studies have employed group designs, comparing drug dependents to non-drug dependents. These studies have revealed that drug dependents discount the future to a greater extent than normals. The fact that this observation has been made for a variety of drugs across drug classes suggests that the increased discounting is fundamentally related to drug abuse, as opposed to any one particular drug.

Several studies have examined temporal discounting rates among heroin abusers. Madden *et al.* (1999) and Madden *et al.* (1997) used a procedure developed by Rachlin *et al.* (1991) to measure discounting in both heroin addicts and matched control normals. Participants were presented with two hypothetical choices. One choice was $1000 at a specific delay and the other choice was a smaller amount available now. This smaller reward amount was varied in order to find the point at which the subject was indifferent between the larger later and the smaller sooner reward. Seven delays were examined (ranging one week to 25 years) and discounting functions were determined by fitting the seven obtained indifference points to Eq. (1). In addition, a similar analysis was conducted with choices between $1000 dollars worth of heroin and a smaller amount of heroin, so that discounting for the drug itself could be evaluated.

Results in both studies revealed that opioid-dependent subjects discounted money significantly more than normals, and opioid dependents discounted heroin more than money. Figure 3 shows that for control subjects, $1000 lost 60% of its value when delayed by five years, while for opioid-dependent subjects, $1000 lost 60% of its value in only one year, a five-fold difference. Additionally Figure 3 shows that, among opioid dependents, heroin lost 60% of its value in only one week, a 52-fold difference compared to their discounting of money. Another study by Kirby *et al.* (1999) replicated the finding that heroin addicts discount money more than normals. But unlike the two studies mentioned above, the choices in this study were not purely hypothetical. Out of all choices made, one choice was randomly determined, and the subject had a one in six chance of receiving the selected reward on this choice. Finally, Odum *et al.* (2000) examined temporal discounting across subgroups of heroin addicts. In-treatment opioid-dependent subjects were categorized in two groups based on self-report: whether the subject would or would not engage in needle sharing with a friend if no clean needle were available. Needle sharers discounted money rewards to a greater extent than those who would not share needles. No significant difference was found between the groups for discounting of heroin. However, as in previous studies, both groups discounted heroin more than money.

A few studies have also examined temporal discounting in tobacco cigarette smokers. Mitchell (1999) used a choice procedure to examine the temporal discounting for money reward in regular smokers and subjects who had never smoked. The choices here were potentially real. Subjects could win one reward, selected randomly, from among the choices made during the experiment. These two groups were also compared on various personality and behavioral measures of impulsivity. Smokers discounted future rewards to a significantly greater degree than never-smokers. In addition, smokers scored more impulsively than never-smokers on the other behavioral tasks and most of the personality tasks. Bickel *et al.* (1999) also examined smokers' temporal discounting. This study compared current smokers, never-smokers, and ex-smokers in discounting for $1000. Discounting was also measured in current smokers for the amount of cigarettes the subject

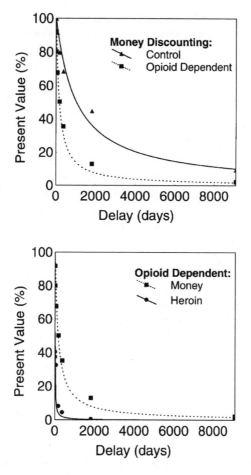

Figure 3: Group indifference points and hyperbolic (Eq. (1)) discounting curves for money and heroin. Opioid dependents and control subjects are compared with money in the top panel. The bottom panel compares discounting of heroin and money within the opioid-dependent group.

could purchase for $1000. Current smokers discounted future money rewards significantly more than never-smokers and ex-smokers; however, no significant difference was found between money discounting for never-smokers and ex-smokers, suggesting that increased discounting in the cigarette smoker may be a reversible phenomenon. In addition, the current smokers discounted cigarettes significantly more steeply than money. Thus, as was demonstrated in heroin addicts (Madden *et al.* 1997, 1999), the abused drug is discounted more than the money needed to purchase that drug.

Temporal discounting has been studied in alcohol drinkers using a choice procedure (Vuchinich & Simpson 1998). Two studies were conducted: one comparing heavy vs. light drinkers, and one comparing problem vs. light drinkers. These studies found that both problem and heavy drinkers discounted future money consequences more than light drinkers. These studies also compared the groups on questionnaires designed to study impulsiveness and time orientation. Light drinkers were found be less impulsive than the other groups; however, there was no strong correlation between these measures and the discounting rate determined via the choice procedure.

Two additional studies examined temporal discounting in heterogeneous groups of substance abusers. Ainslie & Haendel (1983) compared inpatient substance abusers and a group of employees of that inpatient facility. The patients discounted delayed money significantly more than the employees. Petry & Casarella (1999) compared problem gambling substance abusers, non-problem gambling substance abusers, and non-problem gambler non-substance abuser controls. Substance abusers discounted money to a significantly greater extent than non-substance abusers. Moreover, problem gambling substance abusers discounted money more than non-problem gambling substance abusers. These results suggest that, even among substance abusers, temporal discounting rates are sensitive enough to discriminate among subgroups.

Collectively, the studies reviewed in this section suggest that steep discounting is associated with drug abuse in general and risky drug injection practices in particular. Additionally, these studies suggest that both drug dependent and control subjects discount hyperbolically, but differ in the degree of discounting. If discounting is shown to be related to the development of drug abuse, then this may suggest a normal source of pathological behavior. An interesting and potentially important implication of these studies is that steep discounting may provide both a marker of risk and a target for risk.

Discounting and its Relationship to Dependence Processes

There are several phenomena that are related to drug dependence that have yet to be adequately explained or understood. Among these phenomena are the risk for drug abuse among youth, the maturing out of drug dependence, the increasing prevalence of drug dependence throughout our century, and the loss of control associated with drug dependence. We will consider each of these phenomena and their relationship to discounting below.

Drug use and dependence typically start in adolescence and end spontaneously as the drug dependent matures and ages. Let us consider the natural history of heroin dependence as an exemplar. The age of first drug use in the heroin dependent, which is usually marijuana, is approximately age 14. By age 16, in the typical life course of the drug dependent individual, he or she has been arrested, and has had considerable school difficulty. The age of first use of heroin is approximately 18, with the first signs of dependence exhibited at around age 20. The heroin dependent individual's age at the time he or she first seeks treatment is age 26. These data on the life history of heroin dependence are somewhat dated, and may be less relevant today in the emerging epidemic of heroin dependence, where adolescents are trying heroin and becoming dependent at ever-earlier ages. The other phenomenon is that drug dependent individuals often mature out of drug dependence. More specifically, the drug dependent often stop using drugs in their 40s and 50s. The exact reasons for these two age-dependent phenomena have never been adequately explained, nor adequately addressed in any theory of drug dependence.

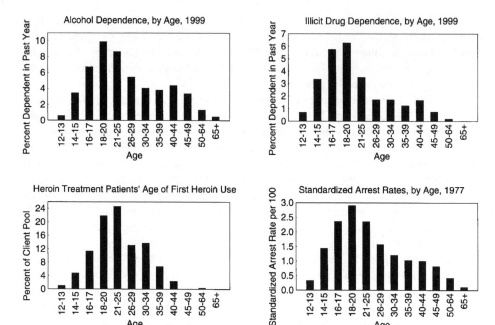

Figure 4: The upper-left panel shows percent alcohol dependent in last year by age in 1999 (Department of Health and Human Services 2000). The upper-right panel shows percent illicit drug dependent in last year by age in 1999 (Department of Health and Human Services 2000). The bottom-left panel shows age of first heroin use by percent of client pool among opioid-dependent patients in 2001 at the University of Vermont's Substance Abuse Treatment Center. The bottom-right panel shows standardized arrest rates by age in the United States for 1977 (Hirschi & Gottfredson 1983).

One way to make sense of these two phenomena is to first recognize that they appear to be related to the life course of many other behaviors. Consider the graphs presented in Figure 4. Each of the panels shows the frequency of individuals engaging in drug use, criminal behavior, or homicides as a function of age. Each graph for all intents and purposes is similar in form. These graphs suggest that the likelihood of engaging in these behaviors increases dramatically in early adolescence, reaching a peak in the early 20s and declining thereafter. The fact that these age-dependent functions are so similar across behaviors suggests that we are looking at a phenomenon that may be dampened or increased by particular cultural forces, but is unchanging in its underlying biological process.

Delay discounting is one process that may account for these phenomena. As was discussed earlier, delay discounting is a developmental phenomenon in which children and adolescents discount the future the most. Perhaps this is a risk factor for drug use and dependence. For example, perhaps those adolescents that discount the future more are the adolescents that are at greater risk for engaging in all sorts of behaviors that provide brief intense reinforcement. If so, drug of dependence would certainly be one set of events that could provide brief intense reinforcement.

Based on our review earlier we also established that degree of discounting decreases as one grows older. Perhaps the drug dependent show the same age related decline in discounting, but tend to discount more than peers of equivalent age. If so, then this may provide a basis for the commonly observed pattern of the drug dependent discontinuing drug use at an older age. Perhaps this "maturing out" phenomenon is a consequence of gaining sufficient temporal perspective.

The third phenomenon we would like to address is the effects of culture on drug dependence. In the section on culture above, we noted that culture's influence on delay discounting could be considered an inverted U-shaped function where greater discounting is more likely to occur in contemporary times because of our consumer culture. If that is true and if greater discounting relates to a greater likelihood of becoming drug dependent, then we should observe that the likelihood of becoming drug dependent increases as a function of birth cohort in the 20th century.

Increasing drug dependence as a function of when an individual was born in the last century is in fact observed. This was shown in a study reported by Warner *et al.* (1995). They assessed the prevalence of drug use and dependence in over 8,000 individuals, comprising four U.S. birth cohorts. Four 10-year cohorts were assessed for five different 5-year age intervals (ages 4, 9, 14 19 and 24), including Cohort I (born 1966–1975), Cohort II (born 1956–1965), Cohort III (born 1946–1955) and Cohort IV (born 1936–1945). Results indicated that Cohort IV (born pre-WWII and modern society) had the lowest prevalence of drug use, with drug use tending to increase with each successive generation. Of course, these data may simply reflect the fact that drugs have become increasingly more available throughout the century. What is important for our point is that this study looked at the probability of becoming drug dependent if the individuals had used the drug. Looking at the probability of being drug dependent amongst those that had used drugs in part controls for drug availability. The data show a more robust effect when the probability of drug dependence increases with successive cohorts throughout the century. Other similar effects have been noted in the drug dependent (Bickel & Marsch 2000). Similar birth cohort effects have been noted in criminal behavior, depression, single mother births, obesity, and childhood behavioral problems (see Bickel & Marsch 2000 for a review).

The fourth phenomenon of drug dependence that may be related to discounting is "loss of control"; that is, drug dependent individuals may state a preference for the larger, more delayed reward, yet nonetheless later choose the smaller, more immediate reward, thus demonstrating a reversal in preference. For example, drug dependent individuals may express a strong preference for employment or participation in relationships with family and friends over drug use. However, a short time before a drug becomes available the individual may choose using drugs instead of going to work or spending time with their family. Similarly, intravenous drug users may prefer using clean needles, yet may willingly share needles when offered the opportunity to use drugs (e.g. Abdul-Quader *et al.* 1987). Also (to the consternation of treatment providers), many drug dependent individuals voluntarily participate in outpatient drug treatment programs, but continue to abuse drugs (Milby 1988). Some of these patients declare a preference for not using drugs upon entering treatment, but nonetheless relapse to drug use at some later point in treatment, indicating a reversal in preference.

Hyperbolic discounting can account for preference reversals and this is illustrated by the familiar depiction of preference reversal due to hyperbolic discount curves (see, e.g. Ainslie & Monterosso, Chapter 1, this volume). One reward is a sooner, smaller magnitude reward, and the other a delayed, larger magnitude reward. Note that these two rewards are separated by time. The two curves indicate the present value of the rewards as a function of time until their availability. Importantly, they are hyperbolic in shape and cross each other. Thus, in this example, the larger reward has the greater value to a subject than the smaller reward at a time point long before either reward is available. However, as time progresses and the smaller reward becomes imminently available, the value of the two rewards reverse and the smaller reward has greater value (i.e. an impulsive choice is made). This reversal in preference occurs even though the objective magnitude of the rewards and the time between their availability remains constant. Hyperbolic discounting of delayed rewards suggests that when the events in question are temporally distant, choices are made that could be referred to as "self-controlled," "rational," and consistent with the objective magnitude of the rewards (e.g. "I want to work, be with my family, and not use drugs"). However, as the smaller sooner reward becomes available, preference reverses resulting in a choice that could be described as "impulsive," "irrational," and inconsistent with both the objective magnitude of the rewards and the prior expressed preference. Thus, not only does delay discounting account for the seemingly irrational behavior of drug dependents when they "lose control," but it also accounts for experiences of non-drug dependent individuals, e.g. the change in reference demonstrated when setting an early alarm the night before to get more work done, and then hitting the snooze button in the morning (Rachlin 2000). This suggests a normal source of pathological behavior.

This section has shown discounting to be potentially applicable to several phenomena in drug dependence. In particular, we speculated about the relationship of delay discounting and the age-dependent entry and exit from drug dependence, and the role of culture in rendering individuals more at risk for drug dependence and a wide variety of other behaviors. Moreover, we demonstrated how hyperbolic discounting could predict preference reversals that are used to diagnose the drug dependent. Of course, this section speaks mostly to the potential of delay discounting to account for these interesting phenomena. Further research will be necessary to determine if such speculations are supported by the facts.

Is Increased Temporal Discounting in Drug Dependence a Reversible Phenomenon?

Two interpretations of the group differences between drug dependents and matched control normals exist. One explanation is that individuals who have higher temporal discount rates, whether this is a consequence of genetic, cultural, developmental, or a combination of influences, tend to be the ones who start abusing drugs. An alternative explanation is that active drug abuse shortens temporal horizon and actually causes increased discounting. And, of course, both explanations may be true. That is, those who have higher discount rates may tend to start abusing drugs, and then drug abuse may tend to make these individuals discount the future even further.

In a recently completed study from our laboratory, we attempted to explore the causal direction of drug dependence and temporal discounting (Bickel *et al.* under review).

Specifically, we have taken cigarette-dependent individuals and randomly assigned them to two groups. Both groups perform a procedure measuring temporal discounting rate for $1000 on a Friday. During the following Monday through Friday, one group must come into our laboratory and give a carbon monoxide (CO) breath sample (an indicator of recent smoking) three times daily. If the reading indicates that a participant has not smoked, he or she is immediately rewarded with $10 in cash. The control group is asked only to follow their regular smoking patterns during this time. On the Friday of this week (one week after initial discounting assessment), delay discounting is once again measured for $1000 in both groups.

Analyses indicate that subjects assigned to the abstinence group have statistically lower temporal discount rates after the week of abstinence than before, i.e. more self-control. No such change is observed in the control group. No difference is detected between groups at the beginning, but the abstinent group is more self-controlled than the control group at the end session. These findings suggest that increased temporal discounting may be a reversible consequence of cigarette dependence, and perhaps drug dependence in general. Importantly, these results suggest that cigarette dependence causes an increase in discount rate, but does not rule out the other potential relationship, that those with initially high discount rates are the ones that tend to go on to abuse drugs.

Conclusion

In this paper, we have made several points about discounting and its relationship to drug dependence. First, we showed that discounting appears to be an evolved psychological mechanism (qualitatively fixed) that appears to have been exapted in the process of drug dependence. Second, we show that discounting has a developmental course that coincides with the onset of drug dependence and with the maturing-out phenomenon often observed in the drug dependent. Third, we have made an argument that discounting may be influenced by culture and that this notion is consistent with the increases in the prevalence of certain disorders observed across the 20th century, especially drug dependence. Fourth, exaggerated discounting is directly observed in the drug dependent. In particular, drug dependent individuals discount future monetary rewards more than matched controls and drug dependents discount the drug of dependence more than money. Fifth, discounting can theoretically account for reversals in preference, often termed loss of control, which are considered indicative of drug dependence. Sixth, we showed data from a recent study in which discounting appeared to be a reversible effect of drug use. Collectively, these observations support the notion that discounting is a behavioral process that may be driven by evolutionarily old brain systems selected to secure vital resources, and these processes appear to be commandeered in drug dependence. Indeed, as a commandeered process, discounting could be a normal source of pathological behavior.

Acknowledgments

This research was supported by National Institute on Drug Abuse grants R01 DA11692, R37 DA06526, and T32 DA07242.

References

Abdul-Quader, A. S., Friedman, S. R., Des Jarlais, D., Marmor, M. M., Maslansky, R., & Bartelme, S. (1987). Methadone maintenance and behavior by intravenous drug users that can transmit HIV. *Contemporary Drug Problems, 14*, 425–434.

Ainslie, G., & Haendel, V. (1983). The motives of the will. In: E. Gottheil, K. Druley, T. Skodola, & H. Waxman (Eds), *Etiology aspects of alcohol and drug abuse*. Springfield, IL: Charles C. Thomas.

Bickel, W. K., Green, L., & Vuchinich, R. E. (1995). Behavioral economics. *Journal of the Experimental Analysis of Behavior, 64*, 257–262.

Bickel, W. K., & Marsch, L. A. (2000). The tyranny of small decisions: Origins, outcomes and proposed solutions. In: W. K. Bickel, & R. E. Vuchinich (Eds), *Reframing health behavior change with behavioral economics* (pp. 341–391). NJ: Lawrence Erlbaum Associates.

Bickel, W. K., & Marsch, L. A. (2001). Toward a behavioral economic understanding of drug dependence: Delay discounting processes. *Addiction, 96*, 73–86.

Bickel, W. K., Odum, A. L., & Madden, G. J. (1999). Impulsivity and cigarette smoking: Delay discounting in current, never, and ex-smokers. *Psychopharmacology, 146*, 447–454.

Bizot, J. C., Le Bihan, C., Peuch, A. J., Hamon, M., & Thiebot, M. H. (1999). Serotonin and tolerance to delay of reward in rats. *Psychopharmacology, 146*, 400–412.

Burroughs, W. (1953). *Junky*. New York: Penguin Group.

Buss, D. M. (1999). *Evolutionary psychology*. Boston: Allyn and Bacon.

Butsch, R. (Ed.) (1990). *For fun and profit: The transformation of leisure into consumption*. Oxford: Oxford University Press.

Cherek, D. R., & Lane, S. D. (2000). Fenfluramine effects on impulsivity in a sample of adults with and without history of conduct disorder. *Psychopharmacology, 152*, 149–156.

Chisholm, J. S. (1999). *Death hope and sex*. New York: Cambridge University Press.

Christensen, J., Parker, S., Silberberg, A., & Hursh, S. (1988). Trade-offs in choice between risk and delay depend on monetary amounts. *Journal of the Experimental Analysis of Behavior, 69*, 123–139.

Cosmides, L., Tooby, J., & Barkow, J. (Eds) (1992). Introduction: Evolutionary psychology and conceptual integration. *The adopted mind*. Oxford: Oxford University Press.

Crum, R. M., Lillie-Blanton, M., & Anthony, J. (1996). Neighborhood environment and opportunity to use cocaine and other drugs in late childhood and early adolescence. *Drug and Alcohol Dependence, 43*, 155–161.

Department of Health and Human Services (2000). *Summary of findings from the 1999 National Household Survey on drug abuse*. Rockville, MD: NCADI.

Diamond, J. (1997). *Guns, germs, and steel: The fates of human societies*. New York, NY: Norton & Company.

Geronimus, A. T. (1987). On teenage childbearing and neonatal mortality in the United States. *Population and Development Review, 13*, 245–279.

Geronimus, A. T. (1996). What teen mothers know. *Human Nature, 7*, 323–352.

Gould, S. J. (1991). Exaptation: A crucial tool for an evolutionary psychology. *Journal of Social Issues, 47*, 43–65.

Gould, S. J., & Vrba, E. S. (1982). Exaptation — a missing term in the science of form. *Paleobiology, 8*, 4–15.

Green, L., Fisher, E. B., Perlow, S., & Sherman, L. (1981). Preference reversal and self control: Choice as a function of reward amount and delay. *Behaviour Analysis Letters, 1*, 43–51.

Green, L., Fristoe, N., & Myerson, J. (1994). Temporal discounting and preference reversals in choice between delayed outcomes. *Psychonomic Bulletin and Review, 1*, 383–389.

Green, L., Fry, A. F., & Myerson, J. (1994). Discounting of delayed rewards: A life-span comparison. *Psychological Science, 5*, 33–36.

Green, L., & Myerson, J. (1993). Alternative frameworks for the analysis of self control. *Behavior and Philosophy, 21*, 37–47.

Green, L., Myerson, J., Lichtman, D., Rosen, S., & Fry, A. (1996). Temporal discounting in choice between delayed rewards: The role of age and income. *Psychology and Aging, 11*, 79–84.

Green, L., Myerson, J., & McFadden, E. (1997). Rate of temporal discounting decreases with amount of reward. *Memory and Cognition, 25*, 715–723.

Greene, M. B. (1996). Youth and violence: Trends, principles, and programmatic interventions. In: R. J. Apfel, & B. Simon (Eds), *Minefields in their hearts: The mental health of children in war and communal violence* (pp. 128–148). New Haven, CT: Yale University Press.

Harrell, A. V., & Peterson, G. E. (1992). *Drugs, crime, and social isolation: Barriers to urban opportunity*. Washington, DC: The Urban Institute Press.

Hill, E. M., Ross, L. T., & Low, B. S. (1997). The role of future unpredictability in human risk-taking. *Human Nature, 8*, 287–325.

Hirschi, T., & Gottfredson, M. (1983). Age and the explanation of crime. *American Journal of Sociology, 89*, 552–584.

Horowitz, D. (1985). *The morality of spending: Attitudes toward the consumer society in America 1875–1940*. Baltimore, MD: Johns Hopkins University Press.

Horowitz, J. K. (1991). Discounting money payoffs: An experimental analysis. *Handbook of Behavioral Economics, 2B*, 309–324.

Howe, D. W. (Ed.) (1976). *Victorian America*. University of Pennsylvania Press.

Johnson, M. W., & Bickel, W. K. (2002). Within-subject comparison of real and hypothetical money rewards in delay discounting. *Journal of the Experimental Analysis of Behavior, 77*, 129–146.

King, G. R., & Logue, A. W. (1992). Choice in a self-control paradigm: Effects of uncertainty. *Behavioural Processes, 26*, 143–154.

Kirby, K. N. (1997). Bidding on the future: Evidence against normative discounting of delayed rewards. *Journal of Experimental Psychology: General, 126*, 54–70.

Kirby, K. N., & Marakovic, N. N. (1996). Delay-discounting probabilistic rewards: Rates decrease as amounts increase. *Psychonomic Bulletin and Review, 3*, 100–104.

Kirby, K. N., Petry, N. M., & Bickel, W. K. (1999). Heroin addicts discount delayed rewards at higher rates than non-drug using controls. *Journal of Experimental Psychology: General, 128*, 78–87.

Kotlikoff, L. J., Spivak, A., & Summers, L. (1982). The adequacy of savings. *American Economic Review, 72*, 1056–1069.

Lancaster, K. (1963). An axiomatic theory of consumer time preference. *International Economic Review, 4*, 221–231.

Land, K. C., McCall, P. L., & Cohen, L. E. (1990). Structural covariates of homicide rates: Are there any invariances across time and social space? *American Journal of Sociology, 95*, 922–963.

Lawrance, E. C. (1991). Poverty and the rate of time preference: Evidence from panel data. *Journal of Political Economy, 99*, 54–77.

Lee, R. B., & Devore, I. (1968). *Man the hunter*. New York: Aldine Publish Co.

Lewis, O. (1966). The culture of poverty. *Scientific American, 215*, 19–25.

Lynam, D. R., Caspi, A., Moffit, T. E., Wikstroem, P. O., Loeber, R., & Novak, S. (2000). The interaction between impulsivity and neighborhood context on offending: The effects of impulsivity are stronger in poorer neighborhoods. *Journal of Abnormal Psychology, 109*, 563–574.

Madden, G. J., Bickel, W. K., & Jacobs, E. A. (1999). Discounting of delayed rewards in opioid-dependent outpatients: Exponential or hyperbolic discounting functions? *Experimental and Clinical Psychopharmacology, 7*, 284–293.

Madden, G. J., Petry, N. M., Badger, G. J., & Bickel (1997). Impulsive and self-control choices in opioid-dependent patients and non-drug control participants: Drug and monetary rewards. *Experimental and Clinical Psychopharmacology*, *5*, 256–262.

Maital, S., & Maital, S. L. (1994). Is the future what it used to be? A behavioral theory of the decline of saving in the west. *Journal of Socio-Economics*, *23*, 1–32.

Mann, J. J., & Arango, V. (1999). The neurobiology of suicidal behavior. In: D. G. Jacobs (Ed.), *The Harvard Medical School guide to suicide assessment and intervention* (pp. 98–114). San Francisco, CA: Jossey-Bass.

Mazur, J. E. (1987). An adjusting procedure for studying delayed reinforcement. In: M. L. Commons, J. E. Mazur, J. A. Nevin, & H. Rachlin (Eds), *Quantitative analysis of behavior, the effect of delay and of intervening events on reinforcement value* (Vol. V, pp. 55–73). Hillsdale, NJ: Erlbaum.

Mazur, J. E., Stellar, J. R., & Waraczynski, M. (1987). Self-control choice with electrical stimulation of the brain as a reinforcer. *Behavioural Processes*, *15*, 143–153.

Meyer, R. F. (1976). Preference over time. In: R. L. Keeney, & H. Raiffa (Eds), *Decisions with multiple objectives: Preferences and value tradeoffs* (pp. 473–514). New York: Wiley.

Milby, J. B. (1988). Methadone maintenance to abstinence: How many make it? *Journal of Nervous & Mental Disease*, *176*, 409–422.

Mitchell, S. H. (1999). Measures of impulsivity in cigarette smokers and non-smokers. *Psychopharmacology*, *146*, 455–464.

Navarick, D. J. (1987). Reinforcement probability and delay as determinants of human impulsiveness. *Psychological Record*, *37*, 219–226.

Nestler, E. J., & Landsman, D. (2001). Learning about addiction from the genome. *Nature*, *409*, 834–835.

Odum, A. L., Madden, G. J., Badger, G. J., & Bickel, W. K. (2000). Needle sharing in opioid-dependent outpatients: Psychological processes underlying risk. *Drug and Alcohol Dependence*, *60*, 259–266.

O'Malley, M. (1996). *Keeping watch: A history of American time*. New York: Viking Penguin.

O'Rand, A., & Ellis, R. A. (1974). Social class and social time perspective. *Social Forces*, *53*, 53–62.

Petry, N. M., Bickel, W. K., & Arnett, M. (1998). Shortened time horizons and insensitivity to future consequences in heroin addicts. *Addiction*, *93*, 729–738.

Petry, N. M., & Casarella, T. (1999). Excessive discounting of delayed rewards in substance abusers with gambling problems. *Drug and Alcohol Dependence*, *56*, 25–32.

Poulos, C. X., Parker, J. L., & Le, A. D. (1996). Dexfenfluramine and 8-OH-DPAT modulate impulsivity in a delay-of-reward paradigm: Implications for a correspondence with alcohol consumption. *Behavioural Pharmacology*, *7*, 395–399.

Rachlin, H. (2000). *The science of self-control*. Cambridge: Harvard University Press.

Rachlin, H., Raineri, A., & Cross, D. (1991). Subjective probability and delay. *Journal of the Experimental Analysis of Behavior*, *55*, 233–244.

Richards, J. B., Mitchell, S. H., de Wit, H., & Seiden, L. S. (1997). Determination of discount functions in rats with an adjusting-amount procedure. *Journal of the Experimental Analysis of Behavior*, *67*, 353–366.

Rosenzweig, R. (1983). *Eight hours for what we will: Workers and leisure in an industrial city*. New York: Cambridge University Press.

Smith, E. A. (2000). Three styles in the evolutionary analysis of human behavior. In: L. Cronk, N. Chagnon, & W. Irons (Eds), *Adaptation and human behavior*. New York, Aldine de Gruyter.

Strathman, A., Boninger, D. S., Gleicher, F., & Baker, S. M. (1994). Constructing the future with present behavior: An individual difference approach. In: Z. Zaleski (Ed.), *Psychology of future orientation* (pp. 107–119). Lublin, Poland: Towarzystwo Naukowe.

Symons, D. (1992). On the use and misuse of Darwinism in the study of human behavior. *The adapted mind*. Oxford: Oxford University Press.

Thaler, R. (1981). Some empirical evidence on dynamic inconsistency. *Economic Letters*, *8*, 201–207.

Tooby, J., & DeVore, I. (1987). The reconstruction of hominid behavioral evolution through strategic modeling. In: W. G. Kinzey (Ed.), *The evolution of human behavior: Primate models* (pp. 183–187). Albany: SUNY Press.

Vuchinich, R. E., & Simpson, C. A. (1998). Hyperbolic temporal discounting in social drinkers. *Experimental and Clinical Psychopharmacology*, *6*, 292–305.

Warner, L. A., Kessler, R. C., Hughes, M., Anthony, J. C., & Nelson, C. B. (1995). Prevalence and correlates of drug use and dependence in the United States. *Archives of General Psychiatry*, *52*, 219–229.

Whitrow, G. J. (1989). *Time in history: Views of time from prehistory to the present day*. Oxford: Oxford University Press.

Wilson, M., & Daly, M. (1985). Competitiveness, risk taking, and violence: The young male syndrome. *Ethology and Sociobiology*, *6*, 59–73.

Wilson, M., & Daly, M. (1997). Life expectancy, economic inequality, homicide, and reproductive timing in Chicago neighborhoods. *British Medical Journal*, *314*, 1271–1274.

Comments on Bickel and Johnson

Keith Humphreys

This is a rich and ambitious paper. I particularly enjoy reading articles like this one that combine detailed research findings with wide-ranging conceptual analysis. (Too many papers we write include only one or the other, I think). On the empirical side, Bickel and Johnson present compelling evidence that drug dependent people discount future rewards to a much greater extent than do non-users. Further, they establish the clinically important fact that smokers apparently can return to a normative level of temporal discounting if they cease using nicotine. Bickel and Johnson place their intriguing laboratory findings in three conceptual contexts that I will comment upon here: evolutionary, developmental, and historical.

The Evolutionary Context

To begin with the evolutionary context, Bickel and Johnson argue that, in humanity's hunter-gathering period, temporal discounting was disadvantageous and impulsivity advantageous in the process of natural selection. Obviously, a species that never listened at all to its impulses, for example refused to eat even when starving, would die off in a generation or two at most. But beyond that truism, I think Bickel and Johnson may be focusing on the wrong human characteristic in their evolutionary argument. Rather than try to explain why humans don't value the future rationally and perfectly, I think we should direct our analysis towards explaining what makes us different from other animals — namely, that we can consider future rewards *at all*, even at a discount. For example, earlier today Dr. Ainslie asked members of the audience to choose whether they would rather have a dollar for themselves or give everyone else in the room a dime. My thought about my answer as he went around the room was, "Well, were I a rat or a pigeon, I'd take the dollar. But because I am a human I will vote that everyone receives a dime. This is because I think about the future. Specifically, I know that one year, two years, maybe even five years from now, one or more of the scholars in this room is going to be on a grant review board and see a proposal with my name on it, and I don't want their reaction to be 'Here's where I pay back that cheap bastard who stole my dime!'"

Levity aside, Bickel and Johnson's wonderful charts show that homo sapiens discounts the future far less than any other species we have studied, and contrary to Bickel and Johnson I believe that this trait was genetically advantageous even during our hunter-gatherer period. Imagine two hunter-gatherers named Jumpy and Pokey. Jumpy is impulsive and never met an immediate gratification he didn't like. In contrast, Pokey often delays smaller, sooner rewards for later, larger ones. Who does better at Darwin's grand game?

When Jumpy gets angry at his children, he gives in to his impulse to strike them with the nearest object to hand, or he simply abandons them. In contrast, when Pokey gets angry he takes a long slow walk around the campsite to cool off before disciplining his progeny in a way that would not put his genes at risk.

After a long day's hunting, Jumpy gives in to his immediate desire to sleep, whereas Pokey forces himself to stay up an extra hour each night tanning hides. Come winter, Jumpy freezes to death while Pokey stays warm and comfortable.

When Jumpy is out walking and sees a strange new fruit or vegetable, he eats it immediately. Though just as hungry, Pokey waits to see whether or not Jumpy dies before he partakes. If Jumpy lives, Pokey knows he can eat safely. And if Jumpy dies, he can go home to comfort Jumpy's widow, thereby gaining another chance to spread his genes.

Similar examples of temporal discounting being adaptive also come easily to mind if one shifts the level of analysis from individuals to groups (e.g. tribes, bands, etc.). For example, the jumpy Great Plains tribe would focus its buffalo hunting on baby buffalo because they are slower and easier to kill, and in a year or two the tribe would starve as the herd disappeared. In contrast, the Pokey tribe would focus its hunting efforts on the old male buffalo, knowing that next season this year's baby buffalo will come back as a larger potential food source.

My perspective that temporal discounting gave an evolutionary advantage in hunter-gatherer societies also escapes what I believe is a logical problem within Bickel and Johnson's argument. They maintains that impulsiveness was genetically advantageous prior to the advent of agriculture. But if natural selection was making humans more and more impulsive and temporal discount-oriented with each generation, we should have developed Nintendo and MTV rather than farming 13,000 years ago. In contrast, if one assumes that valuing delayed rewards was advantageous and therefore its genetic component was becoming more and more prevalent in humans over time through natural selection, the emergence of agriculture is much easier to explain.

The Developmental Context

I found Bickel & Johnson's developmental analysis more persuasive, especially their observation that young people both discount the future more and use drugs more than do older adults. They note that this may stem from the young facing a more unpredictable future than do adults. This observation seems sound as a general proposition, but may not be sufficient to explain extreme temporal discounting among those young people who perceive their future as predictably short and painful. This is a sadly common phenomenon among low-income youth who live in violent cities such as Moscow, Rio de Janeiro and Chicago (cf. Kotlowitz 1991), to which Bickel and Johnson allude by commenting, "Considering one's future may seem a fruitless endeavor for individuals who may not expect to experience the future." Low-income adolescents who are convinced that they will die before the age of 40 or 50 actually have an extremely high amount of certainty about a future, at least compared to their middle income counterparts who expect a much longer and varied adulthood. Given this certainty about the future, why are young, low-income inner-city dwellers prone to temporal discounting? In the same vein, who has heard of a prisoner facing the electric chair who ordered a final meal of tofu, egg beaters, skim milk and dry toast? Yet the future of such a person is quite predictable. At different points in their paper Bickel and Johnson seem to take different perspectives on this issue, so I would just ask them to clarify his view: do they believe it is predictability per se or *predictable future rewards* that reduce temporal discounting?

The Historical Context

Finally, let me praise in unqualified terms Bickel and Johnson's efforts to place temporal discounting in an historical and cultural context. To use classic public health language, a genetic predisposition for extreme temporal discounting could be construed as a risk factor, and the current culture's view of time and gratification as an exacerbating or protective factor. The combination of these individual and environmental forces influences the host's vulnerability for temporal discounting and, by extension, drug use. Under this argument, those individuals with "jumpy" genes would be at even more risk in a culture such as the Roman Empire, which as Bickel & Johnson note emphasized the value of the present rather than the future. Indeed, many Western languages include a word describing people and events that operate at a painfully slow pace or show an intolerable lack of impulsiveness and spontaneity. (In English, it is "cunctatory"). These words derive from a Roman insult, originally applied to Quintius Fabius Maximus because he refused to rush in and take on Hannibal directly (Plutarch, 75/2002), preferring instead a series of small delaying actions in the hope that a better opportunity for victory would arise later. He was branded as "Cunctator" (delayer) and kicked out, whereupon the new consul general sent the army marching straight into Hannibal's forces at Cannae, thereby converting 80,000 Jumpy Romans into elephant pavement.

I agree with Bickel and Johnson that the spread of Christianity made Western culture less supportive of temporal discounting. The obvious example is the idea that one's humble hard work and suffering on earth will be compensated for in heaven (Brown 1997). The Egyptians believed in an afterlife, of course, but it was still going to be much better for the Pharoahs than for the starving masses, who lived under no more encouraging parable than, "Yea, the sleek shall inhibit their girth." In the Christian vision, everyone is equal in the eyes of God, such that every person who subscribes to the faith can have a comparable expectation of a large, delayed reward. Bickel & Johnson's trenchant comments on how modern consumer culture make any individual-level temporal discounting tendencies stronger becomes even more compelling when one considers that the post-WWII rise of consumerism has been accompanied by a sharp drop within developed nations in belief in Christianity and in heaven (Wilson 1999). Bickel and Johnson argue that whatever jumpiness we brought forward from our evolutionary history may be expressed more strongly at this historical moment than in previous ones. For society's sake, I wish they were wrong on this point but believe that they are right, an ominous sign given that substances that provide short-term rewards at high long-term costs have never been more widely available.

References

Brown, R. E. (1997). *An introduction to The New Testament*. New York: Doubleday.

Kotlowitz, A. (1991). *There are no children here*. New York: Doubleday.

Plutarch (75/2002). *Life of Fabius*. J. Dryden (Trans.). Available on-line at http://www. barca.fsnet.co.uk/

Wilson, A. N. (1999). *God's funeral: The decline of faith in Western Civilization*. New York: Norton.

Reply to Humphreys

Warren K. Bickel and Matthew W. Johnson

> It is not the strongest of the species that survives, nor the most intelligent;
> it is the one that is most adaptable to change (Charles Darwin, as cited in
> Augustine 1997).

Humphreys provides a careful analysis of our paper, and raises some important concerns that may be shared by other readers. Here, we will focus on addressing two of these intriguing questions. Humphreys argues that natural selection should have favored less impulsive choices and that uncertainty of the future does not always cause impulsive choice. We will address each in turn.

Should Natural Selection Favor Less Impulsive Choices?

Humphreys argues that natural selection should favor self-controlled choice over impulsive choice. He vividly illustrates these options with his two characters, Jumpy (impulsive choice) and Pokey (self-controlled choice). Our view is that the language of dichotomies can be both constraining and misleading. Instead, the discounting of delayed reinforcers refers to a continuum that is bounded by impulsive and self-controlled choice, but permits many more subtle shades between those extremes. Thus, instead of the dichotomy proposed by Humphreys' example of Jumpy and Pokey, we suggest that hunter-gatherers may exhibit behaviors that could be described as jumpy in some circumstances, and pokey in other circumstances. Furthermore, in some situations the human may behave in a slightly jumpy manner (i.e. a relatively high degree discounting), and in other circumstances behave in a very jumpy manner (i.e. an even higher degree of discounting). Natural selection would operate on individuals who display a variety of these behaviors, and may favor those whose behavior tends to reside along one area on the continuum vs. another only if the environment consistently favored one end or the other of the continuum. In inconsistent environments, humans that could dynamically change their discounting may be selected. As may be suggested by Darwin's quote above, flexibility in one's discount rate may be a key to survival.

Our proposition is not that humans never faced circumstances where delayed reward was the adaptive choice. In fact, Humphreys suggests several excellent examples of such circumstances. Extremely impulsive choices (e.g. eating great amounts of a novel food) would, of course, have a selective disadvantage. Our proposition is, however, that the hunter-gatherer environment selected for *relatively* high discounting rates, and perhaps selected for flexibility within this limited range.

Viewing impulsivity along a continuum also relates to Humphreys' assertion that ". . . we should direct our analysis towards explaining what makes us different from other animals — namely, that we can consider future rewards at all, even at a discount." Particularly with the development of verbal abilities, humans presumably developed a time horizon that extended beyond that of non-human animals in many circumstances (e.g. intertemporal reciprocity between individuals), but so long as humans relied on a hunter-gatherer lifestyle, the time horizon would still be kept relatively short.

Humphreys states that if humans were impulsive 13,000 years ago, we should have developed MTV and Nintendo in place of agriculture. His point is that agriculture seems to be a very self-controlled enterprise, therefore how did these impulsive creatures develop such a system? Humans, although still relatively impulsive from our hunter-gatherer background, were presumably less impulsive than non-human animals in many respects, placing us somewhat more on the self-control side of the continuum. This, along with the notion that agriculture developed through necessity rather than inspiration (Diamond 1987), should explain why we were able to develop a system that necessitated such self-control.

Does Uncertainty of the Future Always Cause Impulsive Choice?

The second point we address by Humphreys is that uncertainty of the future does not always cause impulsive choice. He states that low-income adolescents who are convinced of an early death by 40 or 50 years of age actually have a predictable future (predicting that life will be short). In behavioral ecology, the certainty of ultimate importance is the certainty of gene reproduction. For the low-income youths in question, there may be a great deal of uncertainty on whether they will be able pass on genes, for a number of reasons, including the chance of dying before having children and uncertainty about having the resources necessary to ensure that offspring successfully develop. Humphreys claims that their middle-income counterparts expect a more varied adult life. They may be uncertain as to which profession to choose or automobile to purchase; however, this choice causes less uncertainly over the fundamental question of whether one will survive and leave viable offspring. This would seem consistent with research on risk sensitivity. In some species, when energy gains exceed demands (perhaps analogous to the low-income individual), the animal shows risk-prone behavior in the acquisition of food, but when demands exceed gains (perhaps analogous to the middle-income individual), the animal shows risk-averse behavior (Bateson & Kacelnik 1998). For the current discussion, the relevance of this finding is that uncertainty in the acquisition of a resource necessary for survival and future reproduction can dynamically cause shifts in basic behavioral processes.

References

Augustine, N. R. (1997). Reshaping an industry: Lockheed Martin's survival story. *Harvard Business Review*, *75*, 83–94.

Diamond, J. (1987). The worst mistake in the history of the human race. *Discover*, *8*, 64–66.

Bateson, M., & Kacelnik, A. (1998). Risk-sensitive foraging: Decision making in variable environments. In: R. Dukas (Ed.), *Cognitive ecology: The evolutionary ecology of information processing and decision making*. Chicago: University of Chicago Press.

Part III

Empirical Studies of Addiction

Chapter 10

Rational Addiction and Injection of Heroin

Anne Line Bretteville-Jensen

Introduction

Theories of hyperbolic discounting, melioration, and relative addiction assume that individuals are non-rational in the sense that they do not consistently maximise utility over the life span. The theory of rational addiction (Becker & Murphy 1988), on the other hand, assumes that individuals have stable time preferences and exponentially discount the future. Becker & Murphy demonstrate how a rational consumer may start consuming an addictive good and end up in a situation in which the consumption level of the addictive good is very high and sub-optimal for that user. According to the theory, a high consumption level is a consequence of a series of previous choices, not the result of an "addiction illness," lack of information, or irrational behaviour. The work of Becker & Murphy has been met with both enthusiasm and rigorous criticism.

Traditionally, economic consumer theory has been concerned with individual choices under constraints and a phenomenon like addiction has attained little attention. Based on standard assumptions of utility maximisation, stable preferences, etc., little effort has been spent on examining why people start consuming a certain good or why they eventually stop it. Further, consumption of addictive goods like cigarettes and heroin causing severe problems to the user and third parties, have been discussed more within other disciplines than among economists. As shown in Chaloupka *et al.*'s paper in this volume (Chapter 2), however, Becker & Murphy were not the first economists to show an interest in addiction, but they were the first to launch an addiction theory based on standard neo-classical assumptions. In this paper, one of these assumptions and three derived hypotheses will be examined empirically and discussed.

After a short introduction to Becker & Murphy's theory and a description of the data sets, we examine how the assumption of stable time preferences and the hypotheses of price response and consumption stand after being "tested" against data collected among heroin addicts in Norway. Becker & Murphy's theory of rational addiction postulates that drug addicts have a higher time preference rate than non-addicts, that addicts' drug consumption is sensitive to changes in prices and income, and that past and future drug consumption influences present consumption of the drug in question. In the concluding section we discuss our empirical results, the theory we applied, and possible policy consequences of our findings.

The Theory of Rational Addiction

Rational addiction sounds like a contradiction in terms, but Becker & Murphy claim that even this type of behaviour is amenable to analysis by standard theory. Addiction is defined as a strong complementarity between past and present consumption, i.e. an increase in past consumption causes an increase in consumption of the same good today. Rationality signifies that individuals take into account the interdependency between past, present and future consumption when utility over the life span is maximised in a consistent fashion. Becker & Murphy introduce a utility function specified with continuous time:

$$U(0) = \int_0^\infty e^{-\sigma t} u[C(t), Y(t), S(t)] \, dt \qquad (1)$$

where

$$\dot{S}(t) = C(t) + L(t) - \delta S(t) \qquad (2)$$

$C(t)$ is the addictive good, $Y(t)$ is the vector of non-addictive goods, $S(t)$ is the stock of "consumption capital" and σ is the time preference rate. The rate of change in consumption capital is a function of consumption of C and biographical episodes (L), along with consumption capital depreciated with a rate δ. Two key aspects of the addictive good set certain limits on the utility function and are defined by consumption capital:

- *Tolerance*, $\partial u/\partial S < 0$, that is, the utility of any consumption level today will be lower if the individual had a high consumption level of the good in the past.
- *Reinforcement*, $\partial C/\partial S > 0$, that is, higher past consumption stimulates the wish for high present consumption. Reinforcement means that the marginal utility of consumption today increases the more the individual has consumed in the past ($u_{CS} > 0$). Under certain conditions, this could lead the individual to increase consumption of the good. This inherent dynamic in consumption is peculiar to addictive goods.

Consumption capital therefore has two opposing effects on utility and future consumption and, for a rational utility maximiser who consumes addictive goods over time, the reinforcement effect will be greater than the tolerance effect. Becker & Murphy (1988) show, through maximisation of a quadratic design of the utility function, that a sufficient and necessary condition for this is:

$$(\sigma + 2\delta)u_{CS} > -u_{SS} \qquad (3)$$

The reinforcement implies "adjacent complementarity"; that is, the consumption of the addictive good over different periods is complementary. Equation (3) indicates that the higher the time preference rate, the higher the depreciation rate or the more the marginal utility of C rises with rising S, the greater the potential for addiction. Strong adjacent

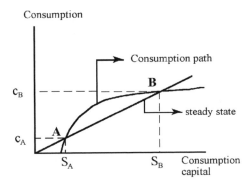

Figure 1: Optimal consumption path for a rational consumer of an addictive good.

complementarity can cause unstable equilibrium points along the optimal consumption path. The existence of this type of unstable equilibrium point is key to the theory because it, inter alia, explains how things like peer pressure, divorce and the like can cause people to develop an addictive condition, as well as explaining how a person's consumption of the addictive good can vary across time despite the absence of any changes in the person's economic environment.

The individual sets his/her optimal consumption of goods on the basis of utility function, prices, income, initial stocks of consumption capital and time preference rate. The "full" price of C corresponds to market price P_C and the value of future costs (including damage to health, loss of social relationships, esteem, etc.). For constant values of the other factors, an optimal consumption path for a variety of combinations of $C(t)$ and $S(t)$ is given in Figure 1.

The consumption path illustrated in Figure 1 (a corresponding figure can be found in Becker & Murphy 1988) is based on a quadratic utility function. The steady state line gives all combinations at $C(t)$ and $S(t)$ where the consumption capital does not lead to any change in consumption ($C = \delta S$). If the optimal consumption level lies over the steady state line, the reinforcement mechanism will cause consumption to rise until equilibrium is reached. If the consumption path lies beneath the line, consumption will decline over time. Point A is an unstable point of equilibrium and B is stable. The optimal consumption path in Figure 1 corresponds to a high time preference rate.

Given that the assumptions underlying Figure 1 hold, the initial value of consumption capital will be the decisive factor in determining whether a person develops a high consumption level (addiction) of the good. The initial value will be ≥ 0 since biographical events are also included in S (cf. Eq. (2)). If the agent's consumption level is low ($S \leq S_A$), s/he will be either to the left or at the unstable point of equilibrium. And there s/he may remain for a time. However, should a life crisis or similar life-shaking events occur, the agent may fall out of or be ejected from this state of unstable equilibrium, move towards the right along the consumption path and end up in a stable equilibrium state with a significantly higher consumption level (B). A consumption level equal to C_B will be suboptimal for the person if the long-term negative effects of past consumption exceed the immediate gratification of a high present consumption rate. For a change to occur and consumption to be lowered, consumption capital needs to fall. A reduction in consumption capital is distressful in the short run and, with much emphasis on the immediate future, the person will not be willing to reduce utility on a provisional basis to increase it in the long run. When the individual arrives at equilibrium B, s/he will remain "imprisoned" there and only changes in the exogenous variables will be able to "liberate" the person.

Heroin Addicts in Norway

The data sets used to test Becker & Murphy's theory are based on interviews with heroin injectors. The interviews took place in the vicinity of a needle exchange service in the centre of Oslo. Three types of data were collected: (1) anonymous interviews, conducted on a regular basis from June 1993 to September 2000, with drug users who attended the needle exchange service; (2) re-interviews with a group of attendees one year after the initial interview (individual panel data); (3) interviews with "non-attenders"; a control group (non-addicts) with similar characteristics to a group of attendees and interviews with a group of former addicts.

The first data set is based on the regular interview sessions that took place first on a monthly basis, then quarterly, from June 1994. A total of 3,039 questionnaires were completed. There were 2–4 interviewers working 2–3 nights for each data-collection session and people were approached after they had used the needle exchange service. As many as possible were asked to participate, but asking everyone was impossible because people often came and left in groups. Except for a short period in 1997, when we were granted special authorisation by the Norwegian Data Inspectorate, the interviewees were anonymous. Thus, it was not possible to register participants in order to help recognise them from one interview session to the next. Some individuals will therefore have been interviewed more than once, but precautions were taken to prevent this from happening during the same interview session. The mean age for the whole sample was 31.6 years (29.6 for females and 32.5 for males). The youngest person was 16 years old and the oldest 59. Females constituted 32% of the sample.

The representativeness of the current sample is difficult to ensure and can be questioned as follows. First, are the drug users attending the needle exchange service representative of all drug injectors in the area? Second, are the individuals included in the sample representative of the attendees? These questions have been discussed elsewhere (Bretteville-Jensen & Biørn 2003a) and, based on a comparison of variables like gender and age distribution etc., with what is known about this group from other studies, the sample may be assumed to be fairly representative of injectors in the Oslo area.

Out of the total of 3,039 completed questionnaires, 2,595 addicts reported that they mainly injected heroin. The remaining group of 444 consisted of people who mainly injected amphetamine, injected both drugs equally frequently, mainly injected other drugs (morphine, methadone, etc.), or did not respond to this particular question. Injecting is an extreme way of consumption. Even if other routes of administration, like sniffing and smoking, appear to be less dramatic, Norwegian heroin users seem mainly to prefer injection. We decided to include only heroin users in the present sample. Some questionnaires were excluded due to missing information on age, gender, ranking of income sources, or prices of the drug injected.

The second data set, containing individual panel data, was based on a group of drug users interviewed in the regular data collection who were asked if they would consent to being interviewed with the same questionnaire in about one year's time. Those who agreed were asked to identify themselves so that they could be contacted by the interviewer twelve months ahead. Out of a total of 286 persons interviewed from March to September 1997, 171 agreed to participate in the panel data study.

It is possible that, for various reasons, those who agreed to participate in the panel data study differed from those who declined to take part. As it happens, this does not seem to be the case and statistical testing showed that the two groups did not differ significantly. When comparing the 171 drug users in the panel data sample with the 115 who only took part in the first regular quarterly data collection, we found a markedly similar distribution among variables such as age, gender, education, age at first injection, number of hiatuses in drug career, income, amount of heroin per injection, and total amount of heroin consumed in the previous month.

Drug injectors constitute an unstable group with respect to where they live, how much and what types of drugs they consume, how they obtain money and so on. They often report poor housing conditions as many live on the streets, provisionally with a friend or in bed-sits in apartment blocks. They are often in prison, a treatment institution, or hospital. Thus, drug injectors are generally very hard to trace for re-interview. So, even though we had their address at the time of the initial interview, we spent a great deal of time later searching for those who had agreed to participate. As we regained contact with our sample, we began to re-interview those who were interviewed in March 1997 in March the following year, and by the end of 1998, 138 of the 171 drug users had been traced (retrieval rate of 81%) and re-interviewed. Among the group of 138, only 84 persons (61%) were still active drug users. Fourteen (10%) were in prison; 11 (8%) were in residential treatment institutions; 10 (7%) were dead; 10 (7%) did not want to give a second interview; 8 (6%) had stopped consuming illegal drugs; and one person (1%) was in hospital.

Comparisons between those who were active heroin injectors both in 1997 and 1998 and those who injected heroin only in 1997 showed few differences between groups regarding the variables we are able to control for. Of the initial sample of 171 drug injectors, 156 reported that they mainly consumed heroin, and 78 out of the 84 re-interviewees reported the same. The final analyses of this second data set are restricted to the group of 78 heroin injectors.

The third data set covers three groups of people: G1 is a group of 110 heroin injectors who answered an additional set of questions when they responded to the regular questionnaire; G2 is a case control group of 110 non-injecting people with characteristics similar to G1 with respect to gender, age, and education. In accordance with discounting theory, we assumed that it was age and education in particular that we should control for. The non-abusers were approached in the street, shopping centres etc., and were randomly selected from passers-by. In addition to questions on the discount rate, respondents were asked about their consumption of intoxicants over the last year. G3 consists of 50 former drug abusers. This was the group that was hardest to find. In the main we employed the "snowball method": on the basis of our acquaintanceship with a few former abusers, we were able to make contact with others. A person was defined as a former abuser if they stated that they had previously been a long-term abuser of either heroin or amphetamine. By including the latter group it was assumed that we might get an indication of the stability in preferences within a group of people who had all been seriously addicted. In contrast to the face-to-face interviews for the groups above, the interviews for this group of former users were mainly conducted by telephone. The questionnaire used here was the same as for the group of non-users.

The Questionnaire

Interviewees we contacted at the needle exchange service were asked to give details about their levels and sources of monthly income, levels of drug consumption and the prices they had paid for the different types and quantities of drugs. Initially, concerns regarding the response rate in these outdoor interviews put constraints on the feasible length of the questionnaire and only a few socio-economic variables (gender and age) were included. After some time, however, we decided to add questions like age at first injection, education, number and total length of drug-free periods, housing conditions, experience with non-fatal overdoses, etc.

Income: Respondents were asked how much money they got from six possible sources: work, state benefits, stealing, sale of drugs, prostitution and "other" sources. This involved two stages: individuals were first asked to rank the six possible sources of income in proportion of total income; then they were asked to estimate the amounts acquired from each source. Besides social benefits, drug dealing among men and prostitution among women were the most frequently reported income sources.

Information on income was far from easy to obtain. Most interviewees responded to the ranking exercise, but some failed to give an estimate of their monthly incomes from the different sources. To avoid possible bias due to non-response, we imputed the missing values. For example, an individual who reported drug dealing as the second most important income source could be assumed to have obtained the average amount reported by others who ranked dealing second. This allowed us to assign an income value to 44 heroin users who had only responded to the ranking exercise. In addition, it increased monthly income for some who had not completed the questions for all income sources they had ranked. The interpolation raised slightly the sample's average income (from 38,000 to 44,000 Norwegian kroner or 4,270 to 4,950 US$).

Consumption: For heroin users, a combination of three variables was used to estimate monthly consumption: quantity of drugs for last injection; number of injections during previous day; number of injecting-days in the previous month. The wide variation in the amount-per-injection was only recognised after some time into the interview period, but a question to pin down the exact amount was then included in the questionnaire. Heroin dealers reported consuming more of the injecting drug than their non-dealing counterparts. Females consumed more heroin than males.

Most respondents also reported extensive use of other intoxicants. The number of drug-taking/drinking days for the month leading up to the interview was available for alcohol and cannabis. We constructed a dummy variable for each of these which we set to unity in cases of 20 or more days of use, since we assumed that this consumption frequency would be needed in order to classify a potential substitute or complementary good to heroin.

For pills, we only have information on consumption or non-consumption in the previous month and the corresponding dummy variable was set to unity if the respondent reported consumption.

Prices: Price data were obtained by asking people what they would have to pay for different types and quantities of drugs. Dealers were asked how much they had paid for the last quantity of drugs they had bought (at least partially) for dealing purposes. The number of units into which a gram of heroin was "cut" declined over the period and we have taken account of this in calculating equivalent unit prices for those who buy in grams. The price of heroin decreased throughout the study period. For heroin users not reporting any amphetamine price, we constructed a variable where dealers and non-dealers were given the average price reported by amphetamine dealers and non-dealers in the corresponding interview session.

The market purity of drugs could be an important determinant of the price-responsiveness of consumption, and trends in market prices should ideally be presented in quality-adjusted terms to reflect the possible effects of purity changes on behaviour. Police seizures indicate large variations in heroin purity at the wholesale level, though it is somewhat more stable at the retail level. However, the purity is often unknown to the buyer at the time of purchase, so quality-adjusted prices may not be very useful after all. In any case, it was not possible to collect any purity data here.

Testing the Addiction Theory of Becker & Murphy

Implications of the theory have resulted in several testable hypotheses such as the following: (1) consumption of the addictive good will have a bimodal distribution in the population; (2) addicted persons will cease consumption suddenly (cold turkey); (3) addicts will be sensitive to changes in economic factors; (4) adjacent complementary implies that current consumption will be positively correlated with past and future consumption; (5) long-term price elasticity will be greater than short-term price elasticity; (6) the effect of expected price changes will be greater than the effect of unexpected changes: (7) the effect of permanent price changes will be greater than the effect of temporary changes; and (8) the time preference rate (TPR) of addicts will, on average, be higher than for non-addicts (high σ gives, ceteris paribus, higher likelihood of addiction). We will examine (3), (4), and (8) in addition to exploring the assumption of stable time preferences.

Hypotheses Regarding Individuals Time Preference Rates[1]

The four theories of addiction discussed in this volume are all to some extent concerned with the time aspect of addiction and, thus, with people's discounting. Time preferences reflect how individuals view utility at different times and a discount function gives the present value of utility obtained at some later point in time. People's discounting is linked to addiction in that addiction is a consequence of a series of choices made over time and their impact will often reverberate far into the future. (Severe health problems from smoking can take decades to materialise.) The rational choice theory assumes that individuals have stable preferences, i.e. it is assumed that their time preference rate is constant and that they discount the future exponentially. A departure from this assumption allows for the possibility of non-rational agents.

Becker & Murphy claim that people with high preferences in the present are more likely to end up with sub-optimal consumption levels corresponding to C_B in Figure 1. The full cost of current consumption includes possible negative consequences occurring at later points in time, but with heavy discounting these negative consequences are given less weight. The time-preference rate contributes to determining where the path of the optimal consumption curve will be situated for the individual person and the shape of the graph (degree of curvature). Becker & Murphy make three statements about consumers' time preferences: (1) time preferences are stable; (2) there is great interpersonal variation in the size of the TPR; and (3) people with a high TPR are more likely to become addicted, that is, a high TPR is assumed to be a contributory cause of addiction. The "pure" TPR (σ) is here conventionally defined as the marginal rate of substitution between present and future utility and the corresponding discount factor is $1/(1 + \sigma)$. The higher the value of the TPR (and the lower the discount factor) the higher the preference for the present.

Empirical estimations of how people balance utility between different periods are, however, difficult to make and no single method has yet been agreed upon. Analyses of both revealed and stated time preferences are commonly based on people's consumption (Deaton 1992) and may at best be taken as indicators of true TPR. The method of stated preferences in response to hypothetical questions has been employed here.

To examine the time preference rate, respondents were asked to imagine that they had bought lottery tickets and had won a specified amount of money. They were asked to give an estimate of how much they would be willing to sell the winning ticket for now if the prize money was not going to be paid out until one year ahead. In other words, we aimed to pin down the amounts that would give the respondents equal utility if they obtained the money now, compared to the utility the lottery prize would give them at some later point in time. The calculation of the discount rates was carried out as follows:

$$r = \frac{1 - (x/y)}{x/y} \tag{4}$$

where r represents the annual discount rate; x is the amount the respondents state they would sell the winning ticket for if the winnings were to be paid out in one year's time; and y is the amount won. Discount rates were estimated for all respondents and the mean values for each of the three groups are presented in Table 1.

Becker & Murphy's theory considers "pure" time preferences and the estimates obtained here are assumed to be indicators of this, but the empirical rates will additionally be affected by other factors such as individuals' income and wealth, life expectancy, and the extent of uncertainty and risk involved:

$$r_j = f_j(\sigma_j, \boldsymbol{\pi}_j) \tag{5}$$

where r_j is the estimated discount rate for person j; σ_j is the "pure" TPR representing individual j's balancing of utility in different periods; and $\boldsymbol{\pi}_j$ is a rate vector of all the other factors.

Table 1: Average of estimated annual rate and corresponding discount factor for the groups of active users, non-users, and former users of hard narcotic substances.

	Annual Disc. Rate (r)	Annual Disc. Factor $[1/(1+r)]$	Size of Sample (n)
Active	0.90 (1.77)	0.53	110
Non-users	0.05 (0.13)	0.95	110
Ex-users	0.15 (0.24)	0.87	50

Standard deviation in parentheses.

Variations in estimated discount rates will be caused by individual differences in either σ_j or π_j. If, however, π_j has a low inter-group variation, any difference found in the mean value for the three groups could be assumed to stem from differences in the "true" TPR. The effect of differences in income, wealth and credit restrictions on the estimates of the discount rate is difficult to evaluate. One could argue, however, that the reported differences in Table 1 may partly be influenced by differences in π_j, but that these differences cannot fully explain the observed variations in discount rates.

A second method was used to elicit participants' time preferences. In order to take account of the special, often acutely felt, financial circumstances in which drug abusers may find themselves, respondents were asked to choose between two ways of having the winnings paid out. Both methods of payment provided a daily sum large enough to cover the purchase of a single dose of heroin or amphetamine (200 Norwegian kroner). The choice was between two ways of payment, in which the first would provide 400 kroner daily for the first half-year and 200 kroner daily for the second half-year, while the other method gave 200 kroner the first half-year and 600 kroner the second half-year. For the addicts, the decision could be seen as a choice between two "free" daily doses of narcotics the first half year and one "free" dose the next vs. one dose the first half year followed by three daily doses for the rest of the year. By choosing the first method of payment, in which the larger sum came in the first half-year, they would end up with a lower total sum when the payment year was over (110,000 kroner as against 145,000 kroner). Impatience would therefore mean a loss in the total amount paid out. For each group the percentages choosing the two possible payment plans were calculated and the results can be seen in Table 2.

Table 2: Percentages opting for the two possible methods of payment of winnings.

	Proportion Choosing A $(\%)$	Size of Sample (n)
Active	32% [23.3, 40.7]	110
Non-users	8% [2.9, 13.1]	110
Former users	8% [0.5, 15.5]	50

Confidence intervals in brackets.

The average of estimated annual discount rates in Table 1 differ significantly among the three groups. Comparisons between the groups show that former users vs. non-users and active users vs. former users both differ significantly at a $p < 0.001$ level.

Non-users in Table 1 quote an annual rate roughly corresponding to interest rates for large capital deposits in the market. The corresponding rate for former abusers lies somewhat higher, but in the vicinity of the level for non-users.

The difference between the estimated discount rates for active users and non-users can be said to conform with Becker & Murphy's theory. Table 1 shows that the active users state that they have a significantly higher discount rate. The high discount rate and correspondingly low discount factor (0.53) is consistent with what Becker *et al.* (1994) report in a study based on a data set of annual per capita cigarette sales for 50 states plus the District of Columbia for the period 1955–1985. By applying the rational addiction framework the authors obtain estimates of the discount factor ranging from 0.31 to 0.64 for different empirical models. However, Becker and his colleagues find their point estimates to be implausibly low and put forward the unrealistic assumption of perfect foresight as an explanation for their finding.

The great difference between the rates of active and former users, on the other hand, does not seem to accord with Becker & Murphy's (1988) assumption of stable preferences. If high discounting is a contributory cause of drug abuse, one would expect former users also to have a high value on their discount rate. According to the theory, consumption capital will be reduced when the consumption of addictive goods ceases, but the actual discounting ought to remain unchanged.

The percentages choosing to have their money paid out under method A (a larger daily sum for the first half-year, but a lower total amount) and method B (a larger daily sum for the second half-year and a larger total sum) are shown in Table 2.

Here too, a multiple comparison indicated that the groups differed significantly, and we find that active users are more impatient than the groups with whom the abusers are compared. The difference between active vs. non-users and ex-users is significant at a $p < 0.001$ level. As many as 32% of active users say they would have chosen method A, while the corresponding figure for non-users and former users in both cases is 8%.

Both Tables 1 and 2 provide estimates that tell the same story, namely that active users' discounting differs significantly from the discounting that is quoted by the groups of non-users and former users.

Does the assumption of stable preferences set forth by Becker & Murphy actually hold? Two possible explanations may be given for the differences between active and former users reported in the tables above.

(1) The estimated discount rate may be lower in the group of former users if there is a *selection mechanism* at work. Given that active users as a group have a relatively high level of discounting, there will probably be large individual variations within the group. If giving up the habit is not a matter of chance, it seems probable that individuals with a relatively low discounting level will have a better chance of controlling their addiction.

(2) Alternatively, active users may have a relatively high discount rate because addiction to intoxicants by itself has changed their discounting. Addiction could influence people's

balancing of future and present income through changes in their "pure" time preference (σ), or through changes in other factors (π) influencing inter-temporal balancing discussed in relation to Equation (5). High discounting may be a consequence of addiction if physical dependence influences inter-temporal balancing. Craving and abstinence pains may, perhaps, make people less able and willing to think in terms of future scenarios and stick to chosen strategies. The present may be given more weight. Abuse of substances such as LSD may, in addition, change their perception of reality and ability to think rationally and thus change their "pure" time preferences. Furthermore, the lives led by abusers of hard narcotic substances involve a heightened morbidity risk, something which, according to discounting theory, will make actors less willing to postpone consumption to later periods. Abusers are also uncertain as to whether they will be in a position to experience tomorrow's consumption on account of the risk of overdosing, imprisonment, etc. With a lower life expectancy they will have fewer years over which to discount, something that in itself will reduce the empirical discount factor.

If drug abuse itself influences discounting, this may contribute to explaining why the rates were so different for active and former users, since this influence, wholly or partly, will cease when the abuse ends.

Former users also report a somewhat higher discount rate than non-users (Table 1). This may simply reflect that those with a lower preference level for the future were those who became drug abusers in the first place. However, the difference in the rate value may also turn out to be a consequence of addiction if the influence on time preferences mentioned above does not totally disappear after the cessation of drug use. A small, but lasting, increase in the risk of diseases and early death may, for instance, have occurred during the period of abuse. In addition, economic prospects may be less promising for former users than for the group of people who have never been addicted to narcotic substances.

Given that the estimated discount rates in this study can be taken as rough indicators of the time preference rate, the results largely confirm variations in TPRs among people with different experiences of addiction. Active users had a significantly higher discount rate than non-users. This is in line with the hypothesis of high TPR as a contributory cause. Ex-users' significantly lower discount rate could be caused by a selection mechanism, *but* it could also be that the assumption of stable time preferences does not hold.

Addicts are Sensitive to Changes in Economic Factors

Michael Grossman, who has been involved in much of the empirical testing of Becker & Murphy's theory, writes (Grossman 1993: 93): "Indeed, in my view the main contribution of Becker & Murphy's (1988) model of rational addiction is to suggest that it is a mistake to assume that addictive goods are not sensitive to price. Even if one does not accept all the aspects of their model, one can examine this proposition in the context of the standard theory of consumer behaviour." This will now be done here.

First, a switching regression model will be applied on the cross-sectional data set from heroin injectors. The main aim is to examine whether drug users respond to changes in economic factors in accordance with standard economic theory, i.e. whether they increase their consumption when prices decrease or incomes increase. A problem with applying the cross-sectional data set, however, is that it is impossible to take the special features of addiction into account as a one-period model cannot take cognisance of possible effects on subsequent periods. We have therefore also used the panel data set to estimate the effect on heroin consumption of changes in prices and income. By following the same individuals over a period of time, the panel data allow us to incorporate aspects of addiction when estimating price and income elasticities. The latter data set will also be employed below when we attempt to examine the possible effect on current consumption of past and future consumption of heroin. In the present section, however, only contemporary effects are in focus.

In modelling heroin consumption, one needs to recognise the fact that consumption patterns of dealers differ from those of non-dealers. Due to dealers' dual role as supplier and consumer, any price changes affecting heroin will have two conflicting effects on their own consumption. Further, user-dealers have more ready access to the drugs they sell, have better knowledge of purity and may be able to buy on credit. Consequently, dealing status itself may have a separate influence on people's heroin consumption. Thus, even if dealing income is treated no differently than income from other sources, the "dealer impact" may be of some importance. As dealing is a frequently reported income source by drug users (46% in the sample report some income from dealing the month prior to the interview), models of heroin consumption should differentiate between individuals according to their dealing status.

An appropriate method needs to allow for the fact that heroin consumers *choose* whether or not to become dealers and the most efficient method is to apply a switching regression model (Greene 1995: 668). The procedure takes account of a situation in which the whole consumption function may differ between dealers and non-dealers. (A fuller description of the method is given in Bretteville-Jensen & Biørn 2003a.) The independent variables applied are prices of heroin and amphetamine, income, gender, age, education, consumption of other drugs (alcohol, cannabis, pills).

As mentioned, the panel data approach provides an opportunity to incorporate aspects of addiction in the estimations. Physical and psychological "stocks of habits" accumulated by previous heroin consumption are potentially important factors when attempting to explain observed heroin consumption. This habit effect may be considered an additional effect to the standard observable economic factors, sociodemographic variables, etc. In a dynamic model of individual behaviour, the addiction to heroin can be represented by a *time-dependent* variable incorporating the "stock of habits" determined by each individual's past heroin consumption (cf. Grossman & Chaloupka 1998). Unobserved habit effects can alternatively be considered as individual "properties," represented within a static model as (components in) time invariant, latent variables (individual specific). The latter approach may be the most convenient when individual data in the form of short panels from a sample of individuals are available. It should be noticed, however, that estimates of the variation in the latent variable will also represent variations in genetic dispositions, attitudes towards health risks, and other valid explanatory variables not specified in the model.

Heroin consumption is here explained by three kinds of variable. The first is a vector of variables that vary across individuals and time, e.g. income and price. The second is a vector of variables that vary only across individuals, e.g. gender. Third, the additive latent variable specific to the individual contains, inter alia, the psychological stock of habits attached to the drug and affects all observations of individual i's consumption of the drug. Two static panel data models are considered, i.e. one random-effect and one fixed-effect model. (More details about the procedure are given in Bretteville-Jensen & Biørn 2003b.)

As the hypothesis of current interest is the possible influence of economic factors, only the estimation results for heroin price and income are reported here. The price and income elasticities in Table 3 indicate how much the consumption of heroin would change in response to a 1% increase in prices or income, respectively.

As can be seen from Table 3, all model variants attain negative and significant price elasticities and all, except one, attain positive and significant income elasticities. In line with the hypothesis, the estimates indicate that consumption would increase substantially if the price of the drug decreased. In two of the three models, dealers seem to be less price responsive than their non-dealing counterparts. The income elasticities vary to a larger extent in the panel data models than in the switching regression model between the two groups of heroin injectors.

The effect of including a latent, time invariant variable representing addiction on the estimated elasticities seems to be small when comparing the results for the switching regression model and the panel data models. Further, when applying the random effects model, the estimated indicator of addiction (not reported in Table 3) was smaller than one a priori would expect. This might partly be explained by possible measurement errors, the low number of observations, the sample consisting of only heroin users (not including non-users), and, perhaps most importantly, the one-year interval between the two observations. A one-year gap between the interviews may be large in relation to the usual "habit cycles" for this damaging drug. We might therefore expect that the estimated strength of the habit formation would have been larger if the drug addicts had been observed at, say, a monthly or quarterly interval.

Although the estimated coefficients vary across the models, the results in Table 3 clearly show that heavy drug users are also responsive to changes in economic factors. Both the results from the SRM and the two static panel data models paint the same picture. As expected, the price responsiveness of dealers and non-dealers differs in every model, although not all the results point in the same direction. A more thorough examination of a subset of the data also reveals that there are gender differences in price responses (Bretteville-Jensen 1999b). Females have a higher price elasticity than their male counterparts. The larger response may indicate that females are more likely to judge other commodities as close substitutes for heroin or that reducing consumption through treatment seems more attractive to them. As the female injectors report consuming more heroin on average than male injectors, the latter result is surprising.

The results in Table 3 are basically in line with previous studies which show great variations in estimated values. Silverman & Spruill (1977) obtained, in an indirect manner, an estimated long-term price elasticity of heroin [−0.25], and van Ours (1995) presented an estimate of −1.0 for the long-term price elasticity of opium demand in the Dutch East Indies. Saffer & Chaloupka (1999) estimated a participation price elasticity for heroin from a national household survey in the USA, and by assuming that elasticity of demand is roughly twice that value, they obtained an estimate of [−1.60, −1.80].

Table 3: Results from a switching regression model (SRM) and two static panel data models.

Variables	Switching Regression Model ($n = 1311$)		Panel Data Model ($n = 78$)			
			Random Effects Model		Fixed Effects Model	
	Dealers	Non-dealers	Dealers	Non-dealers	Dealers	Non-dealers
Heroin price	−0.49 (0.13)	−0.97 (0.12)	−0.56 (0.25)	−0.94 (0.50)	−0.87	−0.72
Income	0.51 (0.06)	0.58 (0.05)	0.78 (0.11)	0.48 (0.21)	0.64	−0.12

Dependent variable is heroin consumption. Variables are in log form. (More results can be found in Bretteville-Jensen & Biørn (2003a, b).)

Current Consumption is Influenced by Previous and Future Consumption

The last hypothesis derived from Becker & Murphy's theory to be examined here suggests that past and future consumption of the addictive good is positively correlated to current consumption. In this section we follow Grossman & Chaloupka (1998), whose point of departure is the empirical testing of the rational addiction model found in Becker *et al.* (1994). The inclusion of both past and future consumption among the regressors distinguishes the derived demand equation from other approaches. A positive and significant estimate of the past consumption coefficient is interpreted as the drug in question being addictive, and a positive and significant estimate for the leaded consumption coefficient is taken as an indication of addicts acting in a rational or foresighted manner.

Grossman & Chaloupka (1998) assume that consumers maximize a lifetime utility function given by:

$$V = \sum_{t=1}^{\infty} \beta^{t-1} U(Y_t, C_t, C_{t-1}, \varepsilon_t) \tag{6}$$

in which β is the time discount factor, ε_t reflects the effects of measured and unmeasured life cycle variables on utility, and Y_t and C_t are as previously defined. Assuming a quadratic utility function and a rate of time preferences corresponding to the market rate of interest, the following demand function is derived:

$$C_t = \theta C_{t-1} + \beta \theta C_{t+1} + \theta_1 P_t + \theta_2 \varepsilon_t \tag{7}$$

Ideally, individual panel data for at least three periods should be available properly to test the hypothesis. Unfortunately, such data do not exist in the case of heroin injectors. There are, however, two other sets of data available: first, the genuine panel data set where the same individuals have been interviewed twice; second, we take advantage of the fact that the interviews in the regular data collection procedure are collected over a seven-year period with 28 quarterly interview sessions. For every session a mean value for each of the relevant variables is estimated in constructing aggregate time series.

With only two observations per respondent available in the panel data set, it is not possible to apply Equation (7) as it stands. Instead, we split the analysis by first estimating only the effect of previous consumption on current consumption (disregard C_{t+1} in (7)) and assume on that basis that individuals ignore the future (a myopic model). We then estimated only the effect of future on current consumption without including possible effects of previous consumption (disregard C_{t-1} in (7)). We estimate the two reduced versions of Equation (7) by a two-stage least squares (2SLS) method. This is because past and future consumption may be correlated with the error term and an OLS approach would thus lead to biased estimates of the parameters of interest. As in the previous section, we run separate estimations for dealers and non-dealers.

By calculating the average of each of the relevant variables for dealers and non-dealers in each quarterly interview session, we obtained the other data set to be employed here — the time series. We can now estimate the effect on current consumption of both previous and future consumption simultaneously. For the same reasons as described above, we again employ a two-stage method as an OLS approach could lead to biased estimates. We instrument

C_{t-1} and C_{t+1} by using the predicted values obtained in a first step by regressing these two variables on: (i) income and drug prices; (ii) income and drug prices in addition to the full set of explanatory variables (age, gender, and dummies for heavy use of alcohol, cannabis, and tablets) in the corresponding quarters as instruments. The effective number of quarters in the estimation is 26. Separate models were applied for the two groups of heroin users.

For both estimation procedures, we follow Grossman & Chaloupka (1998) and assume that predicted future variables equal actual variables. The results from the estimations based on the re-interviewed sample are reported in Table 4.

The "myopic" model with lagged heroin consumption indicates that heroin is addictive, as the estimate of the lagged coefficient is positive both for dealers and non-dealers. However, it is not statistically significant at the 5% level for either of the two groups. Also, the lead estimates are positive and insignificant. The parameter values, especially for dealers, are relatively low. In spite of the low number of observations, most of the price and income elasticities are significant at the 5% level and had the expected signs.

Splitting the analysis by estimating the effect of previous and future consumption separately does not constitute a satisfactory test of the rational addiction theory as the theory predicts that both variables influence current consumption simultaneously, i.e. it might create an "omitted variable problem". Becker *et al.* (1994) and Grossman & Chaloupka (1998) both report results from myopic versions of their models corresponding to the first two columns of Table 4. They find that the parameter values of the myopic versions differ to some extent from those obtained from the full model, as the price elasticities are smaller for the myopic versions. The difference was not statistically significant, however. Still, the finding suggests that the omitted variable bias has caused the current estimates to devalue their real value and the low number of observations may explain why these coefficients, both for dealers and non-dealers, are insignificant.

Table 4: 2SLS for dealers and non-dealers with separate inclusions of a lagged and a leaded variable for heroin consumption.

Variables	LAG		LEAD	
	Dealers ($n = 26$)	**Non-dealers** ($n = 48$)	**Dealers** ($n = 38$)	**Non-dealers** ($n = 40$)
Heroin price	−1.09 (0.42)	−1.68 (0.73)	−1.51 (0.45)	−0.93 (0.82)
Income	0.38 (0.22)	0.57 (0.19)	0.26 (0.13)	0.78 (0.37)
Lagged heroin consumption	0.11 (0.07)	0.34 (0.20)		
Leaded heroin consumption			0.02 (0.19)	0.10 (0.23)
Adjusted R^2	0.28	0.49	0.39	0.53

Dependent variable is current heroin consumption. Variables are in log form. Standard deviation in parentheses. (More results can be found in Bretteville-Jensen & Biørn (2003b).)

Table 5: Estimations based on the constructed time series ($t = 26$ observations).

Variables	Dealers		Non-dealers	
	Model (i)	Model (ii)	Model (i)	Model (ii)
Heroin price	−0.00546 (0.00165)	−0.00599 (0.00275)	−0.00243 (0.00102)	−0.00141 (0.00082)
Income	0.000014 (0.000004)	0.000015 (0.000007)	0.000015 (0.000007)	0.000016 (0.000007)
Lagged consumption	0.03222 (0.03327)	−0.01089 (0.03637)	−0.00019 (0.02629)	0.00213 (0.02834)
Leaded consumption	−0.02814 (0.00926)	−0.01720 (0.01155)	0.01052 (0.00763)	0.00538 (0.00755)
Box-Pierce stat.	3.3433	0.8944	1.5211	1.9212
Box-Ljung stat.	4.3827	1.1718	1.8447	2.3735
Price elasticity	−0.61	−0.67	−0.79	−0.46
Income elasticity	0.42	0.45	0.50	0.53

Dependent variable is current heroin consumption. Standard deviation in parentheses. Model (i) is based on the full set of regressors, model (ii) is based on just income and prices as regressors in the first step of estimating instrument variables.

Positive and significant estimates for future consumption have been used as an argument for rational versions outperforming myopic versions of addiction models. In line with this, the positive, although insignificant, estimates reported in Table 4 give some support to the rational addiction theory. Whether a positive correlation between current and estimated future consumption is the result of a utility maximization as described by the theory may, however, be discussed.

The main results from the time series models are presented in Table 5. The estimated coefficients confirm that heroin consumption is negatively related to own price and positively correlated to income. The estimates in the first four rows of Table 5 are not directly comparable to estimates in Tables 3 and 4 as we have applied a different functional form here. Price and income elasticities are calculated on the basis of variable means, however, and are reported in the last two rows of Table 5.

The results do not unambiguously support the hypothesis of a positive influence on current consumption of previous and future consumption. Two of the four coefficients for previous consumption are, on the contrary, negative, although insignificant. Also future consumption comes out with two positive and two negative coefficients (both for dealers) and one of them is significant at the 5% level. Keeler *et al.* (1993) have tested the Becker–Murphy theory with aggregate time series for cigarettes and Olekalns & Bradsley (1996) have applied aggregate data for coffee consumption. These studies, as well as others that have applied individual and aggregated panel data for addictive goods, report support for the rational addiction theory, i.e. they report positive and significant coefficients for the lagged and the leaded consumption variable.

Our results, especially the negative estimates for past consumption, are surprising. If there is an effect of previous consumption on current, one would expect it to be positive. The above-mentioned works based on time series data have been criticised for not taking sufficient account of the trend in the data, hence causing possible spurious results (Gruber & Köszegi 2001; Skog 1999). We have aimed at avoiding this pitfall. In the last estimation, however, we have applied the same functional form as the other studies. Thus, if we are to believe Becker & Murphy's theory, we cannot explain the findings of a negative relationship between past and present consumption other than by claiming that aggregated data are not well suited to explaining individual behaviour.

Discussion

In Becker & Murphy (1988) it was emphasised that even addictive behaviour could be analysed within a frame of classical economic theory based on stable (time) preferences. The nature of the data and methods applied here, however, do not give sufficient evidence for either a rejection or a confirmation of the assumption of stability in preferences, but the analysis indicates that there may be reasons to question it. The significant differences in estimated time preference rates between active and former addicts are difficult to interpret within rational addiction theory. One possible explanation is that addictive behaviour itself may change an individual's time preference. A high time-preference rate may be one among several causes of addiction, but great impatience and short-sightedness may also arise as a result of addiction. Endogenous time preferences in the case of addiction will contribute to undermining Becker & Murphy's theory.

That greater impatience can arise as a result of addiction is mentioned in a more recent paper by Becker & Mulligan (1997). Their point of departure is that endowed time preferences are excessively high and that rational people will, to varying degrees, have incentives to invest in "future-oriented capital" in order to reduce the size of their TPR. As Skog (2001) argues, however, their theory is about enhancing future utility and not about increasing patience, which is a very different phenomenon. Allowing for an endogenous determination of the TPR is nevertheless a very different starting point than the one that was taken in the Becker & Murphy (1988).

An approach in which the assumption of stable preferences is less binding may, however, be more fruitful in discussing the relationship between addiction and discounting. The fact that, in terms of Becker & Murphy's theory, individuals seem always to act in accordance with their own, long-term interests is contrary to the understanding of many professionals in the addiction field (see, e.g. Heather 1998). The assumption of stable time preferences leaves no room for individual vacillation, impulsive acts, relapses, etc. The other addiction theories discussed in this volume are better capable of incorporating such features of the addiction phenomenon.

Previous conventional wisdom said that the demand for addictive goods is unlikely to be responsive to price (cf. Koch & Grupp 1971, 1973; Rottenberg 1968; Stigler & Becker 1977). There are, however, studies that have estimated individuals' responses to changes in economic factors. Not many of them have done so by also attempting to incorporate the special features of addictions. Some, however, have followed the Houthakker & Taylor (1966) approach and included past consumption in the demand function through a "stock of habits" representing the depreciated sum of all past consumption. Others have tested whether there are asymmetries in price responses of addictive goods (Pekurinen 1989; Young 1983). Becker & Murphy explicitly underline the importance of addiction as an independent influence on the consumption of addictive goods within a time-consistent framework and derive several testable hypothesis of the relationship between consumption and price. They even claim that addictive goods would be more price responsive than non-addictive goods in the long run.

The results reported in above confirm that addicts too are sensitive to price and income changes. The estimated values vary across the models and data sets applied. Even the estimations based on the low number of observations in the panel data set, however, arrive at significant price and income elasticities. Estimates of drug price and income elasticities indicate how drug users respond to changes in economic factors and, hence, should be of interest to policy-makers and others who deal with the drug problem. The legalization debate is an example where estimates of the consumers' price response may have an important role to play. De-criminalizing and/or legalizing consumption and sales of drugs that today are illegal will cause the full prices of the goods to fall and, for dealers, income also. Consumers' responses will be of importance when evaluating the consequences on individuals and society from such a policy change.

What does it mean to say that the demand for heroin is sensitive to price? Generally, the larger the elasticity, the larger the scope for substitutes or alternative means to meet the need. Other drugs are obvious candidates as heroin substitutes. Even though drugs like heroin and amphetamine have fundamentally different physiological impacts, heroin users may turn to amphetamine if the price of heroin increases sharply. As many as 42% of the interviewees who reported mainly injecting heroin in the month leading up to the interview stated that they also had injected amphetamine during the previous four weeks. Reducing the amount consumed or stopping consuming drugs altogether, either by professional help or by oneself, is, of course, another strategy that may be chosen if prices rise. Additionally, the need can be met by other means, like better socialisation, as suggested in the relative addiction theory (Rachlin 1997). In any case, the relatively high price elasticity reported here indicates that there are alternatives to heroin injectors' continued drug use in adverse circumstances.

The current analyses have suggested that heroin injectors have both a relatively high price elasticity and a high time preference rate. The combination of the two is in accordance with Becker & Murphy's theory which claims that younger, less educated, and lower income persons will be more responsive to price changes than others. The finding of addicts' sensitivity to price changes is also in accordance with the relative addiction theory (Rachlin 1997) in which individuals are assumed to substitute consumption of addictive goods with other activities like socialisation. The theories of hyperbolic discounting (Ainslie 1992) and melioration (Herrnstein & Prelec 1992) are more concerned with individuals' ways into and out of addiction and are not explicit on active drug users' probable price responses.

The interdependency of future and current consumption is a special feature of the rational addiction theory. Neither of the two data sets applied here for testing the interdependency hypothesis are ideal for the job. The genuine panel data have only two observations for every individual and the total number of individuals is relatively low. Aggregated time series data, on the other hand, cannot be expected to adequately fit a model of individual behaviour. The coefficients for the leaded variable in Tables 4 and 5 are insignificant and in two models also have the wrong sign. As mentioned earlier, however, Becker and colleagues have previously employed aggregated data when testing the theory and their results generally seem to support the hypothesis (Becker *et al.* 1994).

Are the results in Tables 4 and 5 only a consequence of poor data quality or are there other possible explanations? To what extent should we expect future consumption to positively affect current consumption of heroin? Some objections could be made: (1) In an illegal market like the one for heroin, price fluctuations are perhaps more unpredictable than in a market for legal goods, and factors like available resources for buying the drugs, the availability of heroin in the market, the likelihood of apprehension, etc., may contribute to making future consumption an especially uncertain variable. Furthermore, employing actual values instead of predicted future values in the estimations is problematic econometrically and there are reasons to question the interpretation of the model's coefficients (see Wangen 2002 for a discussion of these latter points); (2) Even if future variables could be predicted relatively precisely, is it likely that optimal future consumption imposes a significant influence on current consumption? According to the theory, an expected price rise in some time periods ahead lowers the corresponding optimal consumption level and will also cause current consumption to fall. To what extent will heroin addicts take expected future price changes into account and how will future dispositions be balanced against the acutely felt need for present consumption? It will surely be optimal for addicts to reduce their current consumption in line with the theory, but will it actually happen? The theory assumes that people decide on an optimal path for the future and follow it without problems. No struggling, no impulsive actions, no relapses, no weakness of will, etc. Thus, even if data from this study, in addition to other empirical studies, support some parts of the theory, there are still parts that are highly questionable. There may be reasons to examine certain implications of the theory another time.

To sum up, by applying data collected among addicts attending the needle exchange service in Oslo we have tested some hypotheses derived from Becker & Murphy's theory. We found that heroin addicts act in accordance with the theory regarding the responsiveness to changes in economic factors. The finding of a larger time preference rate among active addicts is also in line with the theory. We did not, however, obtain support for the assumption of stable time preferences. Nor could the data give significant support to the hypothesis of future consumption being a positive influence on current consumption. More research, preferably analyses of individual panel data, is needed, however, before firm conclusions can be drawn about the theory.

Note

1. This section of the paper is partly based on Bretteville-Jensen (1999a).

References

Ainslie, G. (1992). *Picoeconomics: The strategic interaction of successive motivational states within the person.* New York: Cambridge University Press.

Becker, G. S., Grossman, M., & Murphy, K. M. (1994). An empirical analysis of cigarette addiction. *American Economic Review, 84*(3), 396–418.

Becker, G. S., & Mulligan, C. B. (1997). The endogenous determination of time preference. *The Quarterly Journal of Economics, 112*(3), 729–758.

Becker, G. S., & Murphy, K. M. (1988). A theory of rational addiction. *Journal of Political Economy, 96,* 675–700.

Bretteville-Jensen, A. L. (1999a). Gender, heroin consumption and economic behaviour. *Health Economics, 8*(5), 379–389.

Bretteville-Jensen, A. L. (1999b). Addiction and discounting. *Journal of Health Economics, 18*(4), 393–407.

Bretteville-Jensen, A. L., & Biørn, E. (2003a). Do prices count? A micro-econometric study of illicit drug consumption based on self-reported data. Forthcoming in *Empirical Economics.*

Bretteville-Jensen, A. L., & Biørn, E. (2003b). Heroin consumption, prices and addiction: Evidence from self-reported panel data. Forthcoming in *Scandinavian Journal of Economics.*

Deaton, A. (1992). *Understanding consumption.* Oxford: Clarendon Press.

Greene, W. H. (1995). *LIMDEP version 7.0, User's manual.* Econometric Software.

Grossman, M. (1993). The economic analysis of addictive behaviour. In: M. E. Hilton, & G. Bloss (Eds), *Economics and the prevention of alcohol-related problems* (pp. 91–123). Research Monograph No. 25. U.S. Department of Health and Human Service.

Grossman, M., & Chaloupka, F. J. (1998). The demand for cocaine by young adults: A rational addiction approach. *Journal of Health Economics, 17,* 427–474.

Gruber, J., & Köszegi, B. (2001). Is addiction "rational"? Theory and evidence. *Quarterly Journal of Economics, 116*(4), 1261–1303.

Heather, N. (1998). A conceptual framework for explaining drug addiction. *Journal of Psychopharmacology, 12,* 3–7.

Herrnstein, R. J., & Prelec, D. (1992). A theory of addiction. In: G. Loewenstein, & J. Elster (Eds), *Choice over time* (pp. 331–360). NY: Russell Sage Foundation.

Houthakker, H. S., & Taylor, L. D. (1966). *Consumer demand in the United States 1929–1970.* Cambridge, MA: Harvard University Press.

Keeler, T. E., He, T.-W., Barnett, P. G., & Manning, W. G. (1993). Taxation, regulation, and addiction: A demand function for cigarettes based on time-series evidence. *Journal of Health Economics, 12,* 1–18.

Koch, J. V., & Grupp, S. E. (1971). The economics of drug control policies. *The International Journal of the Addictions, 6*(4), 571–584.

Koch, J. V., & Grupp, S. E. (1973). Police and illicit drug markets: Some economic considerations. *British Journal of Addiction, 68,* 351–362.

Olekalns, N., & Bradsley, P. (1996). Rational addiction to caffeine: An analysis of coffee consumption. *Journal of Political Economy, 104*(5), 1100–1104.

Pekurinen, M. (1989). The demand for tobacco products in Finland. *British Journal of Addiction, 84,* 1183–1192.

Rachlin, H. (1997). Four teleological theories of addiction. *Psychonomic Bulletin & Review, 4*(4), 462–473.

Rottenberg, S. (1968). The clandestine distribution of heroin, its discovery and suppression. *Journal of Political Economy, 76*(1), 78–90.

Saffer, H., & Chaloupka, F. J. (1999). The demand for illicit drugs. *Economic Inquiry, 37*(3), 401–411.

Silverman, L. P., & Spruill, N. L. (1977). Urban crime and the price of heroin. *Journal of Urban Economics, 4,* 80–103.

Skog, O.-J. (1999). Rationality, irrationality, and addiction — notes on Becker & Murphy's theory of addiction. In: J. Elster, & O.-J. Skog (Eds), *Getting hooked: Rationality and addiction* (pp. 173–207). Cambridge University Press.

Skog, O.-J. (2001). Theorizing about patience formation — the necessity of conceptual distinctions. *Economics and Philosophy, 17,* 207–219.

Stigler, G. J., & Becker, G. S. (1977). De Gustibus Non Est Disputandum. *American Economic Review, 67*(2), 76–90.

van Ours, J. (1995). The price elasticity of hard drugs: The case of opium in the Dutch East Indies 1923–1938. *Journal of Political Economy, 103*(2), 261–279.

Wangen, K. R. (2002). *Patterns in household tobacco consumption.* Dissertation, Department of Economics, University of Oslo, Norway.

Young, T. (1983). The demand for cigarettes: Alternative specifications of Fujii's model. *Applied Economics, 15,* 203–211.

Comments on Bretteville-Jensen

Michael A. Morrisey

I will preface my remarks by noting that while my wife claims I am addicted to economics, I am not an addiction economist. The distinction is important. To understand the functioning of markets it is important to understand the institutional "details" of how the market functions. Some might say one needs to know the culture and mores of the society. Economists would tend to say we need to know the incentives and constraints. All this is to say that, if what I say sounds silly or naive, it probably is!

Anne Line Bretteville-Jensen's paper (hereafter B-J's paper) is very ambitious in undertaking three sets of complicated analyses. I particularly like the unusually thoughtful discussion that accompanies the analysis. It presents alternative explanations and suggests reasons for unexpected results. I was less pleased with the absence of full regression results that underpin each of the component of the study. Their absence makes it difficult to appreciate the work, to fully understand the empirical specifications, and to glean additional insight.

The paper undertakes three separate studies using related data sets. It examines differential time preferences of addicts, former addicts and non-users; it examines the price sensitivity of addicts to differences in prices and incomes; and it examines the interdependence of future and current consumption of heroin. All are efforts to test the rational addiction model of Becker & Murphy (1988) and all essentially rely on in-person interviews with heroin addicts conducted in Oslo, Norway between June 1993 and September 2000.

The third study, focusing on interdependent future and current consumption, is the least satisfying. The theory argues that past and future consumption of an addictive good is positively correlated to current consumption. Unfortunately, as B-J notes, the data are not up to the task. In her true panel, she only has two periods of observation. The absence of the third period biases the estimation and the results often lack statistical significance, perhaps because of the scarcity of observations. Her efforts to overcome this in a time series of aggregated responses is problematic in that the results vary across regressions and often have the wrong signs. More fundamentally, she is forced to make aggregate data speak for individual behavior.

On the other hand, her second study, examining price and income sensitivity, is strong. I think she is right in separately analyzing drug dealers and non-dealers and in treating dealer status as endogenous. Dealers and non-dealers may have very different preferences for heroin and may operate in very different markets. B-J's results indicate that non-dealers are more price sensitive than dealers. This is consistent with a view that non-dealers have better substitutes for mind-altering substances. This would seem to square with a view that they are not as dependent upon a single type of drug.

However, the empirical result may be driven by variables for which the study is unable to control. Perhaps most importantly, the price and quantity data are not adjusted for drug quality. One would expect that dealers have a better sense of quality. If so, one would also expect that they would have higher quality adjusted price elasticities than would those with less knowledge. In as much as price may proxy for quality in the empirical specification, the differences in elasticity may reflect the non-dealers' lack of quality discrimination.

The nature of the dealer's purchasing "network" may also be imbedded in these price elasticities. If a dealer serves as an independent broker in a wholesale drug market, one would expect that he/she has access to a wide range of supply. As such, one would expect the dealer to have better substitutes in supply and, therefore, greater elasticity of demand. On the other hand, if the dealer is essentially a "franchisee" who is tied to a single source of supply, then the "franchiser" may not allow purchases to fully reflect differences in the wholesale price. Future work should focus on some mechanism to quality adjust the price and quantity measures. It may also be fruitful to better understand the workings of the supply network.

B-J uses sources of income in this analysis to identify dealers and non-dealers. This is obviously a successful approach. However, these data suggest additional research that could focus on the various sources of income and their effects on use. From a policy perspective it would be very useful to know the effects of government subsidies, for example, on heroin consumption. Knowledge of the links between prostitution and stealing as sources of income and heroin consumption would be useful to allow consideration of the indirect effects of changes in policing efforts on these behaviors and their indirect effects on drug use.

The first B-J study offers some clear insight into the question of whether addicts have different discount rates than former addicts and non-users. She finds that they do. She uses a fascinating set of questions dealing with the hypothetical willingness to trade-off lottery winnings over time to obtain estimates of time preference. This is innovative although there is an empirical literature in economics on hypothetical and actual personal discounting (see Warner & Pleeter 2001 for a discussion). B-J's results indicate that addicts have a very high discount rate, in the neighborhood of 90%. Former addicts have a much lower rate, 15%, and non-users had five percent discount rates. She interprets this as suggestive that the rational addiction model is incorrect. The model hypothesizes that addicts will have higher discount rates. The lower rates for former addicts, in her view, are inconsistent with this theory.

This may well be true, but there are other explanations that should also be considered. First, there is substantial variance in the reported discount rate among addicts. The standard deviation reported in Table 1 is nearly twice that of the mean. It is conceivable that the definition of an "addict" is too broad. It may include people who are not actually addicts but who nonetheless completed an interview at the needle exchange center. If the theory is correct, these erroneously coded folks will have the lower reported discount rates within the cohort of "addicts" and actually may have much more in common with "former addicts" than with true addicts.

A second alternative explanation has to do with the nature of the personal capital market opportunities the respondent has available. B-J has argued that the process of addiction may lead one to have higher and higher discount rates as one spins deeper and deeper into addiction. In this view lower discount rates of former addicts may reflect their re-emergence from addiction. Suppose instead that addicts do have stable and high discount rates. They would not necessarily report these high internal rates of time preference to the interviewer. They may have many sources of capital from which to obtain funds over the course of a year. They could borrow from friends, from a bank, from a credit card, from a pawn shop, or from a loan shark. If they could borrow from a credit card at 18%, one would expect that they would list something like 18% as the relevant trade-off between obtaining the lottery proceeds today and next year. The point is that the time preference rate for a spiraling addict may remain constant, but the social decline in the addict's ability to interact with friends and with markets may foreclose low cost opportunities to borrow. From this perspective, the relatively low discount rate reported by former addicts may reflect a process of re-attachment to the labor force. Indeed, if the results of the second component of the B-J study are to be believed, and addicts do respond rationally to differences in prices and incomes, then they would also be expected to respond rationally to differences in the personal capital market.

All this said, a better way to test the theory would be to take advantage of the interview/re-interview nature of the ongoing research effort. In future waves of the interview in which the respondent has agreed to be identified, the investigator can again ask the lottery question. This would allow a much cleaner test of the constant, high discount rate hypothesis.

Overall, Bretteville-Jensen has provided a well done and thought-provoking set of studies. Like all good studies it raises as many new questions as it answers. The exciting feature of this investigation is that the unique and ongoing data collection effort provides the opportunity to investigate many of the new questions.

References

Becker, G. S., & Murphy, K. M. (1988). A theory of rational addition. *Journal of Political Economy*, *96*, 675–700.

Warner, J. T., & Pleeter, S. (2001). The personal discount rate: Evidence from military downsizing programs. *American Economic Review*, *91*, 33–53.

Reply to Morrisey

Anne Line Bretteville-Jensen

I greatly appreciate Michael A. Morrisey's comments on my paper. He demonstrates that it is more than sufficient to be addicted to economics — it is not required to be an addiction economist — to understand the core of areas under discussion. His comments highlight a need for clarification of certain points, he suggests alternative explanations for some of the findings and he also points to weaknesses in the analyses. Further, Morrisey says he misses the full regression results that underpin each of the components. The reason for omitting the full sets of results is, of course, due to space; the paper would simply have been too long for the purposes of the conference. The complete tables of results are naturally available to anyone upon request. Morrisey has some remarks on each of the three studies, and I will start with those related to the hypothesis of addicts' time preference rate.

Morrisey suggests that other explanations underlying the substantial difference in estimated time preference rates between active, former and non-users of hard drugs should be considered. He notes the presence of wide variance in the reported discount rates among active and former addicts and suggests that the definition of "addict" may be too broad in that it might include people who are not actually addicts but who nevertheless completed the interview at the needle exchange service (NES). If that were the case, these erroneously coded people would have lower discount rates than "real" addicts and may have more in common with former addicts.

In the study, people are defined as active drug users if they stated at the interview when frequenting the NES that they had injected heroin and/or amphetamine in the four weeks leading up to that point in time. Out of the 110 individuals coded as addicts, 91% reported injecting on a daily or almost daily basis. People defined as former addicts reported on average their most recent injection as being about six years ago (mean number of months was 73 with a standard deviation of 73.0). Therefore, the high proportion of drug users injecting on a daily/almost daily basis and the relatively long period since former addicts' most recent injection indicate that the problem of coding would probably not have influenced the results to any large extent. Further, if people had been coded erroneously, a corrected estimate of the time preference rate (TPR) for former addicts would increase, but so would the new estimate for average TPR for active drug users. Consequently, it is not certain that the gap between the two groups would have narrowed anyway.

Morrisey proposes a second explanation for the findings and, admittedly, I cannot exclude the possibility that at least parts of the differences in estimated discount rates between former and active users might be explained by better opportunities to borrow money for the former group. The estimated discount rate, r_j, will, however, be influenced by both σ_j (the "pure"

TPR representing individual j's balancing of utility in different periods) and π_j (a rate vector of all the other factors influencing r_j, cf. Equation (5) in the paper). If the high value of estimated discount rate among addicts is just a result of an increase in π_j, due to worsened conditions in the credit market, and the "pure" time preference rate has remained unchanged, then the estimate of former addicts' discount rate is to be taken as the relevant estimate for all addicts. In that case, the revealed difference in time preference rates between addicts and non-addicts is not very large any more, especially since there are reasons to believe that addicts' π_j-vector has a larger influence on r_j than non-addicts'. If the time preference rate is stable, the data will give less support to Becker & Murphy's hypothesis of a high time preference rate being a contributory cause of addiction than indicated in the paper.

When commenting on the second analysis, Morrisey reminds us of the possibility that the price elasticity estimates could be driven by variables that I am unable to control for. He is especially concerned that the price and quantity data are not adjusted for drug quality. Although it definitely would have been advantageous to have access to such information, I do not believe it represents a problem of great importance for the estimation of non-dealers' price elasticities. This is because non-dealers, at the time of purchase, do not possess such information either.

The data reveals that the market price paid by non-dealers for the smallest unit of heroin was very stable across individuals within the same interview session, although it varied substantially over the study period from 1993 to 2000. It is possible, therefore, that if we had had the chance to test heroin purity in real purchases, quality-adjusted prices would have biased the estimates if the quality had varied substantially without being reflected in the market's retail prices. What seems generally to be the case in the Oslo heroin market, however, is that fierce competition between dealers at street level is "forcing" suppliers to offer a certain standard of quality. Even if cheating (selling heroin of very low quality) occurs, chemical analyses of small-unit seizures, performed at the National Bureau of Crime Investigation back in the 1980s, indicate that dealers at this level adjusted the quantity of heroin per unit according to purity of the drug. The National Bureau found that the content of heroin per unit sold at the street level remained surprisingly stable. Unfortunately, due to budget constraints such analyses are not carried out any more. A relatively stable price and purity level of units sold to non-dealers suggest that quality-adjusted price and quantity data would not necessarily contribute to improve price elasticity estimates for non-dealers.

On the other hand, Morrisey's argument may be more relevant for the estimates of dealers' price response, as it might be more likely that prices at the wholesale level are quality adjusted. In contrast to purchases at street level, wholesale purchases are normally based on mechanical weighing in the presence of the buyer. With quality-adjusted prices, one would expect dealers' price elasticities to be smaller than for those who deal in "quantity-adjusted" prices. If units at the retail level are quantity adjusted and at the wholesale level quality adjusted, this may partly explain the observer differences in price elasticities among dealers and non-dealers. There are, however, theoretical reasons to expect additional differences between dealers' and non-dealers' estimates as a price change will have two conflicting effects on dealers' own consumption, while non-dealers will only experience the direct price effect.

Morrisey's last point regarding the interpretation of the reported price elasticities I do not quite understand. He says that the dealer's purchasing "network" may be embedded in the estimates as the elasticities will be influenced according to whether the dealer serves as an independent broker or as a "franchisee." Morrisey argues that a broker would have better supply substitutes and therefore greater elasticity of demand. I do not see his point here as the prices both dealers and non-dealers are asked to report are the prices they have to pay for the drugs they consume. Whether a dealer operates as a broker or a franchisee should not make any difference to how s/he responds to a given price increase with respect to own consumption of the good. A related but still different topic, however, is the question of whether income really is an exogenous variable. If addicts respond to price changes by adjusting not only their consumption but also their income, the estimated price elasticities will be biased upwards provided that the income elasticity is positive. Future work should focus on the relationship between income and price responses.

I agree with Morrisey when he says that the third study, focusing on interdependent future and current consumption, is the least satisfying as the data at hand are not ideal for the job. The absence of a third period biases the estimations based on the two-wave panel data set. As mentioned in the paper, however, similar analyses including only lagged variables are also reported by Becker *et al.* (1994) and Grossman & Chaloupka (1998), in addition to their results from the full models. In both studies the estimates for the lagged variables had a smaller value in the myopic version compared to the full model, indicating that the bias caused by the absence of a third period tends to underestimate the value in the former type of models. If that is the case also in the present estimations, the estimates reported in Table 4 understate the true value to some extent.

Further, I share Morrisey's scepticism towards letting "aggregate data speak for individual behaviour." Many of the empirical tests of Becker & Murphy's theory found in the literature, however, including the authors' own test (Becker *et al.* 1994), are based on aggregated data. The last analysis is therefore meant as a comparative exercise and the functional form applied there (the economic variables were not log-transformed in this case) corresponds better to the previous analyses.

Finally, I want to thank Michael Morrisey for his constructive criticism. He also pointed to new research questions and I will probably look into some of them in the near future.

References

Becker, G. S., Grossman, M., & Murphy, K. M. (1994). An empirical analysis of cigarette addiction. *American Economic Review, 84*(3), 396–418.

Grossman, M., & Chaloupka, F. J. (1998). The demand for cocaine by young adults: A rational addiction approach. *Journal of Health Economics, 17*, 427–474.

Chapter 11

Social Interaction and Drug Use: Rachlin vs. Schelling

Hans O. Melberg

Introduction

Howard Rachlin has written that "addicts are addicts *because* they are lonely" (Rachlin 2000: 145, emphasis in original). This claim is part of his "relative addiction theory" and the purpose of the first section of this paper is to present and evaluate some aspects of that theory. To that end I use findings emanating from a survey of about 500 drug users in treatment, as well as large surveys of the general population. The use of this evidence in turn raises the question of what, if anything, can be learned about the causes of addiction by asking drug users. For instance, Davies (1997a, b) claims that such surveys shed very little light on the causes of addiction and the second part of the paper discusses this view. In the third section I focus on social interaction, not as a variable in an explanation (as Rachlin does), but as a mechanism in the sense used by Elster (1998) and Schelling (1998). I exemplify this by exploring a small model of two mechanisms: observational learning and the dynamics of social stigma.

Rachlin's Theory of Relative Addiction

The theory of relative addiction presents addiction as the outcome of a process whereby a person is driven by a constant (inelastic) need for something — for instance, anxiety reduction or mood elevation — that can be satisfied either by social interaction or by drug use (separable substitutes). The choice is assumed to be governed by the relative return of the two activities. The relative return, however, is not constant. More and more drugs are required to produce the same effect and, in this sense, it becomes more and more expensive the more the individual has used drugs previously (price habituation). Social interaction, on the other hand, is assumed to be analogous to playing classical music or doing sports, in the sense that the more one does it, the easier and/or more pleasurable it becomes. So it could be said that social interaction, unlike drugs, becomes cheaper and cheaper the more one

Choice, Behavioural Economics and Addiction
© 2003 Published by Elsevier Ltd.
ISBN: 0-08-044056-8

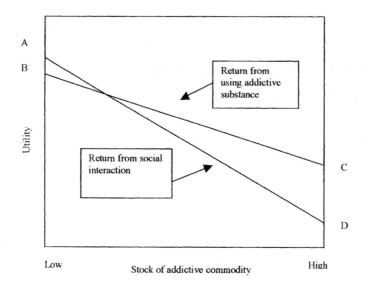

Figure 1: Relative Addiction. The curves indicate the instantaneous utility of using drugs or engaging in social interaction. Individuals to the left of the intersection will tend towards *A* (no consumption of addictive commodity), but a shock that increases the price of interaction will shift the return curve (for interaction) down and an individual who previously was to the left of the intersection, might find him/herself on the right, in which case s/he will use more and more drugs (tending towards *C*).

engages in it (price sensitization). These differing effects on instantaneous utility can be illustrated by letting the utility of drugs decrease the more the individual uses drugs (within a given time window) and the net return to social activity increase the more social activity he or she has engaged in (see Figure 1).

Runaway addiction can follow when a change in the direction of more drugs increases the price of drugs less than it increases the price of social activity, i.e. the curve describing the return to social activity is steeper than the curve for drug use (relative price sensitization). For instance, the loss of a friend makes social activity more costly (shifts the curve down) and makes the use of drugs cheaper relative to social activity. Faced with this change in prices the person may opt for more drugs. Assuming relative price sensitization, this change makes it even more costly to engage in social interaction, so the person will use even more drugs. In short, without enough social interaction to satisfy the undefined need, the person will compensate by using drugs and, given the dynamic consequences of using drugs (making interaction even more difficult), this may create a situation in which the best perceived alternative is to use even more drugs.

The theory of relative addiction is related to several well-known theories of addiction. It is compatible with the view of Herrnstein & Prelec (1992) that agents tend to choose the alternative that has the highest local or instantaneous utility as opposed to the overall best alternative, but it is also well suited to illustrate the phenomena of adjacent complementarity that is important to Becker & Murphy's (1988) theory of how people end up as excessive consumers of some goods. Building on Stigler & Becker (1977), it also provides an account of how properties of a substance may lead to excessive consumption but, unlike Stigler and Becker, the properties are justified in more detail by Rachlin and the resulting theory is compatible with evidence that the demand for drugs is elastic. Rachlin also argues that the theory can explain the shuttling between abstinence and relapse that is characteristic of many addicts. As they consume more and more drugs they are increasingly driven by a need to avoid pain (the behaviour is increasingly negatively reinforced). If people dislike being driven by negative reinforcement, they may eventually reach a point where the feeling of negative reinforcement has such a high cost ("I am a slave") that they decide to quit. A similar story but in reverse explains why such a person may start to use drugs again (Rachlin 2000). In sum, the theory of relative addiction presents an account of why and how people start, continue and stop (and start again) to use alcohol, tobacco and illegal drugs. The question is, how we should evaluate this theory?

An explanatory theory can be evaluated both by the realism of its crucial assumptions and the truth of its implications. Instead of trying to explore all kinds of evidence relevant to all assumptions and implications, I shall concentrate on a limited range of aspects of the theory based on limited evidence. This will allow me to go into greater detail about the relationship between loneliness and addiction, but it also implies that a wider view may contradict the picture that emerges from my narrow pool of evidence.

Evaluating the Assumptions

The assumption that you need larger and larger doses of drugs to achieve the same effect rests on the phenomenon of tolerance or the increasing negative side-effects of using drugs. One might, of course, ask whether the process is as nicely behaved (linear) as Figure 1 might indicate, and Rachlin himself has noted some minor exceptions, but these complications do not seem essential to the argument and in any case they are not the focus of this paper.

The same applies to the assumption that social interaction grows rusty unless it is practiced. A person with few or no friends may have a hard time engaging in social interaction, but he may also have a very high reward from the few interactions that he does have. Moreover, we do not know whether the skill grows rusty in a nice linear way. However, once again, as a first approximation, it would seem acceptable to assume that engaging in social interaction is easier and/or more pleasurable for people who have engaged in much social interaction in the past.

It is far less obvious that social interaction and drug use are separable substitutes. To argue his case, Rachlin (1997) relies on a summary of the relationship between smoking and social interaction as summarized by Fisher (1996). The evidence shows, for instance, that people with little social support smoke more than those with much social support, that smoking increases after losing social support and that attempts at cessation work much better if accompanied by social support. Rachlin also cites evidence to the same effect for alcohol and heroin. Finally he argues that the price elasticity of alcohol and other drugs is indirect evidence for substitutability.

There are several problems with the evidence cited above. First of all, substitutability between two goods is measured by their cross-price elasticity, as opposed to the own price elasticity of one good. Second, evidence of correlation — even of the type that treatment is more successful for those who have social support — must be treated with caution as long as it is not accompanied by a discussion of possible third variables that could exert an impact. Finally, even if we grant the assumption of (strong) substitutability, there is still the question of separateness. Why should we assume that *only* social interaction or drugs are able to satisfy the undefined need?

It is important to note that Rachlin's argument not only relies on the common-sense notion that social support can be helpful in order to beat the habit of using drugs, or that losing social support — e.g. after a divorce — sometimes can lead to more drug use. The claim is much stronger than that because, he argues, loneliness is *the* cause, and additionally that loneliness causes a particular form of drug use in which social interaction and drugs are separable substitutes for some undefined deeper need. Indeed, it is the strong claim which makes the theory interesting as a general theory of addiction. To argue that that social support is often helpful when trying to quit drugs — or to avoid starting drug use in the first place — is neither surprising nor amounts to a general theory.

Strong Implication: All and Only Lonely People Use Drugs?

The theory of relative addiction implies that there should be some kind of relationship between use of drugs and loneliness. If we really assume that social interaction and drug use are the *only* activities that can satisfy an undefined and constant need, then individuals who have much of one must have little of the other. Hence, when an estimated 1.9% of the Norwegian population claim to be "very lonely" in a large survey from 1998 (Lunde 2001), we would expect this group (and only this group) to have a high consumption of various drugs. In short, an implication of the strong version of the theory is that all addicts should be very lonely, but no one else.

It is not difficult to throw doubt on the strong version of the theory. For instance, in a large survey of addicts in treatment, 25% denied that they had felt lonely "at all" during the past week (see Table 1). Hence, it seems that many people use drugs even if they are not lonely. Moreover, many lonely people do not use drugs of any kind. In a survey of health among all the inhabitants of a county in Norway ($n = 65,400$), 17% of those who were most lonely did not smoke or drink alcohol at all (data from same source as in Table 2). Not only are there significant numbers of abstainers among those who are lonely, there are relatively

Table 1: Feelings of loneliness among drug users. (How much have you been bothered by feelings of loneliness during the past week?)

	Not at All	A Little	Moderately	Quite a Lot	Very Much	No Answer
(%)	25.3	28	18.0	17.4	10	1.2

Source: Survey of 482 drug users in treatment organized by the Cost-Benefit Project under the National Institute for Alcohol and Drug Research in Norway. Data collection organized by Edle Ravndal and Grethe Lauritzen.

Table 2: Feelings of loneliness, smoking and alcohol consumption by gender and age.

Age	Male				Female				Overall
	20–49	50–69	70+	Total	20–49	50–69	70+	Total	
I have been very lonely during the past two weeks	3.2	4.2	7.8	4.1	3.3	5.0	14.3	5.4	4.8
Do not drink alcohol (teetotallers) (%)	4.3	9.4	22.4	8.5	6.8	20.4	47.9	17.5	13.3
Smoke cigarettes daily (%)	30.4	29.6	17.7	28.1	37.0	30.1	10.8	30.4	29.4
Drink alcohol several times a month (%)	82.2	66.2	36.3	70.5	66.2	41.8	12.8	50.2	59.8
Average number of times per month drinking alcohol	3.7	4.3	4.2	3.9	2.9	3.5	3.4	3.1	3.5

Source: The Nord-Trøndelag Health Study (HUNT). A comprehensive survey of health in a Norwegian municipality 1995–1997, $N = 65717$, 70% of those invited responded.

more abstainers among those who are lonely than in the general population. There were 9.8% abstainers from both alcohol and tobacco in the general population compared to the afore-mentioned 17% abstainers among those who were the loneliest.

Supporters of relative addiction theory can make at least two possible responses to the criticism above. First, they can question the interpretation of the evidence. Second, they could weaken the assumptions slightly in order to make the theory fit better with the evidence.

One interesting way to question the interpretation of the evidence would be to argue that since the theory assumes that drug use is a substitute for social interaction, then the feeling of loneliness is muted by drug use. In other words, the person would be lonely if he were not using drugs but when he is using drugs the feeling goes away. The situation is analogous to the relationship between amphetamine and hunger. Amphetamine is said to reduce the feeling of hunger. For this reason some people have used the drug partly in order to avoid feeling hungry (e.g. when trying to lose weight). In this case, hunger is clearly part of the reason why they take the drug, but when asked whether they are hungry, they would say no precisely because the drug has muted their sense of hunger. In the same way one might argue that all drug users really are lonely, but that it does not show in the survey since the feeling is eliminated by the drug.

Unfortunately, such an interpretation is not compatible with the fact that many drug users also report being lonely. If drug use really mutes the feeling of loneliness, then we would not expect 27% to report that they feel quite or very lonely. Moreover, the theory of relative addiction assumes that drug use and loneliness are connected through an undefined deeper need. Hence, the analogy with amphetamine is misleading since, in that case, drug use and hunger are directly related. Finally, claiming that reportedly non-lonely drug users really are lonely (they just don't know it themselves) is not compatible with other indicators of loneliness. For instance, when asked about number of close friends, 78% of the drug users said they had one or more close friends. Although this is lower than the national average (84%), it seems difficult to argue that the existence of not-lonely drug users can be explained away by arguing that they "really are" lonely individuals with no friends.

Is it possible to reconcile the theory of relative addiction with the existence of addicts who have friends (on average they claimed to have between two and three close friends in our survey) and do not feel very lonely? Rachlin argues that the observed social activity of addicts is only "pseudo social support." It "is not a source of social support in the sense that a family or community is. The opium addict does not go to the opium den for the social support (if any) to be found there" (Rachlin 2000: 156). In this case the cause of drug use is lack of social support, not loneliness, and we need some kind of operational definition of social support — other than feelings of loneliness and number of friends — to test the theory. I have no such definition or data that could be used to distinguish between good and bad friends. Rachlin, too, ends up by appealing to common sense in the quotation above, but he relies on the most plausible case (heroin). The intuition is weaker when it comes to other addictive substances meant to be covered by the theory, such as smoking which is often viewed as a social activity (but see Ennett & Baumann [1993] for contradictory evidence). As long as the theory is meant to cover addictions in general, it cannot restrict itself to evidence that fits the theory by using heroin (and not smoking) to claim the absence of complementarity between social activity and use of addictive substances, while using tobacco and alcohol consumption and not illicit drugs to make the theory fit the age and gender structure of substance use. Also, since the theory operates at the level where all drugs (alcohol, smoking, illicit drugs) are considered to be the same, it cannot explain why some people smoke while others use alcohol.

Implications of a Weaker Version of the Theory

The arguments above may seem too strong. After all, it does seem to be the case that drug users tend to be significantly lonelier than the general population. About 10% of our respondents reported that they had felt "very lonely" during the past week, while — as mentioned — 1.9% of the general population felt the same over the past two weeks. This suggests that there might be something to the claim that loneliness is related to drug use, but we need to weaken the theory to avoid the strong implication that all addicts (and no others) are lonely. Instead the implication should be that addicts *tend to be* lonelier than the general population. This seems like a much more reasonable statement. To arrive at this result we simply substitute the assumption that using drugs and social interaction are *always* separable substitutes with the assumption that they tend to be separable substitutes.

Indeed, one might argue that this interpretation is by far the most reasonable and that the arguments made against the strong version were really attacking a straw man. As Rachlin writes, a "central assumption of relative addiction theory is that addictive activities and social activities are walled off . . . — they are at least *moderately* substitutable for each other but not for any third activity" (Rachlin 2000: 151, emphasis added). Although the implications of the term "moderately" are not explored by Rachlin, one might argue that it is perfectly legitimate to present a simplified theory in which we explore the consequences of strong assumptions, believing that the tendency of the conclusion will hold even if the assumptions are weakened.

I have two arguments against the weaker version of the theory. First of all, there is empirical evidence that is incompatible even with the weaker version. Second, I do not think the move from the strong to the weak version is as innocent as it might seem.

Although drug users in general tend to report being lonelier than the general population, a closer look at the numbers indicates anomalies even for the weaker theory. For instance, the age and gender pattern of loneliness do not match the facts known about the population using illegal drugs. While this population is dominated by young males, loneliness is more predominant among older people and females. The same applies to other drugs; the tendency is that the group that is most lonely drinks and smokes less than the general population. At the extreme, the loneliest group — older females above 70 — both drink and smoke far less than the rest of the population.

To explain anomalies in the pattern of use, the inexact nature of the relationship (not all addicts are lonely) and why some smoke while others use alcohol, one might introduce new variables. For instance, females might have larger barriers against taking drugs as a result of socialization, there might be genetic factors related to willingness to engage in risky behaviour and there are obvious selection effects that explain why older people smoke less than young people. In this way we could maintain the argument that loneliness is the cause of drug use in the face of evidence that the relationship between the two is at best imperfect. The price, however, is a further weakening of the theory by the introduction of a ceteris paribus condition and allowing other variables into the relationship.

The introduction of third variables leads to my second argument against the weakened theory of relative addiction. As soon as we relax the strong assumption of separable sub-stitutes and allow for other variables to enter the relationship, the question immediately becomes why we should focus on loneliness as a cause of addiction as opposed to the other variables. To answer that we need an empirical investigation into the strength of the many different variables that could be related to drug use — childhood experiences, genetic differences, discounting, risk perceptions, income opportunities, and so on. In this picture loneliness becomes one among many possible factors and to claim that loneliness is much more important than the others might be correct, but in the absence of *comparative* empirical investigation it is nevertheless an unsubstantiated one.

The empirical evidence needed to justify the focus on loneliness cannot be satisfied with showing a correlation between loneliness and drug use. We need to demonstrate a causal connection between the two. To illustrate the problem, consider a person who starts to use drugs after his only close friend suddenly dies. Clearly this sounds like a good example of the theory of relative addiction. The causal story — the explanation for the increased drug use — would be that the price of social interaction has increased since the person no longer has a close friend. When one activity (social interaction) increases in price, the person will start to use more drugs in order to satisfy a deeper need for "feeling good" or something else that is satisfied only by either drug use or social interaction. Imagine that we have a group of people like this person and that we have been lucky enough to have data on feelings of loneliness and drug use over a long time period — both before and after the death of the friend. Using these data we find that the death of a friend leads to a great increase in a sense of loneliness and a subsequent increase in drug use, as predicted by the relative addiction theory. Although the correlation in this case is compatible with the theory of relative addiction, we might still question the conclusion that loneliness is the causally important variable. The death of a friend may cause many emotional reactions at the same time — sadness, loneliness, anger, guilt, fear, bitterness. Even if it is true that I am lonely after the death of my friend, starting to use drugs might be a reaction to my guilt or my sadness rather than my loneliness. Hence, what we need is not only evidence that loneliness is strongly correlated with drug use, but that it is causally important in the way specified by the theory of relative addiction.

Is it possible to find this kind of evidence? As a starting point one might try to use the answers provided by drug addicts themselves as to why they started to use drugs. We have already seen that many drug users — but far from all — report that they are lonely. The question is now the extent to which they think this variable played a causal role in the development of their addiction. If the theory of relative addiction is correct, then loneliness should play a very special role and it is not enough that loneliness is an indirect part of the causal chain of events (e.g. death of friend caused loneliness which caused bitterness which caused drug use). The theory of relative addiction explicitly states that drug use is the result of loneliness and it is only evidence of this kind of relationship that would support the theory.

Using Qualitative Evidence to Test the Empirical Relevance of Loneliness

There are, of course, many problems with using and analysing qualitative evidence like the answers we receive from drug addicts when asking, "Why did you start to use drugs?" In an ideal world, we would have a representative sample of drug users who both knew the true reasons behind their drug use and were willing to tell us without self-serving bias. In the real world these conditions are rarely met. The sample on which the analysis below is based is made up of almost 500 drug users who entered treatment (both inpatient and outpatient) in 17 different treatment programmes during 1998. There was no intentional selection of individuals since we tried to interview everyone who was admitted. The 17 treatment facilities, however, were not randomly selected since financial and practical considerations forced us to limit ourselves to institutions in the southern part of Norway. Whether the results can be generalized to all drug users (not only those seeking treatment) all over the world (and not only the southern part of Norway) is obviously an open question.

Even if the sample were representative, arguments based on qualitative evidence are often viewed with suspicion because the biases of the researcher can easily colour the selection and classification of evidence. Stereotypically the researcher presents an argument which is illustrated with a couple of quotations from some of the interviews. This has the obvious disadvantage that the researcher can pick the responses that fit his or her own preconceived notions about the causes of addiction. To reduce the potential for this kind of bias, we could try to code the data into more general and countable categories and present information about the total number of responses in the different categories. However, there remains a lingering suspicion that the coding will nevertheless be influenced by the views of the researcher. In order to reduce these two problems, I have chosen to rely on *quantitative analysis* of the qualitative information using *automatic* (not manual) coding of the data. More specifically, the analysis is based on the frequency of different words in the responses of the individuals. It will become apparent, however, that the reduction in bias from this procedure also has a cost in terms of possible misclassifications and loss of context.

Table 3 shows the result of the frequency analysis of some terms used in answer to the question, "Why did you start to use drugs?" By far the most frequent words in the responses are "curiosity" (mentioned by 34%) and exciting (29%). Loneliness was mentioned by 2.3%. One might, of course, argue that a mere counting of words is too simplistic since many of the answers could indicate loneliness as a cause even if the term itself was never mentioned. For instance, respondents saying that they felt "alone" or that they started to use drugs after breaking with a boy- or girlfriend seem to belong under the general category of "loneliness as a cause." Hence, to compare the relative importance of loneliness and other causes, we need to group the words into more general categories.

The creation of general categories cannot be achieved by simply adding the percentages for each word since the same respondent may have mentioned both. For instance, 10% mentioned both curiosity and excitement. If we want to arrive at the proportion of individuals who emphasised one or both we simply add the percentages for each term and subtract the percentage that gave both answers to avoid the problem of counting some respondents twice. After adjusting for the problem of double counting, the proportion of individuals who replied using terms like curiosity and excitement is 53%. In our criteria for inclusion in

Table 3: Frequency of various words mentioned when asking drug users why they started to use drugs.

Word	Percentage of Drug Users Using the Term in Their Answer (%)
Curious, curiosity	34.0
Excitement, exciting	29.4
Environment	17.2
Friend	9.0
Older	8.2
Gang	7.3
Good	5.7
Moved	4.8
Like	4.6
Insecure	2.9
Lonely, loneliness	2.3
Alone	2.1
Escape	2.1
Calm	2.1
Angst	1.9
Sexual	1.9
Rebellion	1.7
Depressed	1.5
Addicted	1.3
Medication	0.8
Went	0.6
Left	0.2
None of the above	16.1

Source: Survey of 482 drug users in treatment organized by the Cost-Benefit Project under the National Institute for Alcohol and Drug Research in Norway. Data collection organized by Edle Ravndal and Grethe Lauritzen.

the category of loneliness, we might — in addition to loneliness — include all respondents who mentioned words like "left" ("My father left us," "My girlfriend left me"), "went" and "alone." Still, less than 6% of the respondents are in this group.

We could, of course, widen the net to include those mentioning "friends" and "gang." Sometimes this sounds appropriate, for instance when respondents say they started to use drugs because "I had no friends." However, more often replies emphasizing "friends," "gang" and "environment" reversed the causal order. First they joined a special person or a group of friends (sometimes because they were lonely) and *later* they felt pressured or were introduced to the drug by the person or members of the group. That is also why the term "older" came out so high on the list (the fifth most common term, mentioned by 8.2%); many respondents answered that they started to use drugs because an older friend (often an older boyfriend) introduced them to it. At this point the mere counting of words cannot be used because of the necessity for more contextual information to determine the classification of the answer. To solve this it is necessary to resort to manual coding of the data, but given the above-mentioned problem with this kind of coding, this option is closed. Instead, I want to discuss the more general question of whether the responses from drug users can shed any light on the real reason why people start to use drugs.

The (Limited) Usefulness of Drug Users' Own Explanations

One prominent critic of the very possibility of learning anything about the causes of drug addiction by asking addicts themselves is John Booth Davies (1997b). The main message of his book *The Myth of Addiction* (and its sequel *Drugspeak*) is that the answers we receive in surveys are of limited use because they are primarily functional. That is, people will give an answer that is beneficial to them in a given situation and not the true answer. For instance, you are likely to be treated much more sympathetically if you report that your drug use is due to factors outside your control — like a disease ("I am an addict") or an unhappy childhood — than if you simply say that you take drugs because you enjoy the experience. As he writes:

> "From the standpoint of functional attribution, the reasons people give for their drug use are not, and can never be, hard or so-called 'objective' data on why drug use happens. Consequently the use of such statements as criteria against which to validate physiological or other measures, or as factual statements from which to derive diagnostic criteria, is probably misconceived. *The Myth of Addiction* argues that such explanations are primarily functional" (Davies 1997b: vii).

Not only is the answer "I take drugs because I am an addict" functional for the person using drugs, it is also functional, Davies argues, for many non-addicts to accept the answer. Many seem to believe that help and treatment can best be legitimised by labelling the use of drugs as a disease. If it is a free choice, then it seems more difficult to justify spending resources on "curing" a free choice. In this way it becomes functional for people in the treatment system to accept the addiction as a disease explanation. Finally, the addiction label is accepted by most non-professionals because it is functional in that it distinguishes the drug user from the rest of us. "They" are different from us in the sense that they have a disease that we cannot get and this is a comforting thought.

In short, Davies' message is that addiction is a label that is functional both for drug users, for the experts in the treatment system and for the man in the street. It is the functionality of the label that lies behind the popularity of the addiction label and not its truth value; hence the title of the book. The question then becomes: is he right?

First of all one could argue that empirical evidence sometimes contradicts the argument that drug users mainly blame outside circumstances for their own misfortune. Many people simply say "I like it" or "It felt good" to explain their drug use — in contrast to what Davies predicts based on theoretical arguments about the functionality of answers. Somehow people sometimes seem to give at least what they believe is the true answer, despite it being not very beneficial for themselves. This leads to the conclusion that the problem is a question of degrees and not absolutes. There are certainly factors that make respondents twist their answers, but — since they sometimes appear to give answers that are not at all self-serving — there must also be factors that prevent people from always just giving the most beneficial answer. What kind of factors could they be?

Sometimes there is little reason to lie since there are no obvious external sanctions or benefits (as in anonymous questionnaires). Admittedly, there is always the possibility that you need to lie to yourself, but removing external sanctions and benefits at least reduces the problem of possible bias. There is also a need to avoid being seen as stupid, too eager to blame others and, to the extent that norms against lying have been internalized, to avoid psychological costs associated with lying. Theoretical reasoning opens up the possibility of many types of biases, but it alone says nothing about the relative size and importance of these biases. Hence, instead of simply arguing that the above-mentioned problems render all verbal responses suspect to the point of being worthless, we should try to assess the empirical importance of the problem.

We could, for instance, ask the same question in different circumstances to examine if the mechanisms mentioned produce different answers. One such test could be to pose very sensitive questions in face-to-face encounters and compare answers received from more anonymous telephone surveys. *Statistics Norway* has done this and Table 4 shows the responses to three different sensitive questions — about smoking, sex and loneliness — and how they varied depending on whether the interview was done face-to-face or by telephone (Roll-Hansen 2001). As the table shows, the practical significance of the differences is not very great since the absolute differences in percentage points are small (less than 3%). In this case it seems like answers related to smoking and loneliness are reasonably consistent, even though the setting might lead one to expect different answers to be functional.

One could, of course, find empirical evidence that points in the opposite direction. For instance, Davies (1997b) cites research indicating that drug users report higher consumption when confronted by a well-dressed interviewer compared to a more roughly dressed person. There is also a wealth of evidence to suggest that people's responses are sometimes shaped by anchoring, framing, word-switching and many other bias-creating psychological

Table 4: Probability of reporting sensitive information (face-to-face vs. over the phone).

Question	Face-to-Face	Phone
Do you have somebody close to you with whom you can talk in confidence, other than members of your family? (%)	90	88
Do you occasionally smoke? (%)	39	41
Have you had sexual intercourse during the past four weeks? (%)	86	89

Source: Roll-Hansen (2001). $n = 7125$.

mechanisms (Kahneman & Tversky 1982). Moreover, it seems that people are more likely to know whether they have smoked than why they did so. Hence, answers to why-questions may be less reliable than answers to questions of whether a particular form of behaviour has been performed (Nisbett & Ross 1980).

The problem is not only bias. When responding to a why-question people use a concept of explanation, and since there are competing accounts of what it is to explain something, we should not be surprised to receive a list of very diverse answers that do not fit neatly into a list of potentially important causal variables. Some answers cite a situation (e.g. loneliness); some cite an event (e.g. sexual abuse); some point to the effects of the drugs (felt good); some argue that it is best explained by a genetic weakness or some other mechanism that made the person especially vulnerable; and still others argue that they ended up as addicts because they mistakenly believed that they could experiment with drugs without becoming addicted. These answers reveal some of the same disagreements that exist among social scientists and philosophers on the nature of explanation and causation. As Rachlin shows in his contribution to the current volume (Chapter 4), some scientists seek answers by picking (sometimes literally) the brain of the person; others seek the answers in the intentions and beliefs of the individual; yet others believe that we should focus on environmental variables. There is, as Fred Dretske (1988) has argued, no necessary conflict between these perspectives since they are explanations at different levels in the reductionist chain, but, from the perspective of a brain scientist mainly concerned about the dopamine system, a qualitative survey of self-reported reasons for drug use seems of little use. If, however, we believe that causes of behaviour are best explained by assuming that people act on conscious intentions and beliefs, then surveys might be considered useful, providing that the problem of bias can be reduced.

Where does this leave us? There is conflicting evidence on the status and validity of verbal reports as a source of evidence. To some extent we can design questionnaires to avoid some of these problems and we can test the importance of the problem by examining whether we get the same answers in circumstances that are different with respect to the expected functionality of the answers. It is, however, difficult to arrive at any precise kind of estimate of the degree to which verbal reports can be relied on as evidence of why people start to use drugs. This means that it may be better not to use the data as I have done so far, that is, as evidence by counting the frequencies of various types of answers. There is, however, another way we can use the responses: reading answers about why people begin to use drugs can provide us with ideas about mechanisms that *might* be important. Hence, instead of using the data as evidence, we use it heuristically, as a source of ideas. This is what I will do in the next section of this paper.

Mechanisms and Alternative Views of Social Interaction

When discussing the word-frequency approach, one problem was that we needed on occasion more contextual information to determine whether an answer with a particular word should be put into one category or another. For instance, the category for the word "friend" was particularly difficult to determine. This might be an obvious case, but as it turns out it had a particular relevance in the context of social interaction and relative addiction. Conceptually, there is an important difference between those who said they started to use drugs because they were lonely and those who said that started to hang out with "outsiders" because they were lonely and only then started to use drugs. In the first case there is a direct causal relationship between loneliness and drug use; in the second there is an intermediate variable. As argued previously, the theory of relative addiction predicts that the relationship should be of the first type. That is, drug use should be caused by loneliness first, not by hanging out with the wrong people. The second mechanism, however, suggests that drug use may partly be caused by having the wrong kind of friends, which is very different from having no friends. Is the cause "no friends" or "wrong kind of friends?"

Social Mechanisms: Elster and Schelling

There is no general answer to that question. In fact, based on arguments from Elster (1998), we might doubt the very possibility of finding general answers in the form of grand theories which, within a single encompassing approach, claim to explain why people start, continue, and stop (and start again) different kinds of addictive behaviour (smoking, alcohol, illicit drugs). Given the current state of knowledge, Elster suggests that the best we can do is to explore *mechanisms* related to drug use. This may sound like a defeatist attitude, and it raises the question of exactly what a mechanism is and why it might be worth examining.

To explain what a mechanism is and why it is close to impossible to find general laws in the social sciences, Elster presents an example from the well-known alcohol researcher, George Vaillant. At issue is the question of whether there is a social law which says that children of alcoholics also tend to become alcoholics. Vaillant writes that: "Perhaps for every child who becomes alcoholic in response to an alcoholic environment, another eschews alcohol in response to the same environment" (cited in Elster 1998: 45). If both effects are present, there is no general law that children of alcoholics also become alcoholics. The same condition (alcoholic parents) is causally related both to children who become teetotallers (as a reaction to their parents' abuse) and children who become alcoholics (also as a reaction). Now, the argument that there must be some kind of difference between the two that allows us to explain why some ended up as teetotallers and some as alcoholics may be true, but Elster argues that in practice our knowledge is often too limited to discover these factors. There is a multitude of small differences that could work together interactively and non-linearly and sometimes only small differences or relatively accidental events may be decisive. Hence, all we have is knowledge of a mechanism: "frequently occurring and easily recognizable causal patterns that are triggered under generally unknown conditions or with indeterminate consequences" (Elster 1998: 45).

Social laws are useful since they can be used to predict outcomes. Mechanisms, on the other hand, do not claim to have the same predictive power. They are, however, useful in the sense that they can help us to explain an outcome after it has happened. For instance, we do not know in advance whether the child of an alcoholic will also become an alcoholic, but once we observe the outcome (alcoholic or teetotaller) we tend to accept that the alcoholism of the parents played a role in both outcomes.

In the current context Elster's approach seems to capture some of our problems. Social interaction may have both positive and negative effects on drug use depending on the nature of the interaction. Hence to ask whether the cause of drug use is "not enough social interaction" may be too general. Instead of trying to create theories that attempt to explain why people start, continue and stop using addictive substances, we would be better off exploring mechanisms that may help explain (but seldom predict) why some people start using drugs without also claiming that this is the reason they continue or eventually stop or that the mechanism explains the majority of cases.

On the other hand, Elster's account may seem overly pessimistic. After all, it is sometimes possible to get an idea of the relative strength of the various links in a causal chain. For instance, surveys of children of alcoholics can say something about the extent to which they end up as teetotallers or alcoholics. If the tendency is clear, we may have a useful probabilistic prediction (say 70% of the children become alcoholics compared to 5% with non-alcoholic parents). This, in turn, is useful information for policy formulation in terms of suggesting which groups should be focused on to reduce alcoholism. However, the relative lack of such strong and useful relationships in the social sciences suggests that there is something to Elster's argument that we would be better off exploring mechanisms instead of proposing general theories. Hence, I shall first follow Elster's suggestion by exploring a model of two mechanisms that link social interaction to drug use. After doing this, I will discuss whether it is possible to use empirical information to arrive at conclusions about the relative strength of the links and the practical importance of the mechanisms discussed.

Exactly what kind of mechanisms should we explore? Many of the papers in this volume focus on psychological or cognitive mechanisms such as the consequences of different forms of discounting. Because this topic is so well covered I want to follow a different route. The point of departure is Thomas Schelling's definition of a mechanism as a hypothesis that seeks to explain something in terms of two types of interaction:

> I propose . . . that a social mechanism is a plausible hypothesis, or set of plausible hypotheses, that could be the explanation of some social phenomena, the explanation being in terms of interactions between individuals and other individuals, or between individuals and some social aggregate (Schelling 1998: 32–33).

Changing lanes when the next car is less than five feet away is an example of individual-to-individual interaction. Adjusting speed to the average speed of others in the same lane is an example of interaction between an individual and a social aggregate. The definition itself may not seem very revolutionary (and it differs somewhat from Elster's definition) but Schelling's application of it shows that it has the potential to produce original and convincing explanations of social phenomena that are considered to be paradoxical. The main reason is that the aggregate consequences of individual motivations that interact are often far from obvious. For instance, assume people get vaccinated only when they perceive the risk of a disease to be large enough to be worth the effort and cost to get vaccinated. As Schelling shows, the aggregate consequence of such a simple individual decision rule is, depending on the parameters in the model, to create ebbs and flows in the incidence of a disease. When many are observed to be ill, people will get vaccinated. Because of the increasing number of people who get vaccinated, the number of ill people will eventually fall and at some point there will be so few people who are ill that people will not find it worth the cost to get vaccinated But this means that the disease will start to grow again and so the ebb and flow of the disease continues. Hence the apparently simple decision rule is able to suggest an explanation for a larger macro pattern that at first sight looks puzzling (the ebb and flow of a disease). Moreover, the mechanisms in this case have a very surprising implication: if there is a lag between becoming infected and the visible signs of the disease, then one might reduce the overall number of people who become ill by suddenly increasing the number or visibility of ill people! This example illustrates how Schelling's approach can produce both original explanations and potentially important and surprising policy conclusions.

I have so far tried to justify a general approach based on mechanisms in the sense used by Elster (1998). Within this approach I follow Schelling in focusing on mechanisms based on interaction. I also argued that social interaction itself was too general a concept and needed to be broken down. To impose some structure, we can use Manski (2000) who defines and lists three general types of social interaction as follows: "Agents interact through their chosen actions. An action chosen by one agent may affect the actions of other agents through three channels: constraints, expectations, and preferences" (Manski 2000: 118). In the case of drug use, the availability of drugs may be an example of the first (a user moving into a drug-free neighbourhood may remove the availability constraint barring others); learning about the effects of drugs (positive and negative) from existing users may be an example of how other agents' actions may influence somebody's expectations; and if many of my friends use drugs it may change my own preferences on whether or not to use drugs. The change of preference may be shallow (a person doing something not because he likes it but because he prefers to do what his friend is doing) or deep in the sense that you really change your opinion about the value of something after interacting with your friend. Both types of preference are affected by social interaction.

Note that social interaction is here used in a very different sense than in Rachlin's article. Psychologists and sociologists often use social interaction as a variable, trying to measure the quality and quantity of relationships with friends and family. This, in turn, is used as a variable to explain, for instance, drug use. When economists present a model that uses social interaction to explain something they usually do not use interaction as an explanatory variable in itself. Consider, for instance, a model that starts from the assumption that people have a desire to conform and then derives the aggregate consequences of that desire for the level of drug use in society. Moene (1999), who has modelled one such mechanism, shows that individual desire to conform opens up the possibility of multiple equilibria and a tendency for drug use to go up more easily than down. This model is categorized under social interaction because the preferences of the agents are interrelated ("I want to do whatever the others are doing"), not because social interaction is an explanatory variable in itself in the model. There is little point in discussing who has the correct definition of social interaction, as long as one is aware of the difference and avoids being confused.

Using the suggestion from the survey about reasons for starting to use drugs, one might want to explore the possibility that friends influence each others' use of drugs. As it stands, however, this is far too general and vague. What we need is a more rigorous formulation of the decision process and the mechanisms of how friends may affect one another's decision to use drugs. I shall explore two such mechanisms. First there is observational learning in the sense that potential users learn about the dangers (and joys) of drugs by observing the consequences of drugs on existing users. Second, I include a mechanism which implies that the pleasure of using drugs depends on how many others are also doing drugs (a stigma mechanism).

Microfoundation: Observational Learning, Social Stigma and Decision Making

For the sake of argument, let us assume that each individual (i) in time period (t) decides whether to use drugs based on a comparison of his expected utility of using drugs [$EU_{it}(D)$] and the expected utility if he chooses to abstain from drugs [$EU_{it}(A)$]. The underlying assumption is that the behaviour is at least influenced by some kind of calculation, as opposed to purely emotional or norm-based behaviour.

$$\text{Use drugs if}: \ EU_{it}(D) > EU_{it}(A)$$

What are $EU_{it}(D)$ and $EU_{it}(A)$? The latter — $EU_{it}(A)$ — is assumed to be a constant: U^A. To work out $EU_{it}(D)$ we need to consider the possible consequences of experimenting with drugs. For the sake of simplicity I shall assume that there are only two possible outcomes for individuals who experiment with drugs: Either a junkie career (unhappy) or a yuppie career (not so unhappy). This assumption is meant to capture the fact that not all individuals who experiment with drugs end up as stereotypical junkies.

The two possible outcomes of experimenting with drugs — becoming a yuppie or a junkie — result in certain payoffs. A very simple way of formalizing this would be to say that U_{it}^J is the total (discounted) sum of utility you receive if you end up as a junkie (for individual i at time t) while U_{it}^Y is the total sum of utility if you end up as a yuppie. Note that U_{it}^J does *not* represent annual utility as a junkie. It represents the *total* (discounted) sum of utilities if it turns out that experimenting with drugs makes the person a junkie for whatever time horizon the person has. Hence, the formulation is agnostic about whether the time period is considered to be the rest of the person's life or whether the agent is myopic to the extent that the coming year represents his furthest horizon. If the time period considered is the rest of his or her life then it may include some years as a yuppie, some years as a junkie and then, finally, some years as a non-user (treated or natural recovery/matured out). The same goes for U_{it}^Y. It does not only include years as a happy drug user, but also years as a non-user after the "happiness" has worn off.

The individual does not know whether he will end up as a junkie or a yuppie, so when working out the expected utility of experimenting with drugs, he or she has to estimate the probability of ending up as a junkie. One way of doing so would be to use the current proportion of junkies as an input in the estimation of how likely the person believes it is that he will end up as a junkie: $p_{it}(j)$. It is as if the individual looks round to take bearings and if he sees relatively few junkies, then he or she may conclude that the danger of becoming a junkie must be quite small.

Finally, in order to capture the effects of social stigma, I introduce a moral cost of experimenting with drugs (m). One might think about this as the cost of doing something that many people dislike. A stigma parameter like this, however, should vary depending on the number of people who engage in the activity. For instance, when few people were divorced, the associated stigma was large, but in a situation where divorce is common the stigma is lower. Hence, the stigma associated with drugs is assumed to depend on the proportion of people that are junkies (j). Moreover, individuals are assumed to differ to the extent that they care about the stigma or moral cost associated with drugs. In other words, each person has a parameter (θ_i) that indicates the degree to which they are sensitive to social stigma (reflecting, perhaps, a desire to conform). This parameter has a cumulative density function described by $F(\theta)$. This function simply tells us the proportion of individuals with "sensitivity to stigma" less than a certain number (θ) and this, in turn, is the same as the proportion of the new generation that begins to experiment with drugs. We may even allow negative values of θ_i to allow the possibility that some people enjoy deviating from the majority.

Altogether then, the expected utility of experimenting with drugs for an individual at a point in time is the utility he will receive in the two possible outcomes (junkie career or yuppie career) multiplied by their respective probabilities and adjusted for social stigma:

$$\text{EU}_{it}(D) = p_{it}(j)U_{it}^J + (1 - p_{it}(j))U_{it}^Y - \theta_i m(j)$$

One might argue that the formulation so far ignores many issues that are central to addiction. For instance, I do not explicitly model discounting, which many people argue is an important phenomenon when trying to explain addiction. I do not deny the importance of discounting, but the present focus is on something else, namely the effects of interaction through observational learning and social stigma. I want to isolate this and I do not want to bring in more complications than necessary. Moreover, there is a difference between explaining addiction at an individual level and explaining the social level of addiction. Much effort has been invested into tracing the causes of addiction — searching for a golden key variable or set of variables that would explain why some people become addicted. These efforts might lead one to assume that the individual and the aggregate are connected in a simple way: for instance, if loneliness is a major cause of drug use, then societies with much loneliness will have many addicts. Focusing on social interaction between heterogeneous agents makes us aware that this kind of inference from the individual to the aggregate is sometimes wrong and, as a consequence, the answers to "why is the level of drug use X?" or "why did drug use increase by Y%?" need not always be "there was a change in the loneliness factor" or whatever is believed to explain addiction at the individual level. Instead one could point to the dynamics of the aggregate system itself. This aspect has, perhaps, received less attention than the search for a key variable and, for this reason, I find it worthwhile to focus more exclusively on aggregate mechanisms.

There is, of course, a relationship between the aggregate and the individual even if it is not of the simple "representative agent" type. Indeed, it is important to model this, which is why I have made an effort to incorporate good microfoundations. However, the important micro-features from a macro perspective need not be the same as the important features from a micro perspective. That is, discounting may be very important at the individual level, but it need not be important when considering the overall level of drug use or changes in that level. Hence, we must postpone for a later stage a more explicit modelling of discounting.

The Aggregate Result of the Model

So far, all I have is a very general formulation of the decision problem. What I want, however, is an expression of the aggregate result — the proportion of drug users of the total population and how it varies — if people make their decisions based on the microfoundation just described. This requires several assumptions, both in terms of simplifying assumptions and in terms of more substantial assumptions about the mechanisms of aggregation.

In order to make it easier to get analytic results, I now make the following simplifying assumptions:

- $p_{it} = p_t$ $\forall i$ (every individual uses the same probability of becoming a junkie)
- $U_{it}(\cdot) = U(\cdot)$ $\forall it$ (the utility of ending up as a junkie, a yuppie or an abstainer is the same for every individual at all times)

This means that every individual uses the same probability of becoming a junkie and that the utility of ending up as a junkie or as a yuppie is the same for every individual at all times. The decision problem for the individual is then reduced to comparing U^A to the following expression:

$$\text{EU}_{it}(D) = p(j)U^J + (1 - p(j))U^Y_t - \theta_i m(j)$$

How do we get from this individual decision problem to an aggregate result? (The following solution is based on suggestions by Jörgen Weibull on a previous paper that tried to formalize the aggregate result.) In equilibrium there is no incentive to change strategy, so, for the individual at the margin, the expected utility of using drugs must be equal to the utility of not using drugs. Hence, we solve:

$$\text{EU}(D) = U^A$$
$$p(j)U^J + (1 - p(j))U^Y - \theta_i m(j) = U^A$$
$$\theta^*_i = \frac{p(j)^J + (1 - p(j))U^Y - U^A}{m(j)}$$

Or, in plain language, there are some people who will choose to experiment with drugs (those who are least sensitive to social stigma, $\theta_i < \theta^*$), and some people who will not experiment with drugs ($\theta_i > \theta^*$).

In equilibrium, assuming rational expectations, the expected probability of becoming a junkie must be the same as the equilibrium proportion of junkies:

$$j = p(j)F(\theta^*)$$
$$j^* = p(j)F\left(\frac{p(j)U^J + (1 - p(j))U^Y - U^A}{m(j)}\right)$$
$$j^*_{t+1} = p(j_t)F\left(\frac{p(j_t)U^J + (1 - p(j_t))U^Y - U^A}{m(j_t)}\right)$$

Depending on the properties of $p(j)$, $F(\cdot)$ and $m(j)$, we may have one or several solutions. For instance, if the moral cost of using drugs is non-linear, we could have the situation illustrated in Figure 2. To construct this figure I assumed that the distribution of sensitivity to sanction was normally distributed. This means that the cumulative distribution $F(\theta)$ becomes non-linear (it looks like an extended S) and it is this non-linearity that creates the

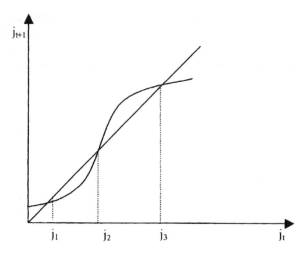

Figure 2: Multiple drug use equilibria in a model of observational learning and social stigma. The number of junkies next year is a function of the number of junkies last year. Possible equilibria (i.e. no change in the proportion of junkies) are located along the 45 degree line (along which $j_t = j_{t+1}$). The S-shaped curve shows the number of new drug users for given values of j_t, i.e. the shape of $F(\cdot)$. There are three possible steady states: j_1, j_2 and j_3. Two of these (j_1 and j_2) are stable in the sense that you will return to these states after a small deviation. j_2 is unstable since small deviations will start a dynamic in which you are moved even further away. Hence, otherwise similar communities may be "locked" in very different (and self-sustaining) drug situations: j_1 (low drug use) or j_3 (high drug use).

multiple equilibria. We could, for instance, have three equilibria, two of which are stable (see Figure 2)

Discussion

One might wonder what we gain from exploring a formal mechanism in this way. It is not an attempt to explain drug addiction in general, so its utility as an explanatory model is, at best, partial. What we have are some plausible assumptions about individual behaviour and the model helps to derive the aggregate consequences of these. These aggregate consequences are not immediately obvious, so in this sense it may be worthwhile to engage in formal modelling of mechanisms. If it turns out that the model captures a mechanism that is empirically important, it may help to explain why some communities seem stuck in a situation with high drug use while others are relatively stable in a low use situation.

Policy implications   The model may also have some surprising policy implications on how to shift from a high to a low-user equilibrium. Traditionally formal models of the spread of heroin and other drugs have used standard epidemiological models as their starting point. In these models a drug user is always "contagious" in the sense that he spreads the habit when he interacts with friends (see, for instance, Hoppensteadt & Murray 1981; Mackintosh & Stewart 1979). The obvious policy conclusion in these models is to isolate the contagious individuals in order to reduce the spread. The problem with the traditional models is that people are linked by assumption rather than by explicit modelling of mechanisms. The models do not say exactly *how* drug use is contagious. And, as soon as we start to think about that, we discover that sometimes drug use may deter as much as it attracts. Watching a friend die from heroin use may sometimes scare friends away from continued use, but hanging out in a group where there is no social stigma attached to drug use (indeed, there may be pressure to conform to use) has the opposite effect. Within this new framework, isolating heavy drug users may be counterproductive since you then remove the "fright" effect. The model developed in this paper takes into account both effects and for this reason the obvious policy implication is not necessarily to isolate the drug users. On the contrary, the model developed in this paper suggests that the visibility of the worst off individuals should be *increased* in order to reduce the aggregate level of drug use. The implication, however, is not very strong in the sense that it depends heavily on the relative strength of the various links. Even if high visibility could increase the belief that drug use is harmful, it could also reduce the belief that drug use is limited to a few outcasts. Thus, unless we have good indications of the relative strength of the links, we are back to Elster's argument that we can use knowledge of mechanisms to explain *ex post*, but not to predict or design policies.

Empirical evidence   One of the main problems in testing theories of social interaction, as discussed by Manski (2000), is the so-called reflection problem. For instance, when students in a neighbourhood behave similarly, it is statistically often very difficult to distinguish whether they do so because they find themselves in the same environmental circumstances or through more direct influences (peer pressure and so on). Rather than looking at aggregate data, therefore, we would be better off trying to explore the empirical plausibility of the microfoundation that went into the model. For obvious reasons, few controlled experiments have been done on peer influence and illegal drugs, but there has been extensive research on the extent to which the amount of alcohol consumed is influenced by the introduction of another person (heavy or moderate drinker, male or female, high or low status). The results from these experiments strongly suggest that people are influenced by their peers (Quigley & Collins 1999). It is, however, much more difficult to pin down whether this is because of some desire to conform to what the rest of the group is doing or some other mechanism. The same goes for the mechanism of observational learning. When asked about their sources of information, many people answer that their most important source is "friends" (Hanneman 1973); there are also studies which show that those with high risk estimates are more likely to avoid smoking than those with low risk estimates (Viscusi 1991). Although suggestive and supportive of the empirical relevance of the mechanisms modelled in the last part of this paper, the evidence relies too much on correlation to allow it to be used as strong evidence for the existence of a causal relationship. The best that can be said is that the correlations at least do not appear to contradict the assumptions on which the model is built. Little can be said about the relative importance of the links at this stage.

Extensions   Within the model, individuals are assumed to be influenced by everybody else. It is as if they observe all other individuals and what they are doing at all times. A much more realistic formulation would be to let people interact more locally in small groups. Instead of observing the number of junkies in the total population, they would observe the number of junkies within their small groups. And, instead of being influenced by a desire to conform to (or deviate from) the whole population, they could be influenced mainly by the members of the group to which they belong. Making social interaction local in this way would produce a much more realistic model, but one of the main results would remain (the existence of multiple equilibria and the importance of visibility of the bad effects of drugs). The same is true for more realistic formulations of how people form beliefs about the probability of ending up as a junkie. Instead of using only the proportion of junkies, they might try to work out the exact proportion of all people who have experimented with drugs who became junkies. While this revision makes the model more realistic, it does not give quantitatively different answers: it is still possible to get multiple equlibria.

Conclusion

The theory of relative addiction is an ambitious attempt to explain why people start, continue and stop/relapse smoking, alcohol and illegal drug use. I have argued that there was only weak support for the statement that loneliness and drug use are separable substitutes. Moreover, the strong version of relative addiction theory was inconsistent with many empirical facts about drug use and loneliness (not all addicts report being very lonely and vice versa). By relaxing the assumption of separable substitutes, we could create a weaker version of the theory, but then loneliness becomes only one of many possible causes. That being the case, we need comparative empirical research to justify the focus on loneliness as the most important cause of addiction. Finally, instead of using the general category of social interaction, we need to distinguish between different types of interaction and how they might affect drug use. This approach, as exemplified by a model of observational learning and stigma effects, represents a new line of research that deserves to be explored because of its potential to produce non-obvious knowledge (the aggregate consequences of several individual level structures are usually not obvious when the agents are heterogeneous). Finally, models that use social interaction as a mechanism sometimes produce policy implications that are often ignored in models that simply assume a representative agent and for this reason it is important to focus on social interaction.

References

Becker, G. S., & Murphy, K. M. (1988). A theory of rational addiction. *Journal of Political Economy*, *96*, 675–700.

Davies, J. B. (1997a). *Drugspeak: The analysis of drug discourse*. Amsterdam: Harwood Academic Publishers.

Davies, J. B. (1997b). *The myth of addiction* (2nd ed.). Amsterdam: Harwood Academic Publishers.

Dretske, F. I. (1988). *Explaining behavior: Reasons in a world of causes*. Cambridge, MA: MIT Press.

Elster, J. (1998). A plea for mechanisms. In: P. Hedström, & R. Swedberg (Eds), *Social mechanisms* (pp. 45–73). Cambridge: Cambridge University Press.

Ennett, S. T., & Baumann, K. E. (1993). Peer group structure and adolescent cigarette smoking: A social network analysis. *Journal of Health and Social Behavior, 34*, 226–236.

Fisher, E. B. J. (1996). A behavioral-economic perspective on the influence of social support on cigarette smoking. In: L. Green, & J. H. Kagel (Eds), *Advances in behavioral economics: Substance use and abuse* (Vol. 3, pp. 207–236). Norwood, NJ: Ablex Publishing Corporation.

Hanneman, G. J. (1973). Communicating drug-abuse information among college students. *Public Opinion Quarterly, 37*, 171–191.

Herrnstein, R. J., & Prelec, D. (1992). A theory of addiction. In: G. Loewenstein, & J. Elster (Eds), *Choice over time* (pp. 331–360). New York: Russell Sage Foundation.

Hoppensteadt, F. C., & Murray, F. C. (1981). Threshold analysis of a drug use epidemic model. *Mathematical Biosciences, 53*, 79–87.

Kahneman, D., & Tversky, A. (1982). Judgement under uncertainty: Heuristics and biases. In: D. Kahneman, P. Slovic, & A. Tversky (Eds), *Judgement under uncertainty: Heuristics and biases* (pp. 3–22). Cambridge: Cambridge University Press.

Lunde, E. S. (2001). Større åpenhet om psykiske lidelser. *Samfunnsspeilet, 5*.

Mackintosh, D. R., & Stewart, G. T. (1979). A mathematical model of a heroin epidemic: Implications for control policies. *Journal of Epidemiology and Community Health, 33*, 299–304.

Manski, C. F. (2000). Economic analysis of social interactions. *Journal of Economic Perspectives, 14*, 115–136.

Moene, K. O. (1999). Addiction and social interaction. In: J. Elster, & O. J. Skog (Eds), *Getting hooked: Rationality and addiction* (pp. 30–46). Cambridge: Cambridge University Press.

Nisbett, R. E., & Ross, L. (1980). *Human inference: strategies and shortcomings of social judgment*. Englewood Cliffs, NJ: Prentice-Hall.

Quigley, B. M., & Collins, R. L. (1999). The modeling of alcohol consumption: A meta-analytic review. *Journal of Studies on Alcohol, 1*, 90–98.

Rachlin, H. (1997). Four teleological theories of addiction. *Psychonomic Bulletin & Review, 4*, 462–473.

Rachlin, H. (2000). The lonely addict. In: W. K. Bickel, & R. E. Vuchinich (Eds), *Reframing health behavior change with behavioral economics* (pp. 145–164). Mahwah, NJ: Lawrence Erlbaum.

Roll-Hansen, D. (2001). Blir du sykere hvis du får tenkt deg om? *Samfunnsspeilet, 4*.

Schelling, T. (1998). Social mechanisms and social dynamics. In: P. Hedström, & R. Swedberg (Eds), *Social mechanisms* (pp. 32–44). Cambridge: Cambridge University Press.

Stigler, S., & Becker, G. S. (1977). De gustibus non est disputandum. *American Economic Review, 67*, 76–90.

Viscusi, W. K. (1991). Age variations in risk perceptions and smoking decisions. *The Review of Economics and Statistics, 73*, 577–588.

Comments on Melberg

Howard Rachlin

I hereby abandon the strong theory of relative addiction. I did not really mean to say that all addicts are (or rather, were) lonely people. Some of my language, I admit, could be taken to imply this strong assertion. What I actually think is that relative addiction theory is a mechanism in exactly the sense that Hans Melberg uses the term. Even within relative addiction theory there are positive addictions other than social support that may substitute for negative addiction: exercising, listening to classical music, reading Trollope, doing crossword puzzles, watching soap operas, collecting stamps, gardening, and so forth. A behavioral theory would be silent about internal events common among all of these activities and addiction, but Fisher's (1996) speculation that they all induce positive mood and reduce anxiety is at least not completely implausible.

Fisher showed that *actual* loss of social support was correlated with increased smoking and that *actual* success in treatment varied with degree of social support. This evidence is only suggestive and far from decisive. But the evidence presented by Melberg does not bear on the issue. It is not even evidence against the strong form of relative addiction theory, let alone a weak form.

First, relative addiction theory is silent on "feelings of loneliness." From the viewpoint of teleological behaviorism, feelings of loneliness would themselves be patterns of behavior. So, it would be possible to observe them. But for that we would have to ask, not the addict, but the addict's friends or relatives, people who live with him and can observe his behavior. But let us drop this idiosyncratic point of view for a moment (I will pick it up again later) and let us suppose that feelings are internal states that addicts can introspect and report on veridically. Even then, such feelings may or may not correlate with actual degree of social interaction. And, even if feelings of loneliness (accurately reported) were indeed indicative of degree of social interaction, relative addiction theory makes no prediction about absolute social interaction over a population of addicts. As correctly and lucidly described in Melberg's paper, relative addiction theory says that *loss* of social interaction in an individual may (if the effect of present choices on future behavior are as they are drawn in Figure 1 and if the loss of social interaction is severe enough to upset the previous equilibrium) lead to addiction, and that a given treatment will work better if it involves increased social interaction than if it does not. Neither of these predictions implies any correlation (positive or negative) over a population, at a given point in time, between social interaction and addiction.

The study in which addicts are asked to speculate about the causes of their addiction and why it is maintained also has serious flaws — but these are described much more clearly and thoroughly by Melberg himself than I could do. From a behavioral viewpoint, it would again have been better to have asked the addicts' friends, relatives, co-clients, co-workers, physicians, and psychologists about the addicts' social interactions than to have asked the addicts. But, absent longitudinal tests on individual subjects, using objective measures, or at least *current* measures such as diaries, it is not possible to directly and decisively test the assumptions underlying relative addiction theory — even in its strong form.

As Melberg says, relative addiction theory does not answer such questions as, Why do some people smoke while others use alcohol? It is true that relative addiction theory does not make distinctions between forms of addiction, and this is a common criticism of it. However, a theory that predicts that a person will move from New York to California need not say whether he will take the plane, train, bus, or car. Such a theory might be useful nevertheless.

One area in which relative addiction theory is silent is the internal mechanisms that might mediate between lack of social support and addiction. I intended the word, "loneliness" to stand, not for an internal state — cognitive, emotional or physiological — but simply for lack of social support. If someone should eventually discover how to measure guilt other than behaviorally, it would not matter to relative addiction theory whether internal guilt, so measured, or internal feelings of loneliness were the mediating factor.

I agree with Davies (1997) that "addiction" is a functional label for people who use the word. It allows them to classify behavior patterns into those that are addictions and those that are not — and this is a very useful distinction to make. That distinction is exactly what many of us here are trying hard to make. But I disagree that this fact makes addiction a myth. If it did, we could with equal justification label as myths: sensation, perception, thinking, as well as hope, love, imagination, and all mental and emotional terms. For a teleological behaviorist, these terms are not labels for ephemeral internal states that we may introspect upon and report. They are labels for patterns of behavior, labels we apply because we find them useful. This, in my opinion, makes them more not less real.

Truth and lying about mental or emotional states therefore depend on the degree of conformity between verbal and non-verbal behavior or between one instance of verbal behavior and other instances of verbal behavior. Telling the truth about your emotions does not depend on a match between words and internal physiological events.

The addiction mechanism presented in the latter half of Melberg's paper is an interesting one but would be even more difficult to test than relative addiction theory. It says that addiction depends on a person's social milieu. A high number of addicts relative to non-addicts in a group will increase the probability of a member becoming an addict in two ways: via the person's desire to conform and via decreased moral condemnation. Moral condemnation would seem to vary oppositely to social support and might be measured. But "desire to conform" is not a behavioral variable. Melberg is correct in not using this term in his utility functions. You could nevertheless ask how desire to conform would be generated and maintained. One possible candidate is by social support. Thus both of the variables said to determine addiction in this model may be traced to social support, which in turn depends on social interaction. And, social interaction can be measured. It would remain then to state how social interaction behaves in this mechanism differently from its behavior in the relative addiction mechanism.

One possible difference is the influence of the group in this mechanism and the focus on the individual in the relative addiction mechanism. A problem arises, however, in determining which of the many groups that every person belongs to determines the critical ratio of addicts to non-addicts. We are all members of our family, our neighborhood, our town, our school, our circle of friends. Ratios of addicts to non-addicts may vary widely from one of these groups to the other. Which one counts?

Finally, I want to express my gratitude to Hans Melberg for taking relative addiction seriously enough to put it to the test. That the tests are not definitive is not his fault; it is mine, for not specifying the theory more clearly and for using such a term as "lonely" in the title, just because it sounded good, rather than "lack of social interaction" which sounds a lot worse but better expresses what I meant to say.

References

Davies, J. B. (1997). *The myth of addiction* (2nd ed.). Amsterdam: Harwood Academic Publishers.
Fisher, E. B. J. (1996). A behavioral-economic perspective on the influence of social support on cigarette smoking. In: L. Green, & J. H. Kagel (Eds), *Advances in behavioral economics: Substance use and abuse* (Vol. 3, pp. 207–236). Norwood, NJ: Ablex Publishing Corporation.

Reply to Rachlin

Hans O. Melberg

In his comments Rachlin argues, first, that the key variable in his theory is social interaction, not loneliness, or its even less relevant counterpart, *self-reported* loneliness. Second, evidence on the relationship between drug use and social interaction/loneliness across a population has no relevance when it comes to testing his theory since the theory is only intended to explain individual changes and not absolute levels of substance abuse in a society. Third is the claim that the theory sets out a useful mechanism even though it does not distinguish between addiction to cigarettes, alcohol and illicit drugs. Finally, Rachlin argues that the model presented towards the end of my paper is compatible with his theory but even more difficult to test empirically. I will respond to each of these comments in turn.

Social Interaction and Loneliness

In his previous articles on the topic, Rachlin writes about both social interaction and loneliness. It is therefore conceptually useful to learn from his comments that social interaction is considered to be the main variable. Empirically speaking, however, it is actually less useful since the term is never operationalized. In order to test the theory we need some way of measuring social interaction or some variable that is related to social interaction. Based on this requirement I used self-reported feelings of loneliness and number of friends as proxies for social interaction. In response Rachlin writes that: "such feelings [loneliness] may or may not correlate with actual degree of social interaction." Against this, I believe that a negative correlation is most likely. That is, on average people who are lonely probably have less social interaction than people who are not lonely. Whether this is actually true is impossible to know as long as Rachlin does not present an operationalized definition of social interaction.

Rachlin also argues that we would be better off having information about other people's perceptions of an individual's loneliness than that individual's own feelings. Speaking in terms of cause and effect, I would argue that it is the subjective feeling of loneliness or lack of social interaction that is important; it is of little help that others believe I have lots of social interaction if I do not feel that way myself. Against this, one might argue that feelings have no place in a behavioural theory in which only observed behaviour counts. Although I disagree with this type of strict behaviouralist approach, this disagreement has far wider ramifications and Rachlin is right in correcting me for introducing non-behaviouralist elements (like feelings) into what was intended to be a strict behaviouralist theory.

A Theory of Individual Change or Levels of Drug Use?

In his comments Rachlin argues that:

> ... relative addiction theory says that *loss* of social interaction in an individual may [...] lead to addiction, and that a given treatment will work better if it involves increased social interaction than if it does not. Neither of these predictions implies any correlation (positive or negative) over a population, at a given point in time, between social interaction and addiction.

This is a much more modest and less interesting claim than the one I believed Rachlin to have made in some of his previous articles. Two of the key elements in the previous theory were, firstly, that there is a constant need for something, and second that this need can only be satisfied by drug use and social interaction (i.e. the assumption of separable substitutes). As he wrote, "A central assumption of relative addiction theory is that addictive activities and social activities are walled off in this way — they are at least moderately substitutable for each other but not for any third activity" (Rachlin 2000: 151). Interpreted in this way, the theory really is linked to aggregate implications. It is true that more assumptions are needed to make the link empirically testable — for instance, about individual differences in the substitutability of the two goods or the urgency of the need for the undefined good — but the major linking assumptions are the ones that are made by the theory itself, i.e. the assumption that there is a constant need and that this need can only be satisfied by two activities (drug use or social interaction), i.e. that they are separable. This necessarily implies that if you have a lot of one, you will have less of the other. Rachlin's suggestion that there might be many other factors apart from social interaction that might have the same effect would, as he correctly argues, eliminate the aggregate implications, but it would also mean that he has to abandon the assumption of separability which was "central" to the original theory.

Usefulness, Mechanisms and Testing

I am in complete agreement with Rachlin that a theory of addiction may be useful even if it does not predict exactly what the person is addicted to (alcohol, tobacco, illicit drugs and so on). My point was only that when trying to test such a theory one should be careful not to use evidence only from the most plausible case to support the general theory.

I would, however, disagree with the more general argument that the theory of relative addiction really is a mechanism in the sense in which I used the term. The defining feature of a mechanism, according to Jon Elster (1998), is that the same type of event — say less social interaction — may lead to both more or less drug use. In the theory of relative addiction, I do not see how less social interaction could lead to less drug use. In the model presented towards the end of my paper, however, this is possible since interaction can both scare people away from drugs (observing its bad consequences if you meet junkies) as well as attract people (peer pressure and/or observing happy and successful drug users). In this way, less social interaction could lead to both more and less drug use and the question becomes not how much social interaction there is, but what kind of social interaction we have.

Rachlin is probably right in arguing that my model is more difficult to test than the theory of relative addiction and I do not make any strong claims about the empirical relevance of the model. Moreover, the two contributions are not on the same footing. The model does not claim to represent a general theory of addiction; the theory of relative addiction does (or at least did).

Conclusion

The theory of relative attention draws attention to a phenomenon that is potentially important both to explain and treat addiction: vicious and virtuous self-reinforcing cycles. Surely, the bad consequences of using drugs can sometimes lead you to consume even more — as when the alcoholic gets drunk to forget the misery caused by his or her alcoholism. It is also an important lesson that to find a self-sustaining treatment we should search for activities that induce positive cycles — that is, activities that become more and more enjoyable the more you do them. Although I share this general interest in the mechanisms that create positive and negative self-reinforcing cycles, I have reservations about the more specific details of the mechanisms proposed in the theory of relative addiction, such as the assumption that there is a constant need for something that only can be satisfied by drug use or social interaction.

References

Elster, J. (1998). A plea for mechanisms. In: P. Hedström, & R. Swedberg (Eds), *Social mechanisms* (pp. 45–73). Cambridge: Cambridge University Press.

Rachlin, H. (2000). The lonely addict. In: W. K. Bickel, & R. E. Vuchinich (Eds), *Reframing health behavior change with behavioral economics* (pp. 145–164). Mahwah, NJ: Lawrence Erlbaum.

Chapter 12

Discounting the Value of Commodities According to Different Types of Cost

Suzanne H. Mitchell

Introduction

Human and non-human animals are continually making choices about which activities to engage in and about which commodities to obtain. Consequently, understanding the factors controlling choice is a fundamental concern for individuals and scientists interested in understanding the processes governing behavior. One area in which there has been considerable interest in choice processes is the area of drug use and abuse. From a practical standpoint, understanding the factors controlling the initial and continued choice of drugs over an abstinence alternative may suggest ways of altering that choice. This, in turn, may help people to avoid beginning drug use and, for current users, help them to end their drug use.

The "cost" of a commodity relative to other available commodities is a major influence on choice. All other things being equal, it is expected that human and non-human animals should select the item that can be classified as the least costly or expensive item from a series of alternatives. Although this statement appears self-evident, understanding what constitutes a cost for an organism and precisely how costs impact behavior is complex. The difficulty of understanding the impact of cost on behavior is compounded because different cost variables often covary, e.g. items that require more time to obtain often also require more effort to be expended to attain them.

This paper will examine three variables that can be viewed as imposing a cost on the acquisition of a commodity. The paper then reviews the experimental and mathematical procedures used to examine how costs impact the value of a commodity, that is, how the imposition of costs results in the objective value of a commodity being devalued or "discounted." The majority of the research examining discounting has examined the impact of the delay before the receipt of a commodity on the subjective value of the commodity (delay discounting). These studies will be reviewed, but in addition, this paper will examine the discounting that occurs when costs other than delay to receipt are associated with a commodity, and possible inter-relationships between different types of cost discounting.

Choice, Behavioural Economics and Addiction
© 2003 Published by Elsevier Ltd.
ISBN: 0-08-044056-8

Types of Cost

The effort required to obtain a commodity has long been known to influence choice: all other things being equal, organisms will select the least effortful/laborious option that leads to reward. In one of many early experiments, rats could obtain food by pulling a string attached to a tray on which the food was placed. Two trays were available that differed in weight, and consequently the energy required to haul them to the experimental chamber. As might be expected, rats chose to pull the lighter tray first, and this preference became more marked as the weight differential of the trays increased (McCulloch 1934). The Principle of Least Effort codified this and similar observations (e.g. Hull 1943; Lewis 1965; Solomon 1948).

A second cost variable thought to impact choice is the time taken to complete a behavior; all other things being equal, organisms will select the option associated with faster reward/less delay to reward. Numerous studies have supported this notion. For example, Chung & Herrnstein (1967) reported data from pigeons responding on concurrent variable interval (VI) schedules. A delay of 16 seconds between earning the reinforcer and its delivery was added to one response option, while the delay associated with reinforcer delivery on the other alternative was systematically varied from 1 to 30 seconds. Pigeons allocated their choices to the latter response option in accordance with the relative length of the delay. Lachter (1984) observed similar time/delay sensitivity. In that study, rats allocated their choices to the response option that required them to press the lever for a shorter duration than to the option that required longer duration presses.

A more controversial cost variable that has been suggested to influence behavior is the uncertainty related to acquiring a commodity. All other things being equal, organisms should select the commodity associated with the least uncertainty about its delivery. Data concerning this prediction are relatively scarce and somewhat equivocal. In many behavioral experiments, uncertainty is varied by altering the number of times an action must be repeated to attain the commodity (a ratio schedule of reinforcement). However, differences in the ratio requirement are ordinarily accompanied by differences in the time taken to complete the requirement and the energy required to complete the responses. Thus, although Herrnstein (1958) and Herrnstein & Loveland (1975), amongst others, report that almost exclusive responding to the smaller ratio develops fairly readily, these data do not necessarily indicate preference based on uncertainty. Experiments examining choice between fixed requirement and variable requirement schedules have indicated that deprived animals usually exhibit a preference for higher levels of uncertainty; for example, Herrnstein (1964) observed a preference for a VI 15-second schedule over a fixed interval (FI) 15-second schedule in food-deprived pigeons. However, non-deprived animals appear to prefer the less variable/less uncertain options (e.g. Caraco *et al.* 1980). Thus, again the impact of uncertainty on choice is ambiguous. In addition, although the organism's sensitivity to nuances of the probability density function, and thus the uncertainty associated with the fixed and variable requirements, has been demonstrated (Taylor & Davison 1983), the psychophysical relationship between schedule manipulations and perceived uncertainty remains undefined.

It is worthwhile noting that, in humans, we ordinarily think of the cost of a commodity in terms of its monetary cost. Given that money is ordinarily acquired through employment, monetary costs can be viewed as related to effort/energy and time costs, although the precise relationship may be complex.

While it is possible to consider the impact of these three types of cost on choice behavior separately, different behavioral disciplines have emphasized different combinations of the costs of commodities. For example, in behavioral economics, expressing the cost of commodities in terms of their unit prices has allowed for differences in the sizes of commodities to be taken into account as well as their cost (e.g. Carroll & Campbell 2000; DeGrandpre *et al.* 1993; but also see Woolverton & English 1997). The concept of unit price interestingly incorporates all three of the costs discussed earlier, i.e. the effort, time and uncertainty costs of commodities:

$$\text{Unit Price} = \frac{E \cdot N}{A \cdot p} \tag{1}$$

where E represents the energy required to complete the response required to acquire the commodity, N represents the number of times the response must be performed, A represents the size of the commodity acquired and p represents the probability that a response will yield the commodity when the ($E \cdot N$) requirement has been completed (modified from Hursh *et al.* 1988).

In behavioral ecology, the ultimate currency of behavior is inclusive fitness, i.e. the reproductive success of an organism; however in food-related activities the immediate currency is assumed to be the net rate of energy gain which presumably impacts reproductive success (e.g. Stephens & Krebs 1986). The net rate of energy gain takes into account the time costs associated with acquiring food and the energy that is expended to acquire the food, as well as the energy derived from the food item:

$$R = \frac{\lambda \bar{e} - s}{1 + \lambda \bar{h}} \tag{2}$$

where R represents the net rate of energy gain, λ the time between successive encounters between food items, e is the expected *net* energy gain from an individual food item (energy gain minus energy cost of ingesting), s represents the energy costs of searching for food items per unit time, and h represents the expected time costs associated with handling the food after it is encountered until it is ingested (Holling's disc equation: Holling 1959). Uncertainty is not explicitly incorporated into this equation.

However, no matter what the currency, the idea is the same. Commodities that are more costly will be subjectively less valuable, i.e. their objective value will be discounted as some function of the associated cost.

Measuring the Extent of Discounting

The following discussion uses examples drawn from experiments examining delay discounting in human subjects. The rationale and methods for measuring discounting occasioned by other cost variables, such as uncertainty or effort, are identical. Animal procedures have been devised following essentially the same logic and hence are very similar.

The extent to which a commodity's value is discounted is typically measured using classical psychophysical procedures, especially the Method of Limits. The "standard stimulus" might be $100 available in 365 days for a human subject. The "comparison stimulus" is a commodity that the experimenter varies in a single dimension — for example, a variable amount of money available after a fixed time period (e.g. immediately). The magnitude of the comparison commodity is adjusted while the subject indicates which is preferred: the standard or comparison commodity. The value of the comparison stimulus at which a subject is indifferent between the standard and comparison commodities is assumed to index the subjective value of the standard commodity. In most animal and some human research, researchers examine choice proportions to identify the indifference point, so that indifference is assumed to occur at a choice proportion of 50%. In other human research, indifference is usually arbitrarily set as midway between the smallest amount of the comparison stimulus that was preferred and the largest amount of the comparison stimulus that was rejected. For example, if a subject prefers the comparison commodity when it is $20 over $100 in 365 days, but prefers the standard commodity when the comparison commodity is $10, the indifference point or point of subjective equality will be assessed as $15.

Perhaps the simplest method to measure the impact of delay on the subjective value of a commodity is derived from the Generalized Matching Law (Baum 1974). Assuming the same rates of reinforcement are obtained for options 1 and 2:

$$\frac{B_1}{B_2} = b \left(\frac{D_1}{D_2}\right)^{SD} \left(\frac{A_1}{A_2}\right)^{SA} \tag{3}$$

where B represents the number of choices of options 1 and 2, b represents response bias for options 1 or 2, D represents the delay to the delivery of commodity 1 or 2, A represents the size of each commodity, S is a parameter representing sensitivity to delay and amount. Equation (3) can be converted to logarithms and rearranged algebraically so that, when preference for B_1 and B_2 is equal, i.e. at the indifference point:

$$\frac{S_A}{S_D} = \frac{\log(D_1/D_2)}{\log(A_1/A_2)} \tag{4}$$

S_A/S_D can be interpreted as signifying the sensitivity to amount relative to sensitivity to delay. If subjects are equally sensitive to both amount and delay, the ratio should equal 1.0. A ratio less than 1 indicates that sensitivity to delay is larger than sensitivity to amount; that is, that subject's choices have been more impacted by the relative delays to obtain the reinforcers than the relative amounts of the reinforcers.

Determining the delay and amount values required for indifference does provide a method to establish individual differences in discounting (e.g. Forzano & Corry 1998; Logue *et al.* 1984, 1990). However, this measure has several limitations. First, it cannot be used to predict preferences when either of the commodities is available immediately ($D = 0$). Of course, one might argue that the delay to receiving a commodity is never truly zero, even when an experimenter offers a commodity that is available "immediately." Second, controls are required to ensure that the results are not misinterpreted due to the impact of bias or the existence of interactions between delay and amount values (Rodriguez & Logue 1986; but also see Ito & Oyama 1996). Further, the sensitivity ratio only provides information about an individual's response for one set of amounts and associated delays. Such a point estimate is not a summary statistic that provides information about the impact of delay in general on the subjective value of a commodity for an individual.

To attain a summary statistic, the indifference points for a commodity available over a range of delays must be obtained using the psychophysical procedure described earlier. Plotting these indifference points as a function of the delay of the commodity creates the discount curve. To quantify the impact of delay on subjective value, functions can be fit or the area under this discount curve can be calculated. There is some discussion as to the appropriate function that should be fit, however, the majority of research has used a hyperbolic function of the form:

$$V = \frac{M}{1 + kX} \qquad (5)$$

where V represents the subjective value of the standard commodity indexed by the indifference point, M represents the objective value of the money available from the standard item (e.g. $100.00), k is a fitted parameter indexing the rate of discounting, and X is the length of the delay to receipt of the delayed money. Some researchers favor variants of the hyperbolic equation, most notably a form in which the denominator is raised to a power, s (Myerson & Green 1995). It is somewhat unclear exactly what s represents other than a method to modify the form of the hyperbola (Myerson & Green 1995: 269). In addition, while this form of Eq. (5) accounts for additional variance, k and s appear to be inversely related, which results in interpretational difficulties.

The use of the hyperbolic function stems from the observation that adding a constant to X delay can result in preference switches. A subject might indicate that they prefer $20 now over $100 in 1 year, however if 1 year is added to the delivery dates for each commodity, making the choice one between $20 in 1 year vs. $100 in 2 years, subjects will often switch their preference to the larger, more delayed commodity. This type of preference switch would not be predicted by an exponential function. Data from Green and his colleagues (Green *et al.* 1997, 1999) may open up this debate once more (see Mazur 2001, for a discussion of this issue). They have presented evidence that the objective magnitude of the delayed commodity may interact with the delay such that the value of k is inversely related to the magnitude of the commodity. For example, $1 million dollars available in a year will be discounted less steeply than $1,000 available in a year.

The area under the curve, as recently pointed out by Myerson *et al.* (2001), makes no assumptions about the function. All areas are fitted using a trapezoidal method to proportional values of the x- and y-axes. Thus, the maximum value of the area is 1, which would be obtained if no discounting occurred. However, calculating the area does make assumptions about the appropriate metric for the abscissa — for example, if one is assessing the area under a discount curve where uncertainty is the cost variable. Rachlin *et al.* (1991) converted probabilities of receiving the reinforcer to odds against receiving the reinforcer ($[1/p] - 1$). This has the effect of changing the discount curve so that a hyperbolic function could be fit. Given the relationship between the probability and the odds against metric, it is not surprising that the area under the curve calculated using probability is correlated with the area calculated using odds against, but the correlation is by no means perfect.

Delay and uncertainty discounting were assessed for 140 young adults using two separate computer tasks (described in detail in Mitchell 1999). Briefly, each task required the participant to answer 137 choice questions, presented one at a time. For each question, participants indicated which of two items they preferred: the "standard" option or the "alternative" option. In the delay discounting task, the standard option was $10.00 available following a delay of 0, 7, 30, 90, 180 or 365 days. In the uncertainty discounting task, the standard option was $10.00 available with a probability of 1.0, 0.9, 0.75, 0.5, 0.25 or 0.1. The

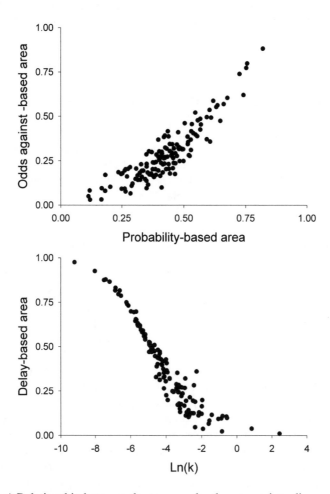

Figure 1: (top) Relationship between the areas under the uncertainty discount curve when the discount curve was fitted for indifference points plotted according to odds against $[1/p - 1]$ and when the curve was fitted to indifference points plotted according to probability ($N = 140$). (bottom) Relationship between the natural log-transformed values of the delay discounting parameter, k, and the area under the curve resulting from that specific discounting function ($N = 140$).

alternative options for both tasks were amounts of money available immediately for sure ($0.01, $0.25, $0.50, $1.00, increasing in $0.50 increments up to $10.50). After completing the tasks, one task was chosen at random, then one choice question was selected at random. The participant received whichever of the two options they had said they preferred when completing the particular task. If they had chosen the delayed $10.00, participants were given an IOU stating when the delay expired and were told to return any time on or after that date to collect their $10.00. If they had chosen the uncertain $10.00, tokens marked "yes" and "no" were placed in a bag with proper proportion indicated by the chosen question, e.g. 5 yes's and 15 no's signified a probability of 0.25. Participants pulled one token from the bag. If they pulled a token marked "yes" they received $10.00; if they pulled a token marked "no" they received nothing. If they had chosen the alternative option in either task, the participant received the amount of money stated in the choice question. Indifference points were then calculated, according to the psychophysical principles described earlier. Examining the obtained data, there was a positive correlation between the areas fitted using odds against and the areas fitted using probabilities ($r^2 = 0.79$, slope $= 0.99$; see Figure 1 top). Further, although the correlation is very good, it is not unity, and there is a hint in the residuals that the relationship between areas may not be linear. For the delay discounting functions there is no discussion about the appropriate metric; delay is expressed in linear units of time like number of days or months. Logically, smaller areas are associated with more choice of the immediate commodity over the delayed one, and so can be expected to be negatively correlated with the steepness of the discount function, the k values. However the relationship appears to be complex when fits were performed for the data from the 140 participants (Figure 1, bottom).

Delay Discounting

A number of studies have indicated that dependent drug users discount delayed rewards more steeply than non-users do: opiate users (e.g. Madden *et al.* 1997), alcohol users (Petry 2001; Vuchinich & Simpson 1998), and cigarette smokers (Bickel *et al.* 1999; Mitchell 1999; see Bickel & Marsch 2001 for a review of these and additional studies). Further, two of these studies (Bickel *et al.* 1999; Petry 2001) indicated that non-users who had never used the drug and former users had similar levels of discounting. This result can be explained in several ways, which are not necessarily incompatible. First, the presence of the drug or the acute neural changes associated with drug use increased the extent to which delayed rewards are devalued. In this case, we might predict that casual, social users might show increased discounting while under the influence of a drug. A study by Richards *et al.* (1999) seems to suggest this is not the case. In that study, social drinkers consumed placebo or alcohol (0.5 or 0.8 g/kg) beverages in counterbalanced order on separate sessions. The experimenters measured changes in the degree to which participants discounted the value of $10 delayed between 2 days and 1 year, and found no effect of alcohol, although the alcohol produced prototypical subjective effects. A second explanation for the similarity of discounting in never and former users lies in a selection issue. Perhaps users who succeed in quitting are those who discount delayed commodities relatively less initially. Bickel *et al.* (1999) presents data compatible with this idea.

In addition to the user-non-user effects, there is some evidence that higher levels of drug consumption may be associated with higher levels of delay discounting. First, Vuchinich & Simpson (1998) presented data suggesting that college students who were problem drinkers discounted a hypothetically available $1,000 or $10,000 more than those who were light social drinkers.

In a second study, Mitchell & Chapman (in preparaton) examined delay discounting in 12 light smokers (6–11 cigarettes/day) and 11 moderate smokers (15–25 cigarettes/day). Participant groups did not differ statistically in terms of their self-reported levels of drug use within the previous 30 days, excluding cigarettes, or in their self-reported lifetime drug experience. The existence of the self-reported differences in smoking was supported by statistically significant differences in breath carbon monoxide levels at orientation as well as the number of cigarettes smoked during a 6-hour ad lib smoking period held as part of the orientation session. In the experimental session, participants chose between different numbers of cigarettes available immediately after the task and $10 available following a delay. Participants were instructed that there was a possibility that one of these choice combinations would be selected, and that they would receive whichever alternative they had selected for that combination. If they had selected the cigarette alternative, they would receive the specific number of cigarettes, and be able to smoke some or all of them during a 6-hour post-task period. If they had selected the money alternative, they would receive an IOU for $10, which could be redeemed by returning to the lab when the specified delay had expired. However, they would not be able to smoke during the 6-hour post-task period. As might be anticipated, moderate smokers chose cigarettes over delayed money more frequently than light smokers did, presumably because moderate smokers expected to smoke more in the 6-hour period after completing the discounting task.

Similar results were obtained in an uncertainty discounting task. When the data from each type of task were converted to proportions, to control for differences in the value of cigarettes between moderate and light smokers, only the delay task revealed differences between the groups. This dissociation between delay and uncertainty discounting implied that moderate smokers discounted the delayed money more steeply than light smokers and these differences were not attributable to differences in the value of cigarettes.

In a third study, Mitchell (2001) examined drug use in young adults, using data pooled from several studies to yield 140 participants (70 male and 70 female) with a wide variety of recent drug use patterns (cigarettes, alcohol and marijuana consumption over the last 30 days) as well as lifetime drug use histories (frequency of recreational use of stimulants, hallucinogens, tranquilizers, opiates, and inhalants). Amongst other tasks and questionnaires, participants performed a delay discounting task in which they chose between variable amounts of money available immediately and $10 available following a delay. As in the Mitchell & Chapman study, participants understood that one of the choice combinations might be selected, and they would receive whichever alternative they had selected. Indifference points were found and the hyperbolic discount function was fitted to each individual's data. As would be expected from previously published studies, delay discounting was more pronounced for smokers than non-smokers. In addition, marijuana users discounted delayed money more steeply than non-users did, i.e. users had significantly larger values of k. Values for alcohol were in the expected direction but

Table 1: k values for the users and non-users of specific drugs.

	All	**Males**	**Females**
Cigarettes			
Users	0.0238^{**}	0.0427^{**}	0.0129
Non-users	0.0134	0.0118	0.0151
Alcohol			
Users	0.0171	0.0215^{*}	0.0108
Non-users	0.0142	0.0051	0.0236
Marijuana			
Users	0.0246^{**}	0.0426^{**}	0.0089
Non-users	0.0135	0.0105	0.0166

Data are also subdivided into users and non-users divided by gender. High alcohol users (>25 drinks each week) were omitted from the analysis so that male and female alcohol consumption was not statistically different. High marijuana users (>25 joints each week) were omitted from the analysis so that male and female marijuana smoking was not statistically different. p-values between user and non-user groups t-test using natural log values of k.
$^{*}p < 0.05.$
$^{**}p < 0.01.$

were not significant. Interestingly, more detailed analyses revealed that these effects held only for male participants, and remained even when differences in levels of use for a particular drug were controlled (Table 1). Further, for male participants only, the number of substances reportedly used was related to the value of k, implying that the more drugs were being used recreationally, the steeper the delayed money was discounted (Figure 2).

It is unclear why female participants did not exhibit the same relationship between drug use and temporal discounting. One explanation that was quickly disproved was that the hyperbolic equation fitted less well for females. On the contrary, the median r^2 yielded by the fits for males was 0.925 and for females was 0.928. However, a number of other explanations suggest themselves. Given that heightened discounting is often interpreted as indicating heightened impulsivity, perhaps initiation and continued maintenance of drug use are not associated with impulsivity in females, e.g. women smoking as a weight control strategy (e.g. Worsley *et al.* 1990), women drinking in response to "emotional pain" rather than the "sex seeking" motivation of males (Beck *et al.* 1995). Another possibility is that any additional factors that influence delay discounting might offset the impact of drug use for females. It is unclear what these factors may be, although gender differences are known to exist for several factors thought to be related to impulsivity, e.g. SES and serotonin-responsivity (Matthews *et al.* 2000), binding capacity of certain serotonin-receptor subtypes in the brain (Biver *et al.* 1996). Interestingly, Waldeck & Miller (1997) reported similar gender differences in the relationship between drug use and questionnaire measures of impulsivity (see also Martin *et al.* 1997).

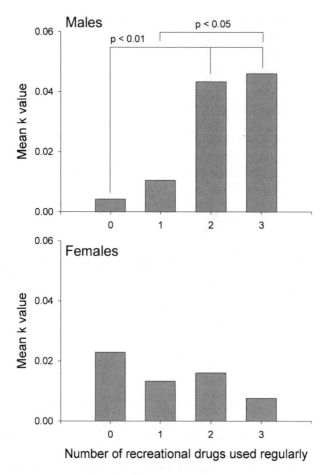

Figure 2: Mean delay discounting parameter, k, values as a function of the number of common recreational drugs used regularly over the last 30 days (cigarettes, alcohol and marijuana) for males and females. One-way between groups ANOVA revealed significant differences in k for males only, follow-up analyses used Tukey's HSD.

Uncertainty Discounting

In contrast to the delay discounting literature, few studies have examined whether drug users discount uncertain rewards differently from never users or former users. Of the handful of studies that exist, the data indicate that substance abusers and non-users do not discount uncertain commodities differently. Vuchinich & Calamas (1997) reported no difference between problem and social drinkers on a repeated gambles task, although there was a robust difference in delay discounting for these two groups. Mitchell (1999) reported similar results for regular smokers (15+ cigarettes/day) compared with never smokers. At face, this lack of difference between users and non-users is surprising from a number of standpoints. First, drug use is often perceived as a risky activity, and so by definition, drug users must be risk takers. To reinforce this point, there is a wealth of literature suggesting that drug use and risk-taking are positively related (e.g. reviews by Bechara 2001; Lerner & Galambos 1998; Yee *et al.* 1995; amongst others). Indeed there are two experimental studies that have yielded results suggesting a link between risk-taking and the extent of delay discounting. Thus, Odum *et al.* (2000) found that needle-sharing (presumably greater risk-taking) heroin addicts discounted delayed rewards more steeply than non-needle sharing addicts. Further Monterosso *et al.* (2001) reported that the steepness of the delay discounting function for cocaine-dependent patients was correlated to their risk-taking on a gambling task, i.e. frequency of choice of decks containing large occasional losses (Bechara *et al.* 1994). Second, several studies have examined the extent of discounting for an uncertain commodity and the extent of discounting for a delayed reward using a within-subjects design and have reported a positive correlation between delay and uncertainty discounting (e.g. Mitchell 1999; Ostaszewski 1997; Richards *et al.* 1999), although it is important to note that the magnitude of this relationship is somewhat uncertain (variance accounted for ranges from 16 to 57%). This positive correlation implies that uncertainty discounting should logically be higher for drug users than non-users.

The existence of a positive relationship between delay and uncertainty discounting is somewhat of a paradox. As noted earlier, in the parlance of the experimental analysis of behavior, the choice of the smaller, immediate reinforcer is an impulsive choice, whereas choice of the larger, delayed reward is a self-control choice (e.g. Ainslie 1974; Logue 1995; Rachlin & Green 1972). Thus, higher rates of discounting signify more impulsive choices, because choice of the immediate reinforcer [impulsive choice] decreases the indifference point. For uncertainty discounting, increased choice of the certain option [risk averse choice] also decreases the indifference point, thus steeper functions represent a relatively higher level of risk averse choices — not more risk prone choices as might be anticipated from the impulsivity approach.

Some authors have suggested that the positive relationship between delay and uncertainty discounting stems from the fact that rewards available probabilistically take more time to obtain, thus to roll a "6" using a die will take longer on average than to flip a "head" using an unbiased coin if each throw or toss occurs at the same rate (e.g. Rachlin *et al.* 1991). Other authors have suggested that uncertainty is the fundamental currency, since events that are further away in time are more likely to be disrupted and not occur than events closer in time (e.g. Sozou 1998). Yet others make the case that both delay discounting and responses to uncertainty are interactive mechanisms that have arisen through the action of evolutionary processes (e.g. Kacelnik 1997). Although there may be commonalities in the mechanisms underlying each type of discounting, there is data to suggest the mechanisms are not identical: Green *et al.* (1999) demonstrated that delay discounting became *more* pronounced as the magnitude of the delayed reinforcer declined whereas uncertainty discounting became *less* pronounced as the magnitude of the uncertain reward declined. Thus, even though it is surprising that drug users and non-users do not differ in uncertainty discounting when they do differ in terms of delay discounting, a disassociation between the two processes is not unprecedented.

Effort Discounting

Although we have a lot of data about delay discounting and, to a lesser extent, uncertainty discounting, we have far less information about the impact of effort requirements on the relative value of reinforcers. This omission is surprising in some ways. Energy expenditure (effort) is viewed as critical by biological theories, where it is assumed that animals have evolved in ways that enable them to maximize the net rate of energy gain.

Data presented by Mitchell (1999) indicated that regular cigarette smokers did not discount a $10 reward more than never smokers when its receipt required effortful responding. To the author's knowledge this is the only paper that has assessed effort discounting and drug use. Mazur has presented several experiments that examined the effects of an effort requirement on delay discounting (procrastination), but these did not disambiguate the delay and effort requirements (Mazur 1998, 1996). However, discounting of effort itself has not been examined widely in any situation. The final portion of this paper presents some data that will address this lack.

In the following studies, the effort requirement was applied by asking participants to squeeze a hand dynamometer (Stoelting Co., Chicago, IL) with their dominant hand for 10 seconds. In this way, effort requirements could be individualized. Prior to signing the consent form, and learning about the effort task, all participants completed a demographic questionnaire as well as a "strength test." The strength test required them to squeeze the hand dynamometer as hard as possible for a fixed time, 10 seconds, thus providing a measure of their 100% maximal voluntary contraction (MVC). This test, along with the demographic information, was ostensibly gathered to ensure that the individual met the study requirements. In reality, the experimenter needed to measure 100% MVC before the participant knew from the consent form that they could earn money for reproducing that contraction, in case participants produced artificially low MVCs so as to ease their effort requirements and enable them to earn the highest monetary reward more easily.

The effort discounting task was similar in all experiments. A computer presented questions one at a time. The experimenter used the first question for each task to illustrate the types of choices in the task and how participants could earn money. For all questions, participants indicated which of two items they preferred: the "standard" or the "alternative" item. The standard item was $10.00 available after squeezing the hand dynamometer for 10 seconds with a certain percent of the MVC measured during screening (e.g. 0, 50, and 100%). The percentages varied for different experiments. The alternative item was an amount of money ($0.01–$10.50) available after squeezing the hand dynamometer for 10 seconds of an MVC equal to the smallest standard value (e.g. 0%). During each task, a standard and an alternative item were selected at random, without replacement, to form the question. Thus, questions were presented in a random order. In addition, the order (first or second) in which the standard and alternative items were presented in each question varied. Participants indicated which of the two items they preferred by pressing "1" or "2" on the computer number keypad. Then the computer asked whether they were sure about their choice. If they were not, there was an opportunity to revise the choice. At the end of the experiment, there was a chance that one question from this task would be selected at random. In this case, the participant received whichever item was preferred for that question (standard or alternative) after they had succeeded in holding the required percentage of MVC for 10 seconds. If the subject could not complete the requirement, they received no money.

Mitchell (1999) reported data indicating that increasing effort did result in a decline in subjective value but this decline was small and did not appear to be a hyperbolic function; only 62% of the variance was accounted for when Mazur's hyperbolic equation was fitted to the data. One question that arose was whether the small decline was due to participants knowing that they could complete the requirement because the highest requirement (100% MVC) had been performed before, suggesting that the curve was determined to some extent by uncertainty about the ability to complete the requirement. To examine this idea, a study was performed in which 20 participants (10 male and 10 female) were asked to rate their confidence of being able to perform and hold an MVC of 0, 50, 100, 120, 135 or 150%. Confidence was rated by placing a vertical mark on a 100 mm line where 0 mm was marked "0% confidence" and 100 mm was marked as "100% confident." As might be expected, participants were relatively confident that they would complete the 0, 50 and 100% requirements (median rating: 99.5, 97 and 73.5% confident respectively). However, at the higher requirements of 120, 135 and 150% MVC, confidence rapidly declined (median rating: 39.5, 21 and 7). These confidence percentages were converted to "perceived odds against performing the behavior that yields money" by subtracting 1 from the reciprocal of the confidence expressed as a probability. When the indifference points were replotted as a function of the perceived odds against, a hyperbolic discount function was obtained (see Figure 3).

In a similar study, data from 90 college students who performed the same effort discounting task were pooled. In this task, participants were asked to choose between an amount of money available with no effort requirement ($10.50–$0.00) and $10.00 available if they squeezed the hand dynamometer with a percent MVC equal to 0, 50, 100, 110, 125 or 150%. For each choice they were asked to rate how certain they were that they could do the work specified. For example, if offered a choice between (1) $5.00 after performing 0% MVC or (2) $10.00 after performing 110% MVC, and the participant chose (1), they would rate their confidence in being able to perform 0% MVC; whereas if they chose (2), they would rate their confidence in being able to perform 110% MVC. Examination of the confidence ratings revealed several interesting results. As in the previous study (see Figure 3), confidence declined as a non-linear function of the MVC requirement. This decline was lower than in the previous experiment, but this was due to participants stating their confidence level only if they selected those options. In the prior experiment, participants were asked about every MVC level up to 150%, even if they had never indicated a willingness to choose or perform that effort requirement. In addition, plotting the indifference points based on the odds against yielded hyperbolic functions similar to those found in the previous experiment (Figure 4). Interestingly though, the relationship between whether a $10 with 100+% MVC option was chosen (and the resulting indifference points) and the perceived odds varied widely for individuals. Several individuals selected the "$10 with 150% MVC" option yet rated their confidence as 0, 1 or 2%. Others seemingly never selected an option that they had less than 100% confidence in being able to perform. Obviously, while confidence rating, or rather the perceived odds against, may account for a substantial amount of variance in the indifference points, the relationship between confidence rating and the ability to predict what an individual will choose is unclear.

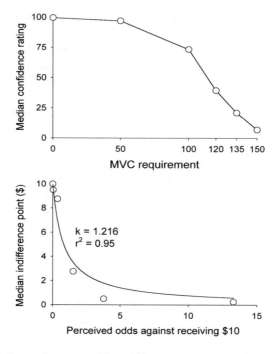

Figure 3: (top) Median ratings from 20 participants who were asked to rate on a scale of 0 to 100% how confident they were that they could complete the specific effort requirement. Note: MVC = 100 was the maximum effort output during the orientation. (bottom) Median indifference points for the same participants plotted as a function of the perceived odds against completing the MVC effort requirement and earning $10. Perceived odds against was calculated using the following formula:

$$\frac{100}{Confidence\ Rating} - 1.$$

Interestingly, indifference points and the confidence ratings appeared unrelated to any recreational drug use measure. Independent groups *t*-tests of dichotomized use variables (use-non-use) for alcohol, nicotine, marijuana, stimulants, hallucinogens, opiates, tranquilizers, and inhalants yielded no significant differences for indifference points or confidence ratings at the six MVC requirements. Further, there were no significant correlations between measures of current levels of use (last 30 days) or frequencies of lifetime use and composite measures of confidence (calculated by summing confidence ratings across the MVC requirements). In other words, drug use did not appear to be associated with a relative overconfidence in what amount of effort could be completed, neither was drug use associated with a perception of being weakened. This lack of significant effects might be due to restricted range effects. That is, a small proportion of the participants were probably nicotine-dependent smokers (10% smoked more than five cigarettes daily) and a proportion regularly consumed alcohol (42% consumed more than five drinks per week

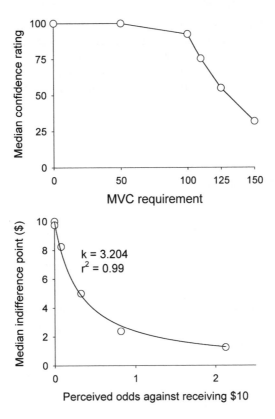

Figure 4: (top) Median ratings from 90 participants who were asked to rate on a scale of 0 to 100% how confident they were that they could complete the specific effort requirement each time they chose the response option that specified that effort requirement. Note: MVC = 100 was the maximum effort output during the orientation. (bottom) Median indifference points for the same participants plotted as a function of the perceived odds against completing the MVC effort requirement and earning $10.

but only 10% consumed more than 20 drinks per week). However, participants were not the same drug-dependent population examined by researchers who reported differences between users and non-users (see Bickel & Marsch 2000 for review).

It would have been interesting to compare the hyperbolic functions for delay and uncertainty discounting with those of effort discounting for these participants, because delay and uncertainty discounting tasks were performed. However this proved impossible. The difficulty arose because, although there were six possible MVC values (0, 50, 100, 110, 125 and 150%), using the perceived odds against on the abscissa led to a smaller number of points available for fitting (only 44 of 90 participants had 6 points for fitting). The number of points was reduced for two reasons. First, if participants never chose a particular MVC, say 125 or 150%, they never rated their confidence and thus no perceived odds against measure could be calculated. Second, a number of subjects would rate their confidence at completing certain MVC values at the same level, e.g. confidence of 100% for the 0 and 50% MVC questions. If correlations were performed for the 82 people who had 4 or more points available for the effort discounting fits, delay and probability discounting were moderately, though significantly correlated ($r^2 = 0.22$), but the degree of effort discounting was unrelated to either of the other two.

Conclusions

The data presented here demonstrate how similar psychophysical methods can be used to measure the amount by which the objective value of commodities is discounted as a function of the delay to their receipt, uncertainty about their receipt, and the effort required to attain them. Further, by appropriate manipulations of the abscissa, the same hyperbolic function appears to apply similarly to indifference points for the three different cost variables. However, the relationship between each pair of cost variables is complex. It seems apparent that any one of the three alone cannot account for discounting in general, e.g. delay discounting cannot be explained solely in terms of uncertainty, although there is shared variance. Although delay and uncertainty discounting are related, it is unclear whether they are also related to effort discounting. Further, only delay discounting appears to be related to drug use, and then only for males. A complete understanding of the role of cost variables in determining the subjective value of commodities, including drugs, must address these issues.

Acknowledgments

Studies were supported by NHLBI 058225. The author thanks Jerry B. Richards for comments on an earlier version of this manuscript.

References

Ainslie, G. W. (1974). Impulse control in pigeons. *Journal of Experimental Analysis of Behavior, 21,* 485–489.

Baum, W. M. (1974). On two types of deviation from the matching law: Bias and undermatching. *Journal of Experimental Analysis of Behavior, 22,* 231–242.

Bechara, A. (2001). Neurobiology of decision making: Risk and reward. *Seminars in Clinical Neuropsychiatry, 6,* 205–216.

Bechara, A., Damasio, A. R., Damasio, H., & Anderson, S. W. (1994). Insensitivity to future consequences following damage to human prefrontal cortex. *Cognition, 50,* 7–15.

Bickel, W. K., & Marsch, L. A. (2001). Toward a behavioral economic understanding of drug dependence: Delay discounting processes. *Addiction, 96,* 73–86.

Bickel, W. K., Odum, A. L., & Madden, G. J. (1999). Impulsivity and cigarette smoking: Delay discounting in current, never, and ex-smokers. *Psychopharmacology, 146,* 447–454.

Biver, F., Lotstra, F., Monclus, M., Wikler, D., Damhaut, P., Mendlewicz, J., & Goldman, S. (1996). Sex difference in 5HT2 receptor in the living human brain. *Neuroscience Letters, 204,* 25–28.

Caraco, T., Martindale, S., & Whittam, T. S. (1980). An empirical demonstration of risk-sensitive foraging preferences. *Animal Behavior, 28,* 820–830.

Carroll, M. E., & Campbell, U. C. (2000). A behavioral economic analysis of the reinforcing effects of drugs: Transition states of addiction. In: W. K. Bickel, & R. E.Vuchinich (Eds), *Reframing health behavior change with behavioral economics* (pp. 63–87). Mahwah, NJ: Lawrence Erlbaum.

Chung, S. H., & Herrnstein, R. J. (1967). Choice and delay of reinforcement. *Journal of the Experimental Analysis of Behavior, 10,* 67–74.

DeGrandpre, R. J., Bickel, W. K., Hughes, J. R., & Layng, M. P. (1993). Unit price as a useful metric in analyzing effects of reinforcer magnitude. *Journal of the Experimental Analysis of Behavior, 60,* 641–666.

Forzano, L. B., & Corry, R. J. (1998). Self-control and impulsiveness in adult human females: Effects of visual food cues. *Learning and Motivation, 29,* 184–199.

Green, L., Myerson, J., & Ostaszewski, P. (1999). Amount of reward has opposite effects on the discounting of delayed and probabilistic outcomes. *Journal of Experimental Psychology: Learning, Memoryand Cognition, 25,* 418–427.

Green, L., Myerson, J., & McFadden, E. (1997). Rate of temporal discounting decreases with amount of reward. *Memory and Cognition, 25,* 715–723.

Herrnstein, R. J. (1958). Some factors influencing behavior in a two-response situation. *Transactions of the New York Academy of Sciences, 21,* 35–45.

Herrnstein, R. J. (1964). Aperiodicity as a factor in choice. *Journal of the Experimental Analysis of Behavior, 7,* 179–182.

Herrnstein, R. J., & Loveland, D. H. (1975). Maximizing and matching on concurrent ratio schedules. *Journal of the Experimental Analysis of Behavior, 24,* 107–116.

Holling, C. S. (1959). Some characteristics of simple types of predation and parasitism. *Canadian Entomology, 91,* 385–398.

Hull, C. L. (1943). *Principles of behavior.* New York, NY: Appelton Century.

Hursh, S. R., Raslear, T. G., Shurtleff, D., Bauman, R., & Simmons, L. (1988). A cost-benefit analysis of demand for food. *Journal of the Experimental Analysis of Behavior, 50,* 419–440.

Ito, M., & Oyama, M. (1996). Relative sensitivity to reinforcer amount and delay in a self-control choice situation. *Journal of the Experimental Analysis of Behavior, 66,* 219–229.

Kacelnik, A. (1997). Normative and descriptive models of decision making: Time discounting and risk sensitivity. In: *Characterizing human psychological adaptations* (pp. 51–70). Ciba Foundation symposium, No. 208. New York, NY: Wiley.

Lachter, G. D. (1984). Concurrent schedules of response duration. *Bulletin of the Psychonomic Society, 22,* 362–364.

Lerner, R. M., & Galambos, N. L. (1998). Adolescent development: Challenges and opportunities for research, programs, and policies. *Annual Review of Psychology, 49,* 413–446.

Lewis, M. (1965). Psychological effect of effort. *Psychological Bulletin, 64,* 183–190.

Logue, A. W. (1995). *Self-control: Waiting until tomorrow for what you want today.* Englewood Cliff, NJ: Prentice-Hall.

Logue, A. W., King, G. R., Chavarro, A., & Volpe, J. S. (1990). Matching and maximizing in a self-control paradigm using human subjects. *Learning and Motivation, 21,* 340–368.

Logue, A. W., Rodriguez, M. L., Pena-Correal, T. E., & Mauro, B. C. (1984). Choice in a self-control paradigm: Quantification of experience-based differences. *Journal of the Experimental Analysis of Behavior, 41,* 53–67.

Madden, G. J., Petry, N. M., Badger, G. J., & Bickel, W. K. (1997). Impulsive and self-control choices in opioid-dependent patients and non-drug-using control participants: Drug and monetary rewards. *Experimental and Clinic Psychopharmacology, 5,* 256–262.

Martin, C. A., Milich, R., Martin, W. R., Hartung, C. M., & Haigler, E. D. (1997). Gender differences in adolescent psychiatric outpatient substance use: Associated behaviors and feelings. *Journal of the American Academy of Child & Adolescent Psychiatry, 36,* 486–494.

Matthews, K. A., Flory, J. D., Muldoon, M. F., & Manuck, S. B. (2000). Does socioeconomic status relate to central serotonergic responsivity in healthy adults? *Psychosomatic Medicine, 62,* 231–237.

Mazur, J. E. (1996). Procrastination by pigeons: Preference for larger, more delayed work requirements. *Journal of the Experimental Analysis of Behavior, 65,* 159–171.

Mazur, J. E. (1998). Procrastination by pigeons with fixed-interval response requirements. *Journal of the Experimental Analysis of Behavior, 69,* 185–197.

Mazur, J. E. (2001). Hyperbolic value addition and general models of animal choice. *Psychological Review, 108,* 96–112.

McCulloch, T. L. (1934). Performance preferentials of the white rate in force-resisting and spatial dimensions. *Journal of Comparative Psychology, 18,* 85–110.

Mitchell, S. H. (1999). Measures of impulsivity in cigarette smokers and non-smokers. *Psychopharmacology, 146,* 455–464.

Mitchell, S. H. (2001) Correlates of heightened impulsivity in college students. Presentation at the annual meeting of the American Psychological Association, San Francisco, August 2001.

Mitchell, & Chapman (submitted for publication). *Delay and probability discounting in light and moderate smokers.*

Monterosso, J., Ehrman, R., Napier, K. L., O'Brien, C. P., & Childress, A. R. (2001). Three decision-making tasks in cocaine-dependent patients: Do they measure the same construct? *Addiction, 96,* 1825–1837.

Myerson, J., & Green, L. (1995). Discounting of delayed rewards: Models of individual choice. *Journal of the Experimental Analysis of Behavior, 64,* 263–276.

Myerson, J., Green, L., & Warusawitharana, M. (2001). Area under the curve as a measure of discounting. *Journal of the Experimental Analysis of Behavior, 76,* 235–243.

Odum, A. L., Madden, G. J., Badger, G. J., & Bickel, W. K. (2000). Needle sharing in opioid-dependent outpatients: Psychological processes underlying risk. *Drug and Alcohol Dependence, 60,* 259–266.

Ostaszewski, P. (1997). Temperament and the discounting of delayed and probabilistic rewards: Conjoining European and American psychological traditions. *European Psychologist, 2,* 35–43.

Petry, N. M. (2001). Delay discounting of money and alcohol in actively using alcoholic, currently abstinent alcoholics, and controls. *Psychopharmacology, 154,* 243–250.

Rachlin, H., & Green, L. (1972). Commitment, choice, and self-control. *Journal of Experimental Analysis of Behavior, 17,* 15–22.

Rachlin, H., Raineri, A., & Cross, D. (1991). Subjective probability and delay. *Journal of Experimental Analysis of Behavior, 55,* 233–244.

Richards, J. B., Zhang, L., Mitchell, S. H., & de Wit, H. (1999). Delay or probability discounting in a model of impulsive behavior: Effect of alcohol. *Journal of Experimental Analysis of Behavior, 71,* 121–143.

Rodriguez, M. L., & Logue, A. W. (1986). Independence of the amount and delay ratios in the generalized matching law. *Animal Learning and Behavior, 14,* 29–37.

Solomon, R. L. (1948). The influence of work on behavior. *Psychological Bulletin, 45,* 1–40.

Sozou, P. D. (1998). On hyperbolic discounting and uncertain hazard rates. *Proceedings of the Royal Society (London), 265,* 2015–2020.

Stephens, D. W., & Krebs, J. R. (1986). *Foraging theory.* Princeton NJ: Princeton University Press.

Taylor, R., & Davison, M. (1983). Sensitivity to reinforcement in concurrent arithmetic and exponential schedules. *Journal of the Experimental Analysis of Behavior, 39,* 191–198.

Vuchinich, R. E., & Calamas, M. L. (1997). Does the repeated gambles procedure measure impulsivity in social drinkers? *Experimental and Clinical Psychopharmacology, 5,* 157–162.

Vuchinich, R. E., & Simpson, C. A. (1998). Hyperbolic temporal discounting in social drinkers and problem drinkers. *Experimental and Clinical Psychopharmacology, 6,* 292–305.

Waldeck, T. L., & Miller, L. S. (1997). Gender and impulsivity differences in licit substance use. *Journal of Substance Abuse, 9,* 269–275.

Woolverton, W. L., & English, J. A. (1997). Further analysis of choice between cocaine and food using the unit price model of behavioral economics. *Drug and Alcohol Dependence, 49,* 71–78.

Yee, B. W., Castro, F. G., Hammond, W. R., John, R., Wyatt, G. E., & Yung, B. R. (1995). Risk-taking and abusive behaviors among ethnic minorities. *Health Psychology, 14,* 622–631.

Comments on Mitchell

Gene M. Heyman

Suzanne Mitchell's paper explores the hypothesis that the various factors that count as response costs can be described by a single, simple mathematical function. This is a novel and potentially powerful proposition. It suggests that quite different procedural operations, such as the length of the delay from response to reward or the force requirement for operating a lever, exact a common underlying bio-psychological effect. Mitchell's new experiments support her hypothesis, and given the idea's organizing power, it is likely that future studies will follow up where her new experiments and review leave off. However, in this response, I want to focus on a background issue that pertains to a subset of the studies that Mitchell discusses. In the delay discounting experiments, the quantitative relationship between delay and preference has proven the same in the various species that serve as subjects in psychological experiments. Pigeons, rats, and people discount the value of future rewards according to a simple hyperbolic equation. Moreover, as Mitchell's review emphasizes, laboratory-established differences in the parameters of this mathematical delay function predict important non-laboratory individual differences in behavior, such as drug use history. This finding implies that the delay procedure can be used to analyze individual differences that contribute to drug use and test new treatments. For instance, if a pharmacological or behavioral treatment decreased "impulsivity" in delay discounting experiments, it should also do so "on the street." However, the delay procedure findings are also quite puzzling, and the puzzle is in their generality.

The experiments that yield the same discount function for people and pigeons differ in ways that under other circumstances make a difference. In the human studies, the rewards are hypothetical and the subjects are not deprived, whereas in the animal studies, the subjects are deprived and the rewards provide essential and, in principle, life-saving sustenance. As these are motivational studies, these differences should matter, but they don't as measured by the shape of the function relating delay to choice. Why the same delay function applies to judgments that have but minor consequences and reinforced responses that have major consequences is the focus of the remainder of this paper.

Why Do Delays Decrease Preference?

The first point to make is that the effect of delay can be distinguished from the effect of a decrease in reward rate. For example, imagine the following study. In one condition, 10 seconds is added to a variable-interval 60 second schedule, and in a companion condition, variable delays are added that have a mean of 10 seconds. Under both conditions the average inter-reinforcement interval is now 70 seconds, but in the second condition the added temporal increments are in the form of a delay (e.g. a blackout between the to-be-reinforced response and the reward). Although this exact experiment appears not to have been conducted, we can predict the results on the basis of similar existing studies (e.g. Chung 1965; Chung & Herrnstein 1967). In the rate condition, response rate will decrease as predicted by the matching law (Herrnstein 1970). For instance, if the experiment involved initially equal concurrent schedules, the decrease associated with the change in reward rate at one alternative would be less than 8% $(70/(70 + 60) - 60/(60 + 60))$. In contrast, in the delay condition, the decrease should be quite large, falling on a point predicted by a hyperbolic (multiplicative) discount function. Chung (1965) made a similar argument and shows in a graph (Figure 5) that the decreases in preference associated with a delay of reward are much greater than those associated with a decrease in reward rate (assuming matching). Indeed, if this were not the case then the preference reversals that are taken as evidence of hyperbolic discounting would not occur.

Thus, delay has a greater impact on preference than does a decrease in reward rate. Why? As is usually the case, we can imagine both a cognitive and a motivational explanation. The delay may weaken the association between responding and reward, thereby decreasing preference. Or the delay may function as a time-out from reinforcement, and time-outs reduce responding in much the same way as punishment. These interpretations are not mutually exclusive, and possibly there are other explanations as well. For instance, delay could be a fundamental parameter that influenced behavior even when the associative links were not weakened and the delay periods were arranged so that reward rates were not reduced. (Imagine an independent reward source that remains available during the delay period.)

Why Do Very Different Experimental Procedures for Measuring the Influence of Delay on Preference Produce Similar Results?

To better appreciate the relationships between method and results in delay discounting, it would be helpful to provide some details on the methods. Chung & Herrnstein (1967) were the first to clearly establish that delaying rewards decreased preference hyperbolically. Their procedure is no longer widely used (see papers by Mazur (2001) and Richards and his colleagues (1997) for more recent methodological developments). However, the relevant issue for the questions addressed in this paper is the range of conditions that promote a hyperbolic delay function, not the current state of animal research.

Food (grain) was the reinforcer. To ensure that the experimenter-arranged reward controlled behavior, the pigeons were put on a diet that reduced their body weight by about 20%. The amount of food earned during experimental sessions was not sufficient to maintain the 80% target weights so that after the experimental session, the birds were given supplementary servings of grain. The free food was eaten instantaneously, indicating that through the course of the session the birds remained ravenous. Thus, the experimental events were important, as measured by the subjects' welfare, and the subjects were, accordingly, highly motivated.

In the experimental chamber there were two buttons. Pecks on both were reinforced according to the passage of time. This was arranged by combining a concurrent variable-interval 60 second schedule with delay requirements. For instance, when a peck was eligible for reinforcement according to the interval timer, the reinforcer was withheld, and the chamber turned dark for a specified period of time. At the end of the blackout, the reinforcer was delivered and the chamber was re-illuminated. Chung & Herrnstein varied the blackout periods (delays) in the hope of determining the mathematical function that best described the relationship between the delays and preference. They found that an equation for a hyperbola did the best job. This result has been replicated numerous times, and as a result, the hyperbola is now widely accepted as the function that best describes the relationship between delay and preference.

Now consider what happens in the typical human study. The subjects are given a list of binary choices. One option describes a smaller amount of money available "now" and the other option describes a larger amount of money available "later," where later can mean an interval stretching from about a day to several years. However, "now" and "later" are in quotes because the rewards are either hypothetical or unlikely. In one version of this experiment, every question is hypothetical; the subject never gets what he or she chooses. For example, Myerson & Green (1995) asked subjects if they wanted $10,000 in 5 years or $6000 now, but the subjects in fact got nothing. In the second version of this procedure, one question from a list of about two dozen questions is selected at the end of the session, and the subject gets his or her choice on that question (e.g. Kirby & Marakovic 1995). For example, if by chance the third question on the list was selected, and on the third item the subject chose $2.00 "now," he or she would get $2.00 at the end of the session. However, for all other questions, the immediate choice could not be said to have precluded the delayed outcome, and vice versa. That is, the "reward" depends on the subject's ability or willingness to imagine receiving $2.00 at the end of the session or $3.00 a month from the end of the session.

Using some of the dimensions that were used to describe the pigeon experiment, it can be added that the subjects in the human studies were not deprived and that no consumption took place during the course of the experiment. It is reasonable to suppose that ingestion, metabolism, and satiation influence reinforcement processes, yet in the human studies the physical consequences of consumption are absent. Also note that delays did not include blackout periods, time-outs from reinforcement, or any factor that would influence associative learning. Finally, the delays in the human and pigeon experiments differ by several orders of magnitude. For the pigeons, 10 seconds was a long delay. In the human studies, subjects were asked to imagine rewards that will occur days, months, and even years into the future. Thus, in the animal experiments the rewards are palpable and matter, whereas in the human studies, the rewards are less palpable and by economic criteria, matter less.

Nevertheless, the results in the human studies follow in precise quantitative fashion the pattern predicted on the basis of the animal studies. Preferences for hypothetical monetary rewards were a hyperbolic function of the nominal delays, just as, in pigeons and rats, response rates were a hyperbolic function of the experienced delays. In other words, the shape of the mathematical function that joined judgments and imagined future events was the same as that which joined peck rates and peck-produced feedings. Moreover, drug users more often chose an imagined sooner, smaller reward than did non-drug users (see Mitchell), just as some pigeons were more impatient than others (see Ainslie 1974, 1975).

The usual research discrepancy is that similar procedures produce different results. But here, markedly different procedures produced similar results. There are either subtle but powerful methodological constraints that yield hyperbolic results regardless of the behavioral processes at hand or the procedures are tapping into highly general and robust biobehavioral processes that play a critical role in animal and human decision-making.

Next are two possible explanations of why human judgments agree with pigeon peck rates. One includes the idea that human judgments about behavior are a veridical reflection of the behavior itself. The other is that behavior, even in the pigeon, has judgment-like properties, with response rates reflecting the value of the reward rather than the strength of the behavior. Most certainly there are other possible accounts, but these two seem the most obvious.

The data make sense if what people say about their preferences in the delay procedures accurately measures how they really behave, and how they behave is quite like how creatures like rats and pigeons behave. This statement involves at least three separable ideas: (1) that the questions regarding hypothetical monetary outcomes activate accurate representations of the quantitative features of past behavior and/or future behavior; (2) that the motivational impact of hypothetical monetary rewards is the same as the motivational impact of primary, consumable rewards like food and water; and (3) that the influence of delay on preference is the same for people and pigeons. These are testable assertions, and the delay literature suggests that there are conditions under which each is true.

Alternatively, human judgments of the value of delayed rewards and the actual behavioral effects of delayed rewards may converge because instrumental behaviors, such as lever presses, are in effect judgments as to the value of the contingent rewards. Put another way, conditioning studies are investigations of the psychophysics of reward, with response rate (on variable-interval schedules) standing as a proxy for sensations and the reward (say its frequency or magnitude) standing as a proxy for the stimulus. Hence, a pigeon's rate of pecking and a human's considered judgment about a hypothetical future event are both statements about the reward value of their respective eliciting stimuli. The competing view is that rewards strengthen or shape a particular response rate, as glue might reinforce a joint. But the strengthening interpretation makes it even harder to understand how reinforced response rates and human judgments can take a similar functional form.

There are two general solutions to the problems posed by this paper. The apparent similarity in the animal and human discount functions reflects similar underlying psychological processes, or, alternatively, the similarities are superficial, arising in quite different ways. To determine which conclusion is correct, the processes that mediate the behavioral level analyses need to be identified. A reasonable strategy would be to develop derivations of the hyperbola, test them in terms of their behavioral predictions, and then identify the attendant biological mechanisms. The second step would be sufficient to answer questions concerning whether the human and animal experiments were in fact revealing the same phenomenon, the third step tells us how nature engineers psychological processes, and the second and third steps together would increase our general understanding of preference for delayed rewards and could also have important clinical applications. Put more generally, as progress is made at the level of behavioral observation, it becomes increasingly important to understand the underlying psychological and biological processes.

References

Ainslie, G. (1974). Impulse control in pigeons. *Journal of the Experimental Analysis of Behavior, 21,* 485–489.

Ainslie, G. (1975). Specious reward: A behavioral theory of impulsiveness and impulse control. *Psychological Bulletin, 82,* 463–496.

Chung, S. (1965). Effects of delayed reinforcement in a concurrent situation. *Journal of the Experimental Analysis of Behavior, 8,* 439–444.

Chung, S., & Herrnstein, R. J. (1967). Choice and delay of reinforcement. *Journal of the Experimental Analysis of Behavior, 10,* 67–74.

Herrnstein, R. J. (1970). On the law of effect. *Journal of the Experimental Analysis of Behavior, 13,* 243–266.

Kirby, K., & Marakovic, N. N. (1995). Modeling myopic decisions: Evidence for hyperbolic discounting within subjects and amounts. *Organizational Behavior and Human Decision Processes, 64,* 22–30.

Mazur, J. E. (2001). Hyperbolic value addition and general models of animal choice. *Psychological Review, 108,* 96–112.

Myerson, J., & Green, L. (1995). Discounting of delayed rewards: Models of individual choice. *Journal of the Experimental Analysis of Behavior, 64,* 263–276.

Richards, J. B., Mitchell, S. H., de Wit, H., & Seiden, L. S. (1997). Determination of discount functions in rats with an adjusting-amount procedure. *Journal of the Experimental Analysis of Behavior, 67,* 353–366.

Part IV

Practical Implications

Chapter 13

Merging Behavioral Economic and Public Health Approaches to the Delivery of Services for Substance Abuse: Concepts and Applications

Jalie A. Tucker and Cathy A. Simpson

Introduction

Behavioral economics is concerned with understanding individual patterns of choice among environmental alternatives that are available under variable constraints. The perspective has proven useful as a model for understanding choices between engaging in substance use or alternative non-drug activities that vary in value, availability, and their short- and longer-term consequences. We propose that the model can be further extended to a public health context that incorporates broader-based, consumer-oriented approaches to the delivery and utilization of services for substance abuse. This issue has considerable applied significance: Over 10% of the U.S. population fulfills clinical criteria for a substance use disorder, but less than 25% of those affected seek help from professional or voluntary services for substance-related problems (reviewed by Tucker 2001). Closing the gap between need and utilization of services will require changes in public policy and in the healthcare and public health systems that are concerned with reducing demand for drugs and drug-related harm. It is our contention that behavioral economic concepts can guide such changes as part of a merger with public health approaches to health behavior change and service utilization.

This paper outlines key areas at the intersection of behavioral economics and public health that merit consideration and development, including: (a) expanding conceptualizations of health and health-seeking behaviors; (b) addressing variations in, and interactions between, open and closed economies that surround patterns of substance use and care-seeking; (c) identifying useful functional units of analysis in the delivery and utilization of services; and (d) shifting from a paternalistic model of service provision to one that is sensitive to consumer preferences and demand for services. Applications regarding the provision of

Choice, Behavioural Economics and Addiction
Copyright © 2003 by Elsevier Ltd.
All rights of reproduction in any form reserved
ISBN: 0-08-044056-8

services to substance abusers are discussed, with an objective of closing the gap between need and utilization, and allocating limited intervention resources in a more cost-effective manner across the population in need. A final section discusses complexities involved in developing suitable methods to support research and applications in open economies.

Finding the Interface of Behavioral Economics and Public Health

An overarching assumption guiding the present discussion is that drug abusers are consumers, be it of drugs or services to reduce drug use and drug-related harm. Behavioral economics directs attention toward finding ways to increase the appeal of non-drug alternative activities, including the utilization of relevant interventions, in relation to drug use. However, viable applications of behavioral economic concepts at the population or community level will need to go far beyond the typically individual level of analysis and laboratory preparations of behavioral economics, and will require concern with natural environments that are not easily controllable, if at all.

Conceptual vs. Methodological Intersection

As a starting point in searching for a viable disciplinary interface between behavioral economics and public health, we argue that the connection should be made primarily at a conceptual level, not at the level of method. There are vast differences between the two perspectives in the scope, level of control, time frames, methods, and goals of analysis that must be recognized and respected for a merger to be successful. Public health approaches bring scale, a broadened perspective, and emphasis on cost-effective allocation of limited goods and services across the population in need. Behavioral economics provides conceptual depth and expertise in experimental methods, model-building, and measurement. Although behavioral economics provides some potentially powerful, simplifying concepts for applied endeavors in public health, the experimental methods of behavior analysis cannot be directly translated at a public health level. Some tolerance for methodological pluralism and non-experimental research is essential for a successful merger.

Fortunately, conceptual connections between behavioral economics and public health approaches to substance use interventions are fairly clear. Both share a common interest in identifying, understanding, and modifying health-behavior relationships (cf. Bickel & Vuchinich 2000). They also share interests in the continuing development of strategies that promote healthy behaviors and reduce high-risk or harmful behaviors. The two perspectives vary, of course, in the adoption of a predominantly individual focus in the case of behavioral economics vs. a predominantly population perspective in the case of public health. The scope and methods of the respective research and practice have varied accordingly. A useful merger will combine behavioral economic and public health principles in ways that are sensitive to population parameters of substance abuse, target and deliver interventions for different risk groups, disseminate cost-effective interventions across communities and populations in need, and promote access to activities that compete with drug-taking. As discussed next, relevant conceptual issues to consider in a synthesis of the two viewpoints include expanding conceptualizations of health and health-seeking, distinguishing open and closed economies, defining useful functional units of analysis, and viewing substance abusers as consumers of goods and services.

Expanding Conceptualizations of Health and Health-Seeking Behaviors

Consistent with earlier work in health economics (e.g. Fuchs 1987, 1993; Grossman 1972), an application of behavioral economic concepts within a public health framework suggests that "health" be operationalized in terms of its functional value. The following questions are relevant to understanding the function of health in relation to choices that individuals make:

Is a given state of "health" a summary variable that predicts access to or loss of future reinforcers? Grossman (1972) argued that good health be regarded as an intermediate state, not an end in itself, that allows engagement in other valued activities by freeing up the necessary time and resources. This directs attention toward characterizing health states in terms of their effects on functional capacity, more so than in terms of the usual biological metrics of medicine.

How do delays in the payoffs for health and health-seeking behaviors affect actions for their attainment? Discounting of delayed benefits is an important conceptual and empirical contribution of behavioral economics, including in applications to substance use and abuse (Bickel & Marsch 2001). The rewards of seeking treatment or making other health behavior changes usually are temporally extended and probabilistic, and different health behavior "bundles" will vary in their probabilities in supporting access to sets of future reinforcers over variable time horizons. A behavioral economic perspective suggests that the appeal and effectiveness of services will depend in part on how sensitive their design is to such discount effects.

What influences behavioral allocation or "investment" patterns in different states of health? The human lifespan involves inevitable changes in "health capital," some of which are predictable (e.g. loss of youthful vigor, women's fertility) and some of which are not. Health capital cannot be saved indefinitely, and good health states afford relatively more opportunities to allocate behavior in ways that promote access to future health states and to future behavioral allocation opportunities. How wisely behavior is allocated when one is healthy will likely be influenced by present investment opportunities and by discounting processes. This view re-frames the goals of behavior change interventions in terms of shifting behavioral allocation patterns in ways that maximize utility over a somewhat uncertain future interval that involves somewhat uncertain health states (Simpson & Vuchinich 2000).

These questions generally suggest that behavioral economics can advance public health strategies by guiding investigation of how individual characteristics, such as health status, family history, and discount rates, interact with broader-based environmental contingencies and interventions aimed at the prevention and amelioration of health and behavioral health problems. Regardless of the specific application, the merger requires an expanded conceptualization of health as a commodity that functions within a broader economic system.

These questions also direct attention toward studying inter-temporal exchanges between behavior patterns that have variable health and other functional outcomes over different time horizons (Simpson & Vuchinich 2000). For example, in a study (Chapman & Johnson 1995) of hypothetical choices between immediately available rewards (e.g. beer, a used car) and reductions in life expectancy, the amount of life expectancy that participants expressed willingness to give up, in order to receive the immediate rewards, was positively related to the monetary value that they had assigned to the immediate rewards. On average, participants were willing to trade five days of life expectancy for a year's supply of beer. As summarized by Simpson & Vuchinich (2000: 195), "these results are consistent with the notion that health is a commodity of malleable value, and that the relative attractiveness of long-term health rewards decreases as the relative attractiveness of competing immediately available alternatives increases." The authors noted that research on such trade-offs suggests that health outcomes are discounted according to a hyperbolic function, as is the case for many other commodities (Myerson & Green 1995; Rachlin *et al.* 1991), including preferences for substance use (Vuchinich & Simpson 1998). However, the value of delayed health outcomes appears to be discounted more heavily compared to commodities such as money. Clarifying these relations is central to using behavioral economic approaches to guide behavior change interventions at individual and public health levels of application.

Open and Closed Economies and Their Relevance to Health and Health-Seeking

Another area of expertise that behavioral economics can bring to a public health approach is an understanding of consumer demand. Put simply, demand is the amount of behavior that a given reinforcer will support. Demand for a given commodity varies as a function of its price (e.g. monetary cost, response requirement), delay to availability, and individual ("taste") variables (e.g. discount rates). A central objective of (behavioral) economics is to determine how demand changes as a function of changes in a commodity's price and changes in other contextual features, such as the availability and price of alternative commodities. *Elasticity coefficients* (ε) express this relationship and are defined as the ratio of changes in the quantity of consumption of a given commodity in relation to changes in its price (*own-price* elasticity) or in relation to changes in the price of alternative commodities (*cross-price* elasticity). Demand curves with slopes between 0 and -1.0 are considered inelastic, and those with slopes over -1.0 are considered elastic (Madden 2000: 10). A value of -1.0, or unity, indicates that each unit change in price results in a unit change in demand.

A related issue of relevance to a merger of behavioral economic and public health principles concerns understanding how demand for goods varies in open and closed economies (Hursh 2000). In closed economies, the availability and price of commodities are relatively fixed. This is modeled experimentally in operant studies that make food or drugs available during experimental sessions according to schedules of reinforcement. Closed economies tend to maintain relatively "steady state" behavior (Hursh 1991). In open economies, the availability and price of commodities is relatively free to vary, and commodity acquisition may be partially or fully independent of completion of prearranged schedule contingencies. This is modeled experimentally in operant studies that make valued commodities available in different settings (e.g. in-session or home cage feeding opportunities) under variable degrees of schedule control.

As economies become more open — that is, as commodities can be obtained across multiple settings and as the schedule contingencies controlling *total* commodity access become more dilute — demand becomes more elastic (Hursh 1980). Seminal animal experiments conducted by Hursh (1978) compared closed economy conditions, during which total daily food consumption was controlled in experimental sessions by variable-interval schedules of reinforcement, and open economy conditions, during which total daily food consumption was the result of schedule-controlled in-session feeding opportunities and supplemental (e.g. home cage) feeding opportunities that were not schedule-controlled. Results showed that demand for food in 80% free-feed weight animals was inelastic under the closed economy conditions and was slightly elastic under the open economy conditions.

Similarly, simulated open and closed economies in experiments with human substance abusers have found that drug demand becomes more elastic as the experimental contingencies become more open (Bickel *et al.* 1997; DeGrandpre *et al.* 1994; Mitchell *et al.* 1994; Shahan *et al.* 2000). For example, Mitchell and colleagues (1994) manipulated the "openness" of the experimental economy for cigarettes in a multi-session study using heavy smokers. Participants completed computer choice tasks to earn points that were redeemable for cigarettes or money. During open economy sessions, varying numbers of unearned ("free") additional cigarettes also were available to participants following the experimental sessions; during closed economy sessions, no unearned cigarettes were available. Mitchell and colleagues' results are shown in Figure 1. In-session demand for cigarettes was less

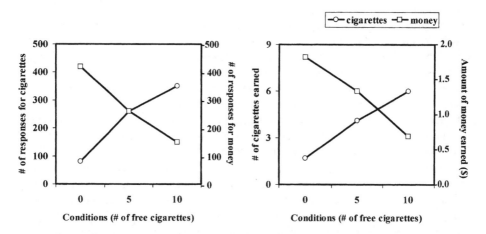

Figure 1: The figure is adapted from data reported by Mitchell *et al.* (1994) and illustrates differences in responding by heavy smokers for cigarettes and money under experimental conditions that modeled closed and open economies (left panel) and total amount of money and cigarettes earned as a function of free cigarettes that participants received post-session (right panel). Responding for in-session cigarettes generally decreased as the number of post-session "free" (0, 5, or 10) cigarettes increased.

elastic ($\varepsilon = -1.29$) when no post-session "free" cigarettes were available compared to when they were provided ($\varepsilon = -1.72$, and -1.55 for the 5 and 10 post-session cigarette conditions, respectively). Moreover, as the number of free post-session cigarettes increased, responding for money increased. These significant changes in responding were achieved with provision of access to relatively modest post-session reinforcers. Providing as few as five free cigarettes during a 6-hour post-experimental period was sufficient to increase elasticity of demand compared to that found in the zero cigarette condition.

In natural environments, open and closed economic conditions can be viewed as operating along a continuum with respect to the extent and variability of restrictions on commodity access in a given environmental setting, including the price and other contingencies associated with obtaining the commodities. This distinction may prove useful in understanding how interventions interact with current and future economic conditions to produce short- and longer-term outcomes. Most public health interventions are designed to operate at the community level and emphasize a broad, cost-effective, low intensity outpatient model of service delivery (Curry & Kim 1999). In other words, they operate in an open economy in which multiple reinforcers are available under relatively minimal environmental restrictions. The same is true for the contexts in which substance use and abuse typically occur. This contrasts with the closed economies in which much of the empirical work of behavioral economics and behavioral analysis has been conducted, ranging from basic laboratory preparations to schools, hospitals, and other institutional environments. Inpatient substance abuse treatment programs also function within relatively closed economies (Hursh 2000). Access to a limited number of available commodities (e.g. local hospital privileges, longer-term ostensible benefits of treatment) occurs in a highly constrained treatment environment and depends on patient adherence to provider- and institution-imposed contingencies.

A fundamental and under-appreciated fact is that open and closed economies typically *co-exist* in the natural environments in which substance use and health-seeking behaviors occur. There probably are complex interactions among economies that range along the continuum from fully open to fully closed, as well as influential differences in their relative reinforcer distributions. Problem health behavior patterns may occur primarily in some environments and not in others, or the environments in which they occur may shift predictably over time. The extent to which the relevant environments include open or closed economies should guide intervention selection or development, and this issue will almost certainly contribute to intervention outcomes.

For example, healthcare systems, especially on the inpatient side, tend to be more consistent with prototypic closed economies. Upon entering that system, one moves functionally from an open to a closed economy with regard to the contingencies that operate on health behaviors and outcomes. In this instance, the social determinants of help-seeking and health behaviors, which are influential in the natural environment and promote treatment entry (Tucker 2001), are likely to give way to a considerable extent to hospital and provider-based contingencies as long as one remains in the hospital environment. Upon discharge, the contingencies largely revert back to the original conditions that maintained problem behavior patterns, and "relapse" is likely in the absence of environmental change. Historically, this well known limitation of institutional behavioral interventions was framed as a problem of generalization of treatment-produced changes. Behavioral economics suggests, instead, that it be framed as an issue of understanding how behavior patterns change during transitions from closed to open economies and how co-existing economies that vary along this dimension interact with one another over time. Addressing the issue is this manner should facilitate a successful merger with public health approaches that routinely operate in open economies.

Units of Analysis

Another issue involved in moving across open and closed economies in the delivery of substance abuse services is selecting one or more units of analysis. Potentially, these units could range from individual behavior to micro-organizations within larger organizations to the larger organization itself. All of these units of analysis can be reasonably assumed to operate both independently and interdependently within a broader economic and cultural context.

Historically, behavioral economics has focused more on individual level analyses, but behavioral issues at the organizational, community, and population levels will be important to a successful merger of behavioral economic and public health approaches. Public health has been more flexible in this area, but leaping from the study of individuals to the study of populations leaves out considerable complexity with regard to intermediate organizational entities, such as a substance abuse treatment unit of a larger healthcare provider system.

As applied to service utilization, effectively defining units of analysis depends on discriminating the functional relations that exist at the various points of contact that consumers have with a particular service delivery system. The scope of the unit of analysis should be compatible with the scope of the functional, consumer-oriented questions being asked. Another complexity is that a given service delivery system may include multiple consumers or stakeholder groups (e.g. patients, physicians, and managed care organizations [MCOs]), each with unique and common utility functions.

For example, it has long been known that providing behavioral health services tends to reduce the utilization and costs of medical services, often to the point of covering the costs of the behavioral health services (reviewed by Fiedler & Wight 1989; Holder 1998). Despite the salutary, "cost-offset" effects of behavioral healthcare, insurance plans historically have covered behavioral health services at levels far less generous than for comparable medical care. As the U.S. healthcare system has moved from a fee-for-service to a managed care model (in which large, for-profit organizations manage comprehensive healthcare), benefits for behavioral healthcare have improved, at least in terms of the number of people who have a behavioral health benefit. Cost-offset effects tend to increase as healthcare organizations deliver comprehensive care to larger pools of patients. So, whether recognized as such or not, MCOs have a greater economic incentive to provide behavioral health benefits compared to when healthcare was largely a provider-controlled, cottage industry (cf. Mechanic 1994).

The above example illustrates how the relevant levels of analysis can change over time and how these different levels potentially interact with changes in the macro-environment. Behavioral economic concepts are potentially applicable across many levels of analysis, but an effective merger with public health approaches will require greater sensitivity to macro-economic parameters that are common in a more open economy.

Service Utilization as Choice

A final conceptual issue involves taking a broader view of substance abusers as potential consumers of intervention services. Until quite recently, U.S. healthcare in general and substance abuse services in particular have been delivered in a fairly paternalistic manner, in the sense that the provider, treatment program, or health plan largely determined the procedures and goals of treatment, independent of patient preferences. A behavioral economic (as well as a health economic) perspective differs in viewing treatment utilization as a matter of demand for a particular commodity from among a menu of commodities available under variable constraints. As economies become more open, this issue becomes more obvious, and customer preferences become a greater concern. Hursh aptly summarized the issue:

> ... outpatient treatment is a necessary step in the treatment or rehabilitation process; successful progress will depend on a realization that outpatient treatment is an open economy in which the benefits of treatment are economic goods evaluated in a competitive market. Innovations that improve the economic utility ... of therapy will serve to swing more clients toward compliance with the outpatient protocol (Hursh 2000: 46).

When this expanded view of service delivery is adopted, the challenge becomes one of making services more appealing and more accessible when substance abusers' motivations shift in the direction of their wanting to stop substance misuse or reduce related problems (Humphreys & Tucker 2002). If substance abusers are viewed as consumers, then it makes sense to assess their needs, preferences, and valuation of different service options and goals, in order to guide the development of more appealing and accessible services that can reach a larger segment of the "treatment market." This strategy is common in public health applications. Social marketing techniques are used to segment populations into risk groups that are receptive to, and in need of, different health communications and behavior change programs (Curry & Kim 1999). It follows that similar market research should be conducted regarding consumer preferences for substance abuse services. To our knowledge, such research is lacking, even though anecdotal reports from the help-seeking literature suggest that many substance abusers find available treatments unappealing or unhelpful (Marlatt *et al.* 1997). Therefore, we are currently conducting a population survey on preferences for, and knowledge about, substance abuse services that includes substance misusers as well as their family and friends, since the latter groups often are influential in promoting or discouraging help-seeking. Although verbal reports of preferences, needs, and knowledge obviously are proxies for measuring utilization patterns of care under various choice conditions, surveying the relevant population seems like a reasonable starting point. Such information can help guide the development of intervention systems in ways that make substance-focused services more appealing and responsive to the heterogeneous needs of the population with problems.

Applications to Services for Substance-Related Problems

Several shared areas of application to substance abuse services readily emerge when a merger of public health and behavioral economic perspectives is entertained. These points are discussed in Humphreys & Tucker (2002) and are summarized here (cf. MacCoun 1998). The general goal is to increase the relative reinforcement value of help-seeking and sobriety in relation to continued substance misuse using concepts suggested by behavioral economics. Pursuing this goal will entail making the system of care more accessible by shifting limited intervention resources away from a near exclusive allocation to clinical treatments for the visible minority with severe problems, toward a more widely distributed, leaner, and lower threshold allocation that better serves the population with problems (Institute of Medicine 1990).

First, interventions should be available on demand when contingencies shift in the lives of substance abusers in ways that support behavior change efforts and help-seeking. Appointment delays reduce treatment utilization rates for substance abuse and other health services and, contrary to conventional views of motivation for psychological services, rapid treatment entry is not associated with higher attrition rates (Tucker & Davison 2000).

Second, abstinence-oriented treatments often do not address the problems of living that are adversely affected by substance abuse and that are a primary incentive for seeking help (Tucker 2001). Interventions that focus on functional problems, rapidly increase access to non-drug alternatives, do not require initial abstinence for entry, and support rapid participation are likely to appeal to a much broader segment of the population in need.

Third, much like mutual help groups, professional interventions should be available for utilization over longer, if not indefinite, periods of time, so that consumers can engage them easily when they move through periods of risk or renewed substance misuse. Given that total intervention resources are finite, of necessity the intervention opportunities will generally need to be less intensive and more "extensive" (Humphreys & Tucker 2002). As discussed by Humphreys and Tucker, the extent of intervention involvement required to initiate and sustain positive shifts in behavior allocation patterns will vary depending on individuals' environmental contexts:

> If the environment is positive and supportive, a brief intervention can be effective. But as the task of change becomes harder (i.e. dependence is greater), and the environment is less supportive, the intervention itself must become more extensive to compensate. Put another way, if the environment lacks positive enduring features, then the intervention must become one. This is what we mean by 'extensity' (Humphreys & Tucker 2002: 128).

Another way of stating this point is that better control of behavior is achieved in closed than in open economies. If the natural environment does not include contingencies to support healthy behavior patterns, introducing extensive intervention opportunities is one way of shifting the economy toward a somewhat more closed direction.

These recommendations target issues that largely reside outside of the therapeutic episode and thus differ from conventional efforts to improve treatment outcomes by

Table 1: Assumptions of behavior therapy approaches to behavior change and re-formulations based on contemporary behavior theory and behavioral economics.

Conventional Assumption	Behavioral Economic Re-formulation
Therapy is a learning experience and provides clients with new skills to resolve problems of living and reduce risky behavior patterns.	Interventions should seek to shift behavior allocation patterns in ways that maximize personal utility over lengthy intervals.
Successful therapy "inoculates" clients against future risk by providing relevant skills, much like vaccinations increase antibodies. Therapy thus can be time-limited, because the effects continue.	Interventions should help create economic conditions that shift behavior allocation patterns to maximize utility. Interventions may need to become permanent environmental features.
Maintenance of change is a generalization process from the treatment to the natural environment.	Long-term outcomes are heavily influenced by contingencies in the post-treatment environment, more so than by treatment or client intake characteristics.
Relapse results from extinction of treatment-produced change or from forgetting processes.	Relapse is one result of transitioning from a closed treatment economy to an open economy in the post-treatment natural environment.

improving technical features of psychosocial treatments. This change seems warranted, given the repeated finding of the equivalence of psychotherapy outcomes, including for substance abuse (e.g. Project MATCH Research Group 1997). As summarized in Table 1, the recommendations as applied to substance abuse involve re-framing the therapy experience and behavior change process using concepts from contemporary behavior theory that supercede older neo-behavioral and medical model concepts that guided early behavior therapy applications. A basic change involves the rejection of intervention models for acute infectious diseases, which emphasize the rapid delivery of time-limited treatments as soon as possible after symptom onset (Tucker *et al.* in press). Substance abuse, with its characteristic periods of recurrence and remission, is more consistent with a chronic disease model. Control of a chronic disease often is a more complex task spread out over longer intervals, and the contributions of behavior patterns to health and disease often are greater (Tucker *et al.* in press). These re-formulations involve a shift away from viewing behavioral interventions as an acute, discrete, and intensive remedy that helps clients learn new skills for better living and inoculates them against future risk. It is instead recommended that interventions be offered in a more extensive manner, in order to facilitate shifts in behavior allocation patterns in the natural environment in ways that promote healthier living.

The Question of Method

Applications of behavioral economic concepts at the population or community level go far beyond the typically individual level of analysis and laboratory preparations of behavioral economics, and involve concern with natural environments that are not readily controllable. Direct topographical extension of the methods of behavior analysis cannot bridge these differences and will likely mislead efforts to connect the two perspectives. This concern applies to experimental and applied behavior analysis. Applied behavior analysis, the apparent heir to applications of behavioral economics, has avoided extensive applications in natural environments and has remained in relatively controllable environments, such as hospitals, institutions for the developmentally disabled, schools, and business organizations (Critchfield & Kollins 2001). It thus has been a barren pathway for applications to substance abuse, including service delivery, that consist of temporally extended behavior patterns in natural environments in which the maintaining variables often are neither obvious nor amenable to experimental manipulation.

Therefore, just as interventions have to operate in a more open economy, so does the research process in a merger of behavioral economic and public health approaches. Experimental approaches often are not feasible, and correlational research is essential. For example, epidemiology, considered the "queen science" of public health, is largely a correlational science. Epidemiologists have developed research designs that vary in the strength with which the findings support inferences about potential causal pathways. The designs (e.g. case-control and prospective cohort studies) have strengths and limitations, and vary in their utility to address different research questions (Tucker *et al.* in press). Methodological pluralism will be required for a successful merger of perspectives, an issue that is beginning to gain recognition in the field of behavior analysis (Critchfield & Kollins 2001).

More generally, a shift is required from viewing interventions as independent variables, as is the case in conventional psychotherapy outcome research, to viewing them as dependent variables, as is the case in health and behavioral economics. This shift is partially apparent in recent debates over the relative merits of efficacy and effectiveness studies (Humphreys & Tucker 2002). Among other differences, effectiveness studies are concerned with intervention outcomes in usual care settings, including how clients come to utilize services, whereas efficacy studies disregard the role of care-seeking by randomizing clients to treatment conditions, which are the independent variables. In contrast to an efficacy perspective that treats clients as passive recipients of care, behavioral and health economics view them as consumers of services, the demand for which is subject to the laws of supply and demand. Given the evidence that psychosocial treatments will not likely be improved by additional technical refinements, focusing on utilization patterns and determinants may be a more fruitful pathway for improving aggregate outcomes, rather than further investment in "therapy tinkering" research (Curry & Kim 1999; Humphreys & Tucker 2002). In other words, by spreading modestly effective behavioral interventions over a larger portion of the relevant population, their aggregate impact on population health can be increased. Behavioral economics can guide how service delivery systems are devised in order to make choices to seek help more appealing across a range of natural environmental contexts and across the heterogeneous population with problems.

Conclusions

Understanding the complex set of variables that influence consumer choice and care-seeking is basic to improving the utilization of substance abuse services and the quality of outcomes. Adequate understanding of this issue will require taking a population perspective on utilization of substance abuse services, as well as explicating the behavioral processes involved at multiple levels of analysis. We believe that the design of systems of care will be improved by collaboration between the disciplines of public health and behavioral economics. Central features of an effective merger will likely involve making connections at a conceptual level with the rich theory and findings of behavioral economics. However, because this knowledge base has been derived primarily from research and applications in closed economies, and because public health operates in open economies, translational research and novel applications will have to consider this basic difference in the economic conditions surrounding behavior change initiatives, and non-experimental methods will be required.

Acknowledgments

Manuscript preparation was supported in part by grants no. 5 R01 AA08972 and 5 K02 AA000209 from the National Institute on Alcohol Abuse and Alcoholism.

References

Bickel, W. K., Madden, G. J., & DeGrandpre, R. J. (1997). Modeling the effects of combined behavioral and pharmacological treatment on cigarette smoking: Behavioral economic analyses. *Experimental and Clinical Psychopharmacology, 5*, 334–343.

Bickel, W. K., & Marsch, L. A. (2001). Toward a behavioral economic understanding of drug dependence: Delay discounting processes. *Addiction, 96*, 73–86.

Bickel, W. K., & Vuchinich, R. E. (Eds) (2000). *Reframing health behavior change with behavioral economics*. Mahwah, NJ: Lawrence Erlbaum.

Chapman, G. B., & Johnson, E. J. (1995). Preference reversals in monetary and life expectancy evaluations. *Organizational Behavior and Human Decision Processes, 67*, 59–75.

Critchfield, T. C., & Kollins, S. (2001). Temporal discounting: Basic research and the analysis of socially important behavior. *Journal of Applied Behavior Analysis, 34*, 101–122.

Curry, S. J., & Kim, E. L. (1999). Public health perspective on addictive behavior change interventions: Conceptual frameworks and guiding principles. In: J. A. Tucker, D. M. Donovan, & G. A. Marlatt (Eds), *Changing addictive behavior: Bridging clinical and public health strategies* (pp. 221–250). New York: Guilford Press.

DeGrandpre, R. J., Bickel, W. K., Higgins, S. T., & Hughes, J. R. (1994). A behavioral economic analysis of concurrently available money and cigarettes. *Journal of Experimental Analysis of Behavior, 61*, 191–201.

Fiedler, J. L., & Wight, J. B. (1989). *The medical offset effect and public health policy*. New York: Praeger.

Fuchs, V. R. (1987). *The health economy*. Chicago, IL: University of Chicago Press.

Fuchs, V. R. (1993). *The future of health policy*. Chicago, IL: University of Chicago Press.

Grossman, M. (1972). *The demand for health*. New York: National Bureau of Economic Research.

Holder, H. D. (1998). The cost offsets of alcoholism treatment. In: M. Galanter (Ed.), *The consequences of alcoholism* (Vol. 14, *Recent developments in alcoholism*). New York: Plenum Press.

Humphreys, K., & Tucker, J. A. (2002). Toward more responsive and effective intervention systems for alcohol-related problems. *Addiction, 97*, 126–132.

Hursh, S. R. (1978). The economics of daily consumption controlling food- and water-reinforced responding. *Journal of the Experimental Analysis of Behavior, 29*, 475–491.

Hursh, S. R. (1980). Economic concepts for the analysis of behavior. *Journal of the Experimental Analysis of Behavior, 34*, 219–238.

Hursh, S. R. (1991). Behavioral economics of drug self-administration and drug abuse policy. *Journal of the Experimental Analysis of Behavior, 56*, 377–393.

Hursh, S. R. (2000). Behavioral economic concepts and methods for studying health behavior. In: W. K. Bickel, & R. E. Vuchinich (Eds), *Reframing health behavior change with behavioral economics* (pp. 27–60). Mahwah, NJ: Lawrence Erlbaum.

Institute of Medicine (1990). *Broadening the base of treatment for alcohol problems*. Washington, DC: National Academy Press.

MacCoun, R. J. (1998). Toward a psychology of harm reduction. *American Psychologist, 53*, 1199–1208.

Madden, G. J. (2000). A behavioral economics primer. In: W. K. Bickel, & R. E. Vuchinich (Eds), *Reframing health behavior change with behavioral economics* (pp. 3–26). Mahwah, NJ: Lawrence Erlbaum.

Marlatt, G. A., Tucker, J. A., Donovan, D. M., & Vuchinich, R. E. (1997). Help-seeking by substance abusers: The role of harm reduction and behavioral-economic approaches to facilitate treatment entry and retention. In: L. S. Onken, J. D. Blaine, & J. J. Boren (Eds), *Beyond the therapeutic alliance: Keeping the drug-dependent individual in treatment* (pp. 44–84) (NIDA Research Monograph No. 165). Rockville, MD: U.S. Department of Health and Human Services.

Mechanic, D. (1994). *Inescapable decisions: The imperatives of health reform*. New Brunswick, NJ: Transaction Press.

Mitchell, S. H., de Wit, H., & Zacny, J. P. (1994). Effects of varying the "openness" of an economy on responding for cigarettes. *Behavioral Pharmacology, 5*, 159–166.

Myerson, J., & Green, L. (1995). Discounting of delayed rewards: Models of individual choice. *Journal of the Experimental Analysis of Behavior, 64*, 263–276.

Project MATCH Research Group (1997). Matching alcoholism treatment to client heterogeneity: Project MATCH posttreatment drinking outcomes. *Journal of Studies on Alcohol, 58*, 7–29.

Rachlin, H., Raineri, A., & Cross, D. (1991). Subjective probability and delay. *Journal of the Experimental Analysis of Behavior, 55*, 233–244.

Shahan, T. A., Odum, A. L., & Bickel, W. K. (2000). Nicotine gum as a substitute for cigarettes: A behavioral economic analysis. *Behavioral Pharmacology, 11*, 71–79.

Simpson, C. A., & Vuchinich, R. E. (2000). Temporal changes in the value of objects of choice: Discounting, behavior patterns, and health behavior. In: W. K. Bickel, & R. E. Vuchinich (Eds), *Reframing health behavior change with behavioral economics* (pp. 193–215). Mahwah, NJ: Lawrence Erlbaum.

Tucker, J. A. (2001). Resolving problems associated with alcohol and drug misuse: Understanding relations between addictive behavior change and the use of services. *Substance Use and Misuse, 36*, 1501–1518.

Tucker, J. A., & Davison, J. W. (2000). Waiting to see the doctor: The role of time constraints in the utilization of health and behavioral health services. In: W. K. Bickel, & R. E. Vuchinich

(Eds), *Reframing health behavior change with behavioral economics* (pp. 219–264). Mahwah, NJ: Lawrence Erlbaum.

Tucker, J. A., Phillips, M. M., Murphy, J. G., & Raczynski, J. M. (in press). Behavioral epidemiology and health psychology. In: R. G. Frank, J. Wallander, & A. Baum (Eds), *Models and perspectives in healthcare psychology (Vol. 1, Healthcare psychology: A handbook)*. Washington, DC: APA Books.

Vuchinich, R. E., & Simpson, C. A. (1998). Hyperbolic temporal discounting in heavy and light social drinkers. *Experimental and Clinical Psychopharmacology, 6*, 292–305.

Comments on Tucker & Simpson's paper

Thomas F. Babor

One important benefit of this paper is to move the conference proceedings from abstract theories of addictive behavior to atheoretical abstractions about treatment-seeking behavior. Another benefit is to introduce public health concepts to behavioral choice theory. Although I appreciate the heuristic value of behavioral economics, the addition of a public health perspective is particularly important to anyone interested in using health promotion, disease prevention and organized systems health care to have an impact on addiction problems at the level of the general population. The main message I derive from this paper is that public health concepts could provide a much needed reality check on the relevance of behavioral economics to the delivery of alcohol and drug intervention services. Public health concepts are often applied to communicate a point of view, in part because public health is more a way of looking at things than a particular theory or discipline or methodology. The public health perspective is concerned with: (a) populations rather than individuals; (b) the distribution of diseases and disabilities within populations, rather than the distribution of symptoms or behaviors within an individual; (c) the organization of health care, including clinical preventive services, for population groups rather than the delivery of clinical interventions to individual patients; and (d) the greatest good for the greatest number, rather than heroic treatments for individual patients.

What does this all have to do with behavioral economics? According to Tucker & Simpson, behavioral economics can be applied just as fruitfully at the level of populations as it can at the level of individuals, and its implications for treatment are as valuable and interesting as its implications for the understanding of addiction. To illustrate this point, let me paraphrase the Clinton era mantra, "It's the economy, stupid." The mantra I derive from Jalie Tucker & Cathy Simpson's paper is: "It's the economy of treatment, stupid." And in particular, the economics of treatment access. For more than thirty years, many of us in the addiction field have been dutifully working to discover the magic bullet that would guarantee successful treatment outcomes. Among the proposed pathways to recovery have been the 28-day residential rehabilitation program, new therapy modalities, pharmacological interventions and treatment matching. The results of this labor have been both exhilarating and exasperating. In brief, the alcohol research literature suggests that at the level of the individual drinker, most interventions, regardless of whether they comprise psychotherapy, behavior therapy or pharmacotherapy, lead to reduced drinking or abstinence. There is little evidence that the setting, modality or cost of treatment has any differential effect on treatment outcomes (Finney *et al.* 1996; Holder *et al.* 1991). If this is the case, then the implications are consistent with the observations made by Tucker & Simpson, that is, the key task from a population perspective is to increase access to treatment, not to find the best one. Under this scenario, the value of diverse settings and modalities is not to match clients with the most appropriate setting, intensity or modality of care, but rather to satisfy consumer preferences.

My next comment deals with an important public health concept emphasized in the Tucker & Simpson paper, that is, population thinking. Despite similarities in the effectiveness of different treatment interventions, there has been little attention to the mechanisms of action that would translate benefits that accrue to individual treatment responders (e.g. fewer medical problems) to benefits that accrue to the health of the population (e.g. lower rates of alcohol-related automobile crashes). Unlike clinical medicine, which is oriented almost entirely toward the patient's presenting symptoms, the public health approach implies that treatment should do more than relieve individual suffering to warrant the amount of resources it consumes. It should also influence morbidity and mortality rates at the level of the community and the general population, not to mention the rates of crime and the costs of health care. The real fear that some of us share is that, despite 30 years of clinical research demonstrating modest short term effects of treatment on substance use outcomes, the aggregate effects of all the treatment that is delivered actually add up to zero over a period of time. Treatment interventions may be no more than a substitute for what would already occur as a function of spontaneous remission. And yet contrary to this rather pessimistic view, there is some evidence that treatment has the potential to produce an aggregate-level impact. Smart & Mann (2000) have shown, for example, that the growth of specialized treatment and AA have contributed to the decline in alcohol-related mortality and morbidity in some countries in recent years. Romelsjö (1987) found that the expansion of outpatient treatment in Sweden was associated with the reduction in liver cirrhosis rates in Stockholm. Holder & Parker (1992) found that a substantial reduction in cirrhosis mortality over a 20-year period in North Carolina was related to increased alcohol treatment admissions (both inpatient and outpatient).

These studies do not establish causality, but they do provide correlational evidence to suggest the potential of formal treatment and AA membership to affect cirrhosis rates and other alcohol-related problems at the population level. Several plausible mechanisms have been proposed to account for a population level effect: (1) treatment is removing those with the highest number of problems from the population of users, not just displacing the time that they are using; (2) treatment of heavy users influences the use and problem rates of less heavy users (cf. Skog's 1985 social interaction theory). If these relationships are to some degree causal, the implication is that with greater availability of treatment and AA, alcohol-related problems could be reduced significantly. Moreover, if one broadens the base of treatment to include brief interventions in primary care settings for people who are not severely dependent, but who are at increased risk of alcohol problems because of frequent intoxication, then the population effect of health service interventions could be even more significant at the community level. Similar data on crime rates and other substance drug-related problems could be marshaled from historical changes in drug treatment availability in the U.S. during the Nixon era (Massing 1998). These findings, combined with the evidence showing that different treatments have similar outcomes, indicate that the population level impact depends on how many people access treatment, not the kind of treatment they receive. Unfortunately, individual and population level research on the environmental contingencies that affect the decision to seek treatment is virtually nonexistent. Yet it would seem that behavioral economics could provide a useful framework to study access and availability questions. Some of those are considered in this paper, and others could be suggested. For example:

- Does the retail price of alcohol or heroin affect the treatment-seeking behavior of alcoholics and heroin addicts?
- What is the role of mass media in creating consumer preferences, both for drug and alcohol use, and for treatment and abstinence? At present, the mass media are primarily used by the alcohol and tobacco industries as vehicles of social learning, to portray alcohol and tobacco use as attractive, pleasurable, and instrumental for the achievement of other reinforcers, such as sex and social interaction. Could the media be used to change consumer preferences for treatment through such things as social marketing or direct-to-consumer advertising?
- To what extent do different types and intensities of treatment have different reinforcement values at different stages of addiction?
- Does the coerciveness of treatment for alcohol and drug problems alter the substance use career and the relative value of abstinence?
- To what extent do time costs interfere with treatment entry, and what happens when these constraints are removed?

My final comment deals with the limitations of applying behavioral economic principles to the understanding of addiction treatment from a public health perspective. One major limitation is that treatment entry decisions are often constrained by powerful contingencies that leave little opportunity to manipulate the kinds of environmental reinforcers that behavioral economists are interested in. In the healthcare marketplace, it is often the case that neither the payers, nor the providers, nor the patients are rational about how they make choices and allocate resources. Take, for example, the organizations that pay for treatment. Despite the evidence suggesting that addiction treatment reduces overall health care expenditures, managed care organizations have not been eager to implement clinical preventive services, like alcohol or drug screening and early intervention, or treatment services.

Health care providers, whom one would expect to be interested in improving health outcomes, are often unaware or uninterested in evidence-based treatment approaches for substance abuse. Looking at the addiction treatment system, it seems as though it was designed more to suit the needs of providers than patients, with most of the resources allocated to office-based talk therapies. Even when environmental approaches are used, such as community reinforcement, contingency management or case management, the resources are conveniently concentrated in the security of the provider's office, rather than in the patient's environment.

Like the payers and providers, patients often do not behave like rational consumers. One problem is the relatively closed economies of many of the treatment systems that serve alcohol and drug users. The coercive nature of much addiction treatment, ranging from legal sanctions to more subtle employment and family pressures, may limit the range of behavioral choices that are available to treatment consumers.

Finally, I would be remiss if I did not include addiction researchers in any discussion of irrational consumers. I fear that many of us have been chasing small, immediate rewards rather than larger, distal payoffs. Instead of looking at closed economy treatment interventions that show marginal differences at the individual level, we should be looking at the one factor that is likely to influence mortality and morbidity at the population level, that is, the behavioral choice to seek treatment in the first place. In this vein, this very thoughtful paper by Jalie Tucker & Cathy Simpson helps to focus our attention on the issues that matter to those who are interested in the health of the population as well as the individual.

References

Finney, J. W., Hahn, A. C., & Moos, R. H. (1996). The effectiveness of inpatient and outpatient treatment for alcohol abuse: The need to focus on mediators and moderators of setting effects. *Addiction, 91*, 1773–1796.

Holder, H., Longabaugh, T., Miller, W. R., & Rubonis, A. V. (1991). The cost effectiveness of treatment for alcoholism: A first approximation. *Journal of Studies on Alcohol, 52*, 517–540.

Holder, H., & Parker, R. N. (1992). Effect of alcoholism treatment on cirrhosis mortality: A 20-year multivariate time series analysis. *British Journal of Addiction, 87*, 1263–1274.

Massing, M. (1998). *The fix.* New York, NY: Simon & Schuster.

Romelsjö, A. (1987). Decline in alcohol-related in-patient care and mortality in Stockholm County. *British Journal of Addiction, 82*, 653–663.

Skog, O.-J. (1985). The collectivity of drinking cultures: A theory of the distribution of alcohol consumption. *British Journal of Addiction, 80*, 83–99.

Smart, R. G., & Mann, R. E. (2000). The impact of programs for high-risk drinkers on population levels of alcohol problems. *Addiction, 95*, 37–52.

Chapter 14

Is the Addiction Concept Useful for Drug Policy?

Robert MacCoun

Introduction

The development of behavioral economics, with its prospect of integrating insights from economics and psychology, is surely one of the most exciting intellectual developments in the social and behavioral sciences in the past 20 years. And if any domain could benefit from this development, it would seem to be the domain of psychoactive drug use, where choices are so often pathological.

Thus, one can imagine my surprise and dismay when I was asked to prepare an essay on new policy insights that might follow from the leading behavioral economic theories of addiction,[1] and I discovered that there weren't any. Or, at least, hardly any. In this essay, I present evidence for that assertion, offer some speculative hypotheses about why it is true, and ask whether it is likely to remain true in the future.

Some Evidence

As evidence, I offer the behavioral record — the behavior of professional drug policy analysts in the form of two lengthy monographs on drug policy, both of which were published in 2001. Both monographs were prepared by interdisciplinary teams that included both psychologists and economists. I should emphasize that "the psychologist" in both cases was me.

The first is my recent book with Peter Reuter, *Drug War Heresies: Learning from Other Vices, Times, and Places* (MacCoun & Reuter 2001). The book is a comprehensive analysis of alternative legal policy regimes for controlling marijuana, cocaine, heroin, and other recreational drugs.[2] It is thoroughly interdisciplinary in scope — Peter is an economist, I am a psychologist by training, and our collaborators included the economist Tom Schelling and the historian Joe Spillane. The book includes chapters on economic theory, psychological theory, moral philosophy, history, cross-national analysis, and so on. But in a 479-page

Choice, Behavioural Economics and Addiction
© 2003 Published by Elsevier Ltd.
ISBN: 0-08-044056-8

book, with 44 single spaced pages of bibliographic references, we made almost no use of the theoretical literature on addiction.

The other monograph is *Informing America's Policy on Illegal Drugs: What We Don't Know Keeps Hurting Us* (Manski *et al.* 2001), the final report of the National Research Council's *Committee on Data and Research for Policy on Illegal Drugs*. The monograph was produced by 16 members spanning a host of disciplines. This 407-page monograph devotes several pages to neuroscience and behavioral economic concepts of addiction (though not particular models), yet those concepts played almost no detectable role in the subsequent analyses of supply reduction policies, user sanctions, drug prevention, or drug treatment.

One might respond to these observations by suggesting that behavioral economics simply has a marketing problem — that theorists simply need to more aggressively disseminate and promote their theories. That is almost certainly correct. But I don't believe it is the source of my observations. In neither case did the authors simply overlook these theories in the preparation of the monographs. For example, during the nearly full decade Peter and I spent working on our project, I immersed myself in the neuroscience, economic, psychological, and philosophical literatures on addiction, assembling large collections of papers by the other presenters at this conference. It is riveting stuff, and I learned a great deal in the process. We simply found very little we could use in analyzing the question of the relative benefits and weaknesses of alternative drug-control regimes.

A related response might be that we as policy analysts simply failed to comprehend and appreciate the relevance of these models for drug policy. I am not well situated to assess this possibility; by definition, one cannot assess whether one suffers from miscomprehension or a failure of imagination. If others respond to this essay by demonstrating that I overlooked profound new implications of these theories for drug policy, I will happily concede and judge this essay to have failed in its arguments but succeeded in its consequences.

I will consider a number of alternative explanations for why behavioral economic theories of addiction (henceforth, "BETA") have produced relatively few policy insights. I conclude that the limited policy implications stem from several features shared by BETA: the overlap in the causal factors that motivate "addictive" and "non-addictive" psychoactive drug use; the overlap between the policy implications of addiction theories and more conventional theories of drug control; and the notion that addiction is a unitary phenomenon with one correct theoretical explanation.

Some Caveats

Before I plunge headlong into my arguments, it is worth briefly clarifying what I am *not* arguing:

(a) I am decidedly not arguing against behavioral economics as a scientific enterprise.
(b) I am not arguing that there is nothing interesting or worthwhile about developing behavioral economic models of drug use or other potentially addictive behavior, although I will argue that the addiction construct is a distraction from the most useful aspects of the behavioral economic analysis of drug use.

(c) I am not disputing the existence of drug addiction, or the enormity of its consequences, though I do question whether "addiction" forms a discrete, coherent category. I am not simply echoing the positions of critics like Stanton Peele (e.g. 1996), Sally Satel (e.g. 2001), or Thomas Szasz (e.g. 1974), each of whom have criticized conventional uses of the addiction concept, though for differing reasons. My arguments in some ways overlap with theirs, but I approach the issue from a very different perspective, working backwards from policy analytic considerations rather than working forwards from a set of first principles about human conduct, liberty, or morality.

Why the Addiction Concept May Seem More Relevant Than It Is

What do Policy Analysts Want to Know?[3]

The left column of Table 1 lists the key levers that are conceptually (if not always politically) available to drug policy makers (see MacCoun *et al.* 1996):

Analysis of these policy levers follows two approaches, direct program evaluation (common for prevention and treatment, rare for enforcement) or theoretical analysis. The right column of Table 1 lists explanatory constructs relied on most heavily in recent theoretical analyses of American drug policy (e.g. Behrens *et al.* 2000; Caulkins *et al.* 2000; Kleiman

Table 1: Policy levers and related empirical uncertainties.

Policy Levers	Key Empirical Uncertainties
Drug prevention, education, and rhetoric from the bully pulpit	Cost-effectiveness and cost-benefit ratios of various interventions
Drug treatment	Prevalence and incidence of drug use, and statistical distribution of frequency and quantity of consumption
Criminal sanctions against users	Price elasticity of demand for drugs
Criminal sanctions against dealers	Time sensitivity and/or impulsivity of drug users
Interdiction and source country controls	Dose-response relationship between consumption and its acute and chronic effects
Taxes, advertising controls, and other regulatory mechanisms	Relative contribution of psychoactive effects vs. illegality in producing drug-related harms
Drug testing	Possible substitution, complementarity, and "gateway" relationships among drugs
Bans on employment, welfare, and other benefits	Unintended effects of use-reduction strategies on drug harms, and of harm-reduction strategies on drug use
	Distribution of effects of drug use across bearers — user, family, friends, neighbors, community, taxpayers

1992, 1998; MacCoun & Reuter 2001; Manski *et al.* 2001). It is clear that BETA make contact with these explanatory factors in myriad ways. But in the remainder of this section, I will attempt to illustrate how behavioral economic theories of addiction largely generate policy implications that are redundant with existing strategies. And the novel implications they do offer follow from general principles of self-control rather than a narrow and extreme end state called "addiction."

BETA's Implications for Demand Reduction

Prevention   Some authors have argued that BETA have implications for drug prevention. For example, Herrnstein & Prelec (1992: 357) argue that their model "suggests that society should at least provide people with more information, on the grounds that they are less likely to go down the path if they know where it is headed." Heyman (1996: 573) argues that ". . . the ideas presented here indicate that treatment should attempt to bring drug consumption under the control of overall rather than local value functions. . . . Thus, methods that increase the salience of distant behavioral consequences should move individuals towards more rational use of drugs. This point suggests that persuasion is a potentially powerful weapon in altering people's behavior."

These recommendations fall short on two grounds. First, they restate the obvious; public information campaigns on the risks of long-term drug use have been a staple of American drug policy for over 30 years. Second, they ignore the evidence that such information campaigns have been remarkably ineffective at discouraging drug use (and risky sex) and are generally recognized as insufficient by prevention researchers. (See Manski *et al.* 2001: Chapter 7 for a detailed review and meta-analysis.) In fairness, past anti-drug information campaigns might have been more effective if they had been more credible and less moralistic. In contrast, the prevalence of cigarette smoking fell by half in a generation following the release of a series of highly factual, morally neutral Surgeon General reports. But even there, it is discouraging that tobacco initiation rates among youth have remained remarkably stable.

Treatment   A more likely mechanism by which BETA might contribute to drug policy would be via new and better methods of drug treatment. Behavioral economics research has already made significant contributions to the design of drug treatments. For example, the NRC report (Manski *et al.* 2001: 248) highlighted the behavioral economic work of Stephen Higgins and his colleagues as among the most promising developments in cocaine treatment research. This approach applies community reinforcement techniques and a "token economy" system of vouchers for retail goods to help cocaine users remain abstinent (see Bickel *et al.* 1995; Higgins *et al.* 1995). These studies are invaluable. It is highly plausible, but not very helpful, to be told that drug problems might be reduced by eliminating joblessness and poverty. It is nearly incredible, and extremely helpful, to learn that heavy cocaine users will provide three clean urine samples for a $10 gift certificate.

But while this treatment method is decidedly "behavioral economic," it does not depend in any direct way on a behavioral economic account of *addiction*. The same logic would follow from a behavioral economic analysis of self-control difficulties — or indeed from a more traditional applied behavioral analysis (the contemporary term for behavior modification).

For the sake of argument, imagine that insights into effective drug treatment eventually emerge from behavioral economic analyses that require a notion of addiction per se, rather than a broader analysis of self-control. A radical improvement in drug treatment effectiveness would dramatically alter the drug policy landscape, although I argue later that it would not eliminate our drug problems. But if the improvements were only incremental in magnitude, they would be unlikely to have a noticeable impact at the policy level. It is difficult to detect any major impact of past treatment research on policy decisions (see Reuter 2001). And there is sufficient uncertainty about the true efficacy and effectiveness of treatment that any improvement may fall well within existing error bounds (see Horowitz *et al.* 2002; Manski *et al.* 2001) — and short of the more extravagant claims. Finally, the drug policy budget is an imaginary construction — the funds aren't fungible in the sense that dollars could simply be shifted from enforcement to treatment (Murphy 1994), although there could be a reallocation of funds within the treatment portion of the budget.

BETA's Implications for Supply Reduction

Behavioral economic theorists have also drawn various implications of their theories for supply reduction policy.

Availability Several BETA theorists have suggested the importance of minimizing opportunities to obtain drugs: e.g. ". . . differences in prevalence rates will depend importantly on exposure to drugs . . . it seems likely that increasing the availability of addictive drugs would substantially increase the frequency of addiction" (Heyman 1996: 573). This is surely correct but, like the advice on prevention, redundant. Over half of our annual national drug control expenditures go to supply reduction efforts, roughly a third for interdiction and source-country controls. It is difficult to imagine a more aggressive supply reduction effort than the one we've experienced, and yet student surveys show that drugs remain readily available at schools, and cocaine and heroin prices have fallen to about a third of their 1981 levels after controlling for inflation (see MacCoun & Reuter 2001: Chapter 2).

Prices Changes in prices have little import for addicts' drug-use rates under a traditional "enslavement" view of addiction. (It might, however, influence the number of crimes some addicts commit to finance their habits.) Under that model, addicts were considered to be extremely insensitive to prices. Until Becker formulated his rational addiction theory (e.g. Becker *et al.* 1992), drug experts largely ignored users' "price elasticity of demand" (the percent change in drug use for a 1% change in price). But recent studies (reviewed in Caulkins & Reuter 1996) suggest considerable price sensitivity, with elasticities for cocaine ranging from -0.7 to -2.0. In other words, addicts reduce their consumption when prices rise. The emphasis on drug prices is surely one of the most important contributions of the economic approach to drug policy.

Unfortunately, in a prohibition regime, there isn't much we can do with this knowledge. Prohibition itself keeps prices artificially high, but beyond that, our supply reduction efforts are spectacularly ineffective at influencing prices at the margin. A legal regime would provide considerably more leverage, through taxation, price controls, and other regulatory possibilities (MacCoun *et al.* 1996). Thus, BETA probably has greater potential policy impact in the tobacco and alcohol domains than in the domain of illicit drugs.

Smart deterrence and coerced abstinence   Kleiman (2000, 2001b) has offered a persuasive behavioral economic analysis of ways we might enforce prohibition more effectively. He argues that hyperbolic discounting implies the need to shift our emphasis from severe but uncertain and delayed sanctions to a regime in which sanctions are modest but swift and probable. His "coerced abstinence" model of aggressive drug-testing of probationers offers a radically different way of deploying law enforcement resources for drug control. But nothing in Kleiman's analysis requires the notion of "addiction." Coerced abstinence makes sense if heavy users make impulsive choices; it would make little sense — indeed, it would be inhumane — if they were incapable of choice.

BETA's Normative (Welfare) Implications

There is a third category of potential policy implications that are normative rather than empirical.

Is the state justified in prohibiting drugs?   Do BETA tell us whether government intrusion into private choices is justified? A tradition dating back to John Stuart Mill considers such intrusion justified if an act harms others (see MacCoun & Reuter 2001: Chapter 4). There is overwhelming evidence associating drug use with such externalities, but we still know very little about the relative contribution of three causal mechanisms to this association: psychopharmacological effects of drug use; overlap in the dispositional propensities to use drugs and commit crimes (see below); and criminogenic consequences of prohibition and its enforcement (MacCoun *et al.* in press). Unfortunately, BETA have remained largely silent about this question by focusing on drug consumption but not its consequences.

Is drug addiction an involuntary state?   A second normative question is whether drug addiction is involuntary, such that addicts aren't capable of making rational choices. In theory, penal sanctions are unjust if actors are incapable of controlling their actions. In theory, paternalistic government behaviors are justified if actors aren't capable of protecting their own welfare.

Becker's "rational addiction" model is provocative precisely because it suggests that addicts freely choose their situation with full recognition of its eventual consequences. Analyses by O'Donoghue & Rabin (e.g. 1999) and Gruber & Koszegi (2001) persuasively challenge this extreme characterization. But it isn't entirely clear what's at stake in this debate for the normative choice among policy regimes, since BETA also model addiction as a choice process — albeit a constrained and distorted choice process. From a moral philosophical perspective, the models offer not black or white but shades of gray.

Politically, it might not matter; it is not as if the public is teetering on a moral knife edge where evidence might tip us one way or the other. Americans of a conservative stripe insist on strict norms of individual responsibility; American liberals endorse paternalism for far more trivial consumer choices than heroin consumption (Skitka & Tetlock 1993). Yet Americans of both stripes largely reject the notion that drug dependence is completely involuntary; if the addict doesn't choose today's injection, she certainly chose her first injection (see Mannetti & Pierro 1991; Weiner *et al.* 1988). Hamilton (1980) argues that Americans judge others not by scientific causation but by the question, "could the actor have done otherwise?" It is not clear that Becker and his BETA competitors actually differ in their answer to that question.

BETA's Policy Implications: Summary

To date, most of the proposed policy implications of BETA are either redundant with current policies, or have less policy import than meets the eye. Significantly, almost all the policy implications discussed here were also suggested by Bickel & DeGrandpre (1996: 46–47) in their analysis of behavioral economic principles of reinforcement. This point is noteworthy because that analysis made only a passing reference to the notion of "dependence" and no reference to the word "addiction." This suggests, to me at least, that most of the important implications of behavioral economic analysis don't actually require the concept of addiction.

Possible Explanations for the Limited Usefulness of the Addiction Concept

I am confident in my thesis that BETA have offered few new policy insights, at least so far — a rather depressing conclusion. I am less confident that I know why. Here I offer six speculative explanations, one of which seems unpersuasive and five more plausible.

Theory Where No Theory is Needed?

One possibility is that this is just an example of the classic division between "basic and applied research." On this account, it is foolish to ask for policy relevance from basic science. This proposition might be correct at the extremes, but it is certainly not defensible as a general proposition. There is usually good reason to accept Kurt Lewin's (1951) well-known dictum that "there's nothing so useful as a good theory." And it is clear that at least some major theorists in this area do in fact desire to inform drug policy.[4]

In a classic essay, Milton Friedman (1953) defended an "as if" meta-theory of economics, drawing an analogy to a billiards expert who behaves "as if" solving a complex set of differential equations without actually doing so. One possibility is that a formal model of addiction might yield useful predictions of this sort, even though it is not a valid model of the actual addiction process. It would serve as a valid "black box" model of the functional relationship between causal antecedents and consequences, while remaining mute as to the underlying mediational processes.

Or one might ignore causal antecedents altogether. James Q. Wilson (1983) argued that ". . . one can intelligently make policies designed to reduce crime without first understanding the causes of crime . . ." It is hard to know how seriously to take this quote, since only two years later Wilson published (Wilson & Herrnstein 1985) a lengthy tome on the causes of crime. At any rate, BETA researchers clearly aspire to develop valid models of causal process as well as input-output association, as they surely should.

The Wrong Level of Analysis?

Another possibility is that BETA are framed at the wrong level of analysis to be relevant for policy analysis. Interestingly, George Ainslie (1992) has referred to his BETA as "picoeconomics," as distinguished from microeconomics and macroeconomics. It is often the case that collective social phenomena are more than the sum of individual actions. Indeed, the public health movement has made important conceptual advances by adopting "population thinking" as an alternative to an individual-based clinical perspective. But I would not try to defend the position that good policy analyses can do without a model of the individual actor, and that is surely not what Ainslie has in mind either.

Still, it is conceivably the case that the notion of "addictiveness" might be useful for individuals in governing their own conduct (individual policy), without being useful for the governing of aggregate conduct (public policy). A personal theory about addiction might itself be an important self-control device (Ainslie 2001; Bateson 1971). Ainslie suggests that:

> ". . . people cultivate the belief that street drugs are always irresistible once tried, rather than just making an overt rule against trying them. This cultivation is apt to take the following form: An authority teaches that irresistibility is a fact; you encounter evidence to the contrary, for instance in statistics on ex-users who used only casually; you discount or somehow don't incorporate the contrary evidence, not because it seems to be of poor quality, but out of a feeling that it's seditious" (Ainslie 2001: 109).

Later, he notes that when Ockham, Galileo and Darwin "pointed out that the 'facts' on which people based moral norms weren't found in nature, they encountered violent objections on the grounds that these discoveries would undermine morality" (Ainslie 2001: 112).

Overlap With Other Theories

Another reason why BETA might fail to produce novel insights is that they overlap in broad ways with more popular conceptualizations of drug use, even when they differ radically in their details.

One source of overlap is lay common sense or folk psychology. One can describe heavy drug users as "giving in to temptation," that they are "self-indulgent," "impulsive," "shortsighted," and "selfish," without any knowledge of the subtleties of BETA.

But there is also considerable overlap with contemporary criminological theory. In their highly influential "general theory of crime," Gottfredson and Hirschi argue that:

> Crime and drug use are connected because they share features that satisfy the tendencies of criminality. Both provide immediate, easy, and certain short-term pleasure.... Evidence to support our contention is found in the correlation between the use of cheap drugs, such as alcohol and tobacco, and crime ... [and] by the connection between crime and drugs that do not affect mood or behavior sufficient to cause crime (such as tobacco) (Gottfredson & Hirschi 1990: 41).

Whether Gottfredson & Hirschi's central construct of "low self-control" is isomorphic with the BETA notion of hyperbolic discounting is still unclear. Vuchinich & Simpson (1998) found only weak and inconsistent correlations between personality measures of impulsivity and hyperbolic discounting behavior among light and heavy drinkers. The personality measures were better discriminators of light vs. heavy drinking than were discounting scores, at least in that experimental setting and sample.

A Problematic Construct?

Analytic use of the addiction concept may be hindered by its lack of adequate construct validity, in the psychometric sense of a unitary concept that can be adequately delineated and distinguished from other concepts. One can dispute the usefulness of the addiction construct without disputing the ontological reality of addiction or making snide reference to a metaphysical "ghost in the machine." The question is whether the construct would be more useful if it were disaggregated into distinct features.

The DSM-IV permits a diagnosis of substance dependence when any three of the following are observed in a 12-month period: tolerance, withdrawal, using more than intended, desire to quit and/or difficulty quitting; considerable time spent obtaining, using, or recovering from the drug; interference with other activities; and/or persistent use despite problems caused by use. The DSM-IV definition of dependence has fairly high inter-rater reliability (Heyman 2001), and the inter-item correlations are reasonably high (Feingold & Rounsaville 1995). But a construct can have high reliability without having high construct or predictive validity (e.g. astrological signs).

The DSM items may hold together empirically, but it is not clear that they do so conceptually in a way that makes the best analytic use of the data. At least as currently used (with the "any three" criterion), these items don't form a meaningful Guttman scale, as they would if the components had a logical, cumulative order (e.g. None, A only, A + B, A + B + C, etc.). One can interpret the debate between Ole-Jørgen Skog & Nick Heather at this conference as a debate about what a defensible Guttman scale of addiction might look like (see Chapter 5, this volume).

The DSM-IV dependence checklist items don't look anything like interchangeable, substitutable indicators of a latent construct, in the psychometric "domain sampling" sense. They aren't like items on a personality scale or intelligence test that can be thought of as tapping identical construct variance plus idiosyncratic item error. Instead, each component on the checklist is conceptually distinct. Moreover, the critera confound the condition of addiction with its antecedents, its consequences, and its context, thereby begging the very questions that theory (and policy analysis) need to answer. Finally, epidemiological studies (e.g. Anthony *et al.* 1994) demonstrate considerable heterogeneity in the qualifying criteria displayed across individuals receiving the same "dependence" diagnosis, and even greater heterogeneity across addictive substances (alcohol vs. tobacco vs. opiates vs. cocaine vs. cannabis).

An Overdetermined Phenomenon?

Discussions about the relative merits of addiction theories often seem to accept two implicit assumptions: that addiction is a single, unitary phenomenon, and that it is caused by a single process.

Addiction theorists too often rely on "sufficiency" arguments in favor of their theories (MacCoun 1996). Some stylized facts about addiction are reviewed, and it is then demonstrated that the theory in question can produce such patterns. Even if correct, such arguments show that the theory is sufficient to produce "addictive" behavior; they do not establish that the hypothesized mechanisms actually produce the actual addictive behavior we observe in the world. In essence, behavioral economics theorists have tended to start with the model (rational choice theory) rather than actual behavior; the goal has been to teach the model new tricks — how to act addictively — in the fewest steps possible.

But there are good reasons to believe that real-world addiction is *overdetermined*, with a complex set of interrelated distal and proximal causal antecedents. A very partial list would include factors discussed in detail in this volume: classical conditioning of cues; operant conditioning (especially schedules of reinforcement); tolerance, withdrawal, opponent processes, and other neurochemical adaptations; impulsivity due to hyperbolic temporal discounting.

And many researchers would list additional mechanisms falling outside the theoretical framework of either neuroscience or BETA, such as: biased cognitive expectancies (e.g. Stacy *et al.* 1990; Tversky & Kahneman 1974), including "optimism bias" (the tendency to believe that generic population risks don't apply to oneself, e.g. Weinstein & Klein 1995); sensation seeking (Zuckerman 1994); "social scripts" (automatized behavioral schemata, see Wegner & Bargh 1998); maladaptive self-regulatory strategies for dealing with conflicting goals (Baumeister *et al.* 1994; Baumeister 1997; Carver & Scheier 1998; Tice *et al.* 2001; Wegner *et al.* 1989); attentional control (e.g. Steele & Josephs 1990); self-handicapping and other self-presentational strategies (e.g. Higgins & Harris 1988; Isleib *et al.* 1988).

With such a lengthy list, it seems strange that many experts still consider addiction to be "paradoxical." For example, Elster & Skog argue that: "On a theoretical level, addiction raises the paradox of *voluntary self-destructive behavior*. The challenge is to explain why people engage in behaviors that they know will harm them" (Elster & Skog 1999: 1). This notion of a paradox follows naturally from a rational choice perspective, or from a less sophisticated "folk psychological" theory in which actors are conceived as making coherent, conscious choices on the basis of a stable set of beliefs and desires. But it is less clear why addictive behaviors should be viewed as "paradoxical" from the perspective of contemporary scientific psychology or neuroscience. There is ample evidence that self-defeating behaviors are commonplace among otherwise well-functioning, non-clinical populations (Baumeister *et al.* 1994). Baumeister (1997) notes that none of these mechanisms require any explicit self-destructive motives. They are overdetermined by a variety of fairly normal processes, especially cold, warm, or hot cognitive biases of information processing and/or perverse side-effects of self-regulatory strategies for pursuing conflicting goals.

Self-regulatory models in cognitive, social, personality, and developmental psychology do imply a purposive actor, but they are not built on rational or quasi-rational choice principles. This makes them less rigorous deductively, but the models do make clear, testable predictions that can and have been tested using experimental methods (see Carver & Scheier 1998; Muraven & Baumeister 2000; Tice *et al.* 2001; Wegner & Bargh 1998).

Undue Emphasis on the Extremes

The distribution of drug consumption across users   The proposition that "addiction" is overdetermined has testable implications. "Single mechanism" theories may propose qualitative discontinuities — thresholds beyond which a user passes from "non-addiction" to "addiction." But such analyses are ceteris paribus. Presumably, the multiple mechanisms of "addictiveness" are highly correlated, but they are not isomorphic, so a discontinuity in one mechanism might well be obscured by the operation of other mechanisms. A series of superimposed step functions might collectively form a smoothly continuous function. If so, one would not expect to observe stark discontinuities between "addicted" and other heavy users. In principle, this should be testable using psychometric techniques for empirically distinguishing discrete typologies from continuous, dimensional traits (Meehl 1995).

Some indirect evidence on this point comes from the National Household Survey on Drug Abuse for 2000 (NHSDA 2000).[5] Figure 1 shows the number of days of drug use per year among Americans aged 12 and older who used in the past year, separately for marijuana, cocaine, and alcohol. (Unfortunately, cigarette data are not available for this variable.) For marijuana and alcohol, but not cocaine, the distributions are bimodal. The largest mode is at "1 to 11 days per year" (very casual use), but the second mode is at "100 to 299 days per year," *not* "300 or more" as one might expect given the ease with which we use the label "addict."

Figure 2 focuses more narrowly on past-month users, thereby screening out most of the very casual users. The data for cigarettes match the profile of "an addictive drug," with the modal user using 20 or more days out of the month. But for marijuana, cocaine, and alcohol, even among past-month users, few use 20 or more days a month.

Unfortunately the NHSDA sampling and self-report procedures are thought to under-represent heavy cocaine use. Figure 3 shows use frequencies in a sample arguably less susceptible to such biases — a snowball sample of recent cocaine users in Amsterdam (Cohen & Sas 1995). Despite a very different sampling strategy and a far more tolerant culture, self-reports of use during the last three months, and during the users' first year of use, look quite similar to the pattern in the NHSDA data. Even for the "period of heaviest use," only 20% reported daily use. Compulsive use, in which lives are dominated by drug consumption, is an extremely important part of the policy picture, but it is clearly not the whole picture by any means.

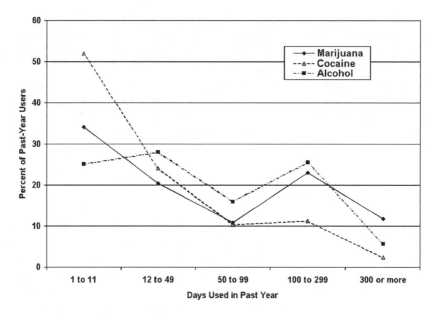

Figure 1: Frequency of use among past-year users.

Loss of information due to the choice of study populations   By treating addiction as a category rather than a continuum, BETA researchers frequently rely on clinical populations that fail to represent the full range of patterns of consumption of a given drug. According to Heyman (2001: 91), "most addicts recover, but this is only apparent if the addicts are

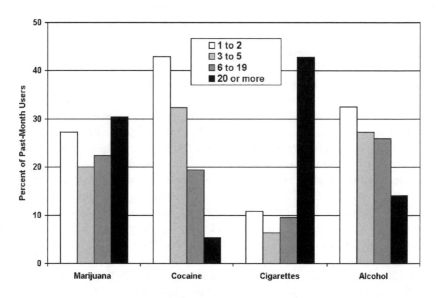

Figure 2: Days of use in past month.

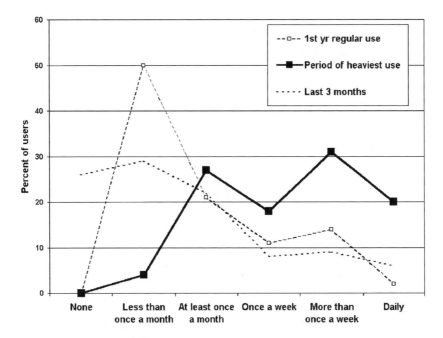

Figure 3: Frequency of cocaine use among Amsterdam users, 1991.

selected independently of their treatment history." Two BETA studies present evidence suggesting that hyperbolic discounting might vary gradually rather than discontinuously between clinical "addict" populations and other users. Vuchinich & Simpson (1998) found that while heavy drinkers and/or problem drinkers showed stronger temporal discounting than light social drinkers, the 75th percentile for discounting among light drinkers fell near the median for heavy drinkers. Bickel *et al.* (1999) found a multimodal distribution of delay discounting parameter values among current cigarette smokers, overlapping considerably at the low end with values for ex-smokers and never-smokers.

Would we eliminate the drug problem if we eliminated addiction? One can reasonably defend a focus on clinically-defined addicts as follows: not all drug use is harmful; a society that values individual liberty ought to concentrate its attention on those users who are harming themselves and/or others. I have much sympathy for this viewpoint. But matters are not so simple; the risks of drug use vary continuously across users with no apparent "step function."

For the sake of argument, let's say we actually cured addiction — i.e. any user who crossed a certain behavioral threshold could be recalibrated — restored to a state of non-addiction, perhaps even one permitting "controlled use" of the drug in the future. Clearly, this would significantly shift American policy away from a primary emphasis on law enforcement to a greater emphasis on treatment; indeed, it may be the only way such a shift could occur given the great political advantages of being "tough on drugs." And the "drug problem" would be reduced dramatically. But not completely. How much of a problem would remain?

The answer depends on some empirical questions that have received some attention in alcohol epidemiology (Edwards *et al.* 1994), but have been largely neglected in the illicit drug domain (MacCoun 1998). What does the consumption distribution look like? What are the dose-response functions that link consumption to various health and safety harms?

We know that the distribution of users by consumption levels is positively skewed. Presumably, addicts are mostly located in the long right tail. We can reduce the harm of drug consumption by either targeting the heaviest users (the right tail) or, as some alcohol experts recommend, by trying to target the great majority of users near the middle of the distribution (see Rose 1992; Skog 1993). Presumably, the greater the share of total consumption due to heavy users, the greater the efficacy of targeting them. So if addiction were cured, would the right tail be eliminated, or just "thinned out?"

A cure for addiction might reduce, but will surely not eliminate, the acute harms of intoxicated driving, parenting, work behavior, and so on. A few facts about alcohol are sobering. It is estimated that teenager drinkers — few of whom are likely to be "addicted" (at least not yet) — account for 11.4% of all alcohol consumed in the U.S. (CASA 2002). In the 2000 Drug Abuse Warning Network study, 12–17 year olds account for 17.7% of all emergency room mentions of alcohol (SAMHSA 2001). Among drivers in fatal accidents, the age 21–24 group consistently has the highest proportion with blood alcohol levels exceeding 0.10 (NHTSA 2000).

Indeed, the literature on "compensatory behavioral responses" to risk reduction (reviewed by MacCoun 1998) suggests that a cure for addiction might actually encourage much intoxication that would not otherwise take place. Existing users might have less reason to fear a binge; non-users would have less reason to fear initiation. Whether these increases would be large enough to offset the sizeable reductions due to the elimination of addiction is not clear.

Much depends on the parameters of the relevant dose-response curves linking drug use to its various consequences. Such curves are usually *S*-shaped. When they are very steep, even moderate consumption levels are risky. Presumably, some "acute" risks are primarily sensitive to dosage per incident (e.g. driving accidents, overdoses, unsafe sex, and what Goldstein [1985] calls "psycho-pharmacological violence"), whereas other risks are triggered more by chronic use over time (e.g. deteriorating health, bad parenting, and Goldstein's [1985] "economic-compulsive violence").

Interestingly, the recent Swiss heroin maintenance trials suggest that these dose-response functions can vary dramatically with legal context (Reuter & MacCoun 2002). Registered addicts who were eligible to receive heroin from government clinics massively increased their daily doses, yet they significantly increased their legitimate work participation and significantly reduced their income-generating criminal behaviors.

Elsewhere my colleagues and I have decried the American tendency to almost single-mindedly equate drug policy with "prevalence reduction" — a reduction in the number of Americans who use a given drug. Arguably, a more sensible overarching goal is "total harm reduction" – reducing the total social harm caused by a given drug. But *total harm = average harm per use × number of users × average amount used*, and the emphasis on prevalence reduction (something we're not very good at) leads to the neglect of two other strategies – quantity reduction and harm reduction (MacCoun 1998; MacCoun & Reuter 2001).

It is surely better to categorize users into "addicts" vs. non-addicted users, rather than mindlessly (and moralistically) lumping heavy users together with extreme casual light users (see Caulkins 1997). But we should be wary of reifying an extreme corner of a continuous, multidimensional space constituted by the dimensions of frequency of use, quantity consumed per use, and harmfulness of conduct while intoxicated. Doing so begs the questions I noted above — the need to know the shape of the consumption distribution and the relevant dose-response functions linking use to harms.

With Friends Like These . . .

It is regrettable that this paper has such a critical tone. My purpose in raising these arguments is not to discourage behavioral economic work on drug use — far from it. But a candid assessment suggests that, at least so far, BETA's insights into drug policy fall into two categories. They are either largely redundant with the conventional wisdom as expressed by existing policy strategies (viz., drug prevention and supply reduction), or they are quite innovative but seem not to require any conception of "addiction" as a distinct state or category of experience (viz., treatment and self-control strategies). The first category is no fault of the theorists, but the second suggests that the addiction concept just isn't that useful. In my view, the value of the behavioral economic comes from its analysis of self-control (a broad category), not from its analysis of addiction (a very narrow one) — in short, from BEAT (the behavioral economic analysis of temptations) rather than BETA (behavioral economic theories of addiction).

Are there policy implications I (and the BETA community) have overlooked? Probably. I can see at least four areas for future development.

(a) Structuring of the very "local" (in time and space) economy to help facilitate better self-control (an idea floated in various ways by several authors of this volume; see Wertenbroch 1998; Loewenstein & Kalyanaraman 1999 for marketing examples).
(b) The development of more psychologically realistic law enforcement tactics for achieving deterrence (Kleiman 2000, 2001b; MacCoun & Reuter 2001: Chaper 5).
(c) The incorporation of behavioral economic principles into analyses of the dynamics of drug epidemics and the strategic timing of interventions (Behrens *et al.* 2000).
(d) A behavioral economic analysis of the triage problem in the design of heroin and other opiate maintenance schemes — deciding who should be eligible, and when (Reuter & MacCoun 2002).

If I can name four, then hopefully readers can come up with many more. I see no reason why an assessment of the policy payoffs of a behavioral economic analysis won't be considerably more upbeat a decade from now.

Notes

1. I take the members of this set to include the recent work of such theorists as Becker *et al.*; Prelec *et al.*; Ainslie; Rachlin; Elster; O'Donoghue & Rabin. Much of this work has been summarized in

various chapters in the recent volumes, *Addictions: Entries and Exits* (edited by Elster 1999), *Getting Hooked: Rationality and Addiction* (edited by Elster & Skog 1999), *Breakdown of Will* (Ainslie 2001), and *The Science of Self-Control* (Rachlin 2000). Note that Ole-Jorgen Skog at this conference (see Chapter 5) questions whether Becker's model is in fact a model of "addiction."

2. The book is the major product of a grant from the Alfred Sloan Foundation to the RAND Corporation's Drug Policy Research Center.

3. This section draws heavily on arguments developed in much greater detail in MacCoun & Reuter (2001) and Manski *et al.* (2001). But many of these arguments were independently developed and presented by Mark Kleiman at a conference on "The Uses and Misuses of Science in Public Discourse," Boston University, April 1, 2000 (see Kleiman 2001a).

4. "To design treatments and policies that will make people quit their addictions or never become addicted in the first place, it is useful to have an understanding of the causes of addiction and relapse" (Elster & Skog 1999: 1). "If economists want to contribute to the police debate over how to deal with addictions, we need to develop a systematic approach to analyzing self-control problems and other errors rather than assume them away. We hope our analysis will prove useful in this regard." (O'Donoghue & Rabin 2001: 37 of preprint version). Becker and his colleagues (1992: 362) consider "highly tentative inferences concerning the effects of legalization . . ." and Herrnstein & Prelec (1992) devote three pages to a section on "policy implications" of their theory of addiction.

5. http://www.samhsa.gov/oas/nhsda/2kdetailedtabs/Vol_1_Part_4/sect6v1.htm#6.2b

Acknowledgments

I thank Jon Caulkins, Mark Kleiman, Peter Reuter, and Sally Satel for helpful comments on a pre-conference draft, and the conference participants for many constructive conversations.

References

Ainslie, G. (1992). *Picoeconomics: The strategic interaction of successive motivational states with the person.* Cambridge, UK: Cambridge University Press.

Ainslie, G. (2001). *Breakdown of will.* Cambridge, UK: Cambridge University Press.

Anthony, J., Warner, L., & Kessler, R. (1994). Comparative epidemiology of dependence on tobacco, alcohol, controlled substances and inhalants: Basic findings from the National Comorbidity Study. *Experimental and Clinical Psychopharmacology, 2*, 244–268.

Bateson, G. (1971). The cybernetics of "self": A theory of alcoholism. *Psychiatry, 34*, 1–18.

Baumeister, R. F. (1997). Esteem threat, self-regulatory breakdown, and emotional distress as factors in self-defeating behaviors. *Review of General Psychology, 1*, 145–174.

Baumeister, R. F., Heatherton, T. F., & Tice, D. M. (1994). *Losing control: How and why people fail at self-regulation.* San Diego, CA: Academic Press.

Becker, G. S., Grossman, M., & Murphy, K. M. (1992). Rational addiction and the effect of price on consumption. In: G. Loewenstein, & J. Elster (Eds), *Choice over time* (pp. 361–370). New York: Russell Sage Foundation.

Behrens, D., Caulkins, J. P., Tragler, G., & Feichtinger, G. (2000). Optimal control of drug epidemics: Prevent and treat — but not at the same time? *Management Science, 46*, 333–347.

Bickel, W. K., & DeGrandpre, R. J. (1996). Psychological science speaks to drug policy: The clinical relevance and policy implications of basic behavioral principles. In: W. K. Bickel, & R. J. DeGrandpre (Eds), *Drug policy and human nature* (pp. 31–54). New York: Plenum Press.

Bickel, W. K., DeGrandpre, R. J., & Higgins, S. T. (1995). The behavioral economics of concurrent drug reinforcers: A review and reanalysis of drug self-administration research. *Psychopharmacology, 118*, 250–259.

Bickel, W. K., Odum, A. L., & Madden, G. J. (1999). Impulsivity and cigarette smoking: Delay discounting in current, never, and ex-smokers. *Psychopharmacology, 146,* 447–454.

Carver, C. S., & Scheier, M. F. (1998). *On the self-regulation of behavior.* New York: Cambridge University Press.

CASA (2002, February 26). Statement by The National Center on Addiction and Substance Abuse at Columbia University. http://www.casacolumbia.org/newsletter1457/newsletter_show.htm?doc_id=103428

Caulkins, J. P. (1997). How prevalent are "very light" drug users? *Drug Policy Analysis Bulletin, 3.*

Caulkins, J. P., Chiesa, J. R., & Everingham, S. M. (2000). *Response to the National Research Council's Assessment of RAND's "Controlling Cocaine" Study.* Santa Monica: RAND.

Caulkins, J., & Reuter, P. (1996). Editorial: The meaning and utility of drug prices. *Addiction, 91,* 1261–1264.

Cohen, P., & Sas, A. (1995). *Cocaine use in Amsterdam II. Initiation and patterns of use after 1986.* Amsterdam: Department of Human Geography, University of Amsterdam.

Edwards, G., Anderson, P., Babor, T. F., Casswell, S., Ferrence, R., Giesbrecht, N., Godfrey, C., Holder, H. D., Lemmens, P., Mäkelä, K., Midanik, L. T., Norström, T., Österberg, E., Romesljö, A., Room, R., Simpura, J., & Skog, O. (1994). *Alcohol policy and the public good.* Oxford: Oxford University Press.

Elster, J. (Ed.) (1999). *Addiction: Entries and exits.* New York: Russell Sage Foundation.

Elster, J., & Skog, O.-J. (Ed.) (1999). Introduction. In: J. Elster, & O.-J. Skog (Eds), *Getting hooked: Rationality and addiction.* New York: Cambridge University Press.

Elster, J., & Skog, O.-J. (Ed.) (1999). *Getting hooked: Rationality and addiction.* Cambridge University Press.

Feingold, A., & Rounsaville, B. (1995). Construct validity of the dependence syndrome as measured by DSM-IV for different psychoactive substances. *Addiction, 90,* 1661–1669.

Friedman, M. (1953). *Essays in positive economics.* Chicago: University of Chicago Press.

Goldstein, P. (1985). The drug/violence nexus: A tripartite conceptual framework. *Journal of Drug Issues, 14,* 493–506.

Gottfredson, M. R., & Hirschi, T. (1990). *A general theory of crime.* Stanford, CA: Stanford University Press.

Gruber, J., & Koszegi, B. (2001). Is addiction "rational"? Theory and evidence. *Quarterly Journal of Economics, 116,* 1261–1305.

Hamilton, V. L. (1980). Intuitive psychologist or intuitive lawyer? Alternative models of the attribution process. *Journal of Personality & Social Psychology, 39,* 767–772.

Herrnstein, R. J., & Prelec, D. (1992). A theory of addiction. In: G. Loewenstein, & J. Elster (Eds), *Choice over time* (pp. 235–264).

Heyman, G. M. (1996). Resolving the contradictions of addiction. *Behavioral and Brain Sciences, 19*(4), 561–610.

Heyman, G. M. (2001). Is addiction a chronic, relapsing disease? In: P. B. Heymann, & W. N. Brownsberger (Eds), *Drug addiction and drug policy: The struggle to control dependence* (pp. 81–117). Cambridge, MA: Harvard University Press.

Higgins, R. L., & Harris, R. N. (1988). Strategic "alcohol" use: Drinking to self-handicap. *Journal of Social & Clinical Psychology, 6,* 191–200.

Higgins, S. T., Budney, A. J., Bickel, W. K., Badger, G. J. et al. (1995). Outpatient behavioral treatment for cocaine dependence: One-year outcome. *Experimental and Clinical Psychopharmacology, 3,* 205–212.

Horowitz, J. L., MacCoun, R. J., & Manski, C. F. (2002). Response to comments regarding the National Research Council report. *Addiction, 97,* 663–665.

Isleib, R. A., Vuchinich, R. E., & Tucker, J. A. (1988). Performance attributions and changes in self-esteem following self-handicapping with alcohol consumption. *Journal of Social and Clinical Psychology, 6,* 88–103.

Kleiman, M. A. R. (1992). *Against excess.* NY: Basic Books.

Kleiman, M. A. R. (1998). Drug policy for crime control. *Policy Options, 19.*

Kleiman, M. A. R. (2000). *Getting deterrence right: Applying tipping models and behavioral economics to the problems of crime control.* Conference on Cognition, Emotion, and Rational Choice, UCLA, April 8, 2000.

Kleiman, M. A. R. (2001a, May/June). Science and drug abuse control policy. *Society, 38,* 7–12.

Kleiman, M. A. R. (2001b). Controlling drug use and crime with testing, sanctions, and treatment. In: P. B. Heymann, & W. N. Brownsberger (Eds), *Drug addiction and drug policy: The struggle to control dependence.* Harvard University Press.

Lewin, K. (1951). *Field theory in social science.* New York: Harper Row.

MacCoun, R. J. (1996). Is melioration the addiction theory of choice? (invited commentary). *Behavioral and Brain Sciences, 19,* 586–587.

MacCoun, R. (1998). Toward a psychology of harm reduction. *American Psychologist, 53,* 1199–1208.

MacCoun, R., Kilmer, B., & Reuter, P. (in press). Research on drug-crime linkages: The next generation. To appear in *Toward a drugs and crime research agenda for the 21st century.* National Institute of Justice.

MacCoun, R., & Reuter, P. (2001). *Drug war heresies: Learning from other vices, times, and places.* Cambridge University Press.

MacCoun, R., Reuter, P., & Schelling, T. (1996). Assessing alternative drug control regimes. *Journal of Policy Analysis and Management, 15,* 1–23.

Mannetti, L., & Pierro, A. (1991). Health care workers' reactions to AIDS victims: Perception of risk and attribution of responsibility. *Journal of Community and Applied Social Psychology, 1,* 133–142.

Manski, C., Pepper, J., & Petrie, C. (Eds) (2001). *Informing America's policy on illegal drugs: What we don't know keeps hurting us* (http://www.nap.edu/books/0309072735/html/).

Meehl, P. E. (1995). Bootstraps taxometrics: Solving the classification problem in psychopathology. *American Psychologist, 50,* 266–275.

Muraven, M. R., & Baumeister, R. F. (2000). Self-regulation and depletion of limited resources: Does self-control resemble a muscle? *Psychological Bulletin, 126,* 247–259.

Murphy, P. J. (1994). *Keeping score: The frailties of the federal drug budget.* RAND Issue Paper IP-138.

NHSDA (2000). *National household survey on drug abuse.* Rockville, MD: Substance Abuse and Mental Health Services Administration, U.S. Department of Health and Human Services.

NHTSA (2000). *Traffic safety facts 2000.* National Highway Traffic Safety Administration, U.S. Department of Transportation.

O'Donoghue, T., & Rabin, M. (1999). Addiction and self control. In: J. Elster (Ed.), *Addiction: Entries and exits.* New York: Russell Sage Foundation.

Peele, S. (1996). Assumptions about drugs and the marketing of drug policies. In: W. K. Bickel, & R. J. DeGrandpre (Eds), *Drug policy and human nature* (pp. 199–220). New York: Plenum Press.

Rachlin, H. (2000). *The science of self-control.* Harvard University Press.

Reuter, P. (2001). Why does research have so little impact on American drug policy? *Addiction, 96,* 373–376.

Reuter, P., & MacCoun, R. (2002). Heroin maintenance: Is a U.S. experiment needed? In: D. Musto (Ed.), *One hundred years of heroin* (pp. 159–180). Westport, CT: Greenwood.

Rose, G. (1992). *The strategy of preventive medicine.* Oxford: Oxford University Press.

SAMHSA (2001). DAWN detailed emergency department tables 2000, Table 2.12. http://www.samhsa.gov/OAS/majorDAWN.pdf

Satel, S. L. (2001). Is drug addiction a brain disease? In: P. B. Heymann, & W. N. Brownsberger (Eds), *Drug addiction and drug policy: The struggle to control dependence* (pp. 118–143). Cambridge, MA: Harvard University Press.

Skitka, L. J., & Tetlock, P. E. (1993). Of ants and grasshoppers: The political psychology of allocating public assistance. In: B. Mellers, & J. Baron (Eds), *Psychological perspectives on justice* (pp. 205–233). Cambridge, England: Cambridge University Press.

Skog, O. J. (1993). The tail of the alcohol consumption distribution. *Addiction, 88,* 601–610.

Stacy, A. W., Widaman, K. F., & Marlatt, G. A. (1990). Expectancy models of alcohol use. *Journal of Personality and Social Psychology, 58,* 918–928.

Steele, C. M., & Josephs, R. A. (1990). Alcohol myopia: Its prized and dangerous effects. *American Psychologist, 45,* 921–933.

Szasz, T. S. (1974). *Ceremonial chemistry: The ritual persecution of drugs, addicts, and pushers.* Garden City, NY: Doubleday.

Tice, D. M., Bratslavsky, E., & Baumeister, R. F. (2001). Emotional distress regulation takes precedence over impulse control: If you feel bad, do it! *Journal of Personality and Social Psychology, 80,* 53–67.

Tversky, A., & Kahneman, D. (1974). Judgment under uncertainty: Heuristics and biases. *Science, 185,* 1124–1131.

Vuchinich, R. E., & Simpson, C. A. (1998). Hyperbolic temporal discounting in social drinkers and problem drinkers. *Experimental and Clinical Psychopharmacology, 6,* 292–305.

Wegner, D. M., & Bargh, J. A. (1998). Control and automaticity in social life. In: D. Gilbert, S. T. Fiske, & G. Lindzey (Eds), *Handbook of social psychology* (4th ed., Vol. 1, pp. 446–496). New York: McGraw-Hill.

Wegner, D. M., Vallacher, R. R., & Dizadji, D. (1989). Do alcoholics know what they're doing? Identifications of the act of drinking. *Basic & Applied Social Psychology, 10,* 197–210.

Weiner, B., Perry, R. B., & Magnusson, J. (1988). An attributional analysis of reactions to stigma. *Journal of Personality and Social Psychology, 55,* 738–748.

Weinstein, N. D., & Klein, W. M. (1995). Resistance of personal risk perceptions to debiasing interventions. *Health Psychology, 14,* 132–140.

Wertenbroch, K. (1998). Consumption self-control by rationing purchase quantities of virtue and vice. *Marketing Science, 17,* 317–337.

Wilson, J. Q. (1983). *Thinking about crime* (2nd ed.). NY: Vintage Books.

Wilson, J. Q., & Herrnstein, R. J. (1985). *Crime and human nature.* New York: Simon and Schuster.

Zuckerman, M. (1994). *Behavioral expressions and biosocial bases of sensation seeking.* New York: Cambridge University Press.

Comments on MacCoun

Charles R. Schuster

The issue addressed by Rob MacCoun's paper is whether addiction theory is relevant to drug policy. Specifically he is concerned in the context of this conference with the relevance of behavioral economic theories of drug addiction to the development of drug policy. His conclusion is that neither behavioral economic theories of drug addiction nor any other theories of addiction are relevant to the major issues that drug policy experts address. His evidence for this conclusion is that neither in his book (MacCoun & Reuter 2001), which I consider a major contribution to the field, nor in the NRC Monograph by Manski et al. (2001) is there any substantial discussion of "theories of addiction." If I understand Professor MacCoun's position correctly this irrelevancy stems from two sources: (1) drug policy experts are concerned with all levels of non-medical drug consumption, not just the use of drugs by those who are addicted; and (2) the fact that behavioral economic theories of addiction are simplistic and make unwarranted assumptions about the nature of addiction.

Let me address these contentions separately. Clearly our society must be concerned with the consumption of powerful mind-altering, performance-impairing drugs whether these drugs are taken once or repeatedly. From my viewpoint as a psychopharmacologist the harms created by drugs are often greatest in inexperienced drug users. I have seen many first-time users of psychoactive drugs enter emergency rooms because of panic attacks brought on by the novelty of the psychedelic experience. Automobile accidents associated with ingestion of alcohol or other performance-impairing psychoactive drugs can occur after the first drug experience. Obviously, the devastation to the individual, their family and community increases as the magnitude of drug use increases, i.e., as the individual makes the transition from drug experimentation to regular drug use and finally compulsive drug use (addiction). Clearly, opportunities for calamitous accidents, and interference with normal work and social relationships increase with the number of incidents of intoxicating drug exposures. However, the numbers making this transition from drug experimentation to addiction is comparatively low for most illegal drugs. Thus, the total harm produced by illegal drugs may be greatest for the myriad of drug experimenters rather than the relatively few who might be labeled as addicted. Therefore, drug policies must be concerned with the prevention of drug-induced social and public health harm to society at all levels of consumption. I agree with Professor MacCoun that we cannot confine our concern only to those that meet some arbitrary criterion that allows them to be labeled addicts. Thus, theories of addiction per se are not relevant as they only apply to a minority of the problems that can be attributed to illicit drug use.

MacCoun lists a number of means which drug policy experts recommend to limit non-medical psychoactive drug use: drug prevention, education, and rhetoric from the bully pulpit; drug treatment; criminal sanctions against users; criminal sanctions against dealers; interdiction and source country controls; taxes, advertising controls, and other regulatory mechanisms; drug testing; and bans on employment, welfare, and other benefits. These interventions are not limited in their application to those who are addicted to drugs. Rather they are aimed at decreasing all non-medical drug use and its associated social and public health consequences.

Similarly MacCoun lists a number of explanatory constructs used in the analysis of drug policy. These include: the prevalence and incidence of drug use; the statistical distribution of quantities consumed and frequency of consumption; the price elasticity of demand for drugs; the time sensitivity and/or impulsivity of drug users; the deterrent effect of drug-law sanctions (certainty, severity, and celerity); the dose-response relationship between consumption of a drug and its various acute and chronic effects; the relative contribution of psychoactive effects of a drug vs. its illegality in producing drug-related harms (criminality, morbidity, mortality, impaired functioning, etc.); possible substitution, complementarity, and "gateway" relationships between the use of tobacco, alcohol, and marijuana, and subsequent use of harder drugs; the unintended effects of use-reduction strategies on drug-related harms, and the unintended effects of harm-reduction strategies on drug prevalence and consumption; the distribution of the harms (and perhaps benefits) of drug use across bearers – the user, family, friends, neighbors, the community, taxpayers (MacCoun, Reuter, and Schelling 1996). Here I can see more potential relevance of theories of addiction, such as behavioral economic theories, to some of these constructs. For example, how does price elasticity change when one progresses from regular drug use to "addiction?" How do individual differences in delay discounting functions predict those who may be at greater risk for progressing from regular drug use to addiction? It is clear to me, however, that the important contributions of behavioral economics in this context are in providing important analytic tools rather than a behavioral economic theory of addiction. I believe that Professor MacCoun and I would agree that although behavioral economic "theories" of addiction may not be relevant to drug policy, the methods of analysis, i.e. the tools provided by behavioral economics, are extremely important for the analysis of drug policy issues.

Let me illustrate this importance. A recent study conducted at Wayne State University looked at the impact of "cost" incurred by patients in methadone maintenance treatment programs for opiate addiction (Borisova 2000). Because of state and federal regulations designed to prevent diversion of methadone, patients early in their treatment must come to programs on a daily basis to receive their dose of methadone. After several months, only those who are showing progress in controlling their use of illicit drugs are allowed to take methadone home for periods up to 2–3 days. Analysis of the "cost" of out-of-pocket expenses, time in transit and waiting in the clinic for medication dispensing were shown to be excellent predictors of retention rates. The higher the cost of daily program attendance, the lower the retention rates of patients. This clearly has policy implications for the location of methadone clinics and other regulatory issues.

I am very excited about the application of the analytical tools of behavioral economics to our description and understanding of drug consumption, drug abuse and drug dependence. I agree with MacCoun, however, that the theories of addiction generated by behavioral economics have not been helpful to me as a drug policy analyst, laboratory researcher or treatment provider. I also agree with Professor MacCoun that the concept implicit in economic theories of addiction that addiction is a unitary phenomenon with one theoretical explanation is overly simplistic. A functional analysis of the pathways leading from drug experimentation to regular use to compulsive drug use reveals that there is no single pathway to addiction. Individuals begin drug use for a number of social and psychological reasons. Whether drug use is continued depends both on individual reactions to the drug, co-existing psychopathology, the social consequence of drug use, and alternatives to drug use that are available, not to mention the public policies in effect within the individual's culture. Psychoactive drugs may attenuate the negative symptoms of various forms of psychopathology and continued drug taking may be at least initially a form of self-medication. Drug experiences may not at first be positively reinforcing and may even be aversive. However, if powerful social reinforcers are contingent upon being part of the drug using sub-culture, this may override the aversive effects of drugs. Tolerance to the aversive effects may develop and the positive reinforcing effects of the drug emerge. Individuals who lack the opportunity or ability to find other positively reinforcing pro-social activities find that the drug-using life style fills a void. Professor David Deitch of University of Southern California, who is himself a recovering heroin user, has asked: "who do you know that wakes up every morning, thinks of their life goal and achieves it every day? A heroin addict" (personal communication). I cite all of these things simply to state the obvious. There is no single pathway to addiction.

Professor MacCoun has alluded to the contingency management interventions for the treatment of substance abuse developed by Steve Higgins and colleagues at the University of Vermont. These interventions have proven to be extremely effective in decreasing illicit drug use. They clearly can be viewed as behavioral economic interventions involving providing robust positive reinforcers for drug abstinence. I would argue, however, that these procedures stem from classic principles of behavioral analysis and not behavioral economic theories of addiction.

Although I agree with Professor MacCoun that theories of addiction in general have had little if any impact on drug abuse policies, I would argue that, to the extent that such theories influence the manner in which the problem of drug abuse is conceptualized, they may be of great importance. My views in this area are based upon my nine years with the federal government during which I was the Director of the NIDA. At the risk of over-simplification I would state that, in regard to federal drug abuse policy makers, there are those who wish to conceptualize drug abuse and dependence as a problem stemming from ethical and moral weakness and those who would conceptualize it as a public health problem. As has been stressed previously (Moore & Gerstein 1981), the most fundamental and important determinant of policy is the manner in which a problem is conceptualized. Policies generally flow from relatively simplified "conceptions" that determine the "governing ideas" from which specific instances of policy are derived. If drug abuse/dependence is conceptualized as the expression of a problem of weak moral constraints leading to unfettered hedonism, then the governing ideas and derivative policies flow almost inexorably. Governing ideas are usually short, easily remembered "slogans." "Drug Free America" or "Zero Tolerance for Drugs" are two examples of governing ideas stemming from a moralistic conception of the drug abuse problem. They lead to an emphasis on punitive approaches to deter drug use and policies such as a ban on needle exchange programs and other harm minimization interventions. One cannot have "Zero Tolerance for Drugs" and make it safer for people to use them. On the other hand, if theories of addiction can amass sufficient, compelling arguments that drug dependence is most usefully conceptualized as a chronic relapsing disorder, similar in its characteristics to other diseases such as morbid obesity or arthritis, the policies adopted to control this problem will be quite different. Clearly, if drug dependence is a chronic relapsing disorder it should be conceptualized as a public health problem. The governing idea flowing from the conception of drug abuse as a public health problem is to treat it as we do any other public health problem. Derivative policies from this conceptualization would be to conduct surveillance activities to determine incidence, prevalence and harmful consequences of drug abuse. Resources would be devoted to the development and implementation of cost-effective prevention, treatment and other harm minimization interventions. I want to emphasize the utilitarian approach that I am suggesting here. Whether drug abuse is conceived of as moral weakness or as a disease has less to do with the *rightness* of the definition of the problem than whether the conceptualization leads to policies and programs which are cost-effective in decreasing the problem of illicit drug use and its tragic consequences. By cost-effective in this context, I include not only the usual cost considerations, but as well, the costs of an intervention to the society's citizens in terms of their loss of civil liberties and freedom from government intrusion.

The complication for the area of drug abuse policy is that, in fact, drug abuse is both a problem of ethics and morality and a public health problem. Thus, both conceptions of the problem are justifiable, but I would argue they are useful at different stages in the natural history of the development of the problem. Moral training can of course deter individuals from ever experimenting with drugs. For instance, adolescents who spend more time in religious activities are less likely to use illicit substances (Johanson *et al.* 1996). There are, however, significant limitations to the role of religious and ethical training as a deterrent to drug experimentation. First, only a minority of youth in the United States has a significant involvement with formalized religion. Further, the high prevalence of psychopathology, especially antisocial personality, found in drug abusers sets limits on the population who are amenable to drug abuse prevention through ethical and moral constraints (Regier *et al.* 1990). Finally, where there is a breakdown in the structure and functioning of the family and community, children may not be given the ethical and moral training that would deter drug use. If such ethical and moral constraints are ineffective or absent, for whatever reason, and the individual escalates from drug experimentation to dysfunctional use and addiction, the problem changes. Then the problem is most usefully conceptualized as a public health issue and the individual as afflicted with the disease of drug addiction. At this stage of drug addiction, moral constraints alone are as likely to be effective as they would be in the treatment of arthritis. Indeed, one goal of treatment for drug addiction could be conceived of as engendering a state in which ethical and moral constraints against illicit drug use can be effective in maintaining abstinence.

In the United States there appears to be a large schism between those who conceive of drug addiction as an ethical and moral problem and those who see it as a public health problem. Unfortunately, I believe that an overly simplistic interpretation of behavioral economic theories of drug addiction may give support to the conception of drug addiction as a problem of morality. "Choice" is a central tenet of behavioral economic theories of drug addiction that can easily be misconstrued to imply that addicts "choose" that life-style. It is not easy to sell policy makers on the notion that there are determinants of choice — not unfettered free will. I think it is imperative that behavioral economic theories of addiction make it very clear that there are biological (genetic) and behavioral constraints on choice which must be considered if we are to develop effective prevention and treatment strategies. To maintain the concept of "choice" without unwittingly giving support to moralistic solutions to the problem of addiction is a serious challenge for behavioral economic theories of addiction.

References

Borisova, N. N. (2000). *Effects of personal cost of methadone maintenance, especially time price, on attendance*. Doctoral Dissertation, Wayne State University.

Johanson, C. E., Duffy, F. F., & Anthony, J. C. (1996). Associations between drug use and behavioral repertoire in urban youths. *Addiction, 91*, 523–534.

MacCoun, R., & Reuter, P. (2001). *Drug war heresies: Learning from other vices, times, and places*. Cambridge University Press.

MacCoun, R., Reuter, P., & Schelling, T. (1996). Assessing alternative drug control regimes. *Journal of Policy Analysis and Management, 15*, 1–23.

Manski, C., Pepper, J., & Petrie, C. (Eds) (2001). *Informing America's policy on illegal drugs: What we don't know keeps hurting us*. Washington, DC: National Academy Press.

Moore, M. H., & Gerstein, D. R. (Eds) (1981). *Alcohol and public policy: Beyond the shadow of prohibition. Panel on alternative policies affecting the prevention of alcohol abuse and alcoholism*. Washington, DC: National Academy Press.

Regier, D. A., Farmer, M. E., Rae, D. S., Locke, B. Z., Keith, S. J., Judd, L. L., & Goodwin, F. K. (1990). Comorbidity of mental disorders with alcohol and other drug abuse. Results from the epidemiologic catchment area (ECA) study. *JAMA, 264*, 2511–2518.

Reply to Schuster

Robert MacCoun

In reaction to Professor Schuster's insightful comments, I offer only two brief clarifications.

First, I agree that behavioral addiction theories probably oversimplify the addiction phenomenon, but I would argue that the main explanation for their lack of policy relevance is their considerable overlap with popular intuitions about low self-control and impulsiveness, which have already shaped our drug policies.

Second, my essay did question the existence of a bright line between addicts and other heavy users. And I did argue that I believe recreational users, because of their large numbers, can contribute substantially to aggregate drug harms — though I think the relative contributions remain an open empirical question. But I would not want readers to believe I see all drug use as equally troubling. Elsewhere, I have decried the American preoccupation with prevalence (drug users vs. non-drug users), which I would replace with a focus on the harmfulness, quantity, and frequency of drug use (MacCoun 1998; MacCoun & Reuter 2001). Bright lines are rhetorically convenient, and may even help individuals control their behavior, but they are not encouraging constructive thinking about strategic drug policy.

References

MacCoun, R. (1998). Toward a psychology of harm reduction. *American Psychologist*, *53*, 1199–1208.
MacCoun, R., & Reuter, P. (2001). *Drug war heresies: Learning from other vices, times, and places.* Cambridge University Press.

Concluding Comments

Nick Heather and Rudy Vuchinich

In these concluding remarks, we will not undertake the herculean task of attempting to summarise the rich and varied contents of this book. Instead, we will confine ourselves to a few comments about theories of addiction in general and about behavioural choice theories in particular, suggest some possibilities for the integration of the four theories represented in the book, and explore briefly some of their implications for the treatment and prevention of addictive disorders.

General Comments on Theories of Addiction

Levels of Analysis

Heather (1998) proposed that theories in the addictions field can be pitched at one of three levels of discourse: (i) The neuronal level. Theories at this level of analysis may be concerned, for example, with a process of neuroadaptation to a substance, or pre-existing differences between addicted persons[1] and others in neuronal response to a substance or activity. (ii) The phenomenal level. Theories at this level may be concerned, for example, with abnormal desire for a drug or activity, such as the occurrence of "craving." (iii) The behavioural level. Theories at this level of analysis may be concerned, for example, with the failure to refrain from ingestion of a substance or performance of an activity despite repeated attempts or resolutions to do so (i.e. "akrasia" or "weakness of will") (see Figure 1). We believe that the most intellectually satisfying and pragmatically useful theories of addiction will be framed at the behavioural level. This is the case because the essence of addiction lies in "a demonstrated failure to refrain from a behaviour despite attempts to do so or a complaint by the person that the behaviour is out of his or her control" (see Heather's comments on Skog's Chapter 6, this volume[2]), and this is the behaviour pattern most in need of modification. The conceptual and empirical work that constitutes this book clearly is most concerned with explanation at the behavioural level of analysis.

An important issue concerning these levels of analysis is whether or not data from one level can be explained by theories pitched at a different level of analysis (Heather 1998). That is, can data at the phenomenal level (i.e. craving) be given a reductive explanation in terms of a theory at the neuronal level? Or can data at the behavioural level (i.e. akrasia) be given a reductive explanation in terms of a theory pitched at the phenomenal or neuronal levels? We think not. That is, a crucial proposition associated with different levels of analysis

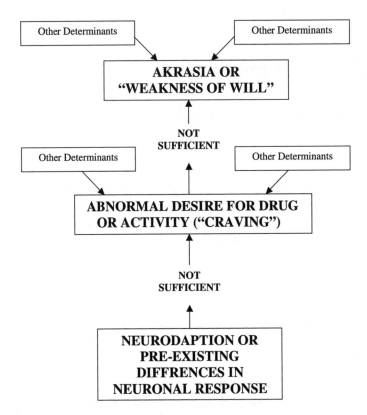

Figure 1: A conceptual framework for explaining addiction (adapted from Heather 1998).

(Heather 1998) is that any theory at the "lower" levels in this framework cannot, in principle, be regarded as sufficient in itself for an explanation of data at "higher" levels. Thus, for example, an explanation of physical dependence that invoked adaptive regulation of drug receptors in the brain (e.g. Littleton 2001) cannot be a sufficient explanation of drug craving. This is the case because persons showing high levels of physical dependence do not always report experiencing craving. Similarly, no theory of drug craving, whether based on classical conditioning, cognitive processes, or some other mechanism (see Drummond 2001), can be a sufficient explanation of the addicted person's failure to control their behaviour. This is the case because, again, relapse to that behaviour often occurs in the absence of reported feelings of abnormal desire for the substance or activity in question. Moreover, people do sometimes escape from addictive behaviour despite continuing to experience occasional craving. A full discussion of the insufficiencies of reductionism is beyond our present scope, but suffice it to say that, with specific regard to addiction, the above reasoning demonstrates that reductive theories can never offer a fully adequate explanation of addictive behaviour.

This is not to say, of course, that explanations of neuroadaptation or of abnormal desires or motivations cannot illuminate or add to our understanding of addictive behaviour, which is implicit in the proposed framework of three levels of analysis. For example, important contributions to an understanding of addiction from neuroanatomy, neurochemistry, and learning theory are made by Cardinal and colleagues (Chapter 7, this volume). However, our rejection of reductionism has two implications. First, addictive behaviour is "the final common pathway" that must be the explanatory aim of any adequate theory, and, second, to be useful a theory need not aim to explain anything other than addictive behaviour itself. From this viewpoint, behavioural choice theories are potentially adequate and useful theories of addiction. This does not mean that any such theory is necessarily valid, merely that it is capable in principle of offering a valid explanation of the defining characteristic of addiction.

Theories of Addiction and Part Theories of Addiction

A recent Special Issue of the journal *Addiction* (Vol. 96, No. 1, January 2001) was devoted to theories of addiction. Although the articles in this Special Issue were of the high quality readers have come to expect from this journal, we submit that none of them is actually a *theory* of addiction, certainly as we wish to define it (see above). Most of these articles are in fact *part* theories of addiction, in that they seek to explain some particular aspect of what is commonly accepted as addictive behaviour and experience or are focused on a particular form of addiction.[3] Thus, Drummond (2001) reviews theories of drug craving, McCusker (2001) describes the cognitive biases associated with addiction, Jones *et al.* (2001) review evidence on outcome expectancy theories of alcohol consumption, and Sutton (2001) provides a critique of the transtheoretical model of change; other articles are concerned with the mechanisms of action of addictive stimuli (Miller 2001; Robinson & Berridge 2001), individual susceptibility to addiction (Buck & Finn 2001), and environmental factors in addiction (Ferrence 2001; Kenkel *et al.* 2001). None of these articles directly addresses the central paradox of addiction and what we see as its defining feature — the repeated return to harmful behaviours despite repeated attempts or resolutions to avoid doing so.

Within the pages of the *Addiction* Special Issue there are two apparent exceptions to the claim that they all propose only part theories. First, Orford's (2001a) model of addiction as an excessive appetite (see also Orford 1985, 2001b) is comprehensive in scope and generalized to a range of behaviours beyond substance use disorders. Moreover, the emphasis on decision, ambivalence, and conflict offers much to admire in its characterisation of addiction, and much that resonates with behavioural choice theories. Nevertheless, we believe that Orford's account is a description of addiction or a perspective on it, not a theory.[4] As West (2001) points out, the definition and attributes of what should count as a scientific theory are debatable. But if one insists that a theory should consist of a formal, more or less rigorous set of statements (postulates or laws) providing a coherent explanation for the occurrence of a designated group of observable phenomena, and from which clear, testable hypotheses may be derived, then Orford's psychological view of addiction, its obvious merits notwithstanding, does not qualify.[5]

The other exception is an article (Bickel & Marsch 2001) co-authored by one of the contributors to this book (Bickel & Johnson, Chapter 9, this volume). This article presents a behavioural economic "understanding" of drug addiction, with particular reference to the ability of the concept of hyperbolic discounting to make sense of the impulsivity and "loss of control" encountered in drug addiction, very close to what we wish a theory of addiction to address. This aim is achieved very well, and the article offers several interesting hypotheses based on delay discounting and important suggestions for future research while falling short of an overall theory of addiction.

Is a Theory of Addiction Possible?

A very different and commonly held view of theories of addiction is to argue that they are impossible, or at least never useful. An argument of this kind is advanced by Schuster in his comments on MacCoun's chapter in this volume (see comments on Chapter 14). Schuster regards as overly simplistic the idea that "addiction is a unitary phenomenon with one theoretical explanation" and insists that "there is no single pathway to addiction". We agree that there is no single pathway, but maintain that to reject the possibility of theory on this basis is to confuse aetiology in the individual case with the task of theoretical explanation. From the point of view of individual causation, it is no doubt true that "there are as many causes of addiction as there are addicts," but this does not prevent us from advancing sets of general propositions that apply to all forms and circumstances of addiction. It is often remarked that Newton's laws of motion cannot fully explain the fall of a single leaf from a tree, but despite this inadequacy have transformed our understanding of the physical universe and radically changed the world we inhabit. More modestly, the same general idea would apply to a valid theory of addiction pitched at a sufficient level of abstraction and universality; such a theory would enable us to improve the prevention and treatment of addiction in general terms without necessarily being able to explain all aspects of every individual occurrence of it.

Characteristics of Behavioural Choice Theories

We have argued that behavioural choice theories are distinguished from most other theories of addiction by being whole rather than part explanations. Behavioural economic and economic theories also can be distinguished on the basis of their use of the language of choice and their focus on the time dimension.

The Language of Choice

Behavioural choice theories obviously employ the language of choice. As described in the Introduction to this book, owing to their origins in a confluence of microeconomics and the matching law from psychology, they see the addicted person as making choices from among a set of behavioural options, including the choice of continuing addictive behaviour. The task of theory is to explain why a particular level of behavioural allocation towards the addictive behaviour is selected rather than a different level of allocation, and to specify the conditions under which such allocations will be made and the conditions under which they may be changed. As also indicated in the Introduction, this marks a sharp contrast to theories that invoke the notion of some disease process from which addicted persons suffer, an idea that has dominated the field of addiction studies for a long time. The language of choice also marks a contrast with any theory of addiction — neurochemical, psychological or sociocultural — proposing that the addicted person's behaviour can be explained by mechanisms or forces beyond their control that compel them to behave the way they do. One problem that all such "mechanistic" theories share is a difficulty explaining how persons can ever refrain from addictive behaviour in the face of the mechanisms that compel them to engage in the behaviour. This raises no difficulty in principle for behavioural choice theories, since the person is seen as always capable of reallocating their behaviour away from the addiction should conditions arise that encourage them to do so.[6]

In appealing to the language of choice as a distinctive feature of the theories under consideration, we should immediately distance these theories from other recent accounts of addiction that reject mechanistic models and see the addict as making choices. For example, in declaring addiction to be a myth, Davies (1992) suggests that what we call addiction is merely an inference from a series of causal attributions used by addicted persons to explain their own behaviour. Such attributions are said to arise especially often in interactions between the "addict" and representatives of the treatment or criminal justice systems, where they are used to avoid responsibility and blame for troublesome behaviour or to benefit in some other way. While causal attributions of this kind probably do sometimes affect the manifestation of addictive behaviour and the addicted person's statements about it, Davies goes further and says that addiction is *nothing more than* a collection of causal attributions, that self-harmful drug use or other self-harmful activity is fully voluntary behaviour like any other normal behaviour, and that addicts take drugs only because they enjoy doing so. Similarly, Jeffrey Schaler reaches the conclusion that ". . . drug addicts are conscious — yes, even calculating — responsible persons, *in full command of their behaviour* (Schaler 2000: 21; italics added). In his book, Schaler usefully criticises common misconceptions about the nature of addiction and its treatment but appears to believe that the only alternative to a disease model of addiction is a "free-will" model. Thus, for both Davies and Schaler, explaining addiction presents no challenge because there is nothing to explain.

As will be obvious from the chapters in this book, views of addiction of this kind are very different from the underlying assumptions of behavioural choice theories. Rather than viewing addiction as a myth and believing that there is nothing to explain, behavioural choice theorists regard it as a very real phenomenon and, moreover, one of the most mysterious facets of human behaviour. That there is something necessary to explain is shown by the fact that addicts complain that their behaviour is in some way out of their control — that they repeatedly resolve to change it but then find that they have failed to do so for reasons they themselves cannot readily describe. These complaints are fundamentally genuine, not mere causal attributions. It is a mistake of equal magnitude to imagine that addicts are completely free to change their behaviour as to assume that they are completely constrained by some form of compulsion. Thus, addicts can be seen as trapped in a special form of behaviour that, on many occasions, they wish they could escape from. All four theories discussed in this book offer accounts of the nature of this trap and how it comes about. As Rachlin (2000a) puts it: "The alcoholic does not choose to be an alcoholic. Instead he chooses to drink now, and now, and now, and now. The pattern of alcoholism emerges in his behaviour . . . without ever having been chosen" (Rachlin 2000a: 4; see also Chapter 5, this volume).

In evaluating the merits of behavioural choice theories, the possible disadvantages for the public understanding of addiction must be borne in mind. Charles Schuster (see Comments on MacCoun's Chapter 14) writes that: "To maintain the concept of 'choice' without unwittingly giving support to moralistic solutions to the problem of addiction is a serious challenge for behavioural economic theories of addiction." This is because "choice," as a central tenet of these theories, can easily be misconstrued to imply that addicts "choose" their life-style. Schuster continues: "It is not easy to sell policy makers on the notion that there are determinants of choice — not unfettered free will. I think it is imperative that behavioural economic theories of addiction make it very clear that there are biological (genetic) and behavioural constraints on choice which must be considered if we are to develop effective prevention and treatment strategies."

Given Schuster's extensive experience in addiction policy-making arenas, these views demand respect. We recognise the challenge that speaking of choice in relation to addicts' behaviour presents, and that there is a danger of being misunderstood. Indeed, despite any efforts to make clear to the public that there *are* constraints on this choice, we think it highly likely that this will sometimes be misunderstood, either by those who genuinely fail to grasp what the theories tell us about addictive behaviour or by those who opportunistically distort the theories' meanings to support moralistic and punitive attitudes. On balance, however, we feel that the risks in question are worth taking and, furthermore, that it is our duty as scientists to take them. This is simply because a genuinely scientific understanding of addictive behaviour, which we believe is inherent in behavioural choice theories, must be in the long-run interests of addicts themselves, their families and communities, and the wider society. After all, no purported science of addiction prior to behavioural economic theories can claim to have had great success in preventing or treating it. More specifically, we are convinced that the disease theory, although it may once have been necessary in the attempt to protect addicts from blame and punishment, has now outlived its usefulness; whatever benefits it may have provided, and these are debatable, they are now considerably outweighed by an inaccurate portrayal of addiction with its misleading effects on public understanding and policy.[7] So something better is clearly needed. To put it bluntly, an awareness of the danger of being misunderstood should never be a justification for retarding scientific inquiry.

The Time Dimension

Another common feature of the theories we have been considering in this book is that they all try to explain the addict's behaviour along the time dimension. That is, the utility derived in the present from engaging in the addictive behaviour or in alternative activities, which presumably is the primary determinant of behavioural allocation, depends on both past and future allocation patterns. This represents an important distinction from other psychological and behavioural accounts of addiction. Although all theories are somehow concerned with past behaviour, the choice perspective's concern with the future is perhaps unique among addiction theories (see Loewenstein & Elster 1992). Although the specifics of incorporating these intertemporal dependencies vary among the four theories, they all rely crucially on some form of interaction between past, present, and future states. More specifically, as Skog (Chapter 6, this volume) points out, all four theories rely on time discounting in one form or another, although the precise function of discounting may differ from theory to theory.

We have also seen that the constructs of ambivalence and conflict are central to behavioural choice theories. Many models of ambivalence and conflict have been applied to addictive behaviour, ranging from the approach-avoidance conflict model pioneered by Miller (1944), through the "decisional-balance" model made popular by Janis & Mann (1977), to the motivational model described by Miller & Rollnick (1991) (see Orford 2001b, Chapter 12: 250–275). But what all these accounts omit, or at least fail to make explicit, is that the addict's predicament entails ambivalence and conflict over time, and this applies whether the ambivalence and conflict is thought to be "simple" or "complex" (see Rachlin 2000a). In other words, the opposing sides of the conflict are not present simultaneously; rather, the addict's stated intentions and behaviour at time 1 are opposed by those at time 2. This, simply put, is the essence of the addicted person's problem and that which any attempted solution to it must resolve. We think it is this basic property of behavioural choice theories that allows them to offer explanations of the addict's situation that approximate to reality.

Possibilities for Theoretical Integration

A primary objective of the Birmingham conference was to decide if, to what extent, and in what ways a theoretical integration might be achieved among the four accounts of addiction under consideration (see Preface). In the interests of providing a modest contribution to this aim, there seem to be at least three components to this task.

First, it may be possible that the four theories, or at least subsets of them, share an essential common ground in their explanations of addictive behaviour. If that were the case, any differences between theories may be mainly terminological and more apparent than real. A second possible means of promoting integration would be clearly to identify points of difference that could in principle be put to empirical test. Is there an experimental or observational study that proponents of at least two theories would accept as a critical test of competing key hypotheses? It would undoubtedly be naïve to hope for agreement on a "once and for all" decider of competing predictions, but a consensus on how critical hypotheses of this kind could be operationalised and investigated would be a major achievement. A third possibility is the suggestion that different theories, or at least parts of them, are concerned to explain different aspects of the way addiction is manifested. This may occur even though all four theories apparently address what we have claimed to be the defining feature of addiction — the repeated return to a certain form of behaviour despite repeated attempts or resolutions to abandon it. In any event, to the extent that the theories under discussion are aimed at explaining different things, they are not inconsistent in principle and could be joined in an integrated theory.

Hyperbolic Temporal Discounting

We have seen that central to all four theories, and arising from their foundations in economics and experimental psychology, is the idea that rewards are discounted over time.

It was also emphasised in the Introduction to this book (see also Chapters 2, 3, 5–7, 9 and 12, this volume) that two different forms of discounting are utilised — hyperbolic discounting, derived from the matching law, in Ainslie's, Herrnstein & Prelec's, and Rachlin's theories, and exponential discounting, derived from neo-classical economics, in Becker and Murphy's theory. Owing to a large amount of experimental evidence with both animals and humans, and also to other, *a priori* objections to exponential discounting as applied to human decision making (see Ainslie 1992, 2001; Ainslie & Monterosso, Chapter 2, this volume), an overall judgement must be that hyperbolic discounting should be preferred as the underlying process applying to temporal discounting and thus to addictive behaviour. In addition, predictions from Becker & Murphy's (1988) theory regarding the behaviour of addicts (see Bretteville-Jensen, Chapter 10, this volume) have fared poorly in observational studies, certainly worse than those derived from the assumption of hyperbolic discounting (Vuchinich & Simpson 1998). The conclusion must be that any kind of theoretical integration should be focused on the three theories based on hyperbolic discounting. It is interesting that this seems also to be the conclusion of Chaloupka and colleagues (see Chapter 3, this volume), the main current exponents of rational addiction theory.

This should not be taken to imply that rational addiction theory has made no contributions to our understanding of addiction, contributions that are summarized by Chaloupka and colleagues (Chapter 3). Neither does it imply that all questions about the respective roles of exponential and hyperbolic discounting in addiction have been settled or that some addicts may not sometimes in some circumstances discount rewards and punishments exponentially (see Chaloupka *et al.*, Chapter 3, this volume). With regard to theoretical integration, Skog's suggestion should also be borne in mind that it may be possible to modify Becker & Murphy's (1988) theory to allow for the inclusion of "akrasia" (Skog, Chapter 6, this volume). Be that as it may, the present conclusion is that any possible theoretical integration should be founded on the assumption of hyperbolic discounting. As will by now be obvious to the reader, the key advantage of this assumption is that it immediately makes possible an explanation for the inconsistency of the addict's behaviour over time — in other words, for "akrasia" or "weakness of will."

The Primrose Path

Common ground between Herrnstein & Prelec's (1992) and Rachlin's (1997, 2000a) theories is the notion of a primrose path along which a substance user becomes increasingly entrapped in addiction. This commonality is made clear by Rachlin (1997) (see also Heyman, Chapter 4, this volume; Rachlin, Chapter 3).[8] In this way, these theories offer an account of the developmental process leading to addiction, in addition to, at the end of the process, an account of the nature of addiction itself. This feature makes these theories different from Ainslie's (1992) theory which is concerned with the state of addiction rather than any process that may lead to it.

Although the Herrnstein & Prelec and the Rachlin theories involve some sort of primrose path, they propose different choice dynamics that produce increasing behavioural allocation to the addictive activity. A critical issue here is whether behavioural allocation is sensitive to local utility or to global utility. *Local utility* refers to reinforcement derived from the response options during their engagement, while *global utility* refers to the sum of the local utilities across multiple response options. Behavioural allocation that is sensitive to the former is termed *melioration*, and is the choice dynamic in Herrnstein & Prelec's theory, while behavioural allocation that is sensitive to the latter is termed *maximization*, and is the choice dynamic in Rachlin's theory (see Introduction, this volume). Although numerous experiments have been devoted to this issue (Heyman & Herrnstein 1986), the question of whether melioration or maximization is the more fundamental choice dynamic has not been resolved empirically (Rachlin *et al.* 1988). But despite the current lack of empirical resolution to this question, and depending on one's purposes, it may be useful to maintain the distinction between melioration and maximization. As noted by Rachlin (2000b: 146), "melioration and maximization are not two competing theories but are instead two alternative modes of explanation — two languages," with the language of melioration couched in terms of behavioural structure and the language of maximization couched in terms of behavioural function.

The Alternative to the Addictive Behaviour

As a result of analyses based on choice, all four theories set up a choice context involving the addictive behaviour and some other behaviour with which it is mutually incompatible. However, in Ainslie's and in Herrnstein & Prelec's theories, this alternative to the addictive behaviour is equivalent to "all other possible activities." The usefulness of this general and amorphous concept for empirical investigation, not to mention developments in treatment and prevention, might be questioned.

Only Rachlin (1997, 2000a, b) has specified in his relative theory of addiction what this alternative activity might be — the "commodity" of social support and the activity of social interaction. The alternative has a special function in the theory in that it is regarded as mutually substitutable, in the economic sense, for addiction, thus accounting for the property that makes substances and activities potentially addictive. This immediately makes Rachlin's theory testable in a way that the others are not. However, it has been suggested by Melberg (Chapter 11) that empirical evidence only weakly supports this particular hypothesis, and Skog (Chapter 6) also argues that it is inconsistent with the accumulated evidence on addictive behaviour. In his reply to Melberg, Rachlin (this volume) straight away rejects the strong version of this hypothesis, that all addicts and only addicts lack social support, but argues that the more general substitutability of addiction and social support has not been disconfirmed. In other places, Rachlin (2000a: 139) has proposed "positive addictions" to be the alternative to "negative addictions." However, should further empirical work lead to the conclusion that neither social support nor positive addictions can sustain the role of the substitutable activity in the theory, then there will be a need to propose some other activity for this role.

Making the Self-Controlled Choice

Another area of possible common ground between the theories is the way they suggest the addict succeeds in overcoming the impulsive choice — in other words, their theoretical account of the process of self-control. There are obvious similarities between Herrnstein & Prelec's (1992) concept of the restructuring of alternatives, Rachlin's (1995) idea of patterning of choices over time, and Ainslie's (1992) notion of the bunching of an extended series of choices, but there are also apparent differences too. An important question seems to be whether these differences are worth worrying about — whether they have important empirical consequences for an understanding of addictive behaviour or whether they are somewhat different ways, perhaps from different epistemological positions, of talking about the same phenomenon. In other words, it is unclear at present whether these concepts can be interpreted to provide different testable predictions in empirical studies of the process of self-control among addicts and, if so, whether such differing predictions have clear implications for treatment principles and methods.

While all three theories assuming hyperbolic discounting address the task of explaining self-control, it is Ainslie (1992, 2001) who has provided the fullest and most detailed attempt at explaining it. At the same time, Ainslie has been much busier than the other theorists in relating his ideas on self-control to everyday examples and clinical phenomena. A question here is whether these ideas, combined perhaps with the more formal offerings of the other two theories, can illuminate and possibly enrich the principles and methods underlying treatment modalities such as "motivational interviewing" (Miller & Rollnick 1991, 2002). This question will be returned to below.

Summary: A Rough Sketch of an Integrated Theory

In summary, what is suggested here is merely a crude outline of a possible integration of behavioural economic theories of addiction. It hardly needs saying that, even if the lineaments of this integrated theory were accepted, many crucial details — concerned perhaps with inter- and intra-individual differences in discounting (see Ainslie, Chapter 2, this volume), the contributions to the choice process of different types of cost (see Mitchell, Chapter 12, this volume), or the relationship between delay and preference under different conditions (see Heyman's comments on Mitchell's Chapter 12, this volume) — remain to be inserted. There is also no doubt of the need, especially in a situation where several epistemological traditions and intersecting academic disciplines are represented, for further conceptual analysis and clarification, thus pointing to the vital role of philosophy in theory building (see Gjelsvik, Chapter 9, this volume). At the same time, we need more development of research paradigms and experimental methods relevant to the study of choice behaviour in addiction (see Mitchell, Chapter 12, this volume). Neither do we claim that the components of the integrated theory we propose here are particularly novel (see, e.g. Skog 1999; Chapter 6, this volume), but we nevertheless hope the proposal may form a basis for progress in theory and research.

We begin with the decision that an integrated theory should be based on the three existing theories (Ainslie 1992, 2001; Herrnstein & Prelec 1992; Rachlin, 1997, 2000a, b) that assume hyperbolic rather than exponential discounting; elements from Becker & Murphy's (1988) theory may come in useful at some stage, and exponential discounting may play some role in addicts' choices under exceptional conditions, but for the reasons stated above an integrated theory should be more or less confined to the three theories mentioned.

We then suggest that the developmental process of addiction should be explained by some form of synthesis between the Herrnstein & Prelec and the Rachlin theories, should such a synthesis prove feasible. If it is not, then differences in the empirical consequences of the two accounts should be identified and, if possible, tested. If it is not possible to identify and test different predictions from these two theories, then the decision which one to incorporate in an integrated theory seems arbitrary and mainly a matter of intuitive appeal. Note that the primary object of explanation here is not the feature of addiction that we have identified as its defining feature (i.e. akrasia or weakness of will) but rather a level of consumption or activity (almost always but not invariably high) at which inconsistent choices over time become an issue.

The next component of an integrated theory, we suggest, would be the specification of some alternative behaviour to represent the alternative that is set against addiction in all three existing theories. Rachlin's (1997) proposal that this alternative is social interaction could be subjected to further research and other hypotheses of this kind could be developed and tested. Whatever the alternative is thought to be, the more basic assumption of Rachlin's theory that addiction and its alternative are separable and mutually substitutable activities could, perhaps, be subjected to research evaluation too. Although Rachlin, from his behaviourist standpoint, eschews the task of identifying the mysterious property 's' that is common to both addiction and its mutually substitutable alternative, this need not presumably be a barrier to investigation from other epistemological positions.

Lastly, an integrated theory would provide an account of how self-control is achieved by some kind of amalgam of those presently offered by the three theories. Again, if these proposed explanations of self-control can be made to yield testable predictions, these should be made the focus of research. Especially important here would be the more detailed descriptions of the self-control process provided in Ainslie's theory which could be evaluated in research, including research among samples of addicted persons undergoing treatment.

Implications for Treatment and Prevention of Addictive Disorders

Another aim of the conference was to explore the implications of behavioural choice theories for treatment and prevention. To assist this aim, experts in clinical, public health and policy issues in the addiction field attended the meeting. Implications for the treatment of addictive disorders were considered by Tucker & Simpson (Chapter 13, this volume) and for public policy by MacCoun (Chapter 14, this volume). The brief remarks here supplement the views given in those papers.

Treatment

It is clear, first of all, that these choice theories can make a good job of explicating the principles and methods of *existing* modalities that can claim some success in the treatment of addictive disorders, using different theoretical constructs from those that originally led to the development of the treatment modalities in question. The most obvious example here is the self-control or "self-management" methods developed in the early 1970s as part of the more general cognitive-behavioural approach to treatment (e.g. Mahoney & Thoresen 1974; Thoresen & Mahoney 1974). The possibility that his own theory can provide a rationale for the principal techniques used in self-management interventions is discussed by Ainslie (1992: 130–133) under the heading of "extrapsychic mechanisms."[9] The further possibility has already been mentioned (see Introduction, this volume) that another category of Ainslie's self-control mechanisms — the preparation of emotion — can accommodate the techniques used in cognitive therapy for addictions (Beck *et al.* 1993) for the control of craving responses. However, the parallels between theory and treatment methods here are used rather to support the validity of theory than to suggest how treatments can be streamlined or otherwise improved. No-one yet, to our knowledge, has extended implications of behavioural choice theories to arrive at a novel form of treatment, let alone implemented it in practice. This remains an unexplored possibility.

A prominent example of the application of behavioural economic principles to the treatment of addictive disorders is found in the work of Stephen Higgins and colleagues at the University of Vermont (see, e.g. Bickel *et al.* 1995; Higgins *et al.* 1995). This applied community reinforcement techniques to the behaviour of cocaine addicts, with impressive results. However, MacCoun (Chapter 14, this volume) has argued that the treatment method that was developed is deducible from conventional applied behavioural analysis and does not rely specifically on principles derived from behavioural economics (see also Schuster's comments on MacCoun's chapter, this volume). The same might well be true if behavioural economic principles were applied to what can claim to be the most successful single modality to have been evaluated for the treatment of alcohol dependence — the Community Reinforcement Approach (Meyers & Miller 2001). Again, behavioural economics may simply provide another way of looking at a recognised treatment approach rather than adding anything essential to it. Thus, the challenge to those who favor the application of behavioural choice theories and behavioural economic principles more generally to the treatment of addictive disorders is to demonstrate that these theories and principles can make a unique contribution to the improvement of treatment outcome.

Arguably the most popular form of psychosocial treatment for addictive disorders at present, and certainly the one that has received most attention recently from addiction specialists, is "motivational interviewing" (Miller 1983; Miller & Rollnick 1991, 2002). In the largest randomised controlled trial of treatment for alcohol problems ever carried out (Project MATCH Research Group 1997a, b, 1998), it was found that a variant of motivational interviewing, known as Motivational Enhancement Therapy (MET), was generally as effective as two more intensive forms of treatment consisting of three times as many sessions. Its apparent cost-effectiveness, combined with an intuitive correspondence to therapists' experience, accounts mainly for the popularity of motivational interviewing. It is now being applied to a whole range of behaviour change problems, essentially those where clients are ambivalent about the need for change, such as all forms of addictive behaviour (Dunn *et al.* 2001). The basic aim is to draw out from clients an increased level of motivation for change without attempting to advise, guide or in any other way impose increased motivation on them; an assumption here is obviously that, once sufficiently motivated, clients are able to effect a change in behaviour on their own, with perhaps a little help from their significant others. This short characterisation of motivational interviewing immediately suggests the relevance of the self-control elements in behavioural choice theories to an understanding of how it works.

There have been attempts to underpin motivational interviewing by employing concepts derived from general psychology — for example, by Miller (1985) himself using principles derived from motivational learning theory and by Draycott & Dabbs (1988) using Festinger's (1957) cognitive dissonance theory. However, the concepts employed in behavioural choice theories to explain how addicts are able to over-ride the effects of hyperbolic discounting and prefer larger, later to smaller, sooner reinforcers — restructuring, patterning and bunching — appear to offer another way to explain how motivational interviewing works. If such concepts can be operationalised and measured, they could be investigated in quantitative studies of the process and outcome of motivational interviewing in clinical samples; qualitative data concerning addicts' experience of the change process could also be useful here. Once more, however, the main objective of these studies would not be merely to explicate motivational interviewing but, by identifying and refining its effective ingredients, to improve it.

Public Health and the Organisation of Treatment Services

As well as implications for the actual conduct of treatment for addictive disorders, be-havioural choice theories also have implications for the organisation of services and, more generally, the public health response to addictions. Implications of this sort have received more attention in the literature so far than the more direct implications for treatment *per se*.

For example, Tucker & Simpson (Chapter 13, this volume) explain how a behavioural economic perspective leads to expanding conceptualisations of health and health-seeking behaviours, with clear implications for improved models of service provision and utilisation among problem substance users. From this perspective, ways of closing the currently existing gap between need and utilisation come to the fore and policies for allocating limited intervention resources in a more cost-effective manner across the population in need are suggested. Perhaps the main advantage of the behavioural economic perspective over other perspectives on service provision is its inherent emphasis on behavioural alternatives to addiction (Vuchinich & Tucker 1998). As we have stressed above, a conceptual innovation of behavioural economics is to view the addictive behaviour as the outcome of a choice. In the same way, applying the behavioural economic perspective to the organization of treatment services views care-seeking and adherence as choice processes (cf. Tucker 1999). From this perspective, in order to facilitate care-seeking and adherence one should attempt to make services more attractive and easier to access, and thus very different from the intense, high-threshold services that have dominated addiction treatment in the past.

Prevention and Public Policy

In his main contribution to this book, Robert MacCoun (Chapter 14, this volume) argues that behavioural economic accounts of addiction lead to no new insights for drug policy at present and are unlikely to do so in future. While not wishing to discourage behavioural economic work on drug use, MacCoun concludes that behavioural economic theories of addiction (what we have called here behavioural choice theories) are either largely redundant in relation to existing drug policy or, to the extent that they do have something to offer, do not require "any conception of 'addiction' as a distinct state or category of experience" (MacCoun, Chapter 14, this volume).

MacCoun's penetrating analysis presents a serious challenge to proponents of behavioural choice theories and, indeed, to anyone who believes the concept of addiction, however, it might be explained, to be relevant to drug policy. This is not the place to take issue with all the many points MacCoun makes and we shall content ourselves with a few general observations on his thesis.

First, it is of course true that the aggregate harm caused by the use of psychoactive substances, and by any form of potentially addictive behaviour such as gambling, exceeds that due to addiction to the drug or activity — violence and other antisocial consequences of intoxication, crime due to a drug's illegal status, and medical damage resulting from regular but not necessarily addictive use, to name only some of these areas of harm. It is possible, as MacCoun appears to recognise, that behavioural economics as a discipline can provide a framework for generating useful policy measures to reduce some forms of harmful behaviour of this kind. At the very least, it could provide an improved public understanding by serving to shed many of the common myths of drug use (e.g. disease states) and relating it to the notions of supply and demand with which the public is familiar. Everyone is familiar with making choices between more or less pleasurable activities, the consequences of which arrive at different times. This could "demystify" addiction in that it would emphasize that one's choices regarding addictive activities are not unlike other difficult choices one faces. Moreover, behavioural economics is perfectly consistent with and could perhaps help to popularise the harm reduction policies that MacCoun favours (see Vuchinich & Tucker 1998). But it is obviously unfair to chastise theories of addiction *per se* for failing to contribute to these goals, since that it not what they are intended for.

Secondly, MacCoun's failure to appreciate the relevance of a concept of addiction to drug policy may result from his rather crude characterisation of addiction itself — what he terms "a narrow and extreme end state called 'addiction' " (MacCoun, Chapter 14, this volume) — that is probably derived from disease-like conceptions of addiction. Defined in this way, addiction is a relatively rare occurrence and can rightly be regarded as of limited relevance to the reduction of total drug-related harm. However, although in these remarks we may have spoken of addiction as though it were a discrete entity discontinuous with normal behaviour, we recognise that, as with the related concept of dependence, addiction exists on a continuum ranging from very mild to very severe.[10] We would go further to say that addiction, in the sense of difficulty in refraining from or controlling drug use, applies to some extent to almost all regular users of psychoactive substances.

In conceding the usefulness of theories of self-control as opposed to theories of addiction, MacCoun misses the point that behavioural choice theories are theories of addiction *because* they offer explanations of how people lose control of their behaviour and how they overcome this loss. More generally, we would argue that it is the property of impaired control in behaviours commonly recognised as addictive that creates special problems for policy-making; if it were not for this "stickiness," policies directed at reducing harm from addictive behaviours would be similar to those applying to ordinary behaviours like failure to wear seat-belts in motor vehicles or littering the sidewalk. To MacCoun's assertion that a concept of addiction is unnecessary for drug policy, we reply that any policy that ignores this concept is unlikely to succeed.

In the end, the best verdict on MacCoun's pessimistic view of the applications of behavioural choice theories is that it is premature. We admitted early in this book (see Preface) that, on the whole, behavioural choice theories have yet to deliver to addiction specialists unique and practical alternatives to the principles and methods they currently use and this applies in varying degrees to treatment, public health, prevention and policy. We remain convinced, at the conclusion of this book, that they are potentially capable of making such an offer. As a last resort in defending the usefulness of behaviour choice theories, as MacCoun himself provocatively suggests (MacCoun, Chapter 14, this volume), we can fall back on Kurt Lewin's (1951) famous dictum that "there is nothing so practical as a good theory." In other words, if a theory provides an accurate and adequate explanation for the occurrence of an observable phenomenon, it must, by definition, contain within it the means of changing that phenomenon. In the case of behavioural choice theories of addiction, time will tell.

Notes

1. Throughout this chapter we refer to "addicts" and "addicted persons" as though these persons' behaviour and experience were considered to be all the same and qualitatively different from the behaviour and experience of everyone else. However, these terms are used only for simplicity and convenience. We are well aware that addiction or "dependence" exists in degrees and that all human beings, or nearly all, must be personally familiar with the addict's predicament as described in behavioural choice theories. Indeed, a major strength of these theories is that they are able easily to relate the processes of "addiction" to those applying to everyday human behaviour and experience.

2. Note that this definition has been criticized by Skog (Chapter 6, this volume).

3. This point appears to be accepted by the editor of the *Addiction* Special Issue (see West 2001) and is probably true of the great majority of the many "theories" of addiction West lists in the tables of his editorial.

4. This is recognised by Orford when he writes: "I refer to the excessive appetites idea as a 'model' rather than a 'theory' since its intended scope is very broad indeed, claiming as it does to provide a coherent account of the whole process of taking up, establishing, and (in some cases) giving up any one of five or so core forms of appetitive behaviour to which people can become so attached that it can seriously spoil their lives, and the lives of those immediately around them" (Orford 2001a: 28). However, his reason for declining to call this account a theory is different from ours. Indeed, the broad scope of explanation he attributes to it is one of the demands we make of any "true" theory of addiction.

5. It might be objected here that Ainslie's (1992, 2001) account of addiction would not qualify as a theory on these grounds either. There would be some justice in this objection but we believe that Ainslie's implicit explanation of addiction *could* be caste more formally and economically as required.

6. Because of this central property of behavioural choice theories, we are puzzled why Miller should describe them as "mechanistic" (see Miller's comments on Ainslie Chapter 2, this volume); despite Ainslie's partial defence of "mechanism" and "reductionism" as applied to his own theory (see Ainslie's reply to Miller, this volume), we see behavioural choice theories as the very opposite of mechanistic in any conventional sense.

7. A sustained critique along these lines of the disease perspective on alcohol problems may be found in Heather & Robertson (1997).

8. The primrose path is also present, although not so named, in Becker & Murphy's (1988) rational addiction theory.

9. The parallels between his theory and Freudian theory, and hence implications for an alternative understanding of the way psychoanalysis works, are more extensively discussed by Ainslie than the parallels with cognitive-behavioural therapy. However, we shall confine our discussion here to methods that have had some success in the treatment of addictive disorders, which psychoanalysis definitely has not (see, e.g. Miller *et al.* 1995).

10. See note 5 above. In rejecting the disease concept of addiction, we would also reject the "drug dependence syndrome" as described in DSM-IV, although it may be useful for some aspects of clinical practice. However, in addition to referring to a discrete and qualitatively distinct syndrome, on a conceptual level the DSM-IV characterisation of dependence is profoundly confused.

References

Ainslie, G. (1992). *Picoeconomics: The strategic interaction of successive motivational states within the person.* Cambridge, UK: Cambridge University Press.

Ainslie, G. (2001). *Breakdown of will.* Cambridge, UK: Cambridge University Press.

Beck, A. T., Wright, A. T., Newman, C. F., & Liese, B. S. (1993). *Cognitive therapy of substance abuse.* New York, NY: Guilford.

Becker, G., & Murphy, G. (1988). A theory of rational addiction. *Journal of Political Economy, 96,* 675–700.

Bickel, W. K., DeGrandpre, R. J., & Higgins, S. T. (1995). Behavioral economics of concurrent drug reinforcers: A review and reanalysis of drug self-administration research. *Psychopharmacology, 118,* 250–259.

Bickel, W. K., & Marsch, L. A. (2001). Toward a behavioral economic understanding of drug dependence: Delay discounting processes. *Addiction, 96* (Special Issue: Theories of Addiction), 73–86.

Buck, K. J., & Finn, D. A. (2001). Genetic factors in addiction: QTL, mapping and candidate gene studies implicate GABAergic genes in alcohol and barbiturate withdrawal. *Addiction, 96* (Special Issue: Theories of Addiction), 139–149.

Davies, J. B. (1992). *The myth of addiction.* Reading, UK: Harwood Academic.

Draycott, S., & Dabbs, A. (1988). Cognitive dissonance 2: A theoretical grounding of motivational interviewing. *British Journal of Clinical Psychology, 37,* 355–364.

Drummond, D. C. (2001). Theories of drug craving, ancient and modern. *Addiction, 96* (Special Issue: Theories of Addiction), 33–46.

Dunn, C., Deroo, L., & Rivara, F. P. (2001). The use of brief interventions adapted from motivational interviewing across behavioral domains: A systematic review. *Addiction, 96,* 1725–1742.

Ferrence, R. (2001). Diffusion theory and drug use. *Addiction, 96* (Special Issue: Theories of Addiction), 165–173.

Festinger, L. (1957). *A theory of cognitive dissonance.* Stanford, CA: Stanford University Press.

Heather, N. (1998). A conceptual framework for explaining drug addiction. *Journal of Psychopharmacology, 12,* 3–7.

Herrnstein, R., & Prelec, D. (1992). A theory of addiction. In: G. Loewenstein, & J. Elster (Eds), *Choice over time* (pp. 331–360). New York, NY: Russell Sage Foundation.

Heyman, G. M., & Herrnstein, R. J. (1986). More on concurrent ratio-interval schedules: A replication and review. *Journal of the Experimental Analysis of Behavior, 46,* 331–351.

Higgins, S. T., Budney, A. J., Bickel, W. K., Badger, G. J. *et al.* (1995). Outpatient behavioral treatment for cocaine dependence: One-year outcome. *Experimental and Clinical Psychopharmacology, 3*, 205–212.

Janis, I., & Mann, L. (1977). *Decision making: A psychological analysis of conflict, choice and commitment.* New York, NY: Free Press.

Jones, B. T., Corbin, W., & Fromme, K. (2001). A review of expectancy theory and alcohol consumption. *Addiction, 96* (Special Issue: Theories of Addiction), 57–72.

Kenkel, D., Mathios, A. D., & Pacula, R. (2001). Economics of youth drug use, addiction and gateway effects. *Addiction, 96* (Special Issue: Theories of Addiction), 151–164.

Lewin, K. (1951). *Field theory in social science.* New York, NY: Harper Row.

Littleton, J. (2001). Receptor regulation as a unitary mechanism for drug tolerance and physical dependence: Not quite as simple as it seemed! *Addiction, 96* (Special Issue: Theories of Addiction), 87–101.

Loewenstein, G., & Elster, J. (Eds) (1992). *Choice over time.* New York, NY: Russell Sage Foundation.

Mahoney, M. J., & Thoresen, C. E. (1974). *Self-control: Power to the person.* Monterey, CA: Brooks/Cole.

McCusker, C. G. (2001). Cognitive biases and addiction: An evolution in theory and method. *Addiction, 96* (Special Issue: Theories of Addiction), 47–56.

Meyers, R. J., & Miller, W. R. (Eds) (2001). *A community reinforcement approach to addiction treatment.* Cambridge, UK: Cambridge University Press.

Miller, C. S. (2001). Toxicant-induced loss of tolerance. *Addiction, 96* (Special Issue: Theories of Addiction), 115–137.

Miller, N. (1944). Experimental studies of conflict. In: J. Hunt (Ed.), *Personality and the behavior disorders.* New York, NY: Ronald.

Miller, W. R. (1983). Motivational interviewing with problem drinkers. *Behavioral Psychotherapy, 11*, 147–172.

Miller, W. R. (1985). Motivation for treatment: A review with special emphasis on alcoholism. *Psychological Bulletin, 98*, 84–107.

Miller, W. R., & Rollnick, S. (1991). *Motivational interviewing: Preparing people to change addictive behavior.* New York, NY: Guilford.

Miller, W. R., & Rollnick, S. (2002). *Motivational interviewing: Preparing people for change* (2nd ed.). New York, NY: Guilford.

Orford, J. (1985). *Excessive appetiies: A psychological view of addictions.* Chichester, UK: Wiley.

Orford, J. (2001a). Addiction as excessive appetite. *Addiction, 96* (Special Issue: Theories of Addiction), 15–32.

Orford, J. (2001b). *Excessive appetites: A psychological view of addictions* (2nd ed.). Chichester, UK: Wiley.

Project MATCH Research Group (1997a). Matching alcoholism treatments to client heterogeneity: Project MATCH posttreatment drinking outcomes. *Journal of Studies on Alcohol, 58*, 7–29.

Project MATCH Research Group (1997b). Project MATCH secondary a priori hypotheses. *Addiction, 92*, 1655–1682.

Project MATCH Research Group (1998). Matching alcoholism treatments to client heterogeneity: Project MATCH three-year drinking outcomes. *Alcoholism: Experimental and Clinical Research, 22*, 1300–1311.

Rachlin, H. (1995). Self-control: Beyond commitment. *Behavioral and Brain Sciences, 18*, 109–159.

Rachlin, H. (1997). Four teleological theories of addiction. *Psychonomic Bulletin and Review, 4*, 462–473.

Rachlin, H. (2000a). *The science of self-control.* Cambridge, MA: Harvard University Press.

Rachlin, H. (2000b). The lonely addict. In: W. K. Bickel, & R. E. Vuchinich (Eds), *Reframing health behavior change with behavioral economics* (pp. 145–164). Mahwahm, NJ: Lawrence Erlbaum Associates.

Rachlin, H., Green, L., & Tormey, B. (1988). Is there a decisive test between matching and maximizing? *Journal of the Experimental Analysis of Behavior, 50*, 113–123.

Robinson, T. E., & Berridge, K. C. (2001). Incentive-sensitization and addiction. *Addiction, 96* (Special issue: Theories of Addiction), 103–114.

Schaler, J. A. (2000). *Addiction is a choice*. Chicago, IL: Open Court Publishing.

Skog, O.-J. (1999). Rationality, irrationality and addiction: Notes on Becker & Murphy's theory of addiction. In: J. Elster, & O.-J. Skog (Eds), *Getting hooked: Rationality and addiction* (pp. 173–207). Cambridge, UK: Cambridge University Press.

Sutton, S. (2001). Back to the drawing board? A review of applications of the transtheoretical model to substance use. *Addiction, 96* (Special Issue: Theories of Addiction), 175–186.

Thoresen, C. E., & Mahoney, M. J. (1974). *Behavioral self-control*. New York, NY: Holt, Rinehart & Winston.

Tucker, J. A. (1999). Changing addictive behavior: Historical and contemporary perspectives. In: J. A. Tucker, D. M. Donovan, & G. A. Marlatt (Eds), *Changing addictive behavior: Bridging clinical and public health strategies*. New York, NY: Guilford.

Vuchinich, R. E., & Simpson, C. A. (1998). Hyperbolic temporal discounting in social drinkers and problem drinkers. *Experimental and Clinical Psychopharmacology, 6*, 292–305.

Vuchinich, R., & Tucker, J. A. (1998). Choice, behavioral economics and addictive behavior patterns. In: W. R. Miller, & N. Heather (Eds), *Treating addictive behaviors* (2nd ed.). New York: Plenum.

West, R. (2001). Theories of addiction (Editorial). *Addiction, 96* (Special Issue: Theories of Addiction), 3–13.

Author Index

Subject Index

addict
  subclinical, 163, 173, 180
  clinical, 163, 164, 166, 180
  happy, 80, 160, 161, 178
  naive, 177, 178
addiction
  as a myth, 413
  definition of, 95, 96, 163, 176
  etiology of, 412
  theories of addiction
    behavioral level, 409
    neuronal level, 409
    phenomenal level, 409
    part theories of, 411
addictive disorders
  organisation of services for, 421
  prevention of, 409, 419
  public policy for, 421
  treatment of, 409, 419, 420, 421, 424
addictive stock, 25, 76, 77
adjacent complementarity, 25, 77, 78, 80,
  148, 282, 310
adolescence, 255, 256, 263, 264
agency, 63, 64, 67, 171, 220, 245
agriculture, 251, 258, 273, 277
alcohol, 8, 13, 18, 22, 23, 25, 26, 37, 41,
  51, 63, 100, 109, 113, 118
alcoholism, 35, 95–97, 103, 151, 157, 172,
  322, 323, 337, 413
ambivalence, 13, 14, 17, 35, 62, 96, 115,
  165, 180, 181, 411, 415
American Psychiatric Association, 96, 98,
  157, 159, 236
anterior cingulate cortex, 184, 194, 199
appetite, recursive model of, 241
approach-avoidance conflict, 62, 415
attention-deficit/hyperactivity disorder,
  183, 192

barter economy, 129–132
Becker-Murphy, 114, 140, 298

behavioral economics, 71, 72, 81, 82, 84,
  85, 90, 91, 151, 152, 251, 341,
  365–368, 370, 371, 374–376, 379,
  381, 383, 384, 386, 392, 403
behaviorism, 139, 144, 145, 150, 152, 332
behaviorism
  Skinnerian, 139, 144, 145, 152
  teleological, 145, 150, 152, 332
boredom, 54

childhood, 254, 255, 264, 316, 319
choice, xiv, xv, xvi, xvii, 1, 2, 5, 9–24,
  35–37, 39, 40, 43, 45, 47–49, 52, 54,
  55, 67, 68, 71, 90, 91, 95, 96, 99, 103,
  104
choice, marketplace model of, 52, 240
cigarette addiction, 100
cigarette smokers, 7, 261, 345, 350, 395
closed economies, 365, 367–371, 376, 381
coerced abstinence, 388
cognitive therapy, 420
cognitive psychology, 43, 90, 142, 144, 240
cognitive-behavioural therapy, 424
commitment, 44, 45, 49, 56, 64, 82, 140,
  141, 178, 179, 229, 233
community reinforcement, 381, 386, 420
compensatory behavioral responses to risk
  reduction, 396
complements, 8, 77, 130, 138, 215, 216
compulsion/compulsive, 51, 52, 95, 96, 98,
  99, 153, 157, 221, 413
compulsiveness, 50, 53
conditioned reinforcement, 185, 186, 192,
  194, 195, 201, 214, 215
consumerism, 258, 274
consumption capital, 26, 282, 283, 290
control of attention, 18, 44
correlates of recovery, 96, 99, 100, 116,
  117
counterfactual definition, 160, 161–164,
  177